An Aslan Book

Mahalia

Laurraine Goreau

Lion Publishing

LION PUBLISHING
121 High Street, Berkhamsted, Herts

First edition 1975 Word Books, Texas, USA
under the title *Just Mahalia, Baby*
First UK edition 1976

ISBN 0 85648 061 4

Grateful acknowledgement is made for permission to use copyright material as follows:

For lyrics from *An Evening Prayer*, on p. 255. Copyright 1911 by Charles H. Gabriel. © Renewal 1939 [extended], The Rodeheaver Co., owner. Used by permission.

For an excerpt from a review article by Whitney Balliett in *The New Yorker*, April 17, 1967. By permission of *The New Yorker*.

For an excerpt from an article by Ralph Ellison on Mahalia Jackson in *Saturday Review*, September 27, 1958. Reprinted by permission of *Saturday Review/World*.

For excerpts from an article by Joe Goldberg on Mahalia Jackson in *Rolling Stone* Issue No. 103, March 2, 1972, as correlated with other direct sources relating to the same event. Rolling Stone © 1972 by Straight Arrow Publishers Inc. All Rights Reserved. Reprinted by permission.

For a brief quotation from an article by Nat Hentoff on Mahalia Jackson in a 1958 issue of *The Reporter*. Reprinted by permission of the author.

For an excerpt from *The Story of Jazz* by Marshall Stearns, published by Oxford University Press. Reprinted by permission of the publisher.

Printed in Great Britain by
Hazell Watson & Viney Ltd
Aylesbury, Bucks

Preface

"You write the real book of me, Laurraines." This charge from Mahalia has been much with me. It opened the way, too, for the scope and authenticity of this book, since Mahalia told key family members and friends, "Laurraine's writing the *history* of me." Mahalia and I had met in 1959, through a week's newspaper conference in Chicago. Our touchstones were New Orleans (our mutual birthplace and still my home), gospel music, and that instant empathy which you will find so often in her story. It was in 1967 that she first suggested I write the "real" book of her, on a wave of dissatisfaction with so much in print which was erroneous. This was not always the writer's fault: references clear to Mahalia could be obscure to the untutored; some inferences were protective coloration. Publicity fancies, confusing reprints, and in-print background errors were often compounded because an exhausted Mahalia waved clippings—"It's all in here, baby"—to save her energy. ("It's only publicity" is a common gospel-world tenet.) Sporadically from 1967 and intensively from early 1971, I made tapes and notes with Mahalia. Her scrapbooks and memorabilia were at my disposal. I shared many of her experiences in the United States and abroad. Immediately after her funeral, I began total research: on the scene in New Orleans, Chicago, St. Louis, Los Angeles, New York; via hundreds of hours of long-distance tapes, and scores of letters, throughout the United States and abroad. Family, executor, doctors, employees, friends, old neighbors, and business, professional and religious associates were generous with recollections, souvenirs, photographs—from the most obscure persons to officials of the Imperial Palace of Japan.

Everyone who knew her well thought he (or she) knew Mahalia's most intimate thoughts and actions. It was increasingly evident that *nobody* knew all of Mahalia. Often the track of fact doubled and turned, or twisted, to be straightened only with yet another primary source. The sorting, the matching, the melding finally yielded a mosaic with all the infinite colorations of Mahalia's extraordinary existence. The dialogue, the thoughts herein are true, thanks to the tape recorder. Mahalia's visions, close-kept, were told me by Mahalia. Her aunts and other closest family have been most generous in assisting and attesting that to them I was "the sole authorized biographer of Mahalia Jackson, to tell her true life story, such being the wish of her family as it was Miss Jackson's expressed wish prior to her death." This manuscript, however, is without any proscription or control by anyone other than the author. Before me is Mahalia's oft-repeated comment when I was the target of flak in endeavoring to assist her with a project: "You know what you doing, Laurraines." I have tried, in all love and honesty.

The sources of information are so many that it would take another chapter to state each, but in the main they are these: Interviews by tape, by letter, or in person with The Rev. Ralph D. and Juanita Abernathy, Mrs. Ethel M. Adams, Steve Allen, William R. Barclay, M.D., Elliott and Ida Beal, Joe Bostic, J. Robert Bradley, Debria Brown, Jerome Burks, Edward Burnette, Sr., The Rev. J. Tallefarra Campbell, Mrs. Rose Duskin Champagne, Mrs. Lillie Chase, Jean and Kenneth H. Childers, Tina Choate, Allen Clark, Sr., Allen Clark, Jr., Mrs. Porterfield Clark, Mrs. Xernona Clayton, Charles Clency, Edmond Castine, Harry Dale, The Rev. Lawler P. Daniels, Thomas A. Dorsey, Duke Ellington,* Mercer Ellington, T. C. W. Ellis, Chauncey Eskridge, Mrs. Mildred Falls,* Leonard Feather, Ella Fitzgerald, Mrs. Geni B. Fox, James Francis, Bernice Durden Franklin, Audrey Franklyn, Sister Evelyn Gaye, Mother Fannie Gaye, Mrs. Sam George, Arthur Godfrey, Russell Goode, Her Royal Highness Grace de Monaco, Richard Grady, Cylestine Fletcher Graves, Dick Gregory, Mrs. Elizabeth Griffin, David Haber, Mrs. Reuben Hack, Tevelda Hall, John Hammond, Yvonne Jackson Harris, June Havoc, Dr. S. I. Hayakawa, George Healy, Jr., Isaac Hockenhull,* Benjamin L. Hooks, Mrs. Mary Ann Hooper, Sen. Hubert Humphrey, Mrs. Marion P. Hunter, Johnny Jackson, The Rev. T. J. Jemison, The Rev. Leon Jenkins, Margaret Aikens Jenkins, Mrs. Mary Lou Galloway Jenkins, Max Jones, Mrs. Lyndon Baines Johnson, Mrs. Bessie Kimble, Thomas King, Sallie Martin Langham, Mrs. Alice Lawson, Mrs. Isabella Lazard, Emanuel Lazard, The Rev. James Lee, Harry Lenetska, Rose Levi, The Rev. James Lewis, Mrs. Gwendolyn Lightner, Mrs. Zenobia Lockett, Corinne Levi'Looper, Mrs. Angelle "Jack" Marshall, Mrs. Harry McCall, Robert McGimsey, John Meston, Amb. Armin Meyer, Marlene Miles, Mitch Miller, Robert Miller, Louis Mindling, Aldus Mitchell, Paulene Myers, Hugues Panassie,*

---

*deceased

Mother Anna Parks, Robert Peck, M.D., Lee Phillips, Robert Phillips, Dave Powers, Della Reese, Col. Jack Reilly, Bertha Nero Reiné, Albertina Walker Reynolds, Henry M. Rightor, Edward Robinson, Mrs. Hannah Robinson,* William Russell, Mrs. Celeste Scott,* Eddie Scott, Annise Jackson Scully,* John Sellers, Gene J. Shapiro, Dinah Shore, Florence White Smith, Ed Sullivan,* The Rev. Jodie Strawther, Mrs. Cecile Taylor, O. C. W. Taylor, Louis "Studs" Terkel, George Thomas, Mrs. Elizabeth Thornton, The Rev. John Thurston, Irving Townsend, Earl Vondrasek, M.D., Mrs. Ernestine Washington, Louise Overall Weaver, George Wein, Granville White, Mrs. Missie Wilkerson, Beatrice Thomas Williams, J. Mayo Williams, Mrs. Rosa Williams, Richard Yancey, Quentin Young, M.D.

Additionally, I received valuable aid in the way of photographs, documents, and other assistance from Mark Lewis, director, Office of Cultural Presentations, Department of State, U.S.A.; Kent Obee, USIA deputy policy officer, Ceylon and Nepal; Daniel P. Oleksiw, director, USIS India; Consul Gen. Stephen Palmer, Madras; Consul Gen. and Mrs. Herbert Gordon, Calcutta; Mrs. William Tolbert, First Lady, Liberia; Mrs. Aristotle Onassis; Daisuku Honda, Protocol Section, Imperial Household, Tokyo; Shigenobu Shima, Grand Master of the Ceremonies, Imperial Palace, Tokyo; Betsy Fitzgerald, American Embassy, Tokyo; Andrew Schlesinger, U.S. Cultural Center, Jerusalem; The Rev. H. A. Townsley, district superintendent, Delhi District, Methodist Church, South Asia; H. C. Schloesser, Pan American Airways, Berlin; Rep. Lindy Boggs, Harnett Kane, Eva Jessye, Pearl Bailey, Victor Olivier, Richard Yancey, Harry Souchon, Irma Thomas; Lylian Kane, University of Chicago Hospital, medical-legal affairs staff; J. R. Taylor, assistant curator, Rutgers University Institute of Jazz Studies; Herman Kogan, book editor, the Chicago *Sun-Times*; Charles W. Corkran, archivist, the Lyndon Baines Johnson Presidential Library; Dave Powers, curator, the John F. Kennedy Library; Ron Juliano, CBS; Leah K. Carlton, Shiloh Baptist Church, Atlantic City; and *Festival International de Télévision de Monte-Carlo.*

Also, I am grateful for help received from the Joseph Regenstein Library, University of Chicago; Chicago Public Library, New Orleans Public Library, Louisiana State Museum Library, Library of Congress, Ocean Springs (Miss.) Municipal Library, West Georgia College Library (Carrollton, Ga.), and the Public Health Library of the Louisiana Division of Health.

For research, transcriptions, translations, and secretarial assistance, my gratitude to my primary assistant, Iris M. Day; to The Rev. A. L. Davis (New Zion Baptist Church, New Orleans), vice president, National Baptist Convention, and his secretary, Mrs. Ellen Lewis; to Mrs. Myriam Guidroz

*deceased

Le Mire; Mrs. Doris Fleming and Audrey Krust, Louisiana Tourist Development Commission; Mrs. Vera Burroughs; the Orleans Parish Board of Education Research Office; the New Orleans Jazz Museum; and the Tulane University Jazz Archives.

Most special thanks are due the members of my family who sustained me throughout this intense, prolonged project: Dr. and Mrs. J. Lincoln DeVillier, Col. and Mrs. Marshall A. Glazebrook, Mrs. Alice Jefferys; to photographer John Donnels, a friend indeed; for extraordinary assistance by Elliott Beal, John Sellers, Mrs. Cecile Taylor, Mrs. Louise Weaver Smothers, Mrs. Jean Childers, and Mahalia's three surviving aunts: Mrs. Hannah Robinson,* Mrs. Alice Lawson, and Mrs. Bessie Kimble; for patient aid by Word Books editor Patricia Wienandt. Most importantly, my unstinted admiration to Mrs. Mary Anne DeVillier, a superb exponent of an often-undervalued field of scholarship, the critical editor, whose diamond-brilliant mind and poet's ear shepherded this work.

LAURRAINE GOREAU

*deceased

1

Mahalia had gone far and her horizons were open. But this time she balked. "Shoot me up with them astronauts? How they going to get somebody heavy as me up in a rocket? . . . Never mind, I'm not going, even for the President."

So much remarkable, and unthinkable, had occurred in her life, she didn't for an instant doubt that her agent meant just what she heard—until, laughing, calling long-distance from Los Angeles, Bob Phillips admitted that all the State Department wanted to beam up was her image. She'd star with the President and several astronauts. They'd zoom live via Telstar to the Congo as the Kinshasa Satellite Special, inaugurating the Congo's first direct television receiving station.

Heady stuff, unless you were Mahalia Jackson, named one of the 20 most admired people in the world; unless you'd veered the course of popular music throughout the world; unless by June, 1971, you'd pioneered so many other firsts that they spilled off your memory; unless within the past 60 days, you'd been with remote Empress Nagasa in Japan and fiery Prime Minister Indira Gandhi in India; private sessions, at their request, which sent their two peoples—nearly one-fifth of all the humans on earth—into a flush of excitement.

And even this couldn't turn your head. Not when you lived with the belief that this mystic force wasn't *of* you, but lived *within* you—a sort of custody, this power drawing the whole sweep of humankind—cleaning woman to king—drawing them right across the walls of ghetto and palace, beyond race, faith, image, politics, life style, money, position. A force that could mesmerize like a guru, transform a life like an alchemist. A power more mysterious than any Telstar and with more dangers—for her.

What was its secret?

Not just a voice. "They got plenty voices like mine down home." Her climb from pauper to plenty? "Money just draws flies." Her visions? Her ESP? "I don't tell people about that."

Her faith? Yet believers are scattered over the earth like the pepper grass Mahalia pulled for supper as a child.

The only extra dimension visible as the world's greatest gospel singer trudged into the dim lobby of Washington's Mayflower Hotel was 50 pounds extra weight. A slim young State Department trainee fluttered after her like a kitetail in a gusty wind.

The wind was blowing the wrong way. She'd come from Chicago weary but willing to do her part for America, only to discover not just a different focus but a different scene: The telecast would be not from the White House but from the USIS studios which made do in an old post office building. The astronauts would be cut in from Houston. Secretary of State Rogers was substituting for President Nixon; he'd be cut in from State. And her bed was too small, cutting into her rest.

"This what I came all the way here for?" she sighed. "They could have cut me in from Chicago."

The narrow bed was dwarfed. That wasn't entirely its fault, nor was it merely Mahalia's bulk. Even lumped like a dumpling, energy drained, this big black woman, natural as the morning, flowed over her surroundings and charged them with a suspenseful current. Her bouffant, curly tower of a wig discarded, only a cap of short, glossy black hair intruded on the rich brown face whose smoothness denied her weariness—until you sought the deep brown eyes, not glistening now. Clouded. Even so, her energy seemed only lightly lidded, plugged in, waiting.

She shifted her bulk.

She shucked her girdle.

Comfort wouldn't come.

Long, tapered brown fingers fidgeted wisps of hair.

One foot nudged off the other's shoe. The sun shone briefly: "See? I wore my comfortable shoes just like you said. But my feet still killing me."

Silence. She should rest.

"Hand me my purse, over there by the dresser, will you, baby? I got to take a pill." The famous contralto deepened: "I'm sorry I got you up here, Laurraine; I thought it would be worth your time."

A sigh. A shake—a monument of a shake. Then she reared, Mother Earth emerging from the waters. "At least we going bring some people closer together. The world can use a lot of that. Gwen, what we going wear? We got to get it pressed. Let me have that Japanese wig; it's in the box under that red—yeah, that's it; let's see what I can do with that mess. Better than that woman in Minneapolis charged me $20. You bring the music, Gwen? And I got to write those people in Canada. When rehearsal?"

She was switched on and running, and suddenly a grin lit the gloom, eyes impish as an oversized elf. "You know, for a minute on the phone they had me believing that about the rocket. How high the moon?"

About 250,000 miles, honey.

For Mahalia, a little farther. She started life six feet below sea level, in New Orleans, where the Mississippi River reached hungry fingers for the land. She was reborn even a little lower than that, in the river itself, still anonymous as a mullet but already leaping.

And New Orleans was a hot town to surface to, in those days.

2

They were seven sisters, the Clarks. Husky, country-strong, bunched together now in the pinch of city urgencies with five offspring in three rooms and a kitchen on the outermost rim of the strangeness of New Orleans.

Only six were afoot. Bessie, 12, was sent outside with her nephew Allen—Isabell's oldest boy, 12 too. He thought Bessie and his mother and all the rest were his sisters. The seventh, Charity Clark, was ready to birth. Big Mahala—"Duke," the natural at command into whose house they'd all crammed—she could tell. So could 'Bell, nursing her own warm brown babe at her breast. Hannah knew, too; she was glad Duke sent her uptown to get the granny before Charity's pains cut too close.

Not that anything could really be uptown from their cottage. It sat squat "front of town," near the northernmost wharfs, a good seven miles from the center of the city along railroad tracks that squeezed the levee, just as the levee itself held the Mississippi's waters close as anything or anyone could until the river got good and ready to roar in and tell New Orleans hello.

The cottage already had kissing acquaintance with the river, too close for comfort: It had come from the other side, the river side of the levee—built on the grassy level of the levee's batture. Like most of its squatter neighbors, the house was a shotgun cottage, aping the architecture popular since the founding French built narrow and deep for safety within their ramparts in remote downtown, more than a century earlier when this was only a cypress swamp: "shotgun" because you could stand at the front door and look out the back, straight as a gunbarrel, through rooms stacked one behind the other. With twin sides, you had a "double-barreled shotgun."

Years earlier, a whole clutch of the weatherworn cypress cottages had squatted on the batture, tolerated by the U.S. Engineers—who thought it was their province—but not by the river, the Old Man, who *knew* it was his, and proved it by swallowing the land bit by bit until the Engineers decreed that to keep New Orleans safe, a stronger barrier—a revetment—must be built. The houses had to go. Scooped up, they were deposited higgledy piggledy on the city side of the tracks on what had been pasture, swamp and tree-claimed land—even, some of it, old sugar plantation acres where Étienne de Boré first crystallized cane syrup into sugar.

The house Duke found had landed on a scrap of Water St. It still faced the river, but in between lay the levee and, first, the busy City Belt Railroad tracks. The house shook now as a train roared by. The next to youngest sister, Alice, went back to check the pot of water boiling on the cookstove. While she was at it, she poked more wood beneath. No bother about enough water; the cistern was full from the rains and with the roof showing day, half the cook pots were full from catching leaks.

Up front, Duke kept an eye on Charity. Charity'd had no trouble birthing Peter, back in Legonier, and the ailment that prompted Hannah to fetch Charity in to New Orleans for treatment at Charity Hospital the year before was all cleared up, thank You Jesus. No, she wasn't worried, but she had a special interest in this child: if it was a girl, it would be named for her. Bell had used up Cecile, their mother's name, on the only girl born to the sisters so far. Now this next name was Mahala, for her—a good Bible name, too. She felt in her bones it was a girl in there kicking. Bell said so, and Bell had the sight. Here the granny. 'Bout time. . . . *Now.*

The Mahala who shot forth eagerly that Saturday, Oct. 26, 1912, was rosy pink on this first day of life, like all Negro children. But her legs were curved as if they questioned existence, and her eyes were red, inflamed, heavily infected. Wiping the mucus that threatened to glue the tiny eyelids fast, Granny Lee shook her head. "You got to guard this baby. Cut that lamp; can't have no light. Keep the room dark dark. This baby liable go blind." Her legs? "That's in the hand of God Almighty."

Whatever else the Clark sisters were short on, it wasn't faith. They'd take care of those eyes: Bathe 'em. Guard the dark. Wasn't much to stumble over in the room but people anyway.

Duke started issuing orders. The rest obeyed. Duke wasn't the eldest—Bell was—but she was undisputed tribal chief by nature: If Duke was around, Duke was boss. The other sisters—good-natured, close-knit—didn't cross her. No man was around to contest her. Nor would there be, in the days and months to come. Halie's father lived just around the corner, on Walnut between Water and Magazine. But already he had another set of children living with their mother in Upper Carrollton, still near the river but on Zimple St.—a "better liver," she was—and he had a boy, older, of yet another mother, living in the Irish Channel. He spent time in Upper Carrollton—a son would be born there a month after Halie's birth and, later, another daughter. He spent time with his parents—stayed by them, in part, in one side of the double-barreled shotgun they owned at 180 Walnut St., his front quarters set up for barbering on Friday evenings and Saturdays after working sporadically on the Walnut wharf weekdays. And he spent time with his sisters, especially Sarah, who lived just down the street. But he spent no more time with Charity.

Actually, Johnny Jackson wasn't running counter to much of the culture. "It was more of a trend at that time to live together and not be married," says an old friend of Mahalia's, educator/choral director Elliott Beal, who grew up nearby. "Most times, the men didn't want to be tied down. Some of them were gamblers on the riverboats. Those big steamboats were running then. Some had work one day, not the next. Some were hands on the boats and barges. They kept themselves loose."

The mainstream of black women weren't always anxious for a white law marriage, either. The lack was no stigma. Only two generations back, civil ceremony for slaves was discouraged, avoided, an entanglement to many of the owners whose chattel property they were . . . the house help often cherished but field hands frequently bought and sold or traded, or at least held available for disposal or breeding—convertible assets, like the crops. In 1912, evolving their own culture, seeking headway, theirs was a matriarchal society. Low wages and big white houses made work far more plentiful for the black woman than the black man. *She* was the steady worker; and don't say "blue Monday" to *her* madam, not if you going to last. Yet any fly husband by the law could spend his money and yours too—by his *right*. A law-married woman in Louisiana couldn't buy much more than groceries without her husband's signed consent. A wife couldn't even make a loan by herself, if it came to that. Even past the grave, he could claim a good piece of anything she had—take it right from the children. That put a red flag up, right there.

Births by law must be recorded, but City Hall custom casually went along with the "open" arrangement: leave the Negroes to themselves. "In the old days," says Elliott Beal, "City Hall let the child take the name of the father even though there was no marriage. The mother's statement was just accepted, without any checking, when she went down to register the birth—or when the midwife went, which was more the custom; like a doctor would file it today."

So Charity made no issue of her newborn, nor any embarrassment in church. She told Granny Lee to register the birth Mahala Jackson, lawful; and she kept her peace. Energetic, rather quiet, naturally sweet, Charity was used to making do. But by now so much Clark make-do was needed, it had to become a mass effort. Shying from marriage wasn't just city style. Back by the plantation, at Legonier, the courthouse wasn't any black magnet either, although work chances were spread about equal. Signing your name to a paper had something fatalistic about it. Paying cash money for a license didn't draw them either. (Besides, the courthouse housed the jail, and white law was chancy.)

So Halie had a big brother, Roosevelt ("Peter") Hunter, almost three now, whom Charity brought with her. Their mother had died—worn out, some said—so Hannah also gathered up young Bessie and Bell's son Allen ("Boy Baby"), whom their mother had raised right along with Bessie. That made a houseful, and Hannah moved them into 268 Audubon St. Finding a place in the waterfront area was no trick: all about equal in size, give or take a room; all about equal in dilapidation; all about the same rent: \$8 or \$9 a month. No indoor plumbing, of course; no electricity. Distinctions were measured in leaks or their lack, in yard space, and the state of the toilet outside. So many were the vacancies, "you could move in a place and let the landlord know when he came," says Allen Clark, Sr.; "they'd just be glad to have it occupied instead of at the mercy of children's mischief." Nearby, Duke had her son, Fred Duskin, 13; she'd brought him with her when she came in soon after childless, venturesome Hannah took the first step at the urging of brother Porterfield, who was getting ahead as a cook on the riverboats. Neither Alice nor Rhoda, who followed, had children. But for all the clan, work was a problem and wages ran but 35¢ to 50¢ a day when you could *get* a day.

With characteristic decision, Duke swept them all into the house on Water St. Then the Atchafalaya in a convulsion so vast, so storied, it went into Gumstump and Clark family annals as "the High Water of 1912," ruined Legonier's cotton and uprooted Bell. With her Celie, 17 months, and new-born Porterfield, there were 13 souls piled together in the three rooms. And the kitchen.

Actually, they loved the being together, and it wasn't so different from Legonier. On the Merrick Plantation—nicknamed Gumstump: "a stumped-over country, plenty gum trees," says Cousin Baby Rosa Williams—their mother had had 11 children before she died at 46. Of the four boys, Cleveland and Harrison died young, leaving only Boston and Porterfield, the youngest. With differences of births and deaths and children's children, a population of 10 or 11 generally bulged the little frame house in the twin row of plantation quarters as the Clark sisters grew tall.

Most Louisiana plantations were built fronting on water to move the cotton or sugarcane or rice, since roads were few and steady rain turned those into mud-traps. In South Louisiana's Pointe Coupée Parish west of New Orleans, Gumstump lay alongside the Atchafalaya River. Tall, wide-bottomed steamboats came to load its cotton bales and fight the current upstream to connect to the Mississippi. Even this long after the Civil War had broken up the slave-labor cotton aristocracy, all life here breathed and fed cotton. It and two adjacent Merrick family plantations were run now by Mr. E. T. Merrick for his father, bluff Captain D. T. Merrick, whose "Captain" hung on long after his Confederate troops had vanished. Now there were field wages to pay, and most garden land was parceled out on shares to ex-slaves and children of slaves. But Paul Clark, the girls' father, didn't have to farm shares. He could rent. Born of some consequence even in slavery—his father the family coachman and his mother the prized cook—when emancipation set young Paul free, he'd clung to familiar territory, like hundreds about him. But when schooling was available, he took it seriously. The Bible did the rest.

Grey-eyed, imposing, with a natural flair for language, Paul Clark became a licensed Baptist minister, a known Bible scholar—and a key man on the plantations: He ran the Merricks' gin on adjacent Belaire which baled for all three plantations, then switched off-season to grinding corn. "Get a head of steam up, you could hear that whistle clear to the next plantation," says Thomas King, a Merrick hand then. There wasn't much pay to it, but Paul Clark was a substantial man in the black community. "You couldn't call at his house without a coat and tie," says granddaughter Cecile Taylor, "and take off your hat at the door."

Sundays, he was often a guest preacher. Of ancient cypress painted white, St. John the Baptist Church stood on Gumstump ground, just a close walk for the Clarks. Weekdays it doubled as the Negro schoolroom—one room, one teacher, grades one to five. If you wanted to learn more, you were on your own. Most didn't, unable to lift their eyes from the "kin to cain't" cycle of grinding back labor from plantation to plantation, eternally in debt to the general store, where nothing ever seemed to pay out. But Sundays, white cloth went over teacher's table, making it again the pulpit. Curtains were back up at the windows (carefully preserved from children's fingers, Sunday to Sunday). Flowers added a final pretty touch. It was now the place of joy.

To his own flock, Reverend Clark was a disciplinarian who never spared the rod—and a heavy rod it could be—but they were proud and deeply attentive to the Bible interpretations he dispensed at church or those times when the cotton or his own place didn't call. Saturdays, he was busy. He barbered hair, mainly for whites (cash too scarce for most blacks to pay out). To his swarm of children, it was an unusual chance to observe, to listen to a variety of white people and sense a world beyond their own.

Legonier was a settled area, held in an intricate lacing of relationships, yet so poor that at Christmas—greatest joy of the year—the main decorations for home and church were newspapers cut into intricate patterns and hung as wallpaper, and as banners from the open rafters. "The houses had no ceilings," explains Thomas King. "If you could get some colored pages from magazines, that made it extra pretty." Fourth of July was the next exciting day. That was the first day you could get ice.

So set was the pattern, there was no way to better yourself. What jobs there were, tended to stay in one family, passed on. For the Clarks, boy or girl, there was nothing to look forward to but working cotton. And that came and went in spells: The men got the plowing—75¢ a day. The rest was for any back—50¢ a day—and the school year flexed to its cycle: planting, new each year, best to get it all in the ground on Good Friday; chopping, careful to cut away the surplus starts until the plants stand one hoe-blade apart and top those so they'll bush out; molding (mound the earth for drainage); scraping, a real fight to clear the weeds in the rich, flood-fed soil; picking . . .

Picking, that was when life picked up too. Down the rows the Clark girls went, blinking away the sweat, narrow yards-long sacks trailing between the rows, plucking the puffy white bolls 'most faster than the eye could follow. You got paid for what you picked, 75¢ a hundred pounds, maybe $1 a hundred if they needed a little extra push. Bell was the family champion. As they grew older, each of the children got to keep something from those earning times, and they learned to squirrel a little against some unknown event, some unknowable great day. No telling what Porter would bring about.

It was he who left first: Porter, fascinated by the turreted steamboats as they churned up to the landing, ready to throw a line just as it was needed; bright, cheerful, a hustler. The men liked him and one became his friend—white Captain Rucker of awesome prestige, who bent to the boy and gave him his ticket to the world: a job on his boat, first as a hand and then as a cook.

New Orleans, that was the place to live. Porter rented a room near the uptown wharfs. Shortly, he married. He worked the river now, clear up to Vicksburg and beyond. But New Orleans was his love, and with his mother dead, he sold his sisters on it, one by one. All but Bell. Even when the Atchafalaya flushed her out, Bell held her doubts. She found city life a cut over cotton some ways, but she meant to go back. This life was risky, mighty risky with the Devil.

Their area was Greenville, although most of the city couldn't have told you it existed. Bunched in a narrow area in the 14th ward, it spilled across the waterfront's shoreward spines—Magazine St. and Walnut—toward Lowerline, and along the levee where the Clarks were clustered. Bright green willow tops waved from the batture side of the levee's slope, itself shaved grassy as a lawn by the U.S. Engineers. One side edged along Audubon Park, dense with tall, mossy oaks and cypress running tangled to the river's edge. But turn around, look down, and the tag ends of a city had been swept to the edge of the railroad tracks, its streets the tailings of criss-crossing dirt streets exhausted at the bend of the levee, making for odd lengths and hidden single cuts with names that went nowhere else. The Clarks were on a little left-over triangle, from where Leake St. petered out. Whites as well as blacks crammed the area, a casual mix common to the city then, poor together. Work for the men was mostly back labor on the busy Walnut St. wharf and its crowded ferries. Work for the women, the respectable black women, was in imposing homes close by, spread like whipped cream next to dark bread.

Somewhere in one of those homes, Charity had to find a place in a hurry. Cash was too scarce. "Baby," she said to the now-brown infant nursing hungrily, encrusted little lids squeezed tight, "you got to help me out." The moment Charity could pull herself out of bed, the resourcefulness Mahalia was to inherit made its move: "Bell, see if my baby will nurse you."

"Oh, sister, I don't think so!"

"Well, see! Son Baby took Mama!"

Gingerly the squirming infant was guided to the new source . . . and instantly clamped on for dear life. A bond was formed that was to last Bell's lifetime, and beyond. Of milk, she had a generous plenty. One breast for Porterfield ("Jack" now), one for Halie, to the daily amusement of a neighbor, a midget lady drawn irresistibly to the sight: Bell stretched full-length on the floor, a pillow under her head, one child on each side, sucking away. With patient tending, Halie's eyes had cleared, and as if to compensate for all the dark, she kept them wide open as she pulled.

On Halie clung. Jack was long weaned. Bell had to get onto a job. She wasn't going to deny the child, but there were known ways:

Pepper on her nipple. Hmph, didn't faze. Vinegar? No different. Well, bitter alum from the drugstore, worse than gall. Halie just pulled away. Bell went into deep thought. Finally she got a chicken feather, wrapped it around her nipple and tied it with a thread. Halie could walk now; a rolling gait. She trotted over, hungry, leaned forward . . . and Bell blew gently on the feather. Halie rocked back, eyes big and staring. Back she came . . . the chicken feather moved . . . she jumped away. Four times, the advance and retreat, woman and child silent in the strange pageant. The fourth time, Halie backed off, stared long, then turned away without a word. Bell closed her blouse. Halie was on her own. From now on, "nursing" was a minding job, left to Bessie and Allen. But those crooked legs!

Charity, worried, had taken her to Charity Hospital. "Got me my own hospital here," chuckled Charity. "Got my name on it!" But the doctor's word left nothing to laugh about. "Sister," she droned, to Bell, "he say they got to operate. Break her bones."

"You let 'em break that child's legs?" flamed Bell. "She could end up a cripple! You let me try!"

Grease from the dishwater was known to have special properties. Morning and evening then, Bell laid Halie on the drainboard and massaged the little limbs, curved as ice tongs; hip to toe, week after month. They believed they could see some straightening.

"What you think, Hannah?"

"Some."

But curved legs and crisscrossed feet didn't still Halie, so self-sufficient soon that neither Bessie nor Allen felt too much called to keep a close eye on her and she found a life outside as rich as the gumbo bubbling on the stove. The Walnut wharf was just two blocks long, but it was a busy funnel you could get into from Water or the important street, Magazine. From the edge of its eddies of men and wagons and barges and dollies and swaying ropes, you could see steamboats and, farther on, giant ships pushing high the sky; crawling over them on mysterious errands were strange looking men, even slant-eyes. Darting in among moored ships and barges with a final bang at the barrier were the Bisso ferries, three on the run and still foot and wagon traffic lined up deep to cross over to Westwego—part of New Orleans but as remote as China from where Halie watched.

Mr. Bisso wasn't a stranger, though, big as he was: Right down from her, on Magazine, Mr. Bisso had a grocery store and bar: a standard combination, the grocery running through to the barroom like a chaser, with the middle door open for a straight shot. Children weren't allowed in the bar unless you were rushing the can—and her mama was no beer-drinker—but you could be sent to the grocery and not miss a look. Besides, wasn't her Aunt Alice working now for one of the Bisso family over on Audubon? Mr. Jung's was close by too—a busy grocery. Took at least one trip every day. A check of ice didn't keep long in the box, and food was important; not just to fill you up but for sociability. Mr. Casserta's drugstore was handy, too. And from the waterfront, the whole stretch of Magazine (from the French *magasin* for warehouse) was all shops and stands and rolling carts selling sundries and trinkets and treats like snowballs—fine-shaved ice mounded and doused with sweet sticky syrup of strong flavors and bright colors. If you had 2¢, you could get one.

Magazine flowed with life any day. "But honey-y," laughed Mahalia years later, "Fridays and Saturdays, payday, the very banquettes—the sidewalks, you know—child, they jumped! Magazine had the only sidewalks around paved smooth with cement. And that street came alive with the gamblers! On their knees they'd be, shaking those dice, or throwing those cards: Pittypat . . . seven could play that; Cotch . . . seven could play that too; Georgia Skin . . . that was like what you call it? Blackjack.

Coon Can . . . just two play that. I don't play cards myself and never did; I don't approve of all that. Those men knew it wasn't right, too: see a preacher come along, they'd jump up and take off their hats and stand 'til he passed by. Preachers today have forfeited much of that respect, and it's a pity, but in that day it was strong even among the gamblers. I was little, but I saw it all."

WATER STREET had nearly emptied now: Duke closer to her job, but no real distance; the others, as they got steady work, setting up in a cluster. Bessie went to Uncle Porter's wife. Bell, with Celie and Jack, was two blocks away, the only black in the 300 block of Walnut. Hannah had Son Baby. Atchafalaya (Fred), at odds with his mother, stayed with Charity but was mostly in for meals—at 16, much too busy to be followed by an adoring Halie or Peter. Anyway, Halie had a bigger preoccupation now. She'd learned "that's your daddy." It wasn't easy to catch a look at him except Saturdays, and then he'd be busy with all those men. She'd watch a long while for a sight of him, laughing, beautiful to look at, from a distance, before she eased up to him on the brick banquette. She could tell he wasn't easy with her, and he didn't much want to talk, the way he'd edge off. But what little he did say was in a nice voice, with a nice way about him, even turning you aside.

She fell in love with her father. If she couldn't visit with him, she could talk to his folks next door. They were nice. Nobody going stop her doing that.

The senior Johnny Jacksons were added to Halie's visiting list. Most times Mrs. Jackson was at home. Years back, the family had left off truck farming at Kenner, just outside New Orleans, and Mr. Jackson had gravitated to the waterfront. As a longshoreman straw boss on the Walnut wharf, he had his crew's hiring and firing. "His word was law on whether a non-union man was bumped when a union man applied," says Edward Burnette, the grandson he reared. Mrs. Jackson kept busy with her house, her church, and the two children of her daughter Jeannette—mostly off in vaudeville as half of the comedy act of Camp and Camp that played the big traveling tent shows, so little Edward could chatter to Halie of Ma Rainey, Bessie Smith, Mamie Smith, Jack Wiggins, King Rastus Brown, Stove Pipe. Remote stars to conjure.

With them, too, lived Mrs. Jackson's mother, Sarah Lemore—an ex-slave who lived to be 104; you could listen to her stories 'til she drowsed off.

Halie learned here that there was another, entirely different kind of church from theirs at Plymouth Rock Baptist. Mrs. Jackson was a Seventh Day Adventist, such an oddity in New Orleans that she had to go clear across town to Delachaise St. to find a church. For her, Saturday was Sunday. That meant you had to be quiet.

Sometimes Halie, Celie, Jack, and Edward played together in Audubon

Park, pulling pepper grass or roasting acorns. But Peter, older, had an even better place to go: Charity took him with her to the Henry Rightors at Millaudon and McCarty. It was an old New Orleans thought, and accepted, carrying your youngsters to work with you soon as they were old enough, especially if there were small children in the madam's family.

Charity had young Henry Rightor's care as the extra on her job, and he and Peter became close playmates. Search for one, you'd find the other, in the dim, cool, two-story house or outside in the side garden or the big backyard with a basketball court.

When Halie had grown enough to keep from underfoot and play quietly, she too got this first sight of a life beyond Greenville. The three Rightor girls were much older, but she could play with Henry.

The Clarks were a force now at the Rightors—a bright, warm, white family who embraced the Clarks en masse: Charity was maid—Hunter, she went by—"and I'm named right, you always got me hunting something." Bell was cook. Bessie and Rhoda came in extra. Papa (Rev.) Clark paid calls when he came to the city. "We really loved them," says Marguerite Rightor Ellis. "All the Clarks were sweet, outgoing, gentle, good-looking people." With a unique sense of justice. Bell fed Halie and Peter lunch one day with the rest of the children. Finished, Halie started to dart away, busy as a bird. "You come back here and play out that lunch!" Bell cried.

"Charity and Bell had wonderful personalities; kind, so quick to laugh," says Mrs. Ellis. "And we liked Peter. But Halie! She was a delight. She amazed us!"

At this point, says Alice Rightor McCall, Halie was "very skinny, very black, very homely." And still so bowlegged that the Rightor children picked up Peter's name for her, "Fishhooks." When she walked, her feet scissored. Long years later, she told a group of crippled children in her audience at Montclair, N.J.—a rare time she mentioned it in public—"When I was little, I was terribly deformed. My legs were crooked and bent. Your young hearts don't understand what has happened to you," she added, looking back. For scrawny little Halie didn't. She beamed. She bubbled. She darted like light. She sang, or she hummed. She was like the mosquito hawks she tried to catch: ugly if you looked at their separate parts, beautiful when they spread their wings. And vibrant as she danced out a song for the Rightors for the sheer delight of it . . .

First you put your two knees together tight,
Sway to the left and sway to the right . . .

A TINY FLECK anonymous on the city's surface, while Halie was soaking up the sights, she absorbed the sounds. Singing came as natural as speech and simultaneously. Her first song was a hymn taught her by an old man who sunned himself on the levee: *Oh Pal Oh God.* But now she was *Balling the Jack.* At some risk. Mama better not catch her. For although New Orleans was a singing, dancing city, a Catholic city with a *laissez faire* which scandalized more sedate visitors, most of the black population was Protestant—especially the ones from the country. Of these, a solid proportion were strict Baptist: no lowdown jazz (jass, so said by some), no cards, no high life. The Clarks were firmly in that pew. Papa had seen to that. But far from leading a dour life, there was laughter in their homes and joy in their churches—mainly Baptist and that even freer offshoot of the Baptists, the Sanctified, or Holiness Church. There, the jubilees were quick to bring the shout, quick to send the members into the high spirit. Sing to the Lord! Shout to His Glory! Dance to His Name! (Dancing was a holy thing if the dancing was in the spirit. Outside, you were stepping with the Devil.) In any four-block square, if there were twice the barrooms you'd expect—and none empty—there were twice the churches . . . little wooden churches, each with its faithful, the pastor subsisting on an outside job and whatever the members could bring from the yard, the garden, the river. Services were Wednesday, Friday, and four times Sunday, and some mustered three choirs: adult, youth, and children's. The solemn hymns were the province of the adult choir; it was the congregation that took out on the jubilees.

At four, with a voice twice as big as she was, Halie ranged before the Plymouth Rock pulpit in its children's choir, singing loud and clear. . . . *Jesus loves me* . . . and *Oh, hand me down my silver trumpet, Gabriel.* . . . On the outside, though, the other sounds you could hear! The strawberry lady, the scissors man, the blackberry lady, the charcoal man . . . whoever moved, made a song. The waist-bare men, muscles rippling, bending to their loads on the wharf. Sweating black gangs laying rails on the tracks . . . a lead man set the beat as he set the stroke, and the songs rang out with the hammers. There were songs for games on the levee: *All of my round, shoo round/ Go choose your lover, shoo round/ Side by side, shoo round/ Back to back, shoo round/ Face to face, shoo round/ Now choose your lover, shoo round.* Even going to the store for your mama had a chant: *Quartee beans/ Quartee rice/* Lagniappe *salt meat/ Make it taste nice.* The shoeshine boy whistled while he snapped his cloth . . . a lone drinker whistled as he wavered through the night. The best bands in town rolled 'round in the day, advertising big dances, fish fries, like of that—black musicians on trucks with the tailgate down so the sliphorn could slide free. Ragtime jazz, they called it. You could hear them on Magazine; Water St. wasn't enough 'count.

The most famous redlight district in America, Storyville—legal and lavish in its fringe entertainment—was distant, downtown, flanking the French Quarter at Basin St., where the great slave market once flourished in Congo Square beyond Rampart and slaves unwittingly rooted jazz in their once-a-week night's release with homemade music. She knew Funky

Butt Hall was down that way on Perdido: the only public dance hall for Negroes. Halie caught the name and the laughter; she couldn't catch all the back-of-hand stories. But Greenville had its own drama, tuned to blues in the night from a doorstoop, or a cranked-up Victrola; the sounds drifting down the block from doorways left open to draw the river air—or erupting in the blare and flash of a fight. Never long near Aunt Duke's door. "Get off my premises with your mess!" Her voice lashed the dark. Halie could hear the scramble as the culprits fled.

There were dance songs, too, reaching out to the sidewalk from barrooms night and day—they never closed—so Halie could pick up on the words and fill in her own steps for the Rightors—

Then you walk around the floor so quick and light,
Hurry up and scurry up with all your might,
Put your loving arms wa-ay out in space . . .

Halie's little crooked legs turned to the sinuous cadence of her voice. . . .

You do the Eagle Rock with style and grace,
Put your left foot forward and bring it back,
Now that's what I call balling the jack!

Wild applause for the dark, glowing mite from the circle of Rightors, her first white audience . . . and her last for many years. For suddenly, mysteriously, Charity died. She was barely 30.

Bell had darkest suspicions. Into Charity's life had come Clement Smith, a small "high yellow" man with a nature at odds with the sisters and heartily disliked by the Rightors, who were drawn into all the Clarks' affairs. "Oh, madam, he poisoned Charity! He did!" sobbed Bell. It was a thought quick to come by. "Not that it applied to Charity, but there was a lot of poisoning known or talked in those days," says Allen Clark, Sr. "People dislike you, they could carry that kind of stuff under their fingernail, drop it in your drink, or in your food, poison you. That was a known way. Bell had cause for it to come to mind."

Of course, nothing could be proved and nothing openly questioned. White law wasn't even a thought. Too chancy; anybody's head could get laid open for no cause. But Bell's words weren't thrown off lightly: Didn't Bell have second sight? (Clement Smith was to die less quietly not long after—in a car which plunged off a cliff "somewhere up North.") Charity herself had known she was going, a month before. On May 12, 1918, Son Baby—18 and just enlisted in the Navy—came to see her. He didn't tell Charity he was being shipped out. Time for that when she was better. Still she burst into tears, startling him; it was so unlike Charity. "I won't see you again, Son Baby. When you come looking, I be gone."

She was right. So Halie's first journey, of thousands to come, was to Gumstump Plantation. She never wanted to go back, but she never forgot. First the sight of her mother in the pine coffin, not with them now on the coach but somewhere. Long hours with clicking sounds and rushing steam on "The Plug." Switching to the L. R. & N., "The Windy," then the climb down at Torras and into a wagon for a mule-pull to the landing. A town, Naples, had once stood there: gone now, cut away by the converging slash of Red River, Old River, and the Atchafalaya. But the landing remained, by custom and convenience of a father and son who operated a flat-bottomed pontoon ferry, a barge, really, attached by ropes to a little gasoline-powered tug chugging its sternwheel indoors. If they weren't on your side of the river, you hollered across. Passengers could stand or sit, as they pleased, outside on the tug; the flatboat was for buggies and wagons, two at a time—or one wagon and a coffin. Halie, Peter, and the grownups climbed into the tug, the engine cranked to a roar, and at the end of the ropes, across the rushing waters, the flatboat moved out behind. Load the wagon again . . . the last mile a lonesome long way for the pine box jiggling the floor as the wheel rims rattle the road to the long rows of Gumstump Quarters.

Finally the house; the white wooden church next by; and Charity joined three generations before her in the churchyard.

A long road.

The way to a new life for Halie and Peter was one short thump. From Aunt Duke. "I'm keeping them," she decreed.

3

When you followed Leake Ave. around the levee from Greenville across Magazine just half-dozen blocks, you were in Pinching Town. It had a character all its own, its very name a wry joke for themselves—an irony, a sly, defensive play on better-living Pension Town over Carrollton way, built up after the Spanish-American War when whites and black landowners sold row on row of houses on 25-foot lots cut deep for a backyard, to blacks with mustering-out pay: "*We* were pinching pennies," explains Mrs. Angelle "Jack" Marshall, Aunt Duke's near neighbor.

"Pinching Town" helped pass over the name they heard from most better-off blacks of other areas: "Niggertown," blotting out the sprinklings of white families who shared their poverty—and their special brand of plenty. Its streets were dirt. So were most New Orleans "side streets," but those in mainly white areas got a spread of clam shells from Lake Pontchartrain. This was bare dirt, land cheated from the river. The slightest rain, and it was mud. A hard pour, and it was a bog. Horses pulling wagons broke their legs trying to wrench free. Trucks and cars churned helplessly, trapped. "Folks used to keep bricks and shovels handy, to help those who got stuck," Mahalia said years later. "But that's the way people used to do everything around there; they helped each other."

Pinching Town itself knew how to handle the mud it lived with for months. "We wore boots," says Mrs. Marshall. "And everything was with the wheelbarrows, even the Jumbo Man." He sold the jumbo bottles of soft drinks, important if you had a sweet tooth, a skinny purse, and a ban on hard liquor. Duke could drink two; so could Bell. On an offer of another jumbo free if she could drink it on the spot, Duke downed a third. She was never one to ignore a challenge.

This was a back pocket of the 16th ward, chopped and patched, no more than a dozen blocks wide and half-dozen streets deep from the cut-tail ends at the levee to—abruptly—the homes of the well-to-do and the wealthy to which many of them went daily to work: maids, cooks, laundresses, gardeners, handymen, and grandest and rare, butlers. Black help, almost without exception. A white domestic in New Orleans was a curiosity, suspect.

Pinching Town whites ran the scatterings of groceries and barrooms or worked the wharves; or otherwise "worked out." As in so many obscure New Orleans neighborhoods then, this was a long-set mold: mainly Afro—some speaking French—laced with Italians, Irish, and Germans, their children flowing in and out of each other's homes, sure of a little something from the kitchen, black or white: spaghetti, or gingercake, or flour biscuits sopped with syrup. Only the elders knew a day would come, inevitably, when "You're too old to play with them now. It don't look right."

The rest of New Orleans could hardly have found its way into the honeycomb. Only the employers knew, come to deliver the cook home in a storm, or worried about a long illness, or drawn to mourn a death or by some other urgency. (Getting the maid's husband out of jail on blue Monday was an accepted obligation of an honorable white employer.) The "Governor Fleet"—the U.S. Engineers—was just over the levee. They wouldn't let you plant on their space, but there were leftover bits of place by the tracks where you could put in a little sugar cane to press for syrup, or a few stalks of corn, or beans: nobody minded.

Except for Boston and Papa—holdouts in Legonier—by June, 1918, when Charity died, the rest of the Clarks had circled in here, including Uncle Porter, shifting with the ebb and flow of whim and vacancy but always close by. Moving was no problem when your biggest possessions were your bed and your mother wit. Young Rhodie had died the year before, cause unknown. But Bell had quit Walnut St. for Pinching Town, settling Celie and Jack at 7471 Esther: a weather-gray building that had been a grocery across the batture but was now lengthwise to the tracks. Bell had two front rooms and a kitchen, $8 a month. She had her eye on something finer, half of 7467 next door, for Duke. Alice, married to Nathaniel Stamps, and Hannah, now Robinson, split a double just around the block, 147–149 Cherokee—Allen living with Hannah, who worked steady on elegant St. Charles Ave. Charity, with Bessie, lived just around that corner, at 7447 Ann. Duke, married to mild Emanuel Paul, a bricklayer and plasterer, was three blocks away in half a double on Gen. Scott, a one-block street whose twin rows of tiny rent houses were packed like soda crackers, gone green: all except high-raised white Broadway Missionary Baptist Church, where Johnny Jackson came. It was to 144 Gen. Scott that Duke had brought Charity, too ill to cope. The half of the double on Esther that Bell's exits faced across her alley opened up right in the Lord's time, as Charity passed. It had a porch, a shadetree, and best of all, a shaded backyard plenty big for chickens and a garden. The roof leaked, but so did Bell's; you set pots and pans. It had once been painted, grayish. What if it trembled from the trains? Bell fixed *hers* so nothing broke. Still, a visitor to the folks behind Bell fell clear out of bed one night, to the children's delight. Life was full of things. In time, Uncle Emanuel would brick the backyard, instead of its being mud; fix everything about the house, in fact, but the roof: he left that leaky to spite the landlord, who wouldn't pay him for any of his work.

'TIL NOW, Halie had been free to run her feet, exploring. With Duke in charge, she thumped against her first wall. Aunt Duke had stern ideas about children, and they didn't include play. No more running the streets. You stay out of trouble. Stay in the house. You old enough to start learning to do. And I won't have worldly songs in my house. Atchafalaya, you be quiet! This is *my* business. Halie, you stay in the path. Church got plenty music. And you mind me. You going to learn to do *right*. And you going to learn how to *work*.

She was five.

Peter wasn't pinned down so easily. He escaped before sunup to Audubon Park, making himself handy by the horses, hunting golf balls, cleaning around the clubhouse, caddying, earning some change. But first, daily, checking out the Governor Fleet. "Can you use a boy?" "What can you do?" "I can be a water boy!" . . . 'til finally, he made it. If Duke pressed him too close, he'd go stay by Aunt Bessie's for a while. "But Halie, she was humble," says cousin Celie Taylor. "A good child!" cries Aunt Bessie Kimble.

Eager, quick to learn, by the time she could see over the ironing board, she'd learned how to pass the heated flatiron over a cedar branch to make it slip, cleaning the iron's face first with a chunk of red brick; learned to sweep to suit Aunt Duke; learned to dust without smudging the soot from the trains and shipstacks, without breaking a thing; learned to scrub the bare cypress floor creamy yellow using brick pounded to dust—rub and wipe, a patch at a time.

But she learned at some expense. "Spare the rod and spoil the child." That's how Duke's papa'd raised *them*. ("He'd whip them pretty fast with anything in his hand, nothing light to whip you with; I come up under that too," says Son Baby. "I guess Duke got some of that from him—she was rough on her own son. I've see her tie him to a bed to whip him, back in Legonier. That was her own belief on how to go about raising children.") Papa's treatment hadn't quenched Duke's spirit. Rather than cry because her hair wouldn't grow long enough to fix pretty like Bell's and Hannah's—a source of real anguish—she regularly launched a fury with fate and her mother. "Duke was such a case," laughs Celie, "mama used to tell me her temper was full-grown before she was, and nobody better cross her."

In the neighborhood, Duke was known as a hot pepper, says Pearl Robinson Hunter. Small, wiry, a compacted force fueling an instinct for righteous rule, Duke was as fiercely protective as she was flashy. Nobody else better raise a hand against Halie. But this child going to *mind*. Forget a job or just set your mouth wrong and out came the cat-nine-tails. Or worse, Aunt Duke grabbed the broomstick. Now kneel in that broke-up brick.

Halie tried to learn not to cry.

Gentle Bell could hardly stand it, yet she dare not interfere. Duke ruled the family. There was one chance. She told Mrs. Rightor, "Madam, they're treating that child something awful! Can't you do something about it?"

Duke worked for Mrs. George Plant, several blocks over on elegant St. Charles. But Mrs. Rightor sensed that wasn't the way. . . . She had an inspiration. A rapt Bell saw her print a letter: "We have heard the way you are treating that child. If you don't stop, we will take steps." She finished with a chilling signature: a Black Hand.

She had struck one sure note of terror. Today we call it the Mafia. Fear of the Black Hand ran through New Orleans like its drainage canals—under every section, black and white, high and low. Especially since June of 1907, when a child, Walter Lamana, was kidnapped, cut up, and dumped in a sack into a swamp, the dread Black Hand signed to the crime. "Papa wouldn't let us go out on the street for a long, long time," says Beth Rightor George. "The Black Hand was the terror of our childhood."

In Pinching Town, the fear thrilled deep. "The Black Hand would come down on you, people would just disappear," shivers Celie. "It kept the children in the house. No trouble making them stay in . . . tell them the Black Hand was out there, we go in the house!"

All of Bell's round bulk glowed when she reported several days later: "Mrs. Rightor, you ought to see how nice they treating that child now!"

It didn't last. Hearing her cries, the neighborhood muttered. If there was time to run hide under Aunt Bell's skirts ("that's the sweetest person God ever put on this earth," Mahalia would remember), Bell might be able to talk Duke out of it. "Whip her next time, Sister; not this time, next time." The decision was Duke's. She ruled not by size—if Bell was 12 o'clock, Duke would be 6:15—but by sheer concentrated force of temper. She's just like those cat-nine-tails, Halie early decided. "Mainly I learned to take my lumps and go about my business."

That business at first was a ragtag Pinching Town tapestry of three bright skeins: McDonogh 24 School, Mt. Moriah Mission Baptist Church, and play with the neighborhood.

School was hardest come by. Not that it wasn't close: on the Pinching Town side of Burdette St., directly off the grandeur of St. Charles. Like the city's forty other McDonogh public schools, its name honored the philanthropist whose bequest had funded much of the dual public school system: the white, and the black elementary system (Negro high schools were just being introduced). The building was wooden, raised high to create a basement, since New Orleans was too wet to dig below ground. Above, two sets of rooms were divided by a wide hall: boys left, girls on the right. (The white schools went further; boys and girls didn't go to the same school.) The basement was divided, too, each side opening onto its separate yard—boys left, girls right, and a high fence to enforce it. "Actually it was one of the better schools for blacks," says Celestine Curtis Graves, a principal now. "Heating was by potbellied stove, but so were every other school's rooms. At least McDonogh 24 rooms were large and bright."

Classes were reading, writing, arithmetic. But the elderly spinsters who taught them dug into their own pay ($45 a month) for classroom aids. Lantern slides projected on the wall or a sheet seemed magic indeed to Halie, hungry for all she could grasp.

Discipline rated high. Principal A. C. Priestley stood at the gate every morning with a strap behind his back, and latecomers got a swat. It created some remarkable runs to get in line for morning inspection—hands, fingernails, hair, ears, teeth. To anybody who didn't pass inspection: "Go home and come *right back!*"

It wasn't being sent home from school that Halie had to worry about. Aunt Duke had her fill the tin tub every night and scrub with Lifebuoy, and she tried to be neat as she could every morning with what she had. No, it was *getting* to school that was the problem. If ironing piled up, or an aunt needed a replacement for being sick, Halie had to miss. She rarely managed a full week. In a perpetual press of trying to catch up, she dug her heels in against the slow backward slide. She learned, too, to swallow something harder: shame. It seared as deep red as the pot-bellied stove she had to stare at, day after day. She had to sit behind it, she decided, because the teacher didn't want to look at her. She was ugly, crooked-legged, ragged, and she must smell bad. Else why wouldn't teacher let her bring her paper up like everybody else, instead of having to pass it up? Besides that, her hair was nappy and too short to plait and tie big bows on, like the other girls. And if she wore those big old shoes—all she had—they went flop-flop. So she didn't. "Mahalia had to go barefoot to school even with icicles!" says an indignant Annise Jackson Scully.

If she just had a pair of tennis!

Ice was rare in New Orleans, but it came, freezing and slippery on the banquette bricks the day Halie quietly made a decision: she'd ask her daddy. Celie came from next door bundled up good before the two cousins headed out. It was Saturday evening—Deep South evening, mid-afternoon. They knew he'd have to be in his barbershop.

He was. So were his four children from Zimple St. Seeing her coming, Johnny Jackson reacted "like he always did when we'd go, like he was frightened to death those other children would see her," says Celie. "He'd try to head her off at the door, speak to her there and get her out before she was in."

But it was icy and she was barefoot. She came in. "Please, daddy, I need a pair of tennis. I got no money. Could I have some money for tennis, daddy?"

"Don't you call him daddy!" exploded the eldest girl. " 'Cause he's *not* your daddy! He's *our* daddy!"

"He's my daddy as much as he's your daddy," flared Mahala. The three girls erupted. "He's *our* daddy!" . . . "Don't you call him daddy!" . . . "He's *not* your daddy!"

"He's all of our daddies," cried Mahala.

"All right, you children, that's enough; you quieten down. Chocolate, I don't have it; you better go."

"All right, daddy," she said quietly and left, Celie trying to fall in with her crisscrossing feet. "Bye, Uncle Johnny," called Celie, to bedevil him.

"Refusing wasn't any different," says Celie; "every time we went, if she asked, he'd say the same thing: he didn't have it. But she never got discouraged from going to see him. She'd even hunt for him when she knew he had to cross our way from Carrollton to come to Broadway Baptist. He was a deacon there. Sometime he'd speak then, on the sidewalk. Then I'd see her feelings collapse—you know the way a child will get its hopes up, against all reason. Sometimes it might be just an ice cream she'd ask. But I never saw him give her a cent."

She never talked it over, then or later. "She would take her hurts and keep them, mostly."

Jeers from the others at school didn't seem to matter one way or the other now. She just whipped them. They'd see. She kept silent as her father's daughter passed her in the hall without a word. They *were* better livers. And she didn't envy Peter—envy wasn't in her—the times she got to go with him to visit *his* father, David Hunter, when he came in from Legonier to visit his sister on Freret St.

Tougher to bear without a shield was when Mr. O. C. W. Taylor, the only male on the faculty, started athletic teams. Basketball. Baseball! "There's be games and practice after school, and I'd see Mahalia with tears standing in her eyes because she couldn't play," says Mr. Taylor. "She could never be on the team because she had a job at this time at the Jewish country club. Somebody her aunts knew must have got it for her. But the tears would really fall when she couldn't *get* to work, when she was kept after school." Her offense: humming. Her teacher couldn't believe she didn't know she was doing it.

She was 10. But tall, passing for older. To get to Lakewood Country Club was an hour's ride by two streetcars, and then a walk. Mr. Taylor met her often on "The Royal Blue Line"—the streetcar whose route ended at elite New Orleans Country Club. (As its assistant headwaiter, Mr. Taylor made more money than he made at school.) "Mostly the child kept her own counsel. She was seemingly very proud. I think she confided in me a bit because I was in the nature of a domestic too. She said her job was moving dishes off and on, and tidying up. She said she needed the job. And she wanted to make something of herself."

WHATEVER HER HURTS, she could throw them off when she headed out to play. She wiggled her schedule, always, to manage that before Duke got home from cooking the Plants' supper. She'd do quiet things with neat, stay-at-home Celie: plait grasses and tie a ribbon around for a doll—she had no other—or make one with corn shucks, "Aunt Jemima," a black scrap sewed on for the face . . . play jacks under the hackberry tree up front . . . make their extra-special treat—dig the insides out of a fat dill pickle and stuff a peppermint stick inside. Peter financed the treats. Second-best was sweet Magnolia condensed milk. She never got enough.

But more often she was the tomboy. Playing ball on the street or up on the levee, she could throw so hard that "I'm not catching if Halie pitches!" announced Annise Jackson (no relation but they passed for cousins). Halie's feet crossed too much to jump rope so she turned, for Mamá and Catherine Hill and Eunice Bonner and Florence White and Bea Thomas. Her "hots" were fearsome. (And maybe a little just-desserts for both her nicknames, "Hooks" and "Black"—affectionate but stinging when Negro social levels were graded by skin tones, with black at the much-scorned bottom.) With George Bonner, Henry Grady, Veedie Jackson, she caught fish and shrimp and crabs in the river shallows, and crawfish in the deep ditches in Audubon Park or beside the tracks. You had to watch out for snakes, but Halie had a reputation of not being afraid of anything—or anyone, except Aunt Duke. They all rolled down the levee curled like barrels—Halie was faster than anyone—or rolling inside an abandoned cistern they'd tipped on its side: high adventure. Sometimes they'd stack bricks and make a fire for roasting sweet potatoes, or corn, or a fish. If she skinned a knee or tore her dress, she'd catch it from Duke—the whip or the broomstick. It didn't stop her. Bright-faced, with a ringing laugh, she was happy to visit with the grownups as she darted in and out of friends' homes (they too fearful of Duke to venture into hers), quick with the smile that was to become the delight of photographers the world over.

When other children—black or white—meddled her, "she'd twist on those hoop legs and pat her behind; that would tell them what to do. She was kicks!" says Mrs. Hunter, watching from her stoop.

Still skinny, never turning down an offer of food, Halie was everywhere. A raggedy, barefoot, hook-legged Pinching Town pet. "Don't you scorn that child!" mothers warned their own; "*you* just lucky; she's a poor little orphan without mother or father to do for her."

Oddly, she was never ill. She might *feel* cold, but she never caught one.

THEN ONCE again her props caved in. For two babes. The children were Atchafalaya's and Sook's (for *Sucre,* sugar; few used her real name, Rose). Atchafalaya—now a handsome, restless high-liver—had taken a wife who "thought the Heavens opened up when she saw him," says Celie. But he was better at producing babies than caring for them, so that Duke, worried over Sook's pregnancy, moved them in with her. That infant, Duke's first grandson, died of pneumonia despite all Duke's ministrations. Sook's second was Isabell ("Doodutz"); the third, Manuel ("Brisko"). At this juncture Atchafalaya decided he was moving out and up—to Chicago; maybe get over to Cincinnati, see how Uncle Porter's making out. All around him, the pass riders were funneling workers into factories of the Middle West and East in a mass relocation which began with World War I, a major shift of southern Negro population taking courage for the move in the company of friends and relatives—the trek made easy by a train pass when enough men were signed up, the move made alluring by word of easy money and sportin' life and sloughing of color restraints. "From down here the place to go was Chicago," says Thomas King; "just as in World War II it was California or Washington, D.C."

Atchafalaya left. For Halie, the sun went down, just like Bessie Smith sang on the record . . . the house dark and the air close without him breezing in and out, having his way no matter what Aunt Duke say; beautiful with his clothes and his friends Duke called shiftless but who laughed a lot. His was the sinful life; she didn't feel any call to follow even if Duke wouldn't've skinned her alive. But this was Atchafalaya, that her own mother had claimed as his Second Mother. "Let him make out," she prayed, on her knees for her nightly prayers.

Sook stayed, but she wasn't to be tied down either. (By Duke, you followed *her* rules. Hadn't Duke carried on 'til Sook changed her baby girl's name from Victoria to Isabell, after Duke's sister? And named her boy Manuel, for Duke's husband?) Sook eased away. "Sook mostly lived to herself and left the children with Duke," nods cousin Allen, Sr. "They were friendly, very close; she just left the children to be raised." Duke's eye had but one place to fall: Halie was taken out of school. She hadn't managed to finish the 4th grade.

To lose both school and Atchafalaya was desperate. But don't waste time on what you can't help. Thing was to get those children in shape and keep them that way and minding, while you got your work done. It never seemed to run out. Sweep and dust every day; scrub the floors every second day except Sunday. (If it was muddy outside, in between, mop against that. Better not have no tracks when Aunt Duke got home or out come the stick.) Empty the ashes from the fireplace and the cook stove and make the kitchen spotless, stove included. ("They'd pass their hand over the stove with their pocket handkerchief," says Celie; "my mama too, except she'd never whip me if I was neglectful; she'd punish me some other way.") Get the charcoal furnace going for the heavy wash in the shade of the chinaball tree out back—not the fig tree; too low and besides, snakes come up in that. Draw the big tub full of water from the cistern and set it on, stir in a little lye to cut the grease, and get the scrubboard going—the rippled tin board had a nice sound to it. When the water got up a good boil, pour in a little coal oil—bring your clothes just as *white*. Got your rinse water on the benches. Now those clothes ready for hanging. See how Aunt Duke like *that*. ("You come through and look at her line, baby, it did you good to see it!" says Aunt Bessie.)

Ironing she caught when she could: fire the furnace, set on bricks in the kitchen so it won't burn the floor; three, four brick-cleaned flatirons heating so one always be ready after you cook the starch for the dresses. If you put a little candle in, or a pinch of sugar, like Annise' mama say, you might not need anything else to slip the iron smooth, but you better not have one lump in it. Cook what Aunt Duke set out, or get it from the garden in back. Seasonal, you and Celie wrap your heads good and muzzle your nose with one hand while you beat the moss pulled from inside all the mattresses, then shake out the moss-dust; now pick clean the moss Peter helped you all pull off the big oaks by the park, and stuff it in the fresh-washed ticking. (The aunts would sew it up; too heavy for small arms.) Trim the lamps. Now what Aunt Duke want at the grocery?

It was an exciting day when Florence flew 'round to say they were getting up a *night* school! ("Halie wasn't the only child pulled from school to tend family," says Bessie. "Plenty like her. You see many a child balancing a bundle of fresh-ironed clothes on her head; mamas took in washing, ironing at home, get 75¢ a big bundle.") For a time she tried. But housework, cooking, caring for the kids—a third, Gussie Hill, left by their neighbor—church, choir, running the track for coal . . . even Halie hadn't enough steam to fuel it all. But how was she going to make something of herself? Get a better living? She *knew* what she wanted to be.

Quietly one day, Halie headed out. It was Friday and she might catch him crossing over from Carrollton. . . . Sure enough. And not a soul around to make him uneasy. "Daddy, please could you put me in the House of Detention where they put the bad girls?"

"Why you want that, Chocolate?"

"They send *them* to *school!*"

He shook his head. "I couldn't do that, Chocolate. It's not for me to say." She stood mute. "I got to go now. You be good, Chocolate."

She turned, rocking in her trot. She hadn't scrubbed the porch and Auntie meant those pots and pans to *shine.*

If the kids got too bad, she'd whip them good and threaten them with another whipping if they told Aunt Duke—who'd beat Mahalie for laying a hand on them. ("We'd keep quiet," says Isabell Duskin Lazard, "because we knew if we talked, we'd catch it next day.") There was one time she could count on them to be still. Atchafalaya had left behind his Grafonola, too bulky to bother with. And what records! Because they were Atchafalaya's—whom his mother adored, though she never gave off trying to change him—Duke wouldn't touch them. But that music wasn't to be heard in her house, now she had the complete saying of it.

By day, though, crank up and who's to say? Best, Mahala liked Bessie Smith. Mamie Smith had a prettier, higher voice, but Bessie's come so full and round. It dug right down and kept at you. You could hear her voice even after the record stopped. *Careless Love, oh careless love. . . .* To the entrancement of Isabell and Brisko, Halie would sing with the record, working her mouth around so she'd get the sounds just right. She didn't dream one day she'd meet that trumpet backing Bessie: Louie Armstrong.

This was a time when people lined up for blocks to buy a new Bessie Smith blues. Might not have coal, but they got more fire out of her. And here was a child sound just like her! Unknown to Halie, a goodly few of Pinching Town regularly gathered on the sidewalk to listen. "You couldn't tell one from the other!" cries Isabell. Those songs were just right for scrubbing to.

Out back in the sunshine, busting suds, she'd be more apt to take out on a jubilee. *Hand me down my silver trumpet, Gabriel. . . .* That made you feel better. And the work fly: Florence and Bea, Henry, Edna Halter, all them waiting to play. It wasn't too often, when Florence looked in back, that she needed to pitch in so Halie could finish up. Tuck Brisko under one arm, grab Isabell and she was ready, wiping the sweat as she went. The neighbors watched from their doorstoops and shook their heads. "That child's the black sheep," sighed Corinne Looper. "They all think Celie's so pretty," said her sister, Rose Monica Levi.

Two occupations were both work and play, so it didn't matter *when* you finished up: drifting wood in, for the cookstove; and for heat, kicking stone coal. Not from the I.C. Their cars had detectives on, so said. But the City Belt.

Slowing 'round the bend, blowing for the turn, finding it necessary to stop often while heading in for the coming stop at Greenville and the sugar cane refinery, the City Belt crew's work somehow required their looking straight ahead, so how could they see the dark little swarm hook on for the ride down—Halie agile as any boy and stronger than many—then swarm up to scuffle the coal, kick off the smaller "nut" coal and throw off the lumps, the prized stone coal, each fall marked by eye, to be claimed later? The stray stalks of cane near the refinery, to chew on, were just *lagniappe.*

Kicking coal was a known Pinching Town province, so when they walked over to the Walnut ferry, while they were down that way, and begged a ride, "Here come the coal hustlers!" hailed Mr. Grannison, the ferryman, agreeing to "One time." It made a nice break, if you could catch it.

Brisko unexpectedly turned into an asset when a white trainman, Hot Lips (they never knew his name, his lips earned him this one) came to a full stop on their curve and watched Brisko showing off with his "elephant dance": Hey! Hot Lips give Brisko a nickel and everybody else! A new "hustling" adjunct was born. Hot Lips would blow for Brisko. After the dance, after the nickels, off Hot Lips would go, coal kickers clamped onto the car "like flies on glue paper," says Edmond Castine, clinging too.

Fair game. Manna for the poor. And in the sharing of Pinching Town, a respectable church woman like Cousin Baby Rosa Williams wasn't ashamed to walk the track. An imposing six feet tall, she had the reach to hoist Halie on top. "I'd put her up on the coal; she get her a basket full—basket she'd begged from the grocery man—she'd throw some down for my sack. Sometime be a string of us, down the track. Usually lots of coal. I helped it be enough, too, if the car was there. Halie and me start to go, I'd holler 'Come back!'—too much in the sack. Halie was strong: I'd squat down, Halie'd help me put it on my shoulder." And glad to. Wasn't Halie welcome to step inside with Cousin Baby's daughter Lena for cake when she made her neighborhood rounds? But after hustling, like as not, "No time! Thank you, ma'am! Church tonight!"

Halie'd found a real home.

4

"Let it out, Mahala! You've got it! Let—it—*out!* Now let's try again." Young Oozie Robinson's withered arm began to jump, a sure sign he was getting worked up at his lead soprano. He tucked it under his other elbow and the Mt. Moriah youth choir started again, Mahala stretching her throat inwardly, ready to let it out. She was entirely blissful.

From first awareness . . . a dark mote against the green willows learning her first hymn; in Plymouth Rock by her mama or on the floor below the pulpit when church was crowded; listening to Papa Clark, in from Legonier . . . right from the first, singing, praying and church were one in her life, immutable, a presence under every other activity. She earnestly loved everything she knew about God and hoped He'd notice her.

"Seek the Lord where He may be found; serve Him in the days of your youth, so when you grow old, He may not depart from you." It was the favorite text of Rev. Clark, who'd chosen Mt. Moriah after checking the half-dozen Baptist churches within blocks, and the Sanctified too, during his long visits after the Merrick cotton was baled. He often took over the Mt. Moriah pulpit then, and held long discussions with would-be preachers at whichever daughter's home he gave his presence to (always an honor).

Halie liked to think of his words when she did her work. But she didn't need to even think when she ran of a Saturday to help the steward ladies get ready for Sunday. Halie loved to make the pews shine and sweep the floor for God. Passing by and hearing Halie's unmistakable voice, Aunt Bessie might look in. "Child, what you doing? 'I'm cleaning the church!' And just laughing. Just as likely, she be on her knees scrubbing—she loved that—while she singing and laughing and talking away."

True, some Sunday mornings she'd get to the church grounds and veer off, start to play, out of sight, she hoped . . . 'til a smack brought her upright or as near as her legs let her, eyeballing Mr. Reuben Hack himself, out from the door and searching for strays. "Inside! Inside!" The Sunday School superintendent kept a firm grip on Halie and Mamá—Annise, her loyal partner in crime—Mamá cringing at Halie's wail. "I don't have no shoes!"

"Never you mind!" A series of smacks had them up the steps and inside. On the bench, with your feet tucked under, it was all right. In church they really didn't care how you dressed, just so you clean and neat. And once the service started, everybody singing, Halie didn't care either.

What was nice was if somebody passed her some easy walkers; then she'd be there early early, hoping . . . and oh joy! plenty times deacon *did* let her press on the lights and ring the bell. It pealed often: Wednesday,

Friday and 6 a.m.-Sunday prayer services, then Sunday School at 10, church at 11, home for dinner and back for B.T.U. (Baptist Training Union, for young people) and night service. Halie made them all. "When they put me in church, they found the right boat," Mahalia would say later. "I could stay in church all day."

Sandwiched between services was a busy social life. The church was a little wooden structure, but at back was a hall which seemed enormous to young eyes. It had a stage and, like the church itself, the hall literally glowed with light—electric! The youngsters organized concerts, apart from choir, complete with costumes and skits. There were fish fries. There were all-day picnics—exciting; you rode a truck clear out to Lake Pontchartrain, into a whole other world . . . but Halie didn't often get in on those: children and chores. When it was dry, there was a ball game every evening by the church or the levee (the streets too ridged and rutted). Halie never missed this. And at good dark they could go inside, put up the light, and have all the fun they wanted. Most Saturday nights, old Mr. Hine came to show moving pictures. Sometimes he circuited Zion or Broadway Missionary, but Mt. Moriah had the largest hall. Everybody welcome, 15¢. Peter often paid her way from caddying (25, 30, maybe 35¢ a time) or his odd jobs: often gave her a little something for herself, in fact; but Halie turned that over to Aunt Duke as she'd been told—squirreling enough for a peppermint pickle. Duke doled it out for Halie's church.

For a long time Mr. Hine showed a serial about Indians, absorbing even if they couldn't really read the words at the bottom. It wasn't about cowboys and Indians but Indian village life, its main character named Warpee. That earned Mahala her third nickname: Warpee, because the Indian was barefoot. Never mind. She loved that show.

Baseball was taken seriously. Fletcher Robinson—"Oozie," their B.T.U. superintendent and choir director, whom they loved—and Mr. Hack regularly played with them, team for team. Shortstop was Halie, playing her heart out. It was her passion. Time and time again Halie risked the stewards' ire and led her buddies with her to the sinners' bench by playing ball on Sunday. Strictly forbidden! laughs Annise, charged years later by Mahalia with telling this sinful chapter of her "real" life. "We'd play on Sunday, get thrown out of church on Wednesday, then have to come Friday night and beg the members' pardon so we could sing on Sunday: 'To the pastor, officers and members of Mt. Moriah Church, I stand before you all and I beg your pardon for playing ball on the Sabbath Day; I won't do it again.' " Then go right back and play next Sunday. "Look like it was a disease with me," confessed Mahalia. "I just couldn't stop."

The expected whipping from Aunt Duke, she took in stride. Begging pardon came harder. "I ain't going beg for them!"

"Then you can't sing in the choir!"

Dilemma. In all the black Baptist churches of the region, music was the lifebeat of the service. In New Orleans, this reached a peak. The Sunday School songs and the senior choir's long and short meters (the "Dr. Watts hymns," after the composer of so many) would have sounded at home in any white Baptist church except for their intensity: those long, sustained notes gave you lots of room for curlicues, hums, whatever you want do with it. But what Halie loved so she could not keep still—body or spirit—were the natural songs from the congregation. Especially the jubilees. Full of hope and expectation, they made you feel so *good*. The long meter could rise the spirit and bring the "Amen!" and "Sing on!" if you put the soul in deep. But it was the jubilee caused you to shout the members and set them dancing in the aisles . . . get happy! . . . get in the service! Sent *you* in the high so you might take off for minutes on end while the members swooned in ecstasy and the stewards raced about with fans—if they too weren't in the number.

Halie couldn't do without that. She begged.

Something irrepressible made her pick up that ball again the next Sunday. "The Devil," muttered Aunt Duke, who fumed and flailed, but didn't forbid. No more than she barred Halie from the Saturday night programs. Given for the church building fund, or the Sunday School—5¢ all under 12, 10¢ all older—these were the youth choir's special delight, their own creation. And for Halie, especially daring. Not *Old Black Joe,* when Barry Jackson tottered across the stage, thin shoulders hunched, while Halie stood off and in a faint voice sang "I'm coming! I'm coming!" Or *Way Down Upon the Swanee River,* another good one to act out. . . . Not *The Star Spangled Banner,* a Mahala solo learned at McDonogh 24 which would one day make her sweat, in Washington. Not their skits, always on religious themes built around a song into which Mahala would insert spoken lines: "God said this . . . God said that. . . ." She felt quite at home with what He'd say. Nor, of course, was it their all-time favorite jubilee, led by Halie: *Hand Me Down My Silver Trumpet, Gabriel*—although they sang that so often, people finally said to let it rest. No, what were downright daring among Halie's solos were such numbers as *My Blue Heaven* and her specialty, *St. Louis Blues*. She tore them up on that.

For the whole chorus, Mahala assigned the parts and sounded them out by ear. For accompaniment, they reached out to Sugar Do, a grown man who could evermore whip a piano and sing too, and to Miss Victoria Walker, who just had to hear a song sung once. Their regular accompanist, Miss Pearl Robinson, refused to play any but church music. Nonetheless the church elders, whatever the scruples, encouraged the programs and all else that might screen their youth from an ever-present danger; a Pinching Town weekend.

A standing affront to the quiet pocket of domestic help in which the Clark sisters lived, so close some areas had to be circled around in Halie's daily business, waterfront dangers ran the gamut with a special New

Orleans flavor. The barrooms, run by local Italian families, were open 24 hours a day, undisturbed by the white law—Prohibition or no—unless called on by the extreme: "Maybe one bad Negro killing up somebody," said Mahalia; "then the police sticks beat on every 'burr head' they could catch, involved or not, no difference. *Any* time you see police be anywhere, even by the poolroom, the people run, jump fences, jump behind doors, scatter like flies, like King Kong coming, anything to get away because they knew they'd be manhandled so bad, and no Negro lawyers to stand in the way or get them out of jail, leastways none known by us. Unless you had a big enough white family would do it, it was the preacher who stepped in; law did show a leniency for the preacher because his position was respected. He's the one went down if a girl gone astray and got put in the House of Good Shepherd, and he's the one a mother went to, to get her boy out of the House of Correction."

Friday and Saturday, especially, men and women reeled in and out of the saloons. "Cherokee and Ann was a notorious corner for killings," says Elliott Beal, warned as a youth to stay out of Pinching Town. Gambling could end up with more than money vanishing. Prostitutes spiced the high life. Churchgoers warned the children against taking money or candy from men who wanted them to "come and get it." Nor were the perils confined to barrooms. What started as a house-rent party—a New Orleans commonplace when you got too far behind the rent: admission charged, refreshments provided—could end up a free-for-all of cracked bones and sliced liver. Same for a fish fry, harder to resist. "Walk through Pinching Town at night, you'd see the lights hanging out to let you know—white for a house-rent party, red for a fish fry," says Mr. Beal. "They'd wrap red crepe paper around a railroad lantern. Or else hang out a red Japanese paper lantern with a candle inside; when the wind blew, many a house caught on fire. They'd have fried fish, home brew, potato salad, French bread . . . that's what drew the people, with some good piano inside. You could smell that fish for blocks away: draw you right out your house. People would be up and down the alley as well as the back yard—it was the children's job beforehand to sprinkle brick dust so people wouldn't slip on the bricks after dew settled, or in rainy weather. It often ended with a brawl, when the brew got to flowing up freely."

Through it all, riffling the streets was ragtime jazz. "Indecent!" cried the church folks. "Music of the Devil!" It didn't help that the Devil had done his work right there in New Orleans, borrowed their own holy beat. They could only hope to pass on their distrust. No way to keep the kids from discovering it—it was on all sides every day. Far more than on Magazine St. ("That area was more numerous with whites," says Celie.) But any day in Pinching Town, black bands who would become legends in Chicago and the East . . . Kid Ory, Kid Foster, Kid Sheik, Kid Thomas, King Oliver, Bunk Johnson, the Tuxedo, Eagle, Eureka . . . any one of them might roll in to advertise a ball at the Merry Go Round, the Bulls Club at 8th and Rampart, the "San Soo" *(Sans Souci)* Hall—colored dance halls open uptown now—or whatever else was big. The band played a sample, then passed around handbills. Sometimes rival trucks at the same junction brought on a "cutting"—a play-down to see who was best. ('Til he left town, Louie Armstrong and Buddy Petit might be cutting each other on trumpet.) The vanquished departed, tailgate between its wheels, to the delight of the clustered adults and children.

Just drifting the streets, they could hear Victrola records, people making work pass easy with Ida Cox and Ma Rainey—both tent shows wintered in New Orleans, so they seemed like home. There might be happy-time jazz coming back from Green St. Cemetery (a forbidden joy that would bring Mahala to abrupt crisis). The Pride of Carrollton and the Buffalo Club each rented a house close by for their "lawn parties"—usually in the backyard. That suited Halie's group fine: Annise's house backed right onto the Pride of Carrollton. Her easygoing father had built a bench around their peach trees where the children could sit and listen as long as they liked. If it got too late for Halie, Mamá's grown-up sister or her mother, Mrs. Elizabeth Jackson, would walk Halie home. The contact point was crucial, minding Duke's "flashy" temper. Annise's was one of the few houses, all close by, for which Halie was cleared to linger. Mrs. Walker's was another. She had a radio she'd let you listen to—not for New Orleans' kind of music, that didn't come on the air, but that's how you could learn songs like *My Blue Heaven* for the programs.

Halie never knew if Auntie learned about that, or *St. Louis Blues,* or the other risky songs. Duke didn't attend the programs, even with Halie as star. Children's foolishness. But when it came to Mt. Moriah's fish fries, *Duke* was the star. To be an assured attraction, a Mt. Moriah fish fry had to have Mama-Duke at the huge iron skillet with Ma-Bell as main helper, both pale to the elbows with their special cornmeal mix for batter, the catfish popping golden brown in the bubbling grease. Since a good portion of their customers also earned their living as cooks, and catfish was a favorite food, the choice was an accolade. The other stewards did the cleaning and dipping, Mama-Duke and Ma-Bell the frying exclusively, " 'cause some people didn't like everybody's frying." Ma-Bell made the potato salad, by acclamation. Halie had nothing to do but enjoy.

Watching with pride, stuffing herself, Halie was happy. Smolder she might over a beating she didn't deserve—not the ones she earned; she expected that—but Auntie sure knew how to do. And Duke was entirely happy, feeding people. No one went from her door hungry. Let Bell raise her flowers—in pots; she had no yard. Duke stuck to vegetables, tended by her quiet husband, known to be draggy sick. Always something coming along: mustard greens, collards, okra, cabbage, string beans, tomatoes, carrots, butterbeans, turnips, beets—eat the green tops too, good as spinach.

Almost always fresh yard eggs and chickens aplenty to wring a couple of necks when you really needed them. In season, you could pull pepper grass from a vacant lot or along the track and boil it up with some salt meat. Not too much more had to be bought. "But listen, baby," says Aunt Bessie, "those days you could take 25¢ to the grocery and feed a whole houseful!" To work this a quite illegal coin flourished in New Orleans: the quartee (aborted from *quatre).* The color of a copper penny, or of brass, the quartee was the size of a quarter and worth half a nickel, one-fourth of a dime. Each grocer had them stamped out with his own store name. Good only at the store which issued it, quartee circulation was brisk. Each would buy a pound of red beans—talk to the man, give you a little bit more; two pounds of rice; pound and a half of cornmeal; quartee salt meat "and the man didn't measure, just cut you off a piece." You could get quartee coffee, enough for two big pots and *strong;* quartee lard (both indispensables) . . . quartee anything. If you craved store bread, you could even get quartee bread—half a grandma bread, a big round French loaf with a crease in the middle to break easy.

Except for staples, the grocers needed the quartee to stir up trade. They had stiff competition from the vendors, who weren't just peddlers but part of the pleasure of the day. *"Blaaaaaackberries!"* The blackberry lady had a voice! People would fall out the door, getting those berries. From the vegetable man, *"Raaabit, lady! Come on with your pan! Come on, get your raaabits, lady!"* His voice would ring in the air. And *"Coons, lady! Got your coons today! Come on, lady, come on with your pan!"* Charcoal man had his own way. *"Charrr-cooaall! Come on! Going freeeeze tonight!"* Or, his wagon rocking in the ruts, mounded high with the green fruit, *"Waaaaa-tuh-melon! Red to the rime!"* Smelling yellow-sweet in the sun, *"Banana, ladeeeee; I got nice ripe banana, ladeeeeee—two dozen a quarter!"*

The children listened and looked . . . food was engrossing . . . unless the railroad cart passed, inspecting the rails, the men singing as they worked it up and down. Then Halie and Celie ran along the track with them, singing too: *"Working on the rail-road, two bits a day, Picking up rocks, just throwing 'em away!"*

"Mama says they make more than 25¢ a day," Celie told Halie. "That's just a song they sing."

A man sold shrimp from buckets laid with ice, and the fig lady came by too. But they felt lucky: their figs came from Duke's backyard, and Halie headed for the river for crabs and shrimp, those necessaries for gumbo. Sometimes Bell brought Duke wild ducks when Mr. Rightor had been hunting. He insisted, too, that Bell bring home *"all* the pan"—whatever wasn't eaten that evening. He well knew how large were the clan's appetites and how many there were. What he didn't know about were the strays, whom Duke never turned away. It was part of her religion.

"People good to each other in those days, yes, indeed, white and black together," says Aunt Bessie. "Feed them right along, whoever there. People need to get to work, stop by and leave their children with you, go on and make a day's work, you feed them with the rest. 'Course when they leave the children, they might leave a little crust to help the pot."

Seated at an overflowing table at night and especially Sunday—seeing all of them stuff to groaning—Duke became downright jolly; Mahala treasured memories of her quips and jokes and generous ladlings long after echoes of Cousin Baby Williams' comforting that Duke was "doing the best she can raising you" had faded away. That Aunt Duke was something!

Mixed into Halie's regard was a strong respect. Not just for Duke's standards at home and as untitled boss of Mrs. Plant's staff—even the pantryman, Halie noticed, working alongside extra. What earned Halie's enormous respect was the factor before which she would always be in awe: knowledge. "Aunt Mahala was a natural philosopher," Mahalia would muse to Roger Winters from a life's plateau of hard-won wisdom. "Even white people used to come tell her things they wouldn't tell another living soul." And Duke's knowledge was of a most special kind. Two kinds, in truth.

5

Since slavery days it had coursed secretly through the subsoil of New Orleans—downtown, uptown, river side, lake side. In the seething underlife of Pinching Town, it boiled close to the surface. Its main effluence lay downtown in the black business strip furrowed by North Rampart St. starting at Canal—*that* broad, proud shopping lane with few exceptions allowed no blacks to try on its dresses, hats, and shoes although they could buy. Just a few blocks off Canal on bustling North Rampart lay the wellhead, a small streetside obscurity that was famous: the Crackerjack Drugstore. So famous (to blacks only) that people journeyed into the city for this one aim: the Crackerjack. Its stock was vast and exotic, little of it on open display. Myriad drawers and recesses held powders ground to secret ritual, herbs of bewildering oddity never meant for *gumbo des herbs* ("gumbo zab" took 13 herbs and greens), elixirs of strange specifics, tiny bones, amulets. . . .

Voodoo.

A stray white would get a blank stare or, at most, a love potion on display or a standard good-luck charm—certainly not even black-cat candles. But what made the Crackerjack exclusive was its darker efficacy. Even today this must be whispered, the shuddering speaker anonymous, the vanished Crackerjack's bones felt not all buried, its hidden powders ready for an ill wind: "All kind of love potions were sold there, but plenty of other kinds too. 'War Water' was a liquid to sprinkle around a home where they were jealous of the people . . . husband and wife would get to fighting, all kinds of things happen to break up this union. But the main and principal thing the Crackerjack was famous for was the other kind of herbs, and liquids, and powdered things . . . snake venom, snail powder, such as that. That's why you have to be so careful with drinking and such: what people can't understand. They had such a powder as powdered snakes; whenever this be put in a drink, from the warmth of your body, after drinking it, snakes would form in your stomach. It has been a mystery, from what you learn; the early doctors couldn't understand. When they'd operate, find snakes inside . . . 'How could it be?'

"Some powders and venom be slow-acting: people eventually be ill, swell up, wouldn't know what was happening. One woman when she did vomit, tadpoles and things came out of her system. And this went on up into the 1930s. And I'm not saying it's all gone now."

For certain needs, Pinching Towners could be served right at home: Swarthy men with straight, shiny black hair, mysterious Turks, came door to door offering wishing oils, charmed perfumes, and more hushed things The flux of hidden knowledge spilled over the levee to the flat batture, where dim squatter houses high on stilts mushroomed again. Here were Readers. All women. Some black, some white. Each had her path but they shared a special province: divination. Today, tomorrow, yesterday. Clairvoyant finders of lost objects . . . perhaps a ring. Previewers of death close at hand. (One gave her customer a description of what proved to be the coffin's accoutrements and the principal mourners.) Sensers of tangled love and hate. Spotters of the source of ill health and misfortune. Many a soul left the batture knowing now of a *gris gris*—a spell—or thinking to set one. "It was known that those people around Pinching Town believed in a lot of voodoo," says Prof. Beal with a shiver; "do a lot of mischievous things. My grandmother used to warn me, 'You go up there, put the double dolleen on Miss So-and-so.' Meant go all around a subject in talking but have no direct connection. Too many evil spells around."

Against just such as these Duke was known for her remedies. It wasn't anything she'd brought from Legonier. You can't *learn* that. It had come to her: a gift. That gift and her cures for more than commonplace ills brought a steady traffic to Duke's door. Halie was supposed to be in bed—"You go hold down those boards," ordered Duke—but Halie eased up to listening distance, quiet as Warpee. Somebody put a *gris gris* on you? No need of Crackerjack or Turk. "Scald a handful of garlic and a bunch of parsley in hot water, pour a cup of sugar in that, then you get in the bath and wash yourself down with that from head to foot. That spell get off you." "And it would, too," says sister Bessie. "That's right." Somebody you need to get rid off, somebody going on at you? "Get yourself a cup of salt, and just as they go out your door, pour that salt on their heel—they never come back no more."

Her romantic streak reached deep. Trying get your girl, or get her back? "Go pull me some fig leaves, then you come back. I'm going dry 'em and make a tea. You get your girl to drink some of this tea, and she'll never leave you again. No, not just the leaves; I'm going put in something extra, a little powder. She can't leave you! But you got to get her to drink the tea. You say, 'Come on, let's have some tea.' You'll see."

Trouble with your man? "Get his socks, and don't wash them. Put them in a jar. Then put you some sugar and some urine in—just a little bit—and you put a top on the jar and set it in your closet. You have your sweetheart *all* the time." When the fig tree was bare, the sock remedy was handy, and stockings would work as well. Warpee drank in every word, from woe to wonder, not believing nor disbelieving, but fascinated.

"People hang around Duke all the time," says Bessie: " 'Mama-Duke, they's such and such a thing.' 'Well, you such and such a thing.' And all that's right, comes true. Make your hair rise on your head sometime. But one thing she wouldn't do was harm anyone, no matter how people pull on her. She too good a woman for that. And she never charged. That was her gift."

"That's right," says Son Baby; "Duke didn't have no dirty heart."

"Sometimes Duke just kicks," says Bessie. "You be too much around her, she say, 'You better go get somebody to wash yourself down, salt you down, 'cause you done got too fresh!' "

Her reputation for cures just as often included quite visible ills. "I'd put Aunt Duke up against a doctor any day." Halie decided that the first time she'd seen Aunt Duke in action: the great flu epidemic of 1917–18. It was awesome. Mr. Betz from the funeral parlor on Zimple St. couldn't keep up with the bodies. Halie's fifth birthday came and went, but her mother had no moment to notice. One and two in every family dead or dying. Hannah, Alice, Bessie had it. Doctors came but their capsules seemed to do no good. With Charity working beside her, Duke pursued her own course. Jimson weed flowers and elephant ears were boiled with hog nails and hog hoofs, the liquid administered day and night. To her own, and to her neighbors. Throughout the city, 1,752 would die, white and black. But for Duke, hog nails barred the coffin. If she lost any patients at all, the fact faded from Halie's memory. Aunt Duke knew what was *what*.

Now she was older, Halie was glad to run to Mr. Luke's drugstore for potash—she liked to help and it was a way to get out. Or, many a night, for blue stone and lard. Blue stone was pretty, but it had a serious use, necessary to Duke's positive cure for syphilis in an era before penicillin. Mr. Luke stocked it.

Halie took things in hand herself one day when she found Celie home from school doubled up with menstrual cramps. "You wait! I be right back!" Voices, then silence. When Halie finally reappeared, she held a steaming stew. It looked good, and smelled good, but somewhat strange. "What's in it?"

"Go on, eat it up. It's going to cure your cramps and they'll never come back." Gingerly Celie tasted. It *was* good. She ate it all.

"Now what was in it?"

"Alligator tails! I caught the lady just passing by."

Celie's cramps vanished. Never to return. And the two girls became devotees of alligator tails, which Halie cooked as often as finances allowed and the lady passed. (She was really the blackberry lady; she didn't cry the tails, the girls decided, because they must be illegal.)

Just once did Halie enter the actual world of spells and potions. Heads together, barred from their heart's desire—Halie to go to a penny party around the corner, her friend to go to Canal St.—the pair pooled their resources and, shivering deliciously, bought some lucky oil from the Turk. Fifty cents! Carefully they sprinkled exactly half around Duke's house; the friend sped off and did the same at home. The friend's house burned down that night. For weeks the two quaked in guilt which they felt would surely be divined.

WHEN SHE HAD something serious in mind, Halie prayed—prayed extra hard. Sometime, God was going notice if she was worthy. 'Course you got to be sensible about what you want.

For something really huge, there was another way. For the requisite nine days, she walked over to the Catholics' big Dominican Convent on Broadway to make a novena. Up the steep steps on her knees. Supposed to be better that way. She was 12. She was praying for a fulltime job.

God must not be ready, she decided. How could Aunt Bell be right?

Back when she was little, just pulled from school, Aunt Bell stopped beside the porch as Halie chucked peas into a pan and jerked Brisko from the edge of a fall. A flock of children were chittering under the hackberry tree, playing with Celie. "Halie," said Bell quietly, "don't you worry. You going be famous in this world and walk with kings and queens." The small dark arms, the hooked legs, the glistening eyes tensed. "You think so, Aunt Bell?"

"That's right, baby. I seen it."

Time and again, in private, Halie questioned Aunt Bell with only Celie to hear. Bell's answer was always, "I seen it." The only remote circumstance Halie could conceive this to be linked to was gone, back after her mother died, when Edward Burnette's mother—her daddy's cousin Jeannette, who got her start at Mt. Moriah and still came when the tent show was in town—asked Aunt Duke if she could take Halie into her act. That child had a voice. She could make you some real money.

Duke took no more time than she did to swat a fly. "The Devil will get no help from this house!" Better bust suds 'til the day she dies.

Halie didn't think to question Duke's judgment. But she wondered if Aunt Bell's dream had somehow got mixed up from that. As the years passed, she put the prophecy away with the other fast-receding dream, the one in her own head. . . .

Besides, she'd thought of a way to make history right here.

6

"The flying horses are strictly for white!" . . . "I don't care. You watch. *I'll* show you how! . . . Halie was at it again. Some nerve! It wasn't enough she passed herself as a boy—pushed that nappy hair under Peter's cap and pulled on his pants so she could go caddy. Unheard of for a girl, but they understood. How else she going get the money for her costumes for the programs? ("I'll get the money, Mrs. Jackson, if you buy the tarlatan! I'll pay you back!" Then Annise's big sister Lily would make Halie's costume too. After all, the child had neither mother nor sister to do it.) But ride the flying horses? Boy *or* girl, if you were black, that was strictly *out*. The group was vague about the consequence, but it stretched infinitely dire.

"I said I would and I will! You wait, I'll be back."

Halie hurried into an old white uniform of Duke's. She'd wash and press it clean again and Aunt Duke never know. Get her a basket. Now find that light-skin child lives on Adam. . . .

The slim, prim nursemaid sauntered through Audubon Park, her fair-haired, light-skinned charge in hand, basket over her arm to amuse the child by pulling moss or pepper grass. Alongside the flying horses—the most alluring attraction of Audubon Park, its horses and chariots and mythical beasts circling endlessly to a calliope—the two stopped. A safe distance in back, behind trees like shadows, a dark scattering stopped too. Breathlessly, they saw Halie bend to her charge, gesture, get a nod and a grin, and the pair mount the best of all, an up-and-down horse, solicitous maid holding the child on her lap. Round and round . . . Halie didn't dare grab for the brass ring that might have won them another ride: just one fare; nursemaid didn't count. But the air had never seemed so sweet as they rounded the circle, on and on, 'til the calliope died; the motion with it.

Off the maid, off the child, to walk primly into the trees, and whoop. "I told you I'd do it. Some day you *all* going do it; but you remember now, I'm the *first colored person* rode the flying horses!"

She had never heard of civil rights.

Now, her fame flared for weeks—almost until Carnival: Beside *that* glittering peak, all else paled. But not everybody clapped. "I'm not going out there. Mama said no. It's dangerous! And I know what Aunt Duke going do to you!"

"That's for you to know and me to find out. I'm going, first thing." At Celie's gasp of alarm, "Oh, ain' nothing going happen to me!"

Carnival had originated with 19th century whites, led by secret groups, as a glorious letting-loose before the ashes of Lent stilled the Catholic city. Blacks had created their own secret parallel (secrecy the very bone marrow of Carnival's being and social status) with its panoply of signs, symbols, and traditions—if fewer strictures. Mardi Gras, the "Fat Tuesday" climax, was the one day when whites came to make obeisance to blacks: The tribes of Indian Chiefs and the Baby Dolls (top-echelon whores) were widely sought as the most splendid in the city, bar none—the costumes usually scrimped for, penny by penny, year-round. The black Zulu parade was topped only by Rex, to white eyes; by none, to black, who on this one day couldn't care less what any white thought. It was Mardi Gras! Masks were encouraged, not to come off 'til sundown. The law looked the other way (it couldn't have coped anyway).

As the city blinked awake, its children knew they were unloved if they weren't hurried into costume and painted and put in position early to watch the parades and all the big "Mardi Graws"—strange beings today, mystifying friends, encircling strangers . . . the air electric, miming made easy as beer and liquor coursed their channels.

Nothing like this in Legonier. Gentle Bell forbid Celie ever to put her head outside. And although Bell had a picture of a soft-eyed Charity in a cowboy hat—so Halie knew her mother used to take her out to see the sights—a scandalized Aunt Duke brooked no such.

Halie ducked out, of course, out before good light. She could take her licks. She wasn't going miss anything. Especially the Indians! Heading out on a long, erratic course from 6th and Willow—at Charlie Brannon's Corner, the barroom where they began to make up at 5 a.m., more or less—some tribes might begin getting here to their streets by six, stomping out a war dance, crying way for the Chief, starting on the chants. One chant Halie could sing along with them—just in her head: wouldn't dare no other way. . . .

Boom boom bah hoo
He he he nah
Me me hah nah
Boom bah—

Tribe on the move! And you never knew. The costumes were new each year, all bright feathers and beads on leather stitched by the Indian himself —no woman to touch the sacred garment. Splendid Spy Boys scouted the streets, a piercing "Aeeeeeeeaaaaaaah! Aeeeeeeeaaaaaaah!" warning Indians on the warpath.

If you don't bow,
When my chief come by,
Chah tah wa tah
Poo nah nay. . . .

A feathered spear is hurled into the dirt street; it sticks there, quivering; the dense crowd backs off, leaving a clear path: Chief coming through, let him have his way. Rival scouts in the block? They must bow-wow. One tribe give and take low? If not, it was spear and knife to first blood.

The chief who struck real terror was Brother Tilman. You knew his tribe by the special glory of their garb, the fierce paint, the special chant. No disgrace for another tribe to take low to Brother Tilman, else first blood could be last.

The sun was so bright nobody wore a coat. The street swirled with masked clowns, cowboys, cowgirls, Indians, bears, bushmen, rabbits, tramps, a man with pop caps head to foot, some ladies like playing cards. . . . And Indian Chiefs. Halie rocked. Brother Tilman!

All out the way!
Pah co nah na,
Get out the way!
Ah no mah na. . . .

Another chant grew. To Halie it sounded like *Two way pack a way, Pock a way*. But she didn't dare voice this one even in her head. Shutter doors were slamming shut; people snatched their children indoors. The street emptied in a flash. But this wasn't Esther St. Halie could only shrink against the closest siding. *"Two way pack a way. . . ."* Stomping and circling. Rivals visible now, standing their ground. *"Two way. . . ."* The moment of wah-wah, a knife flashed in the sun, an agonized scream—war erupted. Halie dove into the grocery bar against which she'd backed. People were packed in, falling all over each other, the smell of whiskey and beer and wine thick even where she was, on hands and knees. Suddenly, fighting here too—not Indians, some private vengeance—Halie trapped, scuttling this way and that until she scrambled through fists and feet and stood outside torn, panting, revolted. What she saw made it worse: bloodied bodies on the ground as the Tilman tribe receded, drunker now with their own glory. Halie raced for home, paced by panic and something more.

A frightened, furious Duke put her out.

She circled the block. "Aunt Alice," the voice small, "can I stay by you?"

By the time Alice walked her home next day, the storm was over; Duke's furies were short-lived as they were sudden. But Halie never faced another Mardi Gras or spoke of it without a shudder. Aunt Duke was right. There was more on her mind, anyway, than murder and vengeance. A window had slipped open in Heaven.

7

The Lord had loomed large in Halie's life from the beginning, His presence as natural as baseball. But now she was shooting up, near grown, she had something to thank Him for that she'd never dared count on; so big that alongside it, the other needs seemed small: Her legs were straightening. Without any doctor. Just with, like Papa said: "Doctor Jesus."

"I am a living witness to the power of prayer," Halie told Aunt Duke's pier glass. She didn't go talking about it outside, but she took the knowing with her every day as she made her way. Increasingly, this was farther afield. Besides working extra at Mrs. Plant's and Aunt Alice's people, she sometimes now could find day's work on her own. She edged up her age, and nobody could beat her for cleaning or ironing, singing as she worked. One whole summer she was at the Audubon Park pool, working in a rent bathing suit they lent her. (It never got wet, except from handling other suits. She'd've been glad to be there early to swim in the sparkling green pool gushing white at one end, but blacks weren't allowed in the water.) One way or the other, with the money she earned, she and Florence White and Bea Thomas (Thompson to Halie) often went all the way downtown on the streetcar to Canal St., shopping. Mostly they just looked in windows and inspected the dresses at Rubenstein's and Krauss's. They couldn't try them on. But slowly the day would come when one or the other had the money to buy: $4—$4.75. None of the three *wore* a new dress or new shoes until the other two had theirs. "Sometimes if Mahala didn't have her money for shoes and I did, I'd let her have my money," says Florence. They were just close.

But for social life, it was harder to join them. Duke still barred the door.

"Can Mahala go to the party? Got a little penny party."

"This is her party, right here, looking at me. *I'm* the party."

Boys called just once. "Who you come to see?"

"I come to see Mahala, I want to talk to Mahala."

"You talking to Mahala. *I'm* Mahala."

"No, the other Mahalie."

"You talking to the right Mahalie. She's not receiving company; she's not *old* enough."

Halie turned to Aunt Alice. Adventurous Aunt Hannah had moved to Chicago in 1922—another shift in the uncertain shoals of Halie's existence. With a boy of her own—Nathaniel Stamps, Jr.—Alice was still around on Cherokee, Bessie beside her in Hannah's half of the double. Aunt Alice was a peacekeeper but with more firmness to her than Aunt Hannah, and much more than Aunt Bell, so there was substance to her help. (Bessie was counted too young to enter in.) "Sometimes I'd talk to my sister if it was something I approved of," says Alice Stamps Lawson, "especially if Celie was going—my sister approved of Celie. But not if I had my doubts, like she asked me about going to a ball at St. Dominic's." ("Ball" in the ordinary of New Orleans, no more than a dance.) "I told her she better stick with Mt. Moriah. 'And try not to get your Auntie in such a high rage. She's trying to raise you.' "

Mostly Halie was docile. When Duke's hand grew too heavy, though, more and more Halie headed around to Aunt Alice or across the street to Mrs. Lizzie and Mr. John—they calling themselves family cousins by closeness. Hardly anybody dared keep her overnight. "It was like coming up against a stone," says Celie Taylor. "And don't let Duke stomp!" Wanting to please, Halie returned each time to the fold, to the family wash, scrub, iron and restraint, to the children. On the quiet, she could count on sympathy from Uncle Emanuel. She was glad he was back. That he'd been allowed to go at all ran a ripple through Pinching Town. "Aunt Duke definitely didn't let him go out unless she went with him," giggles Celie. "She'd see him get all dressed up, watch him all the way to reaching for his hat, then she'd say, 'Where you think you going?' . . . He called her 'Baby Child' . . . 'Baby Child, I'm going to such and such.' 'No you not! No you not!' She standing up in the middle of the floor with both hands on her hips. 'No you NOT! You better not go out that door!' Night time, day time, not unless she was with him. She kept an eye on him, you hear me?"

But he'd gone a pass rider to Chicago with Duke's reluctant consent for the money he promised to and did send back, while Doodutz and Brisko were yet babies, so their introduction to their grandfather was when Duke willed his return, the money not so important as the being there and the garden speaking for his presence at that.

Emanuel Paul was a revelation. "He was wonderful!" says Doodutz. "And he'd tell us things." Halie drank in his stories avidly, as she did every new thing. ("If there was a radio in a roomful of people visiting, she'd edge up to it and listen, especially if there was talking," says Son Baby; "she told me, 'That's one way you can learn something.' ") But Aunt Duke didn't encourage too much conversation about Chicago. She feared it for gangsters and haunts of the Devil. Still, "Going to Chicago in those days was like going to Europe today," says neighbor Corinne Looper. "People find it not what they thought, and come back they still wouldn't tell so as not to run themselves down. You had to find out for yourself." She had. So had Bessie. Shortly after Hannah had moved up, she'd sent for Bessie, who deposited her two little ones—George and baby Alice—with Big Alice next door. Within weeks she was back. "Smoky Town's not for me, honey," Bessie announced, taking back her brood. "They'll put grass on me right here."

In the spring of 1927, though, Chicago scored. Alice pulled stakes to join Hannah, taking Bessie's girl, now 6—Bessie would watch out for Alice's Pudley, 12.

It was a year of shocks. Halie, 14, had hardly got over Mardi Gras and this of Aunt Alice when in the late night, amid the known sounds beyond the door, sounds that faded with sleep, Halie was drawn awake by a strange one. She tiptoed to Aunt Duke's room and it was so. Crying! "Eeeeeee-aaaaaaaahhh . . . " trailing off in a choke. A yellow telegram lay in the lamp's flickers. "What's the matter, Aunt Duke?" Halie gasped.

"Fred's killed, he's been killed! My baby! My only child! Eeeeeee-aaaaaaaahhh . . . "

Halie swam up out of her own pit to help Auntie, to quieten her. It wasn't until she was back in her bed, cold now and she in a sweat, that she could feel her loss.

From a woman strange to them came a letter from Kansas City . . . Fred Clark (his name from Legonier) shot dead by a man, circumstances not told. "We never got the whole story," says Doodutz. "And I didn't know my daddy until after he was brought back."

"Sent back here in a wooden box by that woman called herself wife," says Bessie indignantly. "And you know Atchafalaya always such a good dresser, so particular about the way he looked. We had to buy a casket to put him in."

His burial, though, was all Atchafalaya would have wanted, Halie decided, searching for a satisfaction. Bessie, younger than her nephew, agrees. "Fred had a real crowd, church people *and* sporting people, yes indeed. We waked him at Alice's, and we had *some* food that night. Good thing—people kept a-coming, kept a-coming. All out in the street for the funeral next day, too, at Mt. Moriah, and they had the Tuxedo Band—

that's the band our family always would have. For the men; band is for the men; I have seen just this one woman have a band, an old lady who saved her money for that—craved that band. But friends of Atchafalaya paid; family *never* pay for the band—that's given to them. Then after the funeral all his friends second-lined and goes on to have a good time at the barroom . . . at the biggest one, Cherokee and Ann, down the corner from where he was waked. We could hear them: we been home a long while, time they got there, 'cause of course the family never second line behind your own. Duke didn't like that, anyway. But she never said a word, when the band was for Fred."

Duke, crouching, was hardly able to say anything at all. Iron control gone, her high moans like to peeled the walls. Doodutz and Brisko heard them, lying scared in the dark. Halie heard them too: wide-eyed, silent, tears spilling off her cheeks. But you got to throw it off. All around, there was a busy life to chase: day's work (hunt it, times you didn't have it); the work at home, still Halie's to do and feeling it now an offering, although Duke had donned her old self and her old humor. ("When she'd get the program to go over like she said," says Celie, "she say, 'I'm Mrs. *Paul* and I'm on the *ball*!' She used to just keep you laughing all the time. 'What you say, Auntie?' 'I'm Mrs. *Paul* and I'm on the *ball*. When I say something, I mean *just that*!' ") There were friends to keep up with, and always—work or play, Mt. Moriah or in her head at night—some kind of music. "I hate to see that evening sun go down. . . ." She had *not* the blues . . . but why would Auntie gyrate on about "music of the Devil"? And carrying on about the second line.

EVER SINCE McDonogh 24, the second line had been irresistible to Halie. Zion Travelers was right next to McDonogh 24, so when a big man's funeral began, the schoolrooms vibrated with the solemn boom and brass whose very presence sounded the passing of a big man—a secret-order or a social-club man, or maybe on the sporting side—so Mamá and Barry Jackson, George Bonner, Earlene Garrison, Henry Grady and others eased out with her to join still more, young and old, drawn like honey bees around the band playing slow, slow, and solemn, for the service inside. If it was maybe a Knight of Pythias or an Elk—some really *big* man—the beautiful funeral wagon with the glass sides would be standing, drawn by four white horses. When the body came out of the church, they stepped in tune then, along the crowded, pulsing banquette while the funeral took the street out Allen, across St. Charles, and on to Green St. Cemetery—demure as decorum demanded, hugging the knowledge of what was to come. The last slow, slow note sounded, the body interred, the burial over, the band blew it all out for free on a wide-ranging way back home, rejoicing for the soul in Glory and the money in their pockets—and the second line loosed like a tight-coiled spring: whirling, strutting, dancing, clapping, age lines blurred in the beat and motion, here and there a papered umbrella twirling in an incandescent, ineluctable, all-consuming exclusively black-custom joy.

How you going miss that?

Sometimes if a religious family requested the Young and True Friend Band, which played only hymns, the neighborhood would get up a purse, $60, for an extra band to second-line on the way back, says Celie. "Mama made sure *we* left after the hymns."

Not Halie. A whipping? Small price. "We knew we'd get it," says Annise Scully. "It might be my own daddy marching with the Buffalo, but any day the music coming to Zion, we'd steal out. We'd learn some good songs for our programs, too."

An inescapable hazard, the accepted challenge for the 16th ward was that crossing St. Charles Ave. put you into the 17th: that's where the cemetery was. And if you crossed, their boys were waiting afterwards to fight. Usually it was a boys' scramble, a quick rout for either side and no real damage. But in this 1927 which savaged Halie's being, one of her girl-friends darted in to help a brother in trouble and Halie leaped to help her friend. Fists, feet, butts, scratches, chokes, rips—Halie had really torn it: she was a mess. Lord, what Aunt Duke going say to this!

No avoiding her just desserts. Halie headed home. And into a fury climactic for even Duke.

Duke put her out. Halie crossed to Mrs. Lizzie's; but kneeling to her prayers that night, she felt herself truly wrong. Next day when Duke came home from Mrs. Plant's, Halie crossed to ask forgiveness and be taken back. But "You better ask *God* to forgive you. And you better put yourself on the sinner's bench at church."

CANDIDATES for that bench, in Mt. Moriah eyes, were entirely too numerous: the whole youth choir was being eyed askance. Here was almost a grown set ready for the senior choir and not a one converted. Had the play-acting and worldly music made them light? Of course, all the choir had been duly christened and taken communion regularly. Couldn't miss that. ("Communion was a great day," said Mahalia, eyes alight. "If you weren't right with the Lord, you sat back on the mourner's bench and you meditated, and you got the spirit; then they'd give you communion.") So important was Communion Sunday that there was a "communicating church"—Broadway Missionary, Halie's daddy's church—the service of one shortened on the other's communion day each month so the sister congregation could walk over. Mt. Moriah, in fact, had two communicating churches, Pleasant Green being a split-off close by.

But communion wasn't rebirth. "You have to decide what side you going to be on—the Lord's side or the Devil. If it's not the Lord's, you can't stay in this building. And you know in your hearts, you all possessed by demons."

Abruptly facing their state, the youth choir agreed they all were possessed by demons. They started a revival to pray for conversion. It was one to remember . . . seeking and praying; singing and shouting in the spirit. *Hand me down my silver trumpet, Gabriel.* Jubilees! Happy in the service! Halie in the forefront of the number. But was true conversion on the way? How would you know when it came? At home, Halie got a private chance to ask Cousin Baby Rosa Williams—a churchgoer all her life, but religion in the full sense of the day and of the church had just come; her baptism was this coming-up Communion Sunday. Halie turned on her the glistening, well-deep look the world would learn to know: "How does it feel, Cousin Baby? When a person gets converted?"

"I can't say, child; I can't tell you how it feels but I know it's a good feeling but it's a terrible feeling, when you get real happy . . . you don't know yourself, you don't know what you're doing."

Duke's holler from up front was a trumpet: "Don't you be back there trying to convert Halie! Wait 'til she finds it for herself. She ain't going to go in that water no dry devil, come out a wet one. When she come out, she going have something will carry her everywhere she go—she going carry something she can lay down on and see Jesus with!"

Cousin Baby nodded. "Some people don't have no real conversion; they just think they do, tell theyself they do." Duke loomed. "Halie's not going to *think* it, she's going *know* she has it!"

Halie prayed. ("That was the old way," says Celie. "Today so many just go up and give their hand and say they believe. But in our day, you had to *seek* to *find* the Lord.") Deep within herself, hour by hour, Halie reached with all the ardor of her being, all the compacted intensity used and unused in her seeming long years of being. . . . And Mahala had her first vision. She was traveling through a valley, a green pasture, and she came upon Aunt Bell. "I am seeking for the Lord, Aunt Bell." Bell smiled with all her sweetness. "You just keep searching," she said softly. "Just search among the flowers."

"If I find Him, how will I know Him from any other man?" Halie heard herself ask.

"You'll know Him, because He wears salvation on His brow and He carries a wounded hand."

When Duke found her, she was rapt. "The Lord touched me, Aunt Duke. I have been reborn."

"We'll see."

Halie raced to Bell. "I was not asleep; and I was not awake; I was—"

"—in the spirit."

"You are my gospel mother, Aunt Bell, and you showed me my hymn."

It was a long meter—an old Dr. Watts, one of the scores known to Halie and the choir . . .

Jesus, my God, I know His name,
I wonder where is He—
Go down and search among the flowers,
Perhaps you'll find Him there. . . .

Halie was ready for the water. So were 19 others who eagerly spread the word, each with a hymn given him in prayer just as the revival had adjured they must ask God for—a hymn their own for all time (music so central to true religion at Mt. Moriah). All candidates to speak on Friday, final night of revival.

Pinching Town fairly throbbed. Not Duke. Nor Earlene Garrison's mother. Nor two others who felt the children "didn't have nothing, better put it off and pray." (One boy on the very Friday *played baseball*—so Albert was not reborn; he could just pray some more.)

What had the Lord meant? Without Duke's yes, Halie couldn't go down. Yet her own still waters were full to the brim. She would testify.

Not only the 16's families and Halie's crammed the little wooden church that night. Halie's voice was known from Greenville to Carrollton . . . listened for: when the rest were still ranged below the pulpit, Halie had been called to the loft above—her voice, her power, her motion bursting irresistibly through the formality of the senior choir like fireworks. So all around Mt. Moriah's grounds and every space in the street was crammed this night of the 16—windows and doors opened for the air and the candidates' witness. "We all talked," says Annise, "but Mahala talked the longest, and the loudest. That voice *carry!* She told the story of how she prayed and got converted . . . told her vision, and the moment when the Lord spoke to her . . . how she *knew* she had religion; there was not a doubt. Then she came through with that long meter and she set that church on *fire*."

And Aunt Bell. "My mother weighed 225 pounds and she was tall," says Celie. "That night it took I don't know *how* many to hold her. People couldn't find words to explain it. The spirit of God is too high to explain."

Still Duke withheld. All about, sewing machines were whirring; hearts were thumping over new white shoes and stockings; gangling arms and legs held patient for fittings; mothers' and sisters' fingers were pricked without complaint for the all-important baptismal clothes: all clothing must be new. Pinching Town ached for Halie—collectively, their child. "Don't stand in her way," pleaded the bravest stewards, and some of the deacons too. "She's old enough to *know*."

Duke was not swayed. Finally a group of her fellow stewards paid a formal visitation, Annise's mother among them: *They* were convinced. They had *felt* her. If Mrs. Duke would consent to Mahalie's baptism, they would get her ready. Please, Mrs. Duke, it was *real.*

If they were that sure, sighed Duke, go ahead.

Too late to join the 16, but no matter. Voile or organdy, accepted fabrics for the baptismal dress, were priced about equal, 25¢ a yard. They decided on voile. That was needed too for the white dress-up cap, trimmed in white lace and circled with little voile roses. Cotton batiste, at 15¢ a yard, was needed for the slip, for the long white gown to actually go down in, for the "Baptist tie" (the long white strip to wrap around your head for the water) and for the white piece tied around your waist—the Biblical girdle. The family got her white shoes and stockings.

Halie had never been so splendid. Straight and tall, her brown skin shone with more than the morning's scrubbing as she circled for them to see, all new from tip to toe. Only she and Amelia, Uncle Bos's wife (he finally in from Legonier) were going down this morning. A Sunday never looked so new. And something else—Broadway Missionary was communicating; her daddy would see her.

The block and a half to Mt. Moriah seemed short as they all trooped for service, a guest preacher taking the pulpit so Pastor E. D. Lawrence wouldn't go into the cold water too hot, too wrought up and exhausted. For Halie, seven stewards on that bench—seven who'd got her ready.

Now the long file issues from the church, singing . . . stewards all in white, so white it glitters, deacons in black or as close to black as they can come; the baptizing deacons and Rev. Lawrence marked by close-fitting black cotton caps; and the candidates, the candidates glowing white . . .

Let us go down to Jordan,
Let us go down to Jordan,
Let us go down to Jordan,
Religion is so sweet.

Singing, marching, gleaming, strung out blocks long, rounding the levee to the foot of Magazine where the Mississippi was safe to enter. Down in the water the pastor and one deacon, black robes billowing, the two congregations and more crowding the levee as Halie hands her shoes to a steward. Another steward ties a white string to the tail of her long gown so it won't float up in the water . . . *Let us go down to Jordan. . . .* Blessed, the Mississippi *is* the Jordan now. The two waiting deacons take Halie's arms; they wade in the water. "I baptize you, Mahala Jackson, according to the faith, in the name of the Father and of the Son and of the Holy Ghost, amen!" Eyes shut, a quick plunge . . . time only for a blink . . . not muddy, but clear! clear! . . . red! Halie was clapping her hands as she came up out of the water, reborn, a new creature in Jesus Christ. "Oh, she was a happy soul!" exults Cousin Baby.

Hustled up to a waiting blanket, the hobbling string cut, the march back . . . into the real dress-up clothes to parade the neighborhood, receiving congratulations and sharing the glow. Home to a baptismal banquet from Duke which matched in every degree the one Aunt Alice had given Celie that spring. ("That Duke was a cake-baking thing," says Cousin Baby.) Then the afternoon of callers, congratulations, refreshments, and back to church to receive the right hand of fellowship.

Next day the world was the same but it was not. Not one to air her private feelings, she yet answered a questioning Celie. "I have a new look. I have a desire to serve the Lord in spirit and in truth—"

"You always had *that,*" injected Celie.

"He told me to open my mouth in His name."

That message itself had spread—clear over to Mt. Triumph Baptist uptown where Rev. Curtis pastored. "My daddy said they all felt she had the gift," says Celestine Curtis Graves; "and when they wanted somebody to keep the church where it should *be,* they sent for *her.* Yes, while she was just 14." She couldn't guess that Rev. Curtis would one day watch Halie in far-off wonder, nor that Celestine would see her change a life with a vow.

For now, inevitably the buoyance merged with daily life. To Duke, she was still an instrument to be tempered. She could not seem to please. The broom handle flashed. Her 15th birthday came. The iron will did not ease. Especially of the perils of night: "Don't let dark catch you out, you hear me? Unless it's church and straight back!" Halie chafed in silence. What's the use to talk? Celie had to mind the same from Bell. Be under foot all the time. When their cousin Helen Scriven was burned to death, though . . . Helen home in a rush from seeing her mother, trying so to hurry lunch for her husband that she threw kerosene on the cookstove wood and it exploded . . . when Helen was waked at the Scriven home on Hillery, the two cousins were approved to go. Respects paid, it was still hardly dusk. Halie thought they'd just pass by her married friend on Burdette St., two blocks off the way home.

The house was full of company. Flowering among people, Halie circulated the house and yard. Celie found herself with a strange young man, a student at Lehigh College on St. Charles Ave., who flashed his eyes at her and in time led her back "to where the punch is."

Suddenly aware of the dark, Halie came hunting Celie and found her prim, pretty cousin struggling desperately, face contorted with fear, her short person straining to wrench away from the sure grip, the end not far. Halie hardly broke stride as she snatched up the nearest weapon, the ice pick, and plunged it in. He wasn't hurt bad, the whole house assured her; that blood don't mean a thing. Get on home before you catch it; we'll fix him up.

Sick with the sight, unsure what else she might have done, Halie hurried the blocks so that Celie had almost to trot . . . and as they hit Esther St., both knew the hour with sinking heart: 8:30.

Celie, Bell scolded. But a fury broke over Halie like a typhoon, striking again and again through the beating and beyond. Never mind what happened. What had she told Halie about letting night catch her from home? What kind of a devil was this? She wouldn't have her in her house!

Duke put her out.

Next day while Duke was at work, Halie quietly crossed over, collected her belongings every one, such as they were, and crossed back to Mrs. Lizzie's. Then to Bessie, to tell her story. "All right, baby," sighed Bessie, "if you gone, you gone." She was going *to her self.*

To righteous Duke, home from work and furious . . . accusing Mrs. "Jack" Marshall of helping Halie decamp, so the kindly neighbor pointed out "who put who out" . . . to Duke, it was a contest of wills and she'd never lost one yet. Halie would be back. And better for her lesson.

Days passed. Halie scanned the neighborhood (no thought of quitting that; it was her *place)* and quickly picked a tiny house a block from Bessie—on Millaudon right next to a white lady; $6 a month, one room and a kitchen to itself. From her own stoop she could see Mt. Moriah a block and a half down. Duke was just two blocks off. Horrified. Biding her time.

From Aunt Bessie she got a nice iron bed and mattress. Bessie didn't want her to go housekeeping, "but if she going do it, let her go." Halie scraped up enough to buy her a coal heater; Son Baby would hook it up before it turned cold. Various ones of the church called to contribute . . . see what they could spare. All this hardly skipping a beat in her busy routine. "After she was on Millaudon, Mahala went from different streets, doing day's work," says Cousin Baby, "and you know that's hard. She'd pass and tell me. People still wasn't paying more than $1.50, sometimes not but a dollar. I used to work steady on Oak and Fern, and Mahala worked at different houses around Fern."

Yet Pinching Town couldn't settle down. "We all was grieving for her, all the time, from one house to another," says Bessie. "They knew she was a good girl, they knew she wasn't one to get money any way she can," says Annise. But they were troubled at what could happen to a girl by herself and just turned 15. Edna Posley, the church secretary, wrote Alice—her best friend 'til Alice left; she could tell *her* the whole shoot. Maybe she'd take Halie up to Chicago.

Halie herself wasn't studying about all this. Her serious concern was for a regular job. ("She didn't bother about wishing," says Isabell. "If she could do a thing, she did it; if not, she didn't bother. If she had any wishes, she kept them to herself.")

No sense now in that old dream . . . she'd sing it out.

A steady job came quickly enough but not one to ease any minds: out all night tending a lady's house and little girl for a lady who worked nights.

Had to miss church nights and choir practice. But she had Sundays off and days she could visit around . . . Bea was about to have a baby. . . .

"She came by Sunday morning when I was in labor and she just stayed," says Bea Thomas Williams. "It was my first child. I was 16. She had just got off from her job minding the little girl 'til the mama came home, about 8. My aunt was with me and the doctor came, but Mahalie washed the baby. She just wanted to do that for me. We were very close. And she always was good at doing for people when they were sick." ("Always go along and do things for sick people," nods Bessie, "clean up, help dress them, any way she can give a hand—she just be kind, from a child.")

Turning the rosy-pink boy baby expertly, a whisper of the old dream came inside before she shut it as firmly as she hushed the child's whimper.

"You'll be the godmother," said Bea.

WHEN NEWS came that Aunt Hannah was coming down for Thanksgiving, Halie had been safely on her own for nearly a month. Aunt Hannah would have something to see. Hannah's visits weren't frequent, and always at Thanksgiving, down on excursion fare: $10 for 7 days, roundtrip. (Regular fare was $37.76 one way.) Popular, outgoing, Hannah was eagerly awaited. She could talk! What she had on her mind this time, though, was a surprise: she wanted to take Celie back.

Celie was willing . . . who'd turn down Chicago? But "Hannah might known Bell wouldn't part with Celie—that's her eyes!" says Bessie. "Her only girl! Bell said no. And it was no. Myself, I got hold of Hannah and said, 'Why don't you take Mahala?' My heart was sore for that child." Duke heard and was furious. Leave Halie be! Up with all those gangsters. Trying to *ruin* that girl.

Hannah had always called herself Son Baby's second mother. So she spoke to him about taking Little Allen. "My wife would have a say about that, Hannah, he's pretty young," hedged Big Allen. "Why don't you take Mahala?"

Cousin Baby Williams, who dated far back with the Clarks—Halie's mother and Baby's sister had been thick in Legonier and she'd been fond of Charity too—Cousin Baby's six feet loomed over even Hannah's tallness as she had *her* say. "I wasn't here when Charity died, but they tell me she was good to you younger girls. Now she's in Heaven resting, you do for her child what she can't do for herself: you take her away, up to Chicago. Now don't tell Duke I said so!" she added; "I don't want her mad at me."

Her week almost up, Hannah was standing on the corner in the evening chill listening to Son Baby tell her what had been happening, when Halie came along. Hannah was direct. "Do you want to come to Chicago with me?"

"Yes—I will!"

"Well, go see about getting you a ticket. Talk to Ethel Adams. And you better hurry. You don't have much time."

Halie moved. "Ethel Adams! Ethel Adams!" Her voice came out of the night as she hit the door of 135 Millaudon, where Ethel Adams had moved in just since she'd come on the same train with Hannah. "She had a little brown coat on; I can see this coat on her," says Mrs. Adams. "She wanted to know if I still had my half of my excursion; said Hannah would take her if she could get a ticket in time. People would come down on the excursion, you see, and if they weren't going back—like I was not, this time—then they would sell the return half. I had sold mine to one of the red caps for $4. I was so sorry, because I wanted the best for that girl; she used to, when I be sick, come scrub my floor for me; I'd give her a quarter. Not for pay, she wouldn't ask. Come scrub and stir my beans, just to be nice; she was just that kind of person. 'Go down, see some of the red caps,' I told her, 'see if they have a ticket. They the ones selling to the people going back. Or else, if they don't, go over to the Page Hotel; that's where the Pullman porters stop. Ask for Mr. Allen; he stops there and he has the excursions in charge.' "

Halie was off. Clear downtown off Rampart to the station. No ticket there. Over to Dryades and Howard Ave., to the Page Hotel, heart beating hard. And she got it. "I got it, Aunt Hannah! I got the ticket!"

"Well, get yourself packed and let's make us a lunch, girl. We're going to Chicago."

Thunder muffled the black taxi's rattles next morning as it splashed uncertainly to a stop in the late November dark, but they were all on the porch, Duke's tears meeting the driving rain, Celie's howls rivaling the wind.

"Don't cry; no use to cry, 'cause I'm going, I'm really going."

JUST TAKING a taxi had been new ("Aunt Hannah always did believe in style," says Celie; "wore her corset every *day*"). Now, settling into their own seat on the Illinois Central car—first coach behind the engine—the very prickliness of the green plush on her bare brown legs and the closed-up smell just added to the scary wonderment. Today and tonight and all tomorrow. "Shove these things up on that rack, Halie." She'd believe it when they pulled out. "And keep that lunch where we can get at it, baby. . . ."

"Gone?" cried Annise, cried Earlene, Eunice, Clifford, Herman, Edna Halter. "To Chicago?" cried Florence, Bea, Stella, Henry, Oozie and Pearl. There'd been no time to tell, to talk, to share. . . .

Aunt Hannah wasn't sleeping either.

"Aunt Hannah?"

"What, girl?"

"You think I—you think I could be a nurse?" Said. The dream.

"You be anything, girl, you work hard enough. This is Chicago."

"Ssssshhhhhhh!" cried the steam as they jerked forward and pulled out again through the night. Mahalia Jackson was rolling. She'd be forced to look down, many a time. She would look up, every day. But she would not long look back.

Not that she was sure of that, at first.

8

It was the *strangeness* pressed in on you: not just the station bigness and the bundled-up people's sounds but something else hard to put your foot on. Whoo! the wind took you. Like her coat was a croaker sack. And *this,* the most peculiar yet: riding past dark muddles of big, big buildings, then little lumps of buildings with a white man in his taxi. Law wouldn't allow that, back home. "They're glad to take us," said Aunt Hannah, looking to make sure the man didn't miss their turn. He might not be used to the South Side.

An iron fence with a pretty gate and a high-rise building like people's you'd work for, and it was Aunt Hannah's—her place too now: 3250 Prairie. That didn't seem natural even with the family-ness of Aunt Alice and Bessie's Little Alice in the apartment. A strange girl who didn't have anywhere to stay was in the room Aunt Hannah usually rented out. "I just let her stay until she found a job," says Hannah.

Settling on the sofa, Halie knew just what Florence and Bea and them were doing, and Celie and Bessie. She knew Pinching Town with her eyes closed. She'd have to *think* about doing up here. Find out what you did to be a nurse, for one. Aunt Hannah said she better go finish up grade school, and that she could. That took some switching back. Her first dream was to be a teacher; wear nice clothes like they did. Then she'd gone over to nurse; they wore a clean white uniform. Those were the two high careers thinkable for a Negro girl in New Orleans. And those dreams died. It was peculiar now to suddenly have it all pulled open, up to her. They going let her in school in December? If it wasn't so cold up here. Would she do any good? But she had to *know* more. What year would they put her in, and her so big. These people talk different. Aunt Hannah's was nice; she could do for her. It was what to do outside. Down home, they don't *have* no big buildings like that; no such big houses. And the radio! Just like Aunt Duke foretold. Radio say they let Al Capone back in from Cicero—

don't even *allow* Negro people in Cicero—but he's back in *Chicago,* acting up! "He won't bother us none, girl," Hannah assured her. "You won't even see him on the street. He after them big operators; won't be none of him down the South Side." Halie nodded, troubled. She didn't like it up here. What's the use to even get up?

By Sunday, a worried Hannah acted. "She'd done nothing but lay on the bed all week, moping, missing New Orleans. I said, 'Come on, get up out of there and let's go to church, and you'll feel better.' I wasn't a member of Salem Baptist but I was visiting, with my sister Alice, and that's where we all went, over on So. LaSalle."

The wind whistled through Halie's light coat and sweater like it was hungry for her bones. She was thin, almost skinny, but a full 5′ 7½″, so she could keep up as long-legged Aunt Hannah hustled them past the talkers on inside the big brick church to get a seat. It was packed out. All black. And there was Jesus. There was the cross; there was the Bible. This was Chicago, but this was *church!* God was here too. As the spirit rose up in her, Halie did what she'd have done in any church back home. She stood up to witness, her way.

Hand me down my silver trumpet, Gabriel,
Hand me down my silver trumpet, Lord,
Hand it down, throw it down,
Any way you get it down,
Hand me down my silver trumpet, Lord.
If you get there before I do—
Hand me down my silver trumpet, Gabriel,
Tell all my friends I'm coming too,
Hand me down my silver trumpet, Lord.

Hand me down. . . .

The big Chicago church was transfixed. Not for them the spontaneous outpourings of which Halie was the sum and product . . . not in December, 1927, in this urbane Northern setting with its rigid, formal service not unlike the solemn dignity of the white Baptist church except for the spirituals bred of the bones of their slave ancestors and imprinted in their souls out of the same strivings—but now hemmed by the new-won sophistication which was the cloak and flag of their upward motion. But the wonder of that big voice, the glory of its drive and its emotion were not to be gainsaid. Rev. C. C. Harper welcomed her; the choir director welcomed her. How remarkable this was, she would learn. Yet Halie's first session with the choir surfaced one sorrowful fact: Back home, Oozie Robinson had brought out the others' voices while he was expanding her own (Mahala moving up from her natural contralto as easily as she reached for a drink of cool water); here, the voices were too squeezed down to meet her own. She could only do solos. But these, she'd do. Everything *was* possible; you just had to strike out. This was Chicago. Smoky Town!

She enrolled in school . . . sure enough, she'd have to start back where she'd left off, grown or not; and she could keep an eye on Little Alice, in first. But abruptly, history repeated. Halie had to stop to substitute for Hannah, low sick; it looked like a good long time. The wind felt colder.

Aunt Hannah worked as cook/housekeeper for a white family, the Dr. Siebolts, clear to the north, so you had to get the streetcar in the dark to the El—a scary, high platform business with steps and how you sure this the right one and hardly won't wait a second for you to step on; then clear across town—you watched for your stop and got off to catch the bus. Aunt Alice worked right next, for another white family, so she was there to get Halie on and off; then when one finished work, she'd go to the other's job and wait. Halie was glad she anyway had some company. Still, riding the long cold miles, the elevated's roar the very voice of Chicago over the unknown uncaring vastness, she yearned for the known, the closeness, the friends and helping hands of Pinching Town and tears welled inside, unshed. She worried about Brisko—would he know enough to watch out for trains, running his feet on the levee?

"She liked it down there, she didn't want to be up here," says Aunt Alice; "but anybody, when they first come up to a place, they don't like it. She soon got rid of that."

The day came when she wrote Celie (Celie writing almost every day to please come home) and said don't grieve; it was hard, harder work than back home—"you even have to wash windows"—but she was going to stick it.

One thing helped—and don't dare tell the aunts: Whenever she could, she sneaked around to the Grand Terrace or anywhere she could to hear Fatha Hines and Louie Armstrong, hear a little bit of that Loosiana jazz music, 'cause it reminded her of home.

When Aunt Hannah was well enough to come back—the Siebolts thinking there was nobody like Hannah—they held onto Halie for laundress, to catch up. Then there was a laundress job right by that Aunt Alice got her . . . what you going do? She had to help pay her way, and Chicago was no cheap place; so much to get you, up here. She'd go to school at night.

"She wasn't a bit lazy," says Hannah proudly; "she was very smart. She was never too late and never too early, and it never rained and it never snowed but she went. Anytime they called, she went. Day's work. We stayed by Halie 'til she got on her feet, but she didn't stand to wait until we help her, she went on."

She found work closer by, in the fine section over on Hyde Park Blvd. General housework, $1 a day and carfare. Where all that big pay in Smoky Town? Out of that, now she was regular, $5 a week for room and board.

A hard day's work . . . the drain of adjusting . . . the struggle to swallow self-consciousness (so *big* for fourth grade) . . . the lure of her new center of warmth, Greater Salem Baptist Church: school lost. She'd sing it out.

The three Johnson brothers—Robert, Prince and Wilbur—had welcomed Halie as a kindred spirit to join their singing and playacting for the Salem socials along with Louise Lemon. Hey Mt. Moriah! Right back in the programs. Robert Johnson wrote the scripts, directed, and played the male leads; Mahalia played opposite—at 15, her bearing as mature as his 18: *The Fatal Wedding . . . Hell-Bound . . . From Earth to Glory* . . . she even got to play Mary! All won huge acceptance. So did their quartet, with Prince at the piano. They trooped to Halie's to rehearse, and Hannah and Alice made them welcome. Halie glowed: her very own first guests, ever.

Under this warm acceptance, downstairs in the church basement she bumped against one more lesson of life: A natural worker, at home in a church kitchen, Halie volunteered for every job. She was rebuffed. Puzzled, she tried to blunt the sharp words with a smile and a joke. Must be they have different ways up here. "Then one evening when we were cooking, I realized three of those women actually hated me. Finally one popped out with 'You Loosiana niggers think you can do everything better than anybody else!' That did it. I picked up this big butcher knife and waved it in her face. 'You leave me alone or I'll make Hell a present of you in a basket!' " A wicked glint lighted Mahalia's grin, telling it. "I never had a minute's trouble with 'em after that. But that woman would take the sweet out of gingercake."

Tilts like this Halie could throw off. Too much going on to study *them.* Salem was 10 blocks from Aunt Hannah's but Pilgrim Baptist was close as Mt. Moriah to Duke's. Sunday nights, Rev. J. C. Austin welcomed the tall, eager dynamo. So did his assistant Rev. Seals: *Oh, It's Real,* her impassioned voice would plead in cramped room, hospital ward, reform-schoolroom, cell block. Evangelist A. A. Childs had a huge tent pitched at 33rd and Giles, a block from Pilgrim . . . this was beginning to feel like a neighborhood. Halie eagerly offered to sing for his revivals. When that meant 11 a.m., she let her day's work go: And Rev. Childs held an offering for the singer! Her first church money. *He'll Fight Your Battles* . . . her opening notes drew the people together in mid-morning and often her exultant voice rose like a benediction in the small hours of the next dawn: *When I Wake Up in Glory By and By* . . . Rev. Childs lasted as long as there was any soul coming to Christ or even coming close. And after services, Mahala found herself in a new role: the clear faith with its twin streams of hope and love seemed transfused with a knowing, so the beset were drawn to take her hand, to lay their burdens in her young lap. Aunt Duke, look here now. She told them as it had been told to her, and they seemed comforted. There's a way ahead.

Fired by her outward reach, the Johnson Singers looked for welcome outside Salem, the first organized gospel group to circulate the city, all of it casual as the wind blows a seed. Halie held herself inside the quartet as best she could—over and over they practiced at Hannah's—but in her solos the spirit was irresistible. In the first big church at which she let loose—sang of and to the Lord with her whole heart, being and body as she'd been accustomed—Halie got her next major shock. The pastor rose in wrath. Blasphemous! Get that twisting and that jazz out of his church! Halie ignited. "This is the way we *sing* down South! I been singing this way all my life in church!"

She'd taken on her first preacher. The battle was joined. Fortunately, there was somewhere else to go.

The storefront churches were dim flames in tiny shops, the defunct stores in musty rows with which black State St. was plentifully supplied in 1928 even as Michigan Blvd. rolled with its prosperous blacks and whites. The spenders didn't get too far south—the sector chiefly services, storefronts, liquor stores, quick-food shops.

Many of the flickering little church groups, barely tinder in these cheap-rent sites, were splinters of the Southern groups lured up by visions of good pay, good life, and freedom from discrimination. They'd found only gleams of this smothered in the crammed jammed city but they held onto the Rock, the steady faith in God's guidance. Halie was a fresh wind from the down-home religion. She and her singers *bound* to make you catch fire, reach the Lord. Amen. But worn fingers had little to drop onto the table—the bare wooden table in the black church to which offerings are brought in person while the deacons count and stack.

Aunt Alice and Aunt Hannah had their older affairs, but Aunt Bessie—her way up paid by Alice, her Gold Dust Twin—Bessie went with her when Halie was singing alone, her ardor outstripping the time and interest of the Johnsons and Louise. "Halie didn't care whether it was full, or just a few; she sang on, sang on, let it build up," says Bessie. "She was singing for herself as much as for them."

Bothersome as a fly for Halie was finding that "society Negroes" and some of the other religious singers she began to meet laughed at her talk. "Claim they couldn't understand me," Halie said, looking back. "I did have that New Orleans brogue—and I still have it. Back home, people didn't worry about their diction, or their words. They just went on and sang. If you understood it, you understood it; and if you didn't, well, they had felt it, you see. So I had that to learn."

Visiting from Pinching Town, Ethel Adams remembers "you'd be sitting there and everybody talking and her ear was to the radio—a lot of stories and different things. All that helped educate her."

AMONG THE Southerners who heard Halie—not at a storefront but at neighborhood Pilgrim Baptist, his church—was a man who didn't yet know he'd make history: Atlanta-born Thomas A. Dorsey. When they met, in 1928, he wasn't long out of his role of "Georgia Tom," pianist/arranger/composer for major tent shows—primarily for Gertrude "Ma" Rainey. Ill, with $10 in his pocket, in 1925 he'd come to try Chicago again: 1916–19, he'd played house-rent parties and buffet flats while he tried to get his jazz and blues published. This time he got work transcribing on paper the singers' blues J. Mayo "Ink" Williams cut for Paramount Records—a job the bigtime white arrangers wouldn't bother with: New York would hardly bother with "race records" at all; most blues was cut in Chicago. Dorsey wanted to get into spirituals but there was no market. "The upper-crust black market didn't buy spirituals much; they bought blues," he says. "But I believe it's a little bit off to use the power of music just for entertainment; there's so much power to be drawn, you can get your message across so well, it seems it ought to be reserved for the Book." He spent a 2-cent stamp for a Baptist magazine with church addresses, borrowed money to print 500 sheets of his first song, *Some Day, Somewhere,* sent out 3400 inquiries—and the gospel mail order business was born: in his bedroom. "It was in this time that I heard Mahalia. She had a voice that nobody ever had or anybody ever will have . . . the trills, tones, the spirit. She enjoyed her religion—that was the key, the core." He asked Mahalia to sing his songs. And would she sell them? He'd give her something. Sure, Mr. Dorsey. "She was the only singer who would take my music, then, but Mahalia would stand on a street corner and demonstrate it; then we'd sell a batch: 10¢ each. She was actually about the only gospel singer, besides Sallie Martin when she came in." That was 1929. "A girl brought one of his songs to church," says storied Sallie Martin Langham. Discovering Dorsey appeared every Saturday night, 10 or 12 music sheets in hand, at the home of a Mrs. Dennis who was coaching gospel style so he could put together a group, she promptly joined, and in time it was Sallie who was prime soloist for the group traveling the state as they could, and sometimes outward: was, in fact, gospel's first traveling salesman, since resourceful Dorsey sent her to sell and demonstrate in, "say, Cincinnati—stay three weeks, sell the music," says Dorsey. By then, for Mahalia, some mountains had been burrowed, some rivers had been crossed.

"Mahalia and I kind of got around together on programs," explains Mr. Dorsey; "not *together,* but what was important to me was that she sang some of my songs. Otherwise, she was singing out of her little *Gospel Pearls.* In those early days, not only did the ministers object to her, some would object to any gospel songs. It was something new to them. The South was different; they knew. But these people up here, all they understood was 'evangelistic songs,' up to the 1930s . . . 'You can't *sing* no gospel, you can only preach the gospel.' Preacher throw you out, when you come up with that. Yes, we took some knocks." And often not much more, when they *were* allowed: "10¢, 15¢—a quarter was big money. All in church. Sometimes, people listen, give you nothing."

Yet his music began to sell. And for Halie, the singing was pure elixir. This was what God wanted her to do. He had spoken to her, to use this gift; it was up to her to support herself any decent way she could, to manage it. The big "society churches" might bar her, but the Johnson Singers managed to get heard. Sometimes there was a chance out of town, and if the rest put other obligations first, Halie rattled the train alone, eroding her hoard—or if she didn't have it entirely, Aunt Alice or Aunt Hannah made up the fare, let her go. Once in a town, if she was handed from church to church, Chicago work went by the boards. It was day's-work, anyway—bust suds or slop the mop.

In Chicago, there was Salem or Pilgrim or Ebenezer or some church outside the Baptists—Bishop Childs' Evangelist Temple right at 3140 Indiana—to give her service; her holy dance remembered today; her style so different that young Evelyn Gaye learned to play for her for the pure pleasure of it: "Halie's got something they can clap and rock by." Bishop Childs was a great preacher, says Sister Gaye, "but all you heard something about was her."

She was still working with Rev. Seals among the ill, the possessed. One man who heard her at revival—no church man but drawn inside by the voice—got desperately ill and called for the girl Mahala to receive him into the church. She sent for a minister, but while the two prayed, Mahala sang a soft obligato. Tears streaming down his face, the man professed faith, was taken, happy, into the church, and before he died, baptized. She was 17. She was awed by the event, but the knowledge was armor when soon after, knowing she was in the congregation, yet another minister denounced her from the pulpit—oh, shame! This shouting, and bouncing, and clapping was unseemly in church. Halie leapt to her feet. "I am serving God! You read the Bible—you'll see right there in Psalms 47: 'Oh clap your hands, all ye people; shout unto the Lord with the voice of a trumpet.' I'm doing what the Bible tells me to do!"

She swallowed the scorn and the laughter. It didn't stop her. What you going do? Go on.

Back home, spouting indignation like an orbiting tea kettle, was Mahala's first true satellite in Chicago: Missie Wilkerson, a friend of Hannah's over to see them almost as soon as they stepped off the I.C. track. Her age midway between aunt and niece and with a child of her own, Missie was up from Dumas, Ark.—chocolate brown and big as a minute. Since Halie was skinny in those days, they were about a minute and a minute-and-a-half. The minute was fiercely protective. "I didn't know the *greatness* of Mahala in those days, she was just a girl, a little thing, but her voice spoke to me even when her aunts weren't taking her seriously. I was nobody, but I wanted to be her friend, to help her all I could. The way her life was going, she could use help—there were times I'd say she was treated like a Mississippi mule. We'd get together; and I was the first one started them little dime tickets. I'd pick cardboard off shirts and cut 'em up, make tickets for a dime. Signs, too. Then we'd go tack 'em up, use your shoe, late at night. You weren't supposed to put signs, but we did. On poles, fences, side of a store. It was fun. Mahala was always fun. She had this way she'd look at things. Then the program come, Mahala say, 'Now Missie, don't turn nobody down if they ain't got that dime. I know you—you'll be turning them back.' I say, 'Allll righty'; let 'em on in."

Her life supports swung then between her aunts, the warm hand of Missie, and the firm if undemonstrative approval of Mr. Dorsey. In 1930 she helped him form Pilgrim Baptist's first gospel chorus. She loved his songs . . . studied on them to get his meaning. She had to *feel* a song, else she couldn't make anything of it. Mr. Dorsey, though, that was a great composer; she learned song after song. (Oddly, not *Peace in the Valley*. "I wrote that for her, put her name on it," says Dorsey, "but she never got around to it.") Sometimes now Halie just didn't have time. Something heady as wine had sluiced into her life:

Politics. She wasn't old enough to vote, but black Democrat Louie B. Anderson had seen Halie mesmerize a tentful and sought her for his meeting. *This* was something couldn't be, down South! Wait'll Aunt Duke heard. Pearl Robinson was up visiting, she'd take the news back. Ward headquarters was just three blocks from home, at 3425 So. Indiana. Halie had seen that the Second Ward (biggest concentration of Negroes anywhere outside of Harlem, virtually a city to itself) had its black policemen, black firemen, black-owned stores. Now she realized it had its own government too: a black alderman who sat in with the mayor and had precinct captains and such. Halie, who never did anything halfway, became a fervent voice for Louie B. Anderson. He won. Hallelujah. It was a big thing. Just as it was a big thing, in 1931, to get a chance to sing at a funeral home. She'd get $2 a funeral. The impressive gentleman making the offer was Robert H. Miller, who'd heard Mahala at St. John's Baptist: Owning a funeral home automatically made him an important person no matter how small his place was then. ("Listen, Bob Miller had money when I got off the train," grinned Mahalia, telling it, "and he's about the only one I know, it didn't go to his head.") Poised for flight like a whippet, young Halie was elated. And $2 was $2.

It was about this point Mahala slipped "i" into her name. "It sounded pretty that way." Her aunts liked it; so did Missie, though with her "Mahala" stuck. To herself, she was still Halie, seeking her way.

And in Bob Miller, she found her first enthusiastic ally who could *do* something. "After we'd been talking one evening, she called me up. 'You're my manager,' she said." Mr. Miller proceeded to act like one, between funerals. He used his funeral car to drive her to dates. He got her up a program at a school auditorium—her first outside a church: a rarity, but still a black audience, gospel singing still exclusively within the black church, this whole movement unknown to the white world just as the massive energy of black religious life moved untouched by the currents of the white, and the white record companies' "race records" didn't enter the main stream.

Mr. Miller had his own idea. "We went down to Jackson Blvd. to one of the studios and cut records ourselves. We didn't know about the companies at that time; we were hoping we could sell them at the National Baptist Convention. We'd take our bundle and the master, so we could get additional ones pressed—I don't think we ever did, but we could have. We cut quite a few." It was one of the biggest thrills of a life that would be crammed with the incredible, for Halie Jackson to hear *You Better Run, Run, Run* coming at her from a record shop as she walked down State St. And she'd wanted to go home!

Halie, Mr. Miller, the records, and the handbills he printed on his mimeograph machine rode the funeral car to churches in Freeport, Rockford, Chicago Heights, Danville—wherever they could get to and back in one night: Halie would gladly have forfeited her job of the moment to sing on, but Mr. Miller had a business to run. He also put an impressive price on Halie's out-of-town engagements: 25¢ and 50¢. "Mahalia was always very active; she'd count along with me. Then when I'd turn in the money, she'd say, 'Well, I counted more people than that.' And I'd say, 'I let them in because they didn't have any money.' But she always checked on me, with the count at the door."

What with expenses, every penny *did* count. Things were getting steadily tougher.

DEEP DEPRESSION was grinding in. State St., province of the poor (neckbones were "State St. chicken"), was now strung with bread lines and soup kitchens. Hannah held onto her job. ("I wasn't a worker, I was family," says Hannah with pride.) Big Alice kept hers, too, and she had Pudley up from New Orleans—he helped out. Little Alice could give Hannah a hand after school. So Mahalia's widening search to sing left no hurtful gap. Offerings from the Johnson Singers' church programs had dwindled—just nickels and dimes sometimes. No knowing. But Halie usually managed a day's work around Hyde Park Blvd. and paid her way. With all the mess around she felt blessed: she could eat and she had a good place to stay, with family. She shuddered for the poor people spilling out of those kitchenettes like beans from a busted sack.

"On the South Side they cut up storage buildings and made cubbyholes about 8x10," says Mr. Miller; "called them kitchenettes but there was no kitchen: 20 apartments and one community kitchen, two baths, two toilets. Charge $18 a month. People up from the South to get work jammed whole families in. Only people who *had* money were ones that owned kitchenettes and owned policies."

Evictions were common. Then people turned to "the Reds," who held meetings in the park. "I don't know what else anybody called 'em," says Missie, "we just knew it was 'the Reds.' Whoever couldn't pay the rent, get put out, you go to the Reds. They had their organization go put you back in—landlords wouldn't fool with them."

So you had a place to sleep—what did you eat? Passing the bread line, seeing the sullen shuffling forward to the soup kitchen, Halie could hardly stand it. With $1.75 in her pocket one day, she scooped up the end of the line with a cheerful, "Come on! We'll eat some *real* food." Stop at a market for salt pork and ribs, her trail peering in, hope dawning; then on to a grocery for potatoes and corn meal. Hit Aunt Hannah's kitchen like a dust storm, seasonings flying. Seeing a laden table getting lighter by the second, Halie knew the satisfaction of Duke surveying her strays; of her mother too, so said; and their mother before them. *This* was being Christian.

Elsewhere in the city, restive men began parading, demanding jobs—the Treasury was full of gold, *billions* in Fort Knox. There was talk of forcing a change. On the South Side, few had such energy. No need to set up selling apples, either, like they did downtown: who'd spend a nickel for one apple?

But they'd spend it on policy, the small-time numbers racket that fattened on the poor like weevils on meal but was tolerated, sought, by desperate need. All the more, then, when in 1931, Buddy Bolden—"a gambler, a racketeer, and a little bit of everything else," as Mahalia described it—felt impelled to step inside a revival tent, heard Mahalia, and marched up to "give his heart to God." She *was* an instrument, no matter what those preachers said!

Other singers were coming into gospel, but lacking Halie's dimension, they escaped her fate: Most big churches still didn't receive her work, says Sallie Martin. "Some were very, very much against her—and the other singers looked down their noses at her. The Roberta Martin Singers had organized and they wouldn't seemingly get with Mahalia in any way. I would *go* with her. Once we went over on 45th and I said, 'Now listen, Mahalia, you must get a robe or either something for your lap, because when you get in the pulpit you know you just sit and that's it. I can't be on the pulpit and you sitting there in your dress all up.' So she got something for her lap. She didn't have a robe. "She was about as big as a minnie, tall but thin, very thin; I used to look at her later and say, 'What happened to you?' "

When she could get in a door, be *able* to sing . . . *When I Wake Up in Glory By and By . . . He'll Fight Your Battles* . . . the electricity was like nothing they'd known before. But no getting around it, she wasn't educated. When one of the girls from Salem said she was going up to audition for Prof. Kendricks, see if he'd give her some lessons, Halie went along: $4 each—big money. It was still the South Side, his studio, but she'd never been face to face with so grand a man: the tall, light-skinned tenor holding himself as if he were still on the concert stage. Bolder than her friend, Halie tried first—a spiritual. But the professor's pianist started so slow, Halie had to pull on up, pick up the beat. The great man stopped her. He demonstrated how it should be sung: with dignity—stage presence. Halie started again: the rhythm wouldn't hold back. Prof. Kendricks had enough. "Next! You try it." Ah, this was more to his liking. *"You've* got possibilities, but you—young woman, you've got to stop that hollering. That's no way to develop a voice, and it's no credit to the Negro race. White people would never understand you. If you want a career, you'll have to be prepared to work a long time, to build a voice."

Halie was silent as her friend danced down the stairs. When they hit the street, though, Halie gripped her ground. "I'm not studying about his high-class stuff! I'm not singing for white people! I'm singing in the church, for myself!"

9

If Prof. Kendricks didn't appreciate her voice, somebody else did: Alderman Wm. L. Dawson was running hard for Congress from District 1—1st and 2nd Wards—that summer of '32, and Halie Jackson was running right along with him. "Not only for the big meetings; for all the precinct-captain meetings too—I sang for I don't know *how* many of those different meetings a *night.* I was rather gifted on changing words . . . there was nothing on my mind then *but* music, and I would sing, 'Dawson has brought us all the way, and he carries our burdens. Oh, he's such a wonderful leader, we always got to vote and keep him . . . Dawson has brought us a long way.' And baby, all the politicians would go crazy! Every time I'd go with Fred Dawson, I'd have a new song for him. Fred Dawson, that's what I call him. Fred."

Dawson decided to reward his cheerful young ally with a plum: he'd send her to get an education—or she could be a policewoman, make herself a good salary. Take her pick. School—from where she'd have to start—seemed like a train passed by. Policeman? The pay wasn't nearly so sharp in Halie's mind as the image of that badge shining in flashlight on the South Side at night—rimmed with the memory of police sticks flailing when a Pinching Town brawl brought them in. "Thank you, Mr. Dawson; these children up here too bad."

With August, she had another big enthusiasm: Franklin Delano Roosevelt was nominated for President at the convention in Chicago. "I worked hard for Roosevelt. I went around all the different districts for him, because he said he'd put meat on the table. You know, the Second Ward used to be dead Republican, and Dawson started out Republican too, but he must have seen the way the thing was going, because he switched to Democrat and turned that whole ward." Their very own Dr. Austin from Pilgrim Baptist was on Roosevelt's committee to speak all over the country. Big politics.

When Roosevelt won and closed all the banks not already shut down—many of the South Side banks already collapsed with no new deposits for props—the shaken black people flocked to church even more. What they needed was a *lift:* They went where they could get it. The big black churches began to reassess. Many, flush with the '20s' mirage of ready money—their pews overflowing with the flux from the Deep South—had taken over quarters vacated by white congregations as blacks spread southward from the city's center. Now—tithing shrunk, the whisper of folding money gone from the collection table—the "society" churches became desperate. The one sure solution, the known absolute to bring in money was this Mahalia Jackson, with the Johnson Singers. When she sang, people came. Would pay up front. "That's when the big churches opened their doors," said Mahalia, "when they needed to meet those mortgage notes." The Lord sure knew His business.

All about now, programs flushed together with the flood and slosh of the need. And as acceptance spread over Mahalia, singers lost their timidity or rancor or jealousy or scorn or at least submerged whatever adverse emotions they harbored in the priority of the moment: a multiplicity of singers, a raft of support for whichever voice had captured the pulpit of that hour. Eager, Halie supported them all—and in the doing often somehow there was a rubbing-off, a transmutation. "I've heard a many of them try to sound like Mahalia," says Dorsey, "but nobody could imitate her. And I worked with all the gospel singers. They all wanted to do something with me. This was a time of 10¢, 15¢. It had been tough to make it in 1927–28–29, unless you knew some people, but times got worse. Still, gospel songs helped people get through the Depression. And when a church got into hard luck, *then* it was glad to get the singer to fill the collection box."

Dorsey knew his way around the annual conclave, forum, marketplace of the vast National Baptist Convention, largest religious group in the country—virtually unknown to whites. Neither Dorsey nor Halie could get a spot to sing gospel—the program was reserved for *big* singers, an important mark of distinction in black religious music. But Dorsey—resourceful—and Halie—at the ready—found a gambit for him, if not for her. When Rev. Reuben Hack, now Mt. Moriah's pastor, came home from his first Convention, he disclosed a true wonder: Halie was singing up there! He'd heard her across the big crowd, he exulted: "When I found her, she was selling sheet music at a booth, demonstrating."

"That's how we knew Mahalia was singing," says Ethel Adams. "Rev. Hack said he'd know that voice anywhere; any of us would."

Dorsey was gaining fame now, but Mahalia was on her own as a fish-and-bread singer. They met on trains sometimes, Dorsey with his sheaf of new songs and stacks of successes at the ready for 10¢, sure of sales into the thousands; or so it seemed to Halie, watching, taking whatever the minister handed her for the evening's singing, thanking the Lord, singing for her supper and her salvation. For steady wages, she found work packing dates at a factory on the West Side: Back on the elevated, but it was $7.20 a week, her first job minus the mop or the scrubboard. The empty boxes coming down the line one by one by one were no problem; she was used to working fast. A knife fight between two women was no more than something to throw off after Greenville and Pinching Town, except she knew these people would never be friends of hers. But that sameness. And you didn't even get a taste. ("Mahalia never got to bring home any dates," says Aunt Alice. "But she used to come home, be very tired.") It was the sameness did it. Halie quit. She could do better than *that*.

It took a while, but she found it: a steady maid's job, $12 a week! At the finest hotel Halie had laid eyes on, the Edgewater Beach, high over Lake Michigan. A fancy white people's hotel. No Negro guests allowed and the Negro help fed separate. But that was the way things were. Halie stuck. Over 30 years later, taking a New Orleans friend for a drive in her Cadillac, she detoured to point it out. "Look! I worked there as a maid. And Laurraines, they said I was the best maid they ever had at that hotel." A grin lit her smooth brown skin. "They didn't know that 20 years later, they'd give me a banquet."

There was a special reason the Edgewater Beach didn't slide under the church tracks as swiftly as so many housework jobs, why suddenly Halie had a strong pull to be home. . . .

She fell in love.

10

Ivy was tall, handsome, light-skinned; from New Orleans. Best of all, when Halie brought him home, Aunt Hannah and Big Alice accepted him. The girl was plenty old enough to have a boy of her own.

From her earliest years, and she was 20 now, Halie'd had a need and a talent for loyal friends—boys as well as girls—their give and take direct. But never, even in the hot early run of feelings in passionate New Orleans, never had she had a boyfriend or even yearned the secret teen awakening: a sparing for her with Duke a threat to any youth with an eye on Mahala, and Pinching Town porous as a sieve and as close-contained, so that even a sidewalk look had its substance and was sifted. Since Chicago, since Salem . . . over five years ground into the pot, mixing the need and the seeking and the shoring and the cold and heat and the draining hugeness to finally meet and test and spread to . . . here there had been grateful grasping of such hands as would help and solace but these always less than the task—the grappling—and seeking so late of rest for the body; but restless the mind and the heart, the big heart pouring into the soul its unused emotions. And now there was Ivy. Halie the hotel maid, Halie the day's worker, Halie who sang for the Lord and her supper if He willed, had a man who was music to another, inner ear. She'd see how much singing she could do in Chicago without pushing on out so far. The Johnson Singers were busy. Church nights were moving on up. And there were the funerals.

Bob Miller had started something. Families began to seek her to sing out *their* loss—for love of God and the glory of the passing, not pay. One bright and shining and extraordinary exception came when a co-worker of Missie's died and her boss, Clarence McGowan, gave Missie the body. She got Mr. C. J. Rogers to attend to the funeral, and she got Mahala to sing. Mr. McGowan gave Halie twenty . . . five . . . dollars. It was like a comet bursting, its glow in their eyes long after its substance was gone and she was back to Bob Miller's $2. And right now, this revival in Waukegan.

Walking down 31st St.—just back from Waukegan, heading for home and Ivy—Halie met another male who would instantly loom large in her life. Actually, he was small in almost every respect: height, size, skin stretched thin and tight over his bones, everything except the eyes—large and luminous as he gazed the distance up to Mahalia's own. He was eight. A street urchin. He'd come up behind and tugged. "She was my idol, but I wasn't sure this was her, that particular evening," says noted folk/gospel singer Brother John Sellers, looking down the long street. "I said, 'Are you Mahalia Jackson?' . . . 'Yes, I'm Mahalia Jackson.' . . . 'Well, my pastor wants to meet you—Rev. Bobbie Williams; he's in the restaurant.' So she came on in with us. I had been the one wanted to meet her."

The spindly little boy walked her home, to be back next day and next, a shadow surer than the sun, until "Can I stay by you tonight?"

"Whose little boy is this?" asked Aunt Hannah, searching his face. It wasn't easy to answer. Back in Greenville, Miss., famous tent shows such as "Silas Green From New Orleans" and "Rabbitfoot" came . . . not at county fair time (understood to be for whites) but other times when black revenue was welcome and they, knowing the ways they must mind with none of this written except seared inside and violable at grave peril . . . they came to drive stakes for their guy ropes almost at the door of a tiny one-room shack on the fairgrounds edge such as might hold tools or sloughed possessions but was in fact a dwelling where a little boy sat alone and unseeable had any one of these looked inside, for he was black and it was black and little light seeped past summer's dust and winter's rime on the one window. They had lived in a boarding house in Leland, he and his mother, but in the winter cold with the fire dying in the grate and she not due 'til night, he'd poured gasoline on and it exploded. The owner burst in, knocked the boy down and said they had to get out; so by courtesy and arrangement of his mother's friend Anna May Jefferson, who worked for the white people who had the *saying* of it, John now sat locked into the one room, memory still aching as his burned leg did. "I couldn't move, and the fire would go out, and I'd sit there sometimes all the long day—couldn't turn on a light; didn't have lights . . . just sit there in the dark until she come back, maybe 9 o'clock at night; I don't know what time . . . just look out the window, where I could see a little light."

An aunt home from Chicago picked John up and took him back to where she and her husband lived, his grandfather close by—all three strict Baptists. And this boy around those Sanctified! would *not* stay away! He was no boy of theirs.

"In those days," says Brother John, "the Baptists and Methodists hardly had anything to do with each other, or anybody else. Say segregation—they segregated themselves! To that extent, if you were a Baptist—

I'm a Baptist bred
And a Baptist born,
And when I die,
I'll be a Baptist gone!

So I ended up on the neighborhood. If I got a piece of bread . . . whatever somebody would give me. This now was the fall of 1934 and all year I'd been hearing the Johnson Singers—I saw the plays they did, too. At Ebenezer was the most place, because Rev. Smith liked their singing, used to have them . . .

Looking for the stone that was hewed out the mountain,
Looking for the stone that came a-rolling through Babylon,
Tearing down the troubles of this world. . . .

It was all quartet style in those days, but anywhere the Johnson Singers went, the church be just packed out, 'cause Mahalia was so fiery and *exciting;* had that *excitement* about her. She sang so hard, and she so small, people used to say, 'That woman sing too *hard,* she going to have TB!' "

Just now, to Mahalia and Aunt Hannah, little John looked the more likely candidate. They'd feed him up. He could sleep in the dining room. "And you better go to school," said Mahalia.

He set out for Drake School with Little Alice. "They couldn't figure out why I was so dumb," he laughs, " 'til I told them I hadn't been to school more than once or twice, days, in my life."

Evenings now, when Mahalia wasn't busy with Ivy, her head and little John's were bent together over his books. It eased her mind off Ivy, who was getting restless, talking about heading back South. It came to that, one day, Ivy off for Memphis; if he didn't make it there, he'd head on home to New Orleans.

No way to follow. Let push come to shove, she'd pitched her tent in Chicago and she'd never backed off a struggle yet. Eddie Scott from Salem would drive her around different churches. Mr. Miller and Emma Bell's brother Louis, too. But they weren't Ivy. On her knees, Halie prayed. The Lord was telling her the way. She'd sing it out. Wonder when she'd *ever* get back to New Orleans?

When she did—so soon—she'd have given the whole Mississippi River, Bisso's ferry and Audubon Park combined, not to have that reason to go.

11

First, private things looked up. Not seemingly, those cold spring months after Ivy was gone; but you could throw off what was inside your heart when you were in your own boat. Yet, at the Salem social, bubbling among friends, Mahalia paid scant attention to the steady eyes of the well-dressed gentleman who came across and was introduced: Isaac Lane Grey Hockenhull, from Como, Miss., by way of Pine Bluff, Ark. He seemed older (he was, by 10 years), and sophisticated, among the jostling church crowd, his bearing polished smooth by his ROTC years at Tuskegee Institute, which gave him a graduate's degree as a machinist, and by two years in liberal arts at Fisk University in Nashville, little Athens of the South. His manners were the prettiest she'd ever seen, for a man.

"I loved her the minute I laid eyes on her across that room," says Ike quietly, sitting in a wheelchair. "We talked, that evening, and then I called on her and Hannah and Alice."

There was comfort and a joy and a newness in being courted. Ike brought her candy, and flowers. Even more: Since Warpee days Halie had loved the movies and here were *talkies* scattered like popcorn through the neighborhood so you could take your pick. Sometimes Ike took her on the Jackson Park El—taking her elbow to guide her on the car, so fine—up to the Loop, to the big picture houses grand as palaces and one, the Chicago Theatre, big as a baseball park: 50¢ and not many black people inside (nobody said, but you just went on up to the balcony) but besides a moving picture you got the Pathé News and a stage show, a whole hour, then you could sit there and watch all over if you wanted. All *kinds* of acts, and *colored* people . . . Paul Robeson, Bojangles Robinson, Ethel Waters, Hi-Hat Hattie McDaniels, crazy Stepin Fetchit—Will Rogers generally had Stepin Fetchit. Sometimes they went to the South Side's own big theatre, the Vendome. All the new pictures and the big colored acts too. (Earl "Fatha" Hines got off on the piano so bad you didn't *care* if the Vendome was so grand, you had to shout.) Mostly, though, they went to the Grand right at 31st and State; and Ike agreeably sat there all Sunday afternoon—Halie still thirsty for the sights and sounds—or walked over to another one if Halie wanted to see two: the films not lingering, one night or two in these tailings into the neighborhood houses. Take *The Big Broadcast* with Bing Crosby, the King, got a nice way to him and sing *so* pretty, and Connie Boswell, white girl from New Orleans; and Cab Calloway —all them big singers in there. She could've watched *six* times. Had man or boy said, "You're going to be right there *with* Bing Crosby; he's going to be glad to call you friend," she'd have snorted, "What you talking?" But she'd have wondered. Aunt Bell *had* come out with that. . . . Put all that out your head, girl. The Lord got His ways for everybody.

Sometimes Ike took her to some fancy place come payday, maybe to the Sunset Cafe to hear Louie Armstrong, his horn a letter from home—the Sunset "black and tan," both blacks and whites admitted.

But Ike wasn't too grand to like peppermint pickles. He was just as happy to sit there in Hannah's kitchen, hammer and towel in hand, pounding off the outside, the chewy part, to eat first: the big peppermint stick bigger than a broom handle and near as solid . . . pounding down to the hard part where the pretty red streak would just shine . . . chopping off the likely length for the pickles Halie was reaming to make place for the peppermint core, then munching his share 'til they'd emptied the jar.

Ike had to be after her for herself, Halie well knew: no more on her back than a chicken after a storm. (Let the rest of 'em keep on about her same old dress—let 'em *be* trifling, they'd see.)

Big Alice had a suitor too—Rev. Williams—and when she accepted and moved out, Hannah found fresh walls for her flock at 3225 So. Indiana: got a movie right there on Indiana. Aunt Alice lived half a block off. Across from her was Bishop Childs' revival tent, just down from his temple, and Pilgrim a block over from there. A tight cluster. With an air of anticipation as summer came late to Chicago that year of '35. Papa was coming, sent a ticket by Hannah—Uncle Porter have to wait his turn in Cincinnati. Vigorous and handsome at 83, his voice a rich roll as he interpretated the Bible, in the main his pulpit now was New Orleans so that Bessie could not be budged out of Pinching Town no matter how Hannah urged her. "Leave Papa? I didn't have eyes enough to see my daddy!" cries Bessie. "All of us sisters crazy about Papa, all the family. Yes, you had to mind; he didn't speak to you but once. Learned how to mind and obey, all of us, and how to treat people . . . he believe in Christian practice. When I was small, still at home, people come ask for meal, flour, syrup, sugar, we'd give it to them, by the bucket. My daddy bought his stuff by the barrel."

"What's that smell?" sniffed Papa, arriving.

"Just the stockyards, Papa, over to 47th and Halsted; wind blows this way. You'll get used to it."

A smell was nothing to Papa—lived his life around stock although the steadiness of it did take you. But he had deeper things on his mind. Not just Ike and Missie and the boy John, but Rev. Williams, Rev. Austin, all Pilgrim's young ministers, Bishop Childs, Rev. Petty—all fell under his spell, his erudition. And Papa so pleased to hear her sing! Halie blossomed with pride in her grandfather. And loved him so, she'd put him in the tub and bathe him like a baby. As the day came for him to go, looking so elegant, tip to toe, grey eyes steady under his summer hat, fine lunch ready from Hannah—at work now—for the train, Halie knew what she could do: "Papa, I'll pay for your picture. Little Alice, Pudley, let's take Papa over on Cottage Grove and get the people to make his picture. I got the money!"

Off they hustled, lanky Little Alice and big Nathaniel shepherding Papa . . . into the sun, into the heat wave that had firemen opening hydrants to cool the Black Belt. Studio just a few blocks away. . . .

Papa had a stroke.

All the way in the cab, Halie prayed, John alongside. At County Hospital, they found the people didn't want to take Papa in. Too crowded, they said. Please God, please Jesus, they *got* to. . . . All right, in here, up there, don't crowd, mind the cot, yes you can sit. That evening when Hannah walked in with "Ooh, Daddy's well on his way now," and Alice told her no, he's in the hospital; he had a stroke, "They had to put water on me," says Hannah. It didn't take her aunt to tell Halie it was all her fault—she felt it through her sick, sick heart.

Pretty ill, the doctor said. Low sick, Halie knew. She prayed without cease. God, if You just let Papa get well—If You just let Papa get well, I'll—she searched her heart. What was the most pleasure in the world she could sacrifice, to show God she was sorry, to pay the price for Papa? Not her singing, that was God's work; He'd put her to that. . . . Heart sinking, she knew. Picture shows and vaudeville. God, if You let Papa get well, I'll never go to another moving picture show or vaudeville or a night club again. She got off her knees. Time to go to the hospital.

Papa got well; weak, but well. And Halie kept her vow. She never entered another movie house in her life. Not even to see her own films, and she made three. She didn't speak of it to Aunt Hannah or any of them. Lot of things you don't talk about. You just do.

HALIE BEGGED HIM not to go, to stay on with them. So did Hannah: but "You been too good a daughter for me to die on you—let the rest of them take care of me now."

"You don't have to go home to die, Papa," said Hannah; "you can die here."

"No, Hannah, I want to go home and die with the rest of them."

"Papa, you *well,*" cried Halie. But there was no changing Rev. Clark's word, once given. It was Halie to take him home, he unable or unwilling to make his way unassisted and they wouldn't have taken the chance anyway. Please, God, he's got to be *all* well. Phone poles clickety on the I.C. tracks. Hurry to get him some water, wait her turn at the end of the car; crack the window for some air, close it back now from the draft; get the soot out of his eye; treat him to cold grape pop—take one more now when the man be back; help him make it to the toilet, pass him chicken, bologny, cheese and gingercake; feed him his pills, ask the man what time it is. The two days were long, but it was different, and you could watch people at the stations. Memphis—Jackson—seeing them look like with different eyes, Chicago eyes maybe; when you change? seeing ahead to Duke and Uncle Emanuel on the porch and bound to be Aunt Bell and Celie there and Doodutz and Brisko and Bessie and all them, maybe Peter and Big Allen. . . .

ShhhhhhhhhhhhSH! We here, Papa. Lemme help you up. Just lean on me, Papa. Now let me get down our stuff. We going home in a *taxi.*

As the cab rattled cautiously onto the humps and ruts of Millaudon, Papa took a good deep breath. When it eased onto Esther, his hand was on the handle; and when the taxi pulled to a halt in front of Duke's, Papa leaped out before the engine had stopped, heading for the circle of arms like a moth to the light. "Oh, my God!" cried Mahalia. "I been carrying him on my back all the way from Chicago and here he's running to the porch!"

They were hard put to keep him from going on to Legonier, even Duke unable to impose her will on Papa, who had a mind to sit in his own place a spell, down from the bones of his ancestors. Still, he was glad to give them a few days.

So was Halie. Days flowed by with the eating and talking and the listening, mostly close inside the family or at church, Halie assured in maturity and her new prestige. Still, late of an evening, on the porch with just Celie and the night sounds and the smell of the river, Halie could resist the tug. "It's hard, but I'm going to try to make it; if I make it, that's where I'll make it. Sometime I might be able to do you some good; you can't tell."

She heard her daddy speak at Broadway Missionary on communicating Sunday: "It pays to serve Jesus," he said; he liked that text. And she caught sight of him on the banquette coming from Carrollton: such a beautiful man; little features, skin like black velvet, such pretty eyes. He spoke, in passing.

Three weeks and she was rolling back, her mind on the Johnson Singers—see if Prince going play any more, if not, see if Estelle Allen got more time; on Bishop Childs and Mr. Miller—let them know she's back, see what's coming up; on Ike—looking for her to make up her mind. Emma Bell's brother Louis, he was nice but look like he still hanging on his mama's heel. Missie's brother Sam, he had a way too, but it was noway steady: flash the girls right *with* her; and he wasn't a churchgoing man—take him be like setting an iron kettle in the swamp and watching it rain. Now Ike. . . .

Her eyes softened.

WHEN SHE SAID YES, Ike moved in at Hannah's. He had been living over on Michigan Ave. with his mother, Mme. Hockenhull—broke and ailing now. No distance to go see her and here's a woman with a lot in her head, got more beauty secrets than a tree has leaves: put out "Mme. Hockenhull's," made up the jars herself, starting as a beautician in Pine Bluff, just poked and prodded until she had the hang of the thing and over 200 formulas made up for colored skin, pressed or nappy hair. Made and lost a fortune, never mind how. A woman worth listening to. Halie hadn't much time to pass, though. She had trouble in mind and look like it might be rising. Not the singing—singing going fine: $12 at Bishop Childs' yesterday and revival still going on. Mr. Dorsey back in town with some new songs—got to get with Estelle Allen (her main accompanist these two years). More calls to big churches—be quiet if the big ones don't offer Halie a dime, that's one more against the ones still keeping you out and you have no right *not* to sing; it is a gift of the Lord for His glory. . . .

("These preachers jealous of you, Mahala," sniffed Missie, " 'cause you just a slip of a girl and the people coming to listen to *you*."

"That's all right," said Mahalia, "one sorrow don't make a day; only the Lord make the day.")

No, it wasn't the singing. And she could scuffle up a dime when she needed one. What worried her was the sight of this good man Ike, home from the post office, sitting across the room while she's studying her Bible—and him with the racing sheet. For hours. She hadn't dreamed. Lord, help me straighten this man out. And here John for his lessons. Ike can just help him too.

So smart, so taking was this waif windblown to their door that Aunt Hannah, finding him staring at her one day . . . ("So beautiful; ain't she beautiful; wish she was *my* mama") . . . Aunt Hannah caught his thought. "I'm going to keep this little boy as my godson."

John was in the family. Already Mahalia had him in training, her first protégé. Perfectionist that she was, all by her gift, not knowing why but certain of how, always searching for the way to unfold, the path of the song, unhampered by the thin strictures of notation . . . paper and lines and ink too frail to run the *roam* and hues of melody and meaning . . . Mahalia was no easy teacher. To John, "I don't know . . . you always saying you can't hold one thing. I want to teach you how to sing baritone, and you sing something else; you singing *my* voice, which is contralto." "But I can't *hold* what you give me!"

Still the boy absorbed, and Bishop Childs let him sing at revival those first cold nights of 1937, Mahalia singing by day—no steady job, this deep Depression—and John hard put to stick the school day but doing it, penalty of Mahalia on his hide. Weekends he was at the tent with her, taking up the offering: give what they will or may, for the singer. "Sometimes it would add up to $4, or $2.50. If people give you a dime it was a blessing. Because people were really starving . . . running bread lines."

But Ike had the post office (though he was "temporary"), and she sure knew how to scratch. They'd make out if she could count on Ike not throwing his money away on the horses. Studying his handicaps. She could just hear Aunt Duke. Better not lean on a straw.

12

Abruptly, there it was, the urgent need, this time to find fare to New Orleans. Papa was dead. As far back as last spring, Duke had piled into her new secondhand car and gone to Legonier determined to bring back Papa. But this rock so like her substance could not be budged until his own thought set it in motion, which did not come until January, he confessing to dizziness and triumphantly installed then at Duke's and permitting a doctor, but to that baffled man's face declaring he had better: "Dr. Jesus"; ending, for all that, with Bell, who had known but would not say until Papa recounted his vision; and again, this only after against all counsel and Duke at work, he had taken the notion to walk around the block to Bell's, on Wall St.—got in sight of the door before he collapsed, so that Celie rushed, shrieked to the Bumblebee Bar for the men there who swarmed to help, lifted him with infinite care and caution under Celie's wild-flaring eye into the bed at Bell's, whose door he would then quit only for the journey with two white horses and a glass-sided wagon, face calm, spirit flown, for had he not successfully defied Death standing at the foot of his bed, told him "nay" twice in a ringing tone, sent him sliding into nothingness until *Jesus* should send for his soul? (Calling to Celie, "Daughter, come; Death is here, and I want to tell you what he looks like: he's a big, rawboney man, with blazing eyes; you have to be saved and born again to contend with this man . . . but Death, you have no dominion over me; step aside; you have to wait on King Jesus." Then to Celie, in the moment, "I have been up in the council of elders, twenty and four, and I have answered the questions, every one. King Jesus is ready for me" . . . gave one quick breath, and was gone.)

He was waked at Mt. Moriah, a surging black stream flecked with the whites of Pinching Town who so admired him (where Rev. Clark learned Italian to visit with the family at the grocery a years-long mystery). Mounds of food disappeared and were replenished while the talk, too, flowed—space found for those from Legonier and Uncle Porter having his say but Uncle Bos had stayed the longest with him and knew it well; and the ministers and hoped-for ministers looked their last deeply, drawing strength from this rockbound face, and Halie's tears pooled inside unshed. Oh Papa.

More than enough Clarks, near-kin, Gumstump, ministers, Moriah's deacons and stewards, communicating stewards and deacons led by Mahalia's father (senior deacon now) to overflow Mt. Moriah next day but more must be made room for, could not be gainsaid for peace in Pinching Town so the air was close as time melted into undefinable length, Rev. Hack augmented by all the other ministers impelled to speak well and long for one of their number, all ritual accorded in full and Halie unable now to hold, breaking down, Peter trying to comfort her as whiteclad stewards rushed over with the smelling salts. "She took it some hard," says Celie.

Finally the cemetery. No band, for a minister. A final prayer. Amen.

No lingering now. Back to Hannah's, to Ike, to the freezing search for work—get out and *go;* to the Johnson Singers—shrinking, mostly her and Louise. To a funeral to sing for, not at Bob Miller's but another parlor: for one of Ebenezer's number, so she could expect to and did see, listening intently, dentist Frank J. Hawkins, a big deacon who so loved her singing—had actually called her name from the pulpit the Sunday morning before Papa died; "Ink, I want you to hear Mahalia Jackson." But the dark stranger standing alongside Dr. Hawkins now seemed distracted, swiveling his eyes between her face and the crowd's as her tears mingled for the departed, for the world, for Jesus, for herself, for Papa, the tears of the rest flowing through hers.

Afterward, while people still milled, Dr. Hawkins introduced "Ink" Williams of Decca Records. He'd like to talk to her. Faintly scandalized—such a peculiar place for him to be—Halie listened, lifted, and was enthralled: "I want to put you on records. You had all those people crying. I think we can do something with you."

That night, the next morning, she fingered his card: J. Mayo Williams, Artists and Repertoire, Decca Records, Race Record Division. Then she telephoned. Might as well find out as be sorry. "She wanted to know how much it cost to record," laughs Mr. Williams. "I told her, 'Nothing; just come on down like we said.' "

Get Estelle Allen. What to sing? He said four numbers. How to do? Nobody put gospel on a big commercial label like Decca before. Mr. Williams said so and she knew it was so, gospel so tight it turned around inside itself. How she going make this first one *go?* She'd introduced piano to Chicago's churches for quartet singing ("Wasn't no piano with the singers before Mahalia," says Brother John)—to raise the beat, fill in the long sustains. How about organ? For the slow songs?

"Organ for gospel?" cried Estelle. *"And* piano?"

"You just got to play one at the time. What you think!"

IT WAS THE BIGGEST building they'd ever been in, called the biggest in the world: The Furniture Mart, a blazing whiteness in the sun. "Make ten of anything on Canal St.," thought Halie, saying little as they found their way in. No use spreading nerves.

"Hawkins was there," says Ink Williams, "and Dan Burley; he was on a newspaper . . . had a jive Kodak, pretended to be taking Mahalia's picture but he had no film in it. She'd brought me a box of cigars and a pint of whiskey. Hawkins took the whiskey, and I kept the cigars. She seemed perfectly at ease. I just provided her what she needed and she went ahead."

Put Estelle at the piano for *God's Gonna Separate the Wheat From the Tares* and *You Sing On, My Singer.* (To little John's "How you do that, and you all sing that in a quartet?" she'd said only, "You wait and see.") Shift Estelle to the organ, pumping away, for *God Shall Wipe Away All Tears* and *Keep Me Every Day.*

The small shadow waiting, self-appointed herald, fairly danced all the way to the 20th & Central Bar-B-Que—their celebration. "We didn't none of us have any money," says John, "but Mahalia got two plates and one pop, and she gave me part and saved the rest for Ike. 'Oh, Mahalia,' said the woman heaping up the ribs, 'you're going to be a great singer!' 'No, I don't think so, 'cause I ain't doing nothing.' She wasn't pleased with that first recording. She always did have an idea 'This can be done better.' "

At home, she didn't speak of the session. "She always was one to keep her business to herself," says Aunt Hannah. And her instinct was right.

When Decca released her first record, it got no more motion than a train off the track. Except in the Deep South. There it got some play, sold some few.

But Pinching Town! Alerted that this was a New Orleans singer, the juke box route men for the Negro neighborhoods for the first time put a religious record, *God Shall Wipe Away All Tears,* on the barroom boxes. That day is burnished bright in Pinching Town histories, fingered endlessly as a Catholic's rosary and some Catholics actually among the number that erupted with thc news . . . "Mahalie's on the box!"

"That was the first we knew she had made a record," says Celie; "the whole *family* went to the Bumblebee. Aunt Duke was at work but my mother was broke down to three days a week then (Bell laid off for hard times but offering to come take care of the Rightors for nothing, so they compromised on three days and this not one.) "First time my mother was in a tavern but she was there, Bessie was there, Big Allen, every cousin we had and those who claimed to be, all crowded around, listening. Had it blaring into the street at each corner there was a tavern and honeyyy, it got like Carnival! people was in a rage! just overjoyed! falling out their doors! streets black with people! had to pick the people up! *men* crying, wiping their eyes with towels and handkerchiefs, pounding at the church door to open up! men, women, knocking on more church doors than one, wanting to be baptized! crying 'My God, what a voice!' Young man named Lawrence never been in church before, but he came crying and was baptized that very Sunday."

There was one more who cried. To all within his hearing, "That's my daughter!" cried Johnny Jackson.

13

It wasn't so strange for the jazzman—he'd *sung* in church sometimes, home in New Orleans. And it was New Orleans getting him there now. Back from Europe to Chicago (his home base now, in '37) a new band shaped up, got to check out this girl. Say she's Bessie Smith plus two. Hmmm. . . .

He sat rapt. Slow, slow she sang, deep down in it, moving around the sorrow, pulling on the power, seeking for the Maker . . . Lord God this girl can sing. And here came the tempo, pushing on your feet, driving up the beat, rising in your hands. Clap or shout, but you can't be still!

After church, he sought her out. New Orleans, hello. "Red beans and ricely! nicely! Got you a spot with the band, make you some real green, get to move around. You don't have to show me, I *know* what you can do with the blues."

"I know what I can do with it too, baby, and that's not sing it. Child, I been reborn!"

It was one argument Louis Armstrong lost. His consolation was red beans and rice, his all-time favorite dish, his sister's in New Orleans enough to pull him back by itself. "Baby, I can't stand your beans!" grated Louie, grinning as he dived back into Halie's pot, saving on the stove in reach of the table; "you near Mama Lou."

"Fatha" Hines—same one they'd watched at the Vendome—he came asking too, with no more luck. If Louie couldn't do it, nobody could; and nobody could.

Ike's old argument was loosed, worse now—in their room, in the kitchen—Aunt Hannah neutral. "Why don't you stop this lowdown type of singing and learn to sing right? You straining yourself at all these churches; why don't you *do* something with your voice?"

"Man, I'm doing something right now, I'm doing what the Lord set out for me to do, praise His name with it!

"You have a voice like a cello and a head like a rock!"

"Be glad I don't have a heart like a stone or I'd pitch you out!"

"You can have a *real* career, on the stage, Mahalia, but you can't do it without proper training."

"I *done* that and I'm not doing it!" But to quiet Ike, she went to Mme. Anita Patti Brown, the opera singer, John close behind. Mahalia made no bones about it: "I don't sing opera, honey," she announced. The famous woman, singular for her voice but especially for attaining her goal with black skin in a white sphere, answered, "Just go on and sing; because you can sing." Like God gave it to her. But she'd get some records of Marian Anderson and Paul Robeson to listen to, so these people could understand her diction.

It didn't satisfy Ike. January cold or August heat, they argued. "And you're not helping a bit, me having to contend with these singers and preachers and now those big people at Decca Records!"

New York had told Ink to forget this religious bit; she won't sell: get this woman onto blues. She'll be phenomenal. Make a fortune. "I was privately opposed," says J. Mayo Williams; "I was never in with the preachers, not with me in the blues, but it was against my conscience to switch a religious singer. But I followed orders; I asked." Her no meant it. "Ink, this is a gift of God. I would have no right to abuse it."

Decca dropped her. "But I kept telling those others," says Brother John. "They'd make fun of her singing. I used to *always* get in fights. Robert Anderson and them say, 'Oh, Mahalia can't sing.' 'Yes, she can! Any day she can beat Roberta!' 'No, she can't.' 'Don't talk about that—Ink Williams have Ella Fitzgerald and all them, the Jordans, Cab Callaway, *everybody* black, for Jack Kapp, and Ink Williams told me, "That woman can sing." So don't tell me that!' "

It made no difference to John that young Robert's stance was predictable: Robert belonged to the Junior Gospel Chorus organized for Ebenezer Baptist by Theodore Frye with Roberta Martin (both emerging from Mahalia's church, Salem), from which came the Martin-Frye Singers, dissolving into the Roberta Martin Singers. Sallie Martin (no relation but the two often confused as sisters, to their mutual annoyance, says Sallie) was assembling her own group. These two Martins had separate, passionate camps; Mahalia's and others' partisans also dotted the plain. On the wrong side of the wind at any program, you could get scorched. "There was more rivalry then among church singers than show folk," says Prof. Dorsey.

Such rivalry didn't bar friendship. To Robert Anderson (who would join Mahalia's inmost circle), "back in those days the gospel singers were more as a family. If Mahalia was going to have a concert, all the singers were there; when we have a concert, Mahalia was there."

"When I be up there," Mahalia would say, "I wasn't studying about any of them; I was singing for the Lord."

So immersed were they all in the event, that none of them realized they were making a major turn in the direction of American religious life; knew it but did not *note* it, as slowly their gospel singing began dissolving the icy barriers, the low tight range of cold shoulders between Negro Protestant sects, the erosion as irresistible as the Mississippi River leveling sandbags. In 1937 the barriers were not gone but runnels from the gospel wellhead were flowing through all the intricate networks of Negro churches. "From *no* mixing," says Robert Anderson, "as the different denominations grew interested, their people came for training, and we went around training their different choirs and choruses and soloists; we all did."

In the crossovers, the questing and questioning, Mahalia came to know how much she—how much Mt. Moriah—how all of Pinching Town's encircling Baptist churches had absorbed from the little Sanctified Church—the Holiness Church—shouting the Holy Ghost in the rented house on Aunt Duke's block; knew how this and others like it had drawn in the city's basic beat—a dancing city growing music as free, as pungent, as the pepper grass on the levee; taking its instruments—tambourine, cymbal, steel triangle, drum—and lifting the jubilee to a new pitch for sheer joy in the Holy Ghost and the brilliance of God's glory.

No turning back; why turn back on joy? The gospel tide rolled on. Going to glory. Amen. What church invited whom was watched and guarded, and a minister's announcement of preference was a major moment of ellipsoid consequence, its basic element not always parallel the event and frequently encircling other planes, curves, not necessarily fixed, possible change inherent. It was just such a moment when Halie alone was invited to sing in Buffalo, N.Y., for a whole week. She could stop at the preacher's house.

The three Johnsons were gone about the intense business of survival; Louise Lemon was more and more reluctant to sustain the exploding demands; but ever since Estelle Allen had taken over the piano, Estelle had stuck. She did now. They found a car and driver, bundled against the November cold, and headed East. The church had printed tickets for 25¢: a big piece of change but really 5¢ a night, the Chicago singer at the church five nights running. Halie decided they best see could they get some more dates up here to make out. Just so she got back by Thanksgiving; that was Aunt Hannah's big day to cook.

They just beat the deadline, Ethel Adams with Ike and the rest waiting to see if Halie would make it, when she came in, stomping off the snow. "She told us how well the program went—made a flash. But there was this one man just jumping up with his hand outflung hollering, 'Oh Lord, I wonder what's the matter with me!' She's singing and he's shouting, 'Oh Lord, I wonder what's the matter with me!' Stewards, deacons, nobody could stop him. 'Oh Lord, I wonder what's the matter with me!' "

Big success but no money. What was she going do? City like this, must be some way to find a *career.*

14

"Now we can make it!" Over 200. A *big* stack. Ike's mother had turned over all her cosmetic formulas: they could go into business themselves.

When they bought the ingredients, starting small, Halie was astounded at how ordinary, how cheap was most of what ranged there on the table. No wonder people make a fortune. "Bob Miller, you should see! I'll sell you some, make you beautiful."

They moved around the block to Mrs. Thorne's at 3305 So. Michigan: one good-sized room and a kitchenette where they could set out their stuff. Stir, cook, and pour—John not trusted with this (growing, though, 12 and living with the McIvers, an Irish family, where he worked for his keep)—but able to put the jars in boxes, and help sell.

"Mahalia and Ike would make some stuff up, then me and Mahalia would go: She had a little bag, go this way; I have a little bag, go that way, door to door. Mahalia put it on and tell the people how—rub it on their skin, see how it was. She'd make me do the same thing. And it was cosmetics! Made it up in the kitchen. Ike stirring. I was right there. Sometimes I'd sleep between them in the bed. 'Cause I was young, just coming up."

But mix what they might, the creams, the oils, the powders would not sell. Now if she claimed the oil brought luck . . . hey Pinching Town! Poor fools around here try anything if there's not another nickel in the house—*need* some luck trying to break out of State St. chicken: Must be some other part to the chicken besides the neck.

"We going have neckbones *again?*"

"Yeah, Mr. John, neckbones." No choice.

Since the post office laid Ike off again—not his fault, plenty lost out—look like he couldn't lay his hand on nothing else. ("I just wasn't a man to go up against a WPA shovel," Ike laughs softly.) Busting suds by Hyde Park wouldn't pay the rent and feed a man, not in Chicago, 'specially a betting man. No counting on singing for the pot, either, tight as things was. Even if Missie still cut up shirt boards for tickets, pastor wouldn't always let it go that way: "Give as you may and will for the singer" only *after* the collection for the service. Sixty cents in her pocketbook. What Ike going have when he come in?

He was grinning like a cat got the cream. No, no job, Sugar. No policy. No horse. "What I got here is *your* big chance! A *winner!*" Ike was excited as Halie'd ever seen, waving a piece of paper. "National exposure, Halie! Then you can go on and get some real training. This is it!"

"If you'll hand me that piece of paper instead of fanning me with it, I can see what this all about." The WPA Federal Theatre Project, the newspaper said, was holding auditions for *The Hot Mikado* with an all-Negro cast. Singers welcome to try out. Bring your own music. "This got nothing to do with me."

Ike tried to hold himself in. "Halie, nobody can touch your voice. You've got a *future* in singing. It's not *right* for you to throw it away hollering in churches. You could reach the heights!"

"Gospel wasn't so well thought of then," says Ike softly, a part of him still unconvinced.

"Hollering! Hollering!!" flamed Halie. "I'm singing for the Lord and I got no two minds about that. I don't even know who that Giber and Sullivan is!"

"It's *our* music they're going to use . . . see here, *Hot Mikado* . . . they're going to put in our beat, *your* beat. All they have to do is hear your voice. It's your stepping stone!"

"More like a stone around my neck!"

"Mahalia, you're just being stubborn and ignorant!" They were rarely both mad at once, but this was it. The neighbors at Mrs. Thorne's had no trouble hearing. "Woman, you want to nickel and dime all your life? Look around you. *You* haven't got a job and what can you do? I've left my name all over town and *still* no job and no telling when. Now here's your chance to start really singing and make big money too and you can't bother yourself to go down to see to it. You just don't make sense!"

"Where you going?"

"Out to give you time to think what I'm telling you."

All night she wrestled. "It was the first big temptation of my life. Decca and the blues wasn't nothing to this. I prayed and I cried and I walked the floor. Seemed like I could just hear Aunt Duke . . . singing in something like that was wrong, and sinful, and low-class. It went against all my upbringing. But I could hear Ike, too; I'd never seen him so mad.

"Next day I went down to the Loop to the Great Northern Theatre. I went, but my heart was sore. Felt like I was heading for that French whatyoucallit, take your head off. When I got there, the white woman at the door was nice, she said yes, this was the place, they were all inside, 'But where's your music?' I pulled my little *Gospel Pearls* out my pocketbook to show her. (Mahalia's voice grows mincing.) 'Oh, dear, they won't want to hear that. You need some sheet music, a regular *song.*' Well, whatever I get on, I got to do, you know, so I asked the way to Lyon & Healy, the big sheet-music store, and I didn't know if it was a sign, but what you think they had on the rack? *Sometimes I Feel Like a Motherless Child.* That was me, all right. The piece was right in my own book, but I had to spend my last 50¢ to get the sheet music.

"The theatre was a long, narrow old place, all those balconies reaching up behind you, but they said take a seat down here. The girls were already started singing, calling them up one by one, so I slipped clear to the back. Maybe they'd pick one before they got to me. Finally the man down front said, 'Anybody else?' and I had to get up on the stage, the last one. I tried to act like I'd seen the others do; I handed the man my music. Well, he started in and it wasn't nothing *I'd* ever heard; I looked over to see was he playing my music but he was; somebody had gone and changed it in an arrangement . . . I couldn't tell where to come in. I let him go all through and start again, and this time I had it in my mind and I sang. And honeyyy, I forever more sang it, 'cause I *felt* it. I was chancing my soul for a dollar, and it was just like hot grease popping at me to hear the people in that auditorium applaud. I'd heard the man tell the other girls they'd let them know, so I walked on out of there and looked in some windows to try to take my mind off. Finally I had to go on home, and Ike was already there. Excited again. 'They called next door for you so I took it, honey, and you made it! You're on your way. And you get $60 a week!' That was like $600 today. 'Yeah,' I said, 'for all the good it's going do me.' What would the Baptists think? that's what was in my mind. But to be peaceable, I asked him, 'How'd you do today?' "

"I picked up a little job. Nothing much. Selling insurance."

"Thank You Jesus. I don't have to go on the stage."

"What! Are you at it again?" The bout was shorter this time, especially after Halie marched next door and called to say thank you very much, but I don't believe I'll take the job. Yes, I'm sure; I won't.

Ike got drunk. Drinking wasn't his problem and often Halie joined him in some sociable Scotch, but not this time. She felt like she'd escaped the fiery pit and she better be strictly with the righteous.

Instead she sang herself high in the spirit. Glory Hallelujah!

Of all the pits to follow, she'd be sorely tempted to fall just once more. But that was years and the moon away. Right now, she was determined to show Ike and to realize that better living. She was turning over a plan. It couldn't happen tomorrow, and she had one hill to get over. . . .

TIME OUT FOR Little Alice's wedding—Bessie's baby grown already. Halie was happy to sing *(know* Aunt Bessie bound to bust out crying) . . . to get the family news . . . to show off Ike. She didn't mention the gambling but Bessie got that fast enough: no pleasure to Bessie to hear Ike had a nickname, "Seeing Eye Ike." (Most times sound like he end up the blind man.) Lord Jesus!

There was one extra tie to be told which brought barest "Humph!" from Bessie: Ike had found out Mahalia had a brother at the post office—her father's eldest son, Wilmon. It was peculiar finding him in Chicago, right at the post office: His very existence was news to Bessie.

Ike himself wasn't back on the mail; but he was working at his new job: door-to-door, policy premium 20¢ a week. (When he first said "policy", most folks took the wrong meaning.) Insurance was just a stopgap, he explained; his main business was going to be handicapping the horses. "Not to get too scientific, but—I'm studying out a new system."

Halie herself was studying out moves, but she wasn't one to talk. Less said, soonest mended.

15

The summer of 1938, the pioneer gospel-beat group, the Johnson Singers, quietly vanished: Louise Lemon, sole survivor besides Mahalia, failed to show. "She didn't like a man named Spencer Jackson and Mahalia put him on the program anyway," says Brother John. The church was packed. Estelle was ready. Then and there Mahalia converted all the arrangements to solos, and cast her mold once and for all.

The way was clear. Not that it showed, as September stirred into fall, the air cooler but not inside Ebenezer Baptist, packed out for a *big* program: Ebenezer presenting Roberta Martin; gave her a beautiful robe just for this occasion. Sallie Martin—not so often in town—was the other big gun on the pulpit in *her* robe. Mahalia was sitting up in her same old black dress she wore with a cape. Dorsey was playing for Sallie . . . Helen Green for Mahalia . . . 'Berta for herself, for her group. An outsider couldn't have guessed the drama rippling through the crowd. "They wanted Sallie and 'Berta to go over," says Brother John, "give the program to *them.* So when Mahalia sang, the people just sit on her . . . that's the way they'd do, way of saying you couldn't sing . . . wouldn't do nothing but sit, wouldn't react. But Mahalia kept on—

After while, it will all be over
After while, the sun going to shine. . . .

and one woman in the back say, '*Come* on, Mahalia, you can make it!' Another woman call up 'Yeah, honey, *come* on! You can make it!' Then the crowd pick it up—

It going to shine, Hallelujah,
After a while . . . After a while . . . After a—

'*Come* on, Mahalia, *come* on!' And honey!" grins Brother John, "Mahalia broke up that church. Purely broke—it—up! You hear me? When she got through, everybody just in an uproar!"

"Mahalia," said Dr. Hawkins, "you can *sing.* You'll outlast them; you'll be more famous than they ever were, or they ever dared to conceive!"

"Aw, Dr. Hawkins—"

"You can outsing them all."

Calls for Mahalia—church calls—came in so thick now that she couldn't handle all the demonstrations, it being the custom to sing in the Sunday morning, where the big crowd was, to let the people know what they would get. Now Halie was glad of John's stubborn voice as a big West Side church called (to Missie's delight).

"I got a boy—my boy sound just like me. I'm going to send him over." That Sunday morning, "Mahalia can't be here, but this boy sounds like Mahalia; he's going to be along with Mahalia tonight." They'd break it up. Hallelujah, everybody. Come *on,* Mahalia.

Missie was hard put to scrounge shirt fronts to make the cardboard tickets, but they all clipped away as more West Side churches called. "I had a cousin, Dink Stroud," says Mother Fannie Gaye, Evelyn's mother—of the Spiritualist church; "Dink told me, 'Fan, if Mahalia Jackson was singing down in hell, I believe I'd want to go down there and hear her. I love to hear her just that much.' That got me to go the first time."

"I still hear her singing *If You See My Savior, Tell Him That You Saw Me,*" says Evelyn Gaye. "She sang that so much and the people, look like they were just awed by it, on a higher plane, gone. She had that type of rocking and that holy dance she'd go into—look like the people just *submitted* to it."

None of this was lost on Dorsey. When Sallie Martin made her break, heading far afield, the composer promptly sought Mahalia: He wanted to get to some churches not too much a distance around. He'd play for her, and she could demonstrate his music on her program. Not but in and out, mainly weekends.

That just fit! Singing for the Lord—that was her church work. What she'd been studying was a way to get some fat on the hog . . . and she *knew;* right to her taste: she'd get her a beauty shop. She'd start beauty school right after Baptist Convention. Couldn't get a license to open, without that certificate. Inspector come in, certificate not on the wall—big trouble. Meantime she could be laying up some money, and she could practice on Emma Bell. She already had the hang of it, from watching.

"Mahalia learned on my head," laughs Emma Bell Smothers Pearson; "every Saturday before she ever got any training, she'd fumble in it, mess around in it, style it so many different ways 'til I got tired sitting in the chair: 'You go on and finish, I'm tired.' "

But when she walked over to Apex beauty school at 47th and Park, she got a setback: They couldn't let her in as a regular student—you had to have an 8th grade education. "That's all right," she said at last, "Put me down to come and learn anyway." She'd still have her shop. She'd figured a way.

She had to do *something*. More and more it troubled her: Ike with the racing sheet. And her name coming up with his gambling: Look at the program Mr. Miller got up at DuSable High, big auditorium and Ike and John selling the tickets and what happens? Out to praise the Lord and some man talking *horses* to Ike. Now it's "the track down in Little Rock" and "the Fairgrounds in New Orleans." Horses, stables, jockeys, blood lines . . . like the man had a fever. Her heart beat low. She knew now how his mother lost her fortune: at the track. It *could* be in his blood.

"If you going to New Orleans, you can go meet my daddy. I'll tell you how to get there."

He was still home, though, in September when Halie left for the Baptist Convention—in Buffalo this year. A minister invited her to Cleveland; others linked on, church by church, week by week . . . Estelle sticking at the piano although the day came when she knew she'd lost her secretary job, gone past any boss's endurance . . . Christmas decorations went up in the towns . . . still they strove. . . .

Christmas Eve Ike went for John at the McIvers, "John, you got to help me get something together for Mahalia for Christmas. I got this goose, and I don't know what to do with it."

"While we were fixing," says Brother John, "getting it together in their kitchen, Ike kept saying, 'Now Mahalia should come on home.' The night's passing. 'Now Mahalia should come on home.' We were up all *night*. That goose. I'd never fixed one before.

"Early Christmas morning, Mahalia came in. Ike gave her his present: He'd spent $18, all his money, for a brush set with five mirrors that set up . . . that was *fine,* in those days; she tried to keep that set polished for years, for remembrance . . . then she took a look at that goose. 'All that *grease,* John! That's all right, I'll fix it.' And she did."

Before she could settle down, she had to get something off her mind. She called her politician friend Dawson. "I had Estelle out on the road and we didn't make nothing, and she lost her job. I want to ask you, could you get her a job? If you get her a job, that's all I'll ask you."

Estelle got a job. And Mahalia got a new pianist, Mabel Hamilton. She already knew Halie's style.

16

Good thing she was light on her feet. Week days, classes. She'd shifted to Mme. C. J. Walker's, biggest name in the black beauty world: first to teach black people how to straighten their hair, first to put out a straightening comb, her cosmetics famous. Depression or not, she was a millionaire . . . had a whole block on Oakland: salon, school, everything. John walked over with Mahalia sometimes, and shortly announced he was going do hair too. "You got to do *everything* I do?" cried Halie.

Week nights, hurry, see who got a car—still a fish-and-bread singer but with sponsors for the programs—tickets up to 15¢, singer get a percentage, but some nights, peculiar counting going on. In between, storefront churches—give what you may or will—and the joy of the Holiness service, the Sanctified, Halie bid to preach, to confess the Holy Ghost. ("Mahalia confessed the Holy Ghost before Baptist people ever believed in the Holy Ghost," says John; "Mahalia always said *she had* the Holy Ghost.") And in all that, cook and clean, make those pots *shine,* like we do, down South.

Weekends, catch the train with Dorsey, sing, meet the people, make it back in time for school. No homework. Thank You Jesus! And Ike a peaceable man. Bad enough with this snow and now Big Alice to be seen to, feel so bad. Watch her medicine, the doctor said. They did, Halie and John between them. Big Alice grew worse. Pneumonia, the doctor said. Stay with her then—school have to wait. Halie's anyway; she made John keep on. Hannah was there as she could; weather didn't make for walking. Ike and Big Alice's husband standing around, men in a sick room like a sieve in a pan of water. Everyone prayed. She's dying, the doctor said. "We can't be fooling around with this doctor. We got to use some New Orleans remedies. I'm going to get some hog hoofs, child." No chance of jimson weed, this time of year. Wonder did anybody up here have elephant ears? Never mind, main thing was hog hoofs with the hog nails on.

Not a market had it, not anywhere . . . never heard of such a thing. Halie pulled up short: time was wasting. She'd go to the stockyards. No trouble finding your way; just smell. . . . They didn't want to fool with her, this tall black girl asking for—"sounds like hog husks and nails"—but she used all the wiles she knew with the white man, speak soft, smile sweet, plead, for the love of God and that's the God's honest truth, to save Big Alice.

She hurried home in triumph. John watched wide-eyed as she steeped the brew, fed it to Big Alice hour by hour 'til she turned the bend, showed the signs, flickered back to life, and oh thank You Jesus! one day stood up on her feet.

Now see about school.

COUNT IT UP, talk to the lady, see the equipment, count it up, check for the place, count it— It was enough. Halie announced she was going into the beauty business. To everyone's astonishment, nearly. ("*Told* you she could hang onto a dime," cried John.) The place was right there waiting, a vacant storefront at 3252 So. Indiana next to a barbershop, then the corner drugstore—she wanted Emma Bell to meet Dr. Coleman, the pharmacist; he was nice. Diagonally across was Pilgrim Baptist on the corner of 33rd; Hannah was up in the next block, and Big Alice down around the corner. Plenty room up front for the shop. In back, the storage room was fixed up with a stove—she could put a screen around that—and a toilet and washbasin set off: They could live back there. No bath, but Madame Jordan, the spiritual reader next door, she said they could take a bath there, had a bathtub and everything. And they could always go down to Aunt Hannah.

The storefront didn't ask for frills. Good thing; she was skinning her last dime and some she didn't yet have. But she could make it pretty with blue. And make it shine; no one going to scrub it cleaner than she could. Get her a nice white uniform. New church dress and shoes have to wait . . . get another chair with that. When it was near ready, Missie inspected. "Mahala, it is gorgeous. *Everything* in here that is supposed to be in a shop."

"I'm going have a Grand Opening," said Mahalia.

Excitement ran high. Not every day a girl got her own place, and Emma Bell especially put her heart into it. Hadn't Mahalie learned on her? Still, one evening her mind clearly wasn't set: round eyes in her round face rounder still—a look Halie knew too well. "What?"

"Last night I dreamed—"

"Don't you go dreaming this shop!"

"—I dreamed I saw Jesus ascending in the west, going up. Mama says that means war." War where? "West, I guess."

"Well, we can't study war now, girl; we got to get these handbills *out*." All of them were busier than birds in a box of corn and the South Side didn't notice too much anyway when Hitler invaded Poland. Halie spared it four words: "Girl, you dream too good."

It was hard, this close to opening, to make herself break off and keep her date with Dorsey. But she'd be back in plenty time. She checked about deliveries, fixed up about money, handed out chores, got pledges from Emma Bell and Becky Avery to see it all done with the help of their husbands—and climbed aboard the train. If half done by the time she's back, she be lucky.

So many times programs had died on them, or the set one didn't make offshoots even to clear the fare. Not this time . . . Lord, why You put this on me? No way to face the preacher and say no. Halie's voice was firm when she called Emma Bell long-distance from West Virginia and scared the household. "Emma Bell, you and Becky have the Grand Opening without me. I got to sing. And Emma Bell! Be sure that license on the wall." She'd hired a graduate operator, with license privilege.

For a shop that opened on one leg, business was good. Just walking around, Halie was an advertisement: a beautiful full suit of hair, hot-combed smooth, oiled, and swept up on top with a roll and a deep wave at the front. But then she'd always had a feeling for hair, grown up alongside the fiercest known concentration on it: Duke's. How many times had she seen Aunt Duke take a stand in front the mirror, Uncle speaking soft, so she wouldn't hear, "Oh my God, Baby Chile is getting ready to comb her hair; that's going to be two hours and ain't but a handful." That was the despair. Bell laughed over it with Celie: their mother always able to plait Bell's hair and tie ribbons on the plaits and Duke just carry on, want *hers* like that . . . and not enough to plait. Every Sunday, had a time—show her it was *impossible;* she stomp and carry on. Mother tried all she could to get that little scrub to grow: cook up prickly pear, make a grease of it, saturate the scalp and rub it and rub; never did get over 2½″ long. She had too much of a temper for her hair to grow, Celie concluded.

Too bad that wasn't now. Halie had just the thing. Now *Celie's* took Aunt Bell and Papa, though he was dead and gone: "You know I loved the way that lady down the street did my hair," Celie'd said, "so I could not understand Mama saying don't go no more; that the Lord had showed her I'd regret it. I really did believe she loved me, so I went again and suddenly at home my scalp began just continually itch, itch, itch." Drugstore, doctor, hospital, tests, prescriptions, no remedy worked. Wretched, Celie lay down and put her thoughts on the Lord. And their grandfather came. " 'Daughter'—I was in the high faith—I say 'Yes.' He say, 'Papa wants to talk to you about your head, about further steps. If this was a natural cause, the medicine would have cured your scalp; but it is an un-natural condition; to affect your brain and run you crazy, and it was done through jealousy.' When he said that, the beautician formed herself up at the foot of my bed and looked down with shame. Then Papa finished telling me further steps. And my head grew well. Several months after that, Mother Martha, who used to have the Spiritualist church over here, I met her in the noon hour standing in the block of my house. I hadn't seen her in a long time; she had moved. I said, 'Mother, do you have time? I was going to the grocery but I'll just get the particulars' . . . so she waited. When I unlocked my door, I stepped back and oh! she just got high in the service. 'You have been told about your head from a deceased relative,' she said. 'Yes ma'am, I have—my grandfather.'

" 'The one that done it, she lives right down there'—pointing down the next block. 'Yes ma'am, she does,' I said. 'Hair will be growing on your head when grass will be growing on her grave, and it won't be very long.' That was in the month of November, and in the month of March, the beautician sent for me to confess, and she died, in the month of March."

Show how careful you got to be; beauty shop a *responsibility.*

Halie's own hair, she believed, was a miracle—that and her legs being straight. Nappy and crooked, think people want to see her? listen to her? "Lord, what I have to thank You for!" And thank You Lord for this shop. But I'm not too grateful for being waked up again. "Yeah! I'm coming!"

All hours of the day or night they rang, knocked, hollered. "Be there before light in the day, God knows; but I got up, I needed the business. And they knew I was in back. What you going do?"

Exhausted one day, puzzling a problem in her mind, flung onto the bed while no one was up front, Halie got a shock. She saw Jesus. On the wall. Saw him just as plain, wearing his crown of thorns. "I said, 'Oh no, this isn't true; it's some reflection that's showing in this room.' Then look like I got up out of myself and pulled the shades down and put the room in shadow. Now I'm laying there asleep, but my body got up and did that. But I saw Him still, like a picture. Then when I truly waked up, the room was just like I left it, with the shade up. The spirit left my body to pull the shade down to show me this was no reflection, it was actually so. This was the first time I had seen Him since I got salvation, when I first got to know Him . . . since then we talk, but I very seldom see Him."

A customer. She got up. Another one heading on in. Better get her another operator, regular. And send for Little Allen, 17 and finished high school. He could stay by Hannah. *He knows my heart.* . . . She sang softly as she straightened.

It was interesting for her friends to visit while she pulled hair, nobody minding if instead of Missie or Becky or Emma Bell or Willa Mae Ford Smith, a *great* singer—it was James Lee, from New Orleans, or Eddie Scott or Theo Frye, whom she so respected for starting the early gospel choirs; besides, Frye had such a jolly way to him. They talked churches, singers, Chicago while she was washing; but keep quiet while her fingers were at the hot-comb—a hard press make you drag the comb a half-hour more if there's plenty hair—she studying the face while she's pressing, deciding on the style, then combing it this way and that 'til it's perfect. She loved it. If they'd just let a body take some rest. Enough to lay a mule low.

Who *was* low, low was Roberta Martin. Often as she could, Halie slipped over to where 'Berta stayed with the sister of Rev. Curtis, from New Orleans. "Don't give up, 'Berta, you know the Lord can take care of His own if you truly seeking for Him."

"It was this time, there in my aunt's house," says Celestine Curtis Graves, "that Mahalia encouraged Roberta Martin to make a promise to God: if the Lord would let her get well, she would sing no more blues. Up to then she'd mixed her singing, she did anything; it was hard, very hard to get any kind of spot and there was no money in gospel. But after Roberta got well, though, it was only gospel."

Sometimes now if Mahalia's pianist for the night didn't show and James Lee wasn't there to fill in, "Come on, 'Berta, you play for me." She *asked* to play for Mahalia, for some funerals. 'Berta's rhythm backing Mahala's beat would move a Chinese dragon, says Missie.

The whole pulsing scene was in flux, spreading, rising, better seen backwards than at the time. If Mahalia was busy at the shop, John sang with Emma L. Jackson, Emma selling music and teaching at her own storefront but touring a group . . . Sallie doing all that (her pianist, at 16, was Ruth Lee Jones, not yet become Dinah Washington) and building up her publishing too. Roberta teamed with Sallie, and Martin & Martin Singers took the road, church to church—all this church, black church—Robert Anderson with them, a thickening sheaf of his own gospel songs in hand that he was putting out, making a market, setting up in the Dorsey pattern as were Frye, Rev. Brewster from Memphis, Roberta, and more—chiefly the singers, who would then begin to take in others' work: Chicago only a clap away from a major music industry just as the big wave of New Orleans jazz musicians who'd started up-river to play in the 1920s was rolling on to New York—Louie Armstrong on the crest, back and forth, heading for a Halie-cooked meal whenever he had the time and she had the kitchen.

Mahalia—held to Chicago by the shop except for weekends with Dorsey—found herself with a circle of singers: John always, but now James Lee, Willie Webb, Frye and shortly, Robert Anderson (the two Martins too volatile to stand side by side for long) and more. Fewer women, but among them Myrtle Jackson, Myrtle Scott, Barbara Penson; Emma Bell pitched in too. Halie could usually count on Mabel Hamilton to play—or if not, Ruth Lee Jones, Robert, James, Evelyn, *somebody* came on. Eddie Scott brought in his pretty bride Celeste from Lexington, Miss., and two deep smiles found a singular sisterhood which warmed, chilled, buoyed, grew, frayed, stretched, sagged, but never snapped until death took a hand. Celeste wasn't sure she could sing, but "Sure you can," Mahalia told her, "I'll just show you a few little things."

Often as not what she showed them all was the two-eyes stove in the back. "Mahalia was one of the greatest cooks ever lived," exults Dr. J. Robert Bradley. "I was leader of the Good Will Singers then; we traveled all over the country for the National Baptist Convention but they weren't able to pay us, just our living on the road. So when we were in Chicago, we spent a lot of time with Theodore Frye and Roberta Martin, and Mahalia. They were the ones would give the young people a break. And Mahalia—that was one place you could get a good-sized meal. She could cook anything on that little two-eyes. And she made us welcome—J. Earle Hines, Odie Hoover, all of us."

Mahalia loved the being surrounded: a gospel team, and her pitcher and catcher both—didn't she call the signals? And umpire on Ike. Umpire, send in the relief, send in the everything. Look like his disease nothing but worse and he not *interested* in Dr. Jesus. She was sick of bailing Ike out, she brooded to John. "Seems like every time I see a little bit of money, here comes somebody to take it away from me. I'm scared if I don't pay up what he owes, he'll end up in the river, fooling around with those gamblers. And me preaching the way of the Lord."

HER HEART LEAPED when Ike came with his news. For the first time in 18 years since he'd come to town holding out his diploma, Chicago had work for him as a machinist. War contracts for Europe were pouring in. The unions were opening up. He was in. He was on! With the Interstate Machinery Co. Her heart sank when she heard it all. New man gets the squeak. He'd work at night. That put him all day at the track. No trouble telling which way the day had gone. Walk in quiet, half-smiling, drooping his eyes—lost again. Win too late to lose it, come in head up, big smile, open-hearted, whatyouneed honey? "I need you to stay away from gambling, that's what I need."

The first time he come in saying he'd been robbed: may be. Plenty bad people around. The second time he come with "Robbed" she put him out and went to Aunt Hannah's. ("She always did that, all her life, came back here with me," says Hannah.) And just when she need something to take her mind off, here come this young girl from New Orleans, to get her hair done; look like a flower girl. A teacher *already?* at 17? going to study in

New York! That's the way, honey, don't matter if you *do* be having to scrub clothes to make it, you get your full education. What the preachers up to back home?

The warmth, the eager interest engulfed Bernice Durden for life. At Hannah's that evening they giggled, gossiped, and set off for a storefront church—Bernice resting Mahalia, singing hymns; then off for something to eat, getting the food at the window. Always something, somebody to laugh over. Another night, home so Halie could cook okra with salt pork, sucking a lemon the whole time and still downing a whole pitcher of lemonade. "Look, you want some, better hurry up and get it."

They walked, or if Mahalia got them a ride, even with ministers she knew, "Listen, you tell me things, but don't you tell this girl anything. *I* know how to handle you!" But she couldn't handle the woman at this tiny storefront church . . . Mahalia caught high in the spirit, feeling it surge in, pour out, setting the people up from the benches, into the aisle, "Jesus! Save me! Glory! Amen! Hallelujah everybody!"—clapping, sobbing, a woman out of herself suddenly grabbing Mahalia by the throat, squeezing, Mahalia unable to loose the fingers, iron-held; singing on, loose finally, not letting the people know but cutting the program, getting away. Onto the street, into the air. One cough and spitting blood. "That woman really hurt me!" Up all night, gargling, frightened. Singing again by mid-week.

"She had a perseverance," says Bernice Durden Franklin. "I wasn't so much younger but it seemed so. She had this serious desire to *really* bring Christ to people. We'd talk about that. But still we laughed. Be in church, she'd say, 'See that lady? She always wears good underwear because she knows when she shouts, she's going to pull up her dress.' Or she'd poke me when the women landed in the men ushers' arms: 'They not really shouting; they just want to land there.'

"She had hardly a stitch to her name, and yet I felt she was a queen." (It was a minority view. Still there was something. James Lee's mother felt it, showing it a particular way: washing and ironing her clothes, since Halie had no tub.) Back in town over Thanksgiving, "Flower Girl" and Halie made it through the snow to Liberty Baptist on 46th, Rev. Moss shouting, "Go 'head, Mahalia! Go *'head!*" John and James Lee backing her. Halie on fire. Home with over $30. And Ike in—Ike restored; too good a heart to deny—Ike in with a long tale of being robbed: not just his own money but the insurance premiums. Needed all she got, to turn in. Silently Halie handed it over. Saw him put it safely away. Then pitched him bodily into the snow. "I had to give him that money to cover him, to keep him from losing his job!" she cried, "but I'm mad enough to *melt* that snow."

Outside, Ike just lay there. Next morning she found him, wheezing, sneezing, coughing . . . smiling. "I can't even make this man leave!" But she nursed him well. He did love her. And when she brought Doodutz up for a visit—Isabell turned to a young lady now—she kept her troubles to herself.

LITTLE ALLEN came, that 1940, and fit fine. She'd been sending money down for his schooling—his and his sister Audrey's—and the boy had a soft voice, a pretty way. The women liked his shampooing. And he was a talker. Staying with her sometimes at night while Ike was at Interstate, he could give her all the goings-on.

In the winter, Ike took off for Little Rock and New Orleans . . . went, this time: "I can always get back on, honey, the way they're begging for machinists, and I got this handicapping worked out; *big* money there." When he came back—not broke, expansive, "Hey, my friend!" to Allen, "what you want? what you drinking?"—she found he really had gone up to Walnut St. to meet her daddy. Ike really was not a bad man. But her with the Bible, and him with the racing sheet. Help me, Jesus!

She was paying off some of the equipment and supplies now, getting \$1.50 a head—\$2 if people had curls and things. Maybe she could . . . no, better wait. No telling what Ike would get to.

TRAVELING WITH Dorsey, Mahalia never knew what they'd get to either. She dulled herself to the grime of the trains, the air in the coaches heavy with urine and litter, the soot and cinders making you squinch your eyes and don't hit the seat too hard for the dust. But she couldn't get used to arriving . . . West Virginia, Pennsylvania . . . and finding no program at all, the pastor or church promoter unable to cope with the actuality of preparation so nothing to do but turn around to the station and the weary night; stay awake or sit on the luggage but *watch* it; when the station open, see if they be nice about at least a cup of coffee, finding—law or not—the never-subtle ways of making you unwelcome, not tell you *couldn't* but make it so unpleasant you wouldn't want to eat there, you wouldn't want to be embarrassed. . . .

Or now the program held, the people brought along . . . and nothing for the singer at the door. Dorsey sold his music but that was his.

Home finally, to Ike, Mahalia unburdened. "Dorsey don't want to give me no percentage, he don't want to give nothing, and if you have a pop, he put that down on a tablet, he see that you owe him a nickel!" And Ike, soothing, "Well, Mahalia . . ." at a loss what more to say . . . and John, alongside, supposed to be sleeping but a little pitcher with big ears, John burning with indignation for his idol.

What you going do? Lord, You have put this on me. Dorsey *is* a great man. And here time to open up the shop.

WHEN IT'S ALL you have beyond the push and pull for bread . . . the night life of black Chicago none of yours ("1940, people still scuffling, night life was chitling parties, policy machines, homebrew and bootleg whiskey," says Missie; "been made legal but still felt like bootleg"); when you were a church person, the issue of who was the best singer—gospel singer, gospel having wholly taken over, its very identity now the beat, bounce, body which Mahalia had introduced—this was a juicy bone endlessly gnawed for the passionate pleasure of the act. Loyalties were violently personal, often split within a family (John a piping thunder against his aunt). It was a matter of high interest, that December, 1940, when Mahalia readied a program at Morning Star Baptist. She built her preparations intensely—but as the day neared, she had no pianist. "I don't know where Estelle at," she told John, "and the rest of them don't want to do right, so I'm going take Dorsey. Mr. Dorsey going hit one key here, one key there . . . oh, honey, Mr. Dorsey all right with Sallie and them, but he can't get with *me* . . . but I'm going call him anyway, see will he come."

The big church was packed, rustling with anticipation: the supporting singers first, the crowd on the rise, hands flung high for 'Berta, shouting with Frye, with Celeste. Then Mahalia sang *The Day Is Past And Gone*. Ecstasy swept the church like a wave, people bobbing, rising, running on its crest, even Dorsey, the always-contained Dorsey unable to keep his seat, to still his voice so that he rose from the piano and cried, "Mahalia Jackson's the Empress of gospel singers! She's the *Empress*! The Empress!!"

He wrecked the church.

And the Empress going to get her a place to stay. Been carrying my soap and towel long enough.

Four whole rooms, not but four blocks' walk from the shop—3726 So. Prairie, in Mrs. Williams' building. Not even four to Aunt Alice, five to Aunt Hannah. Right around the corner was St. Luke Baptist. And these were *rooms!*

With reason. At the turn of the century, Prairie was the most glamorous avenue in Chicago, lined with huge homes built by the butcher barons . . . vacated as the barons shifted to even more elaborate lakeshore mansions, and now absorbed by the inexorable black need for housing into well-thought-of apartment and rooming houses.

Put Aunt Duke's whole shotgun in her living room! Now she could cook. Ike hadn't had his full chance to see her loose in a real kitchen. And she could send money to the ones back home to come stay: Doodutz again—wide-eyed to see what Halie had for herself now, delighted with how Halie styled her hair—"Girl, you just have a *gift!* Brisko, like her own—tall, brown, cheekbones like an Indian, excited by the whole wide wonder of Chicago. Big Allen, who liked to go with her to the churches. And Tucker—she had her eye on Tucker—Bessie's son, George Thomas . . . boy got a straight way to him, like to dress and look like he got talent; always beating the side of the house with sticks for drums, Bessie say.

"Black, Halie going to send you to school in New York, to be a musician. How you like that?" (Easygoing Tucker went, but didn't stay, New Orleans pulling him home.) Ike made them welcome but it was Halie who was the chief, looked to for the necessaries and the little something extra to go on, and generally the ticket back if she hadn't got it in the first place. Her purse opened, time on time again, "but don't you think this grows on trees, you hear me?"

No use to ask Aunt Bell—hadn't set foot on a train since Charity was buried. But when all the rooms were just right, bring Aunt Duke, an instant hit on the South Side, her wit and special wisdom carrying the authority of New Orleans. "You want to know how to hold your girl friend? You get you some fig leaves—" John, growing fast, listened enthralled. Duke couldn't stay long—Uncle was sick, *been* sick, "but she came back from that first trip to Chicago with her eyes bugging, couldn't carry on enough about Halie's place," says Celie; "and she didn't see a single gangster."

Nice to have a place now for her good friend Ernestine Washington from New Jersey to stop—there was a singer! fill any church they put her name up in; when she finish, it's doxology—Ernestine of the Holiness people, *home* of the holy dance, the holy beat, the Saints. Rosetta Tharpe came, too, when she was in town; getting a big name since she crossed over into the pop world. For the special visitors, Aunt Alice came over to help with the cooking . . . and even Louie Armstrong had to admit her red beans would "do ricely, nicely," with that nice piece of pork.

Pinching Town friends came too, Bernice and others. Plus one caller who was a complete surprise: Johnny Jackson. Her father's second son. He'd grown tall, with her daddy's way: that soft voice and easy laugh, a quick wit to him. Johnny said he lived in California now. He was stopping with Wilmon, but he'd come by to say hello.

Back home, if she was on the levee when he was heading around to Audubon Park to caddy, if he had the time, sometimes they'd talk. Or if she was playing stickball with the boys at Cherokee and Esther, by Aunt Duke's—if he passed, he might stop and play a while. But a long, long while before she went to Chicago, he was gone. Now she found why: Johnny'd been sent up to Chicago to stay with relatives on through high school, living right there at 2965 So. State—six blocks from where Halie's shop was now and ten from where they sat. He'd finished grade school and gone on to high school at night, working days as a coffee boy, then stayed on that job. Just weeks before Halie had come up with Aunt Hannah, he'd gotten sick and had to go back to New Orleans, to Zimple St. Sitting, liking each other, they thought on the strangeness of it all. And Johnny said how proud their daddy was of her now . . . said he spoke of her often to people on the street.

Wilmon, Johnny explained, was busy trying to be "The Nonchalant

Man," a song and dance solo, writing his own material. She couldn't expect to see too much of him. But he'd be by. Johnny himself had to be off, other places to go and due back in California soon. He stopped by to talk with Halie once more, had thoughts of hitting Chicago again when he could get up the fare, when abruptly all plans, thoughts, actions went sky-high: Dec. 7, 1941. War.

Ike figured he'd have to go . . . better get things fixed up for you to get my allotment, honey. It turned out, though, that his job as machinist kept him from going off. Thank You, Lord. God is good. Those of the singers who were ministers got deferred. John was 4-F from a back injury; also, he was ordained as a Holiness preacher. Some gospel singers got jobs in the war plants—President Roosevelt gave out his personal order that no place could discriminate on jobs by race, creed or color if they wanted government contracts—and who didn't? Still, like almost every other world, the gospel circle was profoundly wracked. Allen had to go. So did James Lee. Halie stuck with Dorsey on the weekend circuits, though trains were harder to get and harder to find a seat on when you squeezed on, and food was downright chancy. The high court in '41 said railroad facilities for black and white had to be "substantially equal," but if there was any betterment, it wasn't noticeable. Still, dates like a church in St. Louis, or Detroit, could be pleasurable and she looked forward to the fellowship. That's why Dorsey couldn't understand, heading out to Detroit this time, why she wanted the very first train back . . . for a reason Dorsey never knew: Back home, getting ready to leave, Ike had walked in from the track with a grin stretched wider than his ears—and a wad of bills he flipped like a deck of cards. "Hold it for me, hon; I don't want to lose it. I had me a good day, a good day, and I don't want to make it a bad night."

"You know I'm going to Detroit."

"Well, you put it somewhere and don't tell me 'til you get back."

Halie waited 'til after supper, 'til Ike had walked down to State, to settle on a hiding place. Smart man like Ike wasn't easy to fool. Finally she rolled up the rug, laid the money flat bill by bill so it wouldn't bulge, and rolled the carpet down. Man like Ike never lifted a rug in his life. "When Mahalie got back," laughs Ike, "that money was gone. I'd found it—I *had* to find it, 'cause I got a chance to buy a horse. My first one." Halie was outraged. "You with all your education! It's not enough to lose your money on horses, you got to feed one too!" Lord, when will You strike this man to his senses? I wish You'd tell me, give me peace.

But she did not hear the voice.

She never spoke of it, the voice. But she did talk visions with her girl friend Emma L. Jackson, over to visit after she shut her music store a dozen blocks away on So. Michigan. Psychic—"I was born with a veil over my face"—Emma told Halie of her sister's recent death in New

Orleans: how clear up here in Chicago she'd felt pins sticking all over her body as it happened and known the loss. Told Halie, too, about Gwen Cooper, the pretty copperskin redhead, just 17, she brought along for company to the shop—how she'd walked, a stranger, into Emma's store; heart set on a classical career but lured into Emma's store for this new kind of music after she'd heard it at Shiloh Baptist—only another customer but causing Emma to get an inner message, on the strength of which Emma hired her on the spot as accompanist and arranger.

Not that Gwen heard this now; she was sent in back to listen to the radio while the two friends talked. ("When that got boring," says Gwen Cooper Lightner, "I was allowed to stand outside the shop or walk up and down but only within view of the storefront window.")

In turn, Mahalia told Emma of the Clarks . . . Papa, who'd prophecized, who'd seen Death and more; Aunt Duke, who had the gift of remedies; Aunt Bell, who saw clear ahead; Aunt Bessie, who had her visions oftentimes; and Celie, too, but nothing to Aunt Bell: When Aunt Bell *said,* you could put your foot on it. (Except—except—Halie didn't speak of the except—clean back to when she was shucking peas on the porch and Aunt Bell turned back to say "with kings and queens." Slipped your foot there, Aunt Bell . . . if it's in this world.)

Back on the coach next weekend, into Pennsylvania to a program in a small mining town. "It was a nice house and seemingly a nice minister," says Dorsey, "but something was funny about the money. We were supposed to stay with the minister and his wife that night, but we got to arguing over that money and Mahalia got enough—we did nothing but go down to the railroad station and wait until a train came that was going our way. Happened almost the same next time in a coal mine town in West Virginia, somebody trying to fool with the money when we knew there was more was our due. We sat in the station through the night, until a train came. The only way to get out then was to go up out of our way 100 miles or so."

Home in Chicago, a weary Mahalia told John, "I'm supposed to be a fish-and-bread singer, but all I'm getting is chips." It could not last. Dorsey knew it too. In parting, that 1942, "I can't do you any good, Mahalia," he said, "but someday, someone will."

Off the train to find Uncle Emanuel had died . . . even Baby Chile's will and wit finally helpless to hold him from slipping off from her. "Nothing in the box"—but Duke saved her tears and waited for Mahalie, who knew this would be so and came prepared. She prayed for them all and paid for the funeral. In Pinching Town this caused no to-do; that's Mahala. But even Rosa Williams was startled when Halie waved a different kind of wand on Esther St. Here come the bundles. Here come the truck. A houseful of furniture, not a stick but brand-new; curtains, spreads, linens, clothes on top of that. A sight to see. Every inch of the dignity that was Mrs

Williams reached out. "I don't see how you do it, myself, but it is wonderful that you do do it, Mahala—come back here and put all those things up in your Auntie's house."

"You know something, Cousin Baby: You and me, we got religion—"

"Lord knows."

"—and if you got religion, you don't hold things in your heart, you can't hold people in your heart for what they do you . . . you throw it off."

"Tell the truth, child, that is the truth, you got to forgive. And in a way, people be strict on you, it makes big people out of you, when you're grown. You wasn't raised any kind of way, and you can't part from it. One thing—nobody trouble Little Halie if they don't trouble Old Halie, 'cause they go up against a mountain. Don't you touch her! Anybody whipping Halie, got to be *her* do the whipping. Still and yet I don't know how you do do and forget."

"I remember. I put it all behind me."

Back on the I.C., New Orleans behind too, tracks clicking . . . look like Daddy didn't make it to the Carrollton stop but that's all right, we had us a visit and Chicago waiting—say South Side, all of Chicago that was of her.

"Open up, Mahalie! Come on, girl—move your butt! I ain't need me but a quick comb . . . won't cost you a minute!" Up meant keep going, no room in the day, except for sweet Jesus—*nobody* going cut Him out. But it was a good business to get into. Son Baby's girl Audrey be finishing high school soon; bring her up then, send her to beauty school; child could get her a license.

SHE HAD a reason for breaking off these coal runs with Dorsey: She'd been offered directorship of the choir at St. Luke Baptist, around the corner from home. And Rev. Grayson wasn't just signifying when he said he wanted her. The job wouldn't have seemed sizeable to anyone outside the church world. But this was a time when the leaders' respect went to those in music who had studied in the white studios in the Loop. It showed in the National Baptist Convention, when President L. K. Williams would say, "Mahalia, you can sing, but—" And Miss Lucie Campbell, real power of the music there, wanted culture put up, didn't want Mahalia in the big programs; pushed her off to the early morning. Frye and Roberta, they had training to be directors; Dorsey too; and even so, the main respect went to the directors of the heavy anthems, such as Mabel Stanford Lewis. Now Dr. D. V. Jemison president, see how he do about gospel; he did like her, she knew that. So did the biggest man in Louisiana Baptists—Rev. A. L. Davis of New Zion: could have stayed many a place, but stayed over with Mahalia when he came up from New Orleans for Dr. Williams' funeral—a shock, the Convention president killed in a plane crash, causing Dr. Jemison to be named at Cleveland.

One thing there showed she was rising: Giving her service at church, not of the Convention but a convention-time program—Elliot Beal came over afterward to give his compliments. Back home, he'd been above her; trained, known as an organist although he was so young somebody had to stand by and pump for him.

Now to St. Luke—she was going make that choir *go*. Energetically she set up a schedule of major programs, one every month. She had Celeste to count the house and the cash, with Little Missionary's help (Celeste's young sister, Margaret, delighted with "May's" name for her). "May never wanted anything funny about the money," says Margaret Aikens. "When we'd get finished counting and adding it up and so forth, she'd always say, 'Now prove it.' I'd say, 'Oh, May, that's the old-fashioned way of figuring! . . . 'Never mind, prove it anyway.' And I'd have to prove it."

She had a good pianist to help—Gwen's big admiration, Helen Green, already with the St. Luke choir and willing to play for Mahalia whenever she was wanted, although she wasn't too much on going out of town. Then she'd get Robert Anderson if she could . . . Robert getting a name as a leading male soloist, composer, and publisher, all that, and generally late to wherever he was due but still he had some of Roberta's beat from being around her and that was the real gospel beat, distinctive, vital for the singer with a range, especially on the long meters . . . gospel often long-drawn, pushing the singer to show what she had and the pianist to weave an intricacy of phrasing to support the singer's every tone, suspension, extension, until the congregation moved upward with them both into a plane of ecstasy that wouldn't let go. Anything less was failure. And Mahalia put the best to the test. "Robert, can't just anybody play for me. You know that."

Besides, Robert and James Lee were easy as soft slippers. She could use some easy, having to crowd train schedules, shop schedules, choir schedules, Ike schedules and now here come Dawson schedules. She felt like a squirrel trying to stuff his acorns in a crawfish hole: stuck and can't hardly back out.

17

Most of the other gospel pioneers had long been ranging on wheels, any they could manage, but Halie wasn't convinced. Too much could happen on the road with may-pop tires and an engine like a Mississippi mule, 'specially down South but don't have to *be* South. Sallie Martin had piled her group into a big old Cadillac, as far east as Washington, D.C., and clear down close to New Orleans: "Baby, plenty a time we had a stop by the road, try to sleep—no place at all to stop for the night or fog catch you, can't go on, and mosquitoes almost take you if you open the window. Then we thought we was stopping at some little *hotel* by Baton Rouge and I'm telling you, I was scared to death. I piled bags and everything else against the door. Gwen crying, pregnant with her first. Me using disinfectant for the bugs. And didn't the woman up me on the price, soon as she looked out and see it's a Cadillac. I'll never buy another Cadillac car!"

"Well, Halie's going tough the train." But when Ike showed up at the beauty shop one day with a quiet "Hon, come see" . . . made her stop right in the middle of a head and come out . . . when she saw that shining new white Buick sitting next the curb . . . it was love. Prettiest thing since God made trees. Halie climbed into the seat and wiggled the wheels. "How much you pay?"

"Had a pretty good day at the track."

"How much you got down?"

"Man let me have it for just the first month, sugar; he knows you. Now don't worry, I'll take care of the car. Just figure you got something now can carry you."

It was wings. Making it go was pure joy. Still couldn't range too far at the time but with this car you sure could take more dates . . . and leave, if nothing but a dark church when you got there. 'Course Ike wasn't keeping up the payments; hadn't since that first time, so she'd taken it on; "and this is *my* car now, Ike, you hear?" But make it to Cincinnati easy; see Uncle Porter and Aunt Berta there. Gospel coming up, tickets 25¢, and some in auditoriums: Cass High School in Detroit on a Sunday. John along to sing, Helen Green playing, and Ike to help drive—he didn't usually make the trips, but Mahalia was just learning the wheel. The place was packed out. "And we just tore it up," says Brother John with relish, "tore—it—*up!* On the way back, and she's driving, she says, 'Oh, we sang today!' Ike's in back sleeping, Mahalia going fast like she always do. Just then the tire blows, Ike jumps up and grabs the wheel from the back, I'm yelling 'Don't touch the wheel, Ike! don't touch the wheel!' and the car's sliding off the road. When it came to a stop, Mahalia said, 'Now you see, Ike, how nervous you is? You woke up all excited. You got to control yourself.' Never letting on one bit if *she* was excited; but she never did let *on*. You never knew! Mahalia could be—you say something to her, she may not say nothing, but she's observing everything you say. And she'd think deep."

One thing she was thinking deep about was her life. Facing Oct. 26, 1942, she talked it out with Sallie: "I am 30 years old, and I haven't done anything in life."

"My dear child," Sallie said from superior years, "you just really stopped wearing those first pants your mother put on you; you ruin yourself being so *over*-anxious."

"I knew I was talking to a rock," says Sallie Martin; "a kind person, but somewhat egotistical—she was so determined." About what, exactly, Sallie wasn't sure.

That was it. What You want me to do, Lord? There's something else.

No answer. Well—in the Lord's time. She got to her feet and went to open the shop. No more to study on there; except you got to watch what's going out to what you taking in. Little Alice need some help now—and Aunt Hannah got doctor bills. At least she didn't have to worry about Tucker; worry about *Bessie* worrying about Tucker off somewhere on a ship, APO Pacific. . . .

"Nov. 8, 1942, war still on," says Bessie Kimble. "I was going to the grocery and my sister Bell heard my voice out there, and she say, 'Celie, that's Bessie. Call her, let me tell her something.' So Celie run to the door. I say, 'Wait 'til I come back from the grocery.' 'She say come *now!*' So I shoved on 'round and went back to her. Bell say, 'Bessie—George going be in here today; George out the service.'

" 'George ain't told me nothing 'bout it. You sure he coming in today?' Bell say, 'I been knowing all week. Wait for him; I seen him.' So I went to the grocery, and you know, by the time I got in that kitchen, my son running up on the steps to surprise me! His ship had been torpedoed, but the Lord spared him and brought him home. Oh, my sister Bell had the visions. Talk all night! sing all night! sing and pray . . . she be sleeping. Awake or asleep, she would reveal."

"Mama," said Celie, "your words are as gold apples in a silver pitcher."

IT WAS MORE BRASS hitting Mahalia's ears now. "Halie, Mrs. Chisholm's behind; can you catch me?" . . . "I *must* be next." . . . "Mahalie, I'm near late to my job!"

"Hold a minute, baby; I'm not a thousand-leg, be everywhere at once."

It was such a day when Rev. Austin crossed over to introduce a tall, nice-speaking girl from up north, a newcomer to his church, Cylestine Belt. A beauty operator. She had a government office job but she'd be willing to come in after work and weekends, if Miss Jackson wanted. Wanted! Thank You, Jesus. Mahalia named her Polly—a born talker, when she had something to say. Polly threw herself at the work so, that Ike took her on the side to caution her. "You are young, but you can't stay up day and night and work."

"No, Mr. Ike, but you don't know me, you don't know what kind of person I am." That capacity, and a front impervious to storms, would one day hold fast when they went through the waters, in currents as remote as the stars from the South Side storefront where they sweated now above the hot comb.

One more caller was Rev. Childs's new organist, James Francis—grew up around Elliott Beal. Blind, yet he'd graduated in piano and organ from Southern University. He didn't have too much of a beat, didn't want to stray from the melody, but he could really play. Promptly "Blind Francis" to Mahalia, James was an unlikely figure to one day throw her a lifeline. But he entered the stream. If underneath Mahalia was a rock, it was magnetic rock; it attracted mettle.

Just so, it was the desire of friendship, to see this girl get ahead, that led her own landlady to put up a big idea: the apartment building next door was up for sale. Why didn't Mahalie buy it? She could get it for a good price. "Oh, Mrs. Williams, I don't have that kind of money, and I got a lot on me."

"Well, you won't have rent on you if you in your own building. And the tenants going to pay it out. How you think I got this one?"

"I'll study on it."

It was out of a dream, that building. Six apartments . . . I could keep the downstairs one for myself, got a living room big enough for a revival. What You think, Lord? Is this my increase?

One morning she rose, satisfied, and bought the building: 3726–28 Prairie. "She didn't ask me," laughs Ike; "I think she thought my mind was too much gone on the horses. And I don't believe the mortgage scared her; she'd prayed on it."

Five rooms now. And tenants to move in, move out, make toe the line on the garbage and the trash: "Don't you people want something nice?" She was five blocks from where she'd lived with Hannah when she first came, a scared 15-year-old. Got to watch close, though. Thank God the last car note was paid, title clear. She was quick to say so when Emma Bell telephoned to ask. Why? "Well, I dreamed your car was taken. You ought to check that title."

"Girl, that car is *mine*."

A few days later Emma Bell was in, the two gossiping by the shop window when Mahalia cried out "Look at those people, bothering my car! Little Alice! go down there and see those people, stealing my car." Allen ran too, and when the pair came back, "They ain't stealing; that's the finance!" gasped Little Alice; "You better go see, 'cause they're jacking it up!" gasped Allen. When Mahalia roared out, righteous, the truth struck hard. Ike had made a loan on the car, owed over $800 with the interest, and hadn't paid a cent. The car was being repossessed. Frantic, Mahalia made herself known—Mahalia Jackson, the gospel singer. Don't haul the car; she didn't have the money but she'd be back with the money; just wait, please. Get Rev. Grayson for her character . . . hurry to another finance close by—"Please, Mr. Johnson, I need the money right *now*" . . . run back breathless, push the money in the people's hands and make them let down her car. *Her* car.

Back to the shop, people buzzing but knowing better than to talk to Mahalia when she looked like that. Coming up thunder. It didn't help that Rosetta Tharpe was visiting with her friend Fosh Allen when Ike strolled in feeling no pain. "I never was a drinker, but sometime I would—we drank Scotch most of the time. And this particular night, I'd had a shot too much," says Ike ruefully. "If it hadn't been for that—

" 'Ike, just get out of here; get out of my sight. Disgraced me! A church person, not paying her bills, pulling her car from right in front her shop! Will you *just get out!*' I said 'Okay.' That was the Scotch. Rosetta and Fosh begged me not to go. I'd used that money for my horse—it costs to train them, feed them, you know. 'What you need is not Alcoholic Anonymous, it's *Gambler* Anonymous!' So I said 'Okay.' If I'd stayed, it would have all blowed over. I still loved her. I never missed a birthday card and Valentine. Never married again. I remember every minute we were together. We separated over nothing."

She had failed in marriage. I tried, Lord; you know I wrestled the Devil for that man. Did I do right? Now You got to help me, Lord, 'cause I'm weak. *"I'm here."* The voice! Halie rose and went to stay by Aunt Hannah's. Seeking for something to cheer her, Hannah said, "Well, girl, you won't have to phone me every day; we can talk right here."

Ike moved just two blocks away. He still visited Alice and Hannah. "When they broke up," says Aunt Alice, "we didn't know no different with him." Still through was through. Mahalia quietly got a divorce.

One thing in this mess had been given her: She must work more for the Lord. Plenty people need to be saved. Polly had a good head on her; she could help with the books. Audrey working out fine, not too long before she be out from school. Let Polly know just where she was, and she could go out of town without fear; Polly would look out for her interests. And there was joy in the Lord! Sometimes, more than expected: "Mahalia got Ernestine Washington down for a big program at St. Luke's," says Robert Anderson, "and that Sunday morning's service, in the demonstration, Blind Francis was playing the organ. Ernestine sang first, Mahalia going behind Ernestine. Well, Mahalia wanted to pick up the beat so she boomped the top like she would, for the signal. She boomp—he gets slower, slower. She —boomp—to pick up; he's putting it down. We can see Mahalia getting disgusted. Well, when that service was over, you ought to heard Mahalia. Just roared, 'I *told* you to pick up! I *told* you!' Francis being blind, didn't know a thing. He just listened, then he said in this calm way, 'Mahalia, you were in your worst voice today.' We cracked up. To dust!"

Besides her own, there were friends' programs to support—including Rev. John Sellers. In turn, John went with his idol to many of the Holiness churches, where she'd preach (something she'd worked in with her singing). She gave her support as well to Salem. But First Sunday, there was one evening service she did not willingly miss. It was famous in black Chicago, like none other. Neither was Rev. Elijah Thurston, chairman of the board of deacons of Greater Salem when the Johnson Singers first formed, and pastor of the split-off congregation, 44th St. Baptist. He was an oak. Resting on Prairie, often she could hear him preach on radio. But First Sunday night: there was a *service*. The witnessing felt like home, only mightier in her soul.

"My father dramatized the communion service," says Rev. John Thurston. "The lights in the church would be dimmed except over the table: that was black. Two of the mothers were stationed at the table. Maybe 10 deacons, all dressed in Prince Albert coats like my father was, for the dramatizing, were lined up from one end. The deacons would pass out the vessels one by one . . . the water, the bread, the wine; and as each one came out, my father would be defining what it meant.

"He had a famous route around the church, based on the fact that when the disciples went into the city to observe the Feast of the Passover, they had a lot of followers behind Jesus as He rode into the city. My father would be walking around the church, deacons following, he telling it all the way around, and the people would just actually surround him, jump on him, and he would continue to walk with them around his neck until he got back to the communion table. The deacons would have to surround him to let him pray over the table. There was hardly a First Sunday but he came home with the buttons of his coat torn off, from the people. And Mahalia was very much a part. I can't ever remember a time that he was praying, that Mahalia didn't give vent to her feelings. There was a lot of singing in this service, and often Mahalia would just pick up the song and go ahead with it—and this was *all* through the years."

Yes Lord! Rev. Elijah was a preacher . . . gave her steam for the days ahead. Shop, building, family—cousins coming up like pepper grass, all needing help; friends, service, programs, in town, out of town—Celeste secretary-singer-companion, with whoever else made up the supporting soloists and musicians as called for . . . James Lee for this first time she'd be presented in the East.

"As far as I know," says Ernestine Washington, "we were the first ones to bring Mahalia to the East, at my husband's church in 1943. That was Trinity Temple, in Montclair, N.J. She was my close, close friend, coming as a friendly gesture, and she was very, *very* well received. We're Holiness people. And people just liked Mahalia for herself—she was free with her friendship; everybody just felt they were a part."

One determined to be was a long-legged, sturdy, brown-skinned girl who fairly vibrated her intent as she knocked at Mahalia's apartment door, unbidden. "I was about 13, and I thought there was nobody like Mahalia Jackson," says Albertina Walker of The Caravans. "When I was a little girl, Mahalia used to come sing at our church; all of her programs that I could go to, I would. So now I'd just show up at her house, and she'd kid me. 'Girl, you just got so much nerves, and you even come up to my house and I ain't even invited you and you just *refuse* to leave! Well, I can afford you because you remind me so much of myself when I was coming up.' But advice! *All* the time. 'You shouldn't do this,' and 'Don't you do that,' and 'Don't you do this—you just *think* you're grown, you want to be grown so bad.' I said, 'No, I just want to hang out with you, that's all.' Then I started singing with Robert Anderson and Willie Webb, so I really *did* get to be a part, because of the programs."

The one coming up right now needed no extra singers, just Celeste to use her talent for keeping people at the job without making them mad. Halie was giving a big program with Rosetta Tharpe, benefit of St. Luke, though plenty in the church world had turned away from Rosetta because she'd gone over to the entertainers, was in fact booked into the Regal Theatre where Mahalia herself couldn't go hear her (but that was Halie's vow; what Rosetta sang and did was between her and her God). Halie gauged well. "The place was so packed out," says John Sellers, "that the fire marshal made Mahalia put some of the people *outside!*"

Mahalia decided to give Rosetta a supper—at a restaurant, to make it special: Morrison's Eat Shop on So. 47th, the evening such a success, the two decided to get their pictures taken out in the side entrance. "Mahalia borrowed a girl named Inez's silver fox fur and put it around her neck and they were shaking hands," says Brother John, "and the picture came out in *The Defender*—said under it 'Mahalia Jackson at the Rum Boogie opening with her friend Sister Rosetta Tharpe.' They was opening a night club right next to the restaurant, and it showed. Well!! Rev. Smith got up and said, 'She'll never sing again at Ebenezer Baptist'—and she used to sing there all the time. Mahalia liked to fainted. Then they tried to make the paper retract it. But people always believe what they read the first time. Rev. Cobb, he wouldn't let her sing either, and he was a big preacher then—on the air. In fact, the churches didn't bother with Mahalia so much then any more."

One minister tried to help. "Rev. Barnes, a little old lady who pastored a Spiritualist storefront but was on radio, she had Mahalia on that night. Mahalia sang *I'm Gonna Tell God All About It One of These Days*. And there was nobody put it in a voice like Mahalia."

Rosetta Tharpe felt bad for her friend—called Jack Kapp at Decca in New York, to see if he wouldn't record her again. Kapp wasn't interested.

Celeste tried to comfort her. "Don't worry, Celeste, one rain don't make a crop." But she sure felt the stones under her feet. She'd ride it out. Truth going to last, lie going to die. She ate a whole jar of pickles stuffed with peppermint. "Mahalia, your lips are purple from vinegar!" laughed Doodutz, up from home. What she was studying on, stuffing herself, was a reaching out for the Lord. She'd go on a revival circuit down South, make the tents one by one, get it up at the National Sunday School Congress

Bring in some souls, ease her own, and show some of these people what Mahalia Jackson meant.

18

1944 . . . 1945 . . . 1946 . . . plying her trade, she plowed for the gospel, mostly heading out from Chicago (then Polly would open up Saturdays and generally keep after things; girl had eyes in the back of her head), Mahalia culling June's National Sunday School Congress and September's National Baptist Convention for dates to bunch into a tour worth the while of a caravan.

That first summer on the wide revival circuit was a major plunge into traveling life for a new youngster in Mahalia's life, Dellareese Taliaferro, 13. Mahalia spotted her at church in Detroit. Here Barbara Penson was sick, got to drop off the tour, and this child with a voice! "I'll look after her like a mother, you know that," Mahalia promised Mrs. Taliaferro.

"Mother" did. It was a tight leash, and sometimes it rubbed. "She was really kind of a stick in the mud when I was 13," laughs Della Reese, "and a pain in the lower posterior, 'cause some of the things a 13-year-old wanted to do, she would not let me do. Even so I loved her. She gave me an opportunity to sing, and being with her, I saw two things: the power of singleness of purpose, and how she was able to *communicate*."

Rolling south after Philadelphia, that power reached into tents, churches, concert halls—wherever revivals were being held. Kentucky, Virginia . . . back into Jim Crow but never mind, the Lord is everywhere, you just got to find Him; hush, child, don't answer the man, just smile and let it be.

Turn on the radio, hear how the poor boys doing in Normandy. Watch your speed; car packed tight, with the girl, wouldn't do to come close like that time Sallie had Robert driving out of Selma, Ala.—Robert, just a boy, pulling to the right to pass a slowed-down car and it was a policeman! Scared even Sallie, he was so provoked with Robert. Nooo, not going happen that way with Halie. Now You got to help me with this thing, Lord . . . all right; Him showing her the way—and her watching the gas tank, wouldn't serve them, some towns. It was a toss-up who was best at mimicking The Man—Mahalia, Celeste or Frye. Find a laugh some way. They were stranded some nights, no decent place to stay and too far or weather too bad to make it on in, but they sang and Halie had everybody pray and nobody meddled them, white or black. Tennessee, Alabama, Mississippi . . . let church roll on. New Orleans . . . hey, everybody! . . . Mahalia Jackson their own. Down Highway 90, a black ribbon of road, of church, of reward across Louisiana but not near Legonier, time past and gone . . . into Texas, into Fort Worth—and Mahalia got a shock.

Revival packed out, that night in Fort Worth, Mahalia was caught by the response, on fire with the spirit, into the holy dance; in *Even Me,* the spirit swept over . . . hard to come down. Drenched with sweat, Mahalia was catching her breath when an excited man came to the edge of the pulpit. She couldn't tell if he was excited or drunk—laughing, crying—he had a funny walk, but—"I can walk!" he shouted, "Great God Almighty! Praise His name! I can walk and you did it! In the singing! Oh, Glory, praise God! I can—" Deacons rushed over, but the people with the man—hardly able to get it out, so struck—they said it was so. He'd been brought to revival paralyzed, and while he was listening to *Even Me,* throwing himself into the spirit, his legs began to move. The first time in 20 years.

A cold chill swept Mahalia, and a surge of awe. "I have not the power to heal you, Mahalia Jackson didn't heal you; the Lord has chosen me as an instrument this night—that is the spirit of the Lord that has blessed you; get on your knees and cry 'Holy' and bless Him every day."

Caught on the road so often with nothing to eat but cold cuts—nobody who'd serve them a hot meal in what looked like a clean place—Mahalia was getting heavier by the day. Long gone, any worry about that thin little thing getting TB; it was the other way 'round—very round. There came a day when Mahalia in the course of an impassioned *I Bow My Knees and Cry Holy* got to her knees . . . and couldn't get back up. Robert was playing. Mahalia said in a hushed aside, music still flowing, Mahalia still singing, "Help me up, Robert" . . . and again, "Help me up, Robert" . . . Robert not hearing, mind wandering on the well-known song. "Help me up, Robert" . . . 'til finally Mahalia shouted, "Help me up, you bubble-eyed nigger!"

"Robert just fell across the piano and hollered," Celeste told everybody when they got home, mimicking them both while Mahalia and Robert joined the uproar. "Help me up, you bubble-eyed nigger!"

"People didn't realize the closeness of Mahalia to me, and James Lee," says Robert. "We were more like her brothers. We did everything with her—even slept in the room with her. And there wasn't a time when she wouldn't call, "Robert, come do this—" or "I want you to do that —" or "Robert, I want you to pray for me."

At the Scott home, Eddie told Celeste, "You just love anything Mahalia does; I don't believe there's anything you wouldn't do for that woman."

"Well, we're just tight; very tight."

Back to politics and Dawson. Back to Aunt Hannah, Aunt Alice, new babies, all the tangled threads of family. Back to the shop—Polly hold that thing *down* while she's gone: Found it stripped clean one morning when she came to open up, the burglar fool enough to do it on a day Polly wasn't heading first to her federal job and Polly picked out the culprit (so close it saddened Halie's heart but what you going do?) and got back every single bit so the shop was running smooth as a ball bearing. That girl *worth* something!

Back to St. Luke. To South Side, West Side programs, preachers giving the matter a second thought; thank You Jesus. To Rev. Elijah's for Communion night service and 11 p.m. broadcast, he preaching, Mahalia singing—*he'd* never turned his back on her. To close-by towns through the snow: Rev. Cole's up near Waukegan, got such nice boys, though Nat was off singing somewhere. Home and to Hannah's in a near-blizzard, so tired but eager to see Bessie, coming in and "Baby! you scared me!" gasped Bessie; "I didn't know who you was! You completely white!" Mahalia rocked with laughter. "That's the closest I'll ever get."

"Well," said Bessie, "you do look more like a bear, come to think of it."

PRESIDENT Roosevelt hadn't been back in office but a month when he declared a midnight curfew. Midnight! sometimes the spirit didn't come that soon!

Then FDR was dead, April 13, 1945. She didn't know much about Harry S. Truman, but D.C. politics was none of hers. Got to get ahead with mother wit and Jesus. Gas scarce, four programs gathered together for New Orleans, Halie rode the I.C. with Rosalie McKenny, her regular accompanist now, and slap! that curtain in the dining car and coach switched up close to the engine. Do those people know what they doing, Lord?

The biggest date was at Progressive Baptist, where Elliott Beal regularly pumped the reed organ. "Even then, she wasn't the main singer," says Elliott, "but that's when we got to be friends. We talked up a dust! Of course in Baptist work anyway, it's like a big revolving circle. She knew Ellen Blount from our church." Another program was reunion: Tulane Baptist, Bernice Durden's. Had the lemonade ready. It was easier to get around with just Rosalie. Visit with Duke, with blessed Aunt Bell; with Celie; with Peter, working the wharf, got a wife but no children. "I'm making it, Halie."

"Remember, Peter, when you gave me nickels to watch Warpee? You got to let me give you a trip to Chicago."

See Son Baby, Cousin Baby, Jack, all the multitude and multiplying of Clarks. See Annise—Hey, Mamá!; that make her mad. Visit with the Jacksons—her daddy, Yvonne, Pearl. Talking with her daddy could make you feel good. "He had a way," says Johnny, Jr., "that you wouldn't lose the edge on life; he'd leave you with something to look forward to: so to speak, 'although it's raining today, it doesn't necessarily mean it will be raining tomorrow, or for the rest of the week.' "

For Mahalia, tomorrow meant Chicago—tend the shop, all the rest. When she got off from it, she could see how much was going on. Main thing, to see where *she's* going with it.

VE Day. How the church bells tolled! Hallelujah! *Ain't Going to Study War No More* . . . that old spiritual said it right. Hit Revival Road. Dates too with some of the gospel promoters who'd been quick to spring up, booking the eager singers on percentage pay (a percentage of the total take); many with one curious, common lack: they couldn't count. "This is what made her become more stern, more dominating, more direct," says Robert Anderson. "She had to speak up because she had no one to speak in her defense when they tried to take advantage of her. She was a fighter."

Mahalia learned to have someone of her own at the collection box; often as not sold tickets herself at the table—or box office, if there was an auditorium open to Negroes—and learned to "prove it" by a quick count of the house. She better; had all these people on her. Some wins, some losses—but never without a fight, and a mark in her memory. Move on . . . almost out of gas in Tyler, Tex.; got the money but the man won't sell them any; won't let them use the washroom, either. Didn't expect it but always hope, always ask, might find a Christian. That was almost the worst; can't relieve yourself like decent folk. Well, the Lord will find us a way. Let's just go on.

War over—the radio said so. And here's President Truman declaring Sunday a day of prayer. Says they need it after two days of nothing but celebrating. Now that is a President. Home to find Emma Bell celebrated *too* much—went and married that man at Ft. Leonard Wood on VJ Day. "Mahalia never liked my second husband," laughs Emma Bell, "wouldn't use his name."

Service at Greater Salem, then Watch Night with well-loved Rev. Boddie, Greater Harvest's bells ringing, service happy through 'til light. Thank You, God, for the blessings of last year; we did all right; and thank You for this new year, this new day. Now I'll strive on, God, You know Halie's going do that. But you got to remember Halie can't think like You do. If there's something You want Halie to do this year, God, You going have to tell me. And remember, Halie's weak.

Home to breakfast with James Lee's mother, and a family feast at Hannah's with just the one big hole: young Allen up in Buffalo with his wife's people—wife and two children and another one on the way. Aunt Hannah voiced it: "Ought to be here." Halie was practical: "Get here through all that snow, they'd have to be penguins."

One family surprise—for Halie—did come soon after: Johnny, Jr., still in his sailor uniform; discharged at Bremerton, Wash., and making it home to New Orleans by Chicago for two days so he could see Wilmon and Mahalia. This time he stayed with Mahalia. He made his Navy time sound funny—easy for Johnny, with his father's way. But there was an extra Thank You, God, in Halie's prayers before she got off her knees that night.

SUMMER REVIVAL, familiar now. The one-day Chicago circuit, then gather up the caravan car and move on out. Hallelujah. Thank You, Jesus. In Detroit, James Cleveland sitting to one side of the pulpit with the others, awaiting his turn, the audience rapt with Mahalia, really bothered. . . . Amen . . . Tell it . . . Sing on, girl . . . JESUS come! . . . Mahalia in the long-meter *Amazing Grace*—most fervent, beloved, and as Mahalia sang it, most prolonged of gospel songs, sustained phrases sending the people into the shout when young James heard—mid-song: *Amazing Grace, How sweet the sound,* James get my pocketbook, *That saves a wretch like me,* James get my bag". . . James so entranced with this that he sat until Mahalia finished and gave him his instruction straight, and strong. The people out front never knew. Didn't know, either, she was carrying several thousand dollars in cash in that big black pocketbook she'd left in the audience where she stopped to visit before the program. She didn't believe in carrying checks. How's a Negro going get one cashed?

She knew the program had gone over well that night in Detroit. How well, she knew when a slight man with a pencil mustache introduced himself and waited to speak 'til they could be alone: Johnny Meyers, *the* most famous promoter in black gospel; from New York City, operating at the Golden Gate—gospel Mecca. He'd like to book Miss Jackson for a date this fall. He'd pay her $1,000.

"You said one thousand dollars."

"Yes."

"In cash?"

"If you want it that way."

Thank You, Jesus!

Time out to visit with Rev. C. L. Franklin—famous on black radio now—and his wife Barbara, her good friend. Can't *believe* little Aretha big enough to have to watch every minute. Must have been just last week Halie changed that child's diapers at Convention. And already singing. "Reverend," said Mahalia, "you got another one there."

It was Della's last tour; 16 needed too much looking after. "But we never lost touch," says Della Reese. "It kept on being Mom—Mother—all my life. And even when I was 30 years old, if I was around her I had that feeling that I shouldn't do whatever it was I had in mind. Whenever I went to Chicago, and I went quite regularly, if I was sitting there she'd say, 'Come on and do this—' and I would come on and do that."

Robert was her regular road accompanist now—always oblige, always say yes, but "Listen, getting you anywhere on time is going give Halie grey hair." Yet, however whichaway, they rolled, car usually full with John Sellers, James Cleveland, James Lee, Barbara Penson (always wanting to go by Mississippi, where she come from). Halie wished it could go on forever . . . and that it wouldn't.

Home, call Aunt Hannah—but don't tell her business. "She just never did to anybody," says Hannah Robinson, who never poked.

And nobody said the pumpkin coach was waiting.

19

In the fall of 1946, few blacks cared to chance a chilly admission or bland refusal—sorry, no space—in most of New York's renowned white entertainment palaces, although management was willing to make money on superior black talent and to seat those few blacks who had a name with lustre, such as the East's first black Congressman, Rev. Adam Clayton Powell. In this world, the Golden Gate shone. Their own. And it led a multiple life: as Golden Gate Ballroom, host for Cootie Williams, Duke Ellington, Count Basie, Lucky Millinder's Band with Rosetta Tharpe, Buddy Johnson with his sister Ella . . . the prestige list stretched long. Seats installed, it became Golden Gate Auditorium, site of the biggest gospel extravaganzas. Presiding over this second realm was bright, energetic Johnny Meyers. To spread his word, he had air time on several radio stations, and for anything big, he paraded sandwich boards over on Broadway. Arriving early for the big night, Mahalia nudged Allen. "See that? Halie never had *that* before!"

It was an omen of the night, and the night's proof was in the pile of green bills Mahalia leafed through on the bed. "Allen, look at that! One—thousand—dollars! Know how long it been taking Halie to get that much together at once? Let's count it again!"

"We stayed up all *night* counting that thousand dollars over and over, different ways," laughs Allen Clark, Jr. They'd have counted it again, but they couldn't stay awake. So, "Here's yours. And yours. Now you people got to let Halie get some sleep. Got a day coming up."

A big one. Bess Berman wanted to see her at Apollo Records. On her knees in the final piece of the night, "God, Mr. Meyers must've thought I sang good, calling Bess Berma, but You got to help Halie now with this thing."

Next morning, waiting for Mr. Meyers in the Theresa Hotel lobby a sturdy Negro boy strode up. "Take a subscription, miss?"—working hard, putting his heart into his pitch for the subscription contest of New York's Negro weekly *Amsterdam News*. Mahalia let him finish, studying eyes shining in a fresh-scrubbed face; then, "What's your name, son?"

"Milton Perry."

"You keeping up with your school?" Yes, he was. He was going to be a *preacher*. "I thought I heard it. I'll take two of those. And you folks here, you going take this boy's paper, aren't you?"

Sarah Vaughan and some of the others obliged. The boy would win his contest. Eight years later, he surfaced to her ken—preaching.

"Now I got to go, son."

THE STOCKY, jowled Jewess confronting Mahalia couldn't have told there was an edgy strand in the body of this good-looking black woman, almond eyes closed, glossy upswept hair beginning to wisp loose as she poured out her song and her soul in Apollo's studio on 45th Street. Mrs. Berman listened impassively. She was owner and president of Apollo Records, a white firm whose product was beamed at the big black market—and that wasn't gospel. Billy Daniel, Arnett Cobb, Charlie Barnett, Babe Gonzales, Eleanor Jackson, Woody Herman, Dinah Washington—these and more like them were making money for her. Apollo was a big blues label. But gospel. At the urging of Art Freeman, Artists and Repertoire Director, Mrs. Berman had just launched an experimental ethnic catchall, a 100 Series into which she was pumping Calypso, Gypsy, Hawaiian, Jewish, Western, Latin, Italian, polka, Negro folk (Josh White)—and persuaded by Johnny Meyers, one session of four sides each with Famous Georgia Peach and The Harmonaires, and the Dixie Humming Birds. Gospel hadn't proved its market to her yet. And this was one woman—a solo. But that voice. "You could sing the blues." Again. "Honey, what Negro couldn't sing the blues? That's the Devil working on you. Sing the blues, what you got? You down in a deep pit, crying for help. You end up—you ain't got it; you where you started. Despair. But gospel. Now gospel might start sad—you down; but honey, you already *know* there's hope; and time you finish, you have found the cure. And so have the people listening. That's singing for the *Lord*. Plenty people like it," she ended practically.

Mrs. Berman stared, heavy-lidded. She conferred briefly with Art Freeman. Mahalia silent, fanning herself. Johnny Meyers shifted restlessly. "All right, we'll try you. Four sides. Mr. Freeman here will take care of the contract. These are the terms—"

Mahalia balked. If you not worth something to yourself, you not worth nothing to them. They compromised. Freeman set up rehearsal time and a session date. "I'll leave the material up to you, Mahalia—though I'll have to okay it, so be ready with some extras. And be on time! Studio costs run by the hour, and I'll catch hell if we run over."

They celebrated at the closest drugstore, Mahalia already meditating on the three other songs to do. She knew what she was going cut first, what she'd auditioned with—*I'm Going to Tell God All About It One of These Days.* It became her first Apollo release, although Bess picked it as the flip side to *Wait Till My Change Comes.*

Honey, Halie's *been* waiting on this record business.

Astute Bess Berman made one more move. She could do a friend a favor —and told him so. Harry Lenetska listened cautiously. Okay, he'd go listen Where? At *church?*

With William Morris Agency, Harry Lenetska had handled Sophie Tucker, Borrah Minnevitch, Ed Sullivan. Earlier, at the Gale Agency, he'd worked with Ella Fitzgerald, The Ink Spots, the top echelon of black talent. Now he was on his own. Searching.

"When I heard Mahalia, in that church," says Mr. Lenetska, "I was thunderstruck. I knew she would be a star—a tremendous star. That voice. That personality. It was like nobody— The only one other that I knew had it—that kind of a personality—was Al Jolson. And Judy Garland. And Mahalia Jackson. To me, she was such a great artist."

But wary of agents. She'd got along so far without one. "So I thought if I took her up to my home, brought her to dinner, and to meet my wife—understand? she may condescend to have me." He had instinctively struck the single best position from which to approach Mahalia. There was one problem: getting her into his building. Colored people weren't allowed in the elevator. He'd risk it. But—lucky; he hadn't said a word to Mahalia—"the color thing didn't come up; we got up, all right—but it did where you'd never expect it."

Dinner was ready when they arrived, so they sat down promptly. Emerging from the kitchen laden with food, the maid—new, up from the South—took one look at the two dark faces among the Lenetskas . . . and ran from the room. "I'm not serving them! I can't serve colored people!" she told a startled Mrs. Lenetska.

"But you're colored yourself!"

"Oh—you can't see!" cried the maid, exasperated.

"You go, then; we'll serve ourselves. But don't come back."

It put no damper on the evening—everyone at the table had learned to rock with the boat—but Mahalia didn't persuade easy. "I can make you a lot of money, Mahalia. What are you making now?" Mahalia heaved a sigh. "Not much, Mr. Lenaska."

No call to tell this strange man her business. ("Probably about $50 a week," Lenetska told his wife later, talking it over.) "I have the connections to book you in the big cafes, and—"

"Waaaait a minute, Mr. Lenaska; you talking to a gospel singer; Halie don't sing in no cafes, serving liquor, playing to the Devil. Halie's singing for the Lord."

"Okay, legitimate theatre, then—I can get you $10,000 a week, playing legitimate theatre."

"Mnh-mnh. Put up all kind of music there. I don't even go *in* no theatre."

"What are you, a saint?"

"No, baby; I'm a sinner like you, but Halie's got something give her by the Lord, and she's not messing with it." Lenetska shrugged, and smiled—you couldn't help yourself, with Mahalia. And who knows? she might change her mind. "Okay, I can get you lots of bookings, anyway, and they'll be by signed contract. I've traveled with the Ink Spots, I know the route. And all I'll take is my 10 percent."

By evening's end, it was an alliance. Harry Lenetska would book her. But she wouldn't sign with him. "What we need that for? Louie Armstrong don't have no signed paper with Joe Glaser. I know what you said, and you know what I said, and if that ain't enough, baby, we better split."

"That's all right, Mahalia; we can do business your way."

HOME TO SOMETHING now: Celie had written the President of the United States . . . had taken matters in her own firm hand for Duke when she found Auntie crying over the Welfare verdict that Duke must sell up what she owned—live off that, before she could qualify for the Old Age pension; Celie then writing President Truman that Mahala Paul had not been treated in a Christian way, that she had been a servant of the State of Louisiana, was born in Legonier and was a cotton picker . . . and lo! the matter was reconsidered. Duke got the Old Age. That's what President Truman had done for them.

It was a family debt Mahalia would soon pay—and gladly.

20

"A woman without a man is like a lost ball in high weeds." She'd heard it from Annise last time home—Mamá making free with it now she was married—but Halie'd said how she going squeeze a man in this life? Got more people hanging on now than a tree has moss.

Joe Mays squeezed in. And Halie fell in love. He was a Chicago barber. He had a grown daughter by his divorced wife and a granddaughter too. But he was tall, brown-skinned, handsome, with nice ways; that wasn't so different from some around her—look at Rev. Joe Branham—"so how you going explain love?" she asked Aunt Bessie, brought up for a visit. "Well," said Bessie comfortably, "from his ways, he looks to be very nice." Aunt Hannah and Big Alice took to him all right, too. And he seemed to fit in with her friends—Ernestine, Celeste, all the rest; her men friends weren't too over-eager but that figured. And he was obliging: always willing to run pick up some of Missie's good food at the little place she was running. Mahalia herself wouldn't go in—wouldn't allow anybody *from* her to go in either. "I was just scuffling to get along," chuckles Missie Wilkerson, pert with the memory, "but Mahalia send somebody for my food, she'd make me send it out to the street!" After that mess with Rosetta and the picture, Mahalia was taking no chances.

Mays was ready to drive her anywhere singing, too, if it wasn't too much time from his shop.

She wanted to see what John had to say. Brother John . . . the name he'd settled on for his professional career (moved over from gospel into folk, had Mr. John Hammond sending for him to New York; a name, been cut on Miracle label, got a booking for a Chicago club and played a run at the Apollo Theatre in New York to the last possible night so he was on a plane for the first time in his life) . . . Brother John was coming in at the airport. She shuddered. Keep me off planes if You can, God.

When she met him, her smile was a warm hug for this boy she'd practically raised; it translated into "Well! you up there making a fool out of yourself singing blues at the Apollo Theatre." Then as the two headed to her car, Mays waiting at the wheel: "I got somebody out here . . . this is my boy; I want you to meet him" . . . and as Mays was dropped off at his barbershop, "How you like him?"

"He's all right."

Wonder when Bess Berma going put out those records? Well, fool wonders; wise man works. Plenty to do at the shop.

It was a great day when she picked up her sample. But there were no more great days for Apollo 110. *Wait 'Til My Change Comes* slipped into the vast graveyard of shellac 78s.

Halie was still waiting. "I don't know about this record business," she told John, disgusted, the two stretched out resting at Hannah's.

"Mahalia, can't anybody beat you singing. You still got the other one to come out."

"Well, I'll sell this one on the road."

It helped, then, to have Mays.

21

Her audiences were still entirely black, still mainly in churches—Harry Lenetska was no Joshua, tumbling walls. But in Chicago, suddenly on stage stepped white actor/author/pioneer DJ Studs Terkel, airing a new program, "The Wax Museum." He used jazz, folk music, opera, everything. "It was primarily for a white audience, but some black people tuned me in because it was the first time they'd heard black artists on radio—I was in a record shop when I happened to hear what this guy was playing and I said 'Oh, wow! Incredible!' So I started playing *I'm Going to Tell God All About It One of These Days."* He learned she was right there in Chicago and found her. "There's a woman on the South Side with a golden voice," he told his listeners over WENR. "If she were singing the blues, she'd be another Bessie Smith. What she sings is called gospel. Listen." He almost wore that first one out. Finally, Bess loosed the second 78. Mahalia thought maybe—

When they'd recorded *I Want to Rest* and *He Knows My Heart,* she insisted on, fought for, a second take; and listening—feeling they could do better—a third. Bess pressed those third takes. Studs spun them both again and again, delighted with his find. But few cash registers rang, anywhere. Bess Berman had had enough. Those two old ladies Johnny Meyers was promoting—The Gospel Keys, with all the grandchildren; one had 67—they were doing better than this. "Drop Mahalia Jackson," she told Art Freeman.

"But that voice! Let me try just once more—"

"No."

"—and if that dies, I won't give you any argument. You know that number I told you about, the one I heard her warming up with—remember? *Move On Up a Little Higher?* I know, you said it was too long but I have an idea: break it, put it on both sides."

Bess balked. Freeman argued. And won. En route to California, they'd stop off in Chicago and cut Mahalia. Just the one number. Minimum costs.

When he telephoned Mahalia, he didn't spell out the situation, but she sensed it.

She'd have Robert to play. Rosalie had cut the others, but she'd gone back to Buffalo to get married and anyway Robert was her regular now, as adept a juggler as Mahalia—when he wasn't late. She thought through how she wanted to sing it, and asked God what He thought. Satisfied, she and Robert rehearsed it before they drove to Kansas City to the Baptist Convention. They'd have to cut Convention short to make the session, but no reason they couldn't, this one time.

That first week of September, '47, it was hard for Halie to concentrate on the huge conclave within which swirled the whole constellation and all nebulae of black Baptist life; in particular, its music, most popular phase of the week-long gathering (besides the fellowship for which it was famous). Robert had no such trouble. It was a good week for his new songs, and for his singing. As the day came for them to drive back to Chicago: "Mahalia, I can't leave; I got these dates come up, and you know I can't pass that by." Well—Robert got to look out for hisself, make it while he can. But they'd come in his car. Train never do it . . . *how* she going get back on time? and get somebody to play?

"Miss Jackson, I'll drive you back." It was Rev. E. J. Jones of Shiloh Baptist—hardly more than an acquaintance among the hundreds of Chicago pastors but a friend right then. She would go to his church whenever he called.

Driving back, she was quiet—meditating; praying—and studying this thing. She was known never to sing a song exactly the same way twice—partly by intent, partly by the spirit moving within her, gripped by the text, restless to improve, never satisfied that good was best. . . . She sat erect. Record with piano *and* organ, for the strength, the richness of it. Get James Francis. And Two-Finger-Picking James Lee on piano. He might not be able to sing so good since he came out the Army, something wrong with his hearing, but he had her beat. They'd have just the one day, but—hey! we all New Orleans! Francis, James and Halie—all three.

For James, the timing was close. "I got in from Brooklyn the night she got in," says Rev. James Lee. "When I checked in, Mahalia had left word to call the beauty shop *immediately*. 'Where you?' she said.

" 'I'm at the Pershing Hotel, with some friends.'

" 'I wish you'd take a cab and come right over here. I have a recording session and I want you to play.'

" 'Want *me* to play?'

"I'd never considered myself a pianist—I sang; we sang duets together—but when the musicians didn't show up, I had to play on the spur of the moment. I said, 'Well, I don't know what you going to record. You ain't told me nothing.'

" 'Come on down here; don't you worry about all that.' "

James Francis was already waiting. Now get Rev. Grayson's permission to rehearse at St. Luke. All day next day, rehearse. And rehearse. And rehearse. It wasn't a new number. Mahalia had it imprinted in her memory from Mt. Moriah ("I was singing it to cheer myself up, give me courage, that first time they heard it at Apollo.") James Lee and Francis had some slight acquaintance with it in the single conventional side by Rev. Brewster of Memphis, making as much stir as a flea in a lake. What they were working on was Mahalia's "head arrangement" with her own interpolations—not written down, but scripture-clear in her heart. "Mahalia sang it slower than anybody else," says James Lee. "And they didn't cut the record until around 3 or 4 o'clock in the morning," says Brother John.

Freeman was pleased. A perfect two sides. All he had to do was convince Bess.

That wasn't in a hurry.

So another peak, another plunge, back to the familiar. But I wish if they going put that record out they'd do it, get it over with. 'Scuse me, God, I'm not complaining, You know that, but I wish they would.

Something else she had to get settled. Estelle Allen, Mabel Hamilton, Helen Green, Wynona Carr, Willie Webb, Harold Smith, Rosalie McKenny, Robert Anderson—been more pianists revoluting around her than the flying horses. James was there, on Prairie, the two having a bite. "Look, James, Halie can't fool around with these pianists no more. I need somebody who can stick, and I mean stick their behind in that seat, so don't say Robert to me; Robert can't handle what he got now, and did Halie that dirty trick."

"I know a girl," James said quietly; "Mildred Carter. I *been* knowing her, from school days; she's a good, good friend of mine, got a good fist to her. She's playing at Big Mt. Moriah right now, over on Dearborn."

"That girl's been coming around me already."

"I think she'll do, Mahalia. You want me to send her to you?"

"Let me think about it." If Emma Jackson was just here . . . Emma come back from California ailing and passed over in *no* time. Emma kept up with the pianists. . . . She called John. "I need somebody who'll stick, John; somebody who can get my style."

"Well, Mildred Falls . . . used to be Mildred Carter when she worked parttime at Emma's store, when I was singing with them . . . she's the one went out to California after Gwen and Emma fell out, played for Emma there. She stayed on, but she's back now. 'Course I don't know, now; can't everybody play for you."

Halie'd got her message. She would make other calls, other moves, but the job was Mildred's: partial product of two colleges, talented, restless, in and out of a marriage and yet another alliance, in Mahalia she found her vocation. The job would be Mildred's for two decades until, tragically, she foundered. But first, "Robert, you got to break this girl in. She's got it, but she hasn't got it *yet*."

FALL BROUGHT no record, but it did open the Golden Gate. This time Johnny Meyers paired her with her friend Ernestine Washington, a star in the East with her followers ready at hand so that Ernestine was called to sing on, sing on; at the last doing *Thank You, Lord* and moving back for Mahalia to have her final say; the night by then having stretched so long that in the middle of *Move On Up a Little Higher*—the lights went out.

"Put the lights out on Mahalia!" says Brother John, with a touch of awe.

"But she said, 'That's all right, I be back.' " It seemed a long way to the Theresa, best of the black hotels in a period when Lena Horne could complain to Broadway columnist Earl Wilson that she starred at the Savoy-Plaza but couldn't get a room, a meal, or a drink there.

And still Apollo held out. Mahalia wouldn't ask. Harry Lenetska did, but it wasn't until he came to Chicago, a Christmas visitor, that he could give her the news, a present: The record would be out anytime now.

Surrounded by the Clarks, expansive in their warmth, in Mahalia's humor, Lenetska teased Aunt Alice, "You know, I'm in love with Mahalia—" Alice swiveled her eyes at Hannah; this was one family didn't hold with white men fooling around with black girls, or the other way around, for that matter. "—isn't that right, Mahalia?"

"You go on."

"My wife and I both, we just love her."

Aunt Alice relaxed.

Merry Christmas.

And a Happy New Year.

How happy, swept over Halie like a flood of gold. *Move On Up a Little Higher* slid onto the market, and streaked like greased lightning. Nothing remotely like this phenomenon had ever hit the gospel field. In Chicago alone, 50,000 records were sold in four weeks. South Side, West Side couldn't keep up with the demand. New York—Detroit—California—Apollo was begging the record plant. Each day a fresh shipment came in —4,000, 5,000 records, whatever Bess could share—and each day Mahalia was there waiting with her car to get them to the record stores. Studs Terkel interviewed her on radio, and shortly, on his new television show, "Studs' Place"; a TV first for gospel. Black air-hero Al Benson, "the Old Swingmaster," seized on it; so did white jazz DJ Howard Miller. "The church people, gospel people, didn't like this too well, criticized her," says Brother John . . . but that time was past. The press awoke in a rush. (The black press, not the white—still no ranger on that snowy slope.) Bulking large among her listeners were non-churchgoers, young blacks pulling away in postwar disillusionment. Lenetska called an excited "Mahalia, *now* we can get some action. I can get you $1,500 a night! I'm sending contracts." Bess issued a hurry call to get up to New York again—they needed some more product. Halie let her friend Frye copyright her arrangement—he had a publishing house. Frye was in such a hurry to push it out, he printed the title with *"I Will"* in front of *"Move On Up"*. Mahalia scratched it out and shrugged—he got straight what mattered: "As Sung by MAHALIA JACKSON of Chicago, Ill."

Dr. D. V. Jemison, Baptist Convention president, topped them all: "Mahalia, I am making you official soloist of the National Baptist Convention." Never *been* such a thing before!

It seemed irresistible. ("There is a riff straight out of early Ellington,"

Ralph Ellison said some years later in a perceptive critique. But Mahalia hadn't yet met the Duke and hardly heard his music—although his name was a black symbol of the summit: where it's at.) *Move On Up a Little Higher* would ultimately sell over 2 million; an unchallenged record in the era of fragile 78s (100,000 constituted the Mt. Everest of the gospel climb) . . . and Mahalia would swerve commercial recording.

Sallie Martin had her own explanation: "It's all those political meetings she goes to."

IF MANY SINGERS now put on their gospel walking shoes, Mahalia hauled on 7-league boots and even—forced to, frightened, praying, asking God not to let her do it, turning her face but yielding to what's got to be done—even got on a plane. Work was piling up in New York, or close to. But Mays was in Chicago. She prayed on it and talked it over with God. Wasn't but one thing to do: move up to New York for a couple of months. Go lean on John's leg a while—been on hers long enough. John had moved to New York ("hadn't no more than got my clothes sorted out," he laughs) and his apartment was right on West 65th, same street as Apollo Records. She piled Frye, Celeste, Mildred and James Cleveland—they'd work two pianos this time—and the luggage into and on top of the Buick and headed for Manhattan. Allen, Jr., joined them. His marriage breaking up, Little Allen brought to Aunt Hannah, he was working for Mahalia again.

There was place with John for Mahalia, Celeste and Frye, but only Allen was in the bedroom when Mahalia said, "John, I want to put something down here—you the only one I'd trust this with . . ." and pulled almost $40,000 in cash from her grip, her stockings, her girdle, her bra, her purse. Allen watched as John counted it, Mahalia counted it, and then, having proved it, put it into John's bottom dresser drawer.

They ranged Manhattan and the boroughs—audiences still black except for a few pale aficionados. Lenetska mainly had to settle for a guarantee against percentage, but sometimes bigger halls hit that $1,000 to $1,500 he talked about—not often, except for the Golden Gate. But if a church wanted her, the scale slipped to what they could afford.

Bess Berman was often at John's now, conferring with Mahalia on promotion, on contacts—and on music, where the going got dangerous. For Apollo, Bess Berman felt *she* knew best. Mrs. Berman was, variously, "direct . . . very precise . . . an eccentric old Jew . . . very dominant . . . no aristocrat." Adds James Francis, "She didn't choose her words, either." In a fight, neither did Mahalia. Sometimes the walls of John's small apartment boomed with the bounce-off. On one song to which Bess was cool, Mahalia was determined. Why, wasn't Bess Berman's business to know; only Celie knew, so far: Halie'd called to tell her. "Celie, the Lord spoke to me; I have been given a song to record, and I want you to know when you hear it: I'm going to dedicate it to you. I was in the bathroom when

He spoke to me." ("When the spirit of the Lord speaks to you," says Celie Taylor, "you can be anywhere. It's just like you hear a person speaking to you, only it's not in your ears; and it's not in your mind; it's in your heart.") A determined Mahalia, especially one with a new contract under discussion, was not to be denied: *Even Me* was recorded. Mrs. Berman countered by making it a flip side—traditionally, a weak song, viewed as one thrown on to fill up—the underside of Mrs. Berman's bet, *What Could I Do.*

Even Me sold more than a million records.

In *Dig a Little Deeper,* Bess heard the ring she'd come to love. Against known practice for singles, the disc was thrown on the market immediately on top of, together with, *Even Me.* It sold a brisk half-million before it leveled to an ultimate near-million.

Johnny Meyers himself came to John's apartment—John elated by these great persons descending, excited by the proximity to big plans. The electricity of Ernestine Washington and Mahalia Jackson pole to pole had registered with the astute promoter; he was pairing them again. With Mahalia so close for promotion, he pulled out the stops—air time, press, "and greaaaat big old signs up and down Broadway," said Mahalia. "Johnny Meyers made me famous in New York." The program became "The East and West Battle."

In the ripping and running, John himself brought another great visitor, one wanting to meet Mahalia Jackson: Mr. Hammond.

"I came out of the Army really excited about gospel," says John Hammond, "but of course I was already into black jazz and folk long before. I was writing for a newspaper in New York and I was the only white critic who got the so-called race records." Scion of the Sloan and Vanderbilt families, young Hammond had promoted the first racially mixed group to tour the U.S., the Benny Goodman Trio, long before he became Benny Goodman's brother-in-law—was, in fact, giving exposure to every black musical talent of any stature he could get on stage, or on records. Although he was vice president of Mercury Records now, he simply wanted to meet Mahalia. John was happy to oblige.

"I'd actually heard those Decca records of Mahalia's. But it was those wonderful Apollo records of hers I was crazy about."

APRIL 11, 1948. The Golden Gate bulged. As supporting soloists, Mahalia had John, Celeste, Frye, J. Robert Bradley (such a beautiful baritone voice the Baptist Convention was paying his music studies in New York). Ernestine had her own. But if it was a battle ("I didn't even know he'd said that," says Mrs. Washington mildly; "that was publicity")—it was no contest: *Move On Up* broke it up.

Gospel had a superstar.

At a directors' meeting of the NAACP (which had a number of active white members), John Hammond, on the legal advisory board, suggested to chief legal counsel Thurgood Marshall that to raise some money they give a concert by Mahalia Jackson. "Thurgood Marshall—that's Justice Marshall, you know—he looked at me sort of stonily," laughs Hammond, "and said, 'What? All that shouting and carrying on?' To kid him, I said, 'What are you, some kind of Episcopalian?' And he said yes! So I found out then the Negro bourgeoisie weren't for gospel at all: gospel was a dirty word."

Harlem's Apollo Theatre, the black Olympus of commercial music, had other ideas. They'd like to have Miss Jackson, pay her a good price. "Thank them kindly," she said to Lenetska, "but Miss Jackson doesn't mix gospel with that kind of pop music they put up there." And privately, "I'm not forgetting my vow, God, don't You worry about that. But ain't they making me wrestle the demons!"

Still, when she pulled base, even with the paying all her own people, John's dresser drawer gave up close to $58,000. John, Mahalia, and Celeste sat on the bed with the cash spread out. Each counted it apart, getting up the total, 'til they came to the same thing. Then she slipped John his.

Back to Chicago to check the shop, see Mays, see Hannah, Alice, play some dates (Mays to drive), see Studs Terkel . . . and take a call from Decca Records. Did they have Miss Jackson's permission for Sister Tharpe to record her version of *Move On Up a Little Higher?* They did not. "Come to find out, Decca had already cut it!" cries Brother John; "started right out getting it on the juke boxes," Rosetta was already a big name there. "Well, I won't worry about it," Mahalia said; "I'll get the royalties."

Mrs. Berman made her own move: She got Mahalia booked for the juke box dealers convention in Chicago. "And that was the end of Rosetta's record; they all switched to Mahalia," crows John. And the sales rolled on.

Settle the family, leave a final flurry of requests, admonitions and instructions to Polly about the shop, to her new roomer Georgiana about the building, and they were off again. Away from the heady wine of New York, it didn't feel too different—she, Robert, Mildred, John, barreling down from Chicago toward Washington, going to sing for Rev. Smallwood Williams—her first time in the capital . . . and the car went off the road. John's head sank over the wheel. "Pastor, is you asleep?"

"I'm *going* to sleep."

"Let me get up there and drive this car before you kill all of us." Car felt a little heavier to handle—with reason: every spare inch was crammed with records to sell along with Frye's and Dorsey's songs and her pictures. Bought wholesale, the records meant a tidy profit, especially since "Don't bother making change for no 89¢," Mahalia told Robert and John, "sell them for $1." At intermission, watching the two in the aisles, "Here, give me some of them; I'll show you all how to sell." Work was work in the eyes of the Lord. Thank You Jesus. Sow and ye shall reap.

Hurry back to Chicago. She and Frye were busy on an ambitious creation: a Music Convention within the Baptist Convention. Dorsey had started the National Convention of Gospel Singers some years back but that was mainly for the gospel choruses and besides, with over 4 million members, look like the Baptist Convention should have its own.

Frye was enthusiastic. Impressed, Dr. Jemison extended his presidential blessing: "Mahalia, I'm going to make Frye official, too, so you'll both be official." *Oh clap your hands, all ye people! Shout unto the Lord with the voice of a trumpet.* Hadn't David said it? Nothing going stop them now.

Long drives for short-notice dates with Mildred and Blind Francis, Mays to drive, Mahalia spelling him. Back from Muskegon with Atlanta ahead, Mahalia balked: "We going by train. Just get *used* of moving by the baggage when you pass D.C., Mildred. Up goes the curtain. You lucky, James, you can't see it."

Ponce de Leon baseball park in Atlanta, a hot June 6: 21,000 faces—the biggest crowd ever—joyous in the Sunday bright, a black sea shining inside and out, swaying to her voice, to the word of the Lord. Hallelujah. Stay a week, then, stopping with one of Rev. Holmes Border's congregation right next to Wheat St. Baptist; singing two other spots, a hall and a church. Go to service at Wheat St. and at Ebenezer; Pastor Martin Luther King, Sr., such a fine preacher, so educated—a big man in the Convention and the NAACP too—but watch to spread herself now; wouldn't do to slight the other reverends been her friends these many years. Then a weary long ride up to Detroit and three days promoting the big program at the Forest Club, her name and her voice blanketing the city, her preacher friends generous with their hospitality in between . . . and back on the train Monday morning after a Sunday-night rousing of the spirit. One to be remembered.

SHE HAD TO give up St. Luke choir, of course; hard enough to keep her hand in at the shop and Stud Terkel calling and people from *The Defender* and *Courier,* and tenants to change, and music to rehearse—where time with Mays—Aunt Hannah not too well, get her to the doctor, and says Little Allen outgrowing his clothes and revival time here and only a week before she's due back in New York, Lenetska signing up dates as fast as they came in, large or small, work the percentages against a guarantee of even $300 if that was the best he could do; she'd pull in more . . . and Max Gordon on the line! Lenetska hurried to the Theresa. "Mahalia, Max Gordon wants to sign you for $5,000 a week at the Village Vanguard—that's a night club and this man is *famous* in New York; a lot of big people would see you."

"Thank the man kindly, Mr. Lenaska, but the Devil won't catch *me* there, singing God's songs in a night club pleasure house. Unh-*unh!*" Plenty else to do. She called James Francis, in Cleveland playing the Sunday School Congress. "Francis, I want you to get on the train, come up to Philadelphia this Sunday—we going into Convention Hall the 4th of July; need a little time to promote it. I'll meet you at the man's house, name of Upshaw; we'll be staying there."

The sky was clear when Francis arrived, but around Upshaw and Mahalia, thunder was rumbling. He wasn't able to get Convention Hall, the promoter said; had to settle for this smaller place, Kennedy Temple, and move over to July 5; couldn't clear near the same money on that. But he knew Ronnie Williams in Newark could use her on the 4th. What you going do? Go to Newark. Arriving, they discovered Mahalia Jackson wasn't an impromptu addition—she was the advertised star of Ronnie Williams' big night; she'd been sold to him by Upshaw. "He had no right to sell me!" flared Mahalia. "The days of slavery are past! Ain't you black enough to know that!"

"He said he represented you out here." . . . "I want to see my money!" . . . "My deal was with Upshaw, Miss Jackson."

"You pay *me* the money or you won't see me." Williams paid, in part, and Mahalia sang . . . even managed to get past these people, get them out from between her and God. Hallelujah. "But you wait. I'll get my money."

Back to Philadelphia Monday afternoon, July 5, Mahalia raining fire, thunder and lightning . . . and Upshaw insisting he had the right to make up his losses. "It ain't in the contract like that!" cried Mahalia, shaking it in his face. Upshaw forked over a portion, a peace offering. They went to perform. Her people knew her too well to think it was over. "That's the first time I was so nervous I couldn't play the organ," says James Francis. "I couldn't even get one good tune out of that great big thing in Kennedy Temple. We knew Mahalia was mad, Upshaw was mad—'cause Mahalia had called the police about getting her money. Then with everything else, it was a small house." A come-lately promoter.

Allen was at his appointed post as spotter, counting the tickets in the box office, when Mahalia strode in, dressed for the street. "I'm going *take* my money!" and in one swift, practiced motion scooped it off the table into her huge pocketbook.

("It's easy to do," says Allen Clark; "I used to do it all the time.")

Upshaw danced with rage. "I'll have you arrested!"

"Well, take me to jail, but I'm keeping this money." She left—Allen, Francis, Mildred, Brother John and James Lee the tail of the comet. On Mahalia's orders, they had already packed. Now they checked into the Chesterfield Hotel, Mahalia grim and silent.

Mildred, James and Blind Francis were at breakfast in the hotel dining room Tuesday morning when Upshaw and two policemen stalked up to them. "Where's Mahalia Jackson? . . . in *what* room?"

They brought Mahalia down in handcuffs. "In handcuffs!" says James Francis. "Mildred and James Lee both crying, telling me what's going on, wailing like they were at Mahalia's funeral."

From jail, she called Rev. W. L. Bentley—an old friend, a close friend, and a big man in Philadelphia: *He* could tell these white people what kind of a person Mahalia Jackson was. Tall, genial Rev. Bentley walked into the jail with a phalanx of fellow ministers. When they left, Mahalia left—with her money. "I wasn't going without it," she said flatly.

Back to the road, take the stone with the peach. Every chance, spend time in Chicago. And crowded or not, make room for Dawson's biggest appeal: "Everybody says Harry S. Truman doesn't have a chance at being *elected,* Mahalia, but I'm going to turn *my* district out. He's been speaking his mind on equal rights to my certain knowledge since 1940, and I want you to sing for our meetings here in Chicago."

Three hundred thousand people heard Truman in Chicago, said the papers. What Mahalia saw and heard, she more than liked. (Dixiecrat J. Strom Thurmond, leading the walkout dividing Truman's support, would say the difference between Truman's and Roosevelt's civil-rights stance was "Truman really means it.") And when Harry Truman saw and heard Mahalia, he recognized a political asset. Would she campaign some places with him? She sure would, and God's going be with you, Mr. President. "I went to three, four places with Truman after he asked me," Mahalia said, "in Ohio, Missouri, Indiana . . . oh, and Illinois."

Some things fell off to make room, but *nothing* interfered with Houston, Tex., Sept. 8–12, 1948. It was the debut of their Music Convention within the National Baptist Convention, proud green satin badges proclaiming "First Session" and matters proceeding as prearranged: "Frye, you be the President; I'm going be *Treasurer* and watch over the money; ain't none of that going astray."

"Mahalia acted as Treasurer, too," says Mildred Falls; "she collected that money herself."

Sweep back to Chicago. She was still the best stylist and the fastest, her regulars keeping a zealous check with Polly on whether Mahalia was going to be in for their time . . . and when she was in, tired or no tired, this to be done and she did it. One thing, she was *strong*. And light on her feet. "You know I used to could iron a man's shirt in 3 minutes? Might take me 4 now," she grinned; "I'm out of practice—thank You, Jesus."

Election night, they sat around her Prairie apartment waiting for returns (hand-counted in the pre-computer age) and righteous victorious! Chicago's black wards, voting in strength, tipped Illinois into "Give 'Em Hell" Harry's pocket. While they were at it, Dawson's forces turned out an impressive vote for a new governor, Adlai Stevenson, and for Gov. Paul Douglas to move on up to Senator. A good campaign. "I worked for all of them," Mahalia nodded, eyes fond.

They would not forget her. Neither did Mr. Truman. "When he was elected, he asked me to the White House. I said, 'Me, going to the White House?' I was scared. I didn't know what to do. They told me, just bow. So I did. The President about walked me to death, showing me the White House. I didn't want to hurt his feelings, but I was glad to stop and get to sing."

22

First, she had to decide about the shop. She couldn't give the business her mind, and she couldn't get it *off* her mind. Even with Cylestine tending to so much on top her own job. . . . God, what You think? I looked for it to be something to lean on, but You changed all that. Seems like it's leaning on me. . . . But I sure do hate to let go. . . . She sold the shop. Polly could still do for her. Charge that girl with something and it got *done*. Not like some. Worth every penny.

Free now to travel, she was like a spring: coiled, in Chicago, compressing all the needs and the wants; loosed by Lenetska—ranging, bending, bobbing, crisscrossing, not singing every night but on the move. Her favorite direction was still New Orleans; her preoccupation still the church. In February she could link the two, booked for a Baptist convocation. Quick, see Aunt Duke, Aunt Bell; take Rev. Boddie—who drove her down—to meet her Daddy: no part of the doings, but "he's a great Bible preacher, Rev. Boddie."

There were joint sessions at night, but by day they spread over various churches for unit talks. Mahalia was on the Mt. Moriah pulpit—Rev. Boddie there, too, an honored guest, when clear above the proceedings she heard Rev. Boddie's voice insist, "That *is* Mahalia's daddy."

"Mahalia let out an 'Ohhhhhhhhh!' " laughs Mildred Falls; "she had a fit . . . she didn't know he was coming; he just slipped in and sat down." After the speaking, and the singing, Johnny Jackson's soft voice told Mildred, "You and my daughter make a good team; I'm proud you're with her. Anything I can do, you let me know."

Two dates in New Orleans, then back to Chicago to change clothes, get the records and songbooks, pick up Lenetska's last-minute dates, and head out by train for the Mid-South boondocks.

Mildred's first tour South. Mahalia didn't seem worried. Probably knew the territory enough to be strong at the right times, soft when it was wrong times, and pray a lot. Mahalia would take the lead. . . . Mahalia got sick on the train. For almost the first time in her life. She couldn't say what was wrong—just in a spell of no strength. Mildred helped her off when the train jerked to a stop in South Carolina—the end of the track for them, a bus ride of some 30 miles ahead to their concert at a Negro college. The train disappeared in the darkening gloom, their luggage heaped to one side, Mahalia leaning on Mildred, and porters not to be seen. Well, get Mahalia over by the bus . . . but step aside, let these white people get on; struggle Mahalia's heft up and into a rear seat, then go back, bring the baggage piece by heavy piece . . . driver snarling to hurry, jerking into motion so that she fell into her seat. Arriving, they managed to find a black taxi to get Mahalia into, then Mildred headed back for the luggage. Two white boys were wheeling up a baggage cart. "I have quite a bit of luggage on the bus," Mildred said in her smallest voice; "would you help me, please?" The two stared hard, then growled, "Who you think you are, gal?" And rolled past. Three trips later . . . the bus driver furious: "Get that stuff off this bus, I got to move this bus!"—nobody able to board until Mildred gave way, unclogged the aisle . . . three trips later she staggered up with the last piece. Negroes were standing around idle, watching, keeping a distance from the cab. Now she'd struggled the boxes and bags, the cab driver didn't want her to put them in, she a marked woman, been uppity—the impasse broken because the luggage blocked his rear wheels, no way to move from the curb but back out . . . "and you better not run over them!" Mildred flared finally, then burst into tears.

Mahalia had been silent. Now, the cab in motion, Mildred sobbing, she said, "Let's stop by the train station. Now Mildred, don't you move from this cab." She came back with a ticket in hand—one way—and the schedule for the first train north. "I don't want you waiting here by yourself, so you come to the hotel with me and I'll send somebody back and you can go home. You not a Southern girl."

"No, I'm not."

"I can see you not."

In silence the Negro driver stopped in pitch-dark a block from the hotel's lights and he and Mahalia left, she clutching him for support. In the dark, in the strangeness, sick to her soul and scared to her stomach, Mildred pulled out the luggage and sat on it. Mahalia wouldn't just leave her.

How long is a few minutes? By the time someone from the hotel arrived, "I aged," says Mildred. She couldn't stop crying. "Mildred, go downstairs and eat dinner. There's a lot of young people down there." She groped her way down . . . and came back, unable to swallow.

"Why don't you take a bath?" Tears joined the water in the tub. In the dark, from her twin bed, Mahalia spoke to the crying. "Now listen, it's getting toward 11 o'clock—get your things on. I see to somebody come out and take you."

At the last, Mildred couldn't leave, Mahalia looking so sick. Yet she couldn't stop the tears. "Mildred—talk. Why don't you talk? Maybe if you talk, you'll feel better."

"Well—I never see anything like this! I've *heard* of it, and . . . you know I didn't say anything when it's 'No, we don't have one' when there's a 'Clean Restroom' sign right in our face; and I've seen them *do* some things . . . but this is the first I've *experienced* of it, this is the *worst:* my own *people* wouldn't help me!" All night. Mildred talking, talking, talking, once she'd started, Mahalia quiet in her answers, explaining the history and the times, the faith and the future . . . then switching to other things. First light, she helped Mildred wash her face and called the desk. "Now Mildred, hold this ice on your eyes. And drink some of this pop. You need something on your stomach."

That night Mildred played, and Mahalia sang the gospel.

IN NEW YORK that March, 1949, a famous figure in France—writer and leader of its jazz cult, founding president of the *hot club de france*—walked into Apollo's anteroom with his pretty blonde collaborator Madeleine Gautier, and his friend Mezz Mezzrow, brilliant jazzman who was spending most of his time in France then. Hugues Panassié wished to speak with Mme. Berman. She'd be a few moments. They were shown into Apollo's audition room. The new releases there could be played. "Mezz had the idea of trying a record by one Mahalia Jackson," says M. Panassié, "and we were immediately impressed by her voice and her style of singing."

Mezz Mezzrow was just as smitten . . . he'd stood entranced listening to Bessie Smith's last performance, in 1936, but *this* girl was something else. They asked Mrs. Berman about Mahalia Jackson.

"But she sings spiritual songs!" said Apollo's boss, surprised at the French jazz guru's interest. M. Panassié emerged with all the Mahalia records on the Apollo label, including her newest hits—the old Dr. Watts, *Amazing Grace;* and *In My Home Over There;* her French admirer had the influence to create one. His weekly program on ORTF (all-France radio) was heard in Great Britain and elsewhere in Western Europe. Immediately upon his return, he played her records . . . and played and played them . . . and some months later, wrote a lead article for his magazine, *La Revue du Jazz,* her impassioned image glowing from the cover. Mahalia had her first all-white audience. Among those who heard, and saw, were the chiefs of *Vogue* records, who released Apollo in France and England. The consequence brought a shout. Going put out her records in Europe! Thank You Jesus.

Apollo was now one of the three big gospel labels of the East, and the most prominent. Roberta Martin, Rev. B. C. Campbell and Congregation, Reliable Jubilee Singers, a dozen more were all selling. Although nobody came remotely near Mahalia Jackson sales—Robert's *Prayer Changes Things* was her latest skyrocket, and her Dorsey numbers never failed ("he's our Irving Berlin")—you never knew. Strange market.

Record, and back to the road: the train to New Orleans with Mildred, then Tucker to drive her around; his G.I. school was out now. "I drove her to Pensacola, to different parts of Mississippi," says George Thomas, "and up to Baton Rouge. Mama drove up to hear her there. ("Baby, you *know* I was proud as a peacock on a sunny day," says Bessie.) Then Peter drove her around for a week. I enjoyed it. Mahalia was always kidding me; she was about the best company I know." In Mobile, George's fuel pump went bad. Mahalia told the man to fix everything else wrong with it. "When she got back, 'Well, they give me my money, then I had to buy George a brand-new car.' That Mahalia was a sweet woman. Good to me."

Good to one, good to all—the hands were out. Except Peter. "When you going let me send you that ticket?"

"We'll see. Don't fret it."

Out to see Celie's new house—*way* out, where she'd never seen, down beyond the Industrial Canal—and hear from Celie herself about her vision. It was a wonder.

"I was led here by the spirit of God, Mahalie. I was. He looked in the form of a man; his color was . . . kind of golden-like; there's no words to describe . . . but He led me to this spot. Twice. How you think I'm going to find my way out here, nothing but cows and horses for company? Me, a city girl. Timid as I am? I just couldn't believe I had it to do. First time was about 3 a.m. That's the hour the vision mostly comes to me, you know. I was walking around in the spirit, He and I were together. When He would walk, it was like a rushing of the wind—I could feel the rushing of the wind; He didn't walk like a natural man and I was just stepping beside Him. 'Right here's where you're going to live,' He told me. When I came to, I had the knowledge of exactly where this spot was. I got my husband to take me in his car. Puddin said, 'Cecile, are you sure you want to live down here?' And my heart was burdened, it was exceedingly sore. We went back, and the tears came streaming down my face; I definitely didn't want to live there. Then I went to bed around the midnight hour, and the Spirit took me back and pointed His index finger to the spot: 'Right here is where you're going to *live*.'

" 'I don't want to live here, Lord.' And all the family, when they saw the spot, they shook their head. When I went down to City Hall, to get the permit, the man looked at me with such astonishment 'til I thought I had purchased restricted ground, where I couldn't build. Then he held up the whole line behind me—landlords jumping up the rents then, and people were coming to ask at City Hall—and he came back with his boss. I said, 'What's the matter, you not going to issue me a permit?' And this boss said, 'Sure, we'll issue you a permit, but we want to be sure—do you really mean it? 'Way down there? Why, we forgot that place even existed.' They were very nice. And I said yes, it had been given to me and there was no way out.

"Now look around you," Celie finished in triumph to Mahalia. "When I came was no water, no lights, nothing but cows and horses and goats and forest, but I had to come down here to bring this city, like Abraham, 'cause you see houses springing up around here like weeds!"

"Celie," said Mahalia, "you have broken the ice for New Orleans, and I'm going to break the ice for Chicago. I'm going back and locate me a home in a subdivision. Any time you can, I can too."

BEFORE SHE left town, there was something else on Halie's mind.

"George, I want you to let me have Irma. Well, let her come to me and see. No, she's not too young. I got some more traveling to do, but when I get home, you send her. I got plans for that child." (Little Irma would be taken down to the station, clutching her mother; take one look at the train, and let loose a wail near to break your heart. They took her back home. Mahalia couldn't have her.)

To New York for Johnny Meyers, Robert with her and forced to his first plane ride to make the date Lenetska booked in Washington, D.C. Safely home—surrounded by company in Mahalia's apartment—"Who was more scared?" "Both of us," said Robert firmly, closing the subject.

The company gone, only Mays prowling around and "Flower Girl"—Bernice, a teacher now—rubbing her feet, a drowsy Mahalia told her, "If this thing keeps up so I can, I'm going do what I told you I wanted to do. Remember? I'm going fix it so children who want to get a high education *can,* in a Christian way. If this thing keeps up."

Would it?

GOSPEL WAS a very way of life now for thousands, an interlacing through the land. When she went to Los Angeles for National Convention, she walked in on friends. "Hey, Gwen!" "Hey, Sister!" Gwen Cooper, who'd kept in touch since she visited the shop with Emma Jackson. And Sallie Martin, a Californian too, for the time. When Mahalia stayed through October, held by a series of church dates, Sallie, Celeste, the whole gospel inner core converged to give her a birthday party October 26. Mid-party, Mahalia remembered something. "Come on, Gwen, come go with me." She chatted of this and that all the way to San Pedro and 54th, where she was staying with a friend—and Gwen didn't feel she could ask—so it was a surprise when Mahalia strode to her room and yanked up a corner of the mattress. "Well, that's all right," she said, picking up a roll of cash and tucking it into her bosom. "Let's get back."

FRYE HAD his own group, but there were gaps in work, so he was glad to go when Mahalia came back and rounded him up with Mildred, Willie Webb, and Emma Bell. Emma Bell was along for the ride. "Mahalia started taking me around after my sisters died. She thought that would help me. Mahalia wasn't a drinking person but I did, and she would like to hear me talk; she thought I was so funny when I did." With Frye and Willie, who liked a laugh too, it was being a good trip. Just for one thing: "Mildred always would stick up under Mahalia so close nobody else could hardly get near her."

Settled in at a motel in Hamilton, Va., due to sing at Hampton Institute, Willie had an idea to level Miss Mildred. "I'm going to stop her from going away leaving her door open." Quietly he carried out every trace of Mildred's luggage, put it into the car, raced the motor, then rushed into Mahalia's room. "Mildred! I just saw somebody coming out your place!"

Mildred rushed out. And dragged back. "She sank down in that chair," says Emma Bell, "just as mournful. 'Somebody has stolen everything I own!' Mahalia *fell out!* And Mildred learned a lesson."

Road wasn't bad, like that.

BUT HOME—that was the place. As Halie, she was at her happiest cooking good Louisiana food for her friends . . . a steady influx and outgo, always a residue to sit to the table and the latest news (the gospel world a living, breathing sponge that soaked in and gave up the smallest events as quickly as they could be squeezed out).

And in Chicago there was Mays.

On the road, she'd thought the idea . . . prayed over it . . . stood off and looked at it . . . waited . . . and got up one morning with her answer. With the money she had, she'd open a flower shop: She'd never felt good about turning loose the beauty shop, except it ran her crazy. No need to study first, either. Been handed enough bouquets, sung at enough funerals, been to enough testimonials to take note of *all* the styles. She could do better than most with one hand tied and falling backwards. People always calling her for funerals—now they could have the decency to get the *flowers* from her: she wasn't charging them to sing. Besides, her name going bring some in by itself. Mays could be manager. Put him up in business, make a good go of that, the two of them together. She could put Audrey to work; Allen, too, when she wasn't using him on the road—and get Becky Avery in; Becky knew flowers. Back when Becky was giving her rides to sing at whatever church would have her, she never dreamed one day her own job would come from Mahala Jackson. Or Halie have one to give. Thank You, Jesus.

MAHALIA'S HOUSE of Flowers was an instant success. Ike came to the big opening—he lived 8 blocks down the street—and she pinned a flower to his lapel. He looked nice. He didn't stay long, though; Mays was looking mad.

As she expected, "some people wouldn't buy my flowers unless I promised to sing, and many of them didn't care how the flowers looked just so I *was* there to sing." Thanks to Missie, she had a big customer in Clarence McGowan, who "buried every one of his workers at his vending-machine place." Mr. McGowan seemed pleased with her work. In fact, when Mahalia made a blanket, it was a marvel to the morning—to the unabashed surprise of many.

She was only 10 blocks from home, at 4657 Michigan Blvd., and she loved working with the flowers: put her in mind of Aunt Bell, with her pots ranged on her side gallery on the alley; and Aunt Duke saying she'd stick to growing what they could eat. Both had their point. Bell didn't have a yard to plant, but she had flowers for Celie to take to McDonogh's statue every year . . . a great day, McDonogh Day, especially if you went to a McDonogh *school*—though the sun got pretty hot standing in those long lines waiting for the white children to finish so they could put theirs on. Halie never did get to go, but Celie said lots of the flowers were wilted by the time they got up to the statue. But it was a great trip downtown; everybody in school go together. . . .

Well! that look good enough to bake.

She stayed just as long as she could before she had to rush to another world, New York. And the end of friendship with her biggest producer, Johnny Meyers. They wrangled about money but that didn't cut any ties, just strained them, until Johnny Meyers took her up to WWRL to Doc Wheeler's "Morning Spirituals" and while she's getting ready to go on the air, he got into an argument with Doc Wheeler over Mahalia. "She's a rotten bitch," said Meyers. "You're not talking about Mahalia Jackson!" cried Wheeler.

Having defended her, Wheeler told Mahalia. What happened then was predictable. "Nothing about Mahalia is small," said Lenetska, getting the word. "She could take a lot," nods Aunt Bessie, "but oh, when you'd get her kind of stirred up, you had something on your hands."

That Mother's Day, 1950, the Golden Gate concert was impressive. Nothing going get between her and her God. No studying at all to say no when Apollo Theatre's manager called with his latest idea: her to share a bill there with Rosetta Tharpe, gone full gospel. And she didn't listen to the clang when Golden Gate slammed shut. Already a key figure had walked in—fate's unknown stranger—and walked out with a daring idea. She hadn't wanted to listen to him either. For another reason.

"That man robbed my peace."

23

She noticed him, because of his peculiar eyes. They cut through you. Not that she paid much attention at Apollo studio that night. She'd come right from the train and she had to put her mind on *Just Over the Hill:* another two-parter. She had in her senses exactly the *result* she wanted, and when she got it, she'd know it. But it wasn't coming out right from James Herbert Francis sitting at that organ. "Francis!" she roared, "we got to get this, and you not *getting* it!" Francis just shook his head, smiling. Let the storm rage; he knew the sun was going to shine. Listening, the outsider was struck with their rapport. "The organist was sightless, and one of the interesting things to me was that she gave him the most violent cursing out and he just reveled in it—because by and large, blind people don't like sympathy and she evidently knew that. He wasn't doing some of the things as she wanted them, and she let him know it." (Mahalia wasn't so pleased with herself. On her knees that night, "God, the demons got me again, didn't they . . . You got to help Halie *wrestle* 'em, God; You know sometimes I gets evil.")

Joe Bostic was interested in his sociological notes; was interested in a great many things. Alert, imaginative, a tan intelligence in the subtly white-washed world of Broadway, he'd been a reporter, then amusements editor in New York in the days when, by unwritten rule, no Negro's picture was run on the front page unless they'd committed a major crime . . . ("Hearst broke that cycle here," says Mr. Bostic, "by having his *New York Journal* run Father Divine on the front page—by the strange reasoning, as press circles had it, that one of Father Divine's tenets was 'no co-habitation'; theoretically, this would mean, ultimately, the extinction of our group.") . . . had then become a press agent: moved into sports as boxing and wrestling announcer, and onto radio as a DJ with a weekly Negro live-talent showcase. Now he hoped for his biggest coup to date: produce Mahalia Jackson in concert at Carnegie Hall.

Mahalia's quiet reply was clear. "You must be some kind of a fool, mister. Now you'll have to excuse me, please, 'cause I got to get me a place to stay."

Immediately after she stopped recording, he'd walked over, made his manners in courtly style, and put his proposition. Her stark refusal was a surprise but no answer, to Joe Bostic—and she'd given him his opening. "Let me get a room for you, Miss Jackson. You're tired, you certainly shouldn't have to bother. I'll be right back. No trouble at all." He returned smiling; she was booked at the Dawn Hotel; he'd see her there, see she was well taken care of.

All the way to Harlem; into the room; into the night he talked, persuasive, cogent. Mahalia didn't budge. "These type of songs are not high enough for Carnegie Hall. *Carnegie Hall!* That's for the great opera singers." There was precedent, he pointed out: Duke Ellington had a successful jazz concert there several years ago. "That's different; Duke Ellington is class."

"Miss Jackson, this will be *done* with class; otherwise I wouldn't be interested."

"Listen, mister, do you know what you trying to do, going into Carnegie Hall? I don't know about you, but I *am* an authority on gospel, and they don't have nothing like me and no gospel song at Carnegie Hall."

"Miss Jackson, I can pack that place out. You're a *star,* surely you know your drawing power? After what I saw at Golden Gate!" ("I was just overwhelmed by her *presence* as well as her projection," says Joe Bostic, "*plus* the talent, which was basic. And there was the one special element, her intensity of spiritual conviction. Mahalia never became so sophisticated that she lost her humility, her relationship with God as a divine being. She never got beyond that point; and many times, many times, you were amazed—at least I was, because she was such a tough business woman.") "Well, I'm not going let you make a fool of me, and have me embarrassed up in Carnegie Hall."

Nearly 5 a.m. His voice kept on. She was so tired of this man. . . . She heard herself say yes.

"I said yes just to get rid of him," she claimed publicly. But privately, to Bostic long later: "You know the reason you was able to get me to come to Carnegie Hall? You got the doggonest pair of eyes I ever seen. The way you look through a person makes them helpless. Strange vibrations . . . strange vibrations when I'm around you."

The yes was still in her head as he leaped to his feet, abruptly jaunty. "You won't regret it, Miss Jackson; I promise you that."

BACK HOME she did, though, and bitterly. She sat down and laboriously wrote a refusal; thank you but she'd changed her mind. A telegram. Reconsider. She didn't answer. Yet she couldn't keep from picking up the yellow sheet time and again; could not throw it out. It would not let her alone even when she was trying her best to rehearse a new Dorsey song. She flicked the yellow sheet away again, contemptuously. "What's that?" asked Mildred.

"A fool," Halie said. "After me to come to Carnegie Hall." "You going?" "I got better sense."

Bostic showed up. "Sign this—you're not going to back out again." Those eyes. She signed.

The second telegram was a confirmation of terms. It lay on the floor where she'd dropped it, more menacing than anything she'd seen since the wire came about Atchafalaya. "Carnegie Hall scared the living lights out of me."

Well! flowers to get up. Funeral to sing. And get ready to ride. But doom was fixed. She'd been fool enough to sign. Is that why You had me to get this florist, Lord?

She said not a word to anybody. Maybe God would spare her. He snatched Daniel from the lions, Jonah from the whale. She reached for her Bible. She still read it daily.

She brightened when Bess Berman sent her two stories from *The Melody Maker* in London. Man named Max Jones started writing about her and ain't even got the Europe records yet. Writing about "the hot Holy Rollers, Sister Rosetta Tharpe and Rosetta Knight," their records selling like hot cakes over there . . . about Ernestine Washington, that's good . . . Goldia Haynes . . . "and a phenomenal 'new' gospel voice—Mahalia Jackson." Look here! "Now we are to hear the 'Mother of Gospel Songs,' as Mahalia is known, on local releases. . . . As for the songs, which she claims to have created"—I didn't say that, I said I *arranged* them my way—"Mahalia says, 'They're not spirituals because they don't have the tradition of slavery behind them. But they express another kind of slavery from which we want to escape' "—Art Freeman got that out; the desire *is* there, he's right—

"And Mildred, look, this one after he got Vogue V301: *In My Home Over There* and *Since the Fire Started Burning in My Soul* . . . oh Jesus! he call it a jazz review; don't let the Baptists see that. . . . He first heard me on Apollo 18 months ago from a collector, got to disbelieving what he remembered and bought hisself *Tired* and *Amazing Grace*. Hah! 'Mahalia has often been likened to Bessie Smith. Whereas Bessie's singing can sound harsh and unlovely, even to jazz students, on first acquaintance, Mahalia's voice is obviously an instrument of uncommon beauty. . . . Mahalia Jackson suggests religious conviction all the time . . . a rapturous quality unparalleled, so far as I know, on records. With her, the accompaniment hardly counts so long as it keeps its place. Her bursts of power and sudden rhythmic drives build up to a pitch that leaves you unprepared to listen afterwards to any but the greatest of musicians.' "

Her eyes crinkled at Mildred. "I believe he likes me."

"Hmph," said Mildred, "I don't particularly like that next to last line."

HIT THE ROAD and make it fast. So much on her mind, hardly time to say thank You Jesus, but contracts got her name: Lenaska can't always make them fit too good; sometimes they want just Mahalia, sometimes she can work some support . . . figure what best to do: ride the train with Mildred to Virginia by way of D.C., catch this church on the way back; get a couple of days in; shop be slacked up then, graduations over, so take Allen to drive and be spotter down to Louisiana and by Texas. A Negro college nearby first; take Boy Baby, her little shadow grown to Rev. John Thurston, finished *his* college education. She so liked to see all those young black people getting their high education and still moved by the spirit of the Lord, want to crowd around after. Listen at Mildred. . . .

Away from the piano, Mildred had slipped into another role: substitute talker. "One thing, I got to keep people off of her," chuckles Mildred Falls. "They didn't want to talk to me that much, but I'd kid—they'd laugh and kid with me—and that gave her a chance to rest."

Something else was happening, strange to young Mildred. The heavy figure, slumped offstage—limp, drained—was changing lives. "Many times it was a perfect stranger who'd outwait me," says Mildred; "young people, singers, preachers too . . . someone who'd come up and say one thing or another was happening in their life and she changed their minds, the way that they were living . . . have a new style and want to come tell her about it. 'Remember you was in this place and you did a song, soandso?' Mahalia say, 'When?' 'I was doing soandso and you was doing soandso and you helped me.' 'When I did that? . . . I did?' Make her feel good. Mahalia say to me, 'You remember that?' 'Sure I remember that.' She say, 'Nobody got a memory like yours.' "

The Virginia run didn't seem like it be nothing to remember. Clickety clackity; poles and rails, how many, Lord; into D.C. and onto the Norfolk and Western . . . you folks have to move up front, now, first car behind the baggage; wonder will Frye remember to check on the badges for Convention . . . maybe Celeste will; wonder what is fully wrong with Mildred's legs; that is a worry . . . what date today . . . that's how many to Carneg— don't think about that, that day is not yet come . . . Lynchburg must be close, if she remember right; never understand the conductor and they don't stay to ask again. . . . "Wake up, Mildred, we here; let's get these bags to the end of the car. How your legs?"

"I'll make it all right, just so I walk slow." Let the porter put the bags off first. "Mildred, I'm going phone these people why they not here to meet us; you stand here by the baggage." Down the platform to the public telephone booth. She could keep an eye on Mildred through the glass.

Here I am by the bags again, thought Mildred, occupying herself watching a lot of people coming off the street, up the steps— "Lady, where you want to go?" The conductor was leaning from the train stoop, looking at her, looking at the people. "Lynchburg."

"This is not Lynchburg! Get on the train, lady. They killed a Negro man here last night and the people are still excited, still angry, see? Get back on the train." The people coming closer; lots of overalls, she noticed. Alarmed, the conductor waved for Mahalia to come quick, waved the train to move, started throwing on their luggage himself. Mahalia saw the action —saw the people—and burst out of the booth at full run. "Hurry, lady!" cried the conductor, swinging aboard, two bags still on the platform, the crowd and the train almost met. Mahalia wasn't about to abandon her bags. She hurled them up, conductor and Mildred dodging—got one foot on the stoop—the conductor leaned down and dragged her aboard—and the wheels rolled away. "Lady, you could have got hurt. Lynchburg's the *next* stop."

"That's what the people on the phone told me, when I tried to call."

Mahalia settled down with a sigh. "Mildred— You'll remember this . . . but try not to keep on remembering it. Put your mind on the gospel we going sing tonight. And remember, there's one God for all."

"Mahalia, I would have got off the train if you hadn't of made it. Had to hurt me too."

"I know that."

BY CONTRAST, New Orleans was a pleasure. Promoter August W. Jackson, Jr., called it a "welcome home," getting up some of the main black Baptist preachers, uptown and down, plus Rev. Hack from Mt. Moriah, Rev. Morgan from Broadway Missionary, and there on the platform with her, her daddy. Introduced. "Mr. John Jackson, Miss Jackson's father." He was pleased, clear to see. Afterward, he took her aside. "Daughter, what you need on Canal Street? Anything you want, it's yours."

Mahalia looked into his eager eyes. "I don't need a thing, daddy—now."

CORPUS CHRISTI, Tex., then, and glory day in the morning, in the audience at St. John's Baptist some white there with the black, except they were bunched apart. From the pulpit Mahalia beamed upon them. "Some of you people up in the balcony might want to come on down here in front, got some seats down here. And any of you folks rather sit back a little from the singing, feel free to take any seat that's vacated." She stood smiling, poised, still, Mother Earth waiting for her seeds to sprout. A hush—a shuffle—then a shifting. Mahalia had integrated her first mixed audience. She started to sing.

Then the big one: Houston, Yates Auditorium. A full-page ad in the Negro weekly: "It Is Believed That More Than 5000 Persons Will See and Hear This GREAT MAHALIA JACKSON." Allen be counting tomorrow night. Now let's get some sleep while there's decent place to get it. "She was getting $300, $400, $500, in a case like this," says Allen Clark; "that was the guarantee, with a percentage above a certain size house. I would take the tickets from the door and count them, see if it would go into the per centage. Then I would see she got that percentage."

From that, hand out the pay due, all around. Nobody ought to wait for their money.

The early June sun was boiling as they pulled out for the long haul to Tyler, Tex. "Allen, watch the gas. This where the man wouldn't sell us any."

Back through New Orleans. "Brisko, how old's little Manuel? I could do something with that boy; you give him to me. Why not? You got another one. You might as well let me have one, I'm paying for both of them."

"Mahalia, you always trying to steal everybody's children."

"Mahalia practically took care of my two brothers all their lives," says

Mrs. Rose Duskin Champagne; "but my father never would let her have one."

CHICAGO, and weddings keeping the shop busy. Mays not too good but Audrey quick to learn, Allen got a knack and Becky really *know,* so they could split up the long hours and still keep up. Go home, catch a little rest. And here her Jackson cousin Edward Burnette, used to pull pepper grass with her in Audubon Park. Him and his wife and mother. Glad Allen let you all in . . . wasn't Little Alice here? She's living upstairs. Yeah, I see Wilmon, he be by sometimes; got an act, writing songs—nooo, baby, not gospel; he don't want no part of that. Look, I'll stretch out just a little, then you all ride with me out to Morgan Park. I'm thinking about buying a place out there—be the first one to move out to a subdivision, clear out by 119th Street. . . .

War in Korea. Where is that? Lord save us, those poor boys got to go again. And me worrying about Carnegie Hall. All right, Halie, it's July; you going through with it?

Sunday, July 2, Celeste with her in Harlem's Rockland Palace on 155th. A big crowd, the spirit on the rise, Mahalia aflame, transcendent. Between songs, she spoke what was uppermost in her heart . . . "You children, if you believe in yourself and have faith in God, you can go to great heights if you get your schooling, and you work hard." Her glistening eyes swept the coalesced swell of uplifted brown faces. "I am a living example! I was nothing, and the Lord put me up! Of course," she added, "now I didn't get the chance you have, to go to school, because you see *I* was born without a mother—"

The sea erupted: a volcano of laughter, Celeste the first to burst, Mahalia rocking with the rest. "Well," she said, wiping her eyes, "you people know what I mean." And she signaled Mildred: *The Last Mile of the Way,* just out on Apollo. Jesus, don't let Carnegie Hall *be* my last mile.

Home and up to Germantown, Pa., the star for a tri-state black Baptist meeting. Mid-concert, she proposed a national day of prayer for all American soldiers fighting in Korea. Send petitions to President Truman. "And get plenty signatures."

August. A week's sweep of the Detroit area—schools and churches; home with a big bronze trophy for achievement, from Rev. Barnes.

September. Philadelphia. National Baptist Convention. Sure enough, Joe Bostic showed up.

Her smile was weak; his, bouncy with assurance. "Just making sure you don't change your mind." Jesus save me. Three weeks. She put it out of her mind. Her own need her now: her and Frye's music convention. No chance anybody at Convention *not* knowing their music one was on: they all wearing red caps. "Mahalia, Frye, Celeste—*all* of them," cries Brother John Sellers, "those red caps on like the Shriners, everyone at the music convention." Willa, too—Willa Saunders Jones, high up, studied music at Columbia University; one of the big choir directors for the Baptist Convention and produced the Black Passion Play every Easter at the Chicago Opera House (Mahalia unable to be in it all these years because she couldn't read music, but Willa her friend right on)—Willa, too, had on a red cap.

There was no way out of Carnegie Hall, so tell it: she was going into Carnegie Hall Oct. 1; a gospel breakthrough. "After everybody picked themselves up off the floor, know what was worrying all my friends? What was I going wear. That's the last thing worrying me, but the first thing worrying them: I should come out with a long trail . . . and this the way Madame Schumann-Heink . . . Lily Pons did this . . . but this the way Marian Anderson done. I say, 'I don't know anything about that, how they come out on the stage; I just got to go out the way I'm used to dress."

She did have an idea. Wait past Detroit, though: "Mahalia Jackson Day" with pictures and interviews and a parade. Bess Berman came and got interviewed too—one pale, plump mote on the shining black sea. Nobody happier than Bess, all those Apollo records playing. "Mahalia, I want you to come back and record."

They cut two sides, but Mahalia wasn't pleased. "Bess, you just got to wait past Carnegie Hall. Can't no good thing come out of Israel until then." Hurry back, ask Bishop G. T. Murphy to come see . . . there, that's fixed: he'd make her a beautiful black velvet robe edged with white—he was a fine tailor when he wasn't being pastor of First Church of Divine Science. She would still feel like Mahalia Jackson. "And I'll come up and dress you, Mahalia, for Carnegie Hall." What else . . . oh, *Ebony!* The magazine, five years old and apex of the black media, was doing its first article on gospel singers. A reporter and photographer were due; better cook those boys some food. It was instant love. Photographer David Jackson even fixed the wave in her hair before he took her picture. She didn't mention Carnegie Hall.

Sunday. One week. Better call up James Francis, let him know when she be in . . . James was gone. To New Orleans for a *month?* You sure? Well, all right, then. No, no message. She sat down heavily. Is this the Lord's work, or the Devil's? Now why would James do me that?

Monday night, Mahalia went to pay her annual installment on an old gift—her first formal gown for a program for Alice Scott: a fund-raising for Antioch Baptist. Hey, Boy Baby. Hey, Lou. Louise Overall Weaver, Rev. Thurston's organist at 44th St. Baptist, come as a guest artist too. When they called on Mahalia, she first made an announcement: gospel was making a breakthrough; she had been asked by Mr. Joe Bostic to give a concert at *Carnegie Hall* next Sunday. Nobody there had ever heard of Joe Bostic. And not many knew of Carnegie Hall, Mahalia could tell, watching their faces. "That's a big concert hall in New York City," she added. "For the opera stars." They took her word for it. No telling where Mahalia would turn up next. What they wanted most now was her to *sing.*

The program over, the aisle was jammed with those trying to get up to the pulpit and those trying to get down, Mahalia and Louise among them. "How you feeling, Lou?" "Fine." Louise said, "I want to congratulate you on going to Carnegie Hall." Mahalia eyed her. "Francis is not going to play for me. Can you go with me?" Go! "Yes!" ("I had never been to New York City in my life," says tiny Louise Smothers, "and I said yes at the same time I was wondering why Francis would tell her no, because he had studied and if you study music, you know what it *means* to perform at Carnegie Hall. My first husband was there but I didn't even bother to ask him; this was my profession.) The crowd was separating them. "Look, you call me tomorrow, or either can I call you?" The crowd was too thick for Louise to write down her number. "I'll call you," said Mahalia.

Tuesday, "Mahalia, let me get myself together." She thought she could leave by Friday. No, she didn't fly. "That's okay," Mahalia said. "The concert's not 'til Sunday." Louise would get there Saturday morning. "Mahalia, I never played for you before!"

"I'm not worried."

Send Little Alice down to the station: One round-trip to New York; and be sure to give the man this clergy book (gospel singers were covered, as missionary work), then he'll ask you full fare for the roomette and here's Louise's name. Just Louise. The rest of us going drive up.

She cleaned the entire apartment Wednesday, singing away . . . "Let the power of the Holy Ghost fall on me. . . ." All by herself, she got happy. Hallelujah!

And then it was Thursday. Great gettin' up day in the morning. Hustle to show Bishop Murphy and Little Alice where to put the bags, round up Mildred—blinking, that girl never ready; and Willa Jones, coming as road secretary and general strength, the one closest to the music of Carnegie Hall . . . with all that, it wasn't so bad. But as the highway stretched ahead, "Do you know where you're going?" Willa asked, wonder in her voice—and Mahalia felt her stomach heave. "Carnegie Hall. *Do you know* what that means? Do you know?" Mahalia rolled down the window in a hurry. "Do you know Caruso . . . Marian Anderson . . . Mme. Schumann-Heink . . . Paul Robeson . . . Lawrence Tibbett . . . Lily Pons . . . *those* are the people who have stepped into the magic circle. Do you know they call it the magic circle? 'Course you don't *know!*"

"Jesus help me," Mahalia gasped, gulping air, "they going to put a woman up to sing in Carnegie Hall don't know a note big as a car—"

"That never had any training," said Willa, shaking her head.

"Slow down, James, I got to throw up again—never mind; nothing left to come." She struggled for air.

"Willa Jones is a great music teacher and a good girl friend of mine," said Mahalia, every mile vivid in memory, "but she had me vomiting from Chicago to New York."

And now Mildred started to moan. Mahalia twisted around. "What you moaning about, Mildred? *You* ain't got to sing."

"I—I think I got food poisoning or something, Mahalia. I—I think I better get to a doctor. Wait! stop the car for me! *I* got to throw up!"

"My God," gasped Mahalia, "help us make it to Jordan."

"THAT'S IT, James—pull in there where its says ambulance." The walls of Bellevue emergency entrance rose around them. The air was a thickness of broken bodies, grief, medication, fear, the antiseptic washing-compound an orderly methodically sloshed on one area. Turrible vibrations in this place. Questions to answer—yes, I'm responsible; forms to fill; Mildred to uphold . . . the need steadied Mahalia's own insides. "Lord, pull her through," prayed Mahalia, "and me too." She drew her flock together. "Come on. We need to get to the International Hotel and we got to find it; 6–8 St. Nicholas Place. They be waiting for us." What her critic friend had said? "Fools rush in where angels dread to trod." Ohhhh Lordy.

"I'M NOT STUDYING 'bout eating," Mahalia told a distressed Harry Lenetska without turning from the 10th floor window. It had been a wearisome day. Check with Bostic. Talk to the Gaye Sisters. See Bess. Go see the piano for Mildred—proudest thing she'd ever seen, a 9-foot ebony Steinway. Get them to send in a Hammond organ for Louise—can't get gospel out of that big pipe organ, too grand. Check out the spaces of the Hall itself—haunted. Go see Mildred: food poisoning, all right, and they wouldn't promise whether she could play or not. "And Bradley, stop carrying on. You got no need to be oppressed." J. Robert Bradley was not to be stilled. "Why you? Why you and not me? Why am I up here *years* studying all this music? They won't take *me* in Carnegie Hall? I might as well jump out of the window!"

"Bradley, I don't know. Honest to God. You've got such a great voice, you could sing about this glass and make a person feel good. I wish it *was* you, 'stead of me."

"You don't even want to go!" Bradley roared. "I'm going to jump out of this window!" Lenetska rushed across the room and flung open the window. "Go on, jump! Jump!" Shocked, Bradley stared. "Go on, jump out!" Bradley subsided, and walked out. Robert Anderson and John Sellers doubled with laughter. "Now let's let Mahalia get some rest," said Lenetska.

"John," said Mahalia from the bed, "you stay and rub my feet."

Friday, an awed Louise arrived—awed from the moment she stepped off the train into Grand Central Station, Mahalia's instructions clutched in her hand. They trooped over to Carnegie Hall to try the Hammond, installed now. Mahalia intended to rehearse with her, "But when I opened my mouth, I had lost my voice; I had a voice like a little bird." She told Louise that one number was enough. They went to check on Mildred.

SLEEP WAS somewhere off with peace. Mahalia stared into the darkness. Why, Lord? Why Bradley can't go, instead of me? He's just a great singer. If he can't get in there, God, why You put *me* up in Carnegie Hall? No answer. Lord, will Mildred be able to play at the program? You know I'm not used to singing by too many different pianists: she knows my arrangements just in her head, without any writing down. Lord, what I'm going do?

Listening, Mahalia dozed. She awoke with a start. 5 a.m. She moaned, and slid to the floor to pray. Jesus, I just got to go; this man got my name in the paper and I'm scared the people will ruin me what I have already accomplished. I'm vexed and sorry this man did this thing, but I'm a determined woman. You know. If I flop, I like to flop big. So I'm going on in there. Just let me, Lord, get through.

She rose and told room service to send hot tea.

One prayer answered. Mildred walked in, wan but composed. "Well," said Mahalia, "I might known you wouldn't miss Carnegie Hall. Want some hot tea?"

It was good and it was bad, as their car neared, to see a line of people a block long, waiting. "And who you think was setting on the step, to get in? Harry Belafonte. To get in to hear me. I'm telling you." All performers had been told to come two hours early. With reason. Backstage was filled with groups a nervous Bostic had surrounded her with. Just sorting them out for order of entrance would take time: the Ward Singers from Philadelphia; two groups from Brooklyn; two from Virginia; the people on Bostic's Sunday WLIB program from the Theresa . . . and the Gaye Singers—Mother Fanny Gaye's children from Chicago plus two from their church—tiny brother Donald, age five, dressed tip to toe as Mahalia had suggested when she got Joe Bostic to listen and add them to Carnegie Hall: shiny patent leather shoes, tails, top hat. "Now Little Preacher *looks* like a preacher," she told Evelyn, giving him a quick hug as she walked through.

Around the Gaye Singers, the whispering was a scratchy rustle to match the brushes of sounds from the auditorium. Out there, the "little people" —dressed in their Sunday best, excited by the riding down in style in a taxi, by the coming into this grand hall thought to be held for whites and the black elite—the little people were passing the word. From one to the next the whisper went: the place is filled with rich folks; want us to be on our best today. Backstage, too, the whisper rounded: *please* don't have none of this type of singing that will embarrass us, disgrace us, with the shouting and so forth; this type of audience is not accustomed to those kind of songs.

Mahalia heard none of it. As the star, the *raison d'être,* she had a star's dressing room. Bishop Murphy was there with the black velvet robe. Not a wrinkle in it. Carefully he dressed her; that had never happened to her before. He settled the robe on her shoulders. It felt like a priest's robe, plain and straight all the way down, with the little edge of white. "It's just gorgeous, Bishop Murphy; it just makes me look like a saintly nun." A wire was tucked into the frame of the mirror. Best wishes from the Mayor of Bronzeville. Mahalia grinned. Bob Miller didn't ever forget. She checked the time. "John, will you go downstairs and tell Joe Bostic send me the rest of my money or come up here and bring it, one." When John was gone, "Now will you pray with me, Bishop?"

IT SEEMED a long time. She knew the groups were going on one by one . . . nothing for *them* to worry about; it wasn't *their* program. . . . Joe Bostic came in, money in hand, excited: "Full house, Mahalia! Mixed—about 20 percent white, I'd say." That's the Gaye Singers now . . . "You're on next, Miss Jackson."

Mahalia meditated, drawn into herself now, outstretched fingers pressed palm to palm in prayer. Is this my trial, Lord? What is a woman like me doing in Carnegie Hall? "Ready, Miss Jackson." She rose.

"I got out there, and stood in that ring, and looked, and thought about allll them people, them great stars standing where I was. Honest to God, I got cold chills; cold sweat come off me. And I sang *A City Called Heaven,* the first one . . . *'I am a poor pilgrim of sorrow. . . .'* Then *I Walked Into the Garden.* These are not—*Walk Into the Garden* is not a gospel song; it's a sort of ballad. And here me, who don't know too much about ballads, I'm out there trying to come up to the standard of Carnegie Hall. I'm singing (mimics quavering voice) 'I wal-lked into the gar-den'—like that, you know. And I got tired of putting out that mess, and I opened my mouth . . . and look like my Daddy whispered to me, 'It pays to serve Jesus.' Baby, I hit out with that song, *It Pays to Serve Jesus . . . 'all the way.'* And honeyyyyy, I began to see that audience turn, and twist, and I began to turn and twist. Then I sang, *'Lord, I hear of showers of blessings that Thou art scattering far and near, and let some drops, Lord, fall on me . . .'* And I knew, when I sang that song; that's a prayer to me. Then I began to put in there some of those bounce songs. I spent a long time working it up . . . but *that's* the thing that gave me the *dignity,* over the other gospel singers. Being scared to death, they thought I had poise and training, and I was just scared, you see. And feeling my way.

"After I sang a couple of songs with tempo, and I didn't sing *them* too fast—that was still *cultured* at that time to the better-class-thinking Negro; the Negro that didn't like *that* kind, was just waiting for me to get back like I do in church. But they would just applaud, 'cause it was Carnegie Hall. Then I sang one of the old meters of the church, *Amazing Grace . . . how sweet it sound . . .*' and baby, it's a doxology in there. People died, they screamed, they walked the floor. They never done that in Carnegie Hall before. And I just lost sight of the people and sang."

Backstage, they crowded around. "Oh, Sister Jackson!" gasped Evelyn Gaye, "you are truly a living legend in your time. You lead us, truly you lead us, you lead us."

"You were all right yourselves, baby, with that *I'm a Soldier*." Joe Bostic thrust in. "Mahalia, there were 8,000 people out there who thought you were *great*."

That was the people. What would the critics say? Had she made a fool of herself? The reception after the concert helped pass the time, but nothing could take away the tension until the papers came on the stands. Never mind what they said, just so she knew. The *New York Times* had three sentences, about two inches, listing "the imposing cast of participants," making the point of how far some had traveled. "The featured singer was Mahalia Jackson," the last sentence said. There was no review. "I know the *Herald Tribune* was there," said Bostic, leafing to the entertainment section. Yes. Francis D. Perkins, concert and recital critic, said Mahalia Jackson "displayed a voice of range and timbre well suited to the character of her music." All right.

What they really were looking to was the *New York Amsterdam News*. They waited in hushed silence while Willa searched it out. "Mahalia Jackson, the diva of all gospel singers," said critic Nora Holt, "was even more electrifying than her fame. Some inner spiritual force has given her the power to tell a story in song with as much passion and rapture as any prima donna who ever graced the stage. . . ." "Mahalia!" broke in Willa Jones. ". . . We have never heard the sorrow-song *City Called Heaven* sung with such an impact of suffering ecstasy. Her voice ranging from the lowest sultry tones to the highest thrill of tonal purity, sent chills of blessed enchantment through the blood of every hearer. A genius unspoiled . . . a great artist. She can grace the most imperial concert hall in the world."

Blessed Lord. Hallelujah. And a surprise—Johnny Gotham's *New York Beat:* "OFF OUR BEAT: That's the way it might seem to hear talk about GOSPEL MUSIC, but after what we heard Sunday at CARNEGIE HALL, we feel it's in everybody's beat. GOSPEL MUSIC, that indefinable area of religion peculiarly Negro in origin, and until now, little known to the 'intelligensia,' had been the property of a vast number of ardently religious members of the Negro race who love it and the people who make it with the same fervor as jazz addicts or symphony lovers. At CARNEGIE we saw in recital the incomparable MAHALIA JACKSON, Queen of Gospel Singers . . . and she reigned supreme! . . . the music . . . has successfully passed from the narrow confines of the GOLDEN GATE into the hands of anyone who wants to hear it!" Mahalia let out her breath. "That's all right," she said.

A powerful white voice added its assessment. "Mahalia has a voice of enormous power, range and flexibility, and she used these with reckless abandon. She has a glowing personality, exuding warmth and religious passion," wrote John Hammond in *The New York Daily Compass.* "There's a man know what he's talking about," said John with satisfaction.

There had been other potent persons in the audience, she discovered, resting at the Theresa (where she'd shifted to Louise's delight: "Mahalia, it's gorgeous! I can *see* it's the best one we've got"). Lenetska was fairly dancing. Ted Steele wanted her for his TV show; "that's an important step, Mahalia; it means you're reaching out." She was wanted for a new play on Broadway. To that, she listened but said no. Thank you kindly. "I didn't want to be sitting up there playing cards." (When it was clear that Mahalia meant no, blues singer Ethel Waters would play the role and make theatre history in *Member of the Wedding.*) Bostic bounced in with word NBC had nibbled on his suggestion that they book her for a half-hour show on either the Red or the Blue Network. Mahalia blinked; he *was* a promoter. Columbia University called. Dr. Grayson L. Kirk, University Provost, had attended her Carnegie Hall debut and asked Clark Foreman, director of its Bureau of Opportunity and Social Research, to schedule a campus presentation. Further, Mr. Foreman wrote, "Your presence will be very inspiring to students training in radio and television, as well as some 17 German students studying here at the invitation of the State Department."

Mahalia's eyes danced. Already, Bostic had announced at Carnegie Hall that there were plans afoot for a series of concerts by Miss Jackson in Paris. She had just received an award from Hugues Panassié, from his *hot club de france*—his ardent sponsorship the takeoff point for the talk of Paris. Now official students from Germany.

"Mahalia," said Lenetska, "we're on our way." It pays to serve Jesus. When she went over to Apollo with Mildred and Louise, it was the first song she got down.

Finally, back to Chicago. Check on the aunts, the shop, on Mays, on the waiting friends crowding her Prairie Ave. living room.

"You going to Europe, Mahalia? *The Defender* says you going to Europe."

"If the war don't get worse."

"Mahalia, they will love you in Europe," pronounced Rev. Cobbs.

"I don't mind going to Europe, but Carnegie Hall was a nightmare."

She would never fear a stage again. Even Columbia University, when she went back to sing for the music students—even the huge white university campus wasn't too much, after Carnegie Hall. The people were nice, they seemed to like her music, and they crowded around to get her records and her autograph at the reception afterwards. Thank You, Jesus. And look like those German boys couldn't get enough of her. Yes, she'd come back for them before Christmas, and yes, they could tape an interview to take the people back home; sure, she'd sing. "Mahalia—" broke in Harry Lenetska.

"That's all right," said Mahalia firmly.

Now call James Herbert Francis to come over here to this hotel and see what happened to *him*. Blind Francis was not the least bit repentant. Shrugged, in fact. "Carnegie Hall—Carnegie Hall—I heard you talking Carnegie Hall in the car after we finished recording—you and Bess, Bostic and them—but I didn't know nothing about it. I didn't even know where it was. Nobody said anything to *me*. I went to New Orleans on vacation."

"Oh, she berated me," laughs James Francis: " 'I naturally assumed you would know to come to Carnegie Hall! Do you know who I am?' 'Yes,' I said. 'Do you know who I am? I don't go where I'm not invited.'

"From that day 'til this," adds Mr. Francis, "they stopped *assuming* about me."

CALIFORNIA ahead, but Chicago first, *Ebony*'s article on gospel singers the big stir. Robert was dubbed "the gospel crooner, the most popular of the new gospel singers"; she had top billing in pictures and superlatives. "But they don't mention Carnegie Hall!" cried Robert.

"They come before that, and I didn't tell 'em. But don't talk Carnegie Hall, Robert. I got something else on my mind."

Would she really have a network show?

Not NBC but CBS seemed the prospect this December, 1950—and not radio, but TV: an all-Negro religious show for Sunday mornings. Ralph Frye, CBS casting director, told Joe Bostic they could fit in an audition Dec. 7. Mahalia was under contract for that date. Well, they'd let him know about another time. Interviewed at the Theresa, Mahalia said she would do her best to perfect a religious show that would be of interest to the general public. She felt she could, she'd put her mind to it just as soon as she finished two important dates—a concert at Brooklyn Academy of Music, and entertaining the German students at Columbia University.

No further audition date was set by the network. Lenetska shrugged expressively; he could learn nothing. Bostic, equally balked, delivered a flat theory: "It's racial. They don't think it will go down South." Mahalia looked at him. It could be. But "How can they sit here in New York and know what will go down South?"

"I'm not finished with it," Bostic promised; "I'm going to keep trying."

"Well, I'll tell you what I sang for those German boys . . . 'I'm going on with the spirit, in Jesus' name.' "

24

Early '51, fight the Michigan snow, wipe the Florida sweat, take the dates where they fall—sometimes so close so far you need the strategy of a troop captain. But "anybody can stand more than they think." Off the road, on to New York. No more than record business, thank You Jesus. Settled into the Theresa, the others about their business, she called John: come over.

She double-locked the door behind him and nudged one of half-dozen suitcases. "Take all that underwear out there." John stared. Underneath the jumble of underwear and cosmetics was a neat layer of bills banded into stacks. "There's $1,000 in each one and there's 60 of them," she said triumphantly. "Now that's what you call money."

"Mahalia, you not afraid to carry all that around?" She grinned. "Nobody going to mess with old underclothes. And they don't think I got that much to worry about. I don't wear mink and I don't wear diamond rings."

She got gold when she went to the Apollo's media luncheon in the Amsterdam Room, but that was for looks—for what it signified: a gold-plated stamper, meaning Mahalia Jackson was in the million-seller class; *Just Over the Hill* was the latest. Willie Bryant, one of New York's reigning DJs, made the presentation, and Celeste, Frye, Bradley, Lenetska, all basked in the glory.

The new wasn't off that, when something else came: *Grand Prix du Disque* of 1950 from the Charles Cros Académie of France for *I Can Put My Trust in Jesus*. The first gospel singer to be so honored by the distinguished institution. For this, Bess didn't at all mind being topped.

Record. Then give Johnny Meyers the one final date, after all—not in a choir robe, but a full-length rose chiffon. Some 10,000 jammed Golden Gate and Jamaica Arena that Sunday, and having to stand in line an hour to get a seat didn't keep many in them when the magic began to work, when the spirit began to rise, when Mahalia gave the message. Hallelujah.

THEY WERE TRYING to work up a 25th Anniversary program to recognize her in Chicago—wanted it for spring but no way Mahalia could stay put long enough to get the thing through in style and she'd mean to supervise the doing of it, they recognized that. All right, October—too many singers out on revivals to think of summer.

It would be a heavy spring. Awake, thinking it through in the night, Mahalia took a long-distance call, made soft sounds of refusal and good wishes, then dialed Albertina Walker. "Tina—me. Who you think just called? Rosetta Tharpe. Going to get married in Griffin Stadium in Washington and sell *tickets,* baby!" Albertina hooted. "She's got money on her mind more than you!" Mahalia roared. "Nobody could understand how I could talk to Mahalia like I did, what our relationship was, by me being so much younger," says Albertina Walker Reynolds. "But I would always signify with Mahalia, talk about her like a dog, and she would laugh—that was just her joy because nobody else had nerve enough to do it; this just killed her. She would call me in the middle of the night, tell me get out of the bed and come go somewhere she had in mind to go."

Right now what was on her mind to do was New Orleans, Florida, Georgia, Nashville, St. Louis, into Ohio and maybe Baltimore. First, make these little Carolina dates Harry Lenaska got. Off with Mildred and James Lee, Allen at the wheel. A stiff drive back—long dark before they pulled onto Prairie Ave., but worth it for a few days' rest, a chance to be with Mays, check on Hannah, Big Alice, the shop, friends, get some decent food. . . .

A thick envelope from Harry Lenetska, forwarded from Fayetteville, stared at Allen as he leafed through the accumulated mail—Mahalia pulling off her tired clothes, James still shuffling luggage. "Mahalia! here's a stack of contracts for Carolina and we just *came* from down that way!" Mahalia checked, Allen was edgy with premonition: "Mahalia, I just ain't going to take that long ride in that car no more."

"I tell you what you all do . . . to make sure, you all leave right out—" Allen groaned; this woman going to kill him "—I'm going take the train; I know they's one in a hour or so. 'Cause I got to *sing*. I'll tell Mildred."

The songbooks, the records, the pictures hadn't yet been unstacked from the trunk of the big black Buick. James and Allen put the clothes back in and left. Allen let James drive. They should get to Reidsville in time to let the promoter know Mahalia was on the train due 10 minutes before curtain time: she just had to step off the train, cross the street, and there was the Armory. They pulled up by 6 p.m. Allen found the promoter. "Miss Jackson will be in just before 8. We're here, but she's coming on the train." The promoter looked worried, and sounded it. "I went on and set up—regular procedure," says Allen Clark, Jr. "Frye's music books, her pictures, records, everything. Then I would sell them." Working, he ignored the mounting crackles from the entrepreneur. 8 o'clock, and no train. "She's defaulted! The whole thing's off!" roared the promoter. "She'll be here," Allen said. At 8:10 p.m. the train pulled in with a whoosh of steam and Mahalia got off, Mildred hurrying to keep up as the three crossed quickly. "This man is raising pure hell, Mahalia; says it's off. The whole thing is, I believe he ain't got your money." She entered the Armory at 8:15 p.m. The promoter had dismissed the crowd. Without a word, Mahalia strode to the front entrance.

"This is Mahalia Jackson," she shouted through cupped hands. "I'm here and I'm ready to sing. If you find a church somewhere—or if you will bring a piano out here on the street, I'll stand here and sing for you for nothing!"

She sang for two hours straight at the Baptist church they opened. "This is a present, I don't want a dime," she announced. When they insisted on taking up a collection, she left it for the church. Then she and Mildred climbed into the car with Allen and James and they drove to Goldsboro.

On her knees for bedtime prayer, ". . . and thank You, Lord, for helping me put that devil to shame tried to ruin me with the people. Amen." But not amen. By evening the Reidsville promoter showed up with an order to impound the car—and the police to do it. His grounds: that he'd suffered great damages from ticket refunds. "Bull," Mahalia agreed with the others, who stood sputtering, worried; everything they had was in that car and more than the rest knew she had . . . "but there's nothing to do 'til after the program. Except Allen, you go to the jail and sit in the car. See if we can take anything out." She called a minister. "I won't be able to do anything until morning," he said, "but we'll get it straightened out then." *I Am a Poor Pilgrim of Sorrow* had a special poignance that night. ("Baby," Mahalia would say, "black promoters oppressed me before white promoters ever got hold of me to do it. Don't talk skin to me.")

Down at the station, the police spoke nicely to Allen and let him sit in the car all night since it was parked in front of the jail. But no, he couldn't take anything out; the attachment was for the car and contents.

If this car had an address, thought Allen—searching the best way to ease his back—it would be my residence.

With morning light, the Goldsboro preacher made good his word.

YOU COULD FEEL the river in the air, she believed, when you got near New Orleans . . . always that anticipation, so you didn't mind so much the slights below the Dixie line—minded, but withstood, for at the end of this road was where you began. Wonder how much all the babies grown.

Stop first to Aunt Duke, in and out so fast that Mrs. Elizabeth Griffin couldn't get her apron off and across before Mahalia was on her way out to Delery St. See Aunt Bell and Celie but first her daddy, he married to Miss Suzie Johnson now and living just six blocks down Celie and Puddin's street; the Lord works in mysterious ways. Pearl there, with a warm smile, and Yvonne, with little Bertha—a pretty child, a nice way of speaking and interested in her education . . . how old you now? 12 already? . . . I'm going keep an eye on *you*.

Well. "Got to be off, daddy; gospel singer got to be about the Lord's business, you know."

"All right, daughter. Now you all be good to one another." A sort of benediction. But his mind was not at ease. Sitting at Celie's kitchen table a Sunday shortly after, having a bite with her . . . Uncle Johnny a man worth listening to, a fine man, a Christian man, he would speak the Power; just for this one thing when they were little . . . tears slipped from his eyes as he confessed how he regretted that. He wanted to recognize Mahalia at the option, he said, and he should have been a demanding father right then, and let them know he was the father of Mahalia like he was the father of them. He wanted to confess this to Celie, he said, it was a burden on his soul.

"Confess it to the Lord, Uncle Johnny," said Celie.

"I have done so, niece," he said, tears standing on the velvet black skin like the dew on mama's flowers.

ROLLING, MAHALIA eased memories that talking with Celie had rubbed bare. God has blessed me and abled me to do for them. And it feel good in being able *to* do. I must be have ways like Aunt Bell. Nonetheless, the ebb and flow was there, so that Nashville was a step away from nearness as she faced herself with the hot iron, touching the waves set into her long, glossy, upswept black hair. (Poor Aunt Duke!) She was the first known beautician could put her wave in with her own hand, just with the mirror. Singing to herself softly, thinking of those days when she was nothing and her shoe soles flapped . . . of the blessings He had bestowed and His bounty she had now . . . of those cornshucks tied for a doll and sewed with a black piece for a face, closest they could get . . . and suddenly Halie got happy. Her voice loosed full force. *"Let the power of the Holy Ghost*—I can buy a doll!—*fall on me*—I can buy a doll!!" On, on she sang, alone in the room but not alone at all, ecstatic, exultant, while outside cars, trucks, buses, passersby, hotel staff, visitors . . . all stopped in wonderment. "I can buy a doll! Hallelujah!" Dimly she grew aware of a pounding on the door. "Miss Jackson! It's Jodie! Hey, let me in! Mahalia! It's Jodie!" Slowly she descended, plane by plane, to Nashville, the hotel, to the door. "Hey, Strawthford! Come on in! I been having myself a time. How you doing, baby?"

She'd met Jodie Strawther, 16, in 1948; he'd sung on a program at an East Chicago school—there because he was staying with his grandmother in Gary. After the service—or so it seemed to young Jodie—Mahalia ran to him. "Baby, you got a voice! Child, what you doing out here, singing like this on Halie's program?"

"Well, Miss Jackson, I hope some day to be a great singer like you."

"He's a preacher already," Mildred injected—she knew Jodie. He wasn't bashful. "Miss Jackson, I'd like to travel with you sometime." Mahalia grinned. "You still a *baby!* You go on to school, and when you come out of school, the Lord might have something *big* for you." She'd seen him the next year in Oakland, Cal., met his mother, fallen on the neck of his mother's good friend Eloise, one of Halie's sometime charges back in Pinching Town days, Eloise Scott now . . . "How's Doodutz? How's Brisko?"

They'd all become close. Now he was a student at American Baptist Theological Seminary in Nashville. Mahalia questioned him on his studies. "We need more preachers who *know* the Bible, baby. You got to stick with it." He promised to, if he could manage the money. "That's when Mahalia started giving me money, to stay in school," says Rev. Jodie Strawther; "that's when she started calling me her child, when we really became tight. And she had been just singing away, happy in the hotel, shouting. 'I can buy a doll!' "

They'd meet again that summer on a program for her friend Rev. Odie Hoover, just establishing himself in Montgomery, Ala., as a pastor. By then, Mahalia had walked into a strange white world, and been peeled and dissected.

25

Prof. Stearns had made it sound easy, when he called and said he'd like her to come up to Music Inn one day, at Lenox, Mass., and show the musicologists what gospel music was all about.

She didn't know what a musicologist was no more than the man in the moon—"less, 'cause I could see the man in the moon; a musicologist could've had two heads and six piano legs, for all of me. And I couldn't have felt more out of place if they had." She didn't let that show. And it was no fault of the pretty white woman, Mrs. Stephanie Barber, showing Mahalia to her quarters on the beautiful old estate in the Berkshires she and her husband Philip were converting to Music Inn. They'd thought to have the work completed by now.

"I see you still got a lot going on," said Mahalia, needlepoint heels sinking into carpenters' shavings as she clung to her hostess's arm. Trailing behind, Harry Lenetska held tight to Mildred so she wouldn't stumble.

"Now here's where you'll stay, Miss Jackson. It's really an old barn—stables, that we're making over into quarters."

"My Jesus," breathed Mahalia, "I thought I had left that type of place behind." Mrs. Barber looked at her swiftly, saw the twinkle in the almond eyes—and the magnet held. They were instant friends.

Marshall Stearns and John Hammond hurried up to greet her. She'd already met the tall, lanky, soft-voiced professor with the friendly face: a big fan of hers since Carnegie Hall. He was a professor of medieval English at Hunter College, but the past was losing out to living history. This year he'd been given the first Guggenheim Fellowship awarded to study jazz—a scholarly field in bitter dispute. This Music Inn affair was his idea as president of the new Institute of Jazz Studies. As vice president, John Hammond was lending a helping hand.

"Informal," Mr. Stearns had said. That meant, Mahalia discovered, that she had not just to sing, but answer questions. For the first time, from Saturday evening, Aug. 26, through Sept. 3, experts in the social sciences (musicologists, anthropologists, sociologists) were joined with top performers in "Negro folk music" and the seminar's other enthusiasts for the primary purpose of hammering out—word by hard-fought word—a basic definition of jazz. Then when they began digging independently, they could know they were each starting from the same point. It was an exciting point: a new field of research lay fallow; so rich, so porous, it could absorb millions of words without overflowing.

They were palefaces in contact with friendly Indians. With one brown-skinned guide: Prof. Willis James of Spelman College, an erudite musicologist but still on the band wagon. As for Halie—listening to Prof. Stearns analyze jazz Saturday evening, she figured she'd wandered into the wrong tribe. Well, it was only for Sunday. She and John Lee Hooker would be singing then. . . .

Prof. James was talking about the street cries and hollers she'd heard all her life, but she couldn't understand a word he said, no more than she'd recognized Mr. Stearns's "overlapping antiphony . . . implied pulse . . . diatonic scale. . . ." Help me, Jesus! what is Halie into. Then it was her turn, and Mr. Stearns introduced her. *She* was the expert here. She and Mildred would show these people what gospel was. She broke off to instruct them how to clap; "no-no, you got to clap on the *off*-beat like this, see?" She started again . . . then she wasn't showing anybody; she was singing for herself, singing to the Lord—

The storm broke. Applause, to which she was accustomed; and questions, to which she was not—not professorial style. "Oh, they were nice to me. They were. But baaby, here all these professors and Ph.D.s picking at my music like birds at a box of corn, asking questions I didn't even understand what they were asking; I was so ashamed. And me got no more sense than to contend with those professors when they telling me what my music was made out of . . . but I *did* know what my foot was doing: it was tapping out 4/4 time and my singing come right out the church, I did know that. Some of them getting excited about blues and jazz. I just flatfooted told them what I *knew,* and what I didn't know, no use trying to hide that. We ended up having us a time. We did."

"Mahalia, you were superb," beamed John Hammond with founder's pride.

She came for a day, and they kept her all week, schedules thrown to the wind while they plunged into the heady hurricane of gospel. Tuesday night

. . . Wednesday night . . . Friday night . . . still she sang. And in the spaces —the closest she had ever come to a vacation—she had her friend Stephanie Barber and the Berkshires. Searching for assessment, Marshall Stearns would write in his *Story of Jazz* that she "creates an almost solid wall of blue tonality. It's not a matter of tempo. She'll sing a slow tune that we all know by heart, *Silent Night, Holy Night,* for example, adding embellishments that take your breath away. . . . She breaks every rule of concert singing, taking breaths in the middle of a word and sometimes garbling the words all together, but the full-throated feeling and expression are seraphic." Not all. "I 'bout drove them crazy Friday with *Didn't It Rain,*" Mahalia laughed.

At dinner, one earnest musicologist reluctant to let the subject rest came over to say, "Miss Jackson, when you come right down to it, doesn't your gospel owe a lot to jazz?" Mahalia eyed him—so young, so pale—and patted his arm. "Baby, don't you know the Devil stole the beat from the *Lord?*

"When you go home, you tell 'em that."

SEESAW IN and out of Chicago, time somehow to sing for some funerals and make the flowers, suggest and veto and approve details for the 25th Anniversary Year Program . . . and, blessedly, record in Chicago for a change: Art Freeman wanted to use Big Bill Broonzy—playing the Blue Note—and a couple of other Chicago rhythm men. Big Bill was a friend of hers, of Brother John's too, and nobody beat his guitar—that fit just fine. It suited the men, too—just for the one drawback of recording with Mahalia. "With some of the other singers," says James Lee, "the supervisors would bring in fifths of liquor, to limber them up. They knew better to even *mention* that to Mahalia. Now she used to allow us to go out on our own," adds Rev. Lee. "What we did, to ourselves, was our business."

It wasn't being straitlaced, for herself. "When you're a leader in the church, you have to watch your Ps and Qs. That's the way I was brought up to see church people." And wasn't she about to be made Illinois State President of the national singing convention? "Yes ma'am, Sister Treasurer," Frye laughed.

"You know I'm going keep up with that." She turned to Studs Terkel, a good friend now and introduced into the rites of Creole gumbo ("You chew the crab claws; let me show you—like that, see?"): "I sing to make the Convention some money, then I see they keep it."

Studs dug for his pencil. You could hardly eat, for the quotes.

SHE WAS THE TALK of New York, she found as she arrived for her second Carnegie concert. Not of just her New York, but of white Manhattan, Broadway, piqued into noticing by the accolade of the reigning national columnist and radio idol, Walter Winchell: "Carnegie Hall will be packed

Oct. 7 to hear Mahalia Jackson. You never heard of Mahalia Jackson? She's merely the world's greatest gospel canary!"

"A very fine artist," echoed rival columnist Ed Sullivan, "Mr. Broadway," who had the edge of being a network TV hero. *Downbeat,* record-industry Bible, woke up with, "Recognized as the top figure in the field during the last decade."

This Sunday Joe Bostic didn't have to ignore about 100 empty seats as he had in his "sellout" insistence of last year. He could have used two Carnegie Halls. Long before the 2 p.m. curtain, he had crammed 300 folding chairs on stage, leaving bare only the magic circle; he ran out of standing room; some 3700 people lined 57th and 7th Ave. hoping some way to get in, for a Moses to smite the aisles. Three busloads from Connecticut, Massachusetts, and upstate New York had to be sent on their way.

The 2nd Annual Negro Gospel and Religious Music Festival featuring Mahalia Jackson had her old friend J. Earle Hines—who with Gwen Cooper first homesteaded gospel in California, Hines training the choirs and Gwen, the pianists. Her protégés James Cleveland and Norsalus McKissick of The Gospelaires were on too. The audience was good to them and the others, but there was a waiting. Then Mahalia walked on; stood silently; began to sing. The house went up. On in glory, the voice that held the critics; high in the spirit went the essence of her being, so that there came finally an overwhelming urge and she raised her arms for quiet, the hall hushed, and arms still reaching, she sang the old hymn that had crossed color lines in the hymnals long, long ago . . . *"Just as I am, without one plea, but that Thy blood was shed for me . . .,"* tears streaming down her face and the faces before her as they moaned with the joy of it all. *"Oh lamb of God, I come, I come."* Ample justification for the words which followed soon in *People Today* weekly magazine: "When Mahalia sings, audiences do more than just listen—they undergo a profoundly moving emotional experience."

She had broken the attendance records set by Benny Goodman and Toscanini. "That's as far apart as you can go in both directions," Bostic chortled.

Now give Bess a session. She already had half-dozen songs backed up for release—including *Silent Night, Holy Night,* for which she'd fought to do her way in spite of Mr. Opera-Trained Bradley telling her how she ought to pronounce the words: "No, no, baby, you *complete* it; Si-*lent* Night, Ho-*ly* Night." Who's recording? *I Do, Don't You* was already keeping Apollo bookkeepers busy. Busy enough? She'd heard rumors. She filed them with some other doubts . . . Mays, for one.

No doubts, though, at her appreciation program. Just the souvenir book was a testimonial: Her life's story as seen by writer Bernice Bass; news stories and pictures from New York, Detroit, Philadelphia, France; the swingmaster himself, Al Benson, as MC; Miss Jackson's staff smiling from a full page: "James Lee, Singer; Mildred Falls, Pianist; Allen Clark, Secretary; Louise O. Weaver, Organist." "Compliments" ads by the score: ministers, choirs, music studios, business houses; by Apollo Records, Joe Bostic, high friends in a dozen states. Looking over her shoulder, "Look like you won't need no more shirtfront tickets, Mahala," said Missie, cutting her eyes at certain people she could name. Ink Williams came, the backstage crowd letting him through to congratulate her. "When you going pay me for those Decca records, Ink?" He laughed. "Look like you ought to pay me, Halie."

No one there missed the message of the chosen opening: not a gospel song; not in the hymnal—a song of which few whites were aware: *Lift Every Voice and Sing,* the Negro national anthem and so stated in Mahalia's program. . . .

"Lord, what wonders You have wrought," she said when they talked in the quiet of the night. "Now You know Halie's a weak woman, so You got to help me to bring some with me; and You got to show me the way."

26

It was an early Christmas present, brought by an exuberant Lenetska: His good friend Ed Sullivan was booking her for *Toast of the Town.* Her first network TV. On everywhere, from Pinching Town to California. "I sent him one of your records before we talked, and he loved it. He's putting you on right away, Jan. 27. There'll be one rehearsal, the morning of the show, and of course I want to take you in to meet him first."

"What you think I ought to sing?"

"He'll tell us. That's the way they do on television."

Joe Bostic, Lenetska, and John Sellers flanked her Sunday morning as she and Mildred and Louise trailed their way across the tangle of fat cables at the CBS studio on Broadway. The building wasn't strange—Bostic rented an office on the 12th floor; they'd gone up there first so she could catch her breath before they went down for rehearsal. And the studio didn't look too different from when she was on Studs Terkel's show in Chicago except bigger, much bigger, and people running around everywhere, setting up. Lenetska knew some of them. "That's Hal Leroy, Mahalia; he's a big dancing star in the theatre. Those girls standing over there, that's Phil

Spitalny's All-Girl Orchestra; you've seen them on TV. Now wait here, I'll go speak to somebody."

No different on the big folks' rehearsal; sit and wait. Mildred and Louise better go check out the piano and organ.

There was no organ. "I got to have an organ."

"Now Mahalia—" began Harry Lenetska nervously. Mahalia was already confronting a man who looked like he was in charge of something, planted so firmly before the harried man that he actually paused. "I'm Mahalia Jackson and I got to have an organ."

"Oh, Miss Jackson! Yes, yes, we'll get to you in just a little—an organ? There's no provision for an organ." Thunderheads. "I *told* Mr. Sullivan I needed an organ."

"I'm sorry, Miss Jackson. Let's see—you're programed with the orchestra. That's Mr. Block, our music—"

"Where's Mr. Sullivan?"

"Oh, Mr. *Sullivan's* in his dressing room, Miss Jackson. He couldn't be dis—"

"Where?"

He pointed numbly, almost a salute; Mahalia unfurled was not to be denied: She set off, John bobbing in her wake. She did knock but she didn't wait; neither could her organ, she told a shocked Ed Sullivan, standing in his BVDs. She closed the door so the two could talk. "She was mad as hell," laughs Ed Sullivan from the safety of fond memory. "I didn't want to give her my only organ." But he did. And a sunny Mahalia charmed Ray Block so that he took her lead.

Dig a Little Deeper was the number Sullivan wanted over Lenetska's protests that it was the wrong song. To this: "Look, Harry, you don't understand television." The unanswerable, from the man on top to the man left behind.

"She sang the wrong song and she wasn't very good," insists Lenetska. "She gave a tre*men*dous performance," says Ed Sullivan. "After Mahalia's first number you knew she could take them all—anybody—and she did. My personal reaction was that she should be in opera, because she was tremendous—tremendous. The audiences liked her instantly. We tried to make sure that we'd have Negro representation on the show and we had, since our second show—June 27, 1948, when we had the Ink Spots. This was a time the Negroes were in an uproar: they said the whites were monopolizing TV, that producers of TV shows were apparently scared to put a Negro on because of the Southern reaction. Well, the Southern reaction was as great as the Northern reaction. We got a lot of mail response and they loved her. We loved her. CBS—all the networks are always very careful to examine the mail from their outlying stations: There wasn't one letter from any station that didn't exult that we had had her on the show. Not a single damned thing.

"She was just so natural; she didn't give a damn whether they were black or white or yellow, she was just so darned kind to everybody. When Mahalia sang, she took command. The band, the stage crew, the other performers, the ushers—they were all rooting for her. When she came out, she could be your mother or your sister. I mean, she wasn't obsequious, you know; she was a star among other stars. Other people may not have wanted to be deferential, but they couldn't help it. This woman was just great. The name that keeps coming to mind with me is Paul Robeson. He was the same type—and they didn't come into the theatre with any inferiority complex. They knew that once the music started playing and they started singing, that was it.

"If there were any problems, she'd never come out on stage in front of the band or the audience at rehearsal. She'd just come down to your dressing room and say, 'Ed, I think the band—' and I'd say, 'Now wait a moment, wait 'til I get Ray Block'; the two of them got along like old chums. She and I became very great friends. A very deep friendship.

"For Mahalia, the single word I have is power."

SOMEHOW, THE MELTING of the icecap which Ed Sullivan was popularly supposed to be left Lenetska dry. After the show, he looked discouraged—and sounded discouraged. Mahalia eyed him in silence. "Well—we'll just go on," she said. "What Bess Berma say about Europe?" He brightened. After more than a year's vague stirrings, Vogue Records in England had taken hold and it looked as though things would actually get set up. "Better get your passport. You'll need it this fall."

Bess confirmed it. Well—Halie'll believe it when she has something in her hand. Meantime there's this radio show to do, some more record promotions: still black, all black, her world, except for these flashes, like white lightning. So back to Chicago . . . and after the food, the shop, the family, and—with Mays—the fights, climb into the Roadmaster and head out.

It was familiar territory, Virginia; many of the faces familiar. But it was distinctly unfamiliar that night in Danville, Va., to see Allen walk on stage at the Armory just as she was about to open her mouth to sing—"Mahalia, your house done burned down! Bess Berma just got me, they been calling everywhere trying to find us, calling all *day,* she said. I told her we'd leave tonight."

"Okay. You wait for me 'til I'm through."

"You going to *sing?*"

There was no way out of Danville until next morning, and that was by plane. The cousins spent a wakeful night at Rev. Dark's house—Mahalia thinking about her house, all her belongings; Allen thinking about that plane: Mildred could ride back with Ted, the boy who was driving, but Allen, Mahalia decreed, was flying with her; she needed him. "I had never been on a plane before," says Allen, "and it was a *little* plane—then we had to change. When finally we got home, I told her I was *scared.* Mahalia said, 'I didn't say anything, but you was white as a sheet.' "

The damage was confined to her side of the building—was mostly, in fact, in her apartment. Of that, nothing was left except a bedstead and one chair. Ike found Mahalia standing amid the ruins of her finery. "How did it get started, Halie?" She just shook her head. Her roomer Georgiana had been in the apartment; Little Alice had been upstairs—but nobody could say.

Mahalia moved into the Jones Hotel over on So. 47th. Aunt Hannah had too much on her with Allen's two boys to pile Mahalia's commotion on top just now, and Mahalia needed some moving room. That Sunday morning at Greater Salem, a neatly dressed, elderly Negro woman scarce-known to Mahalia came up. "Mahalie, I got $34 left from my welfare. I want to give you half, help you with your fire. I just wish it could be more, baby, but that's all I got to my name." With a love that could have melted the snow, Mahalia hugged her, thanked her, and said it wouldn't be needed. Then Mahalia rose and announced to the congregation, "All of you, go out and get you some insurance! That's what is pulling me through this fire. I tell you what I just told our sister here who offered me half of all she had: You take that money you want to give me, and go get you some *insurance.*"

"Amen," rose the chorus. Mahalie told it straight.

Well, fix up the place. This be a good chance to see how Wilmon's son Ted could do. Even so, this place going smell burn to her a long time. She'd really put her mind to seeing about a place in the suburbs. Be the first here to show the way.

She could only start the motions, though; there were dates to keep. Sunshine Sammy—Rev. Holmes—said he wasn't busy, he'd drive her in his car, just for the trip. Taking Mildred, Barbara Penson and Brother John, she left Allen to help Becky in the shop. Audrey had gone on to New York and you couldn't call Mays tending to business.

A burgeoning promoter, a Rev. Jackson whom she knew, had booked her in through Texas—familiar ground—then up into Oklahoma, a new direction. How'd she do? Oklahoma City was first stop. "Mahalia Jackson" in lights outside a stadium seemed all the advance promotion. " 'Mahalia Jackson'!" snorted the lady herself; "who know that? How a sign just say my name going get anybody in?" She was right. The huge place seemed empty. "Where's my money?" asked a wary Mahalia as curtain time neared. Didn't have it, he said. "If you don't pay me by my contract, I ain't going sing. Let me see your pockets. Hm. I'll take that. But remember what you owe me, in Tulsa."

Tulsa, as her foresense had known, was the same story. Grimly, Mahalia paid up the bills for her charges and headed for the next stop on Preacher Jackson's trail—Nashville. She discovered there she was due to sing for a political rally "to work up customers for the night's program"—and she balked. The man, she told a deputation, hadn't paid her what he owed for Tulsa and Oklahoma City and she wasn't going any farther with this thing. She did not sing.

At the hotel that night, a call from a little town close by: "Miss Jackson, are you coming down here tomorrow night? It's for the teachers and we've got the white people over here; everybody will be so disappointed—they've seen you on Ed Sullivan."

"Does that preacher have anything to do with your program?"

"I *guarantee* he's got nothing to do with it."

Next night at the high school some 90 miles away, Mahalia was on stage well into a song when she felt a tug at her robe. A state trooper. "Are you Mahalia Jackson?"—Mildred's piano rose higher—"Well, stop that singing and come on back here."

Like the dimming tail of a comet, the group followed her off. Preacher Jackson was waiting. "That black bitch got my money," he informed the two white troopers he'd brought; "got it under false pretenses. She took a deposit for Nashville and she didn't sing. And she didn't even sign these contracts—that ain't her handwriting; I *know* her handwriting; that's false pretenses right there!" ("Oh, God!" whispered Brother John to Sunshine Sammy; "Allen signed those contracts!") "*You* the one owe me!" Mahalia appealed to the troopers: "I got all these people down here on me and I sang for him in Oklahoma City and Tulsa and he ain't paid me what he owe me there!"

"Well, what are you gonna do, pay Rev. Jackson, or are we gonna have to put you all in jail? The reverend wants $800 he says you took under false pretenses, and I want $300."

"You mean they give you this kind of money for hauling in—"

Hurriedly Brother John pulled Mahalia aside. "Mahalia, no telling what happen in the morning; they lock all of us up, it going to be a big mess here in the morning." The small room off the school stage was an uproar of people by now, including the protests of the sister of the church who'd put the group up for the night.

"We can't settle this thing here," growled the second trooper. "We got to have court."

In the shuffle off, Mahalia managed to slip her money out of her bosom and over to Barbara Penson, who tucked it away in hers. Outside: "Is this your car?"

"Sammy, you better see to your car, 'cause you know that ain't none of my car; they going take your car, Sammy, you don't see to it. Meet us, go on and meet us, but stay with your car . . ." and the car door slammed behind her.

Court was a hardware store. A man rumpled with sleep presided as judge with eight white people ranged around that he called the jury. All present, it seemed, knew Preacher Jackson. The conclusion was foregone. Barbara's bosom yielded Mahalia's hoard—almost $1,000. That was accepted, handed over to the judge; what happened to it then, the group didn't wait to see. Into Rev. Sammy's car—no sunshine now—and off they went on the only highway out. Near Nashville, at a crossroads store, "Let me out here," Mahalia said; "I got to call this preacher." When she emerged, Mahalia had Rev. Holmes haul her bags out beside the car. From one, under a tumbled load of underwear, she dug out a wad of bills as her Nashville friend from Baptist Convention drew up, motor running. "I knew he could find the fork in the road," she said. Then, briskly, "Here your money, Mildred; here your money, Barbara; you, John; you, Sammy. Now you all meet me in Louisville, Ky."

"Mahalia," said John, "you know you not going to Louisville, Ky. Why you telling us to go to Louisville, Ky.?" Mildred shushing him. "Yeah, I'm going to Louisville; be waiting on you all."

SAMMY'S CAR rolled slowly back onto the highway. Even the March wildflowers were shrouded in gloom which at the city's rim solidified into the Nashville police, lying in wait. "Where's that Jackson woman?"

"She ain't here."

"Where is she? We got an order to pick her up." Sammy gulped. "She—well, she went that way—she got another car."

Off they raced in pursuit. But Mahalia had a long edge. The group had no real fear of the outcome although the two girls sniffled some. "Anyway," brightened John, "she didn't let that big black bastard get hold of her *real* money! She got $20,000 or more in that suitcase. Everybody knows her, know she carries all that money around in her suitcase. He just *thought* he'd trick her into Nashville. Halie outfoxed him."

"She outfoxed him!" they chorused—and felt better all the way to Louisville. Waiting there . . . and waiting there . . . "she's not coming," said Brother John. "What I told you?" He called the Jones Hotel. "Hello," said the familiar soft voice with the hint of inquiry. "What the hell you doing laying up in Chicago at the Jones Hotel and us in Louisville?" She'd been waiting on them to call, she said equably. "Mahalia, why did you lie about going to Louisville?"

"You all just come on home, John." What they didn't know, they couldn't tell.

"RIGHT IS right," said Mahalia, hearing it retold once more. "Back when I was in New Orleans on my own, not but 14 and 15¢ meant a lot to me, a man named Daddy Green owed me 15¢ he promised me to wash and iron his shirt. He came for the shirt and took it while I wasn't home—wasn't no locking doors then. I'd see him, but when it looked like he wasn't *going* to pay, *next* time I saw Daddy Green I piled into him, man or no man. And I got my 15¢. Ain't none of them going do me out no more than I can help . . . aside from some stealing going on from people I got reason to expect better from," she added slyly. The current listeners wriggled. She named no names; some knew, some didn't. Keep the peace. Up to a point.

Curiously, the promoter-preacher would get his whipping at the National Baptist Convention when somebody with a grievance of his own gave the preacher a licking right on stage. And got help doing it.

"I'm glad they beat his behind," said Mahalia. But by then, Nashville was only another black mark in a newly crowded ledger: two crises in the making, and her mother's-milk in question.

27

Mildred must really be sick. Before, Mahalia had always been able to talk the girl out of it when she thought she was—get her to get up, go on, she could make it, and she did. Now look like Mildred was weak as a child, like she must have been back when she had polio. The doctors couldn't seem to put a name to her trouble, but no getting around it: *Gospel Train* would have to roll without Mildred. Alex Bradford would go. Mahalia knew Mildred really was sick when even that didn't lift her from the bed. Couldn't even make it for the St. Luke's program June 10—James Lee filled in. Well—plenty time before October.

She let the production people in New York work up *The Nationwide Gospel Train Extravaganza,* only okaying the singers: the Selah Jubilee boys' quintet; the Clara Ward Specials, James Lee—he and Mahalia still sang some duets, and young Rev. Abner Duncans as preacher. It should've been the biggest thing on her mind. But there was *Europe*. She wasn't telling it, but she had to study on it, pray on it, see what God thought. The *Gospel Train* she could just go on and do. First, though, take a good look at little Rose—Brisko's baby, godchild to Big Alice, who'd brought her back to visit. Hannah was keeping her, and Mahalia was *up*keeping her. "I want this little girl to *stay* by me," Mahalia announced. "Allen, when it's time for school, I be out on the road, but I'm telling you now I want you to enroll her, hear? She be just old enough so they'll take her." (Allen would make an attempt, be told a parent's signature was needed, or a guardian's, and give up. When Mahalia returned, she discovered Rose had been sent back to New Orleans with a tag pinned to her dress, in care of Mahalia's friend Walter Odom.)

"Well, right now you come take this call from Missie; she wants to talk to you *now*."

"Hey, Missie." Mays had taken Missie's $26 she'd got up for a whole *blanket* for her grandmother's funeral, said he would cover the casket, and it hadn't even come. "Mahala, he's not doing right, and he's stealing, and he's lying. I want you to know, but I'll go after him myself."

"Don't say anything to him, Missie. Don't. I'll give you the money back myself. And I'm sorry about the blanket." Jesus, help me. What am I going do with Mays? You got to expect some slippage, but—

She left it dangling. Got this tour to start. And Allen to get a letter off to New Orleans for a copy of her birth certificate—Bess Berma said she'd need that, for a passport. Passport! Suddenly Europe seemed just next to real. She tried not to count on it, though, as the tour swung along, big crowds and the spirit in full flare and flame. The jolts they hit were old ones, accustomed—the carhops who ran to take an order, then backed away when they saw the dark faces weren't shadow . . . the little maybe-places who turned out like Tallahassee, where they had to let the people talk so bad—"go to the back door!" and throw the food at them soon as the money passed in. Sitting in the car, Mahalia cried: "Hard as I'm working, my money won't do me no good for something to eat." Now why had she cried? This wasn't the first time people were mean, or the last. God didn't promise a smooth road; just a sure one. Abruptly she began to heave, and heave again, great gasping gulps in, not out—what *did* this mean, just riding in the car, having to *reach* for air? "That's gas, Mahalia," James scolded; "you got to watch more what you eat."

"Must be backed up on me," she agreed as whatever it was went away. It returned again, though, the spasms. And again. Not when she was singing, thank You Jesus. But she better see Dr. Spaulding when they got their rest mid-way. God almighty! Suppose she got to heaving in Paris, what those people think?

Dr. Spaulding would know. But Dr. Albert Spaulding had no ready answer. And it wouldn't happen while she was there, for him to actually see. "Mahalia," said the handsome young *cafe au lait* medic, "all I can tell you is—diet and rest. But I've said that before. You're too heavy and that makes problems. I can't find anything else of any consequence wrong with you except this prolonged menstrual bleeding, and that we're going to have to watch. I'd better see you again in two weeks."

"I'll be on the road, Doc. But I'll be back in September. Maybe this heaving will pass off by then. Halie's a strong woman, you know." Abruptly she grinned, "And Doc, I hate to tell you this, but maybe this other business is because Halie's one year older than she thought. I just found that out. I was born in 1911." Or was she? It was unsettling, and something else to contend with. The copy of the birth certificate that came from New Orleans said 1911. That can't be, said her aunts. "Baby, we was there," said Big Alice; "and your Aunt Bell was nursing Jack same time she nursed you off her other breast, and Bell came out Legonier from the High Water of 1912."

"Maybe there was a high water in 1911," said Mahalia doubtfully, eying the official paper.

"No ma'am," said Aunt Alice positively. "You ask Bell, you ask Duke, you ask your cousin Celie, your cousin Jack—he was *born* 1912." Aunt Hannah nodded. "Atchafalaya River just run over at Legonier the once—1912—had to get the people out," said Aunt Hannah. "And I went for the granny for you—Mrs. Lee, she's the one catch children." She broke off, peering at the paper; "Granny Lee didn't put this through until the next year, in January; don't even say she done it; it's *all* mixed up."

"Well," said Mahalia, "I can't go against the paper. I got to say 1911." (The shift set up conflicts all the rest of her days. Her first European publicity bore the original year—1912—and she was still dating events from it in 1971.) "Anyway," she added firmly, "I'm still Mahalia Jackson."

SOME 50,000 standing in the August sun in Dayton, Ohio, for "Mahalia Jackson Day" agreed. "More people out than they had for President Truman!" exulted local DJ Brother James. It was enough to make a person shout for joy and the goodness of the Lord. And make them forget they were hurting more than a body could hardly bear. Until the Lord came—in the singing, in the sermon she gave forth note by note, in the praying between her and her God; in that, there was no pain. Hallelujah.

James and Alex Bradford did their best to withstand the crowd offstage, to give her a little breathing room when her body reclaimed her. Jesus, help me! The pain would not go away. She took her pills and began signing autographs. If Mildred was here, she could turn these people off without hurting their feelings. Before she'd even gone to see Dr. Spaulding last time home, she'd made a point to call that girl. Mildred was troubling her mind.

"All that long, long time in 1952 while I was sick," says Mildred Falls, "Mahalia's Aunt Hannah would call me, see how I was doing . . . Big Alice would come by in Mahalia's car with Ted, Mahalia's driver, take me out riding. So when Mahalia called—when she came back after a long trip—and said, 'I was just thinking we might come by and pick you up,' I said all right."

"We" was a whole gospel clutch. They went to Washington Park, by the lake; someone went for fried chicken; Allen went swimming, clowning to make them laugh . . . just a nice day. Mahalia got a chance to ask Mildred privately, "How you feeling?"

"Ohh, pretty good. I get up a little while, go back to bed."

"Well, I was wondering how you feeling, because you can go to Europe if you can get yourself together. I'm going to Europe, in October."

"I didn't get back to bed!" cries Mildred. "No, I didn't go back to bed! I got well! That night! I was ready to go back home and pack my clothes! Then when we got ready to go to Europe, *Mahalia* was sick."

NOT MILDRED, not even her aunts knew. With the heaving and the pain and the bleeding on the road, she was ready for trouble when she went in to the doctor again. But she wasn't ready for what he said: hysterectomy. Nothing to worry about—a fairly common female complaint—but it should be taken care of without too much delay. "What do they cut?" That depended, when they went in. Her trouble was in the uterus. "What about the heaving?" Probably a touch of bronchial asthma. But he wanted to concentrate right now on this other thing. "Well—I'll let you know." She produced a chuckle. "I don't know if I'm ready to give up a piece of me, Doc."

Thinking about it, she decided to see the people at the University Hospital—Billings; professors there *teach* the doctors, and they doctors themselves. See what they got to say. About the heaving, too, with Europe coming up. Look at this boy's father went there—was nothing but a nerve this great doctor pulled out, and *that* was what had kept his father sick.

Tests. X-rays. There were little tumors, Miss Jackson—yes, fibroids—in her uterus, and there was some indication—we'll want some more X-rays. . . . The X-rays show a series of nodes in your chest, Miss Jackson—little lumps, like knots. We'll want to make some more tests, possibly a biopsy. . . . My God, look like 20 doctors; what these people doing now! So much to tend to and got her down here all the time . . . at least it was just on West 59th. Well, what they going say this time?

Cancer. Now don't get too alarmed, Miss Jackson. It does seem indicated, and you should know that, but—we'll get rid of some of your trouble site with the hysterectomy. But your chest . . . we're going to try radiation treatments. For the cancer, yes. That may clear up the nodes.

The huge black machine swung directly over her quivering bulk on the table and came down. Now I know how a ant feels under a beetle. But they said the truth, you don't feel the radion at all. Nothing. Just the weights pressing on you and the blackness of the machine and—"You can get up now, Miss Jackson. We'll see you same time tomorrow."

She wasn't responding to the treatments, the consortium of doctors agreed. That was slightly puzzling. Too, there was mixed opinion on the diagnosis: malignancy, yes, but leukemia or sarcoma? It was just possible—better call in Dr. Barclay.

She got good vibrations from him right away. He wasn't taking anything anybody else said, either; he was starting in on tests of his own. His verdict was strangest of all: sarcoid. "What's that, Dr. Barclay?" That took some explaining. Not many doctors understood; and fewer recognized it when they saw it. "I was sort of a specialist on sarcoid at the University," says Dr. William R. Barclay, now vice president of the American Medical Association in Chicago. "After I made a diagnosis of sarcoid, and this was confirmed by appropriate tests, then I took over her whole case. There's no known cure for sarcoid, but we can take certain measures for control."

And hope for the best. "To answer your question, Miss Jackson—all right, Mahalia—we don't know much about sarcoid yet. It's a disease that affects the lymph glands, and there are lymph glands all through your system. Did you live around a lot of pines in the South?"

"No, there was more oak trees around Audubon Park; willow trees by the river; hackberry in the front yard; fig tree in—" He just meant pines. What about dust? "Every year my aunt would make me take those mattresses and wash the moss and stick the mattress and dry it. So *that* dust went inside me." And what about water—was she around much water? "I worked at the Audubon pool one summer; I didn't get to go in but I was around the wet suits. And no telling how much I had my feet in the Mississippi; I used to drift in the wood that would be floating down the river, for wood to have at home." Dr. Barclay went on making notes.

"There were many theories about sarcoid," he explains carefully, "none of which are proven. My questions to Mahalia then involved two of the most common—dust and pine pollen—both of which have broken down. Anytime I got a patient with this disease, I tried to find clues to why the disease occurred."

"Dr. Barclay, I never heard of a black person having sarcoid before."

"Oh, in this country there are more colored than white, Mahalia. But worldwide, more white people have sarcoid: in Russia, in China; it's very common in Sweden; in England."

"Well, at least I got company," said Mahalia with a dimpled, twinkled grin that reached Dr. Barclay's heart, and would never be dislodged. "And I don't have cancer."

"No." He had to decide now how much to tell her. "Mahalia, you and I are going to work on this sarcoid, but it can give you some real trouble. That's what all this fighting for breath is about, as I told you; and you may experience weakness, inertia. Well—I'll keep close watch on you. But we want to get this hysterectomy out of the way as soon as possible."

"Dr. Barclay, I'm a gospel singer; I got to be on the boat for Europe in no time."

"You'll have a rough trip if you go."

"Don't you worry 'bout Halie. I got strength in my mind."

Helpless between the curiously penetrating eyes with their kindness—she was comforting him!—and what not she but he could foresee, he gave her the one thin shield he could offer: a letter to doctors in Europe.

"You can pray for me too, Dr. Barclay."

NO USE. She couldn't make the boat. Try as she might, she could not get out the bed and make that boat. She called Harry Lenetska. "Listen, Halie's not ready yet; got things to do still; just not going be ready to take that boat," she joked, visions of scattered clothes and scattered chores rippling along her voice. "So you tell Bess Berma to send me a airplane ticket, tell her air mail special delivery so it's sure to be here. And you all go on and take the boat."

Next, Mildred. "Listen, child, Halie's got the flu. I'm not getting on no boat to Europe and be sick on that water with the flu. I'll take the plane when I'm able. But you can go on, if you want to."

"Honey, I'm going to *Europe!*" said Mildred gaily. "We'll see you there."

When Louise called—heard she'd missed the boat and knew from their same doctor, Dr. Spaulding, that she had these nodules in her chest—she told Louise that was from the mucous dripping down from her head into her chest, making those knots.

What they don't know, they can't tell. She climbed back into Hannah's bed, exhausted. God, what else You want me do? She looked over at the long velvet gown—not quite a robe—that Bishop Murphy had designed her for Europe; put a beautiful cross on the piece hanging down from the back. Looking at it was like having something to hang onto. . . . She better be hanging onto her Bible. It was handy to her reach.

BARELY 5 a.m. when Mother Gaye got the call to come pray, but she wasn't surprised. She and Mahalia often communicated first without words. What she didn't expect was that Mahalia would be crying. "She had given up, seemed like," says Mother Gaye. "She said, 'Mama, I got a trip to fly oversea and I'm not able. Pray for me, Mama. I can't make it.' "

Mother Fannie Gaye was known far and wide as a woman of great power with prayer. Yet she was a quiet woman, lay hands on you so nice, so soft, pray so quiet. A psychic woman. Close to God. She prayed for Mahalia, whom she dearly loved . . . prayed long; prayed so well that there came a moment when Mahalia "got up out the bed and began to walk the floor praising God.

"I said, 'Mahalia, the Lord say you going.' "

Mahalia paused. "But I'm supposed to go *Thursday.*"

"The *Lord* say you going." The *Lord* say she going! Praise His Name!

WHEN THE S.S. *United States* docked at Le Havre, Mildred was the only sizable black woman coming down the gangway. Young Odile Métayer of *hot club de france* moved forward smiling around the flowers she held out as the emissary of Hugues Panassié: Welcome to France! "This girl was standing there when I got off," says Mildred Falls; "a little young girl with a great big bunch of flowers bigger than she was. Flowers for Mahalia. She said something in French—I don't know what—and here come all the photographers taking pictures and I still didn't say anything. I didn't know what to *say,* just looked bewildered." Lenetska was busy with the press; Bess Berman was busy with the record and concert people. "I just never did say anything," says Mildred, laughing.

MOTHER GAYE took the call. "Mahalia said to tell you she's on her way." New York. And over the water. Don't be scared. Look at God's heaven. God *said* she was going go. So He's watching.

At Orly, Vogue Records had newsmen and critics out in force. Not Panassié—he was still in the southwest of France—but everyone else, eager for a Mahalia instantly buoyed by their warmth. The group swirling around her as they eddied through the huge airport—excited, needing support anyway—Mahalia unwittingly grasped two arms and drew together two men whose amiable conjunction seemed unthinkable: Milton "Mezz" Mezzrow and Charles Delaunay—"protagonists of France's opposite and warring jazz camps," said English critic Henry Kahn, relaying the tale for *The Melody Maker*. Mahalia, he wrote, brought peace. To Parisians, she became "the Angel of Peace."

Concerts were Oct. 25 and 26. Once settled into the Ambassador on Boulevard Haussmann, check on the organist Mildred was to give the gospel beat in a week, handle the publicity chores, inspect the Salle Pleyel, and get a proper organ in time to rehearse. If perceptive newsmen noticed she looked a little—not pale: gray?—she explained she was "just tired, baby, but I be all right. Now tell him that in French." It would wear you out anyway, you couldn't understand nothing they was saying, and having a time with food: Here she could *get* served anything she wanted, anywhere, and she couldn't *say;* had to ask for water with all kinds of motions, and they still wouldn't understand—have to get an English person to come. And her so thirsty; sweating in this cold. Help me, Lord.

She was eager to meet one Frenchman in any language, the man responsible for her getting to Europe, no matter what Bess said: Hugues Panassié. When finally he came with his friend Mezz Mezzrow, two other visitors were waiting in the suite for Mahalia to emerge from her bedroom. As she did, it was with "Which one of you people is Panassee?" When he gestured, she strode across, put her arms around him, and kissed him. "I was very moved," says M. Panassié. The two were instant friends.

Then it was time. Backstage, she felt she was burning up; she was in pain; and worst—she was short of breath. How was she going make it? Her first European audience. "Harry," she said, "read me the 27th Psalm." Gasping, she heard the words she had read a hundred—a thousand?—times as if she had never heard them before: *The Lord is my light and my salvation; whom shall I fear? The Lord is the strength of my life; of whom shall I be afraid?* Abruptly Mahalia sat erect, eyes shining. "Mildred, God spoke, He said, 'You are healed.' I believe it! I am healed!" Still pulling for breath, still fiery with fever, but *believing,* she walked on. Thousands of French faced her expectantly, almost filled the great Salle Pleyel, although her name had been unknown a week ago except to record fans. The French organist wasn't James Francis or Louise Weaver, but he followed Mildred's lead all right . . . and suddenly she didn't know she was ill, she came alive, she gave them the gospel, gave them the word, gave them the Glory from slave-time to '52; got happy and danced; sank to her knees to pour song and soul and hope of salvation up to God . . . and brought the French to their feet in an uproar of applause. Wave after wave. Some wept. "Sensational!" was the summary verdict. "Inspired."

Offstage, she crumpled, brought so low that except for Panassié—who was of *her,* this big warm white man with his soul in his smile—she refused visitors. "I'm just too tired." With one exception—requested as "the girl who met you at the boat in Le Havre with the flowers."

"Let her come in," said Mahalia. Mildred vanished.

Harry Lenetska knew now that Mahalia was ill. But he kept hoping it would go away. He did the one thing he could that he knew would divert her, please her—he recited long passages of the Bible: the Old Testament.

Next night was a repetition of the house—almost full—the coming alive on stage—the collapse when off. (She perked up enough to toast her 40th birthday with French champagne—or was it her 41st? Harry teased that a lady never told her right age anyway.) It was the pattern for Lyon the next night, and Bordeaux the next—except that Bordeaux gave her something extra: When Panassié saw her in Paris the following day, a pleased Mahalia told him, "The people even clapped their hands on the right beat!" French education was advancing. But at some expense. "I'm very tired," she told her French friend. "And she looked like it indeed," says M. Panassié.

She was losing weight.

THEY LANDED in London the night of Nov. 5. The only truly bright things about her were her red fingernails and the sausage curls on top of her head which bounced back the light from photographers' flashbulbs. She managed a smile, but her answers were brief. Just let her get to the hotel—the Piccadilly, with a big suite for the star. And there was Bradley. Like a letter from home. Even if he was living in England now, studying to be grand. "Hey, Brad." It was such a weak welcome, J. Robert Bradley knew something was wrong. "You got to come up here and stay by me, Bradley; ain't none of these people know how to take care." He moved in. Bess Berman tried to help too—came in and shooed them all out and gave Mahalia alcohol rubs, to try to lift her.

The excitement of Piccadilly Circus was just outside; it was a stimulus of sorts before she made her way through a BBC concert. There, a group of youngsters among the autograph hunters gave her a positive lift. Would Miss Jackson be honorary president of their jazz club? Oh, the children were wonderful, all over. "Babies, you take me back to New Orleans; you do."

Another white organist to be trained—Mildred, try to get the man to let loose a little, please—and people due for interviews. Among them was Max Jones of *The Daily Mirror* and *The Melody Maker,* whom she welcomed with open arms as she had Panassié: Those wonderful things he'd written before he'd even see her! Another instant love match. "Mahalia didn't pull her punches," says Max Jones; "yet she had a simplicity, an innocence; and I feel sure her soul was never loused up." Just about everything else in her felt like it was—although she gave no hint. Except to say she'd "caught cold."

Saturday night, Nov. 15, Royal Albert Hall was icy; even the inured English sat in coats, hats, gloves, mufflers. Any other time, the very sight of Big Bill Broonzy would have warmed her. Not this night. She sat shocked and upset.

Louisiana-born Big Bill was a master of Chicago's sound—distilled out of Mississippi mud, a pint of Sweet Lucy, and a South Side woman gone evil on a busted man. At home he'd never graduated from the South Side, where a guitar and a gutbucket growl had to beat out the El to earn your bread. In Europe, he was famous—which was fine. But he was a *blues* man. What in the world these English people thinking of, to put Broonzy and his blues on before her gospel singing *and* a jazz band in front of him. On the same program! "I feel funny myself about them putting me up with you, Mahalia," said Broonzy; "it don't seem right."

"Harry—"

"Mahalia, there's nothing we can do about it. I swear, I didn't know."

One last prayer. What you going do? She struggled to her feet, took a deep breath, and walked on. It was, said critic Ernest Borneman, not only the coldest evening he'd ever spent at Albert Hall but "the weirdest." The hall was half-empty. The mixed bill had affronted fans of each segment, reasoned the critic. The Charlie Galbraith band came and went to the satisfaction of only its young fans. Big Bill was inaudible from the critic's seat. "But Mahalia! The tremendous voice, with a range almost as big as that so-called Peruvian princess's" (Yma Sumac) "and the tone that really is a tone! That incredible sense of beat which swings more with Mildred Falls's lumpy piano—" (Mildred struggling with stiff fingers and fear in her heart) "and Charles Smart's beatless organ clinging to its shirt tails than most jazz bands with four rhythm behind them! That vibrato as broad as Bechet's . . .!" Yet the only time the audience came alive, he felt, was for a few minutes when some attempted to clap, to mark the beat gospel fashion. Peter Leslie of the *Daily Herald* hailed "the soaring beauty and extraordinary tone." Max Jones acclaimed her "strikingly original" interpretation. "When she dances those little church steps at the end of a rocking number, you need a heart of stone to remain unsmiling."

Or hands of ice.

Offstage, Lenetska waited with her coat, and the now-familiar collapse came on. "Wherever you'd put me at, that's just where I would lay, all day," Mahalia said. "And the *strangest* part, when I hit that stage, I became alive."

Southhampton the next night, Oxford . . . Birmingham . . . the group hovered anxious. She was worse. "I had a sense of them pushing her," says J. Robert Bradley; "I said, 'Why don't you stop?' And she said, 'I got to do it. Contract thing.' " Bess appeared from next door, rubbing alcohol in hand. This time, though, Thursday morning—the England sequence through, Denmark ahead on Friday—Mahalia failed to move. Aghast, Bradley brushed off her protests and called a doctor. "He's *got* to be good, Mahalia, he's second in command to the Queen's doctor! He's coming 'cause he's a friend of mine."

"Well, get that letter out my purse from Dr. Barclay."

The doctor finished his examination, gave Mahalia some shots, and drew Bradley aside. "She's pretty far gone, I'm afraid. You'd best be prepared to kiss her goodbye. I doubt she'll make it to Friday."

Bradley thought it his last word to his friend—his bulwark—her cheeks sunken from their roundness so that when he kissed her goodbye, they gave. "The doctor didn't tell her, though—he wouldn't tell her that; she didn't know. I said, 'Well, Mahalia, I'll see you.' "

"Okay, baby."

Shots? Prayers? Something. She rallied once again, took the plane to Denmark, clutching Harry's arm but straightening to meet the Copenhagen press. She kept her commitments; sang on radio the next day: her latest European release, *Silent Night, Holy Night*—which brought 20,000 orders for the record and total sellout of her two performances. Bess perked up; Harry grew hopeful; Mildred remained morose—she saw the wakening Mahalia each morning.

The first concert was in a church, and Mahalia discovered she was to sing from the choir loft—the audience with their backs to her. "That was odd, but it was lovely," says Harry Lenetska; "instead of applauding, they waved their handkerchiefs in the air. No sound, just all the handkerchiefs waving." Next night, in a regular auditorium, the Danes proved how restrained that church had been: They applauded and applauded, sent flowers, presented her with the valued Kronenberg vase as a token of royal esteem.

She could allow no visitors—pain had her almost speechless. But Mildred ushered in one: His hands and feet had been turned to stone by disease, he stammered in English; doctors said there was no hope, he must have amputation to stop the spread. Facing this at home, he had accidentally heard her sing *Silent Night, Holy Night* and was so affected—felt so great a surge of faith—that his illness had been cured. He had walked into the hotel room. He gave her a rare Bible to remember him by.

That was a strange story, Mahalia mused. Lord, did You use me?

She was booked for an extra performance in the fjord country where the audience turned out to be simply one wealthy man's family. "I knew Mahalia would complain about that," shrugs Lenetska, "but I never had anything to do with those things."

Ahead was Rome, the south of Italy, Morocco—but now Mahalia was at crisis point. A doctor was called. Immediately began one of the touching episodes of Mahalia's turbulent life: Each day Mildred opened the door to tiny uniformed bellboys who clicked their heels, bowed, and announced, "Flowers for Miss Jackson." Day-long, the little boys came; and when there was no more room in the suite, they silently lined the staircase. "When I woke up in the morning and came down, the stairs were lined with flowers," said Mahalia, the sight vivid in her mind. "The children had done it. Things like that really *hurt* you, they make you feel so good inside."

She would try to make Rome. She was going to keep this tour if she could, to get her own special wish. "I had not a sick feeling at that time," she insisted later, "but it was ice-cold outside and the sweat popped off me big as a nickel."

Paris was as far as she got. She had lost over 90 pounds and her pulse was erratic. The doctor said she must not be moved. "What they saying," Mahalia asked fretfully. Mildred was informed. "He says you can't be moved; says if they move you, you'll die."

"Well, tell them I'll have to die, 'cause if anything happen to me, I want to be at home."

"Mahalia," said Lenetska, "this is awful; I can't take you any farther—but why don't you have the operation here in Paris? It's only a hysterectomy. Then we could go on with the tour. You could see the whole world."

She eyed him silently. Then she dictated a cable to Chicago. Tell Allen meet her at La Guardia with an ambulance. She would not see the Holy Land at Christmas: that had been her bargain. Lord, You must be not think I'm ready.

Mildred and Mahalia were put aboard the first plane for New York, Mahalia holding onto her Kronenberg vase and her Bible. Harry stayed on a week to tidy the debris of a broken tour. Bess would fly later.

The weather was bad and the prop plane battled winds, but Mahalia was curiously unafraid: a song had been laid into her heart for her direction, she felt. Softly she sang to herself, *You'll Never Walk Alone*. Two hours past schedule, the plane reached La Guardia. The ambulance had left. Mahalia was again near collapse. "We'll go over to Mary's house, she's not far from here," Mahalia decided. Fortunately, her actress friend was at home. "Mahalia, I've got an engagement, but there's the bed, and there's food; you're welcome to both." Finally, home ground. Aunt Hannah's. Oh, it was good to crawl into Hannah's bed. "Mildred, don't tell anybody I'm here; I'm going to hide out 'til I can get in the hospital. But call Mother Gaye, tell her I made the trip and I'm going into the hospital for a rest. Tell her pray for me and come see me—I'll let her know when." To Aunt Hannah, who tucked her in and asked no questions, she said Europe was just fine and the folks had treated her nice, but she had come home to go into Billings. "Just don't tell anybody I'm back."

It was Nov. 26 before Dr. Barclay could get her in, then the team rallied quickly. Just before she was given the anesthetic, she asked for, this once more, the 27th Psalm. . . . *the Lord is the strength of my life; of whom shall I be afraid?* She was ready.

The womb came out. They'd expected that. What surprised Dr. Barclay and the entire team observing—seeing his diagnosis confirmed—was that "we found an enormous number of large sarcoid lymph nodes in the abdomen. We removed a couple of kidney basins full. I had never seen this much involvement of lymph glands in sarcoid before. You couldn't remove it all, of course, because lymph glands are all through the body." So there was no point in chest surgery. "Fortunately, she tolerated her illness very well. She had a very funny kind of—almost childlike—secret impish smile about her eyes; she would say something and you'd find yourself chuckling. Almost anything we talked about, she kept good humor going."

He still had no idea who she was. He knew nothing of gospel music; he didn't have television; he was busy with research. "To me, she was another black person with sarcoid." He did notice that an unusual number of Billings's black staff apparently went to the same church she did: "She was literally surrounded by friends—nurses, aides, secretaries—so besides the three doctors assisting me, and the surgeon, Dr. Harper, she had people at all levels in the structure who loved her as a person and gave her the best of care." That must account for all the cards, letters, flowers he saw; the church.

Belatedly, Chicago's white press had three sentences relating that "Mahalia Jackson of 3728 S. Prairie, gospel singer and recording artist, was reported recovering satisfactorily after undergoing surgery"; that a "bronchial ailment" forced cancellation of a European concert tour; and that she was "official soloist for the 4 million Negroes of the National Baptist Convention."

The black media knew the news value. Virtually everyone whose skin tone was tan to black in Chicago was worried; and most tried to call.

Nobody could get a call into Billings. The lines were tied up with persons asking, without preamble, "How's Mahalie?" The impasse reached to Mahalia, she relayed it to Rev. Clarence Cobbs—one of the few ministers okayed to visit—and Rev. Cobbs took to the air. "If you people don't stop calling the hospital, worrying Mahalia, they going to put her out. The hospital is very upset. I'm told one man wanted to fight because he couldn't see Mahalia. Now you people got to stop that. Mahalia don't *want* that. She wants you to pray."

Well—if Mahalia don't *want* that. They'd pray.

She lay wasted, eyes glazed. When she could summon energy, she thought deeply. She knew what she had to do. Clean house in her personal life, for one thing. "God, if You get me through this, I will re-dedicate my life to Your service; well, I *been* in Your service but I will strive harder; I will strive to be entirely pleasing to You."

Besides the family, the inner circle, some few favored visitors she wanted, and saw. Al Duckett—a bright, ambitious black newsman. Studs Terkel and Pete Seeger, so shocked, she could see, that she tried to cheer them up, mimicking Broonzy at Albert Hall . . . "I told old Broonzy, 'What am I going to sing for those people?' and Broonzy, with that big deep voice of his, he says 'Just go ahead, Mahalia; they won't know the difference' "; and seeing Studs and Pete so tickled, she kept repeating Big Bill's bass tones, mugging it—"They won't know the difference . . . they won't know the difference." Joe Bostic, in from New York and his unspoken fear that she was done for, finished, so palpable that she made the effort for him too. "They took to me in Europe right off, because they say I'm completely American. They say in Europe they get tired of these American opera singers borrowing from them, then playing it back." Rousing, "Myself, I can't stand those ones sound like they're gargling. 'Oooooooooo'—I say, 'What brand of gargle they using, Listerine?' " Bostic was entertained, but not convinced. Even if she pulled through, could her voice survive? She really looked like she had TB.

She had various answers to what was wrong. To the press, bronchial ailment. Robert Anderson reported, "She has nervous exhaustion; she had an attack." Others announced she'd had her appendix out; an emergency operation. Still others felt her surgery was due to having had to hold water so long, all those times on the road—Mahalia herself believed this was partly to blame, although Dr. Barclay said no. Mildred knew "hysterectomy" (nothing of sarcoid) and when John got to town, she told him this much but warned him not to tell her aunts. Mainly Hannah. "You know how hard she takes things, John." She'd had a tumor removed, she told Aunt Hannah. "She never mentioned anything like a hysterectomy; never discussed that she couldn't have children after that," says Hannah Robinson. "But Mahalia kept her business to herself, big troubles especially . . . she have a hard time, nobody know it but her."

Harry Lenetska didn't come. Nor did Bess. But they both called to see how she was.

THERE CAME A DAY, hallelujah. With a glint in her eye long missing, "God has given me a new body! Dr. Barclay says I have made the grade! I got nothing to do but coast!" She checked out of Billings Dec. 12. Coasting wasn't exactly the word for it, those long weeks in Hannah's bed, Big Alice bringing over the lean food the doctor ordered (knowing that prednisone, the sarcoid control, would sharpen an appetite that needed no help). But Missie didn't see where a little fresh greens and hot water cornbread could hurt anybody. "I'd just go talk with her, pet her, tell her she looked good," says Missie; "carry over the greens and bread."

Mildred had news of the gospel world; Boy Baby (young Rev. Thurston), of the preachers; Frye and Willa Jones, the Baptist Convention. Most tried to stay out of Mays' path. He was now rated a mean man, best not to cross or stumble over. Mother Gaye had no thought of him or anyone but Mahalia; she came to pray. "I could *feel* you praying for me, Mother," smiled Halie; "but it's nice to have your soft hands."

There'd been nothing in the Atlanta papers to let John know Mahalia had like to died while he was singing there at the Peacock Club. It was only when he called Chicago to say he'd pass through that he learned the news. He stayed. Stayed at Hannah's and did for Mahalia, slept at the foot of her bed should she want in the night. "You like my son, John," she sighed as he rubbed her feet. "But you don't quit singing in them clubs, I'm going stop putting you on my programs."

John was in the kitchen when Mahalia called. "Come see what I got!" Her voice was so happy he ran . . . and almost ran into the biggest basket of fruit he'd ever seen; almost tall as he was, with a great big red bow on it. "The great Duke Ellington has sent me fruit!" caroled Mahalia; "took three men to bring it in here!"

Already the place was crowded as a post office, with the cards, letters, packages. Now this. "How you going to eat all that fruit?" cried John. "You going have to give some of this away."

"If I turn you loose, you give away everything," huffed Halie. "I'm sick, you not sick. You give it to me." That they hadn't actually met, made Duke's big gift all the better. It was entirely his respects and esteem. "You not going give away Duke, no you not."

In February, she began going to church and having John take her by the flower shop, which was doing well chiefly because of Becky Avery. She wasn't worried about money, anyway. *In the Upper Room* was well over the million mark and still moving, and *Silent Night, Holy Night* had been another big hit (although Chicago's white music stores still so seldom stocked her records that Studs Terkel advised his white readers to contact her black South Side distributor). She had sizable royalty checks to deposit when John drove her over on 39th to the Drexel Bank—there having come a limit to how much bag and bosom could handle. She'd lost her bank book, she told the clerk—white; no black clerks although this was the South Side. But she wanted to draw out $500. "Who are you?" the clerk asked.

"I sing; I'm Mahalia Jackson."

"I know Ella Fitzgerald," said the clerk.

"I'm Mahalia Jackson, I just come back from Europe."

"I never heard of you," said the clerk; "you'll have to talk to the manager."

Outside, money in her purse—the *manager* knew her—John teased, "See, you think you famous? That white boy never heard of you. Them white people don't even know you."

"Yes they do! You see."

Home and swiping some of John's stewed corn and okra with rice, that he'd made for Aunt Hannah, "You better be careful, Mahalia," John warned, "eating this stuff and you sick."

"I'm not sick," she said firmly, dipping away; "I'm 'most well."

And knew what she was going do. She'd give Becky the shop and put Mays from her life. She would take a secretary—"A secretary?" cried John, "how you going take a secretary?"

"You know I got money enough to pay a secretary regular. I'm going take Polly."

"Cylestine?"

"Yeah. She been doing things for me all along, and she been doing them good. I got plenty business for her. Ain't you see her doing errands for me? They think I'm through—Harry Lenetska and them—but I'm not. I'm going take some programs around here first, and then I'll go back. They haven't forgotten me, you'll see. *God* hasn't forgotten me. Know how I know? He told me so. Besides that, I've been thinking what I mainly want, I want to get me a program on the air, once a week—give my concerts that way and not be on the road all the time. I'm going see if I can get that. But I got to get all my business straightened out first. Polly going help me do that."

FREE, AND IT had been so easy; not even a fight. With that, and having a new body—it sure felt like a new body, she assured Dr. Barclay—she was ready. She'd studied on this business of a manager. She couldn't see where Harry Lenetska would do her any good, no more than was coming. Look like he didn't much want her now, anyway. With Polly to do her business, she'd manage herself. All *he'd* ever done was book—but that's all he said he was going do; couldn't go holding that against him. No, he was a nice man. ("We just sort of parted," says Lenetska, "after she got sick. Nothing unfriendly. I called her, and wrote to her, you know. We just—separated.")

She'd go on alone.

She moved back into her own apartment. "You know, John," she mused, John lying on the floor, she in the bed, "If Ike would have done right, stayed away from gambling, maybe we'd be together today. 'Cause he wasn't a bad man."

EARLY MARCH. Young Rev. Jodie Strawther—staying in Gary—was stretched out with her, Mahalia keeping him laughing about Europe's food and milords, when she threw in, "I'm about to take my first program out of town, Strawthford—to Michigan. Norsalus McKissick supposed to go. If McKissick don't go, I want you to go." She went on then to talk of his needs, his plans. "I forgot all about it," says Rev. Strawther, "until she called that morning. 'Strawthford, I'll be by in an hour, take you to Muskegon.' I said, 'My God!' but I went."

There, and her friend James Lewis introducing her—this was it. She began to sing . . . the spirit rose . . . and swept the church. *Sing* it, Mahalia!"

At home, "It's good I was sick, 'cause God showed me His strength," she told Boy Baby. *He*'d be with her on her trips often as he could, but he had his hands full just now shaking up his father's church, driving out the insincere. "I was a controversial figure," explains Dr. Thurston, "because in the early days, it wasn't popular for a Baptist preacher to be highly educated. They had the notion that you'd ought *not* learn how to preach, you ought to be called directly from God. But Mahalia stood behind me 200 percent. She could not be swayed in a religious matter. And she was strong for persons being educated, whatever they were going to do."

IT WAS his education that awed her as she listened to the little man who said he was a semanticist connected with the University of Chicago—the "Doctor" a doctor in English. But he was writing for the *Chicago Defender,* too, approaching Mahalia because he was a jazz buff, was delving into the origins of jazz, and had come across her records—was excited about them. In fact, he said in his oddly formal, lilting voice, he had a little radio program which he would love to have her appear on; they'd just play her records and talk about them?

Looking down into the bright eyes of the round-faced little Japanese in the jaunty tam o'shanter with a pom-pom on top, Mahalia liked S. I. Hayakawa instantly: one of the unlikely close friendships of her life. Actually, they had more in common that surfaced. Hayakawa had experienced the humiliation of color restriction when he'd tried to move into an apartment building owned by the University. "We let you have this apartment, you'll bring in all your relatives." He'd been rejected academically by the University of Chicago. "They wouldn't *have* me," says Dr. Hayakawa; "nobody else would, either. I was working for the University downtown center part-time, and sort of kicking around while I worked on my own semantics thing and studied psychology like mad." Mahalia had heard through her South Side sensors that he'd also helped organize some cooperative housing for blacks (actually, it was a cooperative grocery store and credit union). Altogether, her complex new friend emerged in her mind as an "anthropologist" and would so remain.

Their radio interview, billed as a "Jazz Seminar," was intriguing to Dr. Hayakawa on several levels: for her glimpses of early New Orleans blues-and-gospel culture, painted in soft strokes by that mellow voice; but even more, intellectually, for the instant analyses which this unlettered black woman made of some of the most sophisticated of current American jazz to which he had her listen and respond. Of Duke Ellington's *C-Jam Blues:* (Mahalia moving in to clap with his beat): "It's a little polished, it's not quite as primitive, but I can still hear something from New Orleans trucked-up jazz in there." Of Artie Shaw and the Grammercy Five on *Sad Sacks* (for which her clapping pattern shifted): "There is a church known as the Church of God in Christ . . . organized about 60 or 70 years ago . . . their music is more on that order, fast and (she demonstrated) beat like that. I tell you the truth, most of the music that Artie Shaw and Duke uses is from our churches." Of the Gerry Mulligan Quartet: "I was wondering . . . is that . . . bop, isn't it, they call it? Is that—after the beat, I think it is. I like it. It's smooth." Bebop (the current popular beat) as a whole came straight out of gospel, she told him: "You take *Rock My Brother* and then take bebop . . . it's almost the same."

He got her to talking about sensibilities, about Bessie Smith. "Listening to a song of Bessie, it almost fits into your own plane. She's trying to get free from something. It's like a preachment, even though it's the blues. When I was a little girl, I felt she was having troubles like me."

The psychologist in him was fascinated as Mahalia gave him a cure for oppression: "I sing my gospel songs, I can get a relief from mine; but you continue to sing the blues and you continue to be burdened, all the time."

Off the air, the tiny professor hugged her with delight—all he could reach of her. "Mahalia, you were wonderful!"

"Think so?" she brooded. "I don't know, Doc; when I open my mouth, I never know what's going come out. But I never learned to keep it shut."

He wanted it open—wide as she could—when he took her to California—the "illustrated," along with Bob Scobey's band—of the lecture he gave on jazz at San Francisco State for NAACP. Later, at the home of physicist Paul Byrd, Mrs. Lillie Chase was among a group who settled around Mahalia. One teased her about the non-alcoholic punch she'd chosen. "Mahalia has been a sinner," she answered soberly; "she had done about every bad thing a person could do, and then she went to Europe and got very sick. She was sick before she *left,* but in France, Mahalia got very, very sick. She promised the Lord then that if He would recover her, she would repent and give him back a substantial part of what His love caused to be hers. . . . "

Blonde face leaned eagerly to brown one, Mrs. Chase was fascinated. She had never before heard anyone speak so naturally of herself in the third person—nor so candidly to people newly met. And her tithing! "I was completely charmed," says Lillie Chase.

It was Halie's turn to be charmed when producer Leonard Sillman (whom she'd met in France) came to town: He wanted to "do" something with her. "Mr. Sillman, you got to remember I'm a gospel singer," Halie cautioned. "We'll come up with something," he said—John listening, hugging himself with glee. John took Ike to see Sillman's *New Faces* and they both told Mahalia what a good show it was. But when Sillman offered $5,000 a week minimum guarantee to star in a Broadway extravaganza, Mahalia shook her head. "That's too far out the church for the Devil to even tempt me, Mr. Sillman. Halie'll just pick up her nickels and dimes the way she been; but I thank you kindly."

After he'd gone, John hooted. "Nickels and dimes! You got that man believing you poor."

"I ain't said nothing but the truth. What he thinks is his business."

Bess came then with Art Freeman to record her—if she felt ready? They'd cut Roberta Martin and Alex Bradford and some blues people anyway. Halie sang with *no* trouble and—persuading Bess to record Robert Anderson—came down and directed his session herself. She wanted nothing halfway. All these boys hers. She sat in on Alex's recording, too. Allen was going out as his manager; they ought to do fine. Her own session? "That was all right," she told Mildred—high praise from Mahalia; "I like that *I'm Going Down to the River.*" She grinned, "Baby, I *been;* I'm coming back!" To Bess, "I'd cut some more, but I don't have no more ready; Robert didn't bring me none and Mildred"—fixing a piercing eye in that direction—"she ain't been by *to* rehearse. Call herself saving me. But that's all right, we'll catch up in New York." Bess relaxed. The only million-seller repeater in gospel history was herself again . . . and she was all Bess's.

Home base discovered Mahalia was back *with* voice, in a major concert to which Al Duckett turned his promotion talents so that 10,000 cash customers poured into Chicago Stadium to soar, to shout, to weep. "That Mahalie, she wastes you." And still the audience was black save for Studs Terkel, Doc Hayakawa, Pete Seeger, Win Strache, and a few other white friends and fans among the jazz buffs.

THE GOSPEL TRAIN got back on the track with James Lee, Blind Princess Stewart, Singing Sammy and Jodie Strawther, who preached or sang—sometimes both. No trouble with dates now it was known Mahalia was back. In person, by letter, by phone, they came, Polly at the ready. Polly was working out fine, just fine, but for the one thing she'd taken care of before she left: "Emma Bell, if Polly going be around me all the time, you got to teach her to make your hotwater bread."

They ranged largely through the South and Southwest, where gospel was popular and revival fervor high. She was glad to plunge back into the waters. Hallelujah.

July 1, 1953, they were between Georgia and Florida when Polly tracked her down. Mahalia's father had died. He had never made it to see her sing in Chicago, but he had lived to stand on the stage beside her. She called Elliott Beal to play for the funeral; she would stay with Elliott and Ida. Johnny Jackson was in from California when Mahalia reached New Orleans. "Johnny, I didn't know he was sick. What did he die of?"

"Old age, I guess. He was 76."

She took care of the funeral and the food, and did not mind bowing to the wishes of the wife. But on one point she had her say: no second line. It wasn't seemly. Hadn't he preached from the pulpit many a time, when the pastor was absent?

Out to see Aunt Bell, then, at Celie's. Watching her in the kitchen with her shoes off, eating a pickle, Celie had a thought. "Halie, now you're big and you're prosperous, did you ever think of buying that whole box of Magnolia milk you were always going to get?"

"No, all that left me. I got a new look now."

IN SEPTEMBER, their official soloist looked and sounded like new to the elated National Baptist Convention in Miami . . . and in October, her New York hotel was new too: the Wellington, her first white hotel. Things were opening up in New York; she could have her choice of several, but *having* it, chose this—the most convenient to Carnegie Hall. Excited, Louise and Mildred went exploring while Mahalia did her hair. When Louise came back in alone, Mahalia said quietly, without turning, "I smell death." Louise blanched. "You smell—death?" Yes, she did; "let's pray it's nobody close."

"It wasn't anybody in her family," says Louise, "but it was a friend, someone we both knew."

Sunday, Oct. 4—her 4th Carnegie concert—was another easy sellout for Joe Bostic, acknowledged a producer of stature now. He'd even been able to get Rev. Adam Clayton Powell for "entr'acte remarks." The volatile Congressman—well known to Mahalia from Baptist Convention—lent an extra weight to the event: he was a vocal civil rights man. And astute politician. If Mahalie didn't like him, he'd never been up there on her program, the audience figured.

In to cover the concert for their first major article on the black phenomenon, Mahalia Jackson, an *Ebony* team ran into French newsman Ralph Hofmann interviewing her, speaking of his "great admiration for Miss Jackson's art." She was interviewed for the black "Our Great Americans" series. Joe Glaser, the white agent who booked Louie Armstrong, called: he'd like to sign her; felt she had great potential. Well, thank you, Mr.

Glaser; yes, she knew of him from Louie and some others, she surely did, but she thought she'd just go it alone for a while. But she'd give him some dates.

Close by, at the CBS building which also housed its affiliate, Columbia Records, new talent chief Mitch Miller had a hunch and debated how best to check it out. Just go see her, he supposed.

Halie had a full schedule for this comeback in New York: To promote her records—let them hear Halie in good voice—make a wide circuit of the DJs. Autograph records at stores. Cut for Bess, two sessions. Do another "Toast of the Town," Ed Sullivan beaming a welcome, the whole crew making her feel well loved, Bostic and Duckett standing by. Go with Ed out to St. Alban's Naval Hospital to entertain the wounded—the last Korean prisoners-of-war had been brought home, war officially over. Thank You, Jesus; let it be the last. With Ed, too, to Halloran General Hospital. "She was always ready to say yes," says Sullivan; "we did one for the orphans about then, too."

Just the one thing wrong with TV: they told you what to sing, then they timed the song and it had to be that way. Kept a person self-conscious. Well, you got it to bear. It's a strange world Halie's into. And now the great Mitch Miller!

28

Columbia Records wanted her. Now that *was* a strange world: white white. No gospel singers there. Any black was just the great voices made people forget about color.

When Mitch Miller came by, he'd wanted to know first how closely she was tied to Apollo. He had a feeling— Ah. Her contract just ran to December. Mm-hm! "There's just the one—" She broke off. "Never mind," she said easily; "just tell me again what you got in mind."

"Columbia is prepared to—"

He talked long and earnestly. Mahalia thanked him and said she'd let him know. Miller went back to his office puzzled. He'd thought she'd jump at Columbia and a $50,000-a-year guarantee. But if puzzled, he was also charmed: "She was a very imposing figure, but she had that little-girl quality about her too."

He was determined to get her. It was a question of approach. . . . John Hammond. It was Hammond who'd first got him fired up about Mahalia

Jackson's great voice back at Mercury—although everybody was talking about her now. Hammond was her friend; she trusted him; she knew what he'd done for Count Basie, Billie Holiday, Lionel Hampton, so many black artists—she'd know Hammond wasn't after a cut of her money or anything else. He called his friend at Vanguard, where he was director of jazz classics. When could John have lunch with him and Mahalia Jackson? Yes, Mahalia Jackson. He was trying to get her away from Apollo. He wanted to set up lunch at his place, so Mahalia could get an idea of what he was all about.

At the Wellington, Halie had some deep thinking to do. Columbia was a long step. To shore, or into deep water? She'd fought with Bess Berma from the day they met, but she'd had some big hits on Apollo, made a lot of money, still was. On the other hand, Art Freeman just slipped her the word that, much as she was getting from her actual sales, Bess was cheating her sizably out of her just due. Nothing personal—it was general practice. Still and all, she at least knew the ins and outs of Apollo. What did she know about Columbia? They's such a thing as out of the frying pan into the fire. She called John Hammond. "Mr. Hammond, what about this?" He talked at length, but his summation, says John Hammond, was "Mahalia, if you want to make a lot of money, they'll promote you and take out page ads in things like *Life* magazine, because Mitch believes in promotion. But if you go with Columbia, they don't know anything about your kind of music, and you'll lose your own people." Hm. As to that—"Thank you, Mr. Hammond. I appreciate your talking to me. I'll think about it."

Arriving at Central Park West, Halie could feel the white richness. This, she sensed instantly, was the most elegant place she'd ever been. Glancing casually around the Millers' spacious flat upstairs . . . this is how the really high-up white people live, different from the millionaires' mansions on St. Charles—without the Southness of it. She knew it was the ultimate hospitality, dinner at home—didn't she feel that way herself? And Mr. Miller and his wife were acting just like ordinary people. She relaxed.

When they got down to business, Mitch waxed expansive. "I want to spread your artistry over everything," he said earnestly; "why limit yourself to gospel?" Mahalia broke in flatly, "I don't sing the blues." He didn't necessarily mean the blues; there are other songs besides blues—you'll be wonderful on ballads, classical songs; you've got a lot to say in music—" For the first time, a wary look clouded Mahalia's eyes. "Mr. Miller, we better get one thing straight at the start. What I got to say, I say in *gospel.* Period."

"All right, all right," he said hastily. "You can record gospel, if that's what you want." No point in crowding her.

"And it's $50,000 a year for how many years?"

"Four. Recording four times a year." She rose. He waited expectantly for her yes. "It's been a wonderful lunch, Mr. Miller. And I'll let you know."

BACK IN CHICAGO, she thought about it—not thinking *on* it, but letting the thinking go on without her noticing—and she prayed a lot, put it right on God. "What You think Halie ought to do? And what You going to do, Lord?" She knew she wanted to go to Columbia. She had pioneered the gospel world, she'd waked up gospel recording, she'd stretched into the reaches of the land as far as blacks knew it, and flown the sea to go to Europe. She'd done all that. Now the hand of the Lord had reached out and opened another gate on another plane, almost another world. She had never backed down from a challenge in her life. She was *going* to Columbia. Hadn't the Lord Himself told Israel, "Behold, I am doing a new thing." Problem was: How's she going get Bess Berma to let her go?

Her contract, true enough, ran out in late December. What she hadn't spelled out to Mitch Miller was that every year, then, Bess exercised her option and took out a new contract with an option written into that. It just leapfrogged, one year to the next. How in the world— No way to *buy* her way out. She didn't have the type money Bess Berma would come up with asking. And no way Bess going just give her up, not the kind of money Mahalia Jackson bring into Apollo. And the singers that come to Apollo because Mahalia's there. Well—she'd just wait on the Lord. Maybe He'd tell her. Get up now and go see Dr. Barclay; this eye bothering her. And don't have him come up with Halie needs glasses!

What he told her, was that sarcoid had invaded her eyes, that because sarcoid is a generalized disease—all through your body—it may flare up more in one part than another at times. "Your eyes are taking it right now. We'll step up your dosage," he said easily. It was a bad sign, but— He knew now who she was, and warmed even more to her naturalness. "Don't you worry, Mahalia, we'll keep you pretty." He hoped to God he could. "Now let's have a look at your Aunt Hannah." Get Halie, inherit her family.

NOW SEE her black doctor, Dr. Spaulding.

"You're putting back too much weight, Mahalia."

What you going do when you such a good cook? When one more of her own, young Pat Franklin, came visiting from his new church in Dallas, she gave him a luncheon. "Ask four, five of your friends," she told him. Father Franklin set out. "So Mahalia's in the kitchen cooking," says Robert Anderson. "Spread out all her beautiful silver and so forth. You could see down the hall right straight from her kitchen to the front door, so as they began coming, she just called out, 'Okay, Father, tell your guests to come on in.' She's so busy cooking. I was back there helping her. Finally, 'Okay, everybody, come on; it's buffet style; everybody serve themselves.' Then Mahalia looked down the hall. About 20 or more people out there. 'Good

God Almighty!' she said. 'Where they come from?' Father Franklin had invited every one of his close associations. Oh, she cut up. Well, they all stood in line, and Mahalia had come in from the kitchen. The lady standing in front thought Mahalia was serving, so she said, 'Oh, Miss Jackson, that's too much on my plate.' And Mahalia said, 'No, baby, this is for *Mahalia*. I'm so sick of these folks eating up all my food and I don't get a chance to taste my own cooking, I'm going to *eat* today.' And she took her plate by her room and she turned around and said, 'Whatever's left, you can have it,' and shut her door. I died. I *died!* Lord, we had fun."

Mahalia wished she could just that easily shut her door on Apollo. She hadn't found a way out yet.

It took her mind off to find that Big Alice had gone down and bought a house in New Orleans for Bessie—a camelback; Duke was going move on top with Brisko's boys she was raising. It was on Joliet, a good piece out of Pinching Town. And Halie still on the South Side. If she ever got her mind at peace and some time. . . .

As Christmas neared, the days were heavier; any day, that contract be in the mail from Bess Berma.

It did not come. She waited, the calendar creeping. Stretched the length of the bed, working out the last possible days in her head while Jodie Strawther chatted, suddenly Mahalia sat up, eyes alive. "Miracle come to pass! Hallelujah!"

"What?"

"Bess Berma passed her option! Forgot to renew her contract! The Lord done put her to sleep! I can go!" Go where? Mahalia calmed, abruptly casual. "Columbia Records talking to me. But don't tell it."

WATCH NIGHT in Dallas was a thanksgiving and a wonder. Before Father Franklin had left Chicago, he'd asked her to sing for his big Watch Meeting Feast—music, spirit, and food. At the Sportatorium, Mahalia, said the Negro *Dallas Express,* would alternate with Chicago's Soul Stirrers—the stars to be backed by Bessie Griffin, Rev. Strawther and a 500-voice choir. Rev. L. M. Chambers, Jr., of Chicago, would preach from a casket.

It was a night to remember. The food for all comers wasn't Mahalia's, but it did last the night.

BESS HAULED out the new version of the old contract when Halie cut two more sides for her. Halie tried her best to cushion the blow. But Bess was not just a woman scorned, ready to beat Hell with her fury; her cash register was scorched. "After all I've done for you!"

"Seems like Mahalia's done a little for you, too."

"I'll take you to court!" Mahalia just sat, lower lip bunched up, eyes opaqued. Bess squeezed down her wrath. "Listen, Mahalia, you won't fit in at Columbia. They're not your kind of people. What does Columbia know about gospel music?"

Halie bit her tongue, but—where did Bess learn? And still don't know: Look at how she'd made *His Eye Is on the Sparrow* a flip side, this late, when Halie'd introduced it . . . and can't tell her now that *Walking to Jerusalem* is going be the hit over *What Then. . . .*

"Listen, Mahalia, for both of us— Don't sign yet. Think it over."

Thinks she can put sweet back in gingercake.

Just to be safe, Halie got hold of a smart black attorney who'd still been in law school when he'd first come around: Bob Ming would know the latest law. And she believe he'd tell it to her straight.

By phone and in person, in Chicago, Bess alternated sweet and sour and scalding. Studs Terkel met her in the midst of one go, but she got no comfort there: He liked Apollo's product but not its reputation. Studs also dropped in when Doc Hayakawa was there. Getting him and Doc in the same room amiably was a feat in itself, says Studs Terkel: "Remember Mahalia in Paris, when she became known as 'The Angel of Peace'? Well, that was similar to Hayakawa and me."

Doc wanted to talk gospel and jazz—his way. "I would try to talk to Mahalia in my analytical terms, but I don't really know if she ever fully understood, because she'd *always* say, 'Yes, yes, that's the way it was.' I think she got the impression that since I had this highbrow way of talking about it, I must know a hell of a lot about it!" Let Doc work up his words, what difference it make? It won't change the music. And it makes him happy as a child.

One more assault from a worried Bess Berman. This time Mahalia gave herself the pleasure of telling Bess she knew about the shortchanging on money—"only it ain't change, the way I hear it." Furious, Bess went back to New York and fired Art Freeman: he had to be the leak.

Still, when the Columbia contract came, Halie did not sign. It wasn't Bess. . . .

"Mahalia had a keen inner sense," says Louise Weaver; "she didn't *move* until she had the sanction of the Holy Spirit; to hear, like 'This is right'; or 'You can do this'; or 'No, this is not proper.' When I was there and someone came to the hotel to talk business, she listened carefully but I could tell by the look on her face—she was meditating and thinking. The reason she stood fast against singing the music of the world—she said God told her she was not to sing that type of music. *Told* her so. My mother was a Spiritualist pastor—Rev. Mary L. Overall—and she had a strong ESP going with Mahalia."

Now, reading the Columbia contract—getting in a good light to spell out the small print—Halie sighed. With all her praying, and asking— She stuffed the bulky papers into her purse and checked to see if Polly had finished packing.

THE CARLOAD could tell they were getting farther South by the warmness: First stop St. Louis—Mildred, James Lee, Strawther keeping the talk going, but Mahalia telling their preacher friend—his first time to drive her—to keep his ears on the road and his eyes too. Snow behind by Memphis, so the wheels didn't throw up a mess on her brand-new, sky blue Cadillac—her first. Little Rock, then working the area. And still she pulled out the contract at night and passed her eyes over the pages. Strawthford knew about it, so she didn't mind his being there; besides he was going read her Scriptures for her. "She always had me do that on the tours," says Rev. Strawther; "whenever I was around her at home, too. I'd sit on the floor down beside her bed and read her Scriptures until she'd go off to sleep—this trip, sometimes she'd have that contract in her hand."

Days, weeks slipped by: Dallas—"that's where we changed drivers," laughs Jodie, " 'cause that preacher disappeared with the car for two days." Then a long pull out to Jodie's hometown, Oakland, for Easter.

Singing Easter Sunday—a joy and a glory to the Lord—visiting with Jodie's folks, with Eloise Scott—talk New Orleans, child!—still she returned each day to the California Hotel and fingered the Columbia contract. Jodie kept her close company. Came a day no different from yesterday, in the week after Easter, and suddenly Mahalia reached for a pen and signed all the copies, electrified with her excitement. "Thank You, Lord; *thank* You, Lord," she said over and over, softly. "Now I can do some of the things I have wanted to do in my life. Here, baby, hurry and put this in the mail. Go straight to the post office—don't put it in no mailbox. Oh, thank You, *Lord!* Praise His name."

When they got back to home base—Halie holding her knowledge inside, unspoken and untalked by Jodie either, even the fragment he knew as a witness—Mahalia gave him one more chore. "Go get Ralph Jones, baby; I'm going try him."

Louise couldn't make the long tours—couldn't and didn't want to, already juggling nine balls in Chicago: Blind Francis didn't want to travel; it was too hard on him. Mahalia had tried her best to turn Strawthford from a pianist into an organist, "But I couldn't get my feet to working," says Jodie ruefully, "and that's when she sent me for Ralph Jones."

Jodie knew where to look: Ralph Jones worked for Prophet Wheeler in a little storefront church on So. State at 51st. The slender young organist stared in utter disbelief when Jodie delivered the message. "I can't believe it! *I can not believe it!*"

He was just in time.

IN NEW YORK, delighted with his coup, eager for a commercial breakthrough, Mitch Miller parlayed his bet. He called Lou Cowan, whose agency produced the phenomenally successful network *Quiz Kids* and others through its Chicago office. Columbia's newest star was going to be Chicago gospel singer Mahalia Jackson—why didn't he put together a package for radio? Get an audition tape up to Mr. Paley—CBS President William S.

Paley—and Mitch would guarantee a fast decision. She only sings religious songs so far. But she was a smash in Europe. What's the matter—don't you know what's going on in Chicago?

If Louis B. Cowan had read the multicolumn story just run in the *Chicago Daily News*—her first major Chicago white press—one paragraph might have stopped him: "Her popularity here is confined largely to her fellow Negroes. . . . Most white Chicagoans never have heard her," wrote M. W. Newman, adding that the "handsome 220-pound woman with dancing brown eyes" and "organ tones" hopes for the day when she gets a "wider audience in her home town."

It took your breath away. In a swift circuit that bypassed all the bogs, Lou Cowan taped Mahalia on Monday, and on Friday she was offered a CBS network show: half-hour, out of Chicago. When Mr. Paley himself spoke to her—told her she'd sounded sensational—she answered gravely, "You thought so? I thought I was very bad." Lou Cowan shuddered. But Paley knew what *he* thought.

"That's what you call the power of prayer," she exulted to Joe Bostic and shortly to Sidney Fields of the *New York Daily Mirror*. "I prayed hard."

Mahalia had one condition: If she was going to have a national radio show, she wanted Mr. Stud to be the writer. He knew her, he loved her, she trusted him—"and if he hadn't of kept plugging me, you all might not have known me past 12th St."

For the network, it was a prickly situation. Studs Terkel was a first-class talent as a writer; he also knew the music—which no other writer for radio did. But he was dangerous to handle nationally. Sen. Joe McCarthy was hunting homefed Reds as avidly as a dog after ticks, and "I was blacklisted," shrugs Terkel—"sort of grey-listed, actually; it was not bruited about—because I took part in many things and signed petitions against Jim Crow, etc., and I never apologized. They'd say, 'Aren't you sorry?' 'No, I'm not sorry.' " The industry knew, of course; that's where the list was released, to purify the mainstream of communications. . . .

Studs Terkel was her writer. Without a single crisis session—somehow, it came to be.

Happy, she tried to make Joe Bostic a present; she offered to get *him* together with the Columbia people—"something might come out of it, you don't know"—and when he stiffly asserted his independence, she shook her head. "Well, you keep it in mind."

Hard to put her mind on the summer tour, but they lit out, Ralph Jones making a good team with Mildred. Through New Orleans for a program at Booker T. Washington High—the talk now about the new Supreme Court decision making school segregation unlawful: what would it mean; what would it do? "Can't but be the Lord's work," said Mahalia; "if there's better in their schools, our children will have their full chance."

THE NETWORK broadcast was set for late September and already Studs Terkel was talking scripts and taking notes but visiting, too—one more in the mixing bowl of her Prairie apartment where she stirred as happily as she ladled food into all so inclined, with always a gospel jam session. Some were just passing through, maybe wanting to use her piano to rehearse. Aunt Alice pitched in for Harry Belafonte, Dinah Washington, Louis Armstrong, Billy Williams, Sarah Vaughan—or maybe Chicago's new president of the Baptist Convention, Dr. J. H. Jackson: no kin, but they felt close. ("I didn't mind the cooking," says Aunt Alice; "I'm pretty good at it; and Mahalia could be with them and talk and sing. I just enjoyed their having a good time.") Increasingly an ingredient were the strangers asking advice or money or both. If she'd helped a brother or a sister she knew, why not one she'd just met—if they were real—being the cause was good? The nebulae around her watched this drifting dust carefully; some stuck, and permanently widened the mass.

If for no more than that she was the best cook in the city, Nettie Irving would have called her that day—Nettie one of the new friends, the college-bred young woman active in the United Negro College Fund, the South Side Community Art Center, a half-dozen other causes and still found time to teach and raise her children and be a warm, natural friend, eager to help any way, any time. Mahalia loved her. She had not an instant's hesitation when Nettie said, "I want to bring out a very dear friend for you to meet."

Mahalia knew him when he walked in the door. Duke Ellington. She threw her arms around him, eyes bouncing with glee, and gave him a kiss: "That's for that fruit, Mr. Duke. Biggest thing I ever saw!" He bussed her warmly in return (Duke Ellington never one to neglect a pretty woman), shaved that "Mr." from his name, and one of the deep friendships of Mahalia's life was firmly set. He had all the qualities her being reached out to: keen intelligence, superlative talent, wit, a music-man's ear and voice, warmth, good looks, taste, a dedication to hard work and a pleasure *in* his work, and an easy naturalness which lounged inside a sophistication that just made the natural better. With all this, the Duke had three qualities, she quickly discovered, to which she could wholly respond: the wizard of jazz was a deeply religious man; he had a strong psychic sense; he loved to eat, and knew what he was eating.

After dinner—gumbo and rice, chicken, steak, hamhocks and greens, cornbread, a big salad, cake *and* pie—after the talking, Duke went to the piano and played chords for Mahalia. "That's where he first heard her sing *The Lord's Prayer,*" says Nettie; "he could chord for her and just let her go—he followed. These two beautiful people. That was a night. Duke wasn't acclaimed then the way he is today. But Mahalia, she thought he was the greatest: 'That man, why, he's the daddy of 'em all! People just don't give him credit.' She idolized him. They are similar souls really.

I know him so well. Something would go between the two of them; you could be standing by and sense the current."

MAHALIA FELT the first faint stirrings of another kind of current from a different kind of visitor—and yet was he so different, when you knew how Duke was inside? That this fresh current was stirring at all, caught her by surprise as Rev. Dr. Russell Roberts sat relaxed, one slender hand clasping his Coca Cola, the smooth, handsome face intent on their project—the big benefit Mahalia was staging for the South Side Boys Club and The Christian Youth. The prominent Atlantic City minister had come with his friend, ex-champ Joe Wolcott, as a favor to Mahalia Jackson. She'd known him slightly, lightly, from conventions and singing engagements; never really focused on the vibrations of the man. Now she could pick up on the inner being, on the strength and power. She blinked. She wondered if he had noticed anything. She decided he had. And she liked the way he was throwing himself into this program for the boys—for Gleason. Poor Gleason. . . .

He was nothing but a child, standing at her door that first time. "Come on in, Reverend." He was small but she noticed he walked like a little boxer, this Richard L. Gleason—this pale, tense boy from Ohio she knew had gone unknown into the worst of the South Side, been cut on, got those very colored boys that stabbed him out of jail; been beat on again and stabbed; gone to jail himself, come out and headed back in on the South Side. No one would help him; had their evil thoughts about him. Now someone said go see Mahalia Jackson. She listened while he said in this calm way how he was going to make a South Side Boys Christian Mission if it killed him. (And it just might, Mahalia thought.) So would she help?

"Gleason, why don't you go home to your mother?"

He wouldn't go. And when she saw into his heart, she knew he was real and said she'd help. First thing, she'd send out word this boy Gleason wasn't to be touched—he was with Mahalia Jackson. "And we'll see if we can get you to Billy Graham. He's got an organization; that's what you need. And I'll give you a program—raise you some money. But you got to let your mother come."

Things were moving now. Gleason had brought his mother to her and when she saw Mahalia was there with him, it gave her a little relief—"the poor woman had thought her son was a psychiatric case," laughed Halie.

MATCHING UP Mahalia was a favorite guessing game at National Baptist Conventions. She'd been linked with Rev. Bentley—a catch: tall, good-looking, a successful pastorate in Philadelphia; a man who had it all together. She had been paired with Rev. Joe May, and if he was a little young as a match, look how well their careers went—wasn't May a gospel recording star in his own right? There'd been talk of Rev. Franklin of

Detroit, now he and Dorothy had definitely split, but that was harder to give weight. Seeing Rev. Roberts and Mahalia together now in St. Louis, this September, '54, you didn't have to wait for the sermon to know the text: Russell Roberts and Mahalia were tight. See what comes of it—if Mahalia ever stays put long enough for either one of them to find out.

Her announcement that she would have her own network radio show was not only a sensation—the first gospel singer to make that—it also gave the romantics just the puzzle-piece they needed: She'd have to stay put every week for her show, wouldn't she?

Before she ever hit a CBS mike, though, she had to face her toughest network audience. They weren't listening by choice. Station managers of all the CBS affiliates were in Chicago for their annual briefing, and Mahalia had been asked to entertain along with Marilyn Marlow, Frank Parker, Peter Lind Hayes, Mary Healy, and Robert Q. Lewis as MC. She felt like a Mississippi catfish on a plate of Maine lobsters. Mitch Miller, you get me into this? Or you, Mr. Cowan? Probably both. Well—go on, do your best with this mixup.

None of them suspected by as much as an eyelid that Mahalia felt any strain, any nervousness, and if she didn't eat the dinner, anybody could understand she was dieting. In all the big Edgewater Beach Hotel banquet room, she was the only black guest. She leaned over to Robert Q. Lewis, smiling. "You know, Mr. Lewis, this is the first time I've been in this place since I worked here as a maid." The famous MC dissolved on the instant. Now see what they going make of gospel, all these men tired from the day, highball glasses in their hand.

Mahalia was introduced as CBS's latest radio star, to debut this fall in a half-hour religious program. The ho-hum goodgodwhatsthisdoinghere was almost audible. Well, Lord—it's Yours. Moments later, if the cries were "Encore!" instead of "Hallelujah!" the fervor was the same. The men whistled, stomped, clapped—and after a little coaching from Halie, even got the claps right, off the beat. There was a general stampede to schedule time for this woman. And another hurdle hit the dust.

It was a tired but exhilarated Mahalia that Doc Hayakawa found alone, wonder of wonders, one midweek afternoon. She'd just finished scrubbing her whole place so it shined, pressed her table linens, and was taking some hot tea. He was silent as he sipped with her . . . jaunty air missing as tangibly as his beret on the sofa. Such a little man. But so smart. She smiled and patted his arm. Suddenly, to his own amazement, Hayakawa found himself pouring out his heart. "I told her that my children were grown, and I felt my life was over. Mahalia sort of rose up about two feet taller without leaving her chair and said 'With all you know? All that you possess in *here!* Don't ever tell me you have nothing to do!' Somehow, she jerked me erect, back to myself," says the man whose name would become one of America's most unlikely household words. "It never happened again; it didn't need to."

On his heels came a white jazzman she was more apt to ask for advice, than give it. Lean, lanky, gentle, violinist William Russell—seduced from classical by ragtime—had been into jazz long before Doc Hayakawa more than knew the word—had published an analytical piece in Panassié's magazine in 1938. He was avidly exploring jazz as musician, researcher, producer, writer. He'd cut a lot of New Orleans jazzmen there and in Chicago a dozen years ago . . . he was devoted to Mahalia and her singing, ever since he'd shown up at a high school program with his tape recorder . . . he appreciated Duke Ellington . . . and he had the funniest habit she'd run up against: he went scrabbling on the South Side for old, old jazz records like the Chicago Loopers' 78s; anywhere, so long as it was junky—the Salvation Army, hole-in-the-wall black record shops, secondhand stores, barroom back rooms, even trash boxes on the street. "What Mr. Russell want all that mess for?" Halie had asked Brother John, in town visiting—the two stretched out at Aunt Hannah's. John shrugged. "Hobby, I guess." These two years, Mr. Russell had been a welcome visitor. And now he'd lost his job; not a prayer of getting another for six months. "You can come on out here, Mr. Russell, if you want; I got plenty for you to do." What? "Oh—different things. You can teach me to read music." Was she sure she wanted to? "Yeah, I want to."

He brought his violin and—to keep it safe—his recording equipment, and stowed it all behind her sofa. "Ready for your lesson?" The telephone rang. "Mahalia talked about half an hour; never did get back to the lesson, and that ended it," laughs Bill Russell. Somebody talked her into learning new songs by putting a speaker under her pillow. She tried it one night. "How'd it work?" he asked curiously. "All it done was rob my sleep."

If he couldn't teach her to read music, he'd help her learn by rote. He played the new music through on his violin, with Mildred at the piano, until she got it. "But it never came out the same way it was written, anyway."

Every day for more than a year, when he wasn't working with music, he did whatever was at hand—from nailing posters on poles to washing dishes. And he strode happily with her to programs as never-defined general assistant. Which is how he happened on the The Great Wig Experiment.

With her life like the jar of beans that kept turning in the store window for you to guess the total, her hair wasn't always at its best—that took time. With some urging, she bought a wig (it did save you) and went forth. . . . Into the program . . . *How did I make it over*—words loosed in a roar, face streaming with sweat, head tossed back—and the wig flew off. Mahalia went right on singing—she wasn't *through*—but Willa Jones, on the platform, picked it up and put it on the piano and giggles rippled the house.

Turning, Halie looked at the wig. "Well, I could've lost my head!" she said, rolling her eyes—and the audience roared with laughter—with her.

But nothing in Bill Russell's training had prepared him for the sight of a *soul* gone happy. Sitting beside her—listening to Rev. Elijah Thurston preach, Mahalia drawing it in—suddenly she leaped up shouting "Thank You, Jesus! Thank You, Jesus! Thank You, Jesus!" . . . and was not to be stopped, until she was carried out.

BY FIGURING close, she could get to New York for Rev. Childs—see Mitch Miller, too. She'd take Robert, to team with Blind Francis. Arriving, they went straight to the Bronx Hotel near the church—and discovered that instead of two singles with bath, supposedly reserved, there was one. Just one. "Well," Mahalia said, "this will do for the one night, then we be going over to Brooklyn to Ernestine's." Robert was indignant; he was *past* that. "I'm not gonna stay in no room with you. You get my own room!"

"Now what you trying to do, set up to spend all my money? No, indeed; you been sleeping at the foot many a night and you going sleep at the foot tonight. I'm not going turn you loose and spend my money; I know you!"

Robert crossed to the telephone, called the desk, and calmly requested the first available room. Mahalia listened without comment. He'd no sooner hung up than the phone rang. He picked it up, triumphant—and listened, startled: Duckett, calling from the lobby. "I've been hunting the world over for Mahalia. What's she doing staying at this place?" He broke across Robert's explanation—he'd brought some important people to talk to her— A beautiful thought leaped fullblown into Robert's mind. "Well, she's here." Mahalia was in her gown, ready to crawl into bed. "Who is that?"

"That's Al Duckett. He's got some white people to see you—a man from Columbia Records and *Life* magazine, coming up to see you"—peeling off his shirt as he spoke. "What you doing, bastard?" Mahalia cried in alarm, grabbing for her robe.

"I'm going to sleep."

"You can't do that! These people coming up here! What they think? You trying ruin my reputation?"

She was still arguing with Robert, who was now bare to the waist, shoes off, when the knock came and Robert opened it—as is. Mahalia broke into welcoming smiles and a rush of language. "Oh, you all come on in, children. Oh—this is the great Robert Anderson from Chicago, he's just like my son, my baby. This is—you know, I raised these children and everything; I—" The *Life* man eyed Robert, who was calmly climbing into the bed. "You look full-grown to me"; and to Mahalia—wringing her hands, still talking—"He looks older than you are."

"Oh, no; that's just his looks, that's the God's truth; he's young—we couldn't get reservations, we just sitting up here relaxing—oh, please don't put this in the papers, don't write it—this child, he's only a child, he don't know no better—he's a man but he's off, he don't have no mind, his reflex is gone; listen, he ain't nothing but a child. Al, *you* know—" looking desperately at Al Duckett, standing back—"you all call Ernestine's—Ernestine Washington—they can tell you about it, that I raise this boy, I—you know I'm not having—uh, um, uh—I couldn't have nothing like that; that's a beggar lord—"

The Columbia representative cleared his throat and began talking plans and promotions, the *Life* representative jotting notes, Al Duckett ignoring Robert—the culprit turned in the bed, trying so hard to hide his glee that tears rolled from his eyes. As the visitors rose to leave, Halie fixed piteous eyes on them. "Whatever you do, don't write this, 'cause he don't know no better, he just here playing for me, *believe* me, and he has lost his right mind."

As the door closed, Robert exploded with great whoops of laughter. "I fixed you, with your cheap self! Ha-haaaaaaaa!"

When Halie finished with every word she had ever heard from the Walnut St. wharf to the South Side of Chicago, she called Aunt Hannah. "You know what this dirty lowdown puppy trying do? Tried to ruin Halie's reputation! Come got in the bed and everything!"

Robert Anderson still glows with the glory of it. "That's the onliest time I got away with it, but I fixed her. And that's the first I heard of her signing with Columbia, when they talked that night."

DUKE ELLINGTON knew of it sooner than most: Columbia, New York, had passed the word to Columbia, Chicago—and particularly to promotion boss Granville White. Black, reared in the church, Granny White was delighted. Full of the unannounced news, he was at a trade party where Duke was one of the guests. "We've just signed a new girl; wait 'til you hear her! It's Mahalia Jackson—do you know her?"

"Yeah," drawled the Duke, "she's a great cook."

"No, this is the gospel singer."

"Same girl, same girl. World's greatest cook."

THE STUDIO theater in the Wrigley Building seated about 400. Doors opened at 8 p.m. Friday and within minutes, as if a giant suction was at work, all seats were filled. Doors locked at 8:30, there was one hour to warm up before taping. The audience was ready—or was it? Most of the faces before her were white; the blacks were streaks here and there. After a false start, Halie had a word for the whites. "You all got to learn how to clap, babies; you got to help Mahalia, or Mahalia's scared she's going fall right on her face. Now look—" They loved her for it, making them a part.

To the blacks, Halie addressed herself with a teasing firmness. "Now remember, you all not in church—'though you ought to be. No jumping up and down, no stomping; that interferes with the sounds going out over the mikes. Now you know Mahalia can't have that." Mahalie didn't want that . . . the whisper bobbed like a cork through the dark streaks and capped the sounds. Studs beamed with satisfaction. "She was marvelous. Everyone was pulling for her, the entire CBS staff right down to the ushers." Five minutes for on your mark—get set—and it was go.

She couldn't lose herself. Couldn't seek the spirit. Had to keep her eye on Jack Halloran, the music director, using his quartet to back her. He was the one insisted she learn a song called *Trees* . . . but ah! Mildred and Ralph and these four white boys mixing like a blender . . . then she could forget them all, give over to the songs, even if one part of her had to keep open to the signs: 25 minutes never went so fast.

John Lewellen rushed from the control booth. The veteran manager of Cowan's Chicago office had elected to produce Mahalia himself. A lot had been on the line. "You were a smash! We've got us a show!" Now they could go after a sponsor.

Sept. 26, 1954, was the first Sunday night of her life that she'd been on her feet—not been ill—and wasn't in some church. She felt no joy at 9:30 p.m. as the mellow white tones of the announcer said *The Mahalia Jackson Show* was on the air . . . didn't mind getting up for the doorbell: she felt a sense of *oppression* of what she'd hear. It was Ike. He came in quietly and sat, pleased as they listened. Once or twice she nodded, lips pursed out in total concentration, but when it was over: "I could've been better."

Russell Roberts called; he'd loved it. He'd be coming to Chicago soon as he could. Things were pretty busy in Atlantic City.

THURSDAY Ike was back, trying to look casual but clearly jubilant. She knew the signs. "Your luck brought me luck, honey; we took the purse at Hawthorne in the 2nd. Talk about a beauty—that Topper B!"

"How much the purse?" . . . Besides what they had *on* Topper—the purse was $2700. . . . Yes, he'd split with Nathan Cantrell, his co-owner. Ike hesitated—

"You'll need your part." Ike relaxed. Halie never called your debts Well, this was the start of a real stretch of luck. One day soon—

BUT SOON it was Halie couldn't believe her luck. In her last accolade from Europe—from the prestigious London *Jazz Journal,* more than a year and a half ago—there'd been unconscious irony: Douglas Whitton had exulted that her success in Europe "will add international honors to her already majestic stature in the world of music." That broad world had just waked up. And was trying to throw 25-odd years of Mahalia into one giant splash. Whereas heretofore only *Newsweek,* from its Chicago staff, had run a feature on her, now it took Mahalia and Cylestine both to set up all the interviews. "Mahalia Jackson is being profiled by four national magazines. She's the greatest!" exulted *Sun-Times* columnist Irving Kupcinet, her only Chicago white-press fan of long standing after Studs Terkel. And by the time Kup ran, there were more in the date book. Over and over, the phrases tumbled . . . "deeply religious . . . humble woman . . . dancing eyes . . . child's eyes . . . statuesque . . . piety and commonsense . . . rich vein of humor . . . powerful voice . . . compelling personality." The sophisticate-sated writers and photographers couldn't get enough of this colorful brown-skinned woman from whom quotable quotes rolled richly: "People say 'Oh, they're singing jazz in church,' but David said, 'Make a joyful noise unto the Lord. Clap your hands and come before His presence with singing.' " . . . "The Lord doesn't like us to be dead. Be alive. If you feel like it, pat your feet. Sometimes I dance to the glory of the Lord, because He said so." . . . "The bounce simply means accelerating the beat and putting joy into the voice." . . . "Gospel music rhythms are *not* African in origin, although I know that's what the jazz experts say." . . . "What they call jazz here is not the real stuff at all. Why, compared to the music I heard in New Orleans, it sounds like tin pans. Dixieland music in New Orleans was loud, but it was full and round. It had the melody . . . and the rhythm difference. One thing about playing the real jazz is that you can't count it. When you try to write down the exact note for the exact sound for the exact beat, you lose it. That's what happened to some of our spirituals . . . put a phrase down 4 times, we may say it 12 times if we feel like it, and then we'll come right in on the right beat." . . . "I couldn't sing the blues, sing in a night club . . . I can't let Him down . . . I hope to bring people to God with my songs." . . . "You're blessed if you have the strength to work." . . . "Do you know most of the Jewish songs have the same trend of sadness as Negro spirituals?" . . . "How can you sing of amazing grace, how can you sing prayerfully of heaven and earth and all God's wonders without using your hands? My hands, my feet, I throw my whole body to say all that is within me. The mind and the voice by themselves are not sufficient." . . . "Good music is a mighty and effective force to break down barriers." . . . "I close my eyes when I sing so I can feel the song better. No one else is there for me—I'm singing to the Lord." . . . "To sing is my way of life. Without a song, each day would be like a century." . . . "Everybody doesn't rejoice the same way. Some people rejoice in quiet and others have an emotional outburst." . . . "CBS has just discovered gospel singing and maybe it's new to a lot of people in the North, but everyone in the South is familiar with it."

They delighted in her candor. "People listening to me Sunday nights ought to be in church; it's a bad time." . . . "I'm too fat. I'm a wonderful cook and I like my own cooking." . . . "The trouble with records is that they're too short; in church I'm used to singing 'til the Lord comes." . . . "I'm glad my hands are trained. That spotlight doesn't stay on forever." . . . "How does my family in New Orleans feel about my success? It's the same to them. They thought I was a success as soon as I started paying the bills."

Rhythm and Blues claimed her for its own. Mason Sargent in a scholarly analysis for *Downbeat* proclaimed her the leading classicist of the spiritual. "The standard set by the spiritual," he said, "has been a standard that has called for the most honest communication possible of man's deepest emotions in a musical idiom that is uniquely American, an idiom that did not need, or care to imitate, the musical speech of any other country."

To many European students of music, he pointed out, the spiritual was "this country's first major accomplishment in the creation of a body of important music that was indigenous to America." Spirituals in Europe, he noted, are listened to "with the same depth of attention as is accorded classical music." When "extraordinary vocalists" such as Marian Anderson, Mattiwilda Dobbs and Carol Brice occasionally sing spirituals, he said, it is as part of their art song recitals "translated into the language of European song writing." It is generally agreed, he concluded, that "the greatest spiritual singer now alive is Mahalia Jackson."

Over and over appeared the story of the birth in a shack, which somehow got *between* the railroad track and the levee, fixed into her fast-forming legend along with a score or more entrenched misreadings of Mahalia's sometimes vague and telescoped references. "Look here," she hooted over one, "they got me in a cotton field! Baby, closest I come to a cotton patch was ironing over one—I did *that* aplenty." But what difference did it make? "Those people are sweet," she said with satisfaction, surveying the spate of clippings. "I just love 'em."

It was mutual. And a curious thing had surfaced. Listening to herself explaining gospel, analyzing her people's music, differentiating jazz, expounding her principles, she was amazed. Where did those words come from? A whole other vocabulary inside, ready for these people just waiting on her words. A white press which prided itself on knowing something of everything important going on in the nation learned there was a vast music culture thriving without their getting a whiff of it. "There are 700 or 800 different gospel singing groups being booked around the country *every night*," she told *Chicago American* feature writer Janet Kern; "and this has been going on for years."

Furthermore, "There's plenty more sound just like me down home." She did not add for print what she tacked on later—"they just not willing to work like I did to get there." No use criticizing outside your own house.

For the first time, she was invited to sing for the annual *Chicago Sun-Times* Harvest Moon Festival: Top talent from films, theatre, TV and radio would appear—Saturday night, Nov. 20. Mitch Miller called. Monday morning, Nov. 22, they'd record her in New York. "I'll be there." Been farther for less, in 24 hours.

The *Life* team came—a quick glance relieved her; not the man who saw Robert play the fool. She fixed Duke a big meal for them to photograph, with Marshall Stearns and Frye and Duckett. How was she fitting into network radio every week? She got along fine, she assured them, but of course "I can't let CBS dominate the Lord."

SHE WASN'T being dominated *or* dismayed, just herself and quietly at that, in the quarters crowded with stars and their entourages for the Harvest Moon benefit: Mickey Rooney, Carol Channing, Eartha Kitt, Virginia Mayo, Jim Backus, Sam Levenson, Julius LaRosa, Les Brown—so many. It was a long wait. Finally her turn, for the 22,500 who jammed the Stadium . . . and let their response be known, again and again, until finally MC Irv Kupcinet had to move the show along. "Only a magnificent performer like Mickey Rooney could have followed her," said the admiring Kup. Later the stars were feted at the posh Ambassador East. It was fun for Mahalia—she'd seen these stars on TV and gotten their autographs tonight—but she had a plane to catch in a few hours, she explained, rising to leave . . . and as one, the entire room stood in a spontaneous ovation.

"THIS USED to be a church, Mahalia," Mitch said, showing her around the CBS Studio on E. 30th along with George Avakian, her A&R man. Somebody murmured that it used to be a brewery, too, and Mahalia roared. Mitch was proud that he'd found a new upbeat gospel song for her—*Rusty Old Halo,* about a rich old, mean old, man who didn't rate anything more when he inched into Heaven; Avakian wanted to back that with one he had, *The Treasures of Love*. Mahalia had two new Dorsey songs she liked: *Walk Over God's Heaven* and *It Don't Cost Very Much*. They'd try out a hymn too, see how it went, and there was another gospel with a bounce, *Jesus Met the Woman at the Well.*

Mahalia sat to one side munching grapes, Bill Russell beside her. Fiddling, shifting, testing, balancing of equipment was going on. This wasn't so different from Apollo, except more of everything. Al Duckett was there, and Joe Bostic, and the *Life* boys. Mahalia became oblivious to them all. She seemed to be resting with her eyes closed. Mildred knew she was praying.

"All right, Mahalia, let's try a run-through of *My Faith Looks Up to Thee*. The tape will not be rolling. This is a run-through for sound." Mahalia was just moving into a fine fervor when Avakian called "Cut." Several such break-offs later—*this* was different from Apollo—Mahalia called out, half-joking but hoping he'd take her meaning, "Why you always shout 'Cut' just when the spirit's on me?"

Heading for the hotel and something to eat, Mildred said, "Mr. Miller sold you on *Rusty Old Halo,* didn't he?" Mahalia laughed. "That Mitch Miller is a salesman. He could sell me anything." She cut her eyes at Mildred and added, "except a *new* halo. Halie's not ready for that."

Songs were pouring in to her now. Mildred was writing too. For her latest, *I'm On My Way to Canaan Land* they decided to use a Cuban-African beat: no reason you can't move on out with gospel. It was a living form, and she liked new things if they had a real message.

She put off long as she could going to see Dr. Barclay. "It's my eyes bothering me again, Dr. Barclay—an irritation. You think it's the sarcoids? And to tell you the God's truth, I got these gall bladder pains. What you think—and don't tell me I can't eat!"

He scanned her skin carefully. Sarcoid was common in the skin, lumping and scarring. . . . Thank God. No sign yet. If it came and he couldn't control it, it would end Mahalia as a public figure. She didn't know. "Underneath all the humor, Mahalia was a very apprehensive, anxious woman," says Dr. Barclay. "I never frightened her with possibilities."

There was one other which haunted him—

29

She was eager for it all. Fan mail was coming into WBBM by the bushel from as far away as Switzerland—many unburdening their troubles, telling the comfort, the help they'd drawn from her. Grateful beyond words to Studs Terkel, she bought him a handsome camel's hair coat and when he sputtered "Mahalia, I can't take this!" she countered with an easy "Oh, yes, you can—if it fits." You can't answer a woman like that; he hugged her instead. In less than four weeks, Columbia Records had two singles and the four numbers together on "extended play" pressed and ready. "Another new development being preserved on records," John Hammond wrote for the *New York Times,* "is the music of the Negro gospel singers, up to now available on comparatively obscure labels catering to a small market. Within two weeks, the voice of Mahalia Jackson, one of the great religious singers of our time, will be available on LP." After a quick DJ test, "Get your walking shoes on, Mahalia," said Mitch; "we're sending you on a promotion tour for *Rusty Old Halo.*" Studs had her on his TV show, *Briefcase.* As she could, she sandwiched in out-of-town dates: don't make money on radio like you do on concerts. But she saved time to run revival for Stone Temple Baptist from Dec. 22 through Watch Night, and still got up to Kup Kupcinet's late TV show to sing Christmas Eve. The CBS switchboard lit up like a decoration. Seldom had so many called to praise a star. "Why isn't Mahalia on a network TV show?" Kup wrote. "With her deep religious feelings, she'd be a combination of Bishop Sheen and Dinah Shore!"

The question hung on the midnight air.

NOT HERS, but an even more demanding Chicago question was on stage. Rep. Dawson had been on the Democratic committee that in mid-December dumped second-term Mayor Martin Kenelly in favor of running its chairman, Cook County Clerk Richard Daley. Kenelly was making a stiff fight for the primary. Dawson sounded battle stations. And called Mahalia. After being in the same room with Daley one minute, Haley decided, "That man's engine's turning over; he's going go." Still, things happened as they could because you worked. The magnetic voice which now commanded not less than $1,000 a concert (churches excepted) soared for rally and precinct meeting. Sometimes Dorsey joined in; he'd worked for Dawson off and on since the Republican days. But Mahalia's hidden strength lay in her living room. There was no day when preachers were not visiting Mahalia Jackson. And in Chicago, the reverends controlled a lot of votes.

Throughout the day April 5, 1955, Dawson's vital black wards voted in force. And that night the newly assembled machine of Boss Daley, with one-man-drive, rolled out from the polls.

By then, Halie had mounted her own flying horses and circling, grasped a prize—the first black to win this one—made all the headier because she'd barely caught her breath from being knocked right out of the air.

IT WASN'T EASY to take. After all the fanfare, the critical raves, CBS cut her radio program to 10 minutes. While they were arguing that, the whole show was canceled. Not for lack of listeners. For lack of a sponsor. The consensus was that evidently no national sponsor would touch a show that went South with a black as its star. Mitch Miller was fit to be tied—that beautiful *record* promotion time! Top brass was adamant. Mahalia couldn't believe it. Not the stopping—that was their privilege, hard as she tried to be a success. But don't those people know no more about the South—where gospel *come* from? where gospel is *popular?* Who up there say people who listen to religious songs on a Sunday going hate a sponsor who makes it possible? Lord, don't let the Devil dog you into putting Job's trials on me.

The *most* peculiar thing was that before the radio program was killed, local CBS-TV been looking at her for a show. Kup heard it early as mid-January. She guess now they'd decide she was poison. Show business didn't like a loser. She put it out of her mind and looked at something to make you feel good: *Rusty Old Halo* was a hit. *Variety* rated it a "Best Bet" alongside Perry Como's *Kokomo*. Getting in some strange company. Columbia had it released now throughout the country, with heavy promotion in the stronghold areas where her personal popularity and gospel as a whole made sure of a welcome—the South and Southwest. Hmph. Too bad the different Columbia offices didn't get together, she thought wryly. And put that behind her. No use to hold a thing. Columbia wasn't singling out Dorsey's number for attention, but the black press and black DJs were giving it a big play, to the soft-voiced, pudgy little music-man's delight. "Mahalia," he beamed—at her piano with yet another song (he would write over 400)—"I believe the air is charged with power, all around you; you just have to know how to get it out. And music has a power that nothing else has." She nodded.

"Good thing the Lord snatched you from the demons, Dorsey. Here—let's go over this thing. What we going do for Hayakawa?"

BEYOND THE LIGHTS was her first white Chicago university audience in 27 years' singing. Mahalia turned to Hayakawa, her face grave. "Doc, I have you to thank for this; and I thank you."

The tiny semanticist/jazz-culturist seized his opportunity to lecture his peers. "Just across the road from Cottage Grove Ave. our neighbors have produced this music which has influenced the world. And you darn high people don't know how famous our Negro neighbors are! What a profound cultural influence they are!"

When Mahalia got through, the capacity crowd had joined the world. Just how much influence gospel—and specifically Mahalia's forefront in it—was having was a subject engrossing the industry as well as its writers. To *Billboard* her entry into the general record world via Columbia had brought the field into prominence for the first time. "A big hit in the spiritual market is one that racks up better than 20,000—average is between 7,500 and 12,500 now," said a Steve Schickel survey—"exclusive of the several Mahalia Jackson million-sellers." At Hill & Range music publishers, sensitive antennae rose: Would Miss Jackson be interested in publishing a songbook of her favorites?

Things were picking up. Thank You Lord; I know I never walk alone. She headed for Boy Baby's evening service full of the knowledge. Young Rev. John had followed his father's footsteps. His voice rose and fell as he dramatized the service . . . took his stance for his prayer . . . reached beyond them all—taken by the spirit, pulling them with him; higher, higher, higher . . . "Hallelujah!" Mahalia shouted in the power and glory of the vision and racing past the deacon guard, reached to seize him at the table —seize the source of this joy and the issuance of the spirit—and the microphone knocked the pastor down; Mahalia still so possessed with the spirit and the shout that even as the officers held her, the pastor scrambling to his feet, she stamped with the passion of her feeling and broke both heels.

Next day she called Louise, aghast. "Lou, have you talked to Rev. John? You tell him I said see if I hurt him, and if I did, go to the doctor's—I'll pay for the medical attention. And please, please, tell him I'm sorry; tell him he prayed so, I just couldn't help myself."

"As a matter of fact," says Dr. Thurston, "all I had was a little hicky."

At WBBM-TV, CBS outlet in Chicago, some nail-biting was going on. Everybody *wanted* to do a show with her. . . . "Mahalia Jackson's guest appearance Tuesday on Channel 2's *In Town Tonight,*" Lucia Carter told *Sun-Times* readers, "will be an audition of a sort. A TV show featuring the gospel singer is in the planning stage. Exactly what form future plans will take may be determined by Tuesday's show."

The 10:15 p.m. show depended largely on visiting stars—Studs Terkel had persuaded them to use Mahalia. There was some discussion of how to light her but otherwise rehearsal Tuesday evening went smoothly. Her spot came—chit-chat, then the camera moving in as Mildred and Ralph swung out with the gospel beat and Mahalia poured liquid gold and fire into the air waves. A fascinated Joe Goldberg behind the glass directed his camera into a tight closeup. She was still singing when the switchboard put through a call from the station owner. "Get that big black gorilla off the air!"

They didn't. Not that night, and not later, because the overwhelming response by telephone and card and letter was a roaring tide of approval. The hate showed up, but so light a sprinkling on the sea of delight, it was ignored. They had a show. Two, in fact, because two sponsors turned up: National Credit Clothing wanted 11 p.m. Thursday; and Sunday, 10:15 p.m., was inked by car dealer Martin J. Kelly. Once again it was a Cowan agency package, with her friend John Lewellen in charge. Serious conferences began now, on staff and format. Studs Terkel was the writer—*the* expert on Mahalia Jackson. But who for MC? The brass wanted the urbane *In Town* host. Producer and director wanted Studs. Who better to keep Mahalia relaxed and happy on camera? But there was that black list. The camera was *exposure.* The brass balked. Mahalia was told. She said calmly, "You tell CBS Mahalia don't appreciate that, and she might not sing."

But the *Mahalia Jackson Show* was set—sold! Studs was named show host with a unique compromise: his face must never appear on camera, and his name would not be publicized in the cast. Studs couldn't have cared less. He began his labor of love. He'd keep it simple: Mahalia sings; he—unseen—questions her about the song; Mahalia tells a story about it. She was a born storyteller. And she had radar for what was funny or dramatic: she could ad lib better than Studs or anybody could write it down for her. Besides, Mahalia wasn't going to learn a lot of lines twice a week. They wanted the Halloran Quartet in, to mix it a little? Okay. Period.

As the work moved forward, Halie was in high good humor. Of one studio aide who seemed unable to share their spirits, she whispered to Studs: "I hope that man lasts. He looks like death on a soda cracker." Studs guffawed. Who was relaxing whom?

ON SUNDAY, March 13, 1955, Mahalia, Polly, Mildred, Ralph and Bill Russell got to the Garrick Theatre three hours earlier than the 10:15 p.m. air time. Studs was there. Bill Russell's job was to hold her idiot sheets—prompt cards—off camera. The commercial announcer was getting a run-through. The slide sequence was registering on a studio camera. The Halloran Quartet was rehearsing off to itself. Grips were shifting props and scenery. Electricians flipped cables, stirred equipment. Floormen looked uniformly harried. Mahalia had to break off rehearsing to stand on a blue chalk mark while the men in the production booth debated her lighting: None of them had worked a black TV show before; there wasn't one. It stuck in Joe Goldberg's memory long later, for a *Rolling Stone* interview, that some of the crew were unhappy, off-base because they had nothing to do after the set-up, suspicious that somebody was being conned with this Jesus bit. A game of poker got underway. "Five minutes" call brought required silence—and for Mahalia, a final prayer, a reminder to God that a lot was going on this show for Halie, for black people, for Him—please keep Your eye on this sparrow. Commercials and then a deep breath to let out, be loose, and a Mahalia smiling with the wonder of it all came in view on Channel 2. *I sing because I'm happy. . . .*

The Mahalia Jackson Show was on the air. Studs' voice. Mahalia's response. The singing. The poker game stopped mid-hand; nobody went for coffee or opened a Coke, Joe Goldberg noted. When the show went off the air, everybody applauded her, says Bill Russell.

She took the whole bunch home for red beans and rice.

Next day, one theme sounded and resounded in the Chicago press raves: CBS should start exploring immediately the chances of finding a network TV outlet for Mahalia Jackson. But *TV Guide* cautioned that the smart-money boys contend gospel singers aren't "commercial." Well, Lord, somebody always pulls a peashooter if you get too high up, don't they.

Within two weeks, CBS boss William S. Paley had a copy of her show on its way to him. The staff was elated. Except that she was aging him, says Joe Goldberg—21 then, a fledgling producer. At rehearsal, she sang and he'd tell Studs how much time there was left to talk and sign off. But on the air, Mahalia might remember an extra verse; or skip one, even with Bill Russell holding his cue sheets—and the producer sweat out the prospect of dead time or no time. Mahalia solved it. When Studs introduced the last song, the producer held up fingers to show how many minutes she had to sing. "She never missed it by more than 20 seconds either way," says Mr. Goldberg. "I don't even want to think about how she did it."

SEPARATE AND beyond this whole concentration, her other life was as full of eddies and deeps and sandbars as the Mississippi. In quick order, she did a benefit for her friend Rev. Clay Evans' church; a concert at Evanston High School gym; an early morning service for handicapped workers of Goodwill Industries—which started with the audience as chilly as the Goodwill chapel and ended with the wheelchairs rocking, the crutches tapping. She went over to Rev. Boddie's Sanctified church "to show them I'm not *grand*," she told Bill Russell. At the church, Rev. Boddie spoke out: "Mahalia, we were wondering why you look so light on television?" Quick as a wink: "Rev. Boddie, haven't you heard of the Miracle of Television?" The congregation rocked. Those two were as good as a show. Interviewers came. She recorded again in New York. She got over to Atlantic City briefly to see Russell Roberts. She posed to endorse a jukebox, the ad pitched to equipment so fine you could hear the rare artistry of Miss Jackson with "living realism." Al Duckett prodded her for story material for the black media, his specialty, and kept her name in *Jet*. The 28th Bud Billiken Parade and Picnic asked her to join its stars and prepared a scroll in her honor. *Rusty Old Halo* was so entrenched that *Ebony* used it to key a pungent editorial which noted that Chicago's welcome of the Negro had slipped to indifference, and sometimes hate. Mahalia sighed and called Aunt Hannah; she was worried about Hannah's blood pressure. She got comfortable first—a call to Hannah was at least one hour gone; the two spoke every day. Allen's boys were growing fast—or more to the point, out-growing; yes, she'd pay for it if they really needed the clothes. And send them to see about their teeth. Doodutz came and gave her the home news; somebody always into something, but what you expect with enough cousins now to fill a good-sized church—second- and third-cousins counting equally, Southern style.

Her first album—which Mitch titled simply *Mahalia Jackson Sings*—drew a 5-star rating in *Downbeat*'s Jazz Reviews (Nat Hentoff concurring that "Mahalia Jackson has no visible contenders . . . this one is not to be missed!"). At the opposite pole it won an enthusiastic critique in Classical Reviews for *Record and Sound Retailing*. Everybody's darling. (Bess Berman dug out the lone side she had on hand—*I Walked Into the Garden*, residue of Mahalia's Carnegie nightmare—and topped it with the flip side of Mahalia's first Apollo record, the one which lay unwanted, so that finally *I'm Going to Tell God All About It* had its say.)

No word from Mr. Paley. But "Arthur Godfrey wants you, Mahalia!" said Lou Cowan. The talent king of TV; CBS's own, on more prime time than anybody. Just having Godfrey pick her, Cowan said, would impress

New York. John Lewellen offered to fly her in style in his two-seater plane. Halie? In that? After Bill Russell got blown around in it, had to set down from bad weather? She sang a lot about faith, but she wouldn't overwork the Lord.

She went in Monday—by train—for Columbia. Atlantic City was so close; if she had time to see Russell— She sang a little, thinking. He'd be there.

THEY LIKED each other instantly at rehearsal, says Arthur Godfrey. "I remember that first meeting fondly. I wanted her for her great talent, and when she came, everyone loved her for her sincerity. I admired her natural talent, her capacity for hard work, and her constant pursuit of perfection in performance." He'd had his physical problems, she knew—avid TV viewer that she was—and he offered some advice about one of hers: "I begged her to try to reduce." On the air—giving herself wholly to her singing—the veteran MC was so moved, he cried: "She was very touching." ("That man sure cries easy," Mahalia said affectionately, telling it.) More than that—she was a smash. Socko! said the trade. Socko, said the public. Several thousand wires and cards and calls urged a repeat. Godfrey didn't need that to know he wanted her back—wanted a whole series of dates. They spoke of it before she hurried home for Thursday evening's show.

New York's *Chez Paree* called to book her at their club. The money offered made her blink. "And you can sing whatever you want."

"But I can't sing it in no nightclub. People can't put their minds on the Lord in a place like that. Excuse me—there's nothing wrong with your business, that's just a peculiarity of *me*."

Turn right around to New York for Joe Bostic, who'd sold out Carnegie Hall for Mother's Day long before she'd signed for any Sunday TV. He'd moved his curtain up to 1:30 p.m. "We'll get you back in time." She was glad to be there. But off, she was tugging at sweaty clothes before she was inside her dressing room, changing to board a plane for Chicago and that night's show. Lord, look like Halie would lose weight without no diet. Beside her, Mildred moaned to, please God, keep her off planes. If it wasn't against nature, it was against *her* nature. "Hush, girl can't you see I'm thinking? Just pray." Halie was—hard; but she didn't want to scare Mildred. And she did have to pull her mind together. Willa Jones was going to Europe and the Holy Land, and they were giving her a big appreciation sendoff at Greater St. John Baptist. On a Monday, so Mahalia could make it without all this sweat.

New record material. She wish Bill Russell was still in town. Her first album was all gospel, but Mr. Miller was trying to edge up on her, "broaden her." She told Aunt Bessie about it on the phone—"he wants my records to be more popular." Aunt Bessie's indignation crinkled across the long-distance: "*God* is the most popular person in the world. 'Popular' is God! And remember, baby, He loves you best." Halie wasn't forgetting. She held the line for inspirational songs, from wherever. Hunt for the inside of this new one, find the best place to sing it so Mildred could call the key and George Avakian could have the musicians' arrangements made. Run through the TV program songs. Twice more to the Garrick—hard work but Mr. Stud made it fun. Then ride the train to Detroit.

The *Pittsburg Courier,* titan of the black press, was staging a concert in Detroit with a bill Mahalia was eager to join: Ella Fitzgerald, whom she loved but so seldom got to see; Count Basie, Lionel Hampton, Dinah Washington—that child gone so well now; plus the Clara Ward Singers. The 15,000 who poured into Olympia Stadium Saturday night were ready to have themselves a time. And did. Ella, Hamp, Dinah . . . the crowd yelled, whistled, stomped, danced in the aisles and took to the stage. "But Mahalia!" said the *Courier*'s Gladys Johnson, "Mahalia got the edge with no gimmicks; just flatfooted sang." Stopped the show cold; tied it in a knot.

There was a little visiting time before but hardly any after—yeah, Sunday night TV; Thursday too. Got my own show. It was a wonder to their world.

National Clothing pulled out. She could not get the straight of it. The Cowan agency fished around for another sponsor, came up with empty hook . . . and Thursday was canceled.

"CYLESTINE, see can you find a place to put this." Her walls were lined with scrolls and trophies. It was Festival season. White or black, she was an essential showpiece. She booked them all—some paid, some free if she felt the urge; she shaved Sunday's rehearsal to make the one in Des Plaines at the Methodist Camp Grounds, as sole attraction to benefit underprivileged children. For the huge Bud Billiken Parade, she split honors with Joe Louis, Sen. Everett Dirksen, Lt. Gov. John Chapman, Walter Reuther, Jesse Owen, King Zulu from this year's Mardi Gras, and the new mayor. Rain fell like it was the last in creation, but that didn't stop the parade. About 300,000 people stuck it out. Mayor Daley got a big hand. Mahalia got an even bigger roar of approval, waving hands glistening like smelt crowding the sea. Lord, don't let me lose my voice, she prayed, soaked. As soon as he got the chance, Mayor Daley asked her how she was getting on. "Anything I can do for you, Mahalia, you just let me know."

Whoo! she'd been so busy, there Brisko's child Rose staying with Big Alice and Hannah for the summer and she hadn't seen that child but once. Eight years old and they still wouldn't give her up—Halie had put that out of her mind. Elliott Beal was up from home, too—not staying with her but to Prairie often even though Mahalia made him get on his knees with her, cleaning cracks ("Don't you tell Ida about this; you don't think I do this at home?") when they weren't talking, eating, singing, running over new music. He thought she ought to get into a wider spiritual range with her recordings, too. "Reach out, Mahalia; it won't hurt; it'll help." Elliott was a church-music man, directed two choirs at home besides teaching school. She knew he had her interests at heart. Wilmon came over and Elliott got so touchy about the way he was criticizing her music that Halie had to hush Beal, explain Wilmon was just in a different field of music and didn't understand that people didn't look down on gospel any more. Beal was glad to get out and drive her slowly through the subdivisions, looking for a house.

It took another visitor—Rev. C. L. Franklin of Detroit—for her to meet someone special from right here, and she almost didn't get out to the airport. Couldn't get nobody to drive her car, after he'd taken the trouble to call ahead, and she hated to fight that traffic—but she did—and brought them home with her. "Mahalia and I were friends from right then," says bright, attractive Elizabeth Thornton. "I just lived in Gary—practically a suburb—we saw each other frequently. Sometimes she'd call and say, 'Look, I have a program such and such a date—come and go with me.' And I'd go. Just to go." How far, she couldn't then guess.

It was in a new role that an old friend, Rev. Leon Jenkins, came to see her. Mahalia had been largely responsible for his becoming pastor of Greater Salem. He wanted a Hammond organ for the church . . . would she sponsor a drive? She would. Energetically. For a start, she picked Sept. 26 for "Mahalia Jackson's Gala Musical Festival." Her friends were put to work.

First, though, the giant of them all, the Chicagoland Festival, staged by the *Chicago Tribune;* she'd split star billing with the teens' idol, Eddie Fisher. It brought a reporter to her door. Clay Gowran stayed long, came again, ate with her . . . and found himself with so much to tell that it took three stories.

To him, she spoke publicly for the first time of her heart's desire: to have a big temple in Chicago where gospel could be taught and sung. That it would be a huge, costly project didn't dim the gleam in her eye. "Look at the things that have come true for me."

"GOD WORKS in mysterious ways," she murmured to Brother John, in town and relaxing with her at Aunt Hannah's. Was this one? Not CBS but NBC network had called. She flew to New York to talk. Home for the show and back again with Mildred and Ralph to tape for their audition. Interested. Mm-hm! Return again to check out those tapes herself and see what was doing. Duke's band was playing out at the Aquacade but this was no time to call. Got business on her mind. Lionel Hampton, writing a *Courier* show-business column, leaked that it looked like she had an NBC-TV series set for fall. Al Duckett! did you tell him? (Hamp a Duckett patron too.) *Nothing's* definite with NBC.

No word from Mr. Paley.

A group of Chicago and Detroit ministers, led by young Rev. James Lofton, wired Secretary Dulles urging that—in line with President Eisenhower's new plan to send representative Americans to build bridges of understanding behind the Iron Curtain—Mahalia be sent not only there but around the world on a "peace mission of song." Her impact, they felt, would surpass any words, through "her personality, her powers of persuasion, and her inspiration."

No word from either network. It couldn't be the religion. Bishop Sheen was a big star. Still, this local TV was holding down her income. Good thing her records were moving. Driving her to the bank—fresh from reading yet another story of her rise to fame—John laughed. "These white people think they made you, Mahalia. They don't know black people made your old self rich first."

"Hush. You must be want some."

Still no word by Baptist Convention, first week of September. She didn't know what to do about concert dates. Russell was there and they arranged for her to come to Atlanta one weekend, to take part in his Sunday service. She could get back in time for that night's TV. With record material to learn, dates to sing and a new song to learn that Mr. Kelly, her sponsor, was after her to do—*Danny Boy*—she couldn't be long at Convention—just enough to be official soloist. But even without all that, she might have to leave. She had these sharp pains. Enough to scare you.

B. J. Ross, the daughter of Norman Ross, was announced by executive producer Les Weinrott as the Mahalia show's new producer, on Sept.10. That day, Mahalia was in Billings Hospital. She'd collapsed and been rushed to the emergency room. Dr. Barclay and Dr. Harper—her 1952 surgeon—were called. She had gall bladder colic. "Colic! Dr. Barclay, that's for babies!" Not this; the intense pain coming in waves, over and over and over. And she had gallstones. They'd take the gall bladder out right away and settle the whole thing.

"Ooh, Mahalia's paying for eating those smoked ribs. Well. At least this'll make me a little lighter."

Everyone had left. Just you and me, Lord. She turned to the well-worn page and read and re-read that first paragraph . . . *The Lord is my light and my salvation; whom shall I fear? The Lord is the strength of my life; of whom shall I be afraid?* . . . until the assurance came. Her Bible was tucked under the sheet when they wheeled her down the corridor. In the operating room, before Dr. Barclay's wife gave her the spinal anesthetic, she got them to read the 27th Psalm just this one more time.

She was so fat the needle barely reached the spinal canal.

Then it was Dr. William Barclay's turn to be amazed. "When we opened the abdomen, all of the sarcoid there had disappeared!" That should cheer her up. If he could get her lungs under that kind of control. . . . He knew the sarcoid wasn't gone, just in hiding. Where? There was no cure for sarcoidosis.

SHE PRAYED. Mother Gaye prayed. ("Mama," Mahalia whispered, face smoothed, "I didn't even believe that it was somebody that could reach my peace.") A whole ministerial army prayed. The aunts prayed . . . Aunt Berta, Uncle Porter's wife, came from Cincinnati. Friends, as many as could be admitted—they prayed. And a rejuvenated Halie left Billings on the 10th day and went to Hannah's. A relieved switchboard slowly ebbed to normal.

Now how was she going sing at Salem Sept. 26?

She couldn't. But Harry Belafonte could. He was working in town. It couldn't be announced, but one word on the grapevine was enough. "That was a crowd I won't forget," says quiet Rev. Jenkins. "They were both busy signing autographs." Albertina with her *Caravans* got her share of the glory. And the organ got almost half paid for. She found herself singing around home again. She and Cylestine started rescheduling cancelled dates. She was fine. She called WBBM-TV to tell them she was ready to get back to work.

There was no show. Martin Kelly had dropped her. After she'd sung *Danny Boy* for him. Well—she'd learned Jewish songs for the National, and he dropped first. The Cowan office had heard nothing from Mr. Paley. Silence, too, from NBC. But, dimly, the word sifted down. Cost required a major sponsor, and not one would beam a Negro's show South. It was a period when *Jet* could list a week's total of 4 guest spots for all Negroes scheduled on network radio and one on TV. Lord, when You going open these people's eyes? and hearts? Why don't those New York people go *down* South, take a count?

There was no answer, within or without. Well. The other side of dark is light. Halie blazed the trail. Get back on your known road, girl.

Known—and unknown. Concert audiences were as likely to be white as black, with the whites as enthusiastic—even if they weren't used to letting the spirit come. At Kankakee High School, they broke into applause when she'd no more than opened her mouth for *He's Got the Whole World in His Hands*. She'd tried her best to get Columbia to let her cut that first when it was brought to her to introduce; John had learned it from hearing her and used it in London—and it had taken a boy there to hear it from John and put it on record for a big hit. Experts. New York sure was full of them.

DINNER FOR $25 at the Morrison Hotel's Casino Terrace didn't near come up to her own. It was a delayed Mahalia Jackson birthday celebration, though—really a fundraising for Halfway House, a center that would help girls who strayed. Mayor Daley, sitting next to her, spoke of how proud Chicago was of her. And privately: remember, anything she wanted. He really meant it, this heavyset man with the heavy jaw and the soft voice who looked straight into your eyes. The mayor went with her to the towering, ribboned, decked, curlicued, 50-pound birthday cake Rev. Lofton had given her. Everything was on it, including music notes and a Happy Birthday pillow. What would she have thought back in Pinching Town! And she got a doll. Her mink stole drooped as she bent to accept it from little Rachel

Washington . . . such a pretty doll: tall, with long pigtails, frilly white dress with shoes and sox to match. Big enough to be one of her little cousins. Except the face was white.

It was good to be recording without having to catch a train back the next minute. Mitch Miller and Mr. Avakian were hard workers—they didn't mind how many times you did a thing 'til it was right. Or near as. If she could just pick her own songs. She'd talked and talked and talked to George Avakian until he let her record *Precious Lord, Take My Hand*. It had been in her mind since the hospital. "This is one of the greatest songs Prof. Dorsey has written! This song really has *significance* with people that are oppressed. When you can't do anything else, good God, that's God's time to lead His children on!" When she finished the take, she walked to one side and sat down and cried. They had let her make one of the types of songs she was familiar with and had been singing in the church, instead of wrestling these other things. Thank You Lord.

Home to pitch into the second Greater Salem organ benefit. She'd left everybody with work to do . . . Celeste, Margaret, Ora Lee—all three sisters busy; James Lee, Louise . . . well, things going fine, program building up. . . .

The organ was paid for. Hallelujah. Now to California. Polly and a delegation took her down to the station. But no Mildred. Probably pull up just before the train pulls out. But Mildred didn't. Well, Lord, I got Ralph; I'll get a pianist out there.

Some time later, Mildred Falls was rolled out on the ramp in a wheelchair—knee gone bad—and couldn't believe the train was gone, the track bare. She had an hour! No, lady. Slowly it dawned that in some way she had the whole schedule off by one hour. She was desperate. "Get me out to the *airport!*" she cried. And wired Mahalia she'd meet her in Omaha. She was sitting triumphant in her wheelchair on the Northern Pacific track, a wired acknowledgment from Mahalia in her hand, when the train pulled in. They couldn't get her aboard the compartment now—she'd have to make do in the baggage car. Hoisted aboard, she sent a message back to Mahalia—and looked around as the train pulled out. "I was sitting up there with the *dead*," says Mildred. "Corpses on both sides of me, caskets all around me; some mail in front, baggage behind; and I'm sitting in the wheelchair. I'm the only human in the whole bit. I mean alive. The train stops. I hear a voice, a human live voice say, 'Well, she's on this train—here she is.' It's Mahalia. 'Well, you made it, hm?' I say, 'Yeah.' She looks around. 'Well, I'll see you later.' And she's *gone*. And I'm there. Me and the corpses. She wouldn't say anything right then. She took her ti-i-ime. Oh, she took her time. But she finally got around to it. 'Well! Well! Don't pay attention to what you doing!' Ohhh, did I catch it. She dished me out."

In Los Angeles, she got together with Gwen Cooper. Strange . . . Emma Jackson gone to rest and it's Gwen she's giving her confidences. "I want you to meet Russell Roberts. He's just a special person; a great preacher, and educated, but he's a practical man, too—used to be Jersey Joe Wolcott's sparring partner. And yet he's—*cultivated,* know what I mean? And he'll make you laugh. Honest to God. His folks are from Massachusetts—" she broke off with a self-conscious laugh—"a Southern girl with a Yankee—"

"You serious, Sister?"

Mahalia drew back. "Oh, I don't know about that. We got something going but—he's sure one goodlooking man, though, Gwen . . . taller than me, with nice smooth brown skin and these long, strong hands on him. . . . "Well," she said briskly, straightening, "you'll see."

IT WAS so good to have the time to spend a whole entire day with Belafonte's children—beautiful as their daddy—and when they got the organ ready for dedication before Christmas, he came again to Greater Salem. Word that Belafonte would be there packed the church—a pepper-and-salt mix of expectancy as he mounted the pulpit. But he didn't sing. He spoke. Quietly, eloquently. He was Belafonte the dedicated black, proud and grateful for his heritage of courage, depth, and spiritual power under adversities that would have levelled a lesser people. He was Belafonte the talent, who could and did bring other black talent with him. He was Belafonte the man, proud of his friendship with one of God's special people, Mahalia Jackson—telling some of those things which she would not tell herself. He was Belafonte the board member of the Catholic Interracial Council, dedicated to brotherhood with honor among all men. Beside him on the pulpit, listening to his clear testament of his faith in God as a living instrument, Mahalia glowed with pride in this man. There was more in the air than organ tones when the Hammond rolled forth.

But was her Christmas album sacrilegious? Some of the white world new-come wasn't sure, and some was offended. "It is not only Christmas music, it is jazz," *Sun-Times* critic Charles Piper stated flatly. (The presence of Lionel Hampton backing her lent weight to the point.) "If this had been done by anyone else, the question of good taste would have arisen. But Mahalia could never be accused of being sacrilegious." Well, that was one. Never knew who come up with what next.

Duke opened at the Blue Note Dec. 21. He was going to put on a red suit and play Santa Claus to a bunch of kids at the club, Nettie Irving told Halie. "Don't you want to come? It's got to be the greatest!"

"Tell me 'bout it, baby; you can't catch Halie in no club."

Christmas Day, 1955, surrounded by family and friends and food, torn tissue and bright ribbons, Mahalia promised herself the best present of all. *Then* she could keep that promise she made herself when she was barefoot on the cold boards of Mt. Moriah, staring at the beautifulest thing she had ever seen.

30

Downtown, high in the Loop, attorney William Robert Ming, Jr., shoved aside the William Morris Agency letterhead. Lou Mindling again, wanting to represent Mahalia.

Blond, brisk, Louis Mindling was a veteran of some years with the Morris office in Chicago. The prestige agency handled few Negroes, but those were star-status. Mahalia Jackson would be his coup. Another week. No word from Ming. He called Mahalia himself. He'd like to talk with her about making a lot more money, easier. She gave him an appointment. Never say no 'til you know what you're no-ing.

The man got comfortable before he pulled out figures and names and talked. Maybe it *would* pay to have a manager but she didn't know—she did pretty good by herself. Godfrey had just booked her for some more dates; Ed Sullivan's office wanted one this spring. Still, William Morris was *big*. They represented Duke Ellington; she hadn't heard the Duke complain. And they did a lot of TV. She'd think about it. And pray.

The decision came. She wouldn't sign a contract—one with Columbia was enough—but they could book her exclusively. The head office didn't like it but this was Mahalia Jackson: God! you read about her every time you turned a page. The biggest talent agency in the complex business fine-tuned its dials to pitch this new product. She was like nothing they'd ever seen or heard or handled. After considerable acquaintance, one day when she was in the New York office the clerk who did the bank reconciliations came in to advise that a check to Miss Jackson had been outstanding for about nine months and Miss Jackson reached into her brassiere, shuffled several checks, and showed him one with a pleased smile. "It's all right, baby; I got it."

HER PENDULUM swung wildly. The reverends still claimed their own. And it was the reverends who got her to Canada.

Massey Hall, Toronto, wasn't packed . . . the police concert, Rev. Daniel explained apologetically. But some 1,800 Canadians plus three critics heard the gospel truth. "Few, if any, of those who heard her could resist being caught up in the contagious spirit of happiness Miss Jackson created," said Robert Adams. She taught them how to clap. And she showed the jazz fans among them that after *Jesus Met the Woman at the Well* she could hold them with *The Lord's Prayer*. "God is real to me. This is not put on. He took me from the swamps of the Mississippi to the streets of Paris. Who wouldn't believe in a God like that?"

Critic John Kraglund decided Mahalia "could give a few pointers to some of the current rhythm-and-blues and rock-and-roll styles." When she saw that, Mahalia hmphed. "Don't he know that's just eggs hatched from the chicken?"

Negroes themselves were only now taking a good look . . . she'd come from singing for a Waterloo, Iowa, junior high school's first Negro History Week, trying to tell those children what they *had* in gospel. White music analysts were searching thoughtfully. Gospel had "occasional blue notes." The accompaniment sometimes "inserted an eight-to-the-bar passage" (one of the fundamentals of boogie-woogie) yet it seemed "appropriate . . . without irreverence." . . . Mahalia Jackson had created a new market for "the hymn" by injecting a bouncy rhythm while retaining the cathedral-like tones . . . and in turn, this created a new field for songwriters on pop labels . . . The Ink Spots' *It Is No Secret What God Can Do;* Frankie Laine's *I Believe;* Al Hibbler's *He;* Nashville's *Crying In the Chapel.* Major labels were "jumping on the spiritual bandwagon with increasing fervor."

Mahalia wasn't happy. It hurt, what was happening to gospel. "Some of it is getting into the hands of hustlers meeting a lot of weak-minded gospel singers and trying to make singing 'entertaining,'" she told Nat Hentoff of *The Reporter* with scorn, "Gospel singing is *bigger* than entertainment. . . . Gospel singing doesn't need artificial, unnecessary, phony sounds. Man has to have something to look up to. I do believe gospel singing can be commercial and uplifting at the same time. God is that wide, that broad. He supplies all our needs." She admitted she wasn't too happy with Columbia herself. They'd got her into a new field, all right; they'd got her on TV, and paid her well. "The only thing they haven't been too particular about is my songs. Some of the songs they pick for me I don't understand, and those I couldn't put myself into."

"HOLY ROLLERS again," she murmured. Robert Anderson whooped as he pulled onto the road. She'd made short runs regularly . . . lawyer Bob Ming going along now when he could, expansive in the spotlight . . . but this was her first real sweep since—"since before my radio show, you realize that?" Never mind the cold, in a heated Cadillac. Ohio, Pennsylvania, D.C., Virginia, then on south, Cleveland first . . . Then "Just 'GET ME TO MY CHURCH ON TIME.' I wonder how Strawthford?" . . . "Mahalia, his name is Strawther." . . . "Well, he come when I call."

Jodie had started a little storefront church in Cleveland, but he knew the big preachers would lay claim to her, along with the mayor, the newspapers, TV. He was satisfied to lay eyes on her at the hotel. So young Rev. Strawther was as startled as his congregation—what there was of it—when Mahalia Jackson walked in Sunday to join the singing, work around the altar, shout 'til the Lord came. "Oh, we had ourselves a *time!*" says Rev. Strawther; "it was a boost for me—and Mahalia called it her filling station."

Drive through now; no time for lunch. Mahalia telephoned ahead to the lady sponsor to have some food ready . . . they'd just about be in Harrisburg in time to eat and make the auditorium. "Mahalia, can't we please stop and let me fill this hole?" said Robert. "Stop it with your tongue, baby, 'til we get there. Dorothy have a lovely dinner fixed for us—something worth eating." Dorothy had farmed out the job. "It's not far," she assured Halie, shepherding the tired flock. "Here—this lovely house." In they advanced—and stopped. The table was prettily spread with tuna salad, cheese dip, punch—and they'd remembered she liked hot tea. Mahalia's jaw dropped about the same rate as her stomach.

"Wait a minute, lady. I got to sing tonight—this is air; you're pumping more air down in my stomach and I just had an operation. Give me some *food.*"

"Dorothy didn't tell us until—"

"Well, I'm not going on nobody's program, not until I eat. These folks here is *hungry*— Dorothy knows we folks who like to eat." Turning to that squirming soul, "You all ain't got my money, I *know* that, and I know the best thing I get out of you is something to *eat.*" With that she sat down. "And you know," says Robert, "that woman had to fix a whole meal before Mahalia went on her program? We sure ate."

Down the line and South, nearly a 300-mile drive to Roanoke with TV before the concert. Rain sluiced the road. Robert slowed, struggling to see. "Get past that bus, Robert."

"I can't see to get around it, Mahalia!"

"You getting old," Mahalia taunted; "you can't see, you don't know where you are, you got milked down." Robert swerved out and around while the bus honked indignantly as both rounded the curve. "Don't you come killing me with a bus!" Mahalia cried. He slowed. "Move on, Robert! We got to make the TV." He picked up. But he couldn't crowd enough miles. Mahalia started changing in the car. Just outside Roanoke, "Pull over, Robert! Now fix this girdle up on me." Tugging, Robert zipped it up, sputtering. "That's the reason I hate to be around you; every time I get around you I have to fasten your girdle—pull up your something, whatever you have. And I don't make a quarter the whole month." Straightening her dress as they drew up before the station, Mahalia said, "It's things like this save me from being 'famous.' "

WITH ALL the television, the Southern white people were eager to hear her. "But they didn't want to sit together, as Christians. There would be a side for white and a side for blacks, but I said to myself, this is one step of progress that they are coming to hear me. Then in the middle of the first songs I would make a parable of it: 'We that are here now, some of many colors, races, together but separated, that is not real Christianity' . . . and many immediately stood up, had not been aware they did wrong, and would sit closer to their brother and sister. But I didn't make a big issue of it. Some would obey, some wouldn't; that's the way life is—but that doesn't stop love from being the proper strong medium of getting people together."

Sometimes, though, she felt moved to try the other way. Mildred waited for those times. "Mahalia say, nice and soft but they *knew*: 'Well, if we got to have all this, then you give them their money back, I'll just go on.' That's the last thing sponsors want to hear—'give them their money back'—the *last*. So they open the curtain, 'Everybody can mix, sit where you please.' And lots of white people didn't *want* to be down in front, they moved. Some of my people felt better to sit right down front. Made a better evening. Accomplish without making a big to-do—that was Mahalia's way, before I ever heard of anybody else doing such a thing. For a long time she didn't tell a soul in Chicago; and she never would let *me* say a word."

Do more, talk less. How many times Halie heard that from Aunt Duke? Right now the William Morris office was trying to get an okay for her to go behind the Iron Curtain. Maybe when she went to Washington, she could ask the President. . . .

It was just the ladies. Well, anyway, she was proud to be singing for the First Lady and her mother, Mrs. Doud. Such sweet people. So natural. And polite. The very next day, Mar. 23, 1956, Mrs. Eisenhower took time to write from the White House. Such a nice letter. "You were so kind to bring so much enjoyment to my birthday luncheon yesterday by giving us the benefit of your very great talent. *Swing Low, Sweet Chariot* is, of course, a great favorite of my mother's and mine, and we agreed that your interpretation was especially beautiful and memorable. With my appreciation, and very best wishes always, Mamie Doud Eisenhower."

"Polly, put this letter in my scrapbook before somebody walks off with it."

31

With all the ins and outs, she'd put the thing in the hands of a real estate agent—but that hadn't worked. Thing be done right, do it yourself. She'd started looking in earnest, picking out a direction and driving around slowly searching. It took a while . . . and then it was there: "For Sale" sign in the yard. On the corner of 83rd and Indiana, set back, solid brick, ranch style, seven rooms with good yard space and a chimney rising up—though she

Two famous smiles as Mahalia gives President Eisenhower a birthday present after she has sung a gospel-style 'Happy Birthday' in 1959.

Mahalia joined other stars in a Washington gala for President Kennedy's inaugural in 1961; among them were Leonard Bernstein, Ella Fitzgerald, Bette Davis and Harry Belafonte.

Below Dr Martin Luther King tells Mahalia what he wants her to sing to set the mood for his speech at a great Chicago freedom rally in 1966.

Right A formal photograph in the White House in November 1965 with (left to right) pianist Mildred Falls, Mahalia's husband Minters J. Galloway, Mrs Johnson, Mahalia, President Johnson and the organist and pianist Edward Robinson.

Below right Mahalia meets Indira Gandhi in New Delhi.

Left Duke Ellington helps celebrate Mahalia's sixth Carnegie Hall triumph in 1956; left to right: Elizabeth Lands, Duke Ellington, Joe Bostic and Mahalia.

Below left Bing Crosby and Mahalia make a TV programme together in 1958.

Right Filming: Mahalia with Billy Preston on the set for *St Louis Blues* in 1957.

Below An early recording session with Columbia Records in 1954. Left to right: her friend and helper Bill Russell, Mitch Miller and George Avakian.

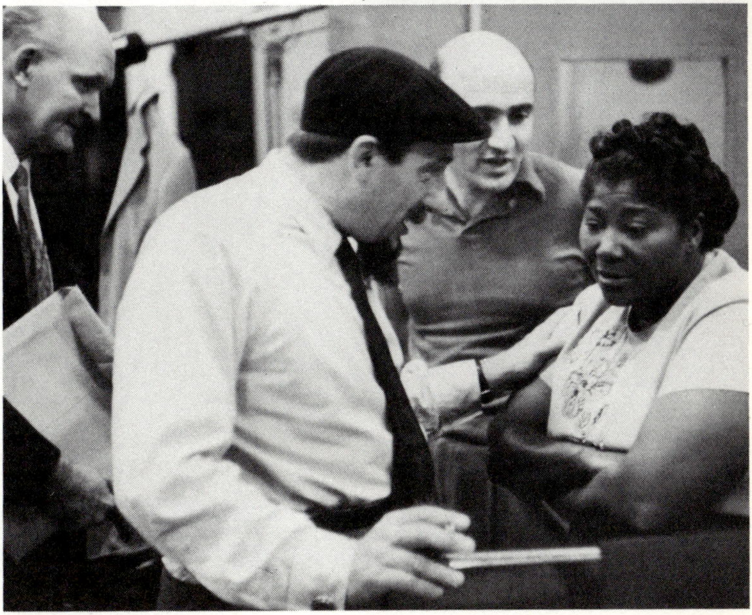

With all

Left Mahalia poses with Princess Grace of Monaco in the palace gardens in 1968.

Below left Mahalia is invested as an honorary doctor of music at Marymount College, New York, in 1971.

Below During her 1971 tour of Japan, Mahalia and her biographer Laurraine Goreau are besieged by reporters at a Tokyo press conference. Together with Gwen Lightner they took time out for sightseeing in Kyoto in cherry-blossom time.

Red Skelton clowns with Mahalia in a 1963 TV show.

Mahalia at her happiest performing with her dear friend Dinah Shore – the first of many sessions for them both.

sure didn't want to build fires again; built-in garage, picture windows so you could enjoy the view, and a side entrance so you wouldn't mess up the living room to get to the kitchen. She could cut that grass herself, maybe she'd lose weight—satisfy Dr. Barclay without this dieting mess. One thing, it had been looked after—the whole neighborhood was looked after, and quiet. And look at all those beautiful trees up and down Indiana, those pretty white children playing so nicely. Now this was the *suburbs*. Chatham Village, the map said.

The owner—a white doctor—knew of Miss Jackson and said he'd be glad to sell to her . . . and thump, it hit Halie: There were no laws, but this was one of those unwritten-law sections; strictly for white. All right. Mahalia can blaze the trail.

The blaze was up and down the streets. Her agent called. Miss Jackson ought to know that if she moved in, she was going into trouble. Block meetings were being held, to protest her moving in: "The block would be tainted; it would injure their investments; hurt their values socially; let one in and they all come." The doctor was holding out for selling, but she'd have to live there.

She cried. After all these high white people been so nice to her, and writing how much they liked her on TV, what a comfort her faith was to them—it had not occurred to her that Mahalia Jackson wouldn't be welcome. The phone calls began. Cylestine could catch some, in the daytime. "Don't answer them back, Polly; just hang up." But late at night, she'd be the one and afraid not to answer—might be somebody sick or died, or important business, show people kept late hours. The worst grated out, "Your songs aren't going to help you when we blow up your house."

Lou Mindling tried to talk her out of it. "It's too much money, Mahalia —$40,000. I'm telling you as a manager, it's a bad investment." Sallie Martin knew about property, and she agreed with Mr. Mindling. Too much. Halie didn't care. "I'm a Negro and they don't want me in that house but I *want* that house."

"Well, if that's the way you want to go, all right; but don't think of paying cash."

"Oh, I can't be bothered with interest, Mr. Mindling. I had enough of that on Prairie. I saved my money." She paid cash. It would take about a month to clear the title, close, and begin redecorating. The calls were vicious now; obscene. The threatening letters felt like acid on your fingers. Lord, what You want me to do? She had to leave for Cincinnati to sing. When she got back, her picture window on 83rd was bullet-splattered. The message from Chatham Village was clear. Mahalia called Bob Miller. He was an alderman now. And when she hung up, she dialed Mayor Daley. Police were there as fast as sirens could bring them. Guards were set up. Chatham Village got the word that the FBI was investigating. The threats stopped but the air was uneasy. The guards stayed on duty. She was casual on the telephone with Aunt Hannah; she told Big Alice she wanted her to "wait 'til things got cleaned up." She felt . . . "so denied," she would tell a reporter, searching the right words. "It's like being put out of a family."

She hired a decorator. "I'm a Loosiana woman, Mr. Hunter; down home I always wanted to have the kind of furniture those white folks had." He helped her pick some solid Louis XIV pieces—Celeste overriding her protests about the cost.

She knew just which room was His. That was a promise she'd made in the hospital. Margaret—"Little Missionary" grown to "Prayer Warrior" —came with Celeste to help dedicate the prayer room. It gave Halie a chance to tell Margaret, "There's a lot I'm up against, baby; the Devil don't sleep. You know they want to take Jesus' name out the title of my songs?" Margaret gasped. "For 'commercial purposes,' they say; want to strike out Jesus. I told them, and I'll go on telling them, 'I want to *praise* my Jesus. Halie's not turning her back.' It's a pitch-down fight in the land of Goshen, and Satan's got prettier coats than Joseph!"

It cost $200 to replace her window.

One of the first things up was a plaque:

DEAR LORD
IN THIS HOUSE YOU ARE WANTED
AND YOU ARE WELCOME

Two Catholic priests came. They said she was welcome. Which offset the one Lou Mindling got mad at, who wasn't very nice. She looked out of her picture window and thought what flowers to plant. Beyond, she could see "For Sale" signs popped up on lawns like daisies. She'd plant her some greens in back; have fresh every day. Even in Eden, they had a snake.

Her first night in her home. About 2 a.m. she called Emma Bell Smothers. "Come out here, girl; I can't stand this, I can't hear nothing but crickets. And they got a something sound like a button on a washboard." Emma Bell dressed and took a taxi for the long ride out. "Woman wouldn't let me leave," says Emma Bell. "Put her clothes on me—and look at the two of *us*: hang on me like a sack and I trip besides. After about two weeks, I said, 'Send me home, or take me home, but I got to get out of your clothes.' And still she said, 'Come on back.' That was the first time, but it wasn't the last."

Thinking things out, talking it over in her prayers, it came to her that she should get her young cousin Steve to come stay. He got a nice even way to him. John Stevens was a second cousin of Clark cousins in New Orleans, but still cousin. "I haven't been with myself in so long," she told Ike—out to see if she was all right—"I get nervous when I'm alone."

Her first concert after she invaded Chatham Village was at Trenton, N.J., sponsored by the White City Rod and Gun Club. They just loved her.

Days later, Gov. Frank Lausche of Ohio had his picture taken with her at the capitol. The state's motto was up: "With God, all things are possible."

HARRY BELAFONTE was one of the first to come see. That Harry was something. "As much as Mahalia weighed, I have never seen another man of his stature just lift her off the floor," says Allen Clark, Jr.—"lift her off the floor and swing her around, so glad to see her. Yes, indeed. When he was in Chicago, he'd stay at a hotel and she'd bring the children out to her house, and take dinner to him."

It was cooking for Harry—sending his dinner down to the Palmer House one night—that again made her a target. Not Chatham fire, but black flak: How come she's toadying to Belafonte when she should have been at the civil rights rally? Halie sighed. How many meetings, how many benefits had she sung when these people forgetting their ABCs? No use saying her tires been slashed—not at home; on the South Side. When you climb the mountain, always somebody want to slide you down to their shelf.

Louie Armstrong came, and loved her new house. "Sugar, how you stand this fresh air?" He liked the way she was getting it to look like New Orleans. "Louie, I ever tell you I used to could hear the jazz from the steamboats coming 'round our bend by my house?"

"I ever tell you I was on that river myself? Might of been my horn you heard, girl." Granville White was content to listen. He'd come to talk record promotion with Mahalia but with the visiting, he forgot: "That was easy to do. She was the only gospel singer we had—and we had kind of cornered the market as far as merchandising a gospel product, at that time. One thing always stuck in my mind with Mahalia, was her constantly trying to do something for young people—it was *great* to see—her eyes would just light up."

She had her say—make them *appreciate* college—when she went over to Gary to help raise money for their United Negro College Fund. Halie Jackson sitting big as life with Dr. Benjamin Mays—president of Morehouse College and a famous preacher; he could rout the demons. Lord, You sure put Halie up. And give her the strength to stay. One good thing —Dr. Barclay live near her now. Come to see her, too, if she can't get down or it's night.

"I didn't normally make house calls, but her house was just a couple of miles away and I had a great deal of respect, very deep affection for Mahalia," says Dr. Barclay. "She had a chronic disease and one I had to see her frequently for. That eye involvement would flare up and die down, and by looking in the eye I could get some idea of just what was going on. In my group at University of Chicago, I had four or five wonderful physicians—Dr. John Kaysick, who went to University of Iowa as head of pulmonary disease; Dr. Albert Niden, who became head of pulmonary disease at Arizona—all of them knew Mahalia and her problems well."

Nobody outside knew. Closest to it was Polly. Certainly J. Robert

Bradley didn't guess, when he came. Bradley had made his debut at the top—opened the Baptist World Alliance in London, and closed it—then got himself off to Paris and Rome and around the world before he came home. Broke. "Give me some money, Mahalia. I need some."

Mahalia eyed him with a glint—this big figure taking his ease in her family room. "You the one just been around the world."

"Yeah, and I need money."

"Bradley, whatever you get, you ain't going have. No."

"Robert Anderson and James Lee and the others can always get money from you 'cause they come 'asking'—you not going see me beg."

"NO!" It was a roar. After a while she got up. "Now let me have all your dirty clothes. Halie's going to wash and iron 'em for you."

"Oh, Mahalia, I can take them to the laundry."

"No-no-no, you need that money; you ain't got nothing." Hours later, when the tide of visitors started in, "Oh, honey, I'm so *tired*. You know the *artist* is in my house, J. Robert Bradley, and I'm the slave; I'm washing and ironing his clothes—his shorts as big as sheets." Seeing her mop her neck, and heave, "people feel so *bad*," says Dr. Bradley; "oh, she'd put coals on me; she'd keep you laughing day and night. And that went on for *years*. 'Bob, baby, don't you stay at nobody else's house when you come.' "

About midnight, when they'd got all the folks out the house, Bradley in bed half-asleep, Mahalia said, "Bradley, look in that drawer—right there by the bed. They's a old check in there . . . what it say?"

Groggy, half-looking by the bedside lamp. "25."

"Look again." He groaned, but he humored her: "Oh. $250."

"*Look* at that thing here."

"Mahalia!" He sat up wide-awake. "This is $25,000!"

"That's from *Si-hi-ilent Ni-hi-ieeeeght*."

He wasn't long gone when Bernice Durden came. So with Alice McLaherty there (a gospel singer needing a room for the summer and Mahalia with all this space) Halie was hardly alone at all. It was fun having somebody around who liked to pound peppermint for pickles. One thing, she had to stop Bernice getting upset about the family, how she'd give over to them, young and old. No use to aggravate. It was something for Bernice to take home when Nat King Cole came to dinner; then Duke Ellington—"you know I always got time to cook for you!" And time, too, to talk the old dream: "Bernice, I'm going have me my temple. See how God works a long ways? Right now, I'm giving scholarships to get some children through college. My temple will be a place to learn, too. I'm working it out in my mind."

Then it was Beal. Mahalia snatched him from Betty Lightsy: "Get your things and come on out here; I need you to go with me and help me with my program." Elliott packed and moved.

"Any of these neighbors speaking to you, Mahalia?"

"Yeah, Beal, they warmed up, some of them . . . I don't see the signs down, though."

Steve was living with her, driving for the short trips. Allen was in town, too, working for her; plenty to keep everybody busy. He'd fallen out with Alex Bradford.

One caller intrigued Elliott Beal above all. "Mayor Daley was in touch with her for a lot of things; not just to sing—political things too, to be in his corner. She didn't go into it, but I could hear some."

MAHALIA HUNG UP and dialed long distance. "Guess who called? They want me to sing for the National Democratic Convention. That's Mayor Daley got me that, that's who."

Mitch Miller was elated. "I'll come down and check on your sound." The Coliseum was by the stockyards—close to where she'd had to plead for hog hoofs for Aunt Alice's pneumonia. It was Daley's first chance to be national convention host. He wasn't happy when the delegates (knowing Adlai Stevenson was their candidate and Dwight Eisenhower was due another term) kept right on talking through his welcome. Sen. Paul Douglas didn't get any closer attention. Mrs. Franklin D. Roosevelt got more notice on one side of the hall giving an interview. Somebody said there might be a fight about the vice presidency; Sen. Jack Kennedy thought he had it, but Sen. Kefauver wanted it and he had a coonskin cap going for him.

Halie just waited. Her part came after the orators "tested their lungs," said Russell Baker of the *New York Times,* "against the oceanic roar of 4,000 disinterested and gabbling delegates." Mitch Miller used the time to check out the networks' control booths, to make sure about her sound. Hundreds of thousands of words had been said but not heard by some 20,000 people in the huge hall by the time she took the podium. Party Chairman Paul Butler rapped his gavel, asked for a moment of silence for the late Vice President Alben Barkley, and announced Miss Mahalia Jackson. It was a surprise. "Very few black artists sang at conventions," says Mitch Miller. In the Alabama delelgation, a wit piped, "I need a washerwoman," which almost provoked a fistfight from Ohio, the whole thing quashed before the hall darkened and taps sounded their lonesome requiem. Slowly, a single pink spot grew on Mahalia and she sang *I See God.* "There wasn't a sound," says Mitch Miller. "You were absolutely in a—didn't dare breathe, it was such a tremendous moment. There wasn't a dry eye in the house when she got through."

Three weeks later, their own convention in Denver talked it up and down. Elizabeth Thornton, Mahalia, Willa Jones and Mildred shared a suite, but Mahalia was so much in demand that she wasn't around when somebody introduced young Rev. Martin Luther King, Jr., to Butch Thornton. He eyed the tall beauty. "This is the lady who never remembers me." It was so, thought Elizabeth, suddenly knowing him: she was in Birmingham with Rev. C. L. Franklin when Dr. King had come from Montgomery to see him; then later he'd almost run over her in a service station. "I won't forget you again," she promised.

While Mahalia went about her Convention business—official soloist, treasurer of the Music Convention, and this still the big marketplace for gospel singers—she and Russell spent as much time together as they could. He wanted Shiloh Baptist to present her in Atlantic City, and they fixed on Dec. 1 for that. She'd be in New York before then—he figured he could be there at the same time.

The Convention watched and wondered.

THINGS HAD sure changed. A Baptist born and a Baptist bred, taken up by Holiness—well, that was a split-off—but by all the Protestants too; had sung for a rabbi, "and here the great Belafonte got me with the Catholic Bishop and the Cardinal!" She sang for the Catholic Interracial Council breakfast Sunday for Bishop Joseph Bowers of British West Africa. Next evening she was special guest as the Council, led by its president, R. Sargent Shriver, Jr., honored Samuel Cardinal Stritch of Chicago. Harry Belafonte gave her a diamond crucifix as his thanks. Never *had* a diamond before! She wore it Sunday for Carnegie Hall—her sixth—with the grandest of "narrators," Duke Ellington. On her knees for *Bless This House,* Mahalia got lost high in the spirit, the audience thrusting there with her. Oh Lord, bless my house. Keep it safe. She'd been singing it through her own rooms for days, getting as happy by herself as she was now at Carnegie Hall. Afterwards, they went up to Joe Bostic's offices to celebrate: Duke, Mahalia, Mrs. Bostic and the slender high school girl to whom she'd presented the first Mahalia Jackson Annual Award—Elizabeth Lands. Hallelujah.

Russell couldn't leave Sunday services to hear her, but he joined her mid-week and she was so glad Gwen was in from Los Angeles—Halie loved showing him off. When they could women-talk, "What you think of Russell, Gwen?"

"Sister, you got yourself something else there. He sure does dress—"

"I knew you'd notice that."

"Well, I just think he has a very beautiful personality. And you have fun together—I like that, a man who likes to joke, kid around; do you good to have somebody tease you, Miss Jackson. And you know my mother's a Loosiana woman, I got some of that blood—I like the way he looks."

"Go on, Gwen."

He came to watch her record. She was glad and she wasn't. She was going to have to take on Columbia. "Mitch, they getting into some more of these songs like *He* and *I Found the Answer*. Now I'm feeling pretty good, maybe I can wrestle with these things, get some suption out of them, but I want to get back more to my good old gospel songs. Mahalie get a weak chest on nothing but this sweetened-water stuff."

"Mahalia, you've got to believe George and I would never do anything to hurt you. I'm broadening you to reach our markets. I want to make you *available*. Everybody's been copying you, and I want to be sure *you're* the one gets completely into the public consciousness."

"Mitch, you just a great salesman, but what *I* want to sell is God. Now please let me do this one—please; this song is so much of my life."

"It just wouldn't go, Mahalia," said Avakian, standing by, hating to turn her down again. She turned to Mitch. "Just let me make this and I won't fight with you again. Not today, anyway," she added, with a droll face. They all laughed. "Please?"

Singing *God Is So Good to Me,* the tape rolling, she forgot Mitch, she forgot Columbia, she forgot everything clear back to drifting wood on the Mississippi and she thanked God as she sang. Released—"There's Mahalia again!" said her DJ friends who'd been the whole way. It didn't make great waves, but that wasn't her pattern now. "What you did, you looked at the end of the year," says Mitch Miller, "and found you'd sold a hell of a lot. And they *kept* selling all the time while others sold a lot for two or three months and then stopped. She was truly a standard artist."

Trouble was, sighed Mahalia, their standard wasn't hers.

Mitch took her to the Ed Sullivan show and stayed to make sure the sound was right for her. He *did* care. Joe Bostic was bitter. "You've got a Mitch Miller syndrome, Mahalia—John Hammond, Benny Goodman, the whole bit. Why do you think Columbia romanced you away from Apollo? Because Miller convinced them he could turn you around. They're all part of this CBS bit—where's your television show, if they think so much of you?"

She didn't have an answer. But wasn't nobody going to turn her around. Too much of that going on right now—and she'd just about had enough of *that* mess . . .

I don't know, but I've been told
Even Adam and Eve did the rock 'n roll.

"Halie," she announced, "is getting ready to fight for God."

She was primed for *Sepia*. Rock 'n roll!

Across the country, the cry was that frankly sexual rock 'n roll would create delinquency. Halie wasn't buying that; children were going to have some wild fad in each generation. What she was against was the rock 'n roll which burlesqued sacred music. "They took the church music and the church rhythms and perverted it to make money." The prospect of newcomers to black church music labeling *it* rock 'n roll was enough to make her pop her girdle. She didn't put that last part in the story.

That off her chest, she could talk to Celeste about Russell. Celeste was her bosom friend—she wouldn't tell it. "Halie's not just too sure what she might be moving into—and she's not moving into anything without a lot of praying." One mistake was bad. Two would be foolish. "Thing is, I'm wondering if he loves me or Mahalia Jackson?"

"Mahalia, you're the only one can answer that. That, and how do you *feel* about him."

At Atlantic City High School, "another eminent performance," said the *Philadelphia Independent*. Then she stayed on, for his services. They were just beautiful working in the pulpit, Mildred thought . . . a beautiful team. "When he got ready to preach, she knew just what to sing. But when he got through preaching and she got through singing, they weren't coordinated, to my way of thinking. Mahalia was a simple, down-to-earth type and Russell Roberts was not. He was a man that would live in his mind very high. And Mahalia didn't. She could fit in anywhere, but the fact that he had more education than she did was the thing that sort of—to me—would make Mahalia not live up to the great Mahalia she was. She would bend a little *too* much. Feel inferior."

In Chicago, Robert thought about it. Can't no man be *strong* enough for Mahalia, he decided—"a woman that independent, and forceful, and dynamic; a woman that self-secure. Couldn't no man equal her."

First chance, Mildred voiced her view to Mahalia. "I just don't think he's for you." Ohhh, what'd I tell her that for, Mildred asked herself when the blast died down. She bit her tongue many a day. . . .

Not on this train, though. Not this time. Say it; *out*. "At least last time we almost got killed we didn't *know* it when we got on the train. What you getting Mildred into now? Say my prayers and get ready to run."

Mahalia let her rattle on. It was nerves more than anything, she knew. *Jet, The Defender, The Courier* . . . they'd been full of the bus boycott for freedom in Montgomery, Ala., ever since a tired-out woman who'd been shopping after her day's work—Rosa Parks—told a bus driver, "I'm not getting up from this seat" when he wanted her to move back for white people. Halie knew just how she felt—her feet and her feelings. Black men, women, and children had been beaten, bombed, cursed, and jailed, but still they persevered, and when Rev. Ralph Abernathy called, she knew just who he was. The struggle had been going on almost a year, said the slow, deep voice. They needed her inspiration, and they needed funds to carry on. Desperately. Dr. King extended his invitation. "I was director of programs under Dr. King," says Dr. Abernathy, "and when we planned this week's observance—which we hoped would reinforce our people's will to continue—I insisted we have one fund-raising night to which we would invite this great gospel singer, Mahalia Jackson. Naturally, I knew her at a distance, but I had never had an opportunity to get very close to her. When I called, I told her we wanted her to lend her presence during several of our programs but I wanted one entire concert in which people would give contributions." Would she come?

"Of *course* I'll come, Reverend—I'll come for whatever service." Ar what would be her fee for the event? "I don't charge the walking people."

When she called Studs Terkel to tell him she was going, he said that was great. But be careful. "They play rough down there." On the train now, Mahalia knew she'd have to be a fool not to be afraid—and she was not a fool. On the edge of her mind were stories she'd heard of Chicago just nine years before she'd come up—the Race Riots of 1918: 34 people killed, about 100 more hurt, houses on the South Side burned and smashed, those paid back on the other side, hate built up that hadn't gone out yet. Mr. Carl Sandburg, the great Chicago writer, he had a book out on it. And all that because a black boy at the public beach swam past the spot so said was *for* black—no line but just as set—and got beat off a raft and drowned by some white boys the policeman wouldn't even arrest. She shivered. Sense flies when demons run. Aunt Duke said a lot of people even in New Orleans now had another, ugly way to them, and Aunt Duke, with her line all the way downtown to the Crackerjack Drug Store, she knew. And here Halie's taking this girl Mildred into who knows what. . . . "I wish I had nerves like you; sit there like tomorrow never come and me scared so, my fingers might shake right off the keys." Mildred making a production now, livening things up, entertaining her. . . . "No need for me to be scared, miss; you enough for two."

Finally "Montgomery!" and craning their necks in the dim lights that were no match for the dark of near midnight . . . there were the men. *Men* to meet you, situation like this.

Mahalia was unmistakable to Dr. Abernathy and—Dr. Martin Luther King. Just a boy. Look like his pictures; those eyes reaching in.

The men drove them to the one hotel available to Negroes, then went their separate ways. The work still to be done this night would be done at home.

"You put her *where?*" Mrs. Abernathy was aghast. She was upstairs checking the front bedroom to make sure Dr. Gardner Taylor hadn't left anything behind. The noted minister, one of their speakers, had left not half-hour ago when her husband came to report they'd checked Mahalia Jackson into the hotel. He had some qualms about it, but again, it was so close to the Kings' house. . . .

Juanita Abernathy stared. Men! The property was owned by a nice black family, but the owners had no control over its use; it was a "transient house," primarily. "Had she been a man—maybe a man could have adjusted to the surroundings. I had certainly never been in it, but I knew she would never get a night's sleep."

She called Mahalia. "I'm coming to pick you up and bring you out here."

"Oh! wonderful!"

There'd been no chance even to change the bed; she fixed the fresh liner while Mahalia kept her company and Mildred sat silently by. "There! Now you can get a good night's sleep." Mahalia Jackson was just as she had ex pected: very down to earth, very regular. It would be a pleasure to have her in the house.

Dr. King's parsonage and church (which served mainly black professionals and faculty from Alabama State) were downtown, directly in the vortex. So was Dr. Abernathy's church—First Baptist, where the National Baptist Convention was organized. But the Abernathy home was a mile and a half off. Still, acid eats its way. Day and night they drove slowly past: the hecklers, and worse. "That church across the street—you can see it from your bedroom window—it was bombed not too long ago," Dr. Abernathy said casually at breakfast. "They assumed it was my church, but it's Methodist."

Mildred stifled a moan.

The area was black, except for one row of white houses whose rears shared an alley to one side of the Abernathys. Immediately beyond that was huge Oak Park. Halie took careful note of that.

The next three days and nights, peace had left the land and no more so than at the Kings' house on South Jackson—phones, people, papers, packages, children, calls, calls, calls. Coretta King looked like she was holding up; slight young thing, she was one of those made out of steel—you might bend it but it won't break, and keeping her family going in this mess and confusion. Well! another meeting to run to—Halie making as many as she could, keeping her eyes and ears open, hauling Mildred through the tense streets—she wouldn't be left—just *facing* the terror out of her. Can't let her know Halie's scared. The ones here seemed not to pay it any mind. "We've learned to live with it," Dr. Abernathy explained, over dinner. That was one thing—Juanita Abernathy knew how to really cook. Halie had particularly asked for collard greens and ham hocks and cornbread today. This civil rights got you *hongry*.

Dr. Abernathy walked in with a white woman. "This lady's from Detroit, from Dr. Henry Hitt Crane's church," he announced with a pleased smile; "she was sent down to study our movement and she missed out on the food at the church." Mrs. Abernathy set another place at the table. Halie eased over to whisper, "Reverend, what you doing? Bring that white lady here! She is *not* going get Mahalia's greens. And I know Mrs. Abernathy don't have no broccoli or asparagus to fix her up."

"Oh, please, Mahalia," begged Ralph Abernathy, entering into the spirit. "Won't you give her a little greens?"

"No." Mahalia sat down to the table, kicked her shoes off, heaped her plate, got her pot likker ready for her cornbread, and piled in. The white guest confessed she'd never seen collard greens before. Mrs. Abernathy immediately got to the kitchen to fix some carrots and string beans. By the time she returned, the white woman had kicked off her shoes, left the silver, and had *her* fingers picking up cornbread, picking up greens. "Now wait a minute, madam," Mahalia said, "these are my greens and I wish you would not eat them all for me." They died; oh! it was good to laugh.

As you moved around in the day, there were barricades and the feeling there might be bullets, but none came. After lunch they went by big St John A.M.E. Church to check the piano for the concert, known as *her* night: the balm of God's gospel going overflow all wounds and a woman of the highest of their race standing before them, serving them, the first big star to join them. The place was packed out and not but midday. Mildred came to life; it was like a tonic.

Only the basement, beyond any hope of hearing, had any space that night, and it was no surprise that the church went up. Glory! Hallelujah! Sing on! Let those outside jeer and threaten. In here was God, and they believed. Intellectual Martin Luther King had come to realize the role of the testifying, the shouting, the service of feeling, of seeking not so much with your mind as with your heart for the path to the soul. Hearing Mahalia this night, he would tell her he now knew fully what gospel music meant.

Mahalia had one more word to say: "The Lord has blessed me. I was nothing and He lifted me up. But the success of one Negro doesn't mean anything if every Negro isn't completely free."

Afterwards, for once, they could all get together—the Kings, the Abernathys, Mahalia and Mildred. Mahalia had listened and looked long enough now to make her observation. Up to now, principal support had come from white liberals up north. "You got to keep this organization alive, Martin," she said earnestly, "and to do it, you got to do two things. Well, the first one you know—to raise money. But the second main one is—you got to get *black* people involved."

Martin nodded, his eyes rarely leaving her face. Theirs had been an instant empathy beyond act or word. Had any been needed—under the banter, under the courage, under the weary coursing of the current of necessity—three words of Martin's gave Mahalia the base of the man whom all week her senses had measured. "God," said Martin, "is personal."

EVEN LISTENING in the night for every car wheel can finally put you to sleep. With the light, it was time to go. As the train shrieked into motion, Mildred drew the shade, as much on the sight as the sun. "Good-bye, Montgomery!"

"Anybody think you was a little scared back there, Mildred."

(Four weeks later a bomb shattered the Abernathys' front bedroom where they'd slept. "Mahalia," Mildred wept, "I feel so hurt, just like I was there!" If she was there, Mahalia assured her, "you'd be *more* hurt.")

Home, she checked on Aunt Hannah, then she called Nettie Irving. "That Martin—well, you can't call him a young man, Nettie; he has a wisdom . . . I can't tell you. I believe he is a black Moses, come to lead his people, and I believe God's going to part the waters." To Butch Thornton, she made a confession after making Elizabeth promise never to let Mildred know: "Honeyyy, when I was down there at Ralph Abernathy's, Halie tried to figure her way out of this bombing. I slipped myself over to that open space —that park got an edge growing as a cornfield—and I sighted my way, and I said, 'Lord, let Halie make it here, and I'll stand like another stalk.'

"And Butch, I wish I *was* a stalk—a little brown shoot, then I could keep the peace and not spoil it for Jesus. What I'm talking? Child, I'm talking Dave Garroway TV, in New Orleans for Christmas."

SHE WENT 10 days early. It would nearly *take* that. First circulate house to house, almost, let Mt. Moriah know she's *Halie* still. It wasn't hard—these folks don't need a doxology. She explained she wasn't going let TV make a show out of church; what she wanted was to let the world in on a Mt. Moriah service. And she'd need lots of voices.

Annise Jackson was enthusiastic.

"Oh, yeah, *you* got to be in there, Mamá!" The tiny figure bristled on cue, and Mahalia laughed and hugged her. "Okay, Jackson. But I'm too old to be in the youth choir. Better sit me in the congregation."

Halie was staying with the Beals in their shotgun house on White St. White hotels barred Negroes, and the little black ones made her think of Montgomery. Besides, these were her friends, both swept into the project. "This woman going to kill me," Beal panted to Ida, loving it. Ida smiled and shook her head.

With the time, for once, she went down to Canal St. for some of those New Orleans clothes they didn't seem to have in Chicago. She came back empty-handed, and hungry for more than food. Mahalia Jackson could not try on a dress on Canal St., or be served a Coke. The white cabmen wouldn't take her for a fare and she wasn't going to wait on a Negro taxi. She called Ida. She had more relatives to see, trying to be peaceable, before she made the pick: That was the ticklish part. Finally, she called Brisko's wife Edna. She wanted all the kids to be on TV and could Sister —little Velma—be like Mahalia when she was a child?

When their mother gave them the news, the three girls chirped like hungry sparrows. The two boys were living with Mama Duke—they got their word there. "Oh, we were excited!" says Rose Champagne, "We jumped and we shouted." They'd sit up front with the family. "I want all the children dressed up, Edna; if you can't afford to get new clothes, I will, so start getting everything together." Glory. *Everything* new at *once!* Heaven has been made of less. "We told everybody at school," exults Rose. "We were like something special. All the kids—'You gonna be on TV?' And the grown people just flocked to the house."

They lived uptown, by Carrollton, but they knew the way to Mama Duke's, all right. On Pitt St. (all the street names in the area changed, to everlasting confusion), Mahalia was waiting early to inspect hair, nails, shoes. All right. Let's go. It was raining cats and dogs, and had been for a week. The girls had a fit; it was limping their dresses. Mahalia said that didn't matter to the TV and they'd dry, anyway, before they got on the air. Rev. Hack and his wife had helped Halie round up all the old choir and worked every night for a week, right up to the broadcast—sogging through the mud of Millaudon with the boots. Oh, Pinching Town! The television equipment was too massive to fit in the church and get the range —or have any room for a congregation—so much of that had to be satisfied on the flooded street, shooting in through the door and vestry for the long shots. Of all the mysterious men and things, the huge lights were the most exciting. Nobody had suspected they'd be so *big*. On the pulpit, Rev. A. L. Davis, Jr., and some of the other big ministers were sitting up with Rev. Hack. Mt. Moriah had never had such a visitation. All the Clark family and their extensions were ranged across the front . . . the five aunts: Duke, Bell, Bessie, Hannah, Alice; her brother Peter, Doodutz (now Isabella—she'd taken her cue from Mahalia and added the "a" to be pretty when she learned nobody'd ever registered her birth), Celie, George, Allen, Sr., Little Alice, Jack, Allen, Jr., Brisko, Uncle Porter—brought down from Cincinnati; and husbands, wives and children as they could fit. Some Jacksons were seated in the congregation; Yvonne was singing with the group—she had a good voice. Wouldn't you loved this, Daddy! Little Velma was led to a mark below the pulpit. Mahalia was up above. Beal was in the congregation with their friend Ellen Blount; they could see themselves on a TV monitor set. Her old friend Bill Russell was there, too—living in New Orleans now: Imagine him thinking to show up with a Christmas tree, all decorated, to take over to the family! She was going spend some time at Doodutz's now, spread herself out before people got hurt feelings. She had a thought for the old Chicago TV days—*those* people knew what they doing. But this was Sunday, Dec. 23, and she had this thing on her hands *now*. . . . Matters jerked forward, Mahalia tense, willing it right: false starts, extra advice, changes of equipment, wounded feelings, outsiders' ideas, New York cut in, directing—at her church! None of this live, just labor pains. Abruptly Mahalia took full charge. She was going have it *authentic*. The chorus was moved into the congregation, where they would be, singing gospel songs. "Mamá, come on up closer." . . . "Please call me Annise!" already excusing herself please; obeying . . . "Okay, Mamá!" . . . Rev. Hack had his ideas; they didn't jibe with Mahalia's. For a moment Beal thought they were going to tie in like strange bulldogs. Then it was time, or almost. The director's voice said quiet, they were going live on a national hookup. They could hear Dave Garroway. Lou Mindling said a word from up there. "That's Mahalia's manager." Quiet, please. And Mt. Moriah went to glory. *Sweet Little Jesus Boy* . . . she was wasting them, and they trying to be quiet for national TV. Then *Born in Bethlehem,* with its driving beat—and Mahalia broke up church. "That girl got loose and got *singing,*" says Celie, "and the spirit got high! Ask you be quiet, be calm, but honey, that girl was there on the *Lord's* day. Man can say but when *God* move, you just got to go where He want. How can you be still when the spirit moves you? No way in the *world* to be still. Doing the holy dance? Yes, indeed! Who would stand still when Mahalia sing? Indeed they were on their feet. I was in the number. We forgot all about the instruction 'Be quiet.' That was done away with, honey."

In Los Angeles, "That's my sister!" Johnny Jackson was excited, eyes bright, couldn't keep his seat. But not a soul would believe it was, except his own wife: Jackson just claiming, being he was from the same place.

The flood had left and Moriah stood high and near dry when they emerged in the new light of Sunday and on to Isabell's, Bill Russell carrying the Christmas tree. Mahalia felt wound like a clock, but food, family, old ties gradually slipped the knots. Next morning she washed her hair and was doing her underthings, fixing to leave, when Mr. Russell showed up. She was outdone—embarrassed. He just wanted to tell her again how wonderful she'd been, how remarkable *Silent Night* was; had everybody in church in tears. "How do you do it?" Mahalia fixed the full force of her being on him. "DON'T YOU KNOW?" she said in disgust. This man been around her all this much, and don't know her singing's from God.

Collect her things from Beal and Ida—going drive her to the station. Still uptight, Beal could see that. Step easy. She'd wanted it so right. "It *was* right, Mahalia, it was *right,*" said Ida. "Well," Mahalia subsided, "those people saw I was still just Mahalia."

"Yeah," said Beal, "in mink. You notice, Ida, Miss Jackson is in mink these days? Oh my, me. Where'd you get your mink, Mahalia? It's beautiful."

"Josephine Davis helped me pick it out. She's from here, Ida—you met her, Beal; I just came to know her one day when we both in Lytton's, shopping. She's the one got me into mink—'for my image.' " Now quick. Home to her first Christmas in her very own home. Jodie and Rev. C. L. waiting. Home to what she always wanted, nourished the thought of all the way from that first time at Mt. Moriah. . . .

SHE STARED up at the tree. Red, blue, gold, green, silver . . . the draft from the windows made the decorations dance, even the lights, like little spirits in the dim of the church. She was alone, come back as she had every day since it went up this first Christmas with Aunt Duke since her mama died. Up close close, then inch on back to get the whole thing in view with the star on top. When I get to be grown, I'm going have me a Christmas tree . . . I'm going have me a piano . . . and 'lectric lights . . . and a telephone! . . . and I'm going to have *three Christmas trees!!* She gasped with the thought. That was it. The joy was her looking at the tree. It was the most amazing thing she had ever seen in her whole entire life. *Three* Christmas trees!

She had them now, first time she'd had the right place: besides the one here inside, before she left for New Orleans she got her two up outside—one facing 84th, one on Indiana, with the three wise men, fixed like it's just empty up in the air, and you can see the stars. Then all around, the beautiful lights. People were coming around to see, and she hadn't stopped singing since she'd hit home. . . .

Long time ago in Bethlehem, So the Holy Bible say—

Now how could people kick up such a fuss about that? How could anybody think that was sacrilegious, actually bar Harry Belafonte's record from the air two Christmases ago . . . 'course hers was slow and solemn, not like his calypso. She finished dressing with care. Can't look just any way going to a party with Rev. C. L.—man has 35 suits. Harry be there; she hope he like the way she did his song, but she *knew* there was no hard feelings. What Ed Clayton helped her write up to answer those critical people come off all right; she liked the way that boy wrote. Wouldn't the *Courier* be surprised to know the editor of *Jet* wrote a piece for them? Ed's boss, too. Well, they all nice down there at *Jet* and *Ebony*. They all loved her. That's the tiniest little girl Ed brought, like a pretty doll.

XERNONA STRETCHED all 4 feet 11 inches of her to look up at Mahalia. She just hadn't expected the star to answer her own door. "I was only two years out of college but I was dating Ed, so I'd met my share of celebrities; I wasn't in awe of them when Ed called—we had a dinner date—and said he had to go out there; she'd asked him to come write some sort of statement for the press, something she wanted his advice and help with. I was a member of Rev. Joe Branham's church and they were very good friends, personal friends—she'd given him a fund-raising concert—so I was impressed by what I knew of her; but also I had convinced myself that she may or may not be friendly. . . ."

Mahalia's long, loose garment rippled colors around her ample frame as she swung the door wide with a smile to match. "What's a little girl like you doing with a big guy like this? How tall you, Ed—6 feet 4! He will just sit on you and *crush* you!" She led them into her bedroom and overwhelmed Xernona by piling onto the bed as if they were family. The house was warm and snug. "Babe, you know I had to call on my boy," she said, patting Ed; "and don't worry about your dinner—I cooked something Creole for you all."

She told Ed of this fuss about her song—was Mahalia Jackson sacrilegious—and they discussed that a little, then she came to it: She had to make a statement involving Dawson—asking her position in a big political fight—and Ed would know how to do; she didn't want her meaning being twisted around. The two heads bent together. "Now, Mahalia, I think this ought to be—" They shifted to the kitchen so Ed could use the typewriter. He'd work up two statements for her—one for the white press, one for the black. "I like Ed 'cause he's got such a good mind and it's a double mind—talks the white folks' way and the colored folks' way," Mahalia said to Xernona, keeping her company, talking all the while Ed was typing—and he liked quiet. Next time he hushed her, Xernona was going to bring that up—"You don't let me talk and Mahalia can talk." (Ed had his answer: "I just kind of block her out.") When Ed whipped out the second draft and she got a look, her teacher's mind noted that the main difference was putting in some *ain'ts* for the blacks. Oh, well. Mahalia broke off to answer the telephone. Some politician, wanting an opinion. Xernona knew from Ed that Mahalia was a strong political force. "Not as far as the public knew—she was quiet about it; but the politicians knew, because they called her. And Mayor Daley just absolutely loved her." Mahalia said, "Later—" into the telephone—and again, "Later—" then picked up her sentence to Xernona. "—and Babe," she said, "now I want you come see me, hear? You don't have to wait on this big guy."

The two were firmly threaded into Mahalia's life. Sometimes they came for gumbo, or just stopped. "But sometimes she'd call up just to talk: to Ed, or to me; she was just lonesome."

I can't go to church and shout on Sunday,
Go out and get drunk and raise Cain on Monday,
I'm going to live the life I sing about in my—

Halie broke off from cleaning up after the latest lackadaisy of her revolving household help. She was trying. God, You know I'm trying; but Halie gets lonesome here, too. She had Russell on her mind—*there's* one going live the life he preach about. Question is, can we live in each *other's* life? Which? . . . How about when the star-dust dropped? Halie went back to digging out the left-in wax from the cracks. Wait on God's time.

32

In Hollywood, Dinah Shore had been begging. So had Bob Banner, her producer, who was from Texas. They couldn't get an okay to schedule any black performers.

"All right, we'll make it easy for you, with Mahalia Jackson, this great human being; this lady has the pipeline to God, you know; she is perfection itself."

"We both wanted Mahalia Jackson more than anybody," says Dinah Shore. "I wanted her because I liked her, and because it would be a milestone for me to do a program with Mahalia—I thought it might just lay one little brick in the cornerstone of television. I thought it was *terribly* important at that point." Finally, the okay. Grudging, all the way, but okay.

Walking into the studio with Mildred, Mahalia had no qualms. They'd never met; she'd never worked with a woman star before; but she'd seen Dinah Shore on TV.

She was not really prepared for what occurred. Neither was Dinah. "It was an experience—it was a happening," says the blonde star. Greeting, they looked so different—she slight, blonde, youthful; Mahalia brown, ageless, well over her 200 "singing weight." But one thing matched—their smiles. And their vibrations. Those were right—oh, they were right. Now to put a show together.

It wasn't easy. First, Mahalia vetoed the orchestrations. "We had brass in there, and Mahalia said, 'No, no, no, I can't sing with brass; that is not the spiritual quality.' She was very particular about how we orchestrated the songs we did together, because brass was not part of the church. Drums could be, any rhythm could be, violins could be, but to her brass just wasn't genuine and she didn't allow it. And she was right."

Next, Hollywood studio musicians met their first gospel fist, and it threw them. "That one hand of Mildred's was the strongest thing in the whole world. My musicians had never heard *anything* like this. I had, from the time I was a child—if you slip in and listen to a Baptist revival meeting, then you've heard this piano with the one strong hand, and we ribbed the people on our show: 'Mildred's got a left hand, that's what your problem is.' So Mildred plays with *that,* and the foot was stomping . . . and it was an entirely different beat."

That brought on rockets and conflagration: a Mahalia Jackson eruption on the head of a Mildred unaccountably careless with the sudden notoriety. The burst was over as suddenly as a flash flood—Dinah, the whole set, standing by. "I respected her for it. What she demanded from the people around her was the kind of perfection she exacted from herself, and the dedication. She couldn't tolerate ineptitude or carelessness, or somebody who wasn't giving his full measure."

They got back to work. "I've gotta hear this," Dinah said; "I've gotta do it by ear, or they're going to have to teach me my part on the piano."

"Darling, you too?"

"It's a kind of a deliberate, negative snobbism, I suppose," says Dinah Shore thoughtfully, "but I was afraid that if I learned too much about music, I wouldn't be free as I wanted to be—that's what I felt at the time. I knew too many singers who'd come out of choruses who could read parts, and I envied them, but if you're stuck to that piece of paper and you remember the relation of those notes, you're not going to listen as carefully to the chord. Mahalia had this natural thing from childhood, just hearing a gospel song from the time she was yea big, letting her soul and mind lead her away from whatever she had done in her last performance. Both of us took great pride in never doing anything twice the same. Which drove arrangers up the walls.

"Pinning it down *exactly,* you might have technical perfection, but then there was the chance you might not reach the heights you would if you ad libbed a little. It drove the control room up the wall, too, but it was kind of exciting."

He's Got the Whole World in His Hands was all Mahalia's on the air —and she was theirs. Delighted, they watched as a pulsating exaltation gripped her so that she shifted tempo, felt it differently than they'd rehearsed it, Mildred instantly sensing what she wanted and giving it to her, leaving the rhythm section—custodians of the tempo—to follow. "Mildred was stronger than all of them!" says Dinah Shore. "The drums had to come back down with her. And they loved it."

Cue cards moved Dinah into a discussion of the blues, which she'd sung from a child—white blues. "I was talking to Mahalia about it, and I said, 'Well, there's blues in the gospel; you sing the blues in—' 'No, I *don't.* I sing the *gospel;* the gospel of people standing in an open field, thinking of the Lord, praying to the Lord for something beautiful—the blues is a person standing alone in a deep pit crying for help.' And I suddenly thought about it: the blues are exactly what they say they are, although both are based on the 12-bar phrase—underneath, most of them go in the same direction. She was absolutely right, the content and context of the lyrics . . . you can get just as much excitement in the blues but it's blues of necessity. The only way it's ever light is if there's humor in it, whereas gospel is always happy, and 'up.' The blues of necessity must be 'down' in lyric content. And I was amazed—I had never thought about it that way . . . and that was Mahalia's philosophy of life; we got it that night. And that was a revelation."

They moved together for *Down by the Riverside,* and what had been electric was incandescent. They gloried in the song and they reveled in each other. They generated a voltage that reached through the tubes of the nation . . . and sent thousands to their telephones and pens. It seemed to CBS as if the *world* was thrilled. "They were as thrilled in New Orleans and Houston as they were in New York or Kansas City, or wherever it was. Dignity and integrity and a sense of honor that was incorruptible about herself and her work, they were all there with this great talent and the world saw it. Strangely enough, that first show was many, many years ago, and all the incredible shows we did in the years of that whole series, the one that people single out to talk about today is that one we did with Mahalia."

But was she wholly incorruptible? On the heels of the show, a telegram came from Las Vegas: Singing her own material, they'd pay her $25,000 a week. It was a startling, shocking sum. Five years earlier, Danny Thomas had made entertainment history at $10,000. Now, $25,000 to a black woman to sing the gospel in a club! She stared at the telegram. The telephone rang. Las Vegas. If Miss Jackson had objections to whiskey being served while she sang, there would be none served, or orders taken, while she was on.

Not since *The Hot Mikado* had she been tempted but she was tempted now. Through a long night, she wrestled. Lord? Lord? And rose to say no. "The Devil don't ever sleep, honey," she'd say of that night; "he'll keep prodding and pinching and twisting you—he figures to catch you one day, some way."

Not this day, this way.

Home, she carefully positioned the framed 8x10 picture of Dinah on top her dresser. She could see it first thing, and last. She smiled. That is the realest person I know. She told her good-bye when she flew to New York. It was a busy time in New York—the tug and pull of recording, make the rounds of DJs, talk with Joe Bostic, take time for Duke's sister Ruth's luncheon party: Louise and Mildred's first look at a plush Riverside Dr. apartment, Al Duckett squiring them . . . and now go be analyzed again, up at Hunter's College for Negro History Week.

Not to be late, this being Marshall Stearns' college, she got there an hour early. Men were just setting up. She pulled up a chair in the hall. Coming from the prop room, two stagehands passed, talking: "What's going on in here tonight?" . . . "They got some kind of a gospel singer supposed to be—" . . . "Gospel singer?" . . . "Yeah. These folks tried the psychiatrists, they done tried everything; maybe they going to try her. . . ." People were beginning to fill the halls—rich people, poor people, college people. How many here from curiosity? or call it jazz? She wasn't sure even Mr. Stearns understood—in his new book he gave her, kept talking "blue tonality," not finding the heart of the thing, that gospel is the *message*. He loved her, though. Best she heard, what he put about that Sanctified he went with her to upstate, where the woman said, "That Mahalie, she add more flowers and feathers than anybody, and they all exactly right." Ha! no professor got the thing of her that good. She didn't want this business to stretch too long tonight, having to take the train to Atlantic City so early, be with Russell for his services; then make it on home—Martin King going stop over, talk to some people . . . *surely* got to cook that man something with some suption, give him bodily strength to carry on. Then—hm, get Polly to check; she believe that's—

"Mahalia! what are you doing back off here? We've been looking for you." Langston Hughes gave her a tight hug. He was going to be on the program too. Maybe between the both of them, they could get something over.

JOHN SELLERS sat right up from the bed. "You do?" John was staying with Aunt Hannah while he played The Blue Note, where Studs Terkel got him in—getting him everywhere, now John had made a success in Europe. "You *do?*"

"Yeah. I believe I finally got me a man, John. I really love him."

"You told him?" Yeah. "You going to marry him?" Mahalia pushed up her lower lip and fell silent. "I don't know. That's a big step."

She wondered if wrestling with this thing was affecting her health, had anything to do with this shortness of breath. She was going see Dr. Barclay about that. . . .

Dr. Barclay was worried and trying not to show it, but she picked up on his vibrations. She dimpled at him. "Well, you sure can't turn me over your knee and whip me, big as I am." In spite of himself, the physician laughed back. How was he going to save her? "Shortness of breath meant her sarcoid was not completely burned out—was active again in her lungs. That was one of my worst fears. When sarcoid becomes far advanced in the lung, it can make a person a total cripple—confined to a wheelchair. So I gave her rather large doses of prednisone—cortisone—trying to prevent damage to the lung." But she'd have to seriously curb her appetite.

"Now, Dr. Barclay, you don't want me to serve you rabbit food for dinner, do you? I don't think your wife would appreciate that."

"Mahalia, you've got to take this *seriously*."

"She and I constantly battled to try and get her to cut her food down, cut her weight down," says Dr. Barclay. "She also had a psychological problem here: 'If I lose all you want me to lose, people won't think I'm Mahalia Jackson—and *I* won't think I'm Mahalia Jackson.' She associated a lot of weight and good appetite with good health. I had a very difficult time through those years," sighs Dr. Barclay. "As I kept boosting the steroids up to very high levels, her appetite made her gain an enormous amount of weight. The weight made her short of breath; sarcoid in the lung made her short of breath. We spent a lot of time arguing—me encouraging her sometimes and scolding her other times."

"Dr. Barclay, will you please call my lawyers right now and tell them what's wrong with me—tell them I can't do *all* these things people want me to do?"

William Barclay had never had a patient like her. "All right, Mahalia. I'll call them." Already dialing. Aldus Mitchell listened, nodded and hung up. "Mahalia has this problem that's not going to go away, but still it's no danger to her life or anything of that sort. She's just a little short of breath." Chauncey Eskridge and the others—foot troops in Bob Ming's growing legal regiment—turned back to their work. Nothing serious.

Dr. Barclay tried to look severe to his favorite—and most exasperating—patient. "Now Mahalia, remember: *try* not to exhaust yourself in Washington. Let them turn up the microphones."

33

May 17, 1957: high noon of the Prayer Pilgrimage for Freedom at Lincoln Memorial, Washington, D.C. So much was its religious character emphasized that the people tight-packed to Reflection Pool were asked not to applaud *any* of the 14 speakers or the one soloist, Mahalia Jackson. The litany that surged across the brown sealike surf, capped by the booming sonorities, asked little—and all: That men, "without wrath and malice" beseech God "so to turn the hearts of men toward each other that inequalities and injustices may disappear and the spirit of brotherhood may dwell among us." To "arouse the conscience of the leaders of our country."

He was the 14th speaker, but when Asa Randolph said "—Dr. Martin Luther King, Jr.," 35,000 people came alive, thousands upon thousands of white handkerchiefs and programs rippled. He didn't fail them. In this first national speech, he lashed betrayal by government—sparing neither party—and sounded four words which would shift American history: *"Give us the ballot—"* again and again, the brown waves lapping back "Amen" . . . "Amen" . . . a prayer and a joyful song inside Mahalia. She looked around. Not an ear was strayed. There was affirmation, pledge, benediction; but Martin had been doxology. Louise was finally able to reach her as the cluster of friends thinned. "They cried when you sang *I Been 'Buked,* Mahalia."

"I cried some myself. Where's Mildred?" No chance now to visit with Martin and Coretta. "Find her. We got to go to New York."

The expanse of faces night after next was well-groomed, well-fed, white: New York's Town Hall. She sighed. They had her on with a opera star —Martial Singher. Well, Lord, Halie'll see if she can reach them . . . *The Good You Do Comes Back to You* . . . do they take my message? They took something. The *New York Post* next day said, "She weds a blues technique to religious songs"; but Nat Hentoff wrote for *The Reporter,* "She had a strange effect on the secularists present. Most of them were amazed at the length of time after the concert during which the sound of her voice remained active in the mind." He was a nice man, this one interviewing her "in depth," but she loosed some low-lying irritation . . . "I've come up under this in the last few years . . . everything has to be *analyzed;* makes me conscious of what I'm doing." But she tried to help him understand, then Joe Bostic took over, giving *his* explanation of slavery-spiritual and freedom-jubilee. Well, that was close enough for the book.

Afterwards, Joe came on up and they talked. "She tried again to 'do something' for me and I told her no. 'You just too cocky and independent.' No, I told her; 'I have a career, I don't need your largesse.' "

Bostic's words were in her mind while she waited for Russell to arrive. Some men were strong enough that they didn't *want* a woman's—what he say?—largesse. When Russell came and her heart thumped at the sight of him and once again he asked the question, she said yes. "But don't let's tell it 'til we ready." He agreed. There were some basic decisions to make. Where they would live, for one thing. "Some preachers hold two pulpits and commute," said Mahalia. "A singer can live anywhere," said Russell.

At the Sunday School Congress in June, they didn't settle anything, but "Let's go up to Massachusetts first chance," said Halie; "I want to meet your folks."

That chance wasn't now. She had a lot of road to run, summers. At least she wasn't short of breath. Thank You Lord. And Dr. Barclay.

GOOD THING she *did* have all her breath and her weight too, coming up against this. What had Joe Bostic got her mixed up with?

Newport Jazz Festival, 1957. John Hammond had come to Bostic to get together Newport's introduction to gospel with Mahalia as the essential ingredient: the festival prided itself as a forum for only the best. It was Hammond's idea. But a whole afternoon of gospel for sophisticated jazz fans?

First Joe had to convince Mahalia. She was uneasy about how it would look—Mahalia Jackson associating with a jazz festival. Still, she couldn't not. It was a relief to get a letter from a Newport church: Would she come worship with them? Rev. Canon Lockett Ford Ballard, rector of Trinity Episcopal, was pleased to announce that Mahalia Jackson would sing for his Sunday morning services. The Festival was aghast. They were going out on a limb to pay 40-odd gospel people for a new direction—and one of the main attractions was giving it away. First!

"Listen," said Mahalia sternly when she heard, "when you stop singing free in church on Sunday, you not a real gospel singer any more."

She registered into the Viking. She'd missed Louie Armstrong, Ella Fitzgerald, Kid Ory . . . but Doc Hayakawa was there! Hadn't seen him since he went to Frisco to teach. And just a whole gang of musicians. First time she'd been around this much live jazz since they battled bands back home. Some sound good. But some this modern stuff sound like lost little children . . . in New Orleans when they played jazz, the horns *spoke* the music. Behind a bandstand, she found a tent set up for performers. Not too far from revival, one way—and all the way, in another. Seem like a nice thing, though; everybody enjoying themselves and no whiskey bottles she could *see*. She sniffed. "What's that smell?"

"Just grass, Mahalia."

"It sure ain't *pepper* grass." Jesus! if Aunt Duke ever heard such a thing as this, she'd believe her worst fears for Halie had come to be.

"COME ON, everybody, *relax*—and look natural!" coaxed producer George Wein. The photographer had given up. The whole gospel company was massed for pictures in the tent—no room for them all on stage with piano, organ, and sound equipment for *Voice of America* and NBC Radio. Mama Ward and Clara looked rigid, Wein decided; the others, various degrees of uncomfortable . . . all except Mahalia: beaming, easy, right in the middle of the glum. Suddenly Mahalia caroled, "Mother Ward, do you still owe me any money?"

The group cracked up. Out! The photographer got a great picture. "Mahalia," says George Wein, "knew just what she was doing."

Joe Bostic figured Newport people weren't any different from other people and lined up his program accordingly—except for delivering a cram course in gospel. Then in turn he loosed the Ward Singers, with Marion Williams; the Drinkard Singers; the Back Home Choir, 35 strong . . . and then came Mahalia.

It was like leftover lightning. "Mary Lou Williams, one of the most renowned contemporary jazz pianists, came up to me at one point while Mahalia was singing," says Bostic, "and said, 'That goddam woman makes cold chills run up and down my spine.' "

There would be analysis and rapturous rave ("She sang 13 and she could have sung 113," wrote one) but Mary Lou Williams had said it all.

Music Barn after that seemed pretty tame except for the joy of reunion with Step'anie Barber, her pretty blonde friend she hadn't seen since Music Inn '51 . . . that, and watching Elliott Beal take all this in. The company, Beal decided, fully made up for not getting up in time for Newport: all the men in dress clothes—he was himself; the women elegant in formals and furs. This was the first time he'd seen a live dowager holding pince-nez; *that* was something to tell Ida and Doodutz and them. Surveying the grandeur of the reception scene, Beal appointed himself Mahalia's tutor on social protocol. Before their performance, he peeked out—he was playing organ to Mildred's piano—and came back with the ultimate: "Mahalia, there are *tails* out there!"

"I don't care if they's monkeys out there; somebody help me pull up this girdle."

THERE WAS NOBODY to pull up her image but herself, when she saw the *Downbeat* poll. It named her one of the top four jazz vocalists, along with Ella Fitzgerald, Billie Holiday, and Sarah Vaughan. "Jazz! They're beginning to analyze me in a way I don't like!" she roared. "I don't want but one vote and that's from Jesus."

"Now Mahalia," said Mindling, "that won't hurt your rating in Europe at all." She eyed him soberly. "You really going get that thing together?"

"Are you kidding? With what you've got going for you now, it's like shooting fish in a barrel."

"It ain't *fish* I want. And remember—you going end me up at the Holy Land."

That night when Grand Central Station had finally emptied, she lay meditating—and suddenly sat bolt upright. That was just a *great* idea. Thank You Lord. Wait 'til she told Russell!

She swung through the tight-packed schedule of her first big Los Angeles public concert with a buoyance that even Louise Weaver was hard put to match—excited as *she* was: her first trip to California. In between meetings with organizing committees and the promotion rounds, Mahalia and Louise tramped the streets shopping. Mahalia was looking for new curtains and draperies for Aunt Duke, and she was particular. "You sure love your Auntie," Louise said, "the way you're always buying her things."

"She was all the mother I had, growing up."

When the reporters interviewed her at the Statler-Hilton—no hotel problem here—of the three things foremost in her mind, she told them two: that she was planning a tour of Europe beginning in late October—the first since illness caused her to break off in 1952; and she was planning to build an evangelistic temple in Chicago where youth could be taught gospel music.

Her sponsor, Rev. A. A. Peters' Victory Baptist Church, had four other churches lending support. J. Earle Hines was working with 500 voices. Doris Akers—composer, singer, friend—was helping too. Los Angeles knew Mahalia was there, all right: so many poured into Shrine Auditorium that the singing guests (a standard gospel courtesy) had to be moved up on stage. There'd never been a gospel event to match it on the West Coast, and afterward, Dale Evans and Roy Rogers took them to evening religious services in a Hollywood friend's home. ("They have that in Hollywood," Mahalia explained to Louise.)

"Well," Louise said brightly to Mahalia as they left, "now we've got our spiritual food for this week to go on."

"Baby, we better get something else solid to go on, too—'scuse me, Lord, but we got to catch the train."

Squeeze the City Council's citation into a suitcase—stuff soaked up space like milk on oatmeal; send Louise to see for Mildred; count the combined luggage on the sidewalk and on the train platform—Louise, see what you count—supervise it all aboard and pay off the three porters who'd vied to serve her—and she could settle in her seat for the ride upstate. Two more dates, then Convention. She couldn't wait to tell Russell to his face.

Sacramento . . . Richmond . . . backstage—fiddling with her hair, singing softly to herself—she broke off, her jaw dropped at the very name. "Here?" Paul Robeson, the man she revered for his voice. ("I don't know nothing about his politics, except he is seeking to better our people")—this great man was taking his time to come hear Mahalia Jackson. Afterwards he came back to praise her, and said he was starting to rebuild his career, broken in the bitter Senate investigations when he left America rather than submit. She went back to Chicago with his picture, and put it up alongside Marian Anderson and Liberace. Studs Terkel heartily approved her latest—but he couldn't resist. The incongruity of it. "You don't really like *Liberace,* do you?"

"Yes, I do. His fingers are like little silver fish."

Now Louisville. She hadn't so looked forward to Baptist Convention since they made her official soloist. Russell was waiting. They weren't admitting anything, but Elizabeth Thornton's mother, 72, had no doubts. "I don't blame Mahalia," she told Butch with a glint; "that sure is a *sharp* preacher; that Russell Roberts is all right." Rev. Ralph Abernathy couldn't believe they were serious. To him, they were not a match—like a shirt matches a tie; they were not. Roberts was just too—pretty-boy. Didn't even show his age. First chance the pair had at privacy, when they could really be alone for more than one minute, Mahalia told him: Make the European tour their honeymoon! There's this great boat she missed—the *United States*—they could go on that; or they could fly—she wouldn't be afraid crossing the water if he was with her. Russell was delighted. He'd begin to fix his calendar.

"Russell, wait 'til you see how they treat us over there—like kings and queens."

Anybody would have to be fool not to be excited about Europe; it didn't mean he was starstruck, like some said. What did other people know what was inside a man? or a woman?

ELIZABETH'S VOICE was all a-whisper. Russell Roberts had just phoned her—no! he wasn't there; she didn't *have* to whisper—Russell asked her if she wanted to meet Ava Gardner; Ava Gardner was coming in that night to see him but don't tell Mahalia.

"Oh, Butch! don't believe Russell. He wanted you to tell me that."

"He does carry that little clipping around in his wallet."

That man. He know everything he say, Butch coming right and tell me. That's like Clara Ward—John say she's crazy about him, but Russell's not studying her . . . that's some more for me. He's letting me know I might have more money, but he's got something too. They'd make a good team. Big tease.

"Miss Jackson, there's one thing we didn't clear up: we *will* get married before we sail? Otherwise, I—"

"Yes, Reverend, we'll be married. We better! before the —"

Honeymoon. It had a nice sound. She'd never had one.

34

Halie hung up slowly. Polly had hardly finished unpacking her from Convention—and this. Mr. Mindling had been loud and clear. And to tell the truth, she was excited about it herself. She was such a big fan—and thanks to God, television had come for her to enjoy them even respecting her vow for Papa. Lou Mindling was right. It was important to her career and it was the one thing of all of it that *couldn't* wait on her.

Reluctantly she dialed. "Russell, baby, we going have to put off the honeymoon—I got to go to Hollywood and make a movie. It's just a while." She called Kup at the *Sun-Times*. She called Ed Clayton at *Jet*. Might as well get it all over with. "Yeah, with Nat King Cole—*St. Louis Blues*—but don't go say I'm singing the blues! I'm a missionary. Yeah, I got to postpone my trip to Europe; that was going to be my honeymoon . . . yeah, you can say that."

"Her romance with the Rev. Russell Roberts of Atlantic City," wrote Irv Kupcinet, "continues to blaze."

Well. Get ready to go downtown. Some more VIPs Mayor Daley want her to greet. He put her in all that now. "The mayor knew, and I knew," says Col. Jack O'Reilly, in charge of special events, "that with her voice and her sincerity, and above all, *Mahalia,* anyone who heard her would necessarily be terribly impressed. So we asked her whenever any important people came, and there were many—heads of state and so forth."

Cylestine better check her train tickets. William Morris had her on a big CBS-TV spectacular. They did know television. Maybe—

CBS was calling. Funny how it comes at once. Not the network; her old friends at Channel 2. How about getting together on her show again? She'd see. "Got to talk to my agent these days, you know," making it puffed-up, important. She knew they'd laugh.

Mr. Mindling said the DuPont Show people wanted a date too . . . and Steve Allen; and Perry Como—she just loved that man's voice; like warm water on a troubled mind. . . .

AND NOW she was in the movies. The biggest difference she could see from TV was they did a lot more talking before they did anything. That was all right with her. The company couldn't have been better . . . Pearl Bailey, Eartha Kitt, Ella Fitzgerald, Cab Calloway, Ruby Dee, Juano Fernandez—and plenty who weren't names but *so* nice. Nat was a sweet boy . . . and Pearl Bailey! She was already like a sister.

It was Mahalia's first try at acting. "But don't," urged Allen Reisner, the director; "just be Mahalia—aren't you a missionary?" All she really had to do was sing some hymns—including W. C. Handy's own; most people didn't know he'd written any—give a sermon, and sweep the porch. That was about it. No trouble except for one thing: She couldn't laugh when they said, "Laugh." Or what came out wasn't *Mahalia*'s laugh. Finally, Nat called on his secret weapon. "Get Pearl Bailey." Cued, Pearl sashayed over—eyes rolling, words drawling, a hog-jowl accent dripping. "What do you all mean, you can't laugh? Come on, Mahalia, and"—deep in her bass—*"get with it, girl!"*

Mahalia cracked up.

AROUND TAKES, she did a guest spot for Nat on his network show—the first Negro to get one, even sustaining; she sang in San Diego, Palm Springs, San Francisco. But mostly she sang in Los Angeles. That was where Charlie Chaplin came. Charlie Chaplin! It was like she'd touched a bubble and it didn't pop.

Cal Lampley sent some new music from Columbia, said to see if she liked any so he could record her when she got back East. *That* was different. 'Course he didn't know nothing about gospel. But it was nice, what he said: "I am sure you are making a big hit with everyone, just as you always do." He didn't have to say that. "Things are changing around Columbia," she told Gwen Cooper and Dorothy Simmons—not neglecting her own just because she had all this new. "Columbia is a company just naturally *drives* you; it makes young men old. They got to be with them old drunken artists at night—nightclubbing, and then liquor in to record . . . no wonder they get old. George Avakian going into leukemia, I think; he gone, I got this new A&R man. And Mitch Miller, you can't hardly see him." She'd see what was what when she got East. *Something* going on.

She did another Dinah show: icing on the cream puff. They had themselves a ball. Only thing, Mildred showed up with a splint on one finger—to play on network TV! Mahalia was embarrassed. Mildred said she'd fallen out of the upper berth when she came back from visiting her friends. Mahalia had her thoughts about that, but could be, could be; got to be fair to the girl. Still and yet, there she was, pounding with that splint! God, I guess you give me a hairshirt; don't want to let my head get turned.

In the breaks, she and Dinah talked cooking and the South, two subjects neither readily exhausted. Dinah couldn't get over her. "There's nothing so enlightened as an enlightened Southerner, and Mahalia was one. As for me, when you're young, that's the way things are. Then there comes a day when you have to examine the rules and you say hey! that's wrong; people are not different, and they shouldn't be treated that way.

"With this ability of Mahalia's to forget, and the inability to hate, there we were, sitting up there both loving the South. We both agreed we felt hate and resentment are shriveling. Mahalia just couldn't be shriveled. She was too big for that."

"Now don't be talking about my size, darling," drawled Halie, giving her a hug. *Love* this woman.

Before she left Hollywood, she did one more thing: She gave Johnny Jackson some front.

He hadn't been to any of her Los Angeles programs. And she hadn't seen him. When her daddy had been living, when she stopped over in New Orleans he'd always ask, "When you get to California, see Johnny."

Then, Mahalia get back home, says Johnny Jackson, "—no, she hadn't seen me. So this time, in 1957, Mahalia was at a party where Bessie Griffin was. Bessie's from New Orleans and that put Mahalia in mind of me. She asked did Bessie know me. 'No, but one of the girls in my group says her husband says Johnny's his good friend.' So they passed the word along. 'Boy, your sister's in town.' . . . 'Yeah, I saw her on the Earl Grant Show.' . . . 'She says call her.' So she said come to the motel where she's staying—on West Washington right off LaBrea."

"Did you see my name going to be at these various programs?" Mahalia asked a somewhat uneasy Johnny. "Why don't you ever come back? What did I do to you?"

"Nothing."

"Then why you never show up?"

"Because I got two families—two kids in New Orleans, paying alimony for them; two kids here. I have enough money to take care of my end, but I don't have enough money to keep my front. Knowing that I have done nothing to help you reach the stage that you have reached, I thought I would do my little bit by staying away and not embarrassing you."

Mahalia turned to Mildred. "What day do we have an off day?" To Johnny, "What day can you come?"

"Every day, because I work at night."

Mahalia took Johnny shopping. Tip to toe. He filled out before her eyes. "Now when I come to town, I guess you can come up." Johnny nodded, speechless. "I don't know if it be this trip, but next trip, I'm going come over and see your family."

Mahalia had found her brother.

She was sorry for it to end, but eager to pick up . . . get with Russell—they'd just talked, this whole while; she missed that man! . . . see about the new Europe tour be their honeymoon: *nothing* going put it off again . . . and she was so looking forward to seeing Martin. He was making speeches from one end of the land to the other. They were both due at Orchestra Hall—which, in Chicago, certified "important"—on Nettie Irving's panel for the United Negro College Fund.

When Mahalia started to mount the steps to the stage, Martin saw her, leaped up, and rushed to meet her. "It was almost electrifying," says Nettie. "He ran, and she ran, and they met with a huge hug and a kiss. That night, there didn't need to be but two people on that stage—Martin to speak, and

Mahalia to sing: how they longed for her to sing. But no—she spoke; she had come for the cause."

Martin came to the house next day, and Mahalia called Bob Miller: "Martin and Abernathy over here and there ain't nobody to talk to them. Bring a couple of men with you to talk to them while I fix them something to eat."

Martin had talked with Vice President Nixon this June; he was working on Negro voter registration; he and Coretta had been to Ghana for its independence celebration as the new government's guests; his book on nonviolence and justice was due out this September. All this to talk—yet Bob Miller found him the most eager questioner of the group: about conditions in Chicago. "You'll just have to come back, there isn't enough time to tell it all," said Bob Miller, won over.

IF THE PANEL had missed Mahalia's singing, Nettie Irving got to hear next Sunday at young Rev. Joe Campbell's church. Midway, Mahalia broke loose—rapt in the holy dance, up and down the aisles. So gone did Mahalia seem that Nettie began to worry for her, tried to stay close in case she went. Dancing, Mahalia centered an instant in the aisle beside a woman who called, "I know you sure are glad to be back home in church, Mahalie, 'stead of going all around among those white folks." Then catching sight of light-skinned Nettie—"Oh! I'm sorry!"

"Honey, I'm black too," said Nettie. Mahalia collapsed—with laughter.

"But I *wish* I could do that holy dance just the way I want it. I never have yet. But it's in there."

Hearing Mahalia, on the panel, prod the rest by telling how she was supporting education on her own, Nettie'd had an idea. She explained it now: a Mahalia Jackson Foundation. "You let the fund hand your money out; then there'll be more money for the students and less to taxes."

"Now why didn't Chauncey Eskridge ever tell me that?" Mahalia asked indignantly.

"Maybe he thought you wouldn't want anybody else having a say on your money." Mahalia drew in a little. "How much say?"

It would take three years' jockeying before the Mahalia Jackson Foundation was chartered with a board, extensive "advisers," and among the officers a treasurer, Bob Miller. But only Mahalia could sign the checks. "That way I *know* who's getting the money."

But who was getting the business? At Columbia studios, Mahalia looked and listened. There was a new president, Clive Davis. Look like he'd given some new orders.

He had. Engrossed with the rock scene, he'd ordered full emphasis on that. Mitch Miller had little time for Mahalia. He knew that mattered. "Mahalia was—odd. If you didn't completely love her—your mind could have been some place else—she'd want to know what was wrong." But he couldn't keep her. And Cal Lampley was temporary. She was actually going to Irv Townsend. . . .

Mahalia looked at the pale, slender, sensitive young face. He was really beautiful. She had good vibrations about him, and he sounded like *he'd* been thinking about her.

"I feel you should do—and can be doing—the kind of things that are closest to you, Mahalia; that you know best, and love, and have grown up with." Ohhhh, good. "For one thing, I want to record you live at Newport this next summer—last summer was fantastic."

She was the first gospel singer Irving Townsend had ever dealt with, but he was confident he knew how to handle her.

THE PRESENT from Nat King Cole came just when she needed the lift. Her first color TV, in a beautiful walnut cabinet. That's a sweet boy. She called to tell Russell. He was sick again, they said, but he came to the phone. No, it wasn't anything much; he'd throw it off . . . yes, if he didn't, all right, he'd see a doctor, just to please her.

"You *better* hurry up and get strong, if you going to carry me across the stoop."

"I may have to pass."

"If Harry Belafonte can pick me up, Reverend, *you* can pick me up. You better put on those sparring trunks."

Christmas had a hole in it. Even with Mary and Joseph and Jesus. In the coming and going, Celeste got her to one side. "Mahalia, I'm picking you up for the after-Christmas sales. I'll bet you haven't done a thing about you-know-what" (miming trousseau lingerie).

Halie tried to make a joke about getting her man first but it stuck in her throat. She began softly to sing.

35

Yeahhhh, this was going to work out fine, her and Townsend. Great God Almighty, here's a Columbia man wants her to have her say. John Hammond was a Columbia executive himself now, and he spelled it out for the record-liner notes: "To make great records with Mahalia, it is necessary for her to be in complete musical charge of the sessions. She has to believe in the message . . . feel the sincerity of the accompanying choir . . . be moved by the beat of the instrumentalists. . . . Attempts have been made in the past," he added severely—not saying "Columbia" —"to recruit polished and sophisticated background voices and studio musicians, but it was soon apparent that Miss Jackson could not then perform with . . . conviction and vitality." Ha!

It was critic Hammond who said "gospel music is making a profound impression on the tastes of the younger generation." He singled out church-bred Sam Cooke, Chuck Berry, Ray Charles, Dinah Washington, Sarah Vaughan . . . Mahalia nodded with satisfaction; that girl could do *anything*. Mildred, reading, found her own reward. "Mm-mh! 'Mildred Falls . . . the supreme gospel pianist.' How do you like that, Miss Jackson?"

"You still got me to please."

Sidney Po'tier, Belafonte, and Duke were all in town. Sidney had this idea of putting her in his play: if she could make a movie for Nat King Cole, she could play his mother in *Raisin in the Sun*. But "No, baby, Halie can't be putting up in no theater. I had no business acting theatrical and going to Hollywood."

He got Belafonte to talk to her. She couldn't be budged. Now, going to Ed Sullivan's TV theater—that was fine. She hadn't said one thing about that, when Papa was sick; hadn't dreamed it *to* say. She fell to musing on whether she would've included "or a TV theater" that long-off day. . . . Lost thoughts, lost day. Get yourself to Sullivan, Halie. It was a good show. "Two of the Kennedys were in the audience," says Ed Sullivan —"I don't remember which; there are so many Kennedys—and we all went out to dinner together, to Lindy's. You often get fed up, doing TV, but it was so darned nice to see the reaction of the waiters, and the people on the streets. They looked up to her like a great benefactress."

That wasn't the word an exhausted Irving Townsend had in mind, after their first battle.

"Mahalia, occasionally we *have* to do new things. Duke's *Black, Brown and Beige* tells the whole history of the Negro people in music, but all *you* record is the religious part. *Come Sunday*—see?"

"I can't record with no orchestra! I can't read a—"

"I know you can't read music, Mahalia. Just learn it. It isn't long. He's changing the whole damned thing, just to fit you in."

There were more arguments—Mahalia a seething volcano, Townsend a white-hot poker, prodding: "If I have to drag you kicking and screaming, you're going to do it. It's for your own good!" . . . there was Duke calling, admitting he'd put Townsend up to it—encouraging her: "Doll, it's a breeze" . . . and Lord help me there was the music, to be learned. "Mildred! come over!"

Midwest dates and bounce back to New York for Philharmonic Hall—its first gospel. So said, *that* was the top spot now Carnegie had every kind of thing. Searching for the sound—the elusive ultimate—she had decided on *two* organs to support Mildred, and that night, Louise and young Edward Robinson were pushed where they'd never been before. "It was always something else that needed to be done, as far as she was concerned, to push her a little farther—'cause she *had* more," says Mildred. "But she never sang a song the same twice. Never. One thing in rehearsal; get on the stage, do another. Same night! Two things for me to do—wait on her, and just look at her lips. I be all ears and fingers. Not even look at the piano—*can't*. She throw back her head, close her eyes, and I say, 'Ohhhh—'; do the best I can. Afterward, she might say, 'That was pretty good.' She don't want me to get too satisfied," laughs Mildred.

Next day, Mahalia had a chance to unburden herself to Brother John, just back from Paris. "I been wrestling with this thing, John; they want to put me with Duke to sell more for Columbia. How *you* doing?"

"Well, I'm doing, I guess. Best I can. You?"

"Yeah—but I'm so tired running."

"Girl! you ain't started yet," John cried, amazed. Her at the top! "You got a long time to go yet."

"Well, I'm getting mighty tired, though."

"IT'S THE SARCOID, Mahalia. How much has that chest been disturbing you? You don't look like you've been short of *food*."

"Oh, Dr. Barclay, don't start on Halie. She's so tired of ripping and running. Now Salem's moving and nobody but me to give them the decorating. I got to—"

"Mahalia, please don't waste energy. I've warned you. Now let's have another look in that eye."

Ready to leave, she halted; "Dr. Barclay, this musician going call you—" Another one. "I don't know how many black people—some musicians, some just friends—Mahalia brought or sent to my clinic. 'I want you to give him'—or her—'the best care you can and send the bill to me. Don't embarrass them about money. If you have to put them in the hospital, put them in; if you have to get a consultant, get a consultant.' A good part of my practice were people Mahalia had referred to me and picked up the tab totally," says William Barclay.

She sighed, unable to find her peace. If she could just sit in one place like a doctor and bring the work to her. She couldn't go back to TV just downtown—it didn't pay enough to tie her up; she was past that. But she sure wished—

Louis Cowan *president* of CBS? The whole thing? Bostic was positive. "Oh thank You, Jesus. He loves me. Maybe now I'll get my network TV."

"Get William Morris on it, Mahalia."

"I will, when I can put my mind to it. I got to go out to California for *Come Sunday*." Come who? "Never mind. Something I got to do with Duke."

BETWEEN THEM, they still didn't have it. Mildred just couldn't get with Duke. They climbed aboard the morning I.C. and Elliot Beal and Edwin Hogan drove them straight to Beal's piano that night, the two teaching Mahalia note for note when midnight was long gone. They put her on the morning Sunset Limited to Los Angeles still protesting. "She was scared about the music," says Beal, shaking his head, "she was scared about the big orchestra, and she was scared they were pulling her away from her gospel. Poor baby."

"TOWNSEND SAID rehearse over here." Duke bussed her warmly and waved a languid hand to sit down. He was working on some other material here in his hotel suite. Mahalia watched with some exasperation: a week might be a long time for *him* to rehearse, but this *Come Sunday* didn't feel like none of hers. Besides now he's wanting her to get onto these lyrics. . . .

Walking into Columbia studios on Sunset Blvd., "You all trying make me a opera singer," Halie glummed to Townsend, shaking her head. She got through by letting the orchestra take a note or two . . . this was a terrible experience . . . but she got through it; and they all ended up liking it so well, she hummed an extra chorus to move it out. Well! all she had do now was face the music when this "jazz" record came out.

"Sing what?" She couldn't believe her ears. "The 23rd Psalm," said Duke airily. Halie grew still. "I don't know nothing about that." Duke struck a chord. "Open your Bible and *sing,* woman!"

The Lord is my shepherd, I shall not want— Improvising, Duke's group moving in and out as she led, she followed the prayer's path and lost herself in the green pastures. Townsend was awed. "Seldom in music," he would write, "has such an improvisation been accomplished. Seldom in Duke's career has composition and performance been so simultaneous."

"Duke—" said Mahalia, taking, at last, a deep, free breath—"you a terrible man." Just a genius.

"And you—" she beamed at Townsend, "you made me do it."

"Mahalia," said Townsend, "nobody can make you do anything you don't want to do."

OFF THE TRAIN and hello, Chicago. Cut two dates to rescue Kansas City: need that money for a Negro hospital. Catch up, and down to two kinds of warm—weather and a Welcome Home with Beal and a

500-voice choir in her honor at Municipal Auditorium. "Elliott, this is the first time I have been presented at home with any dignity." Just before curtain time, Bill Russell insisted his way backstage and said he'd been put out—police were putting out *all* the white people; would not allow both races under the same roof. "You had business to come see me before, so I could say you my manager—like I did in Memphis, remember?" He had to go. She sat down and prayed over it. She couldn't let Beal down, wreck his program. But her sorrow song had extra meaning that Sunday afternoon.

(It was still on her mind later in Vancouver: "The law should speed integration in the South, but the only way the white people are going to *accept* it is to learn about the Negro and his principles. But you can't learn about anyone unless he's near you." Her songs, she hoped, were one way. "If people like them, that will help them understand.")

She had arrived in New Orleans with a bad cold—so much switching back and forth in temperatures—and that turned into the flu, so Ida had a patient and Beal had tried not to have a fit the morning of the concert: making an errand outside to pass through her room and see how she was—could he get her anything? . . . on the way back—was she feeling any better? . . . 'til Ida heard, "Ida! Ida, will you please get this man out of here so I can talk to my God?"

"Now Elliott," Ida said firmly, "if you need anything outside, pass around through the alley."

The concert that afternoon, then, was another miracle to her—where had that voice come from, when she couldn't even breathe? She had it to spare even now, but her voice was low and private as she turned to young Hogan, whom she'd told to come home with them: "Now Hogan, I heard a lot of you, and I like your playing, but as *long* as you live, and you ever play for me, don't you *ever* play a prelude that long because Mahalia *Jackson* is the star. Now let's see what they got for us to eat."

It took Ida Beal to top it off, with a hat she'd designed herself—in the business now. "Ida," said Mahalia, twisting around at the mirror, "took you to turn my head." She wore it up to Milwaukee—still under snow and ice, but she wouldn't miss this: invited as one of "America's Outstanding Preachers," asked to deliver a sermon in song and stay for a week, working with the churches. The deep nature of it prompted her to speak of something she was wary of mentioning: the claims repeatedly brought to her of direct communication through her singing . . . persons actually experiencing healing while hearing her sing. "I don't claim to be a healer, that can only be done by God; each one must know his own faith, within; but this is a moving experience of my life and only emphasizes the *mystery* as well as the power of God."

It put her mind all the more on her temple. It was taking shape: What she wanted was a nondenominational temple for all races, with a fine group of singers and teachers and all sorts of classes for youth—even train them for show business, if that's what they want, but alongside of God. Her temple would keep straight, too; no crookery like some she could name—as many bad people warming pews as leaning on posts, and that did not have to be. It did not. Her temple was perfectly simple. Why couldn't Col. Reilly understand what she's talking about? She'd go see Daley again about that City Pier when she got back and stood clear—clear as she'd ever be. Wouldn't hurt the City to give it to her.

She called Russell. What a team they going be in the temple! He still hadn't got his strength back. She'd better make a way to get over there. She'd pull him out of it.

In Chicago, a message was waiting to call Granny White at Columbia. Duke was playing the Regal—how about coming down now to get a picture together for the album cover? Mahalia tracked down Nettie: "Come on, go with me. Now."

"I can't!" Nettie wailed; "my hair's all up in rollers; I'm at the beauty shop. Why didn't you give me notice?"

"Baby," said Mahalia, "you know the Reverend don't ever rehearse."

The result, Mahalia decided, was a real ma-and-pa. "Nettie, you got to see this. There won't never be but the one." But never say never, Halie, she thought, looking at the faces in her living room: No novelty to have the children. When she rehearsed, in came the sparrows, hop hop . . . "Well, come on in, babies; I'll sing *one* for you" . . . shooing them then so she and Mildred can get some work done and—whop whop, little fist . . . "All right, you all can come too, just for a minute." White and black. But the parents: get them together took national TV. Ed Murrow, *Person to Person,* with cameras, a mess of cables, lights, and a swarm of folks setting it up. The commotion filled the streets on both corners—"John? stay over there with Hannah; don't bring her into all this—look like Mardi Gras waiting for a parade." Neighbors white and black had come—could they help in any way? Some of them, she supposed, were part of or stood for the trouble when she'd bought the house. Give them the benefit. No use to hold things. She cooked the whole crowd red beans and rice; then she stood to have her picture taken with the officers of the Chatham–Avalon Park Community Council for a real estate magazine.

Within the year, the last white family left Chatham Village.

TENNESSEE, Missouri, Kansas; change clothes; then East—hurry down overnight to see Russell; what *was* it with that boy?—can't talk wedding 'til he picks up. She told them what foods to fix, with some suption. Then California by train. Getting off the train for her last date there, she lost her balance and fell, which put her to bed. She made it to

Kankakee, Ill., only four days late. One more, then change clothes in Chicago and back to California—Beal, Allen, and Mildred in tow. The 2nd Annual Victory Baptist Church Summer Benefit Musical Starring Mahalia Jackson put 40,000 into the Coliseum, including Gov. Goodwin J. Knight. A white friend of Brother John's, Jules Schwerin, came to talk about making a picture of her life, titled *Kinfolk*. Someone else wanted to make a book of her. *Variety* named her *Whole World in His Hands* a "best bet." God was showering his blessings.

When she arrived in San Francisco, though, she believed she better call herself to His attention. She and Mildred had come early, for the press . . . and found all legs, ears, and eyes belonged to Maria Callas. Nothing of Mahalia had been seen or said—nothing to notice. "Marie Callas has stole my concert," she told Mildred. To flop in Frisco. The shame. Emerging from the hotel—slumped, dejected, the weary and worry of life upon her—she heard a cry: "Mahalia!" It was a man she'd met in Washington—head of one of the big newspapers here. She didn't know how he recognized her on the street. He asked how she was, so she told him—"flopping on her face," she said, almond lids low, brooding as a buddha. "We'll do something about that. Come on!" By day's end he organized a media network that could have elected Martin in Mississippi, if such a thing could be believed. She sang to a solid house. "Marie Callas had been forgotten," she said with satisfaction. "That was nothing but God's hand."

It was a sobering thing to sing one last time with Big Bill Broonzy . . . gone to glory. John Sellers had organized a memorial service at Joe Branham's church. Broonzy was a good man. The Lord would be mindful of his soul. Hallelujah. Forgive him his blues. And Lord, please forgive Halie for mixing in Columbia's jazz business. You know it ain't none of mine.

GEORGE WEIN was everywhere, but Duke wasn't. Mahalia got nervous. "Where's Duke?" She'd expressly come early to Newport Jazz Festival to rehearse with Duke. "Tell him Mahalia says when we going rehearse?" Wein dutifully hurried off.

"Recording Duke's piece was one thing," she fretted to Beal, swiveling his eyes in every direction, so much to take in; . . . "they can do all sort of little tricks—cut and patch and fiddle the sound; but this is live. I'm not going disgrace myself—Beal! you listening to me?" Elliott jumped. "There's George Wein over there—see? Ask him did he see Duke."

Both men came back. Yes, and no. "I must have asked Duke ten times that day," says Wein, "because Mahalia kept asking me. All day, 'When?' Duke was not the least bit worried; he knew Mahalia knew it."

"Hmph!" snorted Mahalia, pushing up her lip. "You tell him I'm glad *he* knows it 'cause Mahalia don't know she knows it."

Time, and not one run-through. Help me, Lord. Duke, you gone evil. She got absorbed in the musical tribute to him—the whole evening planned that way. Look like people finally waked up to what genius they have here. Oh-oh. ". . . with Miss Mahalia Jackson!" Ohhh Jesus.

She knew it. She did know it! "It was, in fact, one of the memorable performances; the audience loved it," says George Wein—despite the frowns of critics who liked Mahalia and liked Duke but found her labors unsuited in this vineyard.

With her own night the first minute of Sunday—12:01—she had two whole days in her hands . . . rare treasure. She spent them wandering around Everybody's Park. Mitch was there to record Duke; Townsend, her. Somebody was making a movie—the man explained everybody was working for scale to make it legal but this was for the Newport Festival so would she please sign this release. "I'm glad to help; this is a good thing, to let people hear real jazz without having to sit in nightclubs," Mahalia told him, pleased. There was a holiday feeling among the musicians, so seldom in the same place at the same time. Louie Armstrong in early. Joe Bostic came. This was fun! Only one thing she didn't like: look like drugs taking these children; too many high, or low, or out—Lord, help them. Doc Hayakawa was like a mosquito hawk, he got around so much: had a lecture he was giving. The little professor clung to his friend fondly, whenever he lighted. The writers were all there, glad to see her—Professor Ralph Ellison was going write a big story on her for *Saturday Review*. There was a man any Negro could be proud of—any American, for that—and he couldn't be served a Coke on Canal St. Martin going change that. With God. Soul force, Martin said, and he was right.

Saturday night was dreary, drizzling, foggy, cold . . . typical Newport, thought New Yorker Bostic. Miserable. The people hunched under soggy newspapers could match anybody on stage for singing the blues. Yet nobody left; for 3½ hours they sat, applause warm but nothing else—sat despite the sudden misery of a real downpour in the last set until it was 12:01 and Willis Conover walked on to announce: "Ladies and gentlemen, it is now Sunday and time to hear the world's greatest gospel singer." Mahalia lifted long, slim palms for quiet, threw back her head, closed her eyes, nodded to Mildred, and—to 10,000 people at Jazz Festival '58—she sang *An Evening Prayer. . . .*

If I have wounded any soul today,
If I have caused one foot to go astray,
If I have walked in my own wilful way,
Lord, forgive. . . .

The hush was so thick you could touch it, thought Bostic, not wanting to breathe himself—nobody knows about the rain or the fog or the cold.

"It was the most fantastic tribute to the hypnotic power of great artistry I have ever encountered. Nothing like it have I ever seen in my life. Those people sat . . . they forgot . . . they were completely entranced."

Head bowed, suddenly Mahalia lifted eyes up, lips to Mildred, and sang out *"Didn't it rain, chillun . . . oh, my Lord; didn't it—didn't it—"* and it stopped. The rain stopped. Not to return for the rest of the hour and the encore and the call-back encores demanded by a crowd shouting, screaming, stomping a love letter to a lady until Mahalia finally, drenched not with rain but in her own sweat, begged off. "Those children want to kill me!" she panted happily to Elliott Beal, offstage at the ready with her mink.

By church time, she was inside the A.M.E. (African Methodist Episcopal church, oldest of American Negro church denominations) refueling herself while the rain renewed its own beat. It wasn't until she got home that she discovered that before the gospel court of opinion, she stood accused of singing jazz. "Nettie, you got to fix this thing up. Get hold of Duke, for pity's sake, and have him tell the newspapers Mahalia wasn't singing no jazz." It wasn't easy to locate Duke, but Nettie did. And he called: "Of course she wasn't singing jazz! She sang the 23rd Psalm!"

By then, Beal was left to hold the fort and Mahalia was on her way to TV with Sammy Davis, Jr. So it was Beal who for three days running took calls from Dmitri Tiomkin for Mahalia. He wanted to plead with her to sing the sound track of *Old Man and the Sea.*

36

"There are certain women singers who possess, beyond all the boundaries of our admiration for their art, an uncanny power to evoke our love. We warm with pleasure at mere mention of their names; their simplest songs sing in our hearts like the remembered voices of old dear friends, and when we are lost within the listening anonymity of darkened concert halls, they seem to seek us out unerringly. Standing regal within the bright isolation of the stage, their subtlest effects seem meant for us and us alone; privately, as across the intimate space of our own living rooms. And when we encounter the simple dignity of their immediate presence, we suddenly ponder the mystery of human greatness."

She tried to go on reading Ralph Ellison's beautiful story in *Saturday Review,* but her eyes wouldn't focus and it slid from her hands.

Russell had cancer.

When he hadn't made it to Baptist Convention, she knew it was serious and finally persuaded him to see, please, really see, have tests made there if he wouldn't come see Dr. Barclay; and as soon as she had a free space she'd gone to Atlantic City and arrived in time to get this—which so threw her that it was him trying to cheer her up. "Don't give me up yet, girl—I have to carry you across the stoop." Their touch-phrase.

There was no way to help and she had contracts to fill and life pulled her on. All she could do was take the lonesome road. It took her full circle to where this started: to Hollywood, for Lana Turner's *Imitation of Life*.

So this was how a great star lives. She surveyed the dressing room assigned her. Like a whole apartment—shower and everything. For *St. Louis Blues* they had us out in tents. And this for just me. To sing one song. None of the other Negroes in the picture got anything like this. Halie felt like a visitor herself.

They'd rented Hollywood Methodist Church and hired 1,000 extras to fill it. She sang the 23rd Psalm from the altar. God is real. Then all she had to do was sob over Juanita Moore in the funeral scene. The sobs came easy. Both scenes were involved, technically, and there were callbacks and gaps. Good thing she had other work, and work that cheered her: Bing Crosby's special—first one of only two he'd do this year, and he wanted her. She walked into his ABC studio to a star's reception: six dozen roses, from Dinah Shore. She was ready to work but Bing was acting like she's made of eggshells—she picked up on that. Funny. Suddenly she knew and walked up close. "Bing, you don't have to treat me like a saint, baby—I'm just Mahalia." He gave her a hug. He was so down to earth, such an American. Dean Martin was being nice too . . . that was a lot of baloney about him drinking all the time. Might of known. She didn't see him with liquor one time. Look to her like he's just reaching out for love.

Everybody was seeing who could be the most relaxed and they ended up with Mahalia in a rocking chair to sing *Summertime,* moving into its source, to her way of thinking—*Sometimes I Feel Like a Motherless Child.* Yes, I do.

SHE WOKE with a strong oppression. She called Russell. No; he seemed kind of cheerful—they were starting treatments and he thought he'd generally picked up some. Aunt Hannah? Alice? No. Bell?

Aunt Duke said everybody was all right—pea patch to chicken scratch, but they were making out. Lord, what is it? Almost worse not to know. . . .

In a Harlem store that day—Sept. 20, 1958—a well-dressed Negro woman plunged a letter opener deep into the chest of Dr. Martin Luther King, Jr. He was rushed to Harlem Hospital, rimming the edge of death. The woman, insane, was a total stranger. "My God, my *God,*" moaned Mahalia, fear crystalized. The TV said Mrs. King was flying to join him. No visitors allowed. She sank to her knees.

Oct. 3, he was released from the hospital. All right, they said on the phone; puny, judging from TV. She hoped he'd have sense enough to slow down for a while—not neglect his health, pay attention to Coretta and the doctor.

If she'd just gone at first, taken Russell by the hand and *forced* him. . . .

Russell was not gaining, that she could see. But maybe holding his own was the next thing to turning the corner. Prayer does wonderful things. Wasn't that the very thing she was preaching at revival—starting at Greater Salem tonight? The first in their new home on 71st. If God was really pleased— She'd promised Him a revival when they cut on her in '55, but by her making it *two* weeks— If she rededicated herself, purified and cleansed herself—if she did just a wonderful job of running this revival—God? will you reach out and touch Russell?

> *"Let all who take refuge in thee rejoice,*
> *let them ever sing for joy. . . ."*

THREE CHRISTMAS trees. Jesus and Joseph and Mary on the ass, with the space above to the stars. Cars clogged quiet Indiana to see the sight. Halie looked again at the *Courier* story, meditated, then picked up the telephone: she'd sung for their employes' benefit and the man had said any time he could help. Poor babies, missing their schooling since September, and once you get out of the going— In Farmerville, Va., 1,700 Negro children were locked out of the public schools in yet another spasm against integration. "I want to sing Christmas carols for those children and I can't get down there; I want to phone it to them." He'd see what he could arrange. She called a preacher—was there a mile of Virginia she didn't know a preacher? Get those children to where she could sing to them, and get some ice cream and cake.

Halie had a project. Like she'd told those Fresno folks (their new sanctuary burned out, Halie standing up shaking the hand of everyone in the auditorium who'd come put money in the Dixie cups, the wastebasket, whatever, until one lady brought up a big shopping bag) . . . you can't just sing and say; God wants you to do.

She started something, wrote Wesley South. "Since the school has been spotlighted, whites in the county have formed an organization with stated plans for getting the youngsters back in school." Negroes would be allowed to use the state's Armory for tomorrow's party. Local merchants had volunteered refreshments and gifts. More gifts were pouring in—

mostly from Southern whites. Praise His name. Reporters and photographers flocked to the scene. Network TV, radio both scheduled it: 1,700 come to glory. Hallelujah. Doublechecking the phone people, Mahalia sat jolted. They couldn't *guarantee* her call would go through clearly. . . . Ha! more than one way to butter bread. For three hours that night they worked, DJ Sid McCoy and Mildred and Mahalia—and by the time they walked into the crisp, cold air, there was a radio-quality tape for clear-channel transmission.

Home to messages from Lou Mindling. He called 'most every night, or either in the day. Too bad he didn't know about television.

She was still waiting on Mr. Cowan. Maybe if Russell—say *when* Russell got well, and the two of them in the temple, maybe Lou Cowan could get her a sponsor for their services. She was going broadcast them, if she had to do it herself. Maybe William Morris could increase her fees. Or either Columbia Records.

Too late to call Russell tonight. Take his hand, precious Lord . . . she moved into the old Dorsey plea, alone in the night. Take my hand too, Lord. Feel like I'm slipping in the dark.

37

If Polly left something out, she could get it in New York. She'd be working there at least two weeks, maybe more. And she was actually going on Milton Berle—like George Washington, in television. She was looking forward to him a lot more than she was to Townsend. But it was always like that: she didn't want to and then when she was there, she did. Do her nerves good to get out this house right now: Polly and Butch bickering; Polly picking on Edward and Edward minding it and that's a sweet boy, Edward, do anything for her—rub her, go get her food, anything. And the aunties come fussing to her; won't say, to Polly. Still, Lou Mindling get along fine with Polly; Bob Ming too—takes a strong person to stand up to Cylestine and still appreciate the strength and good of the girl. Jesus! I don't need all this.

"LET'S JUST not fuss so much this time; Mahalia's nerves are bad."

Irving Townsend shook his head. She wasn't a villain. But she sure wasn't a saint. All she thought about was herself, when it came right down to it. "In the first place, that contract doesn't even come up until late this year, and you shouldn't be concerning yourself with business anyway. You're a great singer, Mahalia, and a great show business personality, but financial genius you're not. And you shouldn't be concerning *me* with your business. What you need is a good business manager. I've told you. Not a good full-fledged *manager*—they hardly exist; I could name on one hand *all* the good ones I've ever known—the personal everything from valet to business manager to professional manager, psychiatrist—he's got to be 40 things and 40 good things to be a good manager. But what you desperately need, Mahalia, is a good *business* manager, and *that* I could produce. I've begged you to let me get you one, but you won't trust anybody. I'm not going to get somebody to take on a woman who tucks everything away in a different bank and doesn't tell him how much she's got or how much she earned or anything else . . . the guy would go nuts in six months. *Would* you give him the money and let him take it over, invest it for you—*manage?*"

She sat silent, eying him; it was an old exercise.

"No, you wouldn't. So don't come talking any more business to me." He was thrashing, and he knew it. He was going to do whatever she asked, ultimately, and he didn't quite know why himself. "Almost from the time I started working with her," says Irving Townsend, "Mahalia involved me in every aspect of her life. Her finances, her emotions, her personal life, her employes, her accompanists, every single thing she had. Mahalia used people, to be frank. Used them to the hilt. She had no compunction about asking me for any kind of help conceivable. My job wasn't managing Mahalia, or handling her tours, or handling her finances, or finding her an apartment building, or getting her lawyers, or finding her houses to rent, or getting her bills paid, or a thousand other things. And yet I was involved in *all* of these things over the years because she just called on you to do it. Like Ellington, like a lot of them in show business, she felt that she was the hub that the rest of us revolve around, and it's what *she* wants, not what anyone else wants or feels that matters. In those days William Morris simply was her agency—they didn't give a damn as long as they got their 10 per cent—and Mindling simply booked her. . . .

"You're always going to have troubles, Mahalia, until you trust somebody to be an efficient business manager for you."

"But do you think Columbia would help me with my temple?" Oh, God. He'd *told* her, the corporate set-up— "But will you *ask* them?"

"I'll ask them." Still—he looked at her, and warmed. In many ways they were good, they both did a lot for each other. She could be tremendous. And fun. And tender. And maddening.

"MAHALIA, YOU baffle me. You're as unpredictable about time as you are about everything else. Some people are always late, and some people are always early—but you show up an hour early as often as you do an hour late." She managed somehow, always, to keep him off balance.

Mahalia was serene. She'd waked up in a good mood, ready to sing, so she'd come. What's wrong with that? "There was never anything easy about recording her," says Townsend. "She worked hard and tried hard and was generally very cooperative. So you know, if you like the way she sings—are a fan—you put up with all that stuff. But she wore both of us out. She wouldn't hire a decent person to learn anything—and good and loyal as Mildred was, I was buying her booze to complete albums there in New York, to get the work done, for heaven's sake. And it was very difficult for Mahalia—she learned many things over the years, but they were tough; and we didn't mess around with pop things most of the time, really. She didn't feel it at all. Sometimes she'd have a terrible time . . . exhaust herself over-rehearsing; and some of the people around her were such a problem, she had to spend half her life teaching somebody else how to do something—all kinds of problems. She couldn't pronounce words well, and she couldn't follow any arrangement unless—well, it was very difficult. We divided these albums up into three or four sessions, since she couldn't last more than two or three hours at a time—because she'd never rest, and she'd never stop singing."

And yet, when it was all over, it was good; and she'd sip a drink with him, to come down. He was really her friend—go anywhere with her, high or low. "Come on go with me to ABC for *V.I.P.*"

"I'm not going to sit there and listen to all that crap about you. But I'll go with you to Berle, to hear you sing." That's all right. Bostic wanted to go to *V.I.P.*

"So what is your great and true admirer Louis Cowan doing for you with CBS?" Joe Bostic was bitter. "Look, Mahalia, instead of hanging around hoping for his highness, who is not going to do a damn thing for you, why don't you let me put together a Mutual package? This is my *business,* remember? But I'm not going to move until I know you'll go through with it."

"I'll let you know. You shouldn't fail to be nice to people, Joe; you should remember who he is."

"He doesn't mean a damn thing to me and he shouldn't mean too much to you because if he's for real, he'd get you a network spot."

Ten days jammed with TV; work in the off-hours on new material with Mildred—Townsend could say what he want, she notice he kept handing her these new songs. Then the long ride to Hollywood to sing for the big producers' dinner. Back to record. Hard to put her mind on it and she knew Townsend wasn't too happy but. . . .

He was worse. Days running, when she called, there'd be no encouragement. Finally she had a gap in obligations and went to Atlantic

City and pulled $10,000 cash out of her purse and said, "What can I do? Besides giving you this for the best treatment in the country. What can I *do?*"

Nothing. She took away with her a frail semblance for her heart's ease and a record Russell had made once, that he wanted her to hear. She stayed with Brother John when she came back, and, New York over, took him to Chicago with her . . . "You got to anyway, you might as well come go with me now . . ." and at last was able to tell—tell this boy so like her inner ear. You got to tell somebody, sometimes. Besides God. Somebody frail like us. Help me, Jesus.

It had to be now that Chicago, about the last—yes, the last big city in the country—Chicago found a place for her downtown. Studs Terkel and Win Strache had made the way; she was going into Orchestra Hall—Chicago's Carnegie—on Feb. 13. With John.

"John Sellers!" Willa Jones, Sallie Martin, Frye—all the upper echelon was aghast. Blah, blah, blah: don't even care if he hears, thought John with infinite satisfaction; that was too *grand* for him to be with Mahalia Jackson first time downtown. "Well, it ain't Halie, honey," she said; "it's the white folks want John Sellers on there—Studs Terkel, Win Strache—people that presenting me. Old Town School of Folk Music—you all see them; I can't get you all on there."

She *had* asked for, and got, one person; but that was different. Langston Hughes was coming from New York as a favor, to introduce her. John was taking off from *Gate o' Horn.* He'd never sung with Win Strache and Frank Hamilton, but he promised they'd rehearse the day before. "I'll be there, Spook; I got to see how you going do singing with those white boys."

They were working away—banjo, guitar, tambourine beneath the voices—when she walked in. John was glad she'd made it; she'd tell him like it was; no messing up on *her* program.

She sat silent. When they broke, he walked down to where she sat. "How you doing?"

"Russell passed this morning, John. They called me. Oh, I feel so bad." My God, John thought. Her first time downtown in Chicago.

"Don't tell it."

After rehearsal he took her shopping. She bought a black dress with a cape around it, for the funeral.

Dr. Barclay and his wife came backstage Friday night to give her well wishes. He took a keen look. Better call Polly and tell her to get Mahalia down to see him.

Brother John's group would sing. Langston Hughes would read a paper on spirituals and gospel music. She had time to read her Bible and meditate after the curtain went up.

There was nothing she could do.

Langston Hughes was still talking—she hadn't meant *that* long. Finally intermission and her appearance . . . and Langston Hughes was still talking, plowing every hill and furrow of his acquaintance with and admiration for— A rain of applause in mid-sentence beat him offstage. She knew it was a cold audience, tired from weathering words. She had to work to reach them . . . stopped the first timid hand-claps to explain that was "off-key; this is the way you clap for gospel; come, do it with me . . ." and not even the ultimate fervor, the white heat of *Elijah Rock,* erased her concern so that her last words were to the critics: She didn't know what they could make of this music, "because they didn't come from there."

John, who'd missed her performance—gone on with Josh White to University of Chicago, doubling up—John made his way slowly through the reviews with her. All three men critics for the white papers loved her. The *Defender's* fine arts man acknowledged her appeal but wondered if gospel singers should risk their careers with too many appearances in halls such as this. It was Claudia Cassidy—etched so indelibly into white Chicago's consciousness that she once was picketed for attacking the Symphony—Miss Cassidy it was who drew blood. For the first and only time in Mahalia's life, a critic had walked out. "I don't care what Claudia Cassidy say!" flared Mahalia. "Who is she? I don't know her, no way!"

"Mahalia," said John, "Mahalia, that's not so bad for Friday the 13th."

"I don't care, honey," she said, rising; "one rain don't make no crop."

Miss Cassidy fairly printed a P.S.: Studs Terkel had assured her that for Mahalia, it was the wrong night. Mahalia saw the clipping when she got back from the funeral. She'd asked Sallie Martin to drive with her, but most of the way over and back, Mahalia had been silent. "It's a pity; she's pitiful," Sallie Martin reported to the waiting circle. "He was a straightforward, a very swell and attractive person—but he would have been too strict for her, you know."

At 2 a.m. Nettie Irving's phone rang until it waked her. Mahalia was wracked with sobs. Broken. It was unbelievable—it tore Nettie's heart. How could she console her? She dressed and left the house. Mahalia was in the pink bedroom, the middle one; she had lighted candles by his picture and paced and prayed the night through. Presently she said to Nettie, "Russell seems to be—oh, he's just present, here!" Nettie shivered. "I don't know what it is this man is trying to tell me." She put on the record, to see if she could get something through that. It was a night Nettie would not forget. And it was not the last. For months, if Mahalia was by herself in the house at night, Nettie might be awakened—2 a.m., 3 a.m. "I can't sleep; I wish you'd come down here." And when Nettie came, used to it now, still Mahalia was pacing, praying, blaming herself for not having married Russell back when they could have. "I don't know, Nettie, I don't know," she moaned. "I feel his presence so close. He's here. Russell is here, and I don't know what he's trying to tell me."

38

You pay extra at the top. Not the money. More comes in, more goes out, a fool knows that. You pay in people. Knowing, you pay. "I'm psychic, Laurraines. I can walk into a room and in 30 seconds I'll size up every person in it . . . and I won't be off very often."

But you work with what the Lord puts to your hand.

A widening claque swirled now—newcomers jostling oldtimers—around, before, behind—eager for slivers of favor that conferred status, the smallest chore a bone to be sought, savored, evidence of familiarity and even, vaguely, dependence: "Works me to *death,* Mahalia!" Gold coin on the exchange, with no relation to whether the chore is done, half-done, or vanishes into the mists of intention. . . . So much need that can't be denied, inside. Not the material—though there was this, always, unremitting, from the known and unknown, in and outside her own world—implicit in celebrity some dim-limned responsibility to be a fount from whom blessings should flow to all the thirsty by right of their having participated through membership in humanity in creating the acclaim of the world of which they were a part albeit unseen, unsung, and unproductive. The dues they had paid was existence. Instinct or not, she could not make good will an essential of the way for this army of the weak, losers of their own battles, so that she grew accustomed to shrugging off theft if it was not too much; betrayal, if it was not too great. Which of us is without sin, O Lord? Forced to violate an inbred instinct for privacy with the least of her affairs, she adopted a tactic of never telling any one person all of anything so that it could wholly be used against her. Give everybody a part. As many as you can. And in thus diminishing your expectancy, assign any given project two or three or even six different ways—an exercise in sheer many as you can. And in thus diminishing your expectancy, assign any given asperation for those exceptional intellects who were present and devoted and capable when called. Banishment when finally decreed was implicitly elastic and inevitably reversed, often not so much by decision as by blurring of the record, which then, in the inexorable course of character, was usually blotted again, and again, but always the hope of never more. She wanted to be loved.

In this year of 1959 she plunged into her work: her refuge—her salvation—and irresistibly, world without end, her joy.

The Lord, your God, is in your midst . . .
He will exult over you with loud singing
as on a day of festival!

Night upon night, she rose and went into the pink bedroom, lit the candles, and played the record. . . . And at last the message came clear: Russell wanted her to know that he truly loved her. That he did not want to forsake her. The tears coursed; they might have married. And the record played. My God, my God. . . .

OH! MY GOD. She hadn't wanted to come, had *resisted* it, she told Celie. "The Lord spoke to me once and I didn't want to take it; He told me to go home and buy some cemetery plots. He said 'You're going to need it.' He told me this but I didn't want to hear it—you know?" Celie nodded. She knew so well. "He spoke it to me the *second* time. Then He spoke it the third time—clear, clear—'Go.' So I had to obey. I'm buying two whole sections of plots at Providence Memorial; that's the best open to us."

She'd done it as soon as she stepped off the train. Then she could go see Peter. She knew he was sick. Maybe he'd come on up and stay a while, let Dr. Barclay see him. . . . Peter, too. Oh, my God. She'd found him so wasted, she dogged him into letting her take him to the hospital for tests, and now they'd come up with cancer. Past help.

Peter—Roosevelt, give him his own name now—who made his own way. Peter, who had nickels for hook-legs Warpee . . . Peter, with the walk of a lieutenant, white linen spotless, straw katy tipped on his head so people stood and watched for his coming. He'd never had children either. She sat by his bed and sang for him what he especially liked—*Precious Lord . . . Just a Closer Walk With Thee* . . . song after song; and they talked about the old days of their mother and Aunt Bell at the Rightors, and his own song, *Ter-Henry Ter-Rightor*. He'd stopped by and played it for Henry Rightor not too, too long ago.

She checked on his care. There was nothing else to do.

"BUTCH, YOU want to go with me to Boston?" She hadn't said anything about Worcester, but that's where they headed first—Mahalia explaining nothing except that she wanted to see Russell Roberts's mother and father. She arranged to bring them to Chicago for a visit; and she let them know she would always keep in touch.

"All right, let's go to Boston. Mildred, you sure you got the music?"

She strung cities like beads on an abacus now, up and down, counting them off in her Cadillac, Allen driving her, moaning at the pace. Mammoth auditorium, high school, elite hall, church—church the best, the coming home, drawing it back as she gave: "Hasn't God been good to you?". . . "Yes! yes!" . . . working around the altar to the puzzlement of one reviewer: "She came off stage to sing in the aisles without missing a note" . . . making them a part, introducing Allen from the audience: "He likes to stand—Mr. Clark!" . . . selling her pictures for 50 cents—

"I look real nice; it was taken a few years ago when I was young" . . . praising the sponsors: "They paid me off in front."

I will give thanks to the Lord with my whole heart; I will tell of all Thy wonderful deeds. I will be glad and exult in Thee, I will sing praise to Thy name. . . . The Psalms were wonderful. She fell asleep, a finger stretched to the place.

Baltimore, Pittsburgh, Buffalo, New York . . . home for the benefit promised Willa Jones' preacher husband . . . out again to New England, towns clicking past like posts: climb to glory night by night, strung out every day. Down to circulate the South for *Imitation of Life,* the title truer than the movie: flowers, medals, trophies, keys, but where do we eat? where do we sleep? who will let us use the toilet? *I believe that I shall see the goodness of the Lord in the land of the living*—27th Psalm; her prop, first to last. Little Rock . . . Houston . . . Dallas . . . "the most celebrated musical evangelist of American history. . . ."

The doorman at the Wellington looked like St. Peter opening the gates. They had come to take their rest—or as close as she could come to it.

"MAHALIA," said Elizabeth Thornton, "you need a mink hat to go with that suit."

"Go on, I don't need no mink hat. And I'm tired. I'm not moving."

"You give to anybody else but you won't spend on yourself," said Butch, exasperated. "That's crazy." Mahalia's eyes closed. "All right, where's your credit card; I'll go get one for you."

Butch's feet hurt, so she flagged a cab to get to Fifth Ave. As they pulled into traffic, she saw Mahalia at the curb waving—just *frantic* signals. What on earth? Time enough to find out when she got back.

She couldn't find the right hat, and sorry to disappoint Mahalia—after all her talk—she walked into the room empty-handed.

"Thank You, Lord!" cried Mahalia.

"What were you waving at me for, when I pulled off?"

"I just realized I turned a fool loose with my money."

The very next city they were together, Butch found the hat. Paid $75 for it.

JOE BOSTIC's "jamboree of the religiosos," as *Variety* airily reported it, was news: Gospel was big business—published in seven languages by the Gospel Chorus Union in Chicago and that was just one. But you don't fill Madison Square Garden without promoting, Mahalia agreed—and pitched in. She was the star. She wasn't going let it flop. Between them they pulled out every stop . . . and turned in 11,000 to make the First Annual Gospel, Spiritual and Folk Music Festival a rousing five-hour session. It made, said one reporter, "even the hottest jazz sound like a longhair chamber music concert." Bostic had the Ward Singers piped in by trans-Atlantic wire from Sweden, and Sidney Poitier, star of *Raisin in the Sun,* introduced Mahalia.

Reunions over, food supped, hellos, goodbyes, and your autograph, Miss Jackson . . . it was good to have a bed to lay her head. She journeyed, then, to Worcester, and in the quiet of its auditorium she dedicated her concert to the late Rev. Russell Roberts of Worcester, spoke of his qualities, of their work together, and sang her songs for him, for herself, for God, for them—making them a part. Steve had his role, with *God's Trombones;* and it wasn't all quiet. She rocked in the cradle of her gospel, and found her peace.

Not for long. Start the Cadillac, Steve to drive: down to Virginia, nose headed south. "What I sing depends on what I feel, what I'm facing at the time . . ." *God Will See You Through . . . Lord, Don't Move the Mountain—Give Me Strength to Climb.* Russell, boy, you can rest. Down to Montgomery—streets strangely clear—integrate Alabama State College Arena, so close to where the trouble was; bring the white folks in. Love ye one another. Amen. Steve made a big impression with *The Creation.* She was proud of that boy.

Tampa, Jacksonville, Orlando . . . by train now. Sellouts, the biggest auditoriums, happy white faces with the black, adulation: inside, just inside. One day, oh Lord, I do believe. But how many bags of fruit can a person eat?

Lou Mindling and his wife met her in Miami. Let's go to dinner. Oh, this is Miami Beach— "Mr. Mindling, you better check; we'll wait outside."

The assistant manager didn't know. "Look, this is Mahalia Jackson!" A staff conference. Nobody *knew.* The agent went outside. "Come on, we're going in." . . . "Did they say it was all right?" . . . "Ahhh, nobody in there knows anything; come on." Mahalia was reluctant; she wasn't going in there, be humiliated. "Come on, Mahalia, for God's sake. It's all right." She let herself be persuaded, because it was Mr. Mindling. Mildred followed silently behind. Inside, hands wrung, eyes rolled, but he marched them to a table. Within minutes—surrounded. The waitresses all wanted Mahalia's autograph.

At Coco, Fla., near Cape Canaveral, a towheaded, pink-faced teenager slumped before the TV. He wasn't really paying attention—to that or anything else in the month since a prostitute mad at his father told him that wasn't his father, and his mother wasn't his mother; he wasn't even adopted. That had blown his mind—church—grades, from A to F, what difference. . . . The Miami announcer was interviewing some black woman. She began to sing *When the Saints Go Marching In . . .* not the way you'd expect but slow, kind of on the blues side. Something went right through him. Next day he bought all the records of Mahalia Jackson they had at the one music store. By then Mahalia was on her way to Nashville. . . .

Lou Mindling himself registered them all into the hotel—"See? no trouble"—then he guided the party out to friends. Back late . . . the desk clerk had changed her mind; the Negroes would have to leave. Mindling's voice had been rasped on the streets of Chicago. "Swell. You call the manager—I'd like him to put us out in person; I'd like to be able to call the *New York Times* . . ." That wasn't cutting any ice—"I'd like to sue them; this is a pretty rich group." They stayed. But at 5 a.m., Mahalia left.

And then it was festival season. She was a smash, revered—the star.

When they got to New York, Mindling took her to the Waldorf Towers. "Mahalia, there won't be any trouble. People come from every African country to the Waldorf-Astoria; they're used to it—international. Never mind what it costs." He felt good about the Waldorf. He wouldn't let anybody do anything to her again—and realized he felt "very possessive" about her. That was no bad way.

If she just didn't have this godawful thing about checks. She screwed up more companies, holding checks for months—and having her own bounce from some bank who turned around and called him. He'd got *that* arranged, at least. In her purse right now he bet there was at least one check nine months old if it was a day. And her banks! "Mr. Mindling, would you meet me at the bank at 63rd & Michigan?" The agent had looked around—no looming marble or granite; only dirty little stores, a Chinese laundry, rib places . . . good God: "Bank." This little storefront. She was waiting inside. "Mahalia, get your money out of there before they close." And she had thousands in it. Just another one she'd found. But argue at dinner about who owes 15 cents. She didn't *realize* she could earn as much as $10,000 a night. And she didn't act it. A gentle soul; you could never look on her as someone trying to scheme something.

THREE MONTHS before she could get back to New Orleans . . . Peter holding on but so thin in the bed at Aunt Bessie's. TV wouldn't wait, and she had to sing for NAACP's 50th Anniversary in New York July 19, unless—"Ida, call this number if anything happens."

Pulling up to the hotel with Mildred and Beal—he'd play organ this summer—she kept one eye his way and had the satisfaction of seeing his eyes bug when they walked into the Waldorf. Got him to see his first stage play, too. *She* couldn't accept Sidney's invitation to see *Raisin in the Sun,* but they shouldn't miss it. Sidney said it was going to be a movie—maybe sometime it be on TV. She sang to herself. Softly. Waldorf wouldn't be used to hearing Halie from her room.

That Sunday, she had no warning so she went to the Polo Grounds for the NAACP with an easy mind—and gave 18,000 people what they'd come for: Glory hallelujah! she was the best, and she was theirs. It looked like rain the whole time but the sky obliged 'til she was through. Then it came all at once. They'd have to run but—she looked around; Mildred needed help. That nice boy who'd directed the choir . . . Russell Goode of Chattanooga was pressed into service.

She was at Columbia rehearsing next day when she burst into tears. Now why am I crying? I like that song. She looked at the clock. And knew.

Peter had died. Aunt Bessie called Ida Beal about 5 a.m. About 6, she called Celie, wishing she could quieten the phone; Sister Bell so low sick. "Don't tell her," Bessie whispered, "We don't want her to know." Celie listened—Mama hadn't seemed to heed the phone. Celie climbed back in bed. They didn't want her to go yet, not to suspicion Bell of anything. Held to the bed, Mama didn't even know Peter was bad off. "Celie! Celie, call Bessie. I say call her. Somebody dead at Bessie's house." Celie shook her head. "I spoken with them this morning and nothing happened." Bell reared up in the bed. "Well, *somebody dead* up there, and it's a man, 'cause I seen one man putting teeth in another man's mouth."

"God knows," cries Bessie Kimble, "Peter's teeth was up there, and my *husband* put Peter's teeth in his mouth when he died. And my sister Bell saw it, from her bed. That was her natural gift."

"When Bell says," Doodutz agreed when she heard, "you can put your foot on it."

Ida set the wheels in motion. Mrs. Lockett already had the body before Ida called Mahalia to report. She had little doubt Mahalia knew. Wasn't Mahalia the one got to them all with her "I smell death" . . . made everybody jump up and get away from her and "Child, don't start that stuff," and sure enough somebody would die? Ida could understand—she dreamed real happenings herself. But "smell it"—only Halie had that.

Mahalia would drive down—go ahead and buy the food and stuff and she'd take care of it when she got there. Polly could come with the aunts.

It was a big funeral, at Zion Travelers—Peter's and Bessie's church—but there were far more people in the streets, to see Mahalia Jackson. To think when she first set foot in this church she didn't have a dime, barefoot as a goose—had one dress. She pulled her mink close. Look like she was getting some virus. Getting drenched at the NAACP did that.

"JUST GIVE ME the respect due me, they find me," Beal gasped, closing his eyes against the glare. "Oh Lord! that woman," he said to anybody but nobody listened . . . not Mildred or Polly or her child or Allen; they'd been hearing it since they got onto this desert—"Has Mahalia ever heard of air conditioning? does she know it don't matter about your *throat* if you dead, picking your bones? Just put me out my misery, give me the respect, that's all I ask. . . ." Polly barked at him to shut up. Now what is this woman! Beal gritted, but wouldn't say it aloud; he was almost ready to put her backside up against this car, so cantankerous. "Ice!" moaned Allen. "Put it—that's right—don't you steal none, Beal, you expect me to get you through . . ."

"Now this," said Beal, eying the beaded glasses Doris Akers was bringing in—"this is more like it. No, no," waving a languid hand at Mildred and Mahalia—Polly and her son staying with her own friends—"serve the ladies; I am a gentleman to the end . . . and it nearly was." Mahalia paid him no mind. She'd come on the train and she needed her car. "Did you hear Miss Jackson has give in, played Las Vegas?"

"Shut up, Beal—that was for Allen's son Donald's church that he pastors."

"Yeah," jibed Beal. "Stopped all them people gambling for two hours. We had a nice crowd."

NOT FOR HOLLYWOOD Bowl. Empty, she learned in stunned silence. Canceled. "Mahalia Jackson bombed out," whispered the trade: Was the end beginning? Beal and Mildred walked on tiptoe all the way to Miami for the Columbia convention.

In Los Angeles, budding promoter Audrey P. Franklyn was puzzled. Why would William Morris call out of the blue and offer her Mahalia Jackson?

"THANK YOU, Mr. President." The President of the United States making a presentation to *her* for the White House Correspondents, when it was *his* birthday—69. She was glad she'd brought him a present: Granny White fixed the album-set just beautiful. ". . . And look at here: Took the trouble on the train to Abilene next *morning* after being up late, to write me a thank-you letter. Eisenhower can call on me any time."

OHIO, PENNSYLVANIA . . . *Have you any rivers you think uncrossable?* . . . New England, leaves turning . . . *Tired, So Little Rested* . . . south again—heart sinking: where is the strength? Follow the work. God is real.

Ah, New York. Voice of America. Ralph Bunche showed her around the United Nations and got tickled at her just as the *Jet* photographer snapped his camera. Good. Let people know Bunche not solemn all the time . . . got to take "Uncle Tom" and "slavey" from these niggers. Well—she did too; let 'em talk; fools stew, folks do.

She signed the new Columbia contract. Even if she had a falling out with John Hammond and spoke her mind. They'd make up.

MUST BE toward morning. She'd give Salem another revival, that's what she'd do. Right after Watch Night. She pinched out the candles and turned off Russell's record and went to her knees.

39

She felt good when she woke up. She said, "Lord, You have been so good to me. You have given me everything. And I just want to know, is You going be with me in the shadows of death? . . . I want You to show me the assurance." She dozed. She was walking down a dark, dark tunnel, but on her righthand side—she didn't see Him, but she knew it was the Lord walking with her. She said, "Lord, it's so *dark* down here!" And look like He throwed a *handful* of stars in their pathway. "Oh! You're throwing stars in the pathway of righteousness, for Your name sake!" He said, "Yes." His voice so clear. She wasn't even afraid or nothing. When they got to the end of this tunnel, it was so *bright,* so bright she could hardly open her eyes. There was a river. Across, on the other side—this river so calm and quiet and beautiful, and across the river was nothing but evergreens—beautiful trees. "Lord—" she said, "Lord, is this the River Jordan that I got to cross?" He said, "Yes." But he didn't take her across it. He left her on this side.

She woke.

She was "an American institution," the ad said, and a picture of her was in the Whitney Museum, but that didn't take her off her feet: Revival time. Work, but it fueled her like nothing else and good thing, dates strung like beans on a vine—Arkansas, Tennessee, Kentucky . . . had to call police to help her from the Louisville fans pressing in on the building. A good concert for Broadcast Foundation of America to tape for Japan and Europe and Africa. Indiana . . . circling Kentucky. Home for Rev. Elijah Thurston and Boy Baby's building fund and back rolling . . . Colorado—people turned away in Denver. Take time to talk to the B'nai B'rith women about the color line on housing—"It hurts when it happens to you; but no, honey, it hasn't hurt my faith in humanity; that's just a little part of America's family; families straighten these things out"—and hear a builder boast *his* development lets in colored people. Colorado! One thing, everywhere—from Arkansas on—white and black together for her songs, clapping together, crying together, all seemingly drawn into a current moving like the Mississippi River, hearts speaking what their minds don't yet know.

Twisting with the road, the necessities of sponsors, churches, family, tenants, feuds, needs, hopes, friends tracked her like joggers wired to a guide car. She was fighting a bad cold now. Mildred, Willie Webb, James Lee all worried; but dose yourself and where are my pills my prednisone how can I get up this bed so small . . . yet at night, the returning miracle—power. At Topeka a message caught up that was 50,000 volts: She was going into Constitution Hall. Since the DAR barred Marian Anderson 21 years ago, the name had become a byword for bigotry. Thunderstruck, "I wish to God I could say something important," Mahalia told *Daily Capital* reporter Pat Swanson before she walked on stage. She had once saved weeks to see Marian Anderson. The event was so significant Dr. Martin Luther King, Jr., was asked to comment. "Another great milestone in human relations," said Dr. King, facing his own trial—indicted for income tax evasion by the State of Alabama. Mahalia's lawyer, Bob Ming, was the one going to stand up in court and defend him. Mahalia grinned. Ming always did like the spotlight—and they sure couldn't have anything *on* Martin. Not the way her vibrations read that man.

She got herself on the train to California before Audrey P. Franklyn had a nervous breakdown—or gave her one; that girl sure loved the telephone. But she had to do Townsend first. Percy Faith! Help me Jesus. Wasn't the bit of good to try it with Mildred; she couldn't be 40 men. Lord, You got to help—what is Halie up against? Besides a lot of work.

A lot of work, thought Irving Townsend. In another Columbia convolution, Mitch Miller had left, and as Vice President, West Coast, Townsend had moved to Hollywood—moving Mahalia's recording with him. But Mahalia made a lot of work for herself—like this silly business of not flying —and "I'm no opera star!" As if he was trying to make her one. But. Recording her with Ellington had been unpredictable, off the top of your head, in a way; there was some play in the whole bag. Not for an album with Percy Faith; not 40 musicians. If Mahalia decides to put six beats to the bar instead of four, Mildred can sit there and wait but 40 men won't. Well, he was ready to play Lord High Executioner if they'd get here.

Outside, Percy Faith was approaching the building on Sunset when the two cabs pulled up. One disgorged Mahalia with a hatbox miscellany; the other, Mildred with the major luggage. The orchestra leader was just abreast as Mahalia looked up from counting pieces. "Let me have $5, baby, to pay the cab." She thanked him and walked on in. Only then did she discover who he was. "It could have been *anybody* down there she was borrowing from," the amused leader told Townsend. That's Mahalia, Townsend thought; she needs five bucks, she just asks for it.

NOBODY HAD ever *dictated* the notes to her before. Song by song. Lord! Percy Faith scared her to death but he was great. "We're going to do this until you sing the *note*—not sliding above or below or between but *on* the note." Not angry, just making her do it right, and she was trying—God knows she was trying. "That right?"

To Townsend, *My Country, 'Tis of Thee*—that she'd asked to include so there'd be "one hymn to my country"—emerged like none other ever sung. As silence reclaimed the air came the sweetest sound an orchestra could offer: the tiny beat of violin bows against music stands, traditional tribute to great artistry. Again and again. 'Til the tapes had *The Power and the Glory.*

"WHAT YOU think, Audrey P.?" The two were walking from the last Columbia session: thin, fair, collegiate-fresh Jewish girl beside tired majesty.

"I think it's great and *we* have some work to do."

The fledgling, 23, was clawing her way up. She'd figured it was her Ella Fitzgerald show that got her the call from William Morris; then she learned about bombing Hollywood Bowl—that scared her. *She* had to pay the rent on Santa Monica Civic; it was her show. But this woman was so fantastic, that must have been lousy promotion. She wished she'd got her sooner, but they'd make the days count. "You have to do a lot of running around," she'd warned . . . and when Halie wasn't recording, the young express train was waiting: Visit the press, one at a time. A big banquet at Long Beach for Baptist ministers—their first mix, black and white. Mahalia didn't seem to mind what Audrey asked, or where she was hauled: off to Billy Graham, or to tape at a hot dog stand because that's where Brother Henderson earned his bread when he wasn't being a DJ. "The reason I work so hard," Audrey P. explained as they sagged to a halt, "is because I would hate to go back to bookkeeping."

"You know," said Mahalia, "I feel the same way about ironing."

It was great to open your door at the Bahia Motel and find Xernona and Ed Clayton—shifted from Chicago to build up *Jet*. Thing was, she'd got so hungry waiting 'til she'd eaten some barbecue; but that's all right, plenty room for Ed's short ribs. . . . Sick. Xernona called a doctor they knew. Indigestion and fatigue, he said. Xernona put her into a tub of warm water and bathed her, while Ed stood beyond the door and kept them company. "You know," Halie said, "I really like California more and more."

Santa Monica Auditorium next night looked like it was being stormed—by happy people: until some 1,500 learned there were no more seats. Not one. Helping Mahalia get ready, Babe Clayton picked up the girdle. "Mahalia, this girdle's too small."

"Oh, no, we can get it in there; just take the fat and fold it in." She stood there, feet planted, while tiny Babe Clayton folded and stuffed, laughing so that Babe got tickled too. Finally—"I knew you could do it."

"Yeah, but don't move."

Butch Thornton came (brought in as road secretary), they collected Mildred, and Mahalia left, gulping huge chestfuls of air. At the hall, no fears for a buzzed-up Audrey P. this night. But she seemed to have forgotten something. Halie said nothing; she'd wait and see. . . . Hm. "Butch, go on now up to the box office." On stage, a slow, slow start, as was her wont; drawing them in, drawing them up . . . and *swoop* them, drive them to happy Glory: *The Good You Do Comes Back to You.* Dinah was there—bless her, Dinah.

Out front, at intermission Xernona Clayton grew alarmed. She hurried backstage. "Butch, intermission's so long—is Mahalia sick?"

"No," said Butch with a certain grimness, "she hasn't got the rest of her money, and she's not going on 'til she does. She's been at it too long not to know promoters."

"Mahalia," said Audrey Franklyn, handing over the cash, "you know I would have given it to you; we just didn't have it together yet."

That night at the Bahia—"Russell? You come here too?" She sat long, tears slipping down the smooth brown cheeks the photographers so loved.

Three nights later she was in Phoenix. South Bend . . . Fort Wayne . . . where we go next? Oh my God, she had to go save Jodie. She hung up the telephone, sliced off a television date, and detoured to Cleveland.

Rev. Jodie Strawther's conscience was clear, he said. "Somebody has just put the finger on me, Mahalia. I picked up these policy slips had been left in my little storefront and these policemen came in, as if I was a policy player—and you know, I'm no gambler. Now they have me up for disorderly conduct. I have an attorney to fight it, to try to preserve my name, but I figure you—"

"I'll do it, Jodie. Stop worrying."

She climbed up on the stand, eyes steady, famed voice strong as she attested to this boy's character, been a preacher since he was a child. Three days and many calls later, Jodie stood cleared in court and characterized for the black community.

Boston was waiting. And Constitution Hall.

"MAHALIA'S BREAKTHROUGH!" All seats had been sold for a month in advance. *Variety* lifted a small voice to say that Dorothy Maynor had a recital at Constitution Hall some years back, but that was deafened in the roar of applause for this first integrated audience at the historic hall. They arrived the day before—Mindling torn between protecting her strength and projecting her image. Thursday morning Mahalia sent Mildred and Willie Webb over to check their instruments and the precise positions, and to see the engineer about the sound system. You can't leave those things to the last. Excitement crackled through them all. This was being measured as the most important performance of her career. The list of government, society, and press notables due gave Mildred and Willie shivers. Joe Bostic, Al Duckett, Irving Townsend came to support her, and a cluster of Chicago ministers in chairs scrounged backstage. She'd especially checked with Boy Baby (Rev. John Thurston); he brought Emma Bell and three other preachers with him.

She walked on in a cloud of turquoise blue chiffon, and the audience never let her down . . . or themselves. Said Irving Lowens, for the *Evening Star,* "In less polite civilizations than ours, music was one step in the ladder to ecstasy, the mystic's food. More than 3,800 people felt this frightening power last night." With it, "the craving to participate, to be a part of this enormous, inspired woman gets too big to contain." Finally she was too exhausted to come back for the scores of bouquets coming across the footlights. "Send them to the sick, please," she panted, "to a hospital."

She had been on Capitol Hill and spoken to both houses of Congress; she had taped a show for Voice of America; she was due now at the reception Rep. Chester Bowles and his wife—fans and friends—were giving at their home in Georgetown. "Help me change, baby," she asked Butch Thornton.

Some of them she'd seen that day on Capitol Hill—Hubert Humphrey, James Roosevelt, her old friend Paul Douglas. Some were diplomats: the wife of the Moroccan ambassador had a beautiful flowing gown. Walter Lippman was there, and Justice Douglas. Their lingering excitement recharged hers so that she was happy, laughing easily, making others laugh—Mrs. Bowles showing her off as proudly as a diamond tiara. They understood when she must go—she must be utterly exhausted—and Halie made her way to Alma Hawkins and the eager ladies of her Interdenominational Church Ushers Assn. at *their* big reception. They'd sponsored the concert.

She could sleep, then, but next day came more reporters . . . *Newsweek,* for one, and because he caught her when she'd just called down home, she told him, "I help my relatives and their kids, but they won't give me the kids. I have nobody to come home to. At my age a person misses these things more and more." She was 47 and believed she was 48, although she gave 1912 if she wasn't figuring.

Ten days later she was back in Washington doing something she'd never thought would come: singing for the Republicans' Jumbo Jamboree. "You can't turn them down, Mahalia; it's really for the President," Lou Mindling had said.

"Ohhhh, for the President," beamed Mahalia. "He's sweet; him and his wife just like they people down home."

And he did it again. The very next day the President wrote his thank-you from himself and Mrs. Eisenhower.

ED SULLIVAN greeted her with open arms for his Easter show and she found he wanted her back for November and December—both!—before she went back home, untangled some strings, snarled some others, and made herself see Dr. Barclay about these pains before she went into being sick. The doctor began to lecture her but she started telling him about Constitution Hall and the President and what are you going to do with a patient like this except love her?

"Mahalia, remember the sarcoid affects your whole system."

"Dr. Barclay, I been pulling enough to kill a Mississippi mule."

"Then stop it. And 238 pounds, Mahalia! *That'*ll give you pressure problems. I know I'm partly to blame, because of the prednisone, but we just don't have an alternative to that."

"That's all right, Dr. Barclay," she said, consoling him.

"WELL, BUTCH, I see they got it." She was looking up at the W.C. Handy statue that nearly got her crosswise of the Baptists again, when she'd come down to Memphis to help the people raise money for it: took her out for a banquet in her honor, and it was—

"What is this place Tony's Inn?" Mahalia'd frowned up at the liquor sign outside. "The dining room's in back, Mahalia," said Butch; "they just sell liquor up front."

"Nooo, baby, Halie's not going in there." . . . "But it's your banquet!" . . . "You tell those people to come out here and tell me hello, 'cause I ain't going inside there."

"Folks had to come out and march around the car and shake hands with her," laughs Elizabeth.

Now everything was programed and publicized. After Mrs. Handy unveiled her late husband's statue for the dedication, Mahalia sang Handy's *I'll Never Turn Back*. She meant it. Now let Halie get home to her temple.

More and more, it was engrossing her. She mentioned the temple at every interview. What she wanted was to pick out a space on the South Side and build one to suit. She couldn't get a straight answer about what such a thing would cost; somebody said up to a million dollars, but she didn't believe that. If she could get the whole thing started with her own money, not have other people messing in— She hadn't given up on Columbia, that be *good* because they wouldn't come in, no more than to record. If Mayor Daley would just give her the old Municipal Pier. She *been* speaking about it—asked Bob Miller get behind the thing; he's an alderman, he can scrounch around: "Mayor Daley always call me to do this and that, Bob, and I want this temple and I think he can help; if the ground can be given, we can do these things." She believed Mayor Daley did want to help—said he'd see if there was a way and told Col. Reilly to look into it. "Anything Mahalia wants, we'll try and find it for her," Daley said. Well, she wanted a temple. And Daley's word was *law*. . . .

Col. Jack Reilly listened, but his mind strayed a little. The city's Director of Special Events couldn't decide if this temple was an idea, or something real, or a building, and what she actually needed in it, what space she needed, specific functions—solid facts to work with. He was afraid the people around her were putting her up to something to siphon off her money, and he wasn't going to be a party to that. He had a strong feeling she'd end up broke; if she did, they'd just have to take care of her. . . . "It will be an interracial, nondenominational, nonsectarian, evangelistic temple, and an institution for the teaching and training of young people. And if ever a place needs a little more of the Lord, I think it is Chicago." He looked at her sharply. No, she wasn't being critical. Just being Mahalia.

"We'll talk about it some more, Mahalia. Let me think about what's possible."

"It's been my dream for 20 years but I'm not worried about it," Mahalia said. "When the Lord is ready, I'll get it. And if it's God's will, it's already done."

That's what he meant. Was she serious?

NAT KING COLE off TV—no sponsor—so said because his love songs going into the South. Now *no* Negro had a network show. Was that a better chance, or a worse chance, for her? and the temple?

West, then catch her breath in Chicago before this Sunday School–BTU Congress coming up on her. No use for Rev. Daniels say, 'Just sing, Mahalia'; she knew she'd end up mixed in. What she didn't want to mix in was Sammy Davis, Jr., marrying a white woman—Mai Britt. Naturally all the papers going ask Mahalia. If there was one thing she couldn't see, it was black men leaving behind the black women. Who supported them in the worst? But that was something to say in the family. "You can't stop people from doing what they want to do, no matter what we think about it. Now don't you people want to ask me about the Sunday School Congress? That's why we here. Got 1,000 people rehearsing at Antioch."

"Miss Jackson, how much will you get for singing at Soldier Field?" Still and yet. "I'm not an artist when I work with the Baptists. I'm a Christian."

Oh didn't it rain, children; didn't it, didn't it! Steve had to hold an umbrella over her head—nice enough to let himself be soaked right through his hat and coat—so she could get in the middle of Soldier Field and sing for her Lord and finally she wrapped a blanket around her against the cold wind—in June!—but she sang on, though only about 2,000 people there: got that to take.

But who put that movie on in Chicago right when all the Baptists in? *Jazz on a Summer's Day,* "starring Louis Armstrong and Mahalia Jackson." Tricked into signing that release at Newport, thinking it was for the Festival! Like Beal says, there's a lot of trickeration in this world. And just as she suspected: an A.M.E. bishop came out against her. Halie thundered back. She had sung only God's songs, and always respectfully, and still she had turned down Newport Jazz Festival these last two summers for this very reason of being misunderstood.

She drank a whole pitcher of lemonade before she cooled down. Then she dismissed it. She had something more important on her mind. Martin had been in and out—especially since he'd resigned as Dexter pastor—and she'd given him bed and board and a sounding board; but now there was something solid she could take hold of.

Branch Rickey, Jackie Robinson, and Pittsburgh's mayor were on the stand at Forbes Field June 25, but 18,000 people were growing restless. "Where's Mahalia? Where's Mahalia and King?" Cheers went up as the two appeared. First Mahalia sang, whipping up the crowd . . . hair flung loose, sweat streaming down her face . . . *How I Got Over* . . . "Sing your song!" shouts the crowd . . . *I Found a New Answer* . . . some getting happy. Martin, then—"the little minister from Birmingham," the *Pittsburgh Courier* called him—a big voice and a big mission . . . "We must all live together as brothers or die together as fools" . . . Branch Rickey intent, leaning on his cane . . . "We will rise to sing a new song. Free at Last! Free at Last! Thank God Above Us! Free at Last!" The place went up. Halie's first Freedom Fund Rally. She left glowing.

Her glow for "My country, 'tis of thee" reached right through the tubes of the Emmy Award show, reached the top rating of the evening, caused Arthur Godfrey to cry, and made Townsend shiver with delight. It also caused some question on the Academy board: She just didn't fit in any category. Shouldn't they make a new one?

SERVE BEAL right. Had himself a time in Minneapolis at the Aquatennial, her billed as the star but the whole place a fair-type thing and Beal loose in it. She was ready to stay put once she got on the train, but Beal and Mildred went wandering—get themselves a drink in the club car probably. . . .

Mildred and Elliott were sitting in the diner, hadn't been served a thing yet, when they heard a crash. Beal didn't *feel* a crash, but Mildred was on him, people rolling on the floor . . . what is this? He scrambled up, Mildred still holding, and looked out, trying to see, when a man shouted the train was off the track. "My God!" cried Beal, "Mahalie! She's in the last coach! That's the first one off the rail!"

They fought their way back—Beal fighting, Mildred holding, both halfway between sobbing and fainting, past people and debris tilted every whichway—got to Mahalia's car . . . and it was standing up. They burst into her drawing room. She was just as they'd left her, meditating and praying.

"The train's wrecked, Mahalie! Come get off!"

"Oh, Beal, you so excitable. Train's not wrecked. Mildred, what you hanging on that man's back for?" Mildred was speechless but Beal almost shrieked. "Don't you see the train done hit a truck? Look! Just go look!" She picked up her Bible. "Why don't you all sit down? We be moving out of here." They had almost to haul her up, the two between them, to get her to look. "Oh, God! Beal!"

"She almost fainted!" says Beal with glee. "The train's laying all different directions, people running, ambulances coming, say 33 people hurt; police lights flashing. When the reporter come up, I was running my mouth so bad, before she could answer, I answered—and she screamed! Like to scared the reporter to death. 'I *told* you I'd find out your age!' That made me realize, so I tried to get *her* to talk but 'No, you the star, go on—you done told it all.' "

The engine had hit a trailer loaded with steel: of 15 cars, only two not derailed. One was Mahalia's.

It was good to get home. Oh, her nerves so bad. And Russell not leaving her at peace.

"NO, LANGSTON; no, baby, Mahalia's not going up on your stage in no musical, even *Tambourines for Glory*. I know you got a good show, but you be running in theaters, won't you? Sure you will. And Miss Jackson, in case you forgot, Mr. Hughes, does not enter theaters. Yeah, I made the movies, but I ain't been to see them."

"THE SENATOR would like to speak with you, Miss Jackson." Would she campaign for him, for the Presidency? Oh, Lord, she had so much of her own work to do, and going to work with Martin—"I just don't believe I want to get in all these big politics," she told John F. Kennedy, Democratic candidate, thanking him and wishing him well. Shortly, across the city, Tommy King, Sargent Shriver's assistant at the Merchandise Mart, tracked down Lou Mindling in Florida. "The Senator would like Mahalia to back him."

"Tommy," said Mindling, "I know she'll do it, 'cause she loves the family. And the Roosevelts. But I want one thing from you. Promise me no one else will sing the national anthem before Mahalia in Washington."

"You got it." Mindling didn't tell Mahalia that last. Let the man win first. She probably couldn't stay out of it anyway, Mahalia decided. Not living in Chicago. So she better tend to this for Aunt Duke right away. Strange, she had no thought of Duke, she'd swear, waking up—and the Voice spoke and said go buy her a house. Three times, the Voice spoke. No mistake. She was so struck, she called Brother John to tell him.

If you put your mind to it, in New Orleans it was no trouble to find a house. She located a nice one on Delachaise, a double, enough room for Auntie and Brisko's son Fred and Etta and the children: three already. Look like they could spare one, but no. Selfish. And Isabell can move in the other half. That way they all be close. . . . Oh, but Aunt Duke was happy about that house. With no call to be stern, she had thrown that over entirely and now she almost jigged, there in the upstairs of Bessie's camelback. Taking her ease, Halie watched Brisko's daughter Rose set out the ironing board to press Aunt Mahalia's dress. Mahalia showed her: a light touchup, like this. . . . Look like anything she ask, Rose willing to do—if they'd let her have this child those summers ago. . . . "You go on with it now. I'm going stretch out."

Rose sidled into the bedroom. "Where my dress?"

"Your dress has—had a hole in it."

Mahalia was swift—had a grip on Rose's arm before she could squirm away. "Now tell me the *truth.*"

"The dress had a hole in it."

"I never had that dress on my back. It has never been worn. You going tell me the truth?"

It came out, then: iron too hot, sticking, and lifted—a hole looked big as a ditch. Mahalia relaxed her grip. "That's okay," she comforted the weeping child. "I told you, but you just didn't remember how. Now take this, go buy you an ice cream cone." Better than cat-nine-tails. And look at how jolly Aunt Duke is today. "Yeah, I'm coming!"

When she got home, she was shopping and saw just two beautiful framed pictures, a boy and a girl, light brown, all smiling. "That will be my little boy and girl," she said, and bought them.

IT WAS THREE worlds far and two lives wide, to hit Madison Square Garden, Beal alongside playing host in the dressing room, the whole flux and flow of gospeldom in and out . . . old friends: "Hey, Ernestine!"—there with her big Temple Choir . . . protégés: The Drinkard Singers all over her . . . young Aretha, Rev. C. L. Franklin's child, her first record for Columbia due out with Alex Bradford directing the choir; Butch be so pleased—had carried the girl wherever in New York Al Duckett set it up for her. Mahalia herself was glad—child come to her all distressed, first chance she had to cut some little record off from gospel—afraid of what her father would say; and Mahalia said just ask God's guidance and go on. ("When I first interviewed Aretha," says John Hammond, "she said Mahalia Jackson had been her inspiration from a child. But the style wasn't derivative.")

"All right, people, I think Miss Jackson would like to be alone a while now, to meditate." Beal could act so grand. "Here, Beal, watch my pocketbook. I just got this little piece of singing before intermission—to let them know not to go away—so see can you find us some sandwiches or *something*. I'm empty as a cupboard."

STUDS TERKEL's voice on the telephone was exuberant. "Mahalia, I've been up talking with Paul Robeson, and he can't say enough about you. He brought up your name over and over."

"Ohhhh." An awed whisper. "That's a great man."

"I know." Studs wanted to write a feature about her for *Downbeat;* when could he come out to talk. "You already know everything I think, Stud, but you come on out when you want. Halie's got time for you long as she lives." She canceled out on the Baptists, though—at the last minute: when Chauncey Eskridge (the young lawyer who handled her taxes in Ming's office and worked for Martin, too, since Alabama) arrived to go to Philadelphia with her for his first Convention. She didn't explain, just "Take this $100 and you go on." What kept her home was a mixture of politics, doctor, mood, and mainly, her foundation, and she'd just as soon not go into all that. . . .

She said one last prayer, mulled one last time, and signed her name to create the Mahalia Jackson Foundation. She would found her temple through that. She guess they knew what they were doing.

Lou Mindling wasn't at all sure of that when Erie, Pa., had such unheard-of bad weather for September that they canceled her concert . . . and instead of leaving, she offered to give it this next night. "Mahalia, for God's sake, you're due in Springfield to sing tomorrow night."

"I'm not going let these children down—this is for the crippled children to get a pool, to straighten their legs." Not everybody can have a miracle. "We'll just drive on after—we'll make it in time for the curtain." Mr. Mindling wasn't used to this hardness of the road. He ought to known her before she got up on the hog, before she hit with Apollo.

"INTRODUCING Apollo's New LP 1000 Series," the *Cashbox* ad read. "Might known Bess Berma would find another way to cash in," said Mahalia.

"Well," said Lou, rubbing his hands, "that's just more royalties."

COLORADO, Kansas, Indiana, then a heavy schedule of TV, stars she held in awe so sweet to her, seem to want to set her apart but she wouldn't have it; and sometimes she got autographs. Mrs. Eleanor Roosevelt's "Diamond Jubilee Plus One" special rounded up the most—a chance to see Nat King Cole, Bob Hope, Carol Channing, Jimmy Durante—what a natural man, and Lord she love that Lucille Ball, watch her all the time. But TV. Like putting a watermelon in a teacup. "You've got 1 minute 59 seconds, Miss Jackson"; maybe that song need 5 or 6 minutes to bring its message through. When she was broadcasting from her temple, she'd let the Lord come. . . .

She hoped Mayor Daley was noticing Mahalia was acting like a queen herself, greeting the King and Queen of Denmark: in case he had any doubts whether she could preside over her temple with dignity. Which he didn't, she knew that. Who did she wish most could see her? Aunt Duke, maybe. Aunt Bell! "You will walk with kings and queens." She called home that night. "Aunt Bell, when you say, it might take time, but a person can sure put their foot on it."

Chicago's 400 and its political 600 swirled in elegance that coveted night, hoping for a word, a glance from tall King Frederik XI or fair Queen Ingrid. But to the press's eagle eye, it was Mahalia Jackson who won their hearts. After dinner Queen Ingrid told Mahalia that *Down by the Riverside* made her feel good; and Mahalia, with a twinkle, said it made her feel good herself. "Come to Denmark," urged the queen warmly. "I'm going to do that." She'd still take democracy—and Kennedy for President, she said loud and clear in Chicago as the countdown neared: "He can put a little more sun and a little more hope in people's lives. I'm going to vote for him. You vote for him, too." The black queen had spoken.

Nov. 8, Chicago helped elect John F. Kennedy. Mahalia watched the returns in New York, stretched out at the Waldorf Towers.

She just loved the Waldorf. She'd done an Ed Sullivan show and tomorrow she was going over to Brooklyn to help them get a child care center, but right now she just loved the Waldorf. And said so, on the telephone to Lou Mindling. Mildred and Louise were out. "Know what I wish this minute? I wish I had me some good fish."

"All right, stay right in your room and I'll see that you get it." He called the owner of the King of the Sea across the way and asked him, as a favor, to send the fish over to Mahalia Jackson. Calculating the time of arrival, he waited a margin of safety and called her. "This is the front desk. You're not allowed to cook in your apartment and there's a fish odor in the hall. Some of the guests are complaining."

"Oh, *no*!" came Mahalia's voice, horrified, aghast. "I'm not cooking, honest to *God*. Somebody sent it to me!"

"I'm glad to hear that," the agent said in his own voice. "How's the fish?"

"Mr. Mindling," said Mahalia, "why you do that to me?"

Peter Lawford called soon after. There'd be a big inauguration gala, and President Kennedy particularly wanted her to sing *The Star-Spangled Banner. The Star-Spangled—!* Ain't sung that since McDonogh 24. Why *The Star*—"Tell the President I'll be pleased to come."

Now when Belafonte called, he made her want to dance the holy dance: meet him in Israel and film a television documentary of religious songs on the actual Biblical sites. It couldn't have been more right. William Morris was this minute getting together her first tour of Europe since she'd cut short and almost died, nine years ago. Nine? Seem like twenty. Somebody else talking about a movie, but Europe held her mind—and just been invited by the Queen. Besides— She put the thought away 'til she could meditate on it. Got to pull out now for Constitution Hall. No big thing, going back so soon. Except to Louise, coming to play organ. . . .

Just like she thought. A good, rousing Saturday night. But she got more out of Sunday afternoon, when she rode out to Lorton Reformatory with the Catholic chaplains who'd brought her a gospel song an inmate wrote. They sang the song for her, the boys of the Reformatory Glee Club, and when they finished, for an hour Mahalia sang for them, talking a little in between. "Don't forget God—He's the best friend you got. It's only the help of God keeps us from being tossed on the wrong side. Don't let the Devil win! Hallelujah. How you think I got over? There is no great and no small among us; we great when we got God's love, and we small only when we reject Him. And remember, boys, Devil's not always ugly. He is not! Evil can wear pretty face. You got to *recognize* him . . . with the help of God. Now what's one last song you want me to sing, 'fore I got to go?"

Look like a good gospel song can reach in, where a anthem don't. So tell it city-wide: a city-wide revival. For eight straight nights she sang revival, preached revival, danced and shouted revival, at Pilgrim Baptist. Wait 'til she had her temple!

Since she was known to be home, people popped up like corn. If Polly was there, she guarded the door, but she had her errands and missions—besides, the side way was unlocked, so "Anybody home? Mahalia? Miss Jackson?" Might be a friend, or a stranger bold as brass. The house was full of people when she came back from a concert one night with $5,000 cash in her purse and weariness in her soul. She lifted with the crowd, the conversation; began stirring up something to eat, got to singing—when suddenly something told her go check on her money.

Gone. "I didn't do a thing but make a circuit of my house, then call everybody into one room. 'All right, I have locked every door in this house; nobody gets out; and I'm going to call the police if my money ain't back in my purse in 10 minutes. I'm not moving. You all go do what you want, go on about your business; I'm standing right here.' Child, in 10 minutes by the clock, when I went to that purse and looked, my money was right back where it belonged. That taught me a lesson—not to leave my purse out of my sight, unless I put it in a hand I could trust."

She had plenty use for that $5,000. Specially at Christmas. Missie and her daughter and grandchildren. The family. And this one can't pay the rent; this one need clothes; this one need medicine, Christmas dinner; this one's babies need school. And got to feed Pharaoh's army. Look like Albertina found herself a preacher right at Halie's table. "Talked about me like a *dog* about that," laughs Albertina. "She was a matchmaker, always pushing people together."

Russell, Russell, can't you rest?

WHEN CHICAGO let loose a blizzard, that was it. Traffic blocked. Even if she got *to* a train, wouldn't run, or not on time. And all those people in Memphis been working for voter registration under steady hate, they counting on Mahalie. She called the phone company. "We got to—" For half an hour, from 8358 Indiana, Halie held the telephone and sang to the families gathered at Owens, the Negro college. Joy to the world. Good will to men.

Now Ed Sullivan—there's a man people call frozen, got so *much* good will. She was helping him with the big Catholics: her last Christmas mission before she could join Jesus and Joseph and Mary on the ass. Hadn't even finished decorating yet. But Cardinal Spellman was having a big rally in Madison Square Garden to raise money for a new seminary. Mahalia was a major attraction and never more so than now: She'd just been named one of the most-admired women in the world, in the Gallup Poll.

"Cardinal Spellman, there's one thing I been thinking. I'm going to Europe next year and—you know I'm a Baptist, but I sure would like to meet the Pope."

40

"The Inaugural Committee requests the honor of your presence to attend and participate . . . " "President-elect Kennedy has personally requested that the enclosed invitations be . . . " "In honor of the Governors . . . and Special Distinguished Guests from three to six." "In honor of the Distinguished Ladies . . . three to six." ("Oh-oh," said Mahalia, "the governors and the distinguished ladies going bump.") "In honor of . . ."

"I can't go to all that," said Mahalia, dropping the newest arrival; "we got to rehearse. Okay, Mildred, let's go through again—and don't be trying tell me how to sing *The Star-Spangled Banner;* I been singing *The Star-Spangled Banner* ever since I been in school. Use that last key. I got to wrestle this thing to get the substance."

Sinatra said come Wednesday if you could, so she came—in comfort on Mayor Daley's special train. She and Mildred walked into confusion, found Frank Sinatra—and discovered who *all* was on: Ella Fitzgerald, in from Australia; Berle, Durante, Poitier, Nat King Cole, Frederic March, Tony Curtis, Joey Bishop . . . who all *wasn't* on. Sinatra called places and they all climbed up. Stand-ins were needed for the ones not here yet. Right now, Sammy Cahn, the songwriter, was being Belafonte. Stagehands and electricians were banging and excuse-it-please; men fitting iron pipes for the stands; Halie looked every moment for Sinatra to let loose his famous temper. The weather was miserable and everybody was worried about a blizzard forecast. Her *Star-Spangled Banner* was tomorrow when the whole cast was there, because after she sang, everybody would. But there was the all-company number . . . placement . . . bows . . . rehearsal went on through the night. Mahalia didn't mind; it was a pleasure to watch these people work. And Helen Traubel—"That woman can sing!" Halie whispered to Mildred.

The snow held off Thursday morning and everybody got in. One big black-browed man caught her attention. "Who that?"

"That's the great Anthony Quinn!" Mildred whispered back.

Anthony Quinn overheard. Instant friends, he told Mahalia she'd put him back in his place, and autographed her program "To my love—Your love, Tony Quinn."

One thing—she knew her words. That was more than some could say, from the sound of them backstage. "Why don't they get . . ." "We don't sing this song all the time . . ." "Well, we don't know this . . ." Ooohhhhh, the singers fussing about their *Star-Spangled Banner!* Her cue. She walked on. Mildred started—the band was to come in, this first rehearsal—and Halie began, *O-h, say can you see—* Kay Thompson, taking the music run-through, had given a lot of instructions to the musicians and to everybody and Halie had listened somewhat but the only thing she had to concentrate on was singing this song. *O-h, say can you see—* This woman speaking to Mildred! got some complaint—the key? tempo? Halie caught enough. "Do you want to sing this song!" she thundered. "Do you want to sing this song? *You* come on up here and sing—" Laurence Olivier saw her face and came running. Leonard Bernstein, closer, moved in too; "she doesn't sing," he said hurriedly. "—'cause I'm not pleasing you. You seem to be in charge here and I'm not pleasing you." Olivier spoke to Miss Thompson, then in the nicest way explained the problem to Mahalia . . . oh, this was the most *marvelous* man, so kind; the really great people, they're nice. Bernstein had his say to the woman too, Mahalia saw out of the side of her eye. Coming in here, upsetting everything . . . now she gone over to Sinatra. "GET THE HELL OUT OF HERE!" Oh-ohhhh . . . picked the wrong man. Woman won't bother Halie no more.

Mr. Bernstein explained the music part. "Mildred, I *told* you that wasn't the right way to do that!"—and while she had the chance, she asked Mr. Oliva about some of her diction. He helped her a lot.

It was snowing when they broke, and the blizzard had snarled the entire city by the time they managed their way back to the National Armory—late, but almost everybody else was later. Some who took in the parties couldn't make it to their hotels to dress: came as they were. Most of the audience was later than the cast. They'd never wind up by midnight. At last Bernstein's *Fanfare for Inauguration* sounded, then a brisk *Stars and Stripes Forever*. Backstage, everybody got into lineup position. Now.

Walking Down to Washington—all on stage singing except Mahalia. Then *Anchors Aweigh* to bring in the real stars: the President-elect and the Vice President-elect. The show had started.

"Just leave her alone, let Mahalia be by herself," they'd counseled each other beforehand. She was in a little space made for her—hands clasped, eyes closed. That was Mildred's last view before she went to the piano. Mildred said a little prayer herself. Mahalia walked on alone, stood still, bowed with that special dignity, closed her eyes, and sang *The Star-Spangled Banner*. "Oh, my God," Mildred breathed, awed, "she's come out a different Mahalia!"

"Encore! encore! encore!" They'd never *listened* to the words before. "And Laurraines," Halie said later, with vast satisfaction, "my diction was like an Englishman's.

"But they could have let us sing songs that we had made our thing and got a nice, known person in the neighborhood to sing *The Star-Spangled Banner.*"

At intermission, she'd hoped to say hello to President Truman, but the crowd pressed in so . . . she and Ella Fitzgerald started signing autographs back to back and ended up four people apart. The vice-president's daughters, Luci and Lynda Bird—darling girls—had their picture taken with her. All Halie had before her now was the reprise on *Walking Down to Washington.* Then everybody could get something to eat. Frank Sinatra was having dinner for the cast.

Thank-you, Lord, right where she's staying, the Statler Hilton—but look at the glasses by each plate! "If I drink all that, I'll be drunk," Mahalia told Bette Davis, who'd followed her around all day, it seemed to Halie. The highlight, though, wasn't the food. She was taken up to meet Vice President Johnson and his wife—so Southern—and President Kennedy's family—she knew some of them already, but his mother and father, she hadn't met them. It wasn't until about an hour later, when they were eating, that her eye fell on a face approaching she well recognized: the President himself. He came to tell her how much he enjoyed her singing; he'd admired it since Newport. "And you know what impressed me about Kennedy?" she said, telling it: "His hands. He had the largest hands I ever saw on a man—I first noticed when he took mine: I put both mine in his—and his fit right over." It was his blue eyes that held her, though. They looked deep into hers, and she felt the magnetism. Later she spoke with Mrs. Kennedy. She had the most beautiful voice.

AN OFFICIAL Distinguished Guest on the President's platform. It hit home, now the show business was over. This was the business of America. The governors. The Congress. The military chiefs. There was a happiness, and a seriousness too. She got a chance to speak to President Truman. He was like a little happy boy, now President Kennedy had invited him back. He said he hadn't been back to the White House since he left, and when Mahalia asked why not?—he said he hadn't been invited.

A WEEK LATER was like old times—Sinatra, Belafonte, *plus* Sammy Davis, Jr., Count Basie, Tony Bennett, Dean Martin—just a whole bunch more, backstage at Carnegie Hall with and for Dr. Martin Luther King, Jr. Halie was a happy girl. They'd picked a quotation of Martin's for the program that said it all: "We now fight for the most elementary right of all—the right to have rights." Ah, Martin. He's deep. But he's a natural man; none of this going to his head. And never say nothing in private he won't say in public. Some Negroes talking he don't go far enough, ought to take out after Whitey. But Martin shared with her the center and core of it: You can't hate God—who would dare?—and there is something of God within every man. Even if some take a lot of praying over.

The hall was packed: chairs bloomed on stage. But all the talent didn't get the applause that went up when Martin was introduced. He sounded a cry for help, not to go to jail, or sit-in—"we can handle that"—but for artists to use their talents to help raise money: the crying need. That Friday night, Jan. 27, 1961, they raised $50,000 for SCLC. And Mahalia, without a flaw, sang *The Star-Spangled Banner*.

"Don't you all think I know something else?" she'd demanded beforehand. "Do you know I know *'McDonogh, leeet the trumpets blow'* "—yodeling it, mock-opera style, to Sinatra's mystification. "That's what we sing down in New Orleans, baby."

("I did that to Truman, Laurraines, when we were campaigning," she laughed, "and poor Truman didn't know what I was talking about either!") Monday, Martin was at 8358 Indiana taking his ease. He'd made a talk at Orchestra Hall, and Butch Thornton had called earlier to say she'd like to come fix him a dinner at Mahalia's.

"Go ahead, baby; you know you're more than welcome to do it."

Butch picked out the prettiest of everything—some hadn't ever been used—with Mahalia's best silverware and crystal. Then they learned there was something more than fellowship to celebrate: Coretta and Martin's third child was due. "We all sat around that day and kidded him," says Butch. "And he kept going to the telephone to check." Mrs. King was already in the hospital. "If it's a girl," said Butch, "you're going to name it Elizabeth, after me." Mahalia rared back: "You better name it Mahalia!" The third female of the party, Cordie King (no relation) spoke up. "It's got to have a *part* of my name, Cordia." The poor man was cornered. "I'll tell you what," he said. "I'll let somebody here select a name if it's a girl. But if it's a boy, it's going to be named for my church in Montgomery—Dexter."

They were sitting around having coffee—tea, for Mahalia—when he took a call and came back beaming. "It's Dexter."

She had one week, then, to square off Chicago, and pack. William Morris had outdone themselves: after Ohio and Indiana, they'd booked her into Montana in February—tight-packed bookings that train schedules couldn't meet. "Mahalia, if you'd just *fly*," said Mindling, exasperated.

"Halie don't fly, Mr. Mindling, less she's desperate or too sick to be in her right mind—and she's neither one now." She gathered up Louise and Mildred, with Frye to drive, and they rolled forth in the Cadillac. If the drifts were deep, the audiences were warm and gradually the weather was too, thank You Lord: California.

LOS ANGELES was like a wheel—she could reach out and give a concert close by; she could record, she could do TV . . . and did all three, including one for her dear love, Dinah. ("Why wouldn't you love Dinah Shore and Bing Crosby?" demanded Irving Townsend; "if they paid me as much as they pay you, I'd love them too.") She had a big Shrine date to promote for Audrey P. Franklyn, and the dynamo took her in tow again—with a new caboose: the bitter teenager of Cocoa, Florida, who on an impulse against all reason found Mahalia's Chicago telephone was in fact listed—reached not Polly but her—spurted rapidfire his story, her solace, his yearning to sing gospel, do entertainment, do something. . . . "How old are you?" Mahalia cut across the flood. "Eighteen, but—"

"I tell you what. You get in touch with Pat Boone, Johnny Lange and Dinah Shore, and tell them I said call. I be out in L.A. in March, at the Bahia Motel, and you come see me then, you hear?" Dick Yancey heard. And came. And fell into step. Could he—? He'd be glad to— Audrey P. Franklyn wasn't too sure about this proffered free help. But when he called to say he was on the street . . . the man where he was staying (a New York friend of Mahalia's) had had a heart attack—could she put him up for the night? . . . she did. And only put him out when two months had gone by.

Just another boy trying to stay on top the water, Mahalia shrugged. It didn't hurt Audrey P., and Yancey taking her records around to all these radio stations. Columbia didn't send them out—getting terrible on promotion—and the boy could get himself known. You hardly ever get to win on both ends. She had a special reason for wanting this Shrine concert to really go over: All her part was for the temple. And Europe be, too. Then with the record royalties. . . . Nobody had yet given her a figure she could put her foot on. As soon as she had the chance, she was going study that. The Lord would show the way.

No Sunday afternoons for Audrey P.—her Mahalia concert was Saturday night, to spell Event. The night before, Dmitri Tiomkin and his wife created their own Mahalia happening in the Crystal Room of the posh Beverly Hills Hotel, stamped official by the presence of archrival press queens Hedda Hopper and Louella Parsons. It was a turnout of 100 top Hollywood personalities for the cocktail hour—with no cocktails. No liquor at all, at Mahalia's request. It was, mused one, quite a tribute to the lady. And if the stairs up to the Polo Lounge Bar had unusual traffic. . . .

Mahalia wasn't scheduled to—it was her party—but she was so happy she sang four songs. Hedda Hopper got the best of Louella Parsons, then: she kneeled in tribute before a great lady . . . and made *Variety*.

Next night at the Shrine Auditorium before a crowd big enough to gladden the hungry heart of Audrey P., Mahalia sang Tiomkin's *Green Leaves of Summer*. It wasn't a gospel song, "but it feels like one," she explained to Bing's young wife when Kathy came to her dressing room to say hello. It was the least she could do, for not singing his film score for him.

UCLA's Royce Hall, then, and turned away a multitude. The boy Yancey wanted her to sing *Rusty Old Halo* but she just pushed up her lip; she didn't like that song. "Besides, *my* halo's not going be rusty." But she sang, sang and *sang* for the college people; came back and sang again—soaring, down only for the applause, the bowing . . . and collapse. The alarmed series director hurried into the dressing room with smelling salts. "Mahalia proves her point and then she oversells," Audrey P. told him, disapproving.

Taking her back to the Bahia, Audrey fretted. "Mahalia, why do you stay at an $8-a-night motel like this? You should be at the Beverly Hilton." Mahalia shrugged. "I don't have anything to prove. I might as well stay here close to NBC, doing these shows with Dinah."

With all this, it was Irving Townsend who claimed the lion's share of Mahalia's mind. He was sewing up for them both a TV film project which was utterly, completely to her liking: with a syndicate, he would produce, and she would sing, 85 filmed segments for television, one song each, to be sold as a long-run series; or the segments could be bunched, if desired. They could start, he said, when she was back from Europe and rested—about mid-June. Hallelujah! But she wasn't telling it 'til she saw a camera roll.

Well, finish up this session. Robert Anderson's new song coming out good. He better like it—his song, and him on piano.

Before she left town, she did a Steve Allen show that taught her something. Mid-song, and her wholly taken up with the message, the moving rhythm, she realized she had a piece of tooth on her tongue. It *felt* like a tooth. She managed to get through and sure enough—it was a tooth.

After the show, she showed Steve Allen. "You and your show! You know I broke a tooth out there singing?" No! "You don't believe it? Here's the tooth." Telling it, she laughed. "Look like he could at least give me a dime for my tooth. He was too surprised to think of it.

"And that's the first time I knew I sang with my teeth."

41

Back out of the West: Phoenix, Santa Fe, Gallup, and now Indian territory —the real thing. But this big, modern round center at Window Rock didn't look Indian to Halie, eying its crowded reach . . . and then she saw it, what she was hoping for without knowing it: Navajo women with papooses on their backs. Oh, the babies. Like dolls. Hey, Warpee! She sang gospel from the heart that night, and they knew it, responded—who said Indians sat on you? She bought her some real Indian moccasins . . . not to remember them by, she didn't need that, but because they looked so comfortable and she was going to climb Calvary. Hallelujah!

San Antonio . . . and turn the map toward Chicago. "Frye, you can throw that map away; I know these roads by heart."

Now Europe, that was different: Five countries be all new, and she was in shape to enjoy the whole seven. No more than tired. March 23, she pulled into her driveway. March 27, she'd leave—but she'd have that nice long week on the ship. Uncle Porter was there and he'd stay on, be in the house while she's gone. He never stayed less than a month at a time, anyway. One main person to talk to was Willa Jones: she *been* to the Holy Land. Halie still wasn't sure what all was booked, but William Morris promised she could have two whole weeks in the Holy Land at the end—just sing when she felt like it, for herself, and visit the holy places. "Honey," said Willa, "if you go up to Calvary, you going to start on your knees, and you going to climb the mountain."

"Well," said Mahalia, almond eyes gleaming, "I got my walking stick and I got my walking shoes."

JUST THE LEAVING said '61 was different. In '52 she was too sick for festivities, but this time she had three: all the gospel troupe at Kenneth Morris's house for a big *bon voyage*—a time-and-a-half up to the minute they boosted her on the train for D.C. with Mildred, Nettie, Polly, and Al Duckett, to *bon voyage 2*—undreamed-of by the Halie of '52. . . .

Mrs. Bowles was a wonderful woman. And Mr. Bowles. Under-Secretary of State now and still look at the trouble they gone to, giving her a *bon voyage* and just gave her a big party last year. Some of the same faces . . . didn't Mildred and Al and Nettie and Polly have their eyes popping! Rev. Joe Campbell, too—brand-new in Washington; he was her escort. He'd brought along a lawyer friend, Bill Davis—fine-looking man, remind her of— Ducket better be taking these names; that's his job for the trip, publicity . . . Dean Acheson, Asst. Secretary of State Philip Combs, Sen. John H. Cooper, Humphrey, Justice Douglas, all the ambassadors: Herve Alphand from France, August Lindt of Switzerland, Avraham Harmen from Israel—she could ask him about Gethsemane. *A man's gift maketh room for him, and bringeth him before great men.* Proverbs 18. Jerusalem! "That's the most important thing of my life," she said softly to the reporters, "to walk the streets where our Lord once walked."

Eying her and Bill Davis, Rev. Campbell had a feeling these two were going to be tight. "Don't he remind you of Russell?" Mahalia murmured. Campbell know what she mean—he's the one introduced her to Russell Roberts at Convention. She wasn't a bit tired; maybe they could have them some dinner together. She felt fine. Tomorrow to New York—then Holy Thursday! Lord, You sure with Halie, start her off Holy Thursday for the Holy Land.

Bon voyage 3 was her Eastern own sending Sister off in style. Young David Haber from William Morris, their road manager, had never seen the like: enough fruits, chocolates, and champagne for half the S.S. *United States.* "Dave-honey, you better come on, go with us, stay off that plane," said Halie. David shook his head—he had a desk to clear—but suddenly, looking at the face alight, the eyes crinkling in the rich brown face, he wished he could. He walked her to the ship's rail for the last goodbyes. Confetti flew up from the dock and she pitched streamers of paper serpentine that landed in a widening gap of water as the band played on. The last face she could really make out was Ernestine Washington's.

My Jesus! she better rest. "Mildred, you go on, show Al around. I got a whole week to do it in. Go on—this *your* ship, girl." That's why Halie'd picked it; Mildred had raved on so about what Mahalia missed in '52.

"Mildred! You dirty dog. Why didn't you tell me I'd get seasick! Lord, help me. It wasn't this bad when I almost died. Don't talk fresh air to me, girl; I no more than try to move and I'm over that basin."

"I'm sick myself, Mahalia—everybody's sick. I swear to God, it wasn't like this last time."

"Oooooooooooooh!" Too sick to go meet Jackie Gleason; do that later. Lord, *Lord!* how she going get up Sunday and sing for those people, bring the wonder of the Lord as she promised—as William Morris promised, too, come to that. But Easter! the time of joy, He is risen. *The Lord, your God, is in your midst. . . . He will exult over you with loud singing on a day of festival.* Lord, if I make it, You going have it to do; Halie can't.

They thought it was what the ship's doctor gave her—that and the diet—but she knew it was praying put her on her feet in this salon—shaky, but singing it out . . . *Were You There When They Crucified My Lord*—Easter and she was going to the Holy Land, and to see the Pope.

Cardinal Spellman fixed that. Halie, Halie, look at you . . . No, look at this water. "Even though the water made me sick, quite sick, I would find myself all day watching the sea, and the way the water would run. It never ran the same way; sometimes it was like this, and sometimes like that—sometimes like this—and like that. It keeps you interested all day long, watching which way the sea going turn—whether it's going spread out, or whether it's going drop; all these different forms that it takes. And the sounds it makes. There really is a song of the sea."

BUSTLE OFF Tuesday at Southampton in a cluster of reporters, photographers, David Haber, and the British sponsor's man, get whisked through customs and into a limousine. Riding into London, Halie felt for the first time that she was on tour. Her comeback. She weighed 240 pounds.

First, the press . . . *hey*! Maxie Jones, her old friend. Honors from the

Lord Mayor—Mayor Daley's doings. Next day, sing for the BBC—"Dave-honey, they calling it the *Mahalia Jackson Show!*" She's really thrilled, thought David, elated—her first network special all her own. "And these people *so* nice." Some of them remembered her from nine years ago, when she was the first gospel singer on BBC—and they no easier now to understand. Yes milord, no milord. Well, she *could* make it out. Then the big day, the test—and to make it tougher, Columbia was recording her live. Check out Albert Hall early. The place was warm. They tested the mikes. The iron band eased in her chest. Mildred flexed her fingers and grinned: no organist to fool with this time.

Friday night over 6,000 people crammed every permissible foot of Albert Hall—latecomers turned away. David hurried into the dressing room to tell her royalty was in the box. Curtain. Fantastic! breathed David, watching offstage. God! What a woman. And the audience! Halie was transported. This was an English audience? Clapping, and clapping *correctly*, a current across the footlights she could feel. The joy of it! She went off, finally, to a standing ovation. She was trying to get her wind back before she changed when Princess Alexandra came backstage to tell her she was "absolutely brilliant." The Albert Hall manager was utterly floored, David noticed, when the Princess told Mahalia not to stand.

Outside, the jostling, trampling, eager autograph-seekers were so dense that a squad of bobbies had to make a way. The last foot, David fairly heaved her into the car so they could make their escape, thrusting Mildred in after. "Dave-honey," she panted, "they like to loved me to death that time."

The critics did too. "An extraordinary spell," exulted Noel Goodwin in the *Express:* "Mahalia Jackson sang to *ME* last night." Mike Nevard of the *Daily Herald* had scored a beat by reviewing her records and was ready for the night. "The sheer beauty of her voice, the feeling she puts into every word, make the hair tingle on the back of your neck—whether you be Christian, atheist or agnostic." An "extremely un-British reception," the press agreed. *New Statesman*'s Francis Newton said, "We can congratulate ourselves that she has done us the honor of visiting this country."

But she was due Monday in Germany. There was the Channel to cross, then Belgium into Central Germany, and Mahalia would not fly. She'd had *that* written into her contracts. David suffered in silence; Duckett sputtered. Mildred kept her relief to herself: it *was* trouble, especially the loading and unloading and the waits for schedules, but that's the road, isn't it?

FROM THE OUTSIDE, Frankfurt's *Kongresshalle* looked like postwar German modern but its manager was pompous Prussian. Any request for shifting equipment or improving poor mikes or, worse, the piano was a personal affront. "If he's a Frankfurter, I'll take wienies," said Mahalia. But go on, make do, it's just for Tuesday night . . . which turned into a rousing, stomping, whistling, cheering, won't-stop-applauding reception. They couldn't be understanding her, not her words, and yet "Mah-hahl-ya! Mah-hahl-ya! Mah-hahl-ya!" Her first exposure to the European unison-clap and foot-stomp—like a drum beat and just as insistent. She couldn't *take* another encore. Mildred helped her change into street clothes and still "Mah-hahl-ya!" One more. And just one more.

The crowd at the exit was worth your life. "You got to be strong in Europe to take popularity," she told Mildred, hard put to scurry behind. It was the overture of Germany's passionate romance. Before she set foot on their soil, Mahalia's records had touched something in the collective German soul—some wellhead of yearning—so that over one-third of her whole tour had been booked by her German sponsor and every seat sold far in advance in the five cities. Hearing her now, gaining the greater dimension of her being—the full impact of her *presence*—she was their Valentine of the spirit. They needn't know her language to speak to her of love. Mail, flowers, telegrams poured in, and she exited each stage wading in bouquets. Nothing like the outpouring had been seen in Berlin's huge *Sportspalast* since Hitler worked the crowd into a frenzy with his own religion, leading them on to war . . . but here was their heart, who would lead them into peace.

"Mah-hahl-ya!" Just one more.

Working around two polarities—her command performance at the Three Falcons Theatre in Copenhagen on April 18 and her audience at the Vatican with Pope John on May 3—her schedule yo-yoed in and out, up and down country, and the trains seemed to stop more than they ran. "Fly!" pleaded David Haber. "Fly!" pleaded the sponsor's man. Mildred held her breath. "Nooo, no; you not going to take me up in one of them." Mahalia was rock. Mildred relaxed. Still safe. Sore but safe.

Everywhere, the lord mayors were taking seriously Mayor Daley's letters naming her Chicago's Ambassador of Good Will. She appreciated the formalities and wrote Kup how nice all the Lords were being to her; it showed what a big man Daley was in Europe. But Hamburg was for shopping: a city of water and bridges that was a *crystal* city. Nothing she liked better than buying for her house, unless it was buying for Aunt Duke's house; and here's a good excuse to do both. Couldn't come up against bargains like this in the States. "Dave-honey! look at there! That's some just like Mrs. Plant used to *dare* Halie not to break when I was helping Aunt Duke wash up after they had a party . . . and here some eggshell porcelain china Mrs. Rightor be proud to use." David Haber trailed her contentedly, helping with the salespeople. Watching Mahalia pleased with her pretties was entertainment enough—and he wasn't letting this valuable person out of his sight.

"Mah-hahl-ya!" Friday night at the *Musikhalle* they wouldn't let her go. Encores after the encores and still "Mah-hahl-ya!" She wasn't going stay in these needlepoint shoes another minute, though; not after all the walking today with photographers trailing behind. She came on in her Indian moccasins—and the house roared adoration. "Mah-hahl-ya!" There must be an end—for the next beginning—and there'd be more Germany: Munich and Essen after Paris, and now William Morris adding on Switzerland, squeezing in on her time for Rome.

FIRST, INTO Communist country—14 hours of jolting, bumping, jerking toward Berlin on a train that could only have square wheels, the very ride a penance for sins and the sight of helmeted soldiers checking papers at every train stop making suddenly real all the stories you heard about Communist kidnapings and worse. The sponsoring agent's presence was nothing to ease *her* mind. The soldiers and officials tried to catch her eye but she withheld, willed herself anonymous; "and Mildred, don't you look at them either." She prayed and searched her soul and told her chest to relax. "Oh, Mahalia, fly!" groaned David Haber, making it his prayer. The luggage problem alone was a killer.

From the safety of the hotel Sunday morning, Mahalia completed a phone call. Then she walked in on Mildred. "I talked to my aunt, and Aunt Hannah say it's all right, 'cause she talked to the Lord and it's all right for me to fly."

"You talked to *your* aunt!" Mildred cried, "but I ain't talked to *mine. My* aunt didn't tell me nothing! Your aunt told *you* to fly, it's all right for *you* to fly, but *my* aunt didn't tell me *nothing*!"

"Ohhh," says Mildred Falls, "Mahalia made *out!* She laughed at me 'til she cried. I had to fly on *her* aunt, 'cause *my* aunt didn't tell me nothing. From then on in 'Well, here we go again, flying on Aunt Hannah, 'cause my aunt didn't tell me nothing!' "

As the day ebbed, laughter died; eyes were somber; a cold fear gripped her heart. She tried to duck people coming into her dressing room, although someone always seemed to get through or she gave in and *let* them through, but now here tonight was a letter from home. Oklahoma. A fan. Big strapping fellow. She let him take pictures of her all kinds of ways: hair tied up for makeup, changing into her concert gown, all ways—just before she was due on to sing. She couldn't set her mind to meditate, anyway. And Columbia hooked up to record her "live in Europe" again. What she wanted do was *stay* live. "Lord, I'm mad at myself," she told the man. "Hate to fly, and I got to get up in that airplane tomorrow. Can't think about singing, thinking about that airplane. I'm *scared* of those planes!"

"Aw, Miss Jackson," he drawled, "you haven't got anything to worry about. More people are killed in cars than planes."

"Yeah, and more people *ride* cars, too; they don't talk about that."

He grinned, took one last picture and left. All between her and that plane now was prayer—and this concert.

No one but the Oklahoma man knew what she drew on that night in the *Sportspalast,* when the spirit took over and Halie held church. The pitch of excitement grew. The crowd roared until she gave in and sang *When the Saints Go Marching In*—and it happened: 6,000 people began pouring down on all sides of the arena. "I'm getting out of here—there's going to be a riot!" Mr. Janicke, the sponsor, flung at David as he ran. Mahalia saw them coming—modulated—ended the number, and calmed them with one sure touch: *The Lord's Prayer*—calmed them, that is, enough for wiry David to get an arm around her, Mildred holding on behind, and try to make it through. Mahalia actually greyed with fear, one part of David's mind noted as he thrust and shouted to let Miss Jackson through. David took a solid hit on the jaw but kept his balance; stadium police were trying to reach them, but it was David got her into the car, Halie saw. Duckett wasn't being any help, no more than he was on publicity—she was through with him! Mildred was past speech. Lord, *Lord,* what is this? asked Halie that night on her knees—and her fixing to fly tomorrow. Help me Jesus.

Morning. Nothing for it but to go. She was due in Copenhagen. All Mildred could get on "her aunt" was a lip-smile. It was a long way to Templehof Airport.

"When I came out there next morning," said Mahalia, telling it, "everybody on the field knew Mahalia was scared to get up in the airplane. And that man from Oklahoma was the pilot. He had done told everybody. And he took it on himself to carry me everywhere."

THE WELCOME from their majesties was warm. Lord Mayor Sigward Munk was impressive. But it was the Danes at large who caught the German fever Tuesday night . . . the love pouring across, and more encore calls than there was of her. They kept asking 'til she gave them *Silent Night,* tears streaming down her face. In three weeks she'd be there.

Board SAS Wednesday to Stockholm: a room overlooking the Royal Palace. No strength or time to see the country, but Thursday night, the *Konzerthuset* an elegant place of grace and beauty, packed: every box, every pigeon roost filled . . . and, by intermission, acting like a down-home revival. What did they hear, with this inner ear so far more knowing than the brain? What brought this response in a land so far removed in every direction from the spirituals and gospels which pushed up out of the dark earth of yearnings and strivings, fed on deprivations and hopes?

"Mah-hahl-ya!" The Swedes too. Next day before she left, the sponsor translated the *Expressen* review for her. "She stands on the stage," wrote critic Al Thor, "like a large mammy and the audience a flock of children to be care for."

She eyed Duckett, "Don't you send that to *Jet*."

CUSTOMS AT Amsterdam wasn't near the trouble it would have been by boat, and they'd have been just in time to sing . . . missed all this press—radio—TV. "Miss Jackson, why did you record with Duke Ellington's band when you won't sing jazz music?" Over here! The sun never going set on *Come Sunday*. The press brought flowers, and flowers kept coming all the way to the concert Saturday night—a three-way thing, broadcast and televised too, so the cameras caught her coming down a long staircase with the audience ranged on either side . . . cheering. She felt like the queen in a movie scene—and Lord, You in here too.

And now Paris. They had loved her when she was sick and Albert Hall was cold. It was her Europe homecoming . . . but a strange Paris this Sunday: Orly Airport was shutting down . . . martial law had cleared the streets . . . a pall of fear like smog blanketed the *joie de vivre*. Rumors were like poison gas, in every crevice: Algerian guerrillas were going to drop paratroops into the capital . . . the rebels were laying bombs in public buildings . . . they would concentrate on theaters. Mildred was ready to get under the bed or go home or both, if possible. Mahalia didn't know what to think. Her concert had been sold out for days, but would anybody in their right mind come? *Should* they?

The phone call could never have been more welcome: Hugues Panassié had just arrived in the city, Madeleine Gautier explained; when could he see her? "You all come now and have lunch with me," Mahalia said, suddenly lifted.

"What do you think?" They were sitting over lunch in her handsome suite at the George V, the rosary Panassié had brought around her neck like a talisman, the question of canceling tomorrow night very much in her mind. The French critic tried to persuade her there was no real danger. The rumors were "considerably exaggerated," he said. ("To this day," says M. Panassié, "I'm convinced that all this was made by speculators who wanted to create financial panic at the Stock Exchange and make a lot of money—which they did!")

David was checking, but she knew no sponsor would willingly hand back all that money. She let the talk flow over her a little, meditating, asking. . . . "I'm going through with it," she announced.

"Good," beamed M. Panassié. "And I hope very much that you will sing *Nobody Knows the Trouble I've Seen.*" Mahalia returned his smile; he was thinking only of the old spiritual, not just how right that title was now. As she put a hat on, standing before the mirror, she began to sing the song. "Just by herself, nothing but that beautiful voice," says M. Panassié, cherishing it, "and I was thrilled. Then right in the middle of the song she broke off to tell me, 'But here is how the white people would like me to sing it.' "

The French guests doubled with laughter at her Lily Pons caricature. She had but one interview. That past, she checked with the sponsor and found the latest rumor was not true—people were *not* demanding their money back for fear of a bomb. That settled it. If they wanted to come, she'd trust in the Lord.

She spent a long time on her knees that night. You got to guide me, now. There's still time. Maybe that's why it struck her so in a heap, Tuesday at Notre Dame. She was having a rare luxury: David was taking her sight-seeing, the day clear, thanks to the rebels, and she and Mildred had already checked out the hall—what kind of a place was that? Throw off the thought and look around at Paris in the spring—that's what they sang about and she could see why. The River Seine so peaceful, boats sliding by with hardly a sound—forget the traffic behind; children playing—look there! an organ-grinder man, old-style like you see in schoolbooks, carrying it around his neck . . . the eternal flame at the Tomb of the Unknown Soldier: fire plays such a part in religion—there is some mystery there. Step into the Madeleine Church . . . drive onto the *Ile de la Cité*—Notre Dame on an island? . . . shudder at the gargoyles jutting out from its eaves like devils . . . "At least they being cast out," Halie muttered. A sense of awe and holiness in this place . . . and then is when she was struck in a heap. There was Jesus risen, telling Mary Magdalene like it said in John: go spread the good news to the disciples—spread the gospel.

Well, Lord, You know just when to pick Halie up.

PANASSIÉ and Madeleine Gautier had a tale to encourage her that evening, when they came by the George V early to go with her to the concert. They'd gone to the Bobino Theatre and seen the Peter Sisters' show. Waiting to exit—"Here comes a gang of policemen with guns!" said M. Panassié dramatically. Mahalia was wide-eyed. "A few minutes later, we saw one of the Peter Sisters. 'What happened?' I asked her. 'While we were ready for the last number,' she said, 'the maestro gave us an unusual fast tempo, so I told him, "What's going on?" and the maestro says, "Leave this place as fast as you can, there'rs a bomb under the stage."' But after they go out," Panassié concluded triumphantly, "the police checked carefully and there was *no bomb*."

Mahalia, he could see, felt better after that. But when Lou Mindling telephoned from Chicago, she told him, "The promoter says we might have a little trouble tonight."

Backstage, soon after they'd arrived at the Olympia, Mahalia called Panassié into her dressing room. "What kind of place is this? This is no regular concert hall." He explained that from time to time concerts were given here, "but ordinarily it's a music hall with numbers like jugglers, people walking on a string up in the air, or presenting animals—dancing bears, elephants, dogs, and so forth."

"Why do they make me sing in such a place?" Mahalia looked thunderous. "But it's nothing similar to the Folies-Bergère," he said hastily; "no naked girls . . . nothing bad!"

Mahalia sighed, a deep sigh from her being, brown eyes hooded. Then somebody brought her flowers from Edgar Wiggins, the *Chicago Defender*'s Parisian representative. "That cheered her," says M. Panassié. "Then came a greetings letter from 'Sweet Pea.' "

"Who is Sweet Pea?" Mahalia asked Panassié. He was amused. She knew Sweet Pea very well: Billy Strayhorn. "Ohhhhhhhh!" Duke's right arm—biggest little man she knew.

Panassié offered to leave—she might want to be alone before the concert. "No! Stay with me; you're the only one I know around here."

And then it was time. Halie gathered herself, stood tall, and walked onto a stage which might blow them all to Kingdom Come. The Olympia was packed to the rafters and more standing. If they had the courage to come, she had the courage to sing.

How she sang! M. Panassié—the critic now—was charged with its excitement as he shared the night for *Le Bulletin du Hot Club de France*:

"Her entrance was greeted by a salvo of clapping as long as it was heavy and when she started her first song, *In My Home Over There,* I immediately had the impression that the audience was listening with an attention, a concentration, a fervor, that were absolutely exceptional. The applause started as the last note was barely finished and lasted so long that Mahalia had to start on the next song to make them stop. A little later, when she started (attacked!!) *Down by the Riverside,* she 'swung' with so much intensity . . . more vehement with each chorus, that the audience hailed that song with one of the most formidable ovations that a black artist has ever received in Paris. The spell lasted . . . until the end."

The audience could hardly bear to let her stop singing *Didn't It Rain.* She brought them down with her note by note with a song many of the audience were shouting for—*In the Upper Room.* Then she—"threw herself" was the phrase, M. Panassié decided—into a final, sublime *Nobody Knows the Trouble I've Seen.*

When all the words were in, Panassié's was the ultimate verdict: "Mahalia Jackson is without the shadow of a doubt one of the greatest artists of our era."

SHE HAD BROUGHT them down, but they would not go out—not from outside her dressing room. Mezz Mezzrow, Billy Strayhorn, and two friends of Billy's had to force their way through, tall Mezz running interference; it wasn't much easier for Panassié and Mlle. Gautier, except for the power of the press. That held for Edgar Wiggins too: happy to see her, happy for her. Joy was flowing all around—and so was the crowd. A *mob* was waiting at the backstage exit on Rue Caumartin. "Take the front door!" the manager cried, turning her back. The fans still backstage saw the turn and guessed. *"Allons!"*—racing outside, around the building, the crowd at their heels, there by the time she arrived. "Back to Rue Caumartin!" cried Panassié—Billy, Mezz, the whole chorus, flying after her. Mahalia sprinted as she hadn't since she rounded third base. She got there first and *threw* herself into the car, wheeled into place. David hustled Mildred after. Exit laughing.

Billy and Mezz sat with her at the hotel into the night, talking home.

Flying in all senses, now. Munich: *"Willkommen!"* . . . giving their hearts and hands: "Mah-hahl-ya!" Essen—steel city, fiery hot core of love: "Mah-hahl-ya! Mah-hahl-ya!" beyond encores, beyond endurance, beyond lights, mike, costume . . . "Mah-hahl-ya!" 20 minutes, until she walked on in skirt, blouse, moccasins—leaned against the piano—and in total hush gave them benediction, *The Lord's Prayer*. Playing, Mildred shook her head . . . the time they'd had learning it: Mildred trying to keep her to the words, Mahalia carried away, adding her own . . . "Mahalia, you can't *do* that; this is *The Lord's Prayer!*" "Don't tell me what I can't do!" and she was right, always in the music she was right, it proved to that . . . and she proved it now.

There was still a nervous, twisting 1½-hour drive to Düsseldorf, where they'd stayed to make plane connections; one carful of fans followed right up to the Park Hotel. Next morning, count the luggage; stack the mountain in an extra cab; rush to the airport—and wait. Plane late. Mahalia was silent on the ride out, David noticed; he assumed that was fatigue, or she was meditating. But when the loudspeaker announced the plane would be another 15 minutes late, Mahalia jumped up. "That's a sign from the Lord. I'm not flying."

"Mahalia!" cried David, "the luggage is on the plane!"

"Get it off." She meant it. He dashed to the counter, begged—argued—demanded the luggage off—only for Mahalia Jackson—checked schedules; rounded up a touring car; managed at last with two porters and the driver to get the luggage in, on, over—everywhere but under them; dashed back to a public telephone—thank God! he had the coins—called the Zurich local manager to tell her the new arrangements: cancel the airport press conference; ran back to the car and made sure the driver understood. Only with luck, and skill, could they reach Cologne in time to catch the train for Zurich in time to make the concert. Oh, the local manager would be furious! He shuddered at what would be needed to cope.

They made the train, and when Mahalia got off, "So glad to meet you," she dimpled at each one, in turn. Everybody loved her. And there was still time for U.S. Consul-Gen. John B. Holt to entertain them. One of his aides could tell her about Jerusalem, too. But the most fun was meeting Ladybird's sister-in-law—Mary Johnson, the vice consul, wife of the President's brother, Sam Houston Johnson. She was like a letter from home when she made herself known, and laid herself out to be nice. She did. The concert that night was Halie's thank-you to them, and to her Lord, 'cause tomorrow, my Jesus, Halie will be in Rome. A Baptist born and a Baptist bred, and when—she didn't care; she wanted to meet the Pope.

A MONTH BEFORE she sailed, she told Cardinal Spellman she'd be glad to sing for Pope John, so he could hear gospel. Just for himself. Maybe with all the people around him, he never got the word—she knew how that was—and if she had the chance today, she was going tell him she was at his disposal, if he had the time . . . that would give him an out; he was such a busy man; but she'd offer. She checked for her black lace mantle—it seemed more *right* than a hat—and she was ready to go to Vatican City for her audience with Pope John XXIII. Their audience: she'd insisted place be made for Mildred and Duckett and David Haber, too—Jew or not. He hadn't been exactly enthusiastic about it—which cost him his first real irritation from Halie, for his lack of *history*—but he wasn't letting Mahalia out of his sight, so he came.

Entering St. Peter's Piazza, she wasn't prepared for the bigness. It took a person right down to size before ever you mounted the steps of St. Peter's. From then on, from the moment you passed the Swiss Guards at attention, you knew this was a moment in memory—a bookmark in your soul. Their credentials checked, they stepped into the world's largest Christian church . . . into the most richly filled museum of religious art anyone could dream of . . . and into one of the biggest crowds Halie had ever deliberately joined. This was semi-private? Poor man. She wondered what passed for privacy—and when they'd start forming into lines; she didn't see how else they'd get any order into this crowd so they could meet the Pope. It was already past the time. The only order now was a path kept clear by guards—even some of the nuns and priests were crowding, craning to see if anything was happening down the open aisle.

"Papa!" The roar was deafening. The crowd surged.

"Papa! Papa!" Screaming, weeping, joyous—a thrill swept Halie, Baptist born, Baptist bred. He was coming now, higher than the crowd—a big, rounded man in a plain white robe and little white skullcap, wearing the most glorious smile she believed she had ever seen, borne on a golden throne set up on a platform so the 12 tall, strong men in crimson damask held it easily on their shoulders, moving quickly up the aisle. Shortly, from the distance, came a murmur, magnified; then they could see Pope John giving them all—and each—his blessing. The crowd began to break. That was it. The audience was over.

Later that day Lou Mindling called from Chicago. "Well, how was it? Did you get to see the Pope?"

"Well, really," Mahalia said slowly, "there were so many people—"

"Mahalia," said Mindling, "just sit tight. Take the extra time. I'll get you to meet the Pope." Lou Mindling was of Jewish parents and proclaimed no religion ("living's my religion") but most of his friends were Catholic and among them was Bishop O'Donnell, whose friend Msgr. Marcinkus—from Cicero, Ill.—was on the Pontiff's staff. "Tell him all four of us, Mr. Mindling."

For two days, they waited. David shepherded them to the Colosseum, Halie's senses attuned to the Christians whose faith withstood even the lions. To the Catacombs, feeling its spirits brush you with their memories in the dank dark where a candle snuffed out—how?—stopped your heart 'til someone came back for you. They walked a road where Peter walked. It was almost as if the Lord was preparing her in this unexpected time, stepping back through the early struggles.

Finally, the impressive documents came for admission next day to the Pontiff's apartments: Saturday, May 6, a private audience at Vatican Palace: see Archbishop O'Connor. Usually limited to 25, they had been added and apparently one or two more; there seemed to be over 30 people gathered. The group was directed up a long staircase but Mahalia was spared for a reason so frivolous she was embarrassed—people recognized her and started asking for autographs. She was quietly sequestered with Mildred, David, and Al. In due course they went up by elevator to join the others—decorum firmly reestablished. Then a sequence of arrive and wait . . . first one room, then another; then—*the* room.

It was a room to make you gasp, thought Mildred. Deep red brocade on the walls and door; a wide, wide golden door frame, gleaming in the soft lights; golden candelabra—not lit, maybe they didn't want them dropping wax; that wonderful clock taller than your head, so beautiful it was hard to tell the time—nearly 11 a.m.; and this carpet! Covered most of the long room, all swirling medallions with the Pope's crown woven in, taking up most of the center. Matching strips alongside this special central rug told you without having to be told that this was the walkway to keep to.

Pope John was coming in, flanked by his attendants in long red robes. Mahalia watched intently. He wasn't near as tall as he had seemed on the chair, and his face was heavy; yet there was a beauty there, a *substance.* The carpet showed his big jewelled crown with the cross on top—that must be heavy—but he was wearing the plain little cap not so different from a rabbi's, only his was white. Maybe that signifies he's at home. . . . He was ready. Emphasizing the informality, the intimacy of the occasion, he spoke his native Italian. Then he stopped for his translator, and she could understand: "The Vatican, this building, seems to me like a mother, stretching out her arms to her children. . . . I have been ill. I do not feel good every day. I do the best I can. But I am reminded of this always when I look at the Vatican—she is stretching out her arms to the whole world, as her children, to come into her breast."

I'm going to write that in my book before I forget, thought Mildred, used to remembering. The beauty of it made you ache, thought Mahalia. He was a saintly man; and yet a natural man.

They filed by, kneeling, each. He gave his blessing.

She *felt* blessed. And mysteriously purified, for the Holy Land. Lord, You cast seven devils out of Mary Magdalene. Maybe You can work some more on Halie?

David's mind was already on his arrangements for getting them to Naples: they'd missed their ship to Beirut, and he didn't know anything about the *Esperia*. He wouldn't rest easy until they were aboard. And he hoped he could then.

42

No! She was struck in a heap. This first day out, she had her first space of mind to really think about her time in the Holy Land and she'd come up against the biggest bump of her singing life: Suddenly she realized that in going to Israel, she'd signed to sing Christian gospel to the Jews. They crucified our Lord for that. A lot had changed, but what kind of concert would this be? Would she be crucified a different kind of way? Should she sing at all? But she'd signed. That contract meant *somebody* wanted her enough to pay good money on deposit.

Israel had robbed her peace. She'd have to face it—and throw it off—whatever came.

For now, look at the water. To look across, the Mediterranean was so deep blue it caused a stirring inside you with the beauty of it . . . then close up, looking straight down, it was more green . . . and white in the wake. No end to the image of the sea; it was in the eye of the beholder.

Evenings, there was an orchestra, and a little nightclub. Halie sat just outside where she could see the people and hear the music. Nothing David said could persuade her to set foot inside . . . "but you go in and dance, Dave-honey—I be all right." David would go in for a dance, then come back on deck. He didn't like to leave her. He was glad when a couple of American kids going to work in a Beirut nightclub got interested in Mahalia and spent time with her—she loved their stories.

EGYPT. The ship would be in port four or five hours, David assured Mahalia; she wanted to see Alexandria, didn't she? Oh, yes! it was famous once as a Christian center. But down the gangway and to the hired car, all her senses got in one sweep was a mess of confusion and people and animals and market stalls and good God! that meat hanging down with the flies. David grew nervous in case the ship loaded faster than expected, but they managed the old palace and a museum full of Greek and Roman and Egyptian things from Old Testament times. *When Israel was in Egypt land* . . . Lord, You going help Halie with the Israelites? Dave said they had to sail up past the Israel coast to land in Beirut, Lebanon, so they could get to Damascus. That's where her pilgrimage was really starting.

HE WOULDN'T have believed it possible but it was, David Haber realized as he tried to calm Mahalia: the Beirut docks were much worse than Alexandria. The noise alone was rather frightening; the heat was intense even this early; and now Customs—what was their problem? Thank God for the American Embassy; it would be all right, all right: his pale, lean hand on Mahalia's ampleness gentled her like a dove.

The Embassy was an oasis. Ambassador Robert McClintock's staff was setting up all arrangements. They could freshen up, relax, have lunch at the Marine mess . . . David grinned at the sight of the men (the Embassy guard) captivated by Mahalia, to a man. Ah, the car. The driver, the staff assured, was a thoroughly reliable guide. It was a point: he'd be with them all the way to Jerusalem. Entering with a flourish, the giant Arab was one of the biggest men they'd ever laid eyes on. He spoke no English. But he spoke French, and so did David.

The veteran car received its load of luggage on top; Mahalia climbed up front beside "Fez" (his name as soon as David told Halie what that little red hat was: like the Shriners), the other three settled in back, and they spurted forward—an omen of the ride to come. They were rolling toward Syria. The Romans had taken this road too—fortified it and built temples, Dave said Fez said. Fez rattled his French like peas spilling on a counter, but Dave was equal. Wherever there was something to see, they got out. Hot or not, it was a relief from the dusty road about as wide as a camel run, with big Fez taking everything like he was heading for breakfast—mountain, valley, desert plain. Halie alternated poking and motioning him to slow down, and twisting around to tell Dave, as Fez finished another of his tales in French (which he enjoyed as hugely as he expected the party to), "Dave-honey, tell this man to keep his hand off my knee." Again. And again. Each time the guide finished a story, he clapped his hand on Mahalia's knee for emphasis . . . or was it? The third time, Dave—secure in his English—hooted, "He's got a terrible crush on you, Mahalia!" She cut her eyes around. "He just wants to get to the U.S.A."

That night in Damascus, the party grew. An American girl said she'd been assigned to cover Mahalia's visit to the Holy Land. It was a surprise to David . . . "she just suddenly appeared" . . . but room *could* be made.

Next morning they were packed like sardines, but the new seating did put David up front: Fez kept both hands on the wheel as they set out to see something of this city taken by David—her David, the psalm-singer—and by Jeroboam, first king of Israel after the division of Solomon's empire . . . Damascus, where on the Street called Straight in the house of Judas, the Lord sent Ananias to restore the sight of Saul of Tarsus after He had blinded him, who was then filled with the Holy Ghost and rose to preach Christ . . . there! in that church . . . and this is where the disciples let him down the wall in a basket when the Jews took counsel to kill him for preaching Jesus in the synagogues . . . oh! Samuel, Kings, Acts: here! here! and this was the beginning. No inch of ground but was in the Bible. She was near to bursting. But they must be off, it was 133 miles to Jerusalem, there was much to see, Fez declared—and off they careened. Desert. A sense of reverence settled on Halie. This was the road where God cried to Saul, "Why persecutest thou me?" and they were near Capernaum, where Jesus dwelt, so that his fame spread through all Syria and they brought him all the sick. In Jordan now. Because Syria and Israel were at war, their route led to Ammon, past the ruins of the beautiful temples of Jerash. They were stopping often—there was so much to see, to visualize; Bible history since Methuselah—and every time their car pulled up, "Honeyyy, those Arabs come out them tents like bees," said Halie, telling it, "and here I am with two Jews: Dave and this girl. I was afraid the Arabs would give them a bad time if they caught them, so I'd point, and make the motions, and I'd say, 'These people just like me: they a little light—'specially him—but they colored too!' " She guessed she got away with it. But she was watching out, without letting Dave and the girl know.

It didn't seem real, how soon they'd be at the River Jordan. "Jerdan," Mahalia called it, David noticed; he wondered why. "That's the way you say it," Mahalia said firmly. Once she'd thought it was just a symbol: now she could wade in the waters. She hummed. Abruptly she gulped, wrenched back to now: the car had stalled. On this road! It had *been* sputtering and puttering but now it was stopped. Fez left it right in the road—God, put out Your mantle, this man going kill us. But he threw up the hood, did something, then climbed in and took off as pleased as if he was a magician. *Take* a magician to get them safe to Jerusalem with this crazy man. Just let me get to the Jordan, Lord, that's all I ask.

Fez pulled the car off the road just short of the Allenby bridge—rickety, wooden, one car wide. This was a Jordan checkpoint, primarily to screen out Jews. Nobody was shooting, but lots of soldiers were around; that was enough to make you unquiet. That and the whole confusion of trucks with oranges, passenger buses, more trucks, all parked around, and people milling about. All Arabs. Jews couldn't be here. Halie looked at David and this girl. She'd work it again, if she had to. She got out of the car and drew away from this confusion, walked off alone to a quiet stretch and down the bank by the riverside.

It was a little river. That was a surprise. It ran fast and not very deep—down a way, some people were in it. But it was muddy as the Mississippi, that the blessing *made* the Jordan, symbolically—Halie all in baptism white and the people behind her singing "*Let us go down to the Jordan*—" She eased down, knees bent, filled with awe; Jesus was baptized by John the Baptist less than a mile from here, in water that flowed by this very spot. She could feel it through her as it flowed across her fingers . . . thank God! she was a Christian. She prayed for another rebirth, closer to His image of righteousness, for His name's sake. . . .

Slowly Halie's eyes became aware of bare brown toes before her. Still squatting, without moving an inch, slowly, slowly she let her eyes travel upward. There stood the tallest, straightest, most beautiful black man she had ever seen. She'd like to scrub him up, shoot him full of penicillin and take him home. *Lots* of penicillin! Her face showed none of this, nor did his expression change when slowly she rose. It was she who stepped away from the river. And panicked. Where was the car?

As Mahalia walked off to herself, David Haber turned the other way with Mildred and Duckett and the writer-girl, who was filling her notebook fast. He knew he should keep his distance, but he meant to keep an eye on Mahalia—and suddenly he wasn't watching Mahalia at all. He was running up the road like a madman, waving his arms, shouting. While David's head was turned, Fez—who had been talking to some soldiers—Fez suddenly roared, "*Je vais retourner*" and drove off. Panic so gripped David at that instant—suppose the man never showed up again? how could he cope?—that he ran screaming across the bridge, waving his arms, and was not stopped by a single guard. He had no idea how he could catch the car. He just had to try.

As he ran, panting with the heat and the hill, behind him a soldier said in French, "He's just gone to have the car looked at." David kept running anyway—and yes, there was Fez, waving, at a garage. David felt such a fool.

Jericho was an oasis. Literally: the only green between the Jordan River and Jerusalem. Tree-protected, lush. Fez took them to where it was thought the fortifications of this ancient city of Canaanland had stood. "*And the walls come a-tumbling down!*" caroled Mahalia, eyes shining. Fez was beside himself with admiration, but Mahalia wasn't even aware of it, David decided. She was entirely in the Biblical world. "Oh, Dave-honey, isn't it wonderful?" And sensing his reserve, "You ought to be feeling this," she scolded; "this is *your* country, boy, the origins of your people, as it is given in the Old Testament."

"Mahalia," said David curiously, "do you believe Joshua actually brought the walls down with trumpets?"

"I believe Joshua did pray to God, and the sun stood still," said Mahalia, tall, exalted; "I believe everything."

They were less than 20 miles from Jerusalem, but Fez said they should wait for daylight; and once on the road they could see why. Halie had thought the desert was always flat but this was mountains, up and down, bare, bare through rocky, pitted, twisting passes with dirt blowing, dust swirling, Fez barreling forward. Mahalia was frightened, hardly dared breathe—and the Spirit spoke: "If Joseph could bring Mary over these mountains on a donkey, why do you fear?" It was a real rebuke. "I'm sorry, Lord," she murmured.

The hills of Galilee—and Bethlehem. David arranged for a guide. They were led to the spot where once was the manger, and was now a church. *Sweet little Jesus boy* . . . Halie was in a reverie, her joy intense so that it almost hurt . . . and there were no words as she kneeled beside a rock said to be the very spot in the cave where Christ was born. One tiny babe, and what He wrought. Who wouldn't want to sing at His birth? And keep on singing. Her very prayer felt like a song.

Back up the stone stairs into light, to more of this blessed city where David, too, was born. And beautiful Ruth lived. She couldn't get it all close *enough!*

On foot, or by donkey, it would take a while, but even with all the people and animals on the road, by car it was only minutes to the walled Garden of Gethsemane, at the foot of Mount of Olives. The scene of Christ's agony and betrayal, and yet so much of beauty here—flowers, green grasses; on the distant slope, nuns and monks moved about the graves; and these old, old olive trees, some so gnarled it was easy to believe they were here for Christ and the apostles and had twisted with His agony. None of the others intruded as she roamed off on her own . . . up the mount to the shrine commemorating the spot where Jesus ascended to heaven. You could look across the deep Valley of Kidron, where Solomon was anointed king, and see where David first created his city; and then higher, on the rock, where his wise son Solomon built his temple. Jerusalem. *Glorious things are spoken of thee, O City of God.* Psalm 87.

When she returned, "Don't you feel it?" she asked Dave quietly.

Now into the old city. Here lay the heart and core and apex of her longing—to climb Mt. Calvary. She had two songs in mind that she might sing at the top—*The Holy City,* probably, but maybe *Lift Every Voice and Sing.* She'd know when she got there.

It was a blow to David to discover their reservations at the King David Hotel didn't exist, and he was upset when they were referred to the YMCA. For Mahalia Jackson! "Don't fret, Dave-honey," said Mahalia; "this is a pilgrimage." Trailing across Julian's Way, they discovered the "YMCA" was larger than the King David—actually a hotel. Well, all right.

The Y was full. They were referred to a *pension* owned by an Arab family who promptly succumbed to this warm, this wonderful lady. David breathed a sigh of relief. Mahalia was happy. He could tell—she hummed a lot. The writer was still with them—she wrote a lot.

They could allow three days. Halie wasn't wasting a moment. *I'm goin' to walk in Jerusalem* . . . yes, Lord! She rested just a little, to make sure of her strength, then she put on her Indian moccasins and grasped her walking stick. She was ready for Calvary. Mildred was close behind her as they followed the guide. The path was only alley-wide, in the Christian Quarter but Jordan's territory in the divided city. They pulsed with the noisy, busy street life of the Arabs. The wail of the Eastern music was as mournful as Halie began to feel—all this trudging on stones and up steps and they still hadn't started on Calvary; she was getting tired. "Whew," she panted to the guide, "when we going start up to Calvary?"

"We're on Calvary now."

"Oh!" ("That minute," she said later, to Butch Thornton, "I could have killed Willa Jones.")

Now she knew this was the way, her senses reached out. She was walking where Jesus staggered with the cross. These high walls had heard the mockery. The guide stopped and pointed them in: the Church of the Holy Sepulchre, built where St. Helena found the remains of the cross. Candle flickers showed the gold-worked interior. The others hung back as the guide led Mahalia to a marble chapel and beneath an elaborately worked golden altar, he pointed to a small white receptacle, recessed, on a marble pedestal. This was it. Halie sank on her knees. Halie Jackson a living witness to all she had sung about, to the glory of her Lord. The fact that a press photographer was trailing her, snapping pictures, disturbed her not at all.

Of all they saw in Arab Jerusalem, nothing surprised her more than that the Jews' sacred Wailing Wall was the actual stones of a wall of Solomon's temple. The other surprise was that the Arabs' sacred church—the Dome of the Rock, built where they said the prophet Mohammed ascended to heaven on a pure white horse—was inside the very area of Solomon's temple—in fact, on Mt. Moriah! There was some mystery there.

Their last night at the *pension,* the Arab family and their relations flocked to give Mahalia a farewell party. They all looked like King Hussein, David decided. Dates, nuts, assorted sweetmeats were handed around and there was much gesturing. Mahalia gave laugh for laugh, glow for glow. It was so warm a scene that David got the owner to write down the mailing address—he wanted to write a proper thank-you from the States. He stared at the inscription: "Gray House Opposite The Bus Station, Jerusalem." Yes, that was the complete correct address for mail.

In early morning, exodus to the Israeli side meant carrying all the luggage by hand to the one legal passage between the Jordanian and Israeli sectors as divided by the United Nations: the Mandelbaum Gate. Around them, the scene was appalling. A mob seemed stationary, hardly moving Stark against the sun's glare were the shattered remains of an impressive Jewish home whose family name had given this passageway its title. Beyond the crush of people was a gap, not deep but an actual no-man's land, barbed wire rusting at one side. David stood with the luggage heaped around him, the Arab porter waiting patiently, nodding reassurance from time to time . . . a very long time. At last they were through the Jordan formalities. David had been briefed. It took him and the porter several trips to struggle Mahalia's, Mildred's and his luggage to precisely halfway in the neutral strip; Duckett carried his. The writer carried her own. When all was negotiated, the cluster stood at dead center; David waved, and a little boy came from the Israel side and they arrayed all the luggage before the little hut where Israeli officials kept a clear view of the strip. Sweating freely now, David ushered Mahalia to the front to be dealt with first. The Israeli sat straight and impassive, forms before him. His first question was, "Where did you come from?"

It was too much for Halie. She roared indignantly, "YOU SAW US!"

THREE MAIN things she must see now, in Israeli Jerusalem—all close beyond the city wall: Mount Zion, the tomb of David, and the site of the Last Supper. *In the Upper Room* . . . when Halie first sang that, she never dreamed these poor eyes would see the glory. God is real.

Now all thought must turn to Tel Aviv. Mahalia had a concert to give. And suddenly she felt it: tired. She was glad to see how close this place was from Jerusalem. And she was glad to sink onto a bed at Tel Aviv's Sheraton Hotel and close her eyes. It couldn't be for long. "What we got to do, Dave-honey?"

What the local sponsor wanted to do was book her immediately for concerts in Haifa and Jerusalem. He had a Tel Aviv sellout. That answered the question in her mind but all she wanted do was get on the S.S. *United States* fastest way she could. She'd *had* her trip.

The sponsor argued, admitting finally that he'd given some public indication that he would present her in Haifa and Jerusalem. David backed Mahalia; she had one agreement, and one only. Tempers ran high, pressures were brought to bear. It was suggested with some bitterness that she had consented to one concert in Israel merely to provide her with opportunity to visit the holy places in Jordan. Another visitor expressed disappointment that the troops would have no opportunity to hear her; there had been hope— All right, said Mahalia, she'd go to a studio and *record* a concert for the troops; they could play it for them anytime they wanted to. It was no time for a reporter from a Jewish newspaper to arrive and ask what message she was bringing Israel from America. The same message she always had, she said—songs of Jesus, *gospel* songs—and gave him a lecture on Christianity.

The *Jerusalem Post* fared better. By then she'd taped a half-hour's interview and songs at the Kol Yisrael studios "for the troops" (it ended as a commercial broadcast), and David had taken her and Mildred shopping. Moccasins gone, needlepoints on; Halie was in the city—a city with stores to make your mouth water, things from all over this part of the world. ("*That's* where damask linens come from—Damascus!") So the *Jerusalem Post* reporter found an amiable, joking Mahalia who told him about Negro spirituals and gospel that came natural as the rain from her people. "To me," she confided, "singing's just like after taking a good dose of medicine. To tell the truth, I sing better 'round the house."

Wednesday she rested for the night. And prayed. She'd used big words on that first reporter and she'd sing her same songs—but how would they take them? She hated to spoil a wonderful trip. Are You with me, Lord?

They were mesmerized. That was the word that kept recurring to the stringer for *Time* magazine. Mann Auditorium held only 2,000 seats, but everyone who could crowd in for standing room did. She started them slow with her standby opening, *In My Home Over There;* she sang the song she'd had inside since Calvary—*The Holy Bible;* she sang *Ain't Gonna Study War No More* and *Didn't It Rain;* she sang and sang 'til she came to a tumultuous climax in the place best calculated to appreciate *Joshua Fit the Battle of Jericho* . . . and Mann Auditorium almost came tumbling down with the frenzy. No letting her go. Again and again, until a panting, beaming, electrified Mahalia put Mildred back on *Ain't Gonna Study* and improvised *Mahalia's Not Gonna Sing No More.* The laughter broke the spell; they could leave.

And so could Halie's party. Hallelujah! David counted luggage—checked tickets—got his flock to Jaffa airport—through Customs—aboard the Israeli plane. Now all they had to do was change at Athens to a Greek plane which stopped at Rome.

Minutes slipped away. Late to Athens. Late out of Athens. Late into Rome. He watched his watch and calculated. As the Rome layover dragged, he got lira and called Paris. Finally, take-off. Now if nothing happens. . . . Land at Orly; find the luggage; try to hurry Customs; try to hurry his three . . . the walk out had never seemed so long; try to prod the porters without making them mad—they'd walk off; cram everybody and the luggage into the car he had waiting at the curb and speed for the dock. The *United States* sailed at 12:05 midnight. They were aboard—just. If David had had any weight to lose, he would have lost it.

43

Gone seven weeks—eight, time we land and Lord, Halie needs this ship if no more than to rest her *sense*. Russell, babe, please don't bother Halie while she's taking her rest. I'm all right. . . .

Five photographers at the dock and she was off and running. Get home, check on the family, on business, on—

Mindling was gone. Left William Morris, while she was in Europe. "All the money we been making for them, Mr. Mindling! What they mean, throwing you out! Mahalia don't appreciate—"

"Wait a minute. They didn't kick me out. I'm taking over as entertainment director for the Arlington Track, the whole complex. I—"

A race track! Just saving his face, poor man. "Mr. Mindling, you sit tight. Mahalia's going to talk to William Mor—"

"Mahalia, don't. It's settled. I have a five-year contract. It's a very good job, really. That's why I left."

"She didn't ever really believe me," says Lou Mindling; "but I told her anything I could do for her, I'd do, as a friend."

Now Halie's got to get with William Morris on who's minding her business. Peace runs like the sea; this way and that, but it's never still. She had three weeks to get ready to shoot 85 TV segments in— "How long you say?"

"Two weeks, Mahalia." The soothing voice belonged to Television Enterprises Corp. president Harold Goldman.

"Two weeks to get down 85 songs?"

"You can do it, Mahalia; we'll start at 9 in the morning and run to 5 p.—"

"That's ten days' working time." . . . "I know, but—" . . . "That's—wait a minute—that's over eight songs a day." . . . "But they're only 3½ minutes each; actually less, in running time. You can—" She fingered the mail Polly had put on the bed beside her. More Europe: "You have changed my life since—" . . . "The beauty of your voice has—" "What Mr. Townsend say?"

"Look, Mahalia, just come on out and we'll set it up. We're not going to make you do anything you can't do."

Actually, she owned 51 percent of Songs of Praise, Inc., set up to make the T.E.C. series. Goldman had 29½ percent; Irving Townsend, 19½ percent. But Mr. Goldman was in charge. "I know you won't, Mr. Goldman. God is good." She turned to the rest of the mail. From a Jew in Israel, "I don't know much about your Savior, but we love your songs."

Thinking of the series ahead and how to handle it, for the first time Mahalia did not feel defensive about not being able to read music. Did the first singers read music?

SHE PUT ON her moccasins and sighed with pleasure. Halie and her tribe. She had Butch Thornton as secretary, Mildred and Edward Robinson to alternate on piano, Louise on organ. She even had a stand-in, her friend Dorothy Simmons. There was a lot of standing. And those *strong* lights. She wore dark glasses 'til the film rolled.

They were working at a studio leased from Paramount, on Melrose. The director was young Larry Peerce, son of Jan Peerce. He really liked her singing. "Mahalia! You could have been an *opera* star!"

"People keep telling me that, babe. But Halie got her marching orders from the Lord."

They had Barney Kessell on guitar, Red Mitchell on bass, Shelly Manne on drums: good musicians, but Halie had to get them with the *gospel* beat —fingers snapping, clapping, whipping them into it—or singing the bass part, head down, eyes flashing, 'til Red got it. "How many times," Townsend asked himself, "have I seen her take an hour to do just that at Columbia while a whole session waits, then 'Come on, baby, let's make it.' And she's paying for the session."

There were just five musicians now; keeping costs down. "This studio doesn't come cheap," Goldman reminded them. If that's what held off the orchestra, Mahalia was glad of it.

Dorothy Simmons, Doris Akers, Gwen Cooper—make Gwen a part—had rounded up singers from different churches and trained them by Halie's specifications. . . . "Trained them!" Townsend muttered. "They can't read a note, not any of them." Or if they could, they didn't act like it; *no* discipline.

Mahalia felt pleased, but she was tiring. Saying "3½ minutes" for television film was like a movie—might take 4 days in a movie to get 3½ minutes. This wasn't that bad; it was just Mahalia they had the camera on, in the one beautiful cerise robe; so why did they have to stop and go back so much on lighting effects and camera angles?

"Dorothy, you take this." She sucked a lemon. And ate grapes. And waited. No way to let the Lord come in 3½ minutes, but she'd get as close to Him as she could.

Where He Leads Me I Will Follow . . . Because His Name Is Jesus . . . Precious Lord. . . . Larry Peerce rushed to embrace her. "Mahalia! Magnificent!" Makeup came and mopped the sweat. *Holding My Savior's Hand. . . .* She fought back the hoarseness. *In the Garden . . . You'll Never Walk Alone . . . To Me, It's Wonderful . . . God Will Take Care of You. . . .*

5 p.m. "Help me off with this girdle, Butch. It's killing me."

"Big" Clayton and Ed took care not to let people know she was coming; she needed just to relax and get some good food. "Mahalia, I can tell you can't stand Ed's ribs. You going to leave him some?"

"What Ed? These *my* ribs. You all found me my house yet?"

The very first time she'd come, a year ago, she'd stayed out on the porch looking at the view a long, long time. They were on the hillside—far and yet close; you could see the "Hollywood" sign. When she came in, "Ed, if you all can find me a placc like this, I'm going buy it and move out here."

The young Claytons had thought she was kidding—expressing the extent of her pleasure. But she must mean it, to bring it up again. They'd look. The bell. "Oh, no!" Xernona muttered. Al. The ex-Globetrotter from the neighborhood. "That man can smell a celebrity, Mahalia," she said apologetically. "He's got vibrations that there's one somewhere."

The Globetrotter settled in. "Why don't you call my house?" he said. "I'd like you to meet my wife." Xernona protested; they didn't want to drag her— "That's nice," Mahalia cut in; "I don't mind—really." Well, it was her decision.

Touring his house, down in the playroom, "Who plays ping pong?" Mahalia asked. "Well," said the athlete, "I try to."

"Let's see if you're good." She picked up a paddle. Kicked off her shoes. Served.

"She's so light!" Xernona murmured to Ed. "She moves around with such *agility*. And such good rhythm!"

She beat the 'Trotter soundly. Another game, no shots barred. Beat him again. And again. The Claytons had to drag her from the room, shoes in hand. But not before she'd accepted dinner next night and another round. . . .

She whipped him again. "And I never even heard her say she could play," Xernona said.

THEY WAITED while Hector adjusted the surrealistic setting for an effect Larry Peerce wanted to try. Ready on camera. "Okay, let's try one for size."

Have Thine Own Way . . . Elijah Rock . . . God Be With You. . . . Five-minute rest each hour. *Just As I Am . . . The Holy Bible. . . .* "Okay, let's break for lunch."

Hold Me . . . It Is No Secret . . . I'm a Child of the King. . . . 5 p.m. Mr. Goldman watched that time, that's one good thing. "Come on, Butch. I'm ready for the bed."

It was really nice, to Butch, being with Mahalia with not a lot of other people messing in, or having to pack and move—just good time to visit. She really had Russell Roberts on her mind. . . . "Not just my mind, Butch; Russell always visits me, you know. 'Specially when I'm not feeling well—but not just then. Every place I go, he's always there."

Lord, Don't Move the Mountain . . . He's Got the Whole World in His Hands . . . I Believe . . . It Don't Cost Much. . . .

It cost her voice. Laryngitis. The doctor was used to nursing Hollywood throats. Don't speak! not a word—write notes. . . . Butch obediently picked up the hat, though she didn't think Mahalia wanted to go out—not even dressed. Mahalia shook her head violently and made motions again. Ohhh! the hairbrush.

Harold Goldman called every day. "Honey," he said—Mahalia held the receiver out so Butch could hear too and answer for her—"honey, you've gotta get well. Do you know how much I'm spending for this studio? $3,500 a *day*. Whether we turn on the lights or not. $3,500 a day," his voice almost reverent, repeating it. Mahalia gestured to Butch. "She's doing everything the doctor said, Mr. Goldman."

Another day, another dawning. . . . "Butch, you the dumbest woman about signs I ever saw. Reach me my pills over there."

"Mahalia, you can speak!"

The Lord's Prayer . . . Just Tell Jesus . . . Joshua— No. She gave Barney Kessell the tempo she wanted. *Joshua fit the battle of Jericho* . . . she'd seen it! . . . *and the walls come a-tumblin' down.* "Mahalia!" cried Larry Peerce, "You're back!" Five-minute rest. *I Asked the Lord. . . .*

"Butch, don't be moving around the room so much, just lay down and get you some rest too. That's right." Mahalia sat up in the bed as Butch settled down. "You know, Butch, Russell ain't going bother me no more."

"He's not?"

"No, he ain't going to bother me no more; he told me so, last night." That instant, the bathroom door slammed. Butch, intent, jumped what felt like a foot high, and a gush of wind came through the room where there'd been none. Butch broke into goose pimples. "Oh, don't be scared," Mahalia said, concerned; "don't pay any attention. That was Russell, leaving."

"Oh, Mahalia!"

"I had this dream about him last night," Halie said quietly; "I went out in the cemetery, it seemed like, to place flowers on Russell's grave—this was my dream—and he got up and just walked right past me. And he said, 'Mahalia, I'm never going to bother you again.' "

There's Power in the Blood . . . Bless This House. . . . They were due to finish June 30, but it ran into July. Good thing she had sense to tell William Morris don't book her before middle of July.

Friday, July 7. Last day, if they could get all the Christmas songs down. "Please, honey," Harry Goldman said, "$3,500 a day."

"We'll do it, Mr. Goldman. Don't worry." *Silent Night*—old Bradley telling her how . . . *Oh, Come All Ye Faithful . . . O Little Town of Bethlehem . . . A Star Stood Still . . . Sweet Little Jesus Boy . . . Joy to the World. . . .*

"You did it!" Peerce was happy, Townsend was happy, everybody was happy. Especially Mr. Goldman. And Lou Mindling. She called him first thing, when she got home: There were contracts and things she wanted his advice about. But Lord! Halie was tired, jumpy, couldn't get her rest and there was this squeezed feeling around her heart. She better go see Dr. Barclay. She *need* to get in shape.

She was in the words of critic Leonard Feather, "at an unprecedented level of world acceptance." Requests for concerts poured in. Mindling was telling her to up her price.

Sunday, July 16, she was singing to over 29,000 people in Madison Square Garden for Joe Bostic, with Albertina's Caravans, Ernestine's Washington Temple Choir, a whole spate of other gospel titans, plus one person new to the Garden: Dr. Martin Luther King—scheduled immediately before Mahalia, to ensure him maximum audience. So strong was her influence that the Garden management made an unheard-of allowance, only to her: they closed their beer concession for the night.

Next day Bostic got a chance to talk about the Mutual syndication. "Cowan's out on his can; CBS doesn't give a damn about Mahalia Jackson —so what's holding you up?"

Ming didn't think it was a good proposition. "Ming! What the hell does Bob Ming know about show business, Mahalia? He's a *lawyer*. Why are you asking *Ming?*" He couldn't get an answer. Not really. Mahalia was more interested in playing with her little godchild, who belonged to Jack Wallace, one of Bostic's fellow DJs. Wendy had run off and said she was Mahalia's, so the child was brought up to her. "I'm going to ask Jack if I can borrow her. I'll take her on the road with me," Mahalia told Butch, "and then I'll bring her back to Chicago."

"MR. MINDLING, these people about to kill me."

"Mahalia, you'd have no problem if you'd fly."

"I flew Aunt Hannah in Europe, Mr. Mindling; I ain't flying Aunt Hannah in America." He didn't know what she was talking about, but let it go.

The minute she got back from Dallas, she dialed Los Angeles. She had an uneasy feeling—"Ed? Look babe, I hope you give those people a lot of help on that Sports Arena. The biggest thing we got to do is get a crowd *in*. We can't have Martin coming out and be embarrassed with a small crowd. And I can't get out there 'til the day before."

Now who else should she call in L.A.? And Long Beach?

The Western Christian Leadership Conference was working hard on the SCLC benefit. It hoped Mahalia Jackson, Sammy Davis, Jr., and this young comedian, Dick Gregory, would draw—but Hollywood had a lot of distractions. Ed Clayton swung to on the promotion. Xernona did her part—call all your women friends and have them call theirs, Mahalia had said.

And because buying a ticket didn't put a warm body into the stadium, they organized some 20 cars to take people out. All to report to the Claytons' house. "When Mahalia checked in, she was so pleased," says Xernona. "She wanted to know if she should come Sunday and go from our house—possibly to make more people show up—but we told her no, because the ministers were going to pick her up at the Statler in a limousine. 'Don't worry,' Ed laughed; 'we'll get our people to church on time.' "

Mahalia turned to her press conference. Still time to make Saturday night TV news and the Sunday papers. Might get *some* more people in.

"WHEW!" puffed Mahalia, following Ed through the door. With Xernona, they'd been at this since 2 p.m. It was 10 now. Their fourth radio station—Los Angeles so spread out, from one to the next could use 45 minutes right there, and they all had steps. "Oh, man, whew!" repeated Halie, looking at the DJ. "I hope *you* the last one." The DJ looked startled; then he burst out laughing. The great Mahalia Jackson had come into his burrow. And the message went out. . . .

Bob Miller was glad Mahalia had prevailed on him to come out early to help and, on Sunday, do whatever Martin needed. He was a firm friend of Martin's now, and of Ralph Abernathy's, since the two ministers had made Mahalia's house their unofficial Chicago headquarters. ("Our second home," Rev. Abernathy called it.) King was the kind of man who'd just pull up a chair and lounge around and talk all afternoon, waiting for that night to come to make his speech. Most often he wanted to spend the time asking information, but now he was enjoying himself getting Mr. Miller to tell him about Mahalia in the early Chicago days.

It made quite a traffic jam, but nobody in the Claytons' caravan of some 60 people minded and Wilshire would survive. Still, it was late when they finally strung out, headed for the Sports Arena. Xernona said a little prayer for Mahalia—she'd be crushed if Dr. King was embarrassed; Xernona would mind herself, after all this work. As they drew near, Babe's heart sank. Must be a game somewhere around the place tonight—all these cars. That was terrible for the meeting. No place to park: Ed had to lead them seven blocks away. When they got to the Arena on foot, the grounds were filled. People were picnicking.

"Is there a game?"

"No, we were turned away. You can't get in the Sports Arena."

They were dumbfounded; then Ed laughed and laughed. "Don't worry," Xernona told the friend alongside her, "*we* can get in, Ed's on the committee." No, said the fire marshal, *nobody* else gets in. Ed was spotted from inside and, reluctantly, finally, admitted alone to do what he needed to do. "Well," said Xernona, all 4′ 11″ bright, "we'll go back to our house and have drinks, and whenever Mahalia gets there, we'll have dinner "

They lost about 20, but 40 trooped up the drive with her. God, she thought, if they all stay for dinner, Ed's short ribs will never go around; he'll have to supplement it. One thing, with that crowd, Mahalia wouldn't be through any time soon.

THEY WERE HAVING themselves a time . . . on stage, in the audience. At intermission, after a little preachment with her songs, Mahalia climbed down with Sammy Davis, Jr., and Dick Gregory and collected money up and down the aisles. "Come on, baby, you can spare it and SCLC can sure spend it" . . . "That's right, honey, you unlock your purse; we got to unlock a few jails" . . . *"I'm on my way—to Freedomland—"* singing a few snatches, happy in the service. Hallelujah.

He didn't mind having to leave, thought Johnny Jackson, maneuvering the parking maze; he understood the necessity and it wasn't often he got to do Mahalia a service. He drove up to the Statler, left the car with the key in it and went into the lobby, secure in his front. He came down loaded with luggage. He thought he knew the way to Wilshire, especially with nobody in the car giving him directions.

Twenty-five people lasted the long hours until Mahalia and the short ribs. Johnny and the luggage arrived—a surprise, but welcome. With 27, what's 28? Some hours later, a Mahalia buoyant and beat (now how does she convey both? wondered Xernona) arrived with Ed, equally pleased. They'd rounded up money by the handsful. "And Mahalia *stayed,* baby, and counted that money. I told 'em before, and I'll tell 'em again—I'll come to any benefit if I *see* SCLC get all the money."

"But Mahalia," asked Xernona in a small voice, "did you have any *people* there?" She broke it up. Dust!

Ed was up very early to put Mahalia on the plane to Chicago. He let Big get a little rest.

ONE THING, no traffic problem if you on the Chicago Police Telethon. Duke, Andy Williams, July London, Pat O'Brien, so *many* stars . . . she hadn't seen Bob Scobey since she was in Frisco with Hayakawa, after her operation. . . . TV was the quickest way to raise money Halie'd ever seen. Look at the work it took to fill Soldier's Field here tonight. Alongside the Sports Arena in L.A., this was the Gulf of Mexico next to the bathtub. And everybody coming to get their feet wet—cold, anyway, with that wind off the lake. Louie Armstrong—*"Hey!* babe"—"Red beans and ricely, nicely, Mahalie!" . . . Risë Stevens, Richard Tucker . . . Halie with the opera stars again, carrying the banner for gospel . . . and who-is-this! "You write *beautiful* music, Mr. Carmichael."

That wind and the huge, huge crowd . . . it cost your throat. It did. But you got to expect that, Festival season. At least it was Chicago and she could seek her rest. Lord, what You want Halie to do? She'd thought it would be more peaceful, but it was *not* peaceful; it was lonesome without Russell coming around. Just empty spaces, Halie and the night. It wouldn't do to go crying like this; started her chest to hurting.

Got to do something about James Lee, now Dr. Barclay say he's over his nervous breakdown but no more singing, no more traveling . . . James could come here to the house; yeah, she could use somebody to keep the house; that be good. 'Specially since Steve gone on about his business; nobody here when she's gone. What You think, Lord? Call James in the morning. What all she had to do tomorrow besides the bank and see those people for Mayor Daley? Who *was* that, again. Polly would have it. Col. Reilly said one-fifth of all the foreign visitors to the U.S. come through O'Hare and she believed it. She'd take Celeste with her to Daley's. Except she want to pick up some curtains for Aunt Alice at Sears and Celeste would go on about clothes—make her spend all her money and not at no Sears. Lord, I'm *trying* to hold on for the temple; the Devil's getting all these people on me, I know. Take Butch, then. Oh, no! Worse than Celeste. Or else put off Sears. Anyway, Granny White coming out about the new album and bring Aretha. Oh, and Eskridge—yeah; Willa Jones had helped her pick Roosevelt University music school for the first Foundation scholarship—be sure Eskridge put down "for black or white." Might have to hold off Margaret coming to work on her song; got a little time on that. Took Robert to tell her who wrote that song she liked so well on the radio. That girl. "I asked her when she phoned me, if she didn't want to take the publishing," says Margaret Aikens, "and she said, 'No, baby; I wouldn't do your song if I didn't think it had a message, and I want the world to hear it.' That one started her to recording my songs—*The Only Hope We Have*."

She knew just how she wanted to arrange it. Her head was full of the project as she rose.

"YOU'RE STILL not feeling well? Check into Passevant; they'll find out what's the matter with you." Lou Mindling's voice was firm. "You know it's a top hospital." Mahalia was reluctant. "Look, just because it's a white hospital, Mahalia, you don't have to worry about getting treated properly—I wouldn't send you there if they wouldn't, would I? Listen, you know Ronald Reagan—his wife's father is on the Passevant staff; he's a brain surgeon."

"Nothing wrong with my brain, Mr. Mindling."

"Mahalia, will you just do what I say? I'll get Dr. Lindberg—Howard Lindberg—to check you in; he's their top internist."

She checked into Passevant. Tests. Tests. Tests. Tests. Finally, a verdict: hypertensive cardiac problems.

"What that means, doctor?" Her heart. Mahalia dressed and walked out

Lou Mindling listened to Dr. Lindberg and shook his head. "She was afraid, I guess; she just didn't want to hear it and she left. 'Cause that's the first inkling of anything like this that I've heard."

At home, Emma Bell and Nettie waited for what she'd report. "Well—" She heaved a monument of a sigh—"What it amounts to, they say I got a tired heart from working so hard; and I got diabetes. That's about what they told me, and me stuck like a pig. All I need is a apple in my mouth and serve me on Sunday."

She could take her rest at home.

She asked Dr. Barclay about cardiac hypertension and he said "Sarcoid." She was tired of hearing that.

MORE AWARDS, more Washington, more concerts—halls, stadiums, churches, prisons, campuses. More talks, people, family, needs, contracts: "Mr. Mindling, they want me for— Mr. Mindling, should I take— And Mr. Mindling, I can't be getting all this help from you without paying. Mahalia's going send you something in the mail from now on."

" 'Something' was regular commission checks," says Lou Mindling, "which I really appreciated."

More albums out—and two she had no hand in: *"Mahalia Jackson Command Performance,* Re-creating Her European Concert Tour, Vol. 1 & Vol. 2." Bess Berma using her old Apollo masters. On top of those four other LPs. Old Bess got the last say. Let's see if she going pay.

Back to Hollywood for a big TV special, *The Sound of the '60s.* André Previn was nice to work with. *Bless This House* got good reviews. Actually she could have done better. . . .

Butch Thornton was trying her best to get Mahalia to buy some of these beautiful clothes they had here in Los Angeles, really fix herself up; she could take all that off her income tax. Mahalia really didn't charge off enough stuff, anyway, to her mind. She could show her— "Butch," said Mahalia, "don't you ever tell me how to beat Uncle Sam, 'cause I don't like striped dresses and I ain't fixing to wear one."

Stay on now to sing again for Dinah, so send Butch and Polly and them back in the car . . . "and Butch, try not to tangle with Polly, please."

"Then tell her not to mess with me." (Driving back, overnight at Flagstaff, it happened anyway—Polly and Butch toe to toe over who charged what on Polly's credit cards she had for Mahalia.)

Halie'd take Babe Clayton with her to Dinah Shore. That little doll-girl was the most *immaculate* person, not going let a hair out of place, or a thread show. Christmas songs again—look like she been singing Christmas all year, but it was a pleasure; she could let the Holy Land float across her mind. She was singing softly to herself, on the sidelines, when her William Morris man came up. Xernona couldn't believe her ears: they'd lost a sizable royalty check of Mahalia's; it must be mixed up someplace; they were looking. "Well," said Mahalia, brown eyes wide, "if you want me to sing this Christmas song with the feeling and the meaning, you better see if you can locate that check."

Xernona held herself in; she wasn't sure she was supposed to laugh.

HOME, AND TAKE the gospel train. Her TV series started in Chicago. *Mahalia Jackson Sings,* five-minute segments three times a day on WBKB. Five minutes! she wish they *had* given her five minutes. *Variety* didn't mind: "Miss Jackson's songs are the stuff that goosebumps are made on," it said, giving Larry Peerce high marks for direction. They'd ended up with 82 shows. How long would that last on WBKB?

It was a wrench to be promised to the White House Press Photographers and have to cut the *Sun-Times* Harvest Festival, because Dinah was coming for it and she'd have made that girl stay over, cook her that meal they been talking all these years. But President Kennedy be there, and you can't disappoint the press; they been too nice to her. Good thing she couldn't get grand. Peacock feathers just fall off. Halie's riding this D.C. road every week now, with one thing and another: got to get right back next week to honor the National Press Club president, and this big Coliseum now, packed *out.*

"Butch—look, I'm tired, now; keep these people off me." Backstage, at intermission, flung back but listening as Elizabeth's voice asks the insistent caller, "Well, may I tell her who's here?" . . . hearing a familiar name, "Yeah, baby! come on in!"

Off in the morning, Frye at the wheel, a concert in Roanoke that night, Frye managed to get himself stopped by a patrolman. And didn't have his driver's license. 'Til this minute Mahalia hadn't known he'd been driving on a beginner's permit and *that* long expired—and her paying him as a chauffeur! Help me Jesus. Turn around, follow the man back to the little town, pull up at the little store. "In there, boy," the patrolman told Frye. "Why here?" Butch was puzzled. "I know," said Mahalia, climbing out. She emerged shepherding Frye before her—Frye still unconcerned. "Do you know this fool nigger in there telling a Southern white man is threatening him, 'Aw, you wouldn't do that.' My God. 'Shut you,' I said and I paid the fine, but Butch, *you* driving this car 'til we get back home."

"He wouldn't have done it," said Frye.

Home—Mindling was fired from the track. He waved his contract but his salary was cut off. He'd fight. "I called to tell Mahalia how grateful I was, because with her sending me commission checks, I was able to fight the track. I had no income problem: she was getting more real work than she'd ever worked—I was getting more money for it. Both of us had a great thing going." He made a proposition and she accepted. And promptly called Townsend to tell him the news "—and Mr. Mindling is just going to look out for *me.*"

DURHAM, THE LAST on this sweep; then—"Oh, I am just going to have the most marvelous Thanksgiving I've ever had in my *life!*" she exulted, eyes shining. The woman commentator was interested. "What are you going to do, Miss Jackson?"

"I tell you, I just can't wait. I—" On she went, stretching it out, holding the interviewer to the outer limit of endurance, then she said, "I'm going to spend Thanksgiving—with the most marvelous man in the world, Dr. Martin Luther King, Jr., in Atlanta."

Elizabeth Thornton relaxed. Why did they always worry when Mahalia gave an interview?

Wednesday, they and a letter arrived almost together—a letter to Dr. King from a minister in North Carolina. "I heard Miss Jackson on the local radio station. As a result, I am sending you a donation for your work."

Next day, an explosion of life and laughter and food and happiness in an oasis in Atlanta. A time to cherish.

C. T. VIVIAN was sticking his neck out, but he didn't to his soul believe it would get chopped off. The pastor of the Cosmopolitan Community Church had a congregation of exactly 78 adults. They'd bought a sizable piece of outlying land with a quonset hut on it which could serve as their church. When young Rev. Vivian looked at that vacant land, in a stretch of Chattanooga crowded with Negroes displaced for urban renewal and not a church within walking distance—he saw a community center, a playground, maybe a school. His *modus operandi,* for starters, was a concert by Mahalia Jackson—her first formal appearance in Chattanooga. Mahalia came in early to help with the promotion, which landed her in the living room of Russell Goode and his mother with some rare free time. The tall, light-skinned, freckled young man who'd shared the rain-shelter at the NAACP anniversary had turned up at Madison Square Garden this past July and visited with her, Mahalia questioning him closely about his studies at Columbia. Since, he'd kept in touch; he was a telephoner. She liked him. "You the only person I know in Chattanooga, Russell, and I feel close to you, boy; so you *stuck* with me." The young teacher was enchanted. He circled about her, quick to every need, drawn to her power.

Friday night she gave C. T. Vivian, his 78 members, and over 3,000 paying customers the concert of their lives. Sixteen songs before ever she stopped for intermission . . . Russell Goode backstage, vying with Butch for services, Mildred too tired to compete . . . then back and another dozen before she was almost restrained from responding yet again to the clapping, stomping, shouting, glory-bound demand.

"One of our more unbelievable mid-century phenomena," said Louise M'Camy of the *Chattanooga Times.* Her baptism in black gospel had been a plunge with no bottom.

Afterwards, Butch, Mildred, Frye (reinstated to grace and license),

Mahalia, and Lou Mindling—in just before the concert—all gathered at the Goode home, relaxing, munching, sipping, listening willingly to Russell. He went regularly now to Atlanta as a volunteer for Martin Luther King, helping in the office at Thanksgiving and Easter holidays. He told them about the letters that came in. Good ones, yes; but the ones you especially remembered were the hate letters. There were plenty of those, Russell shuddered. At 2 a.m., he guided them back to the motel. "Russell," Mahalia said, "I want you back down here at 9 o'clock." That was all. "Yes, ma'am," said Russell. His mother couldn't get over it—much as that boy loved his sleep, Saturday mornings.

"We're ready to leave for Knoxville right now," Mahalia said, letting him in; "I want you to go with me."

"Oh, Miss Jackson! I can't go!" Why not? "I—I haven't had my breakfast!"

"Call your mother and tell her you're going to get your breakfast and—no, I'm going to follow you home; you eat there, 'cause you going be in Knoxville with me *tonight*."

Butch rode with Russell, and he followed Mahalia . . . for the rest of her life.

EMMA BELL was feasting her eyes on the scenery, and she hoped Frye was keeping his on the road. "This," said Mahalia, breaking off her song—"this will be the first time I've been home without some emergency. *I'm a child of the King. . . .*"

It had been a sudden decision. Christmas in New Orleans. Wonder if they still shoot off firecrackers? Well—that was a joyful noise, too, unto the Lord. *Sweet little Jesus boy. . . .* Split up the staying, to keep the peace—first with Ida and Elliott; then with Doodutz; then Ellen Blount. "Baby," she turned to Emma Bell, "you think you have eaten but you going *eat*. And you, Frye, you better behave or we'll throw you to them Loosiana alligators."

"Mahalia," said Frye, "let me drive." *Walking to Jerusalem . . .* "Frye, we not walking to New Orleans, you know. Way you driving, we never get there."

"Mahalia, I'm doing the best I can without going over the speed."

"GET OVER! I'm going to drive."

Just before Jackson, taking the Delta highway straight down the cotton country, the police caught up with her. "That's right—90 miles an hour. Don't argue; we clocked you." Fined her $100. "But we made time," said Mahalia, sliding over for Frye.

MAHALIA HANDED over the grocery list, and enough bills to make the grocer's eyes pop. Aunt Duke was going have her a Christmas party to remember. So was Emma Bell. "Drinks and food! Oh, we had it," cries Emma Bell. "But you all know what I remember most about Christmas in

Mississippi when I was a child?" asked Emma Bell, looking around the table. "It was the time I found Roman candles under the Christmas tree when I stole in that morning, and I thought I'd shoot off just one. I touched it to the fire—and that thing got to swooping and jumping all *over* the room. The *longest,* before my daddy caught it and got it out."

"Emma Bell," said Halie, wiping her eyes, "I believe you."

COLD, COLD in Gary, Ind. Butch answered the telephone. "How's Christmas? How's Russell? Is he having a good time? I'm leaving in the morning; you all meet the train at midnight."

"Emma Bell," said Mahalia, "you ride back with Frye and try not to let him creep. He's got to drive me to Detroit Wednesday morning."

It must be almost 1 a.m., thought Russell, pulling into Mahalia's driveway. By the time the luggage was all inside and he and Mildred and Butch and her friend flung themselves comfortable, Mahalia called from the kitchen. "Russell, come here. The mayor's honoring me in Detroit tomorrow. You want to go?"

"Oh, yes!"

"Well, go get your luggage now."

It was 4 a.m. before Russell was back, what with detouring to pick up his money from where his mother was visiting. He and Mildred were still gossiping when they realized it was 6 a.m. Ought to wake up Mahalia. . . . "Get up! Get up!" Mahalia. They'd dozed off. Ohhhhh. And the phone ringing already. Long-distance collect. "That was Frye. He had car trouble. Russell, call the train station and tell them you traveling with me and we got to get the train to be in Detroit by 1 p.m."

"I'm sorry," the man repeated firmly, "there's nothing I can do for you *or* Miss Jackson. There's just no space to sell. It's Christmas."

"But can't you—"

"Give me the phone, Russell. Hello, this is *me,* this is Mahalia Jackson. Let me speak to the Superintendent of Railroads. . . . Hello, this Halie, and I got to be in Detroit by 1 p.m."

"Miss Jackson, you will be in Detroit. You come on down."

One cab just for the luggage. Russell hastily added on Mahalia's furs—were those *three* mink coats?—and ran to the other taxi. The luggage cab pulled off.

"Where my furs?"

"They've gone in the cab."

"What if he don't take my furs to the station? You *watch* him; keep your eye on him." But the man made a turn off where theirs kept going straight. Russell felt a cold panic. Then they were pulling into the station and the other taxi was waiting and Mahalia was shelling out bills and the Superintendent was shouting "Hurry! You'll have to run!" and Mahalia had trouble running and the train was just *at* beginning to move and there was this step up to take and Halie had not breath left to take it and Russell, frightened—oh, God!—got up behind her and pushed her onto a seat because she could not move.

"Uuugh!" A hoarse, guttural, honking sound. Just one. Russell was scared to death. "Are you all right, Mahalia?" He wanted to cry. Mildred pulled him away and they sat opposite, watching. Gradually she did get breath back; in about a half-hour, it was, but the longest Russell had known. Mahalia sat up. "Oh," she said, breathing deeply, "that was a rough time."

Check into the Cadillac-Sheraton, and the festivities were underway almost immediately. The rest came on and Frye caught up with them eventually. He had three days to do it in, days Halie helped Pentecostal evangelist Byron Lee Wright promote his First Annual Convention of International Teens—existing only on paper so far. By the time she left, the morning of New Year's Eve, he had his teens. And Mahalia had her breath. She used just a very little on the way to Cuyahoga Falls, Ohio, and that was no more than breathing—she was singing to herself.

WATCH NIGHT, '61, in the beautiful round Cathedral of Tomorrow. She liked Rev. Rex Humbard and his wife—they'd worked together before, light and dark sides of the same. Mahalia especially liked the way the pair teamed in the service. . . . Halie, put that from you. That's gone and buried, now.

Mahalia and Stuart Hamblen were the special guests. The composer/singer greeted her with a hug. "You're a legend in your time, Mahalia," he said; "that doesn't come to many. I saw your name on the new Gallup Poll, for Most Admired Women in the World."

She sang every two hours through the night, into the small hours. She let Russell Goode play one number, to make him a part. She was surrounded by old friends and new. Louise Weaver, Willa Jones, who'd driven up with Boy Baby, who was witnessing; Butch, Mildred, Frye—a fine man, a pioneer in gospel, how had he fallen so behind? *How I Got Over* . . . her voice was strong and clear. To make it from one year to the next is quite a blessing. So much had gone on this year and was going on, was even doubling back so she felt like the ark: coming at her two by two.

She didn't dream the *dove* would come.

Just the one.

44

The dove couldn't fly, but it was Halie who was hobbled. She listened to the news from Hollywood with a soaring that went just so high—then pulled back at the way of it: *Mahalia Jackson Sings* (as *"Black Nativity"*) had been awarded a special prize, the Silver Dove, for "the work of quality doing the most good for international understanding," chosen by a panel from—

"*Seventy* countries! Who is it again?"

Harold Goldman was a happy man—suddenly the show was the thing to book. "The International Catholic Association for Broadcasting and Television, Mahalia. They'll give it out at a Grand Ball in Monaco. Big deal: the Prince and Princess, because it's part of their Monte Carlo International Television Festival, see? But Lou Mindling says there's no way you can go. You're tied up tight. So Larry Peerce will go get your dove for you, Mahalia. But isn't that grand news?"

"It sure is, Mr. Goldman. God is real."

It was natural Mr. Mindling would hear it first—he'd moved to Hollywood. Maybe he could— No way, with her dates. She just had time to keep her promise to Greater Salem: made potsful of gumbo—ladling it out herself in the church basement—before she was off to Hollywood. Star with Richard Dyer-Bennett on *Hour of Music* . . . do another Dinah show—nostalgic; the great Chevrolet series had its notice up . . . the *Bell Telephone Hour* with Carol Lawrence, Anna Moffo, Isaac Stern . . . then hit the concert trail. Jan. 30, 1962, she was singing in Oakland, which brought Doc Hayakawa—busy as a slide trombone on San Francisco State College campus—and Rev. Jodie Strawther, trying hard for firm footing on home grounds. "Strawthford," Mahalia said, brown face beaming above her candy-pink gown, "know what Halie's going do? She's going give you a program. We'll work us out a time—and we won't mess with Mindling; this *our* business."

She sang from a full heart that night. Hearing her "recital" was, to critic Stanley Eichelbaum, "like hearing the sounds of the Golden Trumpet, or watching the forces of nature . . . an instrument of miracles." She *told* the audience it wasn't her, it was God. And you sure got to put up with a lot, Lord; look at this *Show Business Illustrated*. She wasn't sure but what they making a mockery of gospel singing. Quoted her right, but talking of her "divining rod"—that was a little too slick. She could hardly blame the magazines, though, the way some gospel singers mingling with the Devil. She had her eye on them.

HOME TO REST—or its semblance—and regroup. Fight with Ming. Check on New Orleans: restaurants integrated; Canal St. opening up. Make Martin and Ralph welcome. See Dr. Barclay—what he *really* say about Hannah. Talk scholarships—so many asking. Launch a few ships. She commandeered like an admiral, the boats bobbing in her wake, content to lave in the troubled waters if they could share when all went well. Northwest now, Mindling bunching the dates. The key to Tacoma and greetings from the governor; Mahalia rated with Col. Glenn's flight as the second big thrill of the month—University of Washington campus had never come so close to revival. Nor Portland, two nights hence. Now drop down to Los Angeles and settle in. There's work to do, children, work for the Lord. Yancey promptly showed up and Mahalia let him in. "That young white boy is crazy about me, Laurraines," she said, with a shake of the head she managed to convey by phone.

Mindling had set up a triple play—not with Audrey Franklyn, but already Audrey P. was turning from producing and she wasn't one to fade: "Let me build your image, that's what you need. I'm not talking about little Yancey getting you on radio shows; I'm talking about building a prestige image. I can give you that."

The two were alone at the Knickerbocker Hotel. Mahalia wasn't really attending to her, but Audrey P. didn't mind; it wasn't the first time she'd talked image and it wouldn't be the last. Abruptly Mahalia reared to full alert, hand plunged into her cleavage. "Audrey P., what did you do with my money?" Eyes darting the room like a squirrel. Audrey wasn't sure it was a rhetorical question. "Mahalia, I'm Jewish; we don't steal," and joined the search. For 30 minutes they looked high and low and finally—"under a bunch of junk in one of the dresser drawers," says Audrey Franklyn—Mahalia scrabbled up a thick wad of bills bound with a rubber band. Her expression, Audrey decided, was like a sorrowful cow. Weakly, "I found it."

Santa Monica, Los Angeles, San Diego, with Ontario, Calif., slivered in. The National Academy of Recording Arts and Sciences, having set up a new category—gospel—awarded Mahalia the first Grammy: a little golden statue like a wind-up gramophone. Days of Atchafalaya. But no time to go get it and be back. It was a good schedule anyway, Butch Thornton thought. And fun to have dinner with ex-champ Archie Moore in San Diego. Mahalia Jackson Day in Ontario had an unexpected extra: Mahalia sang at the prison. Butch found it haunting—a little ruffle of fear edging you until you were safe outside and the doors had locked you out, not in. Night after next the doors were the elegant Los Angeles Philharmonic, Mahalia walking onstage to thunderous applause. *If I have wounded anyone today. . . .* "Her neck is like a swan's," Audrey Franklyn decided; "it's a very, very long neck. If she wouldn't sing so hard, the veins wouldn't pop out."

A day to check Townsend's lawyer, surprise Johnny's kids, look at real estate with the Claytons. Then take a deep breath and shove into four tough days. Johnny Williams was a good leader and he'd written the arrangements himself—but recording with any orchestra was like a girdle. She worked hard at it. She always drives herself, and for what? thought Townsend, as always torn between affectionate distress and executive ire. If they could have a professional chorus, but no—she's got to bring in these semiliterate church singers and kill herself shouting their parts. Look at that, striding back and forth between them and Mildred, getting herself all worked up.

"Oh, my God!" cried Townsend, and rushed to pick her up. Mahalia had tripped over a microphone stand and broken her foot. They'd just have to cancel the sessions.

"No!" said Mahalia from her bed at American Hospital, the cast on her left leg a sharp contrast to the brown hand feeling along it. "I can make it. Just let me get out of here."

Butch saw to a station wagon, and a mattress from the motel so they could stretch her out in back. She finished the sessions. Townsend was pushing her into singing some love songs—inspirational ones, but— She hoped breaking her foot wasn't telling her something.

Frye was very careful driving to Albuquerque, N. Mex. Then they took the long road for San Angelo, Tex. "It's not too bad back here," Mahalia assured them. "Just reach me that fruit, baby." Pulling in at last, Butch got out to call the sponsor, who'd said get in touch when they arrived, he'd tell them where their accommodations were.

Abe Lincoln had gone fishing. "So," Butch told Mahalia, hating to give that poor face the news, "nothing to do but call a couple of motels." Halie nodded.

They'd just left the Sands Motel in Albuquerque, and there was one listed here. Maybe this was a chain. "Oh, yes, we have room," the woman's voice said cheerfully.

Relieved, the safari made its way to the Sands. Elizabeth went in to register and emerged, her hand full of keys. The woman manager came with her, looked into the station wagon—and jerked erect. "Oh, I'm sorry," she said, snatching the keys from Elizabeth, "I made a mistake; those rooms are already rented!" Butch stared; Mahalia closed her eyes. "I don't know how I could have made that mistake." And fled.

A disgust; a confusion; a sickness in your stomach. "I guess she thought I was a Mexican," said Elizabeth.

The group waited at the radio station where the man worked until Abe Lincoln came back from fishing. "Those sort of things happen," he said, shaking his head. Mahalia had sat quiet. Now she fixed him with a steady brown eye. "I come to town as tired as I am, with my leg in a cast and everything, and there's no place for me to stay. I'm leaving this town."

"Oh, you can't!" he gasped.

"Oh, yes, I can. I *will*."

"I'll have an all-points bulletin put out; I'll blockade this town to keep you from going out!" he cried. The group moved toward the station wagon, Frye and Eddie Robinson helping Mahalia along on her crutches. "Do you realize people are here from all over this state to hear you?"

"They all got places to stay," said Mahalia grimly, "and here I am, the one they come to hear, and *I* don't have a place."

Suddenly Lincoln raced to his own car and zoomed it broadside to their bumper. They could not move. "You can't leave," he sobbed, breaking down entirely.

"I want to double-check one thing," Mahalia said finally; "is this audience going to be integrated?"

"Oh, yes; yes, it is; I swear it."

Mahalia accepted a motel in the Negro section without comment. "It's—clean," said Butch.

To get their dinner, Lincoln took Butch inside a big restaurant and had the people put covers over the take-out dishes.

Next night Mahalia sang and the audience loved her.

Oklahoma City—the cast was heavier; she forgot onstage, tried to move. Shawnee—she bought a hammer, and she chipped some of it off. Broad plains on to Tulsa, mattress in the back—they cheered her for her courage, and they called for one more song. Then the wagon angled upward, and they hit Chicago—home.

"KEEP THAT weight off your leg, Mahalia." Doctor's orders. So she wasn't running from church to church like she usually did at home, she explained. The *Jet* reporter let her range where she would and she got a chance to put something on record: "My secretary, Cylestine Fletcher, has been with me for about 18 or 20 years. Any hour of the night you can call upon her. She's a very firm type of person. I *need* that kind of person, not the wishy-washy type. This is what you call 'the power behind the throne.' " That ought to set some certain people straight. All this commotion got to stop. Her foot, she said, was injured in a car accident. *Who* going say she fell over a mike?

She was still on crutches for Ed Sullivan, April 15 . . . for Mayor Daley when she hobbled down to get her Chicago Medal of Merit . . . and in St. Louis the Sunday after Easter for an NAACP benefit where she had to coax them into letting loose with the spirit and the shocked NAACP conservatives argued to pull the curtain. They lost. "Good thing," said Halie; "if they'd pulled that curtain, they'd have had a riot."

Then she was shed the crutches and down in Tennessee. In Nashville, little Gail Jackson of the Junior Youth Crusade sought Mahalia, eyes full. "Am I your little girl?" Halie scooped her up with a hug. "Yes, you're my little girl." Ears perked. The last name *was* Jackson. The seniors of Burnside School in Chicago were just as adoring; Mahalia hung their award among her global trophies.

The National Baptist Convention was due in Chicago this September, '62—start to work on that. Stage a Night of Stars to rescue Joe Branham—

South Shore Baptist having mortgage troubles. Politics. NAACP. More church. Let it all roll on. Hardly time to sit down with the poor man trying to write this book on her; *been,* and keeps coming back. A certificate of merit from Ida Beal's National Beauty Culturists convention—23 years late, a certificate for her wall. Aretha alone in town; bring the girl out for dinner with Granny White. Make a place for this young black lawyer Rev. Jenkins brought, likes to hang around, ask her advice on how to handle people. ("Especially the ones who were bugging me," says Aldus Mitchell; "I needed to learn how to get along 'cause I had a short fuse.") Welcome the boy Russell, teach him gospel. ("Forget about that Bach and Mozart and beat this piano, put something *into* it.") Listen to Mr. Mindling talk contracts. "I'll get them to insert air fare and hotel accommodations, Mahalia—yes, I *did* say air; you can't afford not to."

"Hmph. You don't mean Mahalia."

In Washington, her name was spoken to Russian Ambassador Anatoly F. Dobrynin as a cultural exchange. America would send Mahalia Jackson, with supporting folk singers, for an equivalence of distinguished Soviet folk artists. In Japan, the Japanese Baptist Crusade asked her to lead their revival in March, 1963. And in the White House, President Kennedy told Pierre Salinger he particularly wanted Mahalia Jackson for the ceremonies to commemorate the Emancipation Proclamation, Sept. 22, 1962.

So much in Halie's head, it was rattling across like a bunch of jacks. It was late evening. Eddie Robinson and Mildred were over. They'd been rehearsing the Christmas album. She'd taken to bed now; Eddie was just being quiet; Mildred was going on again about money. No matter what that girl had, it slipped through her fingers some whichaway . . . where? *been* paid good money all these years. The tension mounted, the bearing point was passed, Mahalia was out of the bed, Eddie was trying to restore peace . . . and shortly, Mahalia was on the phone to Townsend. Listening, Irv Townsend groaned; here he was in her troubles again—but this, at least, posed a legitimate problem. . . . "So I won't have Mildred, but if I can get Louise, I'll switch Eddie to piano."

"Don't worry, Mahalia, I'll get you an organist; and calm down, don't be so upset."

"After all these years—"

"I know." Mildred would have her side; he'd hear that direct, soon enough.

"Louise? Me." Louise Weaver knew that voice so well, she sensed something was up; but she *was* surprised. "Yes, I can go. I'll let them know at the Park District that I have to cut Day Camp short two weeks; they can manage."

When Halie reached Irving Townsend at Columbia, he'd already lined up Bing Crosby's organist. "That's all right," said Mahalia; "we can use two organs."

What else. Oh. Answer the President. "I will be pleased and honored to participate in the ceremonies to commemorate the Emancipation Proclamation on September 22, 1962."

That acceptance, and advance word of the program lined up by the Commission for the Civil War observance, shaped a postwar battle which escaped the history books.

45

The battle hadn't broken, the cause wasn't met, when Mahalia joined Mr. Skelton. He was so tall she had to look up at him, even in her needlepoint heels; but it wasn't the looking up, it was his kneeling down that did her in.

They were taping the first of Red Skelton's new hour-long series. He had specified Mahalia as soon as he'd signed; the master craftsman knew just what, and how, he wanted to sing with her. It would be great. But he took his own routines after her solo rehearsal, so that Mahalia could go to her dressing room and rest.

The visitor was unique: Totally bald, standing well below her chin, the bulging eyes in his seamed face had left fans around the world helpless with laughter. Harpo Marx wasn't clowning now. No horn, no curly wig. He was earnestly telling Mahalia how much he admired her singing—and he'd written a song he'd like her to look at, he added shyly. "Ready, Miss Jackson?" She gathered herself to go—"but you stay and keep Butch company." Mostly he wanted to talk about Mahalia. Her voice reached the dressing room. They went out to listen.

"I don't worry too much about the script, Mr. Skeleton," Mahalia had warned him; "I just ad lib, like Pearl Bailey—I just get the basic thought and then I go on with what I've got to say." That could create a problem, but Red Skelton had made the hard, long climb of the nimble wit too; their give-and-take was like pitch and catch . . . "and Dallas has named a street for me: 'Mahalia Drive,' " she concluded, eyes shining. How do you top that?

Now the duet. David Rose struck up *He's Got the Whole World in His Hands.* All went well until *He's got the gamblin' ma-n in His hands*—Red Skelton whipping out dice, rolling his eyes and the dice too, sinking to his knees, throwing those dice. Mahalia burst out laughing, fought to sing, lost—and the orchestra trailed off. Pulling her face straight, eyes stretched wide with the effort, Halie got ready again. *He's got the gamb*— Skelton to his knees, Mahalia convulsed.

"Come on, Mahalia, let's try it again—I won't do that next time." He cut the knees but he rattled and rolled. "Mr. Skeleton," Halie gasped, "you just kill me. I can't sing with you."

They threw out the duet. Ohhhhhh, he was a funny man. She didn't even feel tired when Ed Clayton and Babe came to take her to the Ambassador Hotel, to the Los Angeles Press Club meeting to which she'd been invited, urged; just to say hello. The three friends were going on to dinner, then home to play ping-pong. "There must be 400 or 500 people here," Xernona guessed, and caught her breath: As Mahalia entered, the entire room rose to its feet and applauded like thunder on the mountain. Ed squeezed Xernona's hand. This lily-white club, that wouldn't even consider blacks, gone to their feet, standing like the queen had come. "I have another engagement," Mahalia said, "but I just wanted to come by and say hello."

"Can't you give us a sample? Just one song?" Eager, liking her. She wasn't prepared, she protested; she didn't have her pianist. "Just one? Please?" urged the president.

Looking on, the keen-eyed *Jet* editor searching the faces about him; tiny, elegant Xernona watching Ed watch them (these people could blast the South because nobody was looking at *them* but this had to change, things like this with Mahalia would help, surely), the Claytons heard Mahalia call out, laughing, "Babe! come up here. Come play for me. These people won't let me go 'til I sing."

Introduced, Babe was told by Mahalia what to play—the best she could.

"What key?" Babe asked quietly. Mahalia turned to the audience, planted her hands on her hips, and rolling it out in an exaggerated drawl, "Did you all hear? She up here asking me what key? Babe, I don't know one key from the other. I just sing; I just sing. That's *all*. So you just follow me—or baby, I'll follow you, 'cause I don't *know* no key." The press howled with ecstatic laughter—she wasn't the big star, the Hollywood celebrity; she was their own—just Mahalia, baby.

THE *Silent Night* album was going well—Mahalia mugging *not* tripping over the mike, Townsend laughing, everybody having fun but getting something down. In the first coffee break, Butch approached Mahalia with a stranger.

Elizabeth's Gary friend Ruth Ferguson had learned she was going to California and made Butch promise to telephone her brother this trip; Minters's wife had died six months ago. Last night Elizabeth had called. He was working a band job nights, he said, but he was free days—suppose he came over? Butch invited him to meet her at Columbia. He'd watched the session quietly, visiting with her. A cool, light-skinned man, a sharp dresser. He'd just finished a job in a Rock Hudson movie with his combo, he said, and he did some recording himself—on call, a studio musician. He speaks well, Butch thought. Now she took the opportunity to introduce him. "Miss

Jackson, this is Ruth Ferguson's brother who lives out here—Minters Galloway."

"Minters *Sigmond* Galloway," he said amiably; "I use Sigmond, my middle name."

"Yeah, babe, I know your sister," said Mahalia, smiling, shaking hands warmly. She knew just how she wanted that chorus part to sound. They got back to work. Hours later, the troupe headed for the parking lot. Sigmond Galloway was there. Gallantly, he opened the Cadillac door. Mahalia climbed in, then looked up. "Who is this fine man?"

"Miss Jackson, I introduced you," Butch said; "Ruth's brother."

"Ohhh, yeah," said Mahalia, not disconcerted; she couldn't remember everybody she met. "I'm so tired and hongry," she said to nobody in particular, hoping this man would take the hint, not stand there talking.

"How about coming over to my house, I'll fix you a meal."

"Emma Bell," said Mahalia, "why don't you go, you and Butch—why don't you all go? I'm too tired." To Minters, "You ever eat any Texas greens? Butch, here. You get some Texas greens and let him cook them, and bring me some back to the hotel." And off she went, to her rest. She hoped that man knew what to do with those greens.

Sigmond Galloway came to call at the Knickerbocker twice while they were there but—"Mahalia won't see him," Emma Bell said, widening her eyes. That was her business, said Louise.

And business was on her mind. "Johnny, do you still gamble?"

CALLING this half-brother she'd grown to know so late and like so well, she had a purpose. Johnny Jackson thought he knew what it was. Two years ago, she'd looked over the house where he, his wife, and Doris, Gyrlie Fay, and Bertha Sharon were living. She had asked then, in her fashion—knowing the answers but wanting it brought out: "Do you own this house?" No. "Who cleans up? Who cuts the grass?" He did. "It looks pretty nice. I'm going to help you to help yourself. Can you run a building?" Johnny's jaw dropped. "An apartment building?" He gulped at the enormity. "Well, you run one house; you add a few more. Just like you got one child, you can handle another one; you increase as you go along. Once you get the general picture, you just combine the two."

"Yes," said Johnny, eyes, hopes, lighting up.

For two years, off and on, Mahalia had checked one area, then another for buildings. She had the Claytons looking—her home idea set aside for this—and Townsend's lawyer too. Now the lawyer had located a building he advised as a good investment. Mahalia had looked it over, and "Johnny, do you still gamble?" she asked in a light, offhand fashion, a seeming tangent.

"Yes I do, trying to compensate for what I'm not making on the job. But I think I make a choice. I will look after your building, and you say I won't have to pay no rent, so I will let the rent be my winnings money, because if I continue to gamble, I am subject to lose some of your money."

She bought the Corbett Arms Apartments, 20 units. Johnny Jackson never gambled again.

Now she could go enjoy Nat's party in peace.

The 3,500 people flowing into the Ambassador's Embassy Room to honor Nat King Cole were Hollywood's glittering mainstream. Yet only Mahalia received a standing ovation when introduced, she and the guest of honor. She'd wanted to sing *The Lord's Prayer,* but the committee said it wasn't appropriate; so she sang *Elijah Rock*. The over-entertained, sated professionals sat taut and rapt—then roared their response. Show-business critic Stanley Robertson thought, he said, of "the sound there must have been when the Lord commanded: LET THERE BE LIGHT." It brought another Las Vegas bid: the Flamingo Room, $25,000 a week. No. Old Satan could strive another day, another way . . . although when Irving Townsend offered to buy her a drink which he felt she obviously needed after a tough day and she balked at a bar, he was sure it wasn't the liquor, "just a very shrewd professional analysis of what was good for her career." And not *singing* in a bar had nothing to do with some religious scruple, he thought; "it was smart thinking—she might lose her image and her sales and her career. Forget the saint with wings on her back."

He walked away from the spacious office on whose walls he had just two pictures—Doris Day and Mahalia Jackson.

"NO GOSPEL SONGS on New Mahalia Jackson Album," said the clippings coming in the mail. Was Mahalia turning? Townsend had helped her wrestle it; she'd had the press to answer even before she left L.A.: All right, she told Leonard Feather, she had some popular songs on *Great Songs of Love and Faith,* but *The Rosary* was a Catholic song, and two of Carrie Jacobs Bond's most beautiful songs were on there, and *Because* speaks about the First Commandment, and . . .

She was glad Leonard Feather asked, 'cause it gave her a chance to unburden her mind on what he called "gospel jazz": Taking *I got a home 'way over in Beulah* and making it *I got a woman*. Turn around *This Little Light of Mine* to *This Little Girl of Mine*. "Ray Charles ain't doing nothing but singing those old gospel quartet arrangements but he's not alone —everybody's doing it." Taking *Yield Not to Temptation* and making a blues out of it! And got *When the Saints Go Marching In* so commercial, the Sanctified—the saints—don't want to touch it.

But Lord, she'd be criticized about her record every church she went. Well, she passed her opinion too.

THIS SOUNDED more like a battle, even at a distance, and it *was* a battle, over the Civil War Centennial celebration. And her caught out in the middle. See if she could sit it out, let them settle it, go on about her business. . . .

All right, it had to be dealt with. Bishop Smallwood Williams in Washington was leading the rebellion: As SCLC president, District of Columbia, he was calling for a boycott of the celebration unless more than Mahalia was put on the program to represent the Negro people. The program was "a mockery," he cried. Commission chairman Allan Nevins, the historian, dug in his position and said Mahalia Jackson was indeed enough. Dr. Martin Luther King, Jr., reinforced Bishop Williams's position—there should be a Negro speaker on the program, else Negroes should stay away. A splinter group spoke of picketing. Bishop Williams wired Mahalia: Withdraw from the program.

Two days, some telephone calls, some meetings, some backings and fillings later, newly confirmed U.S. Court of Appeals Judge Thurgood Marshall was announced as an addition to the original participants: President Kennedy, UN Ambassador Adlai Stevenson, New York Gov. Nelson Rockefeller, Mahalia Jackson, poet Archibald MacLeish, and the Marine Band playing a work by Negro composer Ulysses Kay. Mahalia was singing *The Star-Spangled Banner.*

She wanted that air just a little clearer still. Lou Mindling called the President's special assistant, Arthur Schlesinger. On Sept. 18 Mahalia got telegrams from Justice Marshall and the President—expressions of gratification for her participation. "Your contribution will help make this historic commemoration a memorable day for all Americans," said the President.

She hoped everybody was satisfied by the time they took the train. This was a big occasion for Mahala Jackson, granddaughter of Paul Clark born in slavery—sought out by the President of the United States to sing the national anthem to celebrate the freeing of the slaves—and she wasn't going to let some jealous—whoo, better not say that; she did not *know* that. Demons, leave me be.

At Union Station they were met in style. Dr. Nevins greeted her with a framed Certificate of Distinction for her "outstanding contribution to the Civil War Centennial," and Rep. Fred Schwengel, a committeeman, echoed his sentiments. This was going to be a good trip, she knew it, just for the one thing—but put that from you; you cannot argue with the Lord.

Friday Sen. Paul Douglas and his wife gave a luncheon for her at the Capitol, and senators fairly swarmed. Mahalia was kept so busy greeting VIPs that the reporter from the *Washington Star* decided to interview Miss Jackson's secretary—she'd catch Mahalia on the way back to the hotel. Butch had no qualms about her new role; it was easy to talk about Mahalia. "She works too hard; she'll be sick sometimes after a concert and still she'll insist on signing autographs for everyone."

"Mahalia," she said when she saw the *Star,* "I didn't say you practiced every day—I just said you *sang* every day around the house. But I did say this about its being better than a concert to hear you singing up on a ladder washing windows—'cause it is."

Friday night Halie heard what she'd feared and known would come Pudley, Big Alice's son—been around her since she come to Chicago—Pudley had passed. She'd had Billings doing what they could. "Butch, call Mrs. Lockett at the funeral home and then get me Ida Beal—then you better wire those people in New York." She was due Sunday to be honored at interfaith ceremonies with Marian Anderson, Cardinal Spellman, Cardinal Cushing, Joe E. Brown, Billy Graham, David Rockefeller, Lucille Ball, Irving Berlin, and two or three others. But anybody could understand a death in the family.

THE SUN WAS shining on almost everybody Saturday morning, Sept. 22, 1963, when the principals took the front row of seats arrayed on the white marble steps: Stevenson, as principal speaker, closest to the microphone; then Rockefeller, Mahalia, MacLeish, Schwengel, Schlesinger, Ralph Becker (chairman of arrangements) and Atty. Gen. Robert F. Kennedy, who came over to speak with Mahalia. The President wasn't there after all; he was spending the weekend at Newport (boat races, somebody whispered, although that wasn't official) but he'd taped a Centennial message. Too bad; Halie had a gold stamper of one of her albums for him, since he liked her singing so well; she'd give it to him another time. Angier Biddle Duke, State Department chief of protocol, was keeping a professional eye out: a number of UN and foreign embassy dignitaries were on hand. About 3,000 viewers spread in rows down to Reflection Pool.

Louise went to the organ hired to augment the Marine band and eyed the scene with pleasure. Gov. Rockefeller said something to Justice Marshall that made him throw back his head and laugh. Mahalia and Adlai Stevenson joined in the joke—Justice Marshall was her good friend now and she'd *been* knowing Stevenson. Lou Mindling, from a facing seat, watched the rush of politicians to be seen speaking with Mahalia. Butch, beside him, hoped things wouldn't be too late getting started; she couldn't see Mahalia was going to get a bit of rest before long into the night, and Pudley already heavy on her.

Gov. Rockefeller leaned across Justice Marshall to make sure Mahalia knew that, right after the invocation, she was to sing. Now. The Marine Band struck up *The Star Spangled Banner*—and Louise almost froze at the organ: four keys off! Mahalia started to struggle with it—and Nelson Rockefeller leaped across in one sweeping motion and stopped the band entirely. Mahalia sang her *Star-Spangled Banner* with just Louise. ("You have never heard the *Star-Spangled Banner* sung with feeling if you haven't heard Mahalia Jackson," columnist H. I. Phillips would report.)

Now Halie could settle back and enjoy the program. She could almost feel the huge figure brooding behind the white columns as Gov. Rockefeller presented Lincoln's original draft of the proclamation freeing the slaves in the ten states in rebellion—forerunner to the postwar Constitutional Act freeing all—handing the precious document over for a month's loan to the Library of Congress. Papa was freed that day—Sept. 22, 1862. How far they'd come in just a lift of the Lord's eyebrows. And look what was in the making. Without violence—hold onto that; without hate—hold onto *that*; with love—and some leaning. That was the way. Hallelujah.

These important people, thought Louise, they weren't playing; she felt they were sincere. It gave her a kind of happiness.

Then Mahalia sang *America* and the Marine Band knew the key, and speeches were over and benediction loosed a mass of boys and girls eager for her autograph. It was half-hour before she could leave, but she could see Rockefeller was almost as busy as she was. Plop inside the limousine with a breathless "oogh!" and they were off. And stalled. The door next to Butch whipped open and Nelson Rockefeller thrust his head in, smiling—shook her hand with a quick "How de do," looked across and said, "See you, Mrs. Jackson," and vanished. "He thought you were on this side," Butch laughed, "and he was too polite to embarrass me."

Lunch, then, at the State Department, and beside each plate a copy of the poem Archibald MacLeish had composed and read. "He listens for the time to come. . . ." That was the line that stuck with Halie. With space to move around, you could see all the people—William Warfield, the great black singer, for one; Bruce Caton . . . all the distinguished Civil War historians. Dr. Nevins came to congratulate her; and as somebody pulled him away, someone else told her he'd won *two* Pulitzer Prizes and was believed to be the ghost writer on President Kennedy's *Profiles in Courage* —although Dr. Nevins himself had never breathed a word. Into the afternoon and there was just really time to see the people waiting at the hotel and dress for the Centennial Commission's formal dinner. Mahalie was winding down, Butch could see—you had to know her, to realize—and *still* she insisted on going on afterward to the Church Ushers Assn. reception at their new headquarters on 16th St.—"paid for in 13 months mainly through the three concerts you gave for us, Miss Jackson."

They almost *lifted* her with their eagerness, their love, rising like a wave as Dorothy Height, president of the National Council of Negro Women, presented her with a miniature bust of Council founder Mary McLeod Bethune, whose statue would be placed in the capital's Lincoln Park.

Next morning Louise went home, ill; Mildred, Edward and Butch drove down to New Orleans, and Mahalia went by train for the rest. She'd need it, these next three days.

SHE'D CANCELLED Seattle World's Fair, so the others were driving the

Cadillac from New Orleans to Columbus, Ohio—Mahalia would follow on the train next day. The highway took the three through troubled country. This was the time of uproar at Ole Miss, with the troops in because of James Meredith enrolling and the tension spilling out. They didn't stop for gas. At Birmingham, they drew up to the Gaston Motel, where they knew Dr. King was staying. He wasn't back from speaking. The radio just then said he'd been knocked down on the rostrum. "Edward, let's get out of this town," said Butch. In New Orleans, Mahalia heard Ralph McGill, editor of the *Atlanta Constitution,* speak of the situation on TV, and she called to offer her services for whatever interracial cause he might sponsor. "*Anything,* Mr. Gill; you let me know." Then she, too, left for Columbus.

Stalled half-hour in traffic near the auditorium; over 3,000 squeezed in but hundreds turned away; the auditorium "electrically charged with her singing," the Columbus critic said . . . and after, at the hotel, Butch's reporter friend with her again. Halie lifted tired eyes. "Didn't you get enough for your story?" Embarrassed, Bubbles Holloway said yes, he just thought there might be something he could do for her before she retired for the night. "Just rub my aching feet, babe," Mahalia murmured, eyes closing again.

Harrisburg . . . towns clicking off; Mildred being evil to young Edward, in Butch's opinion—poor Edward, pushed around at home by Polly, on the road by Mildred; look now, digging Mahalia to bless Edward out and he so good to Mahalia but don't get in the middle of that.

Home two days, then to Ottawa, sing, and leave next morning for a big day: Friday, Oct. 12, she'd be the first nonclassical soloist into the new Lincoln Center Philharmonic Hall. It wasn't too easy for Butch to understand the Ottawa railway clerk on the telephone—he had such a French accent—but she did make sure that the best and certain route to get them there was to take the fast train to Montreal, then transfer to the express to New York. Good. Except that struggling with the language—how did they end up with all these French people? didn't anybody talk American?—the express to Montreal pulled out while they were waiting beside the milk train and boarding that out of Ottawa, it dragged its wheels, stopped at every village—cows between—so they pulled into Montreal after the last possible train had left which could get them to Lincoln Center. Mahalia was beside herself. "I'll call Gov. Rockefeller! No, this is Canada—I'll call President Kennedy! He'll do something. *Somebody* got to get me there! Who you calling, Butch?"

They ended up in a rented station wagon, and once you accepted it—that this had to be—it was one of the most beautiful rides ever. Fall leaves and sunshine, stopping at little roadside stores for cold cuts, and snicksnacks and pickles by the jar for Mahalia; eating in the car, making time the best way they could and making the best of all that they had. God made a beautiful world.

It was 3 a.m. Friday when they pulled in before the Americana Hotel.

Martin Luther King flew up in time for the concert. William Warfield came back beforehand to say hello. Louise had joined them—Mahalia wanted two pianos and organ. And that evening Halie walked out to turn the predominantly white, elegantly dressed audience into hand-clapping, head-bobbing joiners. When she stopped singing, she gave them a little straight religion. "If you believe in God, He will open the windows of heaven and pour blessings upon you."

"She's treating 'em like a South Side church," Butch murmured to Martin.

ON PAPER it looked good: Saturday through Monday in New York. But hold interviews—talk about her temple; stop by Columbia; see Joe Bostic—she'd sing for him next month; welcome her friends . . . rest time dribbled like a leaky faucet. Monday night they watched the President put Russia on notice that the U.S. would go to war if Russia fired a rocket—anywhere—from its secret Cuban base so close to Miami. And Tuesday they drove to Portland, Me., not knowing whether there would be anything of anything but heading for her first Maine concert with something else of the White House to pray over. This was a peculiar place to be taping her for the most important TV special anybody had put together—Mrs. Jacqueline Kennedy's hour-long preview of the superlative talent America could showcase, if Americans would get behind the National Cultural Center for which Congress had donated the ground. The talent choice, it was understood, was Mrs. Kennedy's. But what was this she had to make do? Wednesday morning they'd walked into Portland's City Hall auditorium into a melee of cameras, lights, mikes, control console, cables—a swirl of organized confusion being brought to bear upon a single mark: her.

Mahalia didn't like the sound of the piano and that pipe organ was out for Eddie. Tune the piano and bring in an electric organ. Now this afternoon they were, supposedly, ready but everything's all wrong, worried Butch; she didn't know if Mildred was going to make it—"Sister, I can't see"—but Butch knew the trouble and so did Halie, which didn't make it any easier to have Eddie's instrument sound more like an ass than an organ. Lord, are You *testing* me? I'm too tired, Lord. Really. Just help Halie so Halie don't come tumblin' down. Butch zipped her up in the turquoise gown which the director had picked the night before. "Ready, Miss Jackson?"

Mahalia killed Take 1 after three bars. Mildred was off. Take 2 was hardly longer—Eddie's organ was off. Take 3 went all the way, but on playback, nobody liked the sound. Adjust the mikes. Mahalia used the time driving tempo into both musicians. Take 4 . . . right to the second! "Unh-unh," ruled Mahalia; "let's make it again." Take 5; 6; 7; 8. Mahalia still not hearing it, director and sound engineer sitting back. Her baby now. "Take 9," droned the aide. Ha! Joshua was *fighting* that battle, surging in his knowledge of the might of the Lord, *and the walls come a'tumblin' down. Hallelujah!* Butch got the shivers, much as she'd heard Mahalia, and the director didn't even move to cut tape for seconds.

Ahead, concerts were knotted pearls strung every other day, city after city, a drive between, down to Virginia and circle back, and some of the knots were in her chest. On the way to Philadelphia, Mahalia and Mildred got into it, front seat to back, 'til Mahalia flung a bitter, "You don't care nothing about me. I found that out in 1952 when you took the boat. That's when I knew you didn't care nothing 'bout me, when you and Bess Berma left me and went off to Europe."

"Oh, Sister!"

"Don't Sister me."

THE REST were Lou Mindling's dates, but Oct. 28 was her gift to Martin—the first of the fund-raisers she'd agreed to do. SCLC was really in need of money, Martin had said, calling Butch, oddly diffident about asking Mahalia direct. Mahalia's one stipulation was relayed back: "That box office will have to be kept as if I was getting the money; I'm not going to let people steal the money; Dr. King is going to get the money. You instruct them to that effect." Wyatt T. Walker, Dr. King's executive assistant, said that would be no problem.

At Hartford, Dr. King got a standing ovation when he rose to praise support given, ask help for the fight ahead, affirm his faith that the non-violent way would triumph. Mahalia got a special citation from SCLC. And Dr. King got all the money. Mahalia and Rev. Walker counted it.

One more date in New England, home for one at Northwestern University, and she was in Hollywood to do the *Bell Telephone Hour* with Carl Sandburg, a long-time admirer; tape a special with Dinah Shore—still together!—and make a guest appearance for Dean Martin. Ruth's brother Sigmond saw in the papers that she was in town and came by, and she took him with her here and there. He was about the politest escort she'd ever had. And when her work day was over and her so tired, he was just as glad to bring her out to the little white frame house he owned on Seventh St., where his sister Emma was taking care of Sigma—not yet three—and cook her a good meal. It was a change from banquets and hotels and she could use some real suption.

She was charging into battle, as defender of the faith. She'd said it in New York, she'd said it in Chicago, she'd say it in Hollywood, and anywhere else she was asked: When gospel music became entertainment, not evangelism—when it was turned into a show for nightclub drinkers to laugh and carouse to—it was a disgrace to the singer and a mockery to God's work.

Since Clara Ward had just launched a nationwide nightclub tour, and lesser lights were equally eager to cash in on "pop gospel," the new entertainment craze, the lines were drawn. Everyone in the church world understood well that, to Mahalia's thinking, Clara had sold out to the Devil. Clara had her defenders, and they spoke up. The press was having a fine time. Mike Connolly of *The Hollywood Reporter* ran an offer from gospel singer Nellie Lutcher saying she was "ready and willing to take any of those Vegas dates Mahalia Jackson doesn't think she should take."

It was the wrong time for the *Playboy* Jazz Poll to list her name again on its ballot. She'd asked those people to please not—what you going do? *The Hollywood Reporter* also printed that Dmitri Tiomkin had talked her into singing his *Natasha Theme.* You sure can't believe everything you read. One thing new in print that was *so* was that *Go Tell It on the Mountain* was such a hit from her album Columbia was releasing it as a single. First new single they'd pressed for her in over two years. "See?" she told Yancey. "You stick with the Lord; He takes care of His own." Yancey had eased into an accepted part of her Hollywood scene, her shadow—pale as he was. He said he wanted to learn everything she knew, and he was willing to do anything she wanted done while he was learning it.

CLARA WAS ON Joe Bostic's Madison Square Garden gospel festival—but that's all right; it was none of her. What *was* of her was this wire from Mr. Mindling putting her right square in the middle: "Don't leave Chicago until you have every penny, or I have every penny and I tell you so." Help me Jesus. From New York, Bostic's response was fury, pure fury, crackling the telephone as she read him the wire. This so-called agent had already forced her price up on him from last year's $3,500 to $7-5-0-0. Unheard of, for gospel! And here it's Saturday. Mahalia *had* to be there Sunday; Madison Square Garden would be torn apart if she wasn't—and Joe Bostic's reputation wasn't going to be ripped with it. He hung up, circled his ticket locations, and wired four installments of $1,500 each—$1,500 short. Mahalia took the train. When she called him from the Wellington, his wife answered. "Dorothy, I have to have the rest of the money befor I can set foot in the Garden." They had the money, Mrs. Bostic said; she'd send a car for Mahalia. Shortly, the driver returned with a message: "Mahalia says, 'Bring the money, and *you* come, because if Joe Bostic brings it, he will not only talk me out of it, he might talk me out of what he's given me already!' "

Dorothy Bostic went, returned with Mahalia—money wadded in her bosom under her high-necked gown—and the three friends enjoyed a laugh. Another round in the gospel game.

STAND BY, D.C. had said. She was due in Washington to do a special Christmas program from America to Europe via the new communications satellite—all three major networks: unprecedented. Everybody was ready but Telstar, the reason for it all. NASA was sure the technical difficulties could be ironed out. Just stand by— Stand by—

Now they'd slacked to "Hold." Halie didn't mind the wait; it was unlooked-for rest: Mr. Mindling wouldn't book anything to risk this—this was *history,* and good for her foreign standing. So there was extra time to get out Jesus and Joseph and Mary on the ass and get more outdoors lights. The flurry about her *Great Songs* had subsided in a rush of praise for her Christmas album, *Silent Night:* "a superb disk," said *Cashbox,* from one "dedicated to the gospel idiom" . . . and *FM & Fine Arts* magazine titled its Christmas story on her, "Why I Sing Only Gospel." Like the sea, it ebbs and flows. That story gave her a chance to point out that "today the white folks in the South come in and sit beside the colored to hear me sing. That's how much these plain old simple songs have accomplished." It didn't please her, then, to see her picture on *Jazz Kalendar*—but that was balanced out with her name on the NAACP Honor Guard.

Another telegram from NASA, this one to Lou Mindling: "Probably read in newspapers about problems. . . . Please reassure Miss Jackson not to worry . . . she at least is standing by in the comfort of her living room, not in the space cone and astronaut suit as John Glenn and the others had to do during their waiting period."

She had her regular Christmas business to be about. No need to get turkeys for Gleason's boys this year—he was getting along fine since he got with Billy Graham. People were underfoot 'til late . . . just visiting, or come with their problems—among the reverends, church problems . . . aunts and cousins in and out—Aunt Hannah better, thank You Lord; Aunt Alice holding well . . . Ike by to say hello but really for a loan—why else he be back so early from the New Orleans track? . . . that man been writing his book about her this long while back again—Uncle Porter could talk to him, she was tired . . . grandchildren brought, and godchildren . . . more urging of her to come to services than there was her to do . . . and still. . . . She fingered the gold brooch Carl Sandburg had given her, "as a token of his esteem," the silver-haired, gentle man had said; in his family for three generations. This would be her—how many? 35 Christmases in Chicago since she left home to be a nurse. She called Celie. Aunt Bell's diabetes had her in the bed and she could lose a leg, though that might be held off. The cousins had an hour's talk. "Sometimes I get lonely, Celie," Mahalia said, at the last. "There is so much on me, but I don't have nobody. Even Adam, when the Lord saw he was lonely, He gave him a companion." That was true, said Celie. "I feel like I would like companionship, someone that really cares—just the thing that I could hardly find."

"If you should," said Celie, "I wouldn't dare be against it; I would shout for joy."

"Celie," said Halie, "this prestige mess is nothing." She hung up and looked at Russell Roberts' picture on her bedroom dresser and went into the pink bedroom and put his record on.

A FINAL BREEZY wire from NASA, old friends now. "Unpack. The relay proved a bust. Christmas show is off." Well—it gave her a good long space of time. At 4 a.m. Christmas morning at Greater Salem, an exultant Mahalia sang the great good news and glad tidings in this hour that Jesus was believed actually to have been born. Christmas Week she was again on the Gallup Poll list of the American people's "most admired women in the world."

Watch Night, '62. So much Lord, we got over. And in seven weeks—a new world.

46

When Missie Wilkerson looked up from her bed in the Providence Hospital ward and saw Mahala sweeping in, it was good as a dose of medicine. Good to see her, good to have what she brought—"*never* failed me with a check; if I got sick, you can see something coming in—a check or whatever have you—even if Mahala was out of *town*. Well, this day she comes into Providence, I was on charity, and when she walked in that hospital and asked for Missie Wilkerson, and who she was, it upset the whole *hospital!* That did me a world of good, 'cause she was so very close to me."

Now pile together the separate parts of her present for Carl Sandburg's 85th birthday, and let's go to New York.

Walking into the big double suite at the Waldorf-Astoria on Sunday evening, Jan. 6, Halie knew this was one of the times you don't need a scrapbook to remember. The newspaper called the dinner "a brilliant literary event," but Mahalia was swept up immediately by those who knew her. Those who didn't, it looked to Elizabeth Thornton, all wanted to. Mahalia and Marian Anderson fell into conversation immediately. Justice Douglas came up. She was introduced to Johnny Steinbeck, who looked big enough to enforce his opinions; to Mrs. Ernest Hemingway, in a beautiful silky-haired white mohair evening dress; and Mark Van Doren, who read a beautiful birthday poem he'd written for his friend. Butch's head wouldn't register all the names, but she took some down: Gunnar Jarring, for one—the Swedish ambassador—there because Mr. Sandburg's parents had been Swedish immigrants. And look how the Lord had lifted him! exulted Halie. They say the way to a man's heart is through his stomach, but I say the way to everybody's soul is through his ear. Hallelujah! She was truly glad of the chance to meet Mr. Sandburg's family. She could see what help his wife was to him: reaching over without a word and rescuing the poor man when he was handed a knife to cut the first slice from his big birthday cake—he probably never did a thing around the house. Then when all the speeches were all over, Halie presented her gift—a song, *I'm Grateful*—and Mildred said some of those people all dressed up in the Waldorf-Astoria had tears streaming down their faces. God is real.

And Lord, You piling Halie's plate higher than she can handle at the time. She was staring at the invitation with the star-circled gold eagle: "The President and Mrs. Kennedy request the pleasure of the company of Miss Jackson—" It had come before she left Chicago, along with the little engraved card she knew the look of by now—the White House in golden tones behind the black letters. It directed her to the East Entrance for admission on Feb. 12, 1963, at 6 o'clock.

The morning of Feb. 13 she was sailing from San Francisco to Hawaii.

JOHN F. KENNEDY's own plate was piled higher than he could readily digest, but he had to let Dave Powers see this. The presidential assistant had been at his side in every political campaign starting with 1946 on the streets of Boston. "The President kept a list of all the people who had helped him before he became President and later as President; and I can still recall his speaking with great pride about Mahalia," says Dave Powers. Now the aide scanned Mahalia's letter with interest. Due to her concert schedule, she would be en route to Hawaii and unable to attend the Emancipation Reception. But "let me reassure you that anytime I can be of service to you, Mr. President, or my country, or the Democratic party, I would consider it a privilege if you would contact me."

Dave Powers grinned and thought that Jackie would be sorry. "Jackie had a great awareness for certain dignitaries who had contributed to the success of the Presidential campaign," says Mr. Powers. "She always had praise and admiration for Miss Jackson."

Nobody was sorrier than Mahalia—but not sorry enough to fly the night of Feb. 12 from Washington to California. Why couldn't it be a day this week? Between Mr. Sandburg and Sunday, she'd even had a chance to go furniture shopping with Butch. She'd *been* booked to sing Sunday at Bethel Temple in the Bronx, where her joy in the Lord so overflowed that TV coverage was titled *Joy Is My Witness*. "She's not singing for them, or for us," thought Butch; "she's up there with God." Next day, Chicago in a blowing cold to sing for the National Conference on Religion and Race.

Every time she walked into the Edgewater Beach with the bowing and the scraping, she thought of the bending and the sweeping when she was a maid upstairs. *Who* going use the front door *then!* A day between and they were signing in again at the Wellington for the *Voice of Firestone*. Wires and calls were thick and fast from Mr. Mindling. Seven Arts was leasing rights to her 5-minute TV series. And so much coming up for Hawaii!

But miles to cross and promises to keep, before ship-time.

South to Baltimore, back for New York, then home in blizzard weather to Martin and Ralph Abernathy—two keyed-up people in search of help. Dr. King had decided upon Birmingham as a demonstration city to sweep away the worst of segregation, and clear the way for Negroes in community affairs. "That's a tough one," said Mahalia gravely. That's why he'd picked it: as a showcase of the might of passive resistance. His insistence on non-violence was losing some of the younger men. "Martin, you know you right. Hold onto the 12th Psalm: *The Lord tests the righteous and the wicked, and His soul hates him that loves violence.* Hallelujah." But exhausted SCLC faced its biggest need yet: for volunteers who'd take training—and for more bail money than they'd ever had. He wasn't getting the support he'd hoped. He was being criticized by black and white. It was a heavy load. "I know the people on the *Sun-Times,* Martin; they'll give you a story." (It was his one interview spelling out the Birmingham plan.)

Halie sang as she fixed something good for Martin and Rev. Ralph to eat. Within an hour, they were all singing. And she made a decision. "Martin, I've *been* wanting somebody big up here, some of these important preachers, to present you in Chicago. I'll get on it before I go to Hawaii."

Call after call. Thunderclouds gathered. Wait 'til she got back from Hawaii! Almost time now. She was eager. But Halie'd have to work her way across. . . .

This was the worst. The blizzard in the Texas Panhandle had been bad enough. Now on the plains of northern New Mexico the howling wind blew the snowstorm straight across. "It's like a dust storm, only snow," Butch muttered to Mildred, the two shivering in the back from Mahalia's open window. She had her head out trying to see for Edward, who was totally blinded, the windshield piled and crusted over. The worst hazard was other cars—off the road on both sides, some stalled in their tracks. They inched forward, the Cadillac's steady hum their only comfort. "And pray," said Mahalia, without turning her head; "you better pray." Finally, dim loomings—and lights. Tucumcari. "I don't care how you say it," Mahalia said; "it spells stop."

There was one room and lucky to get it. They turned out next morning to more snow but the clerk said the road was passable. "Let's hope he's a prophet," Mahalia said. He was, and oh, blessed valley—going into Albuquerque there was no snow. "Well!" said Mahalia, and rolled up her window. But the valley didn't last and the snowstorm claimed the hills—

stole their vision—stole all the world except this narrow ribbon they were trying to hold to, crawling ten miles an hour after hour, into Gallup, into —thank You Lord—a room. Next morning an incoming Greyhound driver said the road ahead was much worse; his bus had been stranded this side of Flagstaff. Mahalia surveyed her troupe. "We," she said, "are going to take the train."

No telling when it might arrive, but the next train west was due about 4 p.m. Butch stretched out across the bed by Mahalia. Mildred and Edward were at it. "You think you are on a pedestal!" Mildred hissed at Edward. . . .

"Butch! wake up—wake up!" Mahalia. "Tell me what a pedestal is."

"BETTER SEE if you left anything, 'cause we not coming back." The weather was still nasty. En route to the station, a woman made a left turn across them, and they collided. Butch leaped from the back and jumped under the steering wheel, shoving Edward over. "Who was driving this car?" puzzled the woman from the other car. "I was," said Butch. "You know you weren't driving this car," said Mahalia. "I was!" . . . "You was *not*." . . . "I *was* driving," Butch said, and got out. Mahalia followed. "Mahalia, Edward doesn't have his driver's license!" whispered Butch. "Oh, my God," said Mahalia.

A policeman came, assessed the situation, and took their statements. "Okay," Mahalia told him, "now I want to be sure nobody's hurt. There's a woman with a child in that car, and I don't want anybody saying this child was hurt." The child was not hurt, its mother said. "She says her child was not hurt," the policeman said, writing it down; "that's enough." No, Mahalia said, "that is not what I want. I want something done about it right now—an examination, or a statement."

"Miss Jackson, I *told* you—" The policeman looked part Indian, and all mad. "I want something done—or in writing," Mahalia said. The two stood toe to toe, a tug of wills. Finally, "Miss Jackson," cried the policeman, past all patience, "I told you it's all right. Now if you don't shut up, I'm gonna put you in jail!"

They were glad to get on the train. They'd just make that ship.

BEAT THE SEASICKNESS. Who *not* going use a new movie camera on this sea. And the ship pretty enough to put in a bottle. She sang the last night with a glad heart. As the *Matsonia* steamed into Honolulu harbor, a plane circled a "Welcome Mahalia Jackson" streamer . . . a dockside committee draped her chin-deep in fragrant pikake leis . . . cheering fans lined the path to her limousine. The Mahalia Happening had come to Oahu.

In the next 11 days, she opened both houses of the 2nd State Legislature to standing ovations—sang two packed concerts in Waikiki Shell—received at a giant reception where she got the recipe for Missionary Punch (guava and grapefruit juice)—bought muumuus by the bale, and Hawaiian records by the box. She autographed albums for hours at four stores; lunched with the Waikiki Business and Professional Women. She listened intently at the early-morning Governor's Prayer Breakfast as Admirals Harry Felt and C. C. Knapp, gold braid sparkling, each read a Bible scripture; Gov. John Burns spoke for International Christian Leadership; Billy Graham gave the main address. Then, unscheduled and for free, she sang. She'd visited earlier with Dr. Graham; his had been the first message she got when she arrived. He was recuperating on Kauai from the flu. Now, chatting after the prayer breakfast—Lou Mindling with the others at her side—she spied the evangelist. "Rev. Graham! Come here! Tell this man that Jesus died on the cross."

"Of *course* he did, Mahalia!" cried Billy Graham—and the two touched each other off. "I thought both of them were going to shout out there on the lawn of the Royal Hawaiian Hotel," laughs Elizabeth Thornton, "but it was wonderful." When they calmed a little, Mahalia said, "I can't convert him. Maybe you can convert him." Mindling shrugged: "He can't do it, and you can't do it, so why don't we all just have a good time."

On Hawaiian TV she talked cooking. She entranced the press. Asked her favorite song, she mused if she had to choose, it would probably have to be *Just As I Am.* She spoke of her temple—"you all come, it's going to be for everybody"—and pressed about financing, said she planned to do most of it before she asked anybody else. She sat in the sun; "I'm trying to get sunburned," she told Lou Mindling. He peered earnestly. "There is a change of pigmentation."

She had 5 pounds to her credit that she'd lost from being seasick and she meant to enjoy every one. Mindling delighted in her pleasure and plied her with all the food she could hold. They stopped at a coconut plantation so Halie could have one chopped fresh from a tree. "We used to do that in New Orleans," she said; "not climb the tree—split 'em open and drink the milk." It was intoxicating—not the drink: the color, the flowers, the scenery, and most particularly the air: God's clean air, yes, but mainly the air of realness in these people's togetherness, all the races mingled. You have to let me see, Lord; it can be.

"GO 'WAY, Edward," said Mahalia without turning from the porthole. "Can't you see I'm meditating? I got a burden on my mind and I'm reaching the strength to pick it up. Baby, Mahalia's getting ready to fight the demons."

It was a serious decision. For the first time in her life—immersed in and brought out of the Baptist church—she was going to defy its sovereign voice in the person of the president of the National Baptist Convention and every other big preacher in Chicago. It would cost friendships, but *she* was going to present Martin Luther King. She called Martin. "Mahalia," he said, "there's only one person *can* bring us into Chicago."

May 27 was the soonest she could hope to work it up, with March already booked up tight. She told Lou Mindling to keep her clear—all except Easter; she'd sing that. And drop Europe he been juggling dates on—talking Sweden, maybe clear on to Australia. Make it—oh, make it some other time. Good thing these three weeks' work was all California; she could be lining up her stars.

THE MOST beautiful fat lady in the world. Art Seidenbaum made a note of it for his story. He'd been sitting in on a Mahalia session since 1 p.m. and it was enough to wear you out, just watching. But watching was too wonderful to walk out. The sight of Mahalia roaring out responses to herself on tape, for *Move on Up a Little Higher* . . . the stomping, tapping, clapping. The three men working with her own accompanists threw themselves into it so that at one point Mahalia held up that long, slim palm and said, "Baby, I know you all great, but unless you ease off on that beat, you going jazz me right out the Baptist church." 5:30. The men packing up, Mahalia still singing, still caught up. She saw the reporter watching her. "I don't do this just to be an entertainment, you know."

Sigmond Galloway brought his Aunt Katie up to the hotel to see her. He seemed to have a nice family.

IN BETWEEN recording for Townsend and radio and press interviews, a concert at Berkeley and one in San Francisco. Back for the American Bible Society. A visit to the City Council of Los Angeles and a citation by Mayor Sam Yorty with a Council resolution commending her "awe-inspiring gift of communicating the original and true meaning of words." A big luncheon honoring her, Mrs. Norman Chandler among the notables—and Halie Jackson found herself standing with a picture in her hands from Her Majesty's Art Studio, Addis Ababa, Ethiopia. *The Trek of the Queen of Sheba.* It seemed to have some force, so that she had to wrench her eyes from it to listen to the speech of presentation to her. She spoke then of how man today is "crying the blues, whether he sings them or speaks them—neglecting to think of, to *use,* the divine power within him which lifts man up. The most wonderful thing about God is that He gives people the intelligence and ingenuity to depend on themselves. Look at me. These old songs I brought up from the South—they're like throwing bread on the waters. It comes back buttered on both sides. I am not a great artist. I am just Mahalia Jackson."

Now to UCLA's Royce Hall. And in and around all this, search talent for the cause.

SHE WAS flaming mad, mad enough to tell it. "The stars keep telling me they've 'already given one benefit.' Well, they have to keep on giving them, 'cause the people keep going to jail and the money gets used as fast as we give it. Me, I'm ready to join a picket line or anything else. Not for Dr. King—for me. Because I have walked all over this world and I'm not free enough to have a decent TV show."

There. She'd have Martin's show and *show* those niggers. Just get her home. And *let* those preachers open their mouths.

47

"In this world, you got to have a made-up mind. No straddling the fence." Mahalia's eyes swept the faces around her. "Lean on the word of God." Amen . . . Hallelujah . . . Tell it, Sister. . . . The response drifted across like a light breeze. "I'm working for two months for Martin without a dime and you all can just do the same. And I don't mean sitting on your behinds and saying you helping Mahalia Jackson. I got no use for dry shells. I want the meat. This thing's going across the country. Celeste—Margaret —just 'cause you singing, that don't let you off. You too, Frye.

"All right now. Here's what we do."

Mahalia was deploying her troops. "And don't nobody go run up any bills and come say you needed it for the work. Ain't nobody but Halie paying these bills, and every dime we collect is going to Martin for the bail money. You need something, you ask Polly."

Down in Birmingham, on April 3, Dr. King's squads kicked off their protest—to meet fire hoses and police dogs. Arrests would run over 2,000. Two thousand bails! All day, every night, 8358 Indiana looked like election headquarters. April 5, they did take time out to vote. Once again, black wards spelled the difference for Richard Daley: 82 percent. Rep. Dawson was a shoo-in.

The Scott family was getting ready to move to California, but Celeste's son Eddie joined his mother and aunt on the clerical assembly line. So did Eddie Robinson and Wallace Smith—Edna Jackson's boy up from home, a college student now. Margaret Aikens enlisted Tevelda Hall, who'd had her own troupe of African singers and dancers but "the Lord began to deal with her," says Margaret; "so by the time Mahalia needed her, she was doing secretarial work. And from the day we brought her, whatever Ma halia wanted, Teevee would do it." A white girl who wrote songs was helping too.

Mahalia coaxed, cajoled, prodded, and pushed everybody she could into donating services and/or wares. Her first stop was the mayor's office: She walked out with 5,000-seat Aerie Crown Theatre in McCormick Place, contributed by the city—operating costs thrown in. The musicians' local waived rules and she got 28 men free. Stagehands, ushers—all free. She drafted Bob Miller to work with her neighbor, Hubert Maybell, who was advising about the business end. Halie wanted everything on top the table, and no mistakes. "Why isn't your godchild here to do some of this ripping and running," she demanded of Aunt Hannah, "instead of jumping around with those kangaroos?" Brother John, at the moment, was giving Down Under its first black gospel.

She gave a kickoff dinner to announce her plans, her goal—$50,000—and to let the press and each other see who was working. Robert Johnson of her old Johnson Singers joined her. Rev. Abernathy flew in from Birmingham to say "Negroes will not be free in Illinois until we are free in Alabama!"

She made John H. Johnson (major black media publisher) and S. B. Fuller (publisher of the *Courier* papers) her undefined co-assistants, along with Mayor Daley, and had no trouble with publicity. Radio was equally generous—if she'd come down and make the announcements. Rev. Al Benson—the leading black DJ—pledged $1,000 in cash besides his air time. The white papers were not overwhelming with space, but they did assist, equating relative news value with Mahalia's hold on their hearts. She spent nothing on ads. The one thing she couldn't get donated, wangle as she might, was the tickets—but she got the price down to $170.

She ducked out, in quick succession, for three things: She helped Jack Paar narrate his Holy Land films on Good Friday. Easter Sunday she sang in Louisville, fighting a cold, sipping hot lemonade backstage, reminding herself she wanted to reach Connie Haines, since she couldn't clear the Easter Week dates Connie had wanted for herself, Jane Russell, and Beryl Davis to give a benefit for the Mahalia Foundation: those girls were *working* Christians.

And she went to the White House.

THE AMERICAN Society of Newspaper Editors was accustomed to having the President speak at one of its convention luncheons. What was new was that the First Lady asked the wives to tea. The men wanted to go too. Now all the editors and their wives were invited by President and Mrs. Kennedy to a reception at the White House. Mahalia Jackson was going to sing. That intrigued George Healy, Jr., editor of New Orleans' *Times-Picayune.* They'd never met.

When they did, it was by introduction from JFK himself. Earlier, through Rep. Hale Boggs, the editor had presented the President a copy of his great-uncle's *Reminiscences of a Portrait Painter*—some nine George P. A. Healy paintings hung in the White House. Now, circulating with Mrs.

Kennedy, the President came to the editor and thanked him. Mahalia happened along at this moment and the three chatted briefly; then, "Why don't you show Miss Jackson around?" the President asked. Mahalia didn't want to say that Truman had shown her around; and Mrs. Eisenhower. Besides, Jackie was making some changes. . . .

Halie found herself sitting in the Oval Room, in the President's chair. They moved on then, but—sitting in the President's private chair. It was a moment Halie never forgot; one of those lifted out of the flux and fixed on the mountain.

NOW WHERE was everybody at? who did what they said? She listened to some good news—and some bad: Some of the ministers didn't want "that man" to come in here were working to make her flop. "The Bible," said Mahalia grimly, "says 'Fear not these faces.' *Who* they going scare off?" She called one culprit and dished him out with a scalding wash of words. Margaret was amazed. "Excuse me, baby," Halie said, "but you don't see the Devil in people like I see them. You think everybody is pure, but people can sometime be full of the Devil and you got to know how to recognize this. Now baby, Halie wants you to pray, 'cause the old Devil gets mad when you're trying to do good. Pray that God will move the stumbling blocks."

The telephone rang constantly, and answering it, trying to spare her, the hovering circle was apt to say Miss Jackson was busy. Mahalia overheard Margaret doing just that.

"Who is it, baby? . . . Let me talk, that's my public." Why did she let herself in for that, why was her number listed, Margaret asked. "I don't have nothing to hide," Halie said, pushing up her lip. "That's for people who hiding. How else people going know how to get in touch with me?"

Lou Mindling got drafted, helping ferret the best routes to free work from the unions—how to scale the house—the angles were endless. Halie decided she should have some help from the Catholic church and called him to get her a monsignor. "Mahalia, for God's sake, you don't 'get a monsignor' like you order half a dozen cans of meat; but I'll call my friend Bishop O'Donnell and ask him if he's got a friendly one who wants to come say something."

Halie wasn't worried; he'd get her a monsignor.

She took an evening out she couldn't refuse: to help Mayor Daley welcome the Grand Duchess Charlotte of Luxembourg, arriving on the arm of U.S. Ambassador William Rivkin. The Duchess invited Miss Jackson to visit. Miss Jackson said she would be honored to. She got home before the typewriters had been covered for the night.

She now had corralled ten ministers—mostly her own young protégés —who were willing to publicly support the night with a $500 pledge each and to help with ticket sales. Dr. John Thurston she'd known she could count on; Rev. Clay Evans had sung with her before he joined the ministry; a significant addition was young Dr. W. N. Daniels—president of the Chicago NAACP, heretofore uncommitted to Dr. King's support. In Detroit, her old friend Rev. C. L. Franklin was among the ten. In Chicago, her senior ministerial support was Rev. Louis Boddie—"the great humanitarian," she said affectionately. From his pulpit at Greater Harvest Baptist, on May 9 she made an impassioned plea. "I'm hot and I'm hurt," she said, pacing the pulpit. "Don't think you're doing Mahalia a favor by coming—you're doing yourself a favor, and you're helping your brothers Down South to help you have the dignity of your identity." She promised "the greatest collection of stars that has ever performed in one night in Chicago."

Exactly which stars, continued to yo-yo.

She talked the telephone company into contributing a special line twice so Dr. King could address her pep meetings of workers—and a week before the benefit, he took the pulpit of Evanston's First Methodist Church for two sermons with comments after each. Press coverage buried a significant stance: "We seek to obtain justice for Negroes, not to reverse the social order. We must not substitute black supremacy for white supremacy—for one is as bad as the other."

THE DAY of the big event, Mindling walked in the side door on 84th. Mahalia had set up a system for ticket sale and accounting designed to ensure absolutely against any finagling—a system so intricate that she'd given him a hurry-call to come straighten the tangle. He searched for her now. My God. She was in the kitchen, on her knees, cleaning the floor. His tap on her shoulder made her look up. "Mahalia, excuse me. You never lie to me, right?"

"I never lie to you, Mr. Mindling; you know I never lie to you."

"Then I just want you to answer me truthfully and briefly."

"What's that?"

"Is white help hard to get out here?"

She collapsed. She whooped. She hollered. And they straightened out the tickets.

When Martin King arrived with his key aides—Ralph Abernathy, Wyatt T. Walker, Fred Shuttlesworth—it was Mahalia's sense of the fitting that they be met by reverends, in force and in style. Bob Miller arranged gleaming black limousines and an open car for Martin; Mayor Daley, an escort of six motorcycle squad cars and "all kinds of escorts, everything we could get on that procession," grins Mr. Miller. "Of course, Mayor Daley would do anything for Mahalia. And one thing, she insisted he just had to stay in his office after hours to receive us."

The czar of Chicago waited while the entourage followed Mahalia's prescribed course: First stop, the *Chicago Defender*—a nicety, since *its* publisher wasn't one of her co-assistants but was generous with space; second stop, Johnson Publications, host to the white press at a general news conference; *then* call on the Mayor.

Richard Daley had been surprised by Mahalia's request, and, apparently, somewhat nonplused by how to handle it. "I wouldn't say it was the warmest welcome Martin ever received, but the mayor received him. He was really surprised that we came by," says quiet Bob Miller, an astute Daley observer as an incumbent of the City Council. Then they were off to the Sheraton Hotel—sirens wailing, horns blowing. It was the finest welcome the SCLC had ever had; now came the crux of the night.

IT WAS a sellout, white and black. They could have filled another 1,000 seats with just those turned away after the decree came that not another living body could enter.

Backstage, Mahalia felt like murdering a couple of people if it hadn't been against her religion. Forgive me, Lord; Halie has provocation. She was trying to press together an amorphous mass into a Hollywood production and it squeezed through her fingers here and there. She was minus late-pullouts Bob Newhart and Shelly Berman. Dinah Washington, Eartha Kitt, Dick Gregory, Gloria Lynn, Aretha Franklin, Al Hibbler—with four MCs and "personages"—formed a small still pool in the turbulence of local acts, 500 from various choirs, ministers, well-wishers, celebrity-seekers, and those trying to do a job. The Mayor was waiting not far from Dick Gregory, only recently released from jail for walking up and down before the mayor's house day after day to protest the school situation. Mahalia pulled the mayor and Martin together with her for pictures. On the edge of it all, Studs Terkel was an amused witness. Mahalia was directing everything, including—one hour late—"Now get that curtain up."

"It was marvelous," says Studs Terkel; "not the show, but the event. All the politicians were there. Sen. Douglas was there, and she announced his contribution. She asked me to introduce Dr. King. I asked, 'Don't you want somebody else?' And she said, 'You just go ahead.' "

"Just seeing the singlehanded support of one committed person, and what can be *done,*" said an awed Rev. Abernathy, and went forth to speak. At the end of his talk, he called for volunteers for Birmingham. No one stood. But ushers passed the baskets Mahalia had ready, and several thousand extra dollars fluttered. Then Mahalia added the full force of her voice before Studs walked on as MC and did the rite.

It was long past midnight when Martin Luther King spelled out the evil, spelled out the cause, praised its heroes, and named some broad remedies —including a call for President Kennedy to sign an executive order outlawing segregation. And if Gov. Wallace stood in the door to bar black students, as he had threatened, "It would be a marvelous and creative act if the President of the United States accompanied Negroes to the door of the University of Alabama." He left them with a challenge: "Chicago is just as much a segregated city as Birmingham," he flung forth. "You must defeat segregation and discrimination in Chicago."

Aretha sealed the night with *Take My Hand, Precious Lord*. She turned church *out!*

2:30 a.m. Martin was whisked away to a reception, but Halie stayed to shepherd the money—only her own most-trusted allowed to help with the counting, bundling, tallying, proving. Finally she saw the cash locked away with the tally of pledges, joining the money already collected from advance sales, program, contributions—she had it to the penny. With all the pledges in, she would top $50,000. She could sleep well.

Waking, she got the money out. Martin was coming for it. Proving it, savoring it, she counted it one last time.

Five thousand dollars was missing.

She counted again, panic rising.

Five thousand dollars short.

When Martin came, Halie—with love, pride, and not another word—handed over to him the whole sum of the original accounting.

She'd been to the bank.

She searched her memory, and she prayed. She buried her strong suspicion. She would not have a scandal. Some day, some way—

JUNE 3 SHE was in Montclair, Calif., surrounded by little white children, trying out a swing—"Think it holds 200 pounds?"—there for the dedication of the children's playground whose equipment her three earlier concerts had bought. That night in nearby Ontario, singing for Montclair again, she looked out over the crippled children given the treat as part of the celebration. "My legs were crooked and bent when I was a child," she told them; "I was terribly deformed. And now my legs are straight as anybody's. I am walking evidence of what God can do."

Now to L.A. recording sessions. A concert at Shrine Auditorium. And pitched, open battle, sword in hand, raised to flame-point by a burgeon of nightclubs whose miniskirted waitresses wore wings, whose tambourines bore drinks. "The Devil is in those singers pandering to this," Mahalia cried. "He's making them destroy the principle of our sacred songs." As for Clara Ward, ensconced at Las Vegas: "I don't know what's got into Clara; like the green bay tree, this will wither and die."

Variety's Joe Price asked her—in the light of this pop gospel foment—how they were treating her at Columbia. "Irv Townsend loves me," she said instantly. "I think he went to Sunday school when he was a boy. I'm very happy with Columbia. I sing what I want, when I want to."

Joe Price forbore to ask comment on what he knew—that Columbia had an exclusive agreement to put its singers into at least three "religious" nightclubs. . . .

Now why did I say that about Columbia, not to make them look bad. Was that me to like them, or them to like me? Oh, this is a big mess. "Laurraines," she said earnestly, "money is the root of—well, not all evil, but enough to keep the demons in buttermilk."

She folded away the issue of *Variety* with Joe Price's interview. It didn't help at all to have the Supreme Court forbid reciting the Lord's Prayer or Bible verses in school. Poor children.

COLUMBIA RECORDS had good reason to give in to Lou Mindling's demands for her new contract. She had just been awarded another Grammy, this one for *Great Songs of Love & Faith*. Now *they* would pay for her recording sessions, not *she*. Usually recording companies make the artist stand the full cost by deducting it from their royalties, a jubilant Mindling had explained; "I'll bet you didn't know that." Yeah, she knew that. "And now if they don't spend X amount on recording you every year, the balance goes into your foundation."

"That's great, Mr. Mindling."

"I threw in something else. If you want to go into some worthwhile investments, they will lend you up to $100,000 at the prime rate—that means the lowest rate going. How about that?"

SHE SAW more of Sigmond Galloway this time. So considerate; so quiet; insisted on doing for *her*. She didn't want him to know too much about her, no more than she was a gospel singer—none of this The Great Mahalia Jackson bunk. Let him tell her where he went to school—his friends in Gary—how he'd worked in his uncle's construction office before coming to California to follow music—about his five-piece combo and their job at Hermosa Beach that lasted ten years—things that happened on the *Bourbon Street* TV series when he played sax and how much everybody liked him; sax was what he ate on, though he loved the flute. He had a soothing voice. And the man went to all this trouble to fix her meals at his house.

Mother Parks was highly amused as she smuggled the dishes into the kitchen, still hot. She didn't live too far away, and she was glad to do it. Minters had been underfoot, her son's best friend, since they were children in Gary. Now all Minters had to do was finish up the touches. He could burn a steak pretty good, but when it came to anything else. . . . She was glad Mahalia Jackson was taking an interest in him. That boy always did like glamor. Now he should let *her* tell *him*.

Mahalia didn't mind. She had a countertheme in the back of her head.

48

She wanted to join these young college people at Carnegie Hall to raise money to teach people to vote, get them registered. But what her mind was reaching to was August. She eyed Ida Beal's hat. Ida had come up for the B.T.U.–Sunday School Congress, and Halie'd made her come here. Then Ida'd stayed on to keep Halie company and cook her some New Orleans food.

It was a good period. Bone-tired and more, Halie'd got Dr. Barclay to call Mr. Mindling and say. Now if she wanted, she could run hide out at Missie's, in the country—take off her shoes, slip on a cotton dress, let Missie cook her greens and cornbread and don't say knife and fork. She decided to give a 4th of July barbecue in her yard. Old friends and new, black and white—Red Saunders, been so nice with the orchestra for Martin's fundraising: she wouldn't want that skin, for sunburn. It was a nice way to let people meet Bertha.

Back in Los Angeles at her Uncle Johnny Jackson's, Bertha Nero had been unburdening herself about her broken marriage. At 24, she felt stranded. Mahalia eyed this trim, pretty daughter of Yvonne's: "Why don't you come live with me?" Bertha had seized at the lifeline. Now Mahalia was turning over what would be a good career for Bertha. The front of her mind was attending to Ida's hat.

"Mahalia," said Ida, "did you see that story in *Jet,* that white girl from Oregon said she got saved listening to your record of *In the Upper Room?"*

"Yeah, that's wonderful; I been knowing that," Mahalia said. "But what I want to know is where's my hat? I'd take the one you got right off you, serve you right, if I didn't like the one better you *supposed* to made me."

"Mahalia, I just—" Ida resigned herself. "I tell you what. I will go down and get the same things and make that hat for you up here, right at your house."

"That'll fix you good, for letting my hat go."

Ida hummed away at her project while Halie attended the major threads of her concerns. Her mind was much on the freedom work, and calls streamed in to sing for benefits. To some she said yes. She went to Dayton for the Congress of Racial Equality, where she explained quietly to the *Journal-Herald,* "I don't support every so-called freedom organization. I'm not about to help any cause that would destroy our country." In Carbondale, "There must be some way to settle these problems as families settle problems—by compromise, conciliation, talk, understanding. Congress is treating us as though we are provoked children. Understanding—that is the key. So many white people talk at colored people, but not to them."

Martin came back to give out the plaques she'd had made for workers in the funds festival. Teevee sent out the letters to everyone who'd helped in any way, and Boy Baby's church was packed with those displaying the badge: "Mahalia Jackson's Salute! to His Honor Mayor Richard J. Daley and All the Good Citizens Who Supported the Benefit Program for S.C.L." The printer dropped the final *C*, but nobody cared. Once again Mayor Daley and Dr. King met in apparent amity, although Richard Daley was known to resent bitterly any aspersion on his beloved Chicago. Halie went off on tour happy. And came home to word more precious than concert kudos: official word—*Billboard*'s—that as quickly as it had blown up, the Great Pop Gospel Balloon had collapsed. Ha! Lord, You fixed the Devil and laid the demons this time. Those buzzards can go back to picking each other's eyes. "And the singers can go back to the church where they belong," she pronounced with satisfaction. "God'll take 'em back. When man stumbles, he can be forgiven. Amen."

"MM-MMH, THAT LOOK good," It was a small, snug hat of purple and brown chiffon leaves with berries in the petals. "If they have any kind of breeze at all," Ida said, "those berries will show. Just be sure you pin it good. You know how you are."

"Washington going know what I mean when I say I got a friend in New Orleans can beat all those hats in New York. Why don't you stay on, Ida, come go with me?"

"No, baby, I'll look at you on TV. Elliott about to kill me now, so jealous of me being up here this long."

They were in the kitchen—Ida, Emma Bell, Frye, Polly, Steve, Celeste, Bertha—when Mahalia rose, her face changing. A hush fell on the instant.

"I smell death."

In the rush of exclamations, Frye turned to Ida. "When this woman start to smelling death, honey, she frightens me."

"Me, too."

"Let me out of here!" Frye leaped up, droll, making them laugh. "You and your smelling death!"

"Frye," said Mahalia, her voice soft in the low hours of early morning, "never mind if I wake you up; I want you to go for a checkup at Billings—yeah, you say you been off, not feeling well, and Halie's going to stand you to a checkup. I'm going call Dr. Barclay and tell him you coming."

"Dr. Barclay—keep him, if you got to. Whatever he needs. This is some good man."

"THEY SAY 100,000, but you never know," Mahalia said.

"How in the world will they be able to control a crowd that big?" wondered Bertha.

Mahalia, Bertha and Polly were with Wallace Smith in his car (Wallace working some for her this summer, since Butch settled into a steady office job in Gary). Willie Webb was driving Mildred and Emma Bell in Mahalia's car. Edward Robinson would meet them in Washington. It was Wednesday, Aug. 27, 1963, and Mahalia was taking them all to The March on Washington for Jobs and Freedom. Designed as a message to Congress, A. Philip Randolph—the grand old architect of civil rights—had slowly, painstakingly put it together with a singular welding of forces—civil, labor, and religious. Next to this, his 1957 Prayer Pilgrimage was a scale model. Still, nobody really knew what the day would bring. She'd check soon as they got in, Mahalia assured them; but things wouldn't get out of hand if A. Philip Randolph had his way, and he had about 1,500 men acting as marshals to keep it *just* that way.

If only the people turned out. In her suite at Executive House, Mahalia tapped her sources. They still figured to get 100,000 out tomorrow—800 or maybe 900 buses had started. She mulled this as James Lee came to take her to Baltimore to see Father Pat Franklin, pastor now of St. Martin's Spiritual Church. Ought to make him give *her* a luncheon, and her bring half of Washington. That would fix his clock. She grinned as she sang.

IT WAS THE SORT of day you're glad you're alive, but little of this emanated from the group leaving Mahalia's suite next morning. There was a pact among the entourage not to tell Mahalia until after the program, but Frye was dead. Mahalia walked ahead in silence. She didn't want to say anything, not to spoil the day for the others, but she sensed—knew—Frye was gone.

Lou Mindling shepherded the whole group out early to get through the traffic. Besides, Halie wanted to see what was going on. The marchers were to congregate at Washington Monument, but Mahalia went directly to Lincoln Memorial, where they'd end up for the program. She'd save her breath. "Mahalia," whispered Bertha, "do you think they'll let all of us on the platform?" They snaked through the crowd. Already the steps were packed, mainly with press and TV. How Frye would have loved this. Such a good heart; and so loved to eat: "Don't give me none of those white innertubes"—reaching for the tripe while he's saying it, back in the old days; always want to make you laugh. Gone. She told Bertha to watch her purse and strode off with her movie camera. The program wasn't due until 2 p.m. Most people brought lunch.

At 9:30 a.m., at Washington Monument, the leaders had started to worry—only about 40,000 had showed up. Then a peripheral logjam was budged apart and 1,500 busloads and 40 special trains and one Hollywood chartered plane disgorged. Walkers and outriders layered in. Ozzie Davis had organized entertainment to keep the crowd happy until march time. It was a giant state fair. Nearly 4,000 police and auxiliaries were on duty. Atty. Gen. Robert F. Kennedy, at his desk in the Justice Department, had nothing to do but relax—although liaison with the Pentagon had been laid on in case troops should be needed. A single burst of sound, a roar, made nerves jerk nine blocks distant at Lincoln Memorial, but it was only the one yell—"Freedom"—asked for on signal.

Then came *the* signal: form to march. Not just walk. March. Blue jeans, coveralls, business suits, shifts, shirtwaists, ties, clerical collars, cassocks, nuns' robes, country Sunday best. Men, women, children. Black and white. Signs and banners bobbed like boats above the sea of heads. In peace and exultation they moved, 210,000 strong down Constitution Avenue, its name and its breadth met for the occasion—the nation's most orderly issuance of moral force.

Seeing them come, singing, holding their banners high, Halie was lifted, excited, exalted. Frye *was* a part of this.

The crowd settled on the grass, into the soil, hats and papers tilted against the sun, and now they were as the mustard seed, past power of counting. What would be planted this day?

"Togetherness, that's the feeling out here," Bertha told herself; white and black together. Doing something *together*. Lena Horne and Sammy Davis, Jr., had seats right before her. Jackie Robinson and his boy a few seats down. Charlton Heston over a ways; Marlon Brando on the steps. Paul Newman, Burt Lancaster. That's already more stars than she saw her entire time in Los Angeles. "James Baldwin," she heard; "William Warfield." And the elegant old lady was the famous Josephine Baker. Belafonte, Poitier . . . Robert Ryan, Tony Franciosa, Faye Emerson, Susan Strasburg . . . James Garner and Diahann Carroll. . . .

The crowd on the platform and steps was dense now. Halie spotted Studs Terkel and waved. She could see him try to push through and give up. About one-fourth of Congress had come, seated mainly in the big section of front seats reserved for them and kept clear of anyone else so that the seats bore witness. On the steps Sen. Hart got across to give Mahalia a big greeting; so did Mayor Wagner from New York. All the politicians trying to be seen with her, thought Mindling.

As the leaders and special guests on the program mounted the platform, Mahalia had a rush of hugs and kisses. All were to say a word or two and no speaker over four minutes, that was the rule. At 5 p.m. the ten cochairmen had an appointment with the President to talk specifics; they'd talked to leaders of Congress while the crowd coalesced.

Four minutes? The speakers were finding it hard to turn loose; so much within, to let out. The program was stretching.

Jammed in his place in the media crowd, Studs Terkel watched the breeze riffle Mahalia's hat and grinned. That was a new hat. Almost three hours now, and she hadn't sung yet. Marian Anderson had. And the choir led by Eva Jessye. Mahalia must be—

She had been placed before the final, climactic speech by Martin Luther King. The two had thought for her to sing his favorite song, *Take My Hand, Precious Lord*. Lou Mindling kept after her to sing something livelier. There'd be just the one song. Now Martin whispered, "Mahalia, sing *I Been 'Buked.*" Mildred nodded. He always told Mahalia what to sing just before he spoke and it was always the right song.

"I been 'buked and I been scorned, I been talked about, sure as you're born—" Singing it into the maze of mikes, into America, out to the crowd, it was not hurt of the past but the now of the future that brought tears of joy to her voice so the vast restless crowd became one listening body, rapt, intent. A plane roared low overhead. Mahalia raised her eyes . . . *I'm going tell my Lord—* "By God," murmured Studs, "she's taking it on, the artist against the machine—and she's *done* it!" She sang it away—face brilliant, glowing, voice vibrant; not while she's telling *her* Lord!—and without a sound the crowd broke out white handkerchiefs, thousands of them waving in the air. With her last note, "More! More! More!" It could not be denied and she rocked them with *How I Got Over*. When she finished—dripping with sweat, panting—she got a standing ovation.

They were ready for Martin. Dr. King had been marking changes in his speech right up to Mahalia's singing. So much, in four minutes—yet what had not been said? It didn't matter. He was cheered before he spoke. They wanted *him* to say it, *his* way, sounding their responses in his every pause, letting him know, lifting him too, so that when the last sentence on his last page was said, he soared impromptu into what was destined to become one of America's most famous pieces of 20th century rhetoric. "I have a dream," he cried—

When he finished, the white handkerchiefs were being used for wet eyes.

As soon as she could get to a quiet telephone, Mahalia called Sis Frye, made arrangements about the funeral, and tracked down James Francis at the Evans Hotel, where she'd stayed when her Prairie apartment was in ashes. "Nigger," she said with the freedom of affection, "I want you to play Frye's funeral."

"How I'm going do that?"—knowing the jealousies, the contending for the honor.

"I don't care; Frye would want you to play."

(Obediently Blind Francis went by the wake, and on Monday he played at the funeral.)

Her calls finished, they all went to unwind at a friend's home. When Dr.

King left for the airport, they returned to Executive House, drained, ready to turn in.

She lay with her Bible a long time that night but her thoughts strayed. She could hardly believe her life was going to take this new turn, but Mr. Newman said it was definitely so. Mahalia Jackson was going to become a doctor.

But first she'd have to sing for her supper, and mend a bowl.

49

She hadn't looked for all this Los Angeles crowd at the station. Johnny Lange with Yancey, Celeste and her people—Celeste crying; her mother just passed (Halie would get her ticket home and help her with that); Mr. Mindling, all of them, and Minnis on the edge. Everyone trying to get his word in first. She looked around and couldn't find him.

"Yancey, where's Minnis?"

He had removed himself, disassociating from the confusion; he was sitting out in the patio, under a tree, waiting.

She didn't blame him. He'd have nothing to do with these people. Still he was nice to everybody. "Yancey, you and Johnny can take Mildred and them and the luggage to the Knickerbocker. I'm riding with Minnis." Nice enough to come meet her when she called him from Chicago. He might like to ride her to the studio when she went to see about the picture. Mr. Mindling could meet her there.

JUST BE HER true self, they said. No different than she'd done for Adlai Stevenson. They were going to use her real name in the movie. There'd be this big dinner at the convention, with Henry Fonda for President, and she'd be introduced and sing and then, "Thank you, Miss Mahalia Jackson," and she was off.

"You going let me eat the steak when I'm through?"

The laugh was a good note to end the conference. She didn't waste much time standing around. She wanted to go talk with Celeste. She and Eddie had moved directly across the street from her building on So. Norton, and Mahalia wanted her to help Johnny keep it filled with the right kind of tenants. Celeste could use the extra change.

IRV TOWNSEND wasn't too happy with the idea, but he'd go along with it to humor Mahalia. He just hoped this guy could read the score, if he was going to sit in with professional musicians. So what if he needed the work. Just when you thought you knew Mahalia, she came up with a ringer. She wanted to make sure you didn't relax. Thank God he could put it off—they weren't using full orchestra for these singles. She might get rid of the guy before the next album. He brightened.

Mahalia was pleased. Minnis was going cook her a steak when she got through, just be quiet with him and the little girl. She was so tired. Thank You Jesus for letting Halie just make these four sides. She wanted to be very particular about *We Shall Overcome*. Did she take her prednisone? Yeah. That's good. Dr. Barclay would fuss.

"THIS IS THE PLACE to see the stars—Hollywood Bowl," she assured Minnis. She'd been waiting for this ever since that cancellation . . . never *had* got the straight of that. But tonight all the big songwriters and orchestra leaders were presenting her, Jack Benny, and Andy Williams in music they'd written or conducted for movies. She was going to do Dmitri Tiomkin's *Green Leaves of Summer* for him, for one thing. Goodness knows what Jack Benny was going to do. He could make a violin squeal between a sick baby and a mad pig. It would be a night. If she could just pull on up from the way she felt. She opened her dressing room and started to back out—must be the florist's. The boy Yancey rushed in and came out stuttering: They were all from Mr. Tiomkin. If they weren't, pity the poor other people; she'd never find their cards. "He must have hired a truck to bring these in!"

Mr. Mindling shooed everybody out and said she had to rest. Well, that was right. Some people here she'd like to tell hello, though.

That Wednesday, Sept. 25, the Bowl was full and the cheers brimmed over and she sang on, sang on, until Mindling wanted to pull her off and Yancey offered to, which got him a quick chill. She came off reaching for breath—the now-familiar gasping, the uuugh! tearing your heart. A doctor was called. A few people had breasted the ramparts, but Mindling was stern about no more. Yet the pale girl outside kept softly *pleading* so, that "I'll see you at least get to shake her hand," Yancey ventured. There was a certain amount of traffic now and Yancey seized his chance and slipped the girl in. At sight of Mahalia, she burst into tears. Mahalia pulled her down beside her and pressed the girl's head on her shoulder. "There, there, baby; tell Mahalia about it; it's all right."

When she could speak, "While my husband was overseas with the Air Force, we lost our baby," she said; "the only thing that kept me from losing my mind was your records. I played them all night, night after night. The doctor *said* that was the only thing kept me from losing my mind, and I know it was."

It was too much for Halie. She burst into tears, the girl burst into tears, and they wept for joy in each other's arms.

When the child left, with her husband, Mahalia rose. Mindling breathed a sigh of relief. All she needed was a little rest. She was her own worst enemy; you didn't have to give them *that* much. He'd kill that kid Yancey, letting people in. In Minnis's Dodge, she sang softly: maybe she *did* hand out a prescription.

DR. JACKSON. It sure sounded funny, but in just about an hour, at Lincoln College, that's who she'd be. She was barely back from Hollywood, hadn't got herself sorted out for this but just go on, Halie wasn't going change anyway—or would wisdom come on her as the doctoral hood came on her shoulders? She wouldn't put it past the Lord. God works in mysterious ways His wonders to perform. Ralph Newman, her sponsor for the honorary degree, was a Lincoln scholar who lived in Chicago, but she'd had to go to Washington to meet him, at the Civil War Centennial.

Lou Mindling shepherded her to the office of the president, Dr. Raymond Dooley, and they found that portly gentleman in time-honored struggle: his zipper was caught on his robe. "Let me fix that thing for you, doctor," Halie said instantly. No trick to fix it, but he was so grateful; not at all grand. It was sort of a nice way to start the afternoon. She felt like a gnat in the cream, walking the corridors, all the education notices pinned to the boards, young boys and girls everywhere with their higher education, passing offices piled with technical books—and she's the one getting the doctorate. Of Humane Letters. It had a nice sound to it.

Gov. Otto Kerner needed no briefing to talk about Mahalia; he praised her as "a great humanitarian." Mahalia was so touched, in this place, among these people, she might disgrace herself. And when Dr. Dooley conferred the honor for her "achievement in human dignity" and her "unique contribution to American culture," she did—broke down and cried as she managed a soft "Thank you."

She wanted to shake the hands of the graduates, then; and Gov. Kerner volunteered to, and did, introduce her to each student: all 400.

At home late that night, she saw it all again—the ceremonies, the festivities, the fellowship, filing past like the graduates. When it all had unreeled, there was a deep space. The quiet of the house rushed in. She lay a little longer, looking at Russell Roberts' photograph on her dresser; then she got up and played his record. Her tears were not for joy.

50

Harpo Marx snatched the blond mop of curls off his bald pate and plopped it onto Irv Townsend. Mahalia rolled, helpless with laughter. When he jerked the startled producer's leg up on his knee, she pounded the dressing table, beyond speech. Off with the mop, and onto hers! She whooped. Now catch Lou Mindling. Hysteria was the note, and nobody wanted to change the key.

She'd hit Los Angeles again after a week's rest with just a steady flow of visitors (including Laurraine up from New Orleans), then four concerts: Ohio, Virginia, New England. So why's Halie so beat? Do all Dr. Barclay say, be no Mahalia Jackson—not with her in L.A. to talk about a TV series for Europe, and do a Danny Kaye show, but first of all record—with Harpo Marx. He was good enough to frame, wrinkles and all. He clowned so—Marty Paich's orchestra bad as the rest of them—even into her dressing room on a break to calm down, and had her about to spill hot coffee on his head—had her so tickled, it was hard to believe this was the same tiny man at his harp now, not at it but a part, loving it, his hands running across like water over rippled sand. He was playing his own song, *Guardian Angels*. God must love him, to give him this power for joy and this depth in his soul.

THE DANNY KAYE rehearsals started the first of Thanksgiving week. Just being around him made it like a holiday. "Danny Kaye is a fine man, Laurraines," she reported; "and is he a nut! He is so funny! And he has this special quality—like a fairy on his toes."

She was content just to watch him, waiting around for her own segments. And when he came, all twinkletoes, and sat with you to visit, you felt like you should get up and take his hand and let him dance you away.

At last. *Just a Closer Walk with Thee.* They'd work on *Deep River* later—the music director had the orchestra arrangement from Marty Paich's session, so if they knew theirs, she knew hers. Cue. *Just a closer walk with Thee* . . . Danny Kaye was moved to some impromptu togetherness: "Dee de doo dee boom de boom—" *Grant it, Jesus, If You plee-ase* . . . "Boom boom de dah boom—" Mahalia broke off. "If you don't shut up, *I'll* have to boom boom!" —and hamming it, taking the edge away, "You white folks just busting up that song." ("Oh, Lord Jesus!" Gwen whispered to herself—sitting in, watching the proceedings—"Sister will say anything.") Danny Kaye shared her joke, and she started again. Alone.

They broke for Thanksgiving Day—"Everybody back Friday, and the same size, please!"—and it was just like the old days on Esther St., so many people in to Mother Parks—a whole gospel crowd, plus Minters.

Mother Parks knew most of them from times back in Chicago: "Remember, Mahalia, at Rev. Brown's church barbecue, when that woman wanted to take over from you?"

Oh, they ate, and Minnis not the least. Mother Parks knew more about a turkey than its mother. They got to singing after, and got happy, and the whole neighborhood stood around and listened.

At 10:30 a.m. Friday, Nov. 22, 1963, Lou Mindling was at the entrance of the Knickerbocker Hotel. He was keeping one eye on his car and the other peeled for Mahalia—set to pick her up for the Danny Kaye rehearsal—when he heard the news: the President of the United States had been shot in Dallas. He rushed upstairs to Mahalia and found her in shock. Sigmond Galloway was with her. Nobody knew what move to make, but Mindling was certain they were due at rehearsal. He started Mahalia down, Galloway following—all stunned, not knowing what to say or think; Mahalia praying. That shirttail Yancey had tagged on but the agent tried to ignore him.

"Yancey, you ride with Mr. Mindling and them; I'm going with Minnis."

Lou Mindling suffered his extra passenger only to the corner of Sunset and Fairfax, then he pulled over. "Is this where you want to get out?" Yancey knew Mindling didn't like him, but it was no skin off his nose. He hopped a bus and made it before Mahalia anyway. They must have stopped off. He'd walk down to get some hot chocolate.

Mahalia had hold of herself by the time Sigmond maneuvered his car into the parking lot. As they paced the studio hallway, Danny Kaye came flying toward them. Mahalia collapsed on his breast. Big as she was, frail as he seemed, he held her, comforted her; then he went on and she and Sigmond walked into the studio just in time to see the TV monitor with the pictures and the words that John F. Kennedy was dead. Mahalia fell as if she'd been shot—and this time it was little Yancey who caught her.

There could be no rehearsal. Mindling was trying to find out something. Everything was a shambles. Mahalia and Sigmond and Yancey went back to the Knickerbocker, Mahalia sobbing inconsolably. In the lobby, "Yancey, you stay with her," Sigmond said; "I'm going home." Little Sigma would be seeing all this, and his sister's nerves were none too good.

They didn't know where Mildred was, or Edward Robinson. Flung across the bed, every time Mahalia's weeping ebbed, a fresh spate of TV reruns touched her off. Inauguration pictures now. Oh, God! oh, God! So young, and so much promise. Poor Jackie. Poor us. Station WBEE, Chicago, called: There was fear of rioting there, as in every other black center where the murder struck home as the killing of the first President who was for *them*. Would Mahalia get on the air? From her bedside Mahalia spoke, tears audible in her voice but pleading for calm, to respect the President's memory with prayers, not fighting; to pray for his soul, for his family, for their country. She believed that's what he'd say if he were here—and she believed she knew his heart.

The switchboard was holding calls now from other cities. Atlanta was next, and again she spoke. Then Irving Townsend had priority—get over to KNXT quickly; they wanted to put her on TV and radio simultaneously, and bring her musicians. Where was Mildred? Yancey called wherever he could think; then while Mahalia tidied herself and he tried to find the one other pianist *he* knew could play for Mahalia, Edward walked in and they left.

The little studio was full of people. Only one camera was available. Irv Townsend was putting it together. Mahalia was placed behind a desk. She walked over and spoke to Edward, then she came back and they went on the air. It was not yet 1:30, California time. Mahalia reminisced. The campaign, the convention, the inauguration; blue eyes and large, warm hands. The MC could see tears welling, and he asked if she could sing a song in the President's memory. Without any comment, she began *Nearer My God to Thee,* there at the desk, not moving, Edward soft behind her.

To a lot of people, thought Yancey, on the fringe, she's like the Pope is to the Catholics.

SATURDAY MORNING they were at Danny Kaye's studio. Only one thing was on anybody's mind, but taping had to be today. The orchestra struck up *Deep River*. It was as if they were all of one deep feeling. Mahalia crumpled into Danny Kaye's arms.

It was years before Halie could sing *Deep River* again—and then only to scale her highest mountain, in a strange, strange place.

51

It was like a homecoming. She'd sung all over the country for SCLC, but never in Atlanta, its headquarters. Now this Dec. 1, 1963, they were all about her—the King families, the Abernathys, the Claytons (Ed on Martin's staff now), all the others with whom she'd shared so much since December, 1956, whose thrust had moved them all so far. It was a proud moment at Atlanta's municipal auditorium when Martin presented her with the award recognizing her special place in the movement.

And now here in New Orleans, for the first time she would sing to a mixed audience in Municipal Auditorium. By right and ruling, the bar should have been dropped in 1962, but legal heeldragging was stretched so far, so fine, that this past summer CORE had quietly bought tickets for, and seated, four Negroes for a Summer Pops concert. No police objection was made. New Orleans' *laissez faire* let what will be, be. The splintered barrier disappeared. Elliot Beal promptly began organizing a major homecoming concert for Dec. 9. Nothing could go wrong this time.

Nor did it. She was installed in the towering Roosevelt Hotel, the city's finest; Ida, Ellen Blount, Zenobia Lockett, Isabell, Brisko, George, all the family and friends could call—and room service at her fingertips. Half a block away, Canal St.'s treasures were at her disposal, beckoning. An excited 25 of Elliott's 500-voice choir met her, Elliott, and Laurraine at WDSU-TV to be exhibited on the air by Mel Leavitt, the city's ace personality. She felt so good, munching grapes right on camera, that when Elliott led his group in one of Laurraine's gospel songs, she made them start again and she joined in. Lou Mindling winced; she'd promised she wouldn't do that, sing for free. Elliott, in turn, was so elated that, telling his experience with Mahalia in the great train wreck, he slipped and told his age on the air.

She was due a gold key to the city and its Certificate of Merit, complete with dignitary to deliver them—but City Hall was slow to join the world. The symbols of its honor would arrive at Laurraine's desk three days late and be delivered—with a wry propriety—by Uncle Sam. But no matter. The concert was packed, the spirit was high, and the flowers poured over —enough for a millennium of McDonogh Days. She was at the old school next day. A new, better edition stood alongside now, but she searched out her old room with school principal Emily Bickman and Celestine Curtis Graves—the child of Roberta Martin days, now principal of James Weldon Johnson Elementary. Halie met the ghost of Hooks-Warpee-Black where the potbellied stove had hidden her, and her shoes had flip-flopped, if she wore them. And in this moment of truth, she told how she'd only really got through the third grade, and all the rest was the grace of God. She told it, a living witness, at McDonogh 24; then again at Celestine's school, the children scattered like rose petals across the floor, faces upturned to the light. "Education is for *keeps,*" she said, imprinting it. "When you can count, and when you keep up with current events—the things that are happening—*then* you can be somebody." But, she added, searching their faces, letting them search hers, "You have to have within you certain kinds of things that make you *want* to learn." Then she walked into their midst and sang, the grandest Pied Piper they'd ever seen.

She grasped the other end of the stick, speaking to the Frontiers Club, hoping to spur these middle-class black business and professional men to stretch out a hand. "I'm happy to hear that Louisiana is now producing Negro lawyers who remain in New Orleans and Louisiana—which is more than some Southern states can say. But I am concerned over whether our Negro youth are getting preparation to qualify them for the various technical jobs that are being offered. I'd like to see you do something about that."

Duty done, she could go see Aunt Duke, who wasn't at all well, had not come to the concert; and to see Aunt Bell, who was worse: She had lost a leg to diabetes. She sounded cheerful, but Halie looked into the dear, dark face and felt her heart wrench. The Rightor children—grown now and with children of their own—had come to see her, and to bring her gifts, Aunt Bell said proudly. "You should have *seen* the way they made over her," cried Celie; "that is our second family." She was loath to leave Aunt Bell, lying there so wasted, no skirts now for a Halie to hide under. She'd be 85, come Christmas. "Aunt Bell," she said, "I'm going to give you the biggest birthday party you ever had. Everything. Spare no expense. I'll get everybody together. And I'll bring my moving picture camera and take pictures."

"Aunt Bell's got something on her mind," Auntie said to her alone, as they parted, "but she'll wait 'til you get back, at Christmas." That was all she'd say. Halie didn't press.

THAT CHRISTMAS, 1963, the little house on Delery seemed to stretch for the ingathering of the Clarks. Happily, it was yard weather. More kept coming; it was always full; and more found space—from Chicago, Cincinnati, New York. Elliott and Ida were there as privileged friends. Halie was everywhere with the color movie camera. They sat Aunt Bell on the side of her bed in an Alice-blue gown, her hair combed like Martha Washington, with a blue satin ribbon tied in. Audrey draped her stole around her grandmother's shoulders. "Now you're in mink!" Celie came marching in with the big cake, candle flames dancing, singing *Happy Birthday to You.*

At nearly midnight, Halie rose from Aunt Bell's bedside—she should get her rest—and started for the hall. "Baby." The voice clear, arresting. "Yes?" "Auntie want to tell you something." Elliott and Ida quietly left the room, wondering, knowing Aunt Bell was psychic. Only Celie remained. Bell's voice was low, for Halie. "Baby, I might not be here the next time you come back. I'm going to tell you something: Auntie want you to watch—fight—and pray. You have a plenty enemies." In particular there was a woman, someone who dealt with her affairs, who meant her no good. "Now all I want you to do now is read between the lines." A lot of pits were being dug; be careful lest she be swallowed up. "That's all I'm going to tell you. Read between the lines."

She fell silent, then she said, "I see something set ahead of you, and if you don't be very particular, you're going to fall into it; and it's not going to be so easy to unwind out of. I want you to be very particular. And remember all I said."

The next night Halie was on the track, rails clicking her back, special delivery to the Chicago postmen's Christmas party—a giant catharsis for the heavy load—with Mahalia Jackson and Jimmy Durante.

On Jan. 27 Aunt Bell died. Halie carried Emma Bell with her to the funeral. She was busy with the tending. Food for the wake, the casket, the music; choose which of the ministers asking could speak; arrange for a doctor to be there to check Aunt Hannah—she wanted Hannah's pulse and heartbeat kept account of. And there were the flowers. Aunt Bell so loved flowers. Halie meant her to have the most beautiful New Orleans had seen. "I want The Broken Reel," she told the florist; "now write this down—besides the blanket, I want The Broken Reel, The Pillow of Rest, The Bird of Paradise."

"They didn't know a one of them," says Celie; "not a florist in New Orleans knew. So Mahalia went and fixed them herself. They was something to see. And she set the pattern in New Orleans because all over now, when they have that type of funeral, you see those designs."

They waked Bell at Mt. Moriah. "Don't tell it; now *don't* tell Aunt Duke." The family was agreed, had the pact and held it—passed the word—Mahala too frail now for the shock; it was too wrenching, to their feeling. But Pinching Town neighbors weren't agreed. Someone sneaked away, carried her to the church, let Mahala see her sister. Duke gave just this little moan—and from then on, *had* that moan; sitting on the porch, moaning like a hymn, "I want to go where my sister Bell . . . I want to go-o-o-o where my sister Bell." The neighbors across the street, it touched their heart.

Neighbors, ministers, congregation more than filled the church for the funeral, but space had been reserved for Marguerite Rightor Ellis, her lawyer son Tommy (who'd grown up in the Rightor home, doting on Bell) and his wife. T. C. W. Ellis looked discreetly around the little church. The three were the only whites present. The ministers seemed to be vying to see who could arouse the crowd more. Then a stir, not so much stir as a palpable knowing, as Mahalia came in, beautifully coiffeured, in full-length mink. Tommy was immersed in his grief, crying, lost in this other world of expressed emotion, when Celie—who had been moaning, wailing, with the ministers and the music—abruptly cried, "Oh God, mama!" and rushed to the casket. Reedlike music stands crashed a-skelter. Someone shouted, "I see the Lord!"—had a seizure. Stout women in white dresses and nurses' caps rushed over and half-carried, half-walked the seized soul to the back to calm her down; in a few moments she was restored, in her seat, none the worse, the service uninterrupted. Already the women were hurrying to another's aid.

Overcome as she was, Celie was aware of Mahalia. Mahalia always used to take them *not* hard, she never was a loud crier, just tears would stream down, but this one time broke through her reserve—it broke *through;* not just that mama was kind and sweet but she was Mahalia's gospel mother, a double portion. Had to get the ushers to get hold of her, give her some smelling salts, fan her, bring her back.

As the Rightor representatives emerged from the church, an elderly Negro woman sitting on the porch next door said to the man beside her, "The white peoples won't even let us go into our graves in peace, they have to follow us all the way."

52

Bereft. Drained. She'd just finished running revival for Rev. Jenkins a week to the day in this 36th year at Greater Salem when Aunt Bell died. They had buried Dinah Washington—Ruth Lee Jones—just before; one of her own. The Kennedy memorial single Columbia had rushed her to cut in Chicago was on the air now: *In the Summer of His Years,* opening her wound the more because it was she who told the story, reliving it. Other editions had been questioned for taste, but not Mahalia Jackson's. She was hailed now as "the preacher of the 20th century—the most acclaimed vocalist in the world."

So hit the road. Sing in New York; join Louie Armstrong, Belafonte, Poitier, James Baldwin, Dizzy Gillespie to support the new Artists Civil Rights Assistance Fund. West—Seattle by the end of February—agreeing, before she left, to be honorary chairman of the Cancer Society campaign. If they only knew. Russell and Peter. Both.

Peter. It might be in the blood.

But at Eastertime, what Christian could not be glad? She took her last date from William Morris (had not cut that off completely, even though Mr. Mindling frowned). It was a happy one—the Jack Paar show for Easter.

LOS ANGELES was picking her up. The political banquet scene in *The Best Man* took intense work. She loved the intricacy, the mosaic, the demand for perfection—if seldom attained, in the instant there was the illusion. Even though she simply appeared as herself, sang her gospel, and exited, the group scene was worked and reworked like choreography. The film's principals were all real professionals—Henry Fonda, Cliff Robertson, Edie Adams, Margaret Leighton, Ida Lupino—the kind you liked to be around, to watch.

The organized confusion at the Ambassador Hotel, where they were filming, broke for something: camera? lights? props? Mahalia was standing around with the rest, chatting, when she was grabbed and wheeled around. Belafonte. She loosed a scream, he gave her a bear hug, she hugged him back, several hundred extras went into squealing confusion—and the cameras missed the best scene of *The Best Man.*

"Susan's Evening" was another kind of best time, and Irv Townsend really couldn't get over it. His daughter Susan had been born with marble bones disease. Its victims faced blindness, deafness, anemia, headaches, early death, and frequently retardation. Yet at 12, although at one time or another every bone in Susan's body had broken, she was a cheerful child busy at her talents—poetry, singing, piano—all realized in a long, expensive partnership with medical research.

Mahalia loved Susie. She and André Previn had produced a star-studded "Susan's Evening" to help fund research and establish a music scholarship. Once again Townsend was baffled by this woman of contradictions. "Demand $10,000 for a concert, and sing free the next night. If anybody needed anything, she was there without a qualm. And yet, 'Give me five bucks for the cab, baby,' and never pay it back." She'd certainly knocked herself out for this show. A real love-in. Irv Townsend guessed he really thought a lot of Mahalia. He wondered about this guy she was showing up with—still.

She was with Minters regularly now. About the most considerate man she'd come across, and she loved little Sigma—a sturdy child, tall for her age. Halie thought she must have been something like that when she was five—if she'd been straight, if she'd had clothes. Getting someplace wasn't just a distance now; it was a ride with Minnis. And if he got a little romantic—well, she was supposed to be a good-looking woman, and a natural woman; she'd have to be dead as a doorstop not to like it. They were in and out of Mother Parks's house; and when she got the chance, Halie questioned the kindly older woman about this man she'd said was a second son. "He was always a very soft, congenial child, easy to get along with," said Mother Parks. "His ambition always was in music. He was good to his wife, far as I could see—I never heard nothing wrong between them, 'til she died of a malignant breast." He *did* have a way of getting along with people—just faded back when the commotion started.

In Yancey's opinion, Sig didn't actually realize who Mahalia Jackson *was*. "I believe that guy's really in love with Mahalia," Yancey said to nobody in particular. "I don't know why else he's so friendly to *us*."

MAHALIA HADN'T fully examined the question until they got to arguing against him. The gospel girls were gathered at Ora B.'s house—Celeste's second sister, moved here too. Mildred was there, a whole covey was there, and by the time Gwen walked in, the roomful had been having at Sister about Sigmond Galloway, with one refrain: "Sister, you don't need to get married."

Gwen walked in on Mahalia saying firmly to one, "Well, *you* can't tell me, 'cause you ain't never been married and you don't know what's happening. Hey, Gwen! Now here comes a child that's got a man, got children; come out to California and made good for herself. I'm going ask *her* what she thinks about it."

Gwen stopped, nonplused, cautious. "What's this all about, Sister?"

"Well, the subject came up about my intentions of marrying Sigmond Galloway. What do *you* think?"

Gwen had met Sigmond a few times, but this was shaky ground. Everyone was waiting.

"Well, Mahalia," said Gwen, "now that isn't a fair question to ask me, because you know you're the one that has to come in after these long weeks of being on the road and look at the four walls by yourself. I *have* a husband, and to tell you not to marry wouldn't be fair, because you—like I need someone, everybody needs someone. The only thing I can tell you to do is like I know you're doing—ask God to direct you; and you decide. Because if *we* tell you and you don't do it, down the road you'll blame yourself, see, like you did about Russell Roberts. You know the man; I don't. I won't tell you to; and I won't tell you not to."

That girl had a lot of sense. And compassion.

Actually, Minnis hadn't asked her. But she meant to have a made-up mind.

She went to Chicago to get ready for Europe. Running over *The Only Hope We Have* with Celeste's sister Margaret—going get that down this time, to record it—the title caught her mind. The only hope we have. Lord, is he?

Nettie would be a good intelligent person to talk to. And she wasn't one to tell it. She'd just say to Nettie she had met somebody out in California, that he had a child—a little girl; Nettie knew she loved children, how she loved Nettie's little girl— "He comes from a very fine family in Gary, Nettie—people in the construction business. He's named for his Uncle Minters." She knew of that family, Nettie nodded; he must be a fine person. "But he's a jazz man!" Mahalia all but wailed.

"Mahalia, don't worry about what anybody says."

"Everybody needs somebody," said Mahalia, slowly.

Nettie saw a thread of doubt hanging. One pull, and it could all unravel.

53

They flew on Mr. Mindling. He had all their air fares written into the contracts—plus hotels and food.

And the whole trip soared. Diet forgotten, she ate her way across Europe, to Lou Mindling's intense satisfaction—it was all paid for, wasn't it?—and she was having such a good time. In London her audience got downright emotional, and she appreciated the way they respected the slow, fervent songs. She sang a command performance in Brussels to an audience of 5,000; and if the king wasn't able to be there after all, the rest of the royal house was: "They liked our American gospel just as well as everybody else," she reported; "it's a real communication around the world." At Amsterdam she was taken to see the John F. Kennedy flower planting in early-May bloom—a remarkable portrait. She knelt and prayed for his peace. The greatest concentration of youth in her life faced her in Utrecht, in Central Netherlands: a mass daytime gathering of its youth Christian society—28,000 of those pretty blond children. They pushed so to get at her afterward, it took a squad of police to get her out intact—or almost. "I thought I was the Beatles," she laughed. That night she sang again, for an audience of 5,000 grownups who acted very nearly like the children in their enthusiasm but didn't pursue her afterward. Thank You Lord. Halie's getting pretty tired.

Mr. Mindling was so happy with the way things were going; he said this time next year he'd have her in Hong Kong.

Only in Sweden did anything go wrong—and that was her own fault. "This sweet young Swedish girl was making over me backstage, and she put a pair of false lashes on me. I don't wear such a thing, but I let her go on and please herself. So I had these false teeth—this bridge—that I had put in just before I left Chicago, and I had *those* on. Well, I'm singing away. So when I first realized my teeth are gone, there's a huge crowd of these pretty young people on stage right up around me—there was *so* many people. So I said to some close by, (imitating a small, cool voice) 'Oh, I believe I lost my teeth. Has anybody seen my teeth?' They answered, just as polite, 'Yes, Miss Jackson, they're right over there.' Oh, I was so embarrassed; but I didn't let on, I just said real sweet and polite, 'Oh? Is that right?' And looked down around on the stage and picked them up. Then one of the children said, 'Miss Jackson, your eyelashes are coming off too.' Sure enough, I'd been so wrapped up in my singing, and so embarrassed about the teeth, I hadn't noticed. They were both coming off; one was hanging by the tip end."

From Paris, she called Sigmond in California—"I just thought I'd find out how you getting along"—and told him when she'd be back in Chicago.

"Called from Paris, France?" cried Sigmond's mother, Mrs. Mary Lou Galloway Jenkins, out to visit him. "Mahalia Jackson? Who is that?" It was an honest question. "I didn't have a record of her or nothing," says Mrs. Jenkins. "I didn't know Mahalia."

"Ruth knows her," said Sigmond.

AND DIDN'T even catch a cold! Singing to herself, she kept her eyes off that stuff out there look enough like cotton to bounce on. Why people think it's great to look out the airplane window? You either lost the ground, or you see just how far you got to drop.

"You ought to be happy flying, Mahalia," Lou Mindling said; "you're up so much closer to that guy you're always talking about."

She sang softly. Through Europe and tired, tired, and yet she had *not* the tired feeling. She knew what it was, but she wasn't so sure she better know. *My* Jesus! Fire in the back compartment and turned on the sprinklers. Halie prayed. Got it out, but that smoke could ruin a person's throat—well, it wasn't too bad. Dropping down to land now. Landing gear stuck! Word came over the speaker system, and stewardesses hurried up and down the aisles trying to act like they wasn't getting you ready to crash-land. Not a thing but the Lord keeping Halie's nerves calm. Well, if You going take me, remember my soul. Just keep my soul. Listen to those two old ladies in front. One crying she don't want to go; other one running her mouth like she want to get all the words she knows out before she dies. Halie put her head back against the rest. It's up to You, Lord. Five seconds later, "We're landing," the captain said. The gear had come loose.

Lord, You telling me to hurry up while I got time? Or are You warning me?

SHE HAD TO BE in Washington for the big Salute to President Johnson May 26. Sort of a substitute Inaugural Ball, poor man. The Democrats trying to make up some money on his like they did on President Kennedy—$100 a ticket for the show, and $1,000 for dinner beforehand, though how anybody was going digest his dinner after paying $1,000 for it, she didn't know—or may be that makes it more precious. Paper said the Democrats getting *millions* in the treasury with this one night and the repeat two nights later in New York.

Oh! she fell low day after Washington. And trying to be ready for the National Baptists in three weeks. She was getting another Grammy Award —this one for *Make a Joyful Noise;* Columbia be happy about that. The League of Labor and Education had an award to give her "for outstanding contributions in the fields of labor and education." Mr. Riddle was calling about staging the big Illinois Rally for Civil Rights at Soldier Field on June 21—Martin, all them be up for that. It wasn't too much hers, mostly a union business—she was supposed just to sing—but they kept calling and anyway she was going make sure there was a good motorcade and drum up the crowd. She'd had to tell Joe Bostic she couldn't make that same date for Carnegie Hall. The Cancer Society was calling. And CORE. All that in mind, but what was *on* her mind was something else.

Minnis was in Chicago. He'd proposed. And she did not have a made-up mind. She talked to Dr. Barclay. He was against it.

DR. WILLIAM BARCLAY wasn't surprised at being asked. Mahalia came to him with many things. He had counseled her over many hours on problems of family and friends. He felt he had become a father figure—and no problem of Mahalia's could be viewed as nonmedical. He'd just seen her too ill to make the Presidential Salute in Madison Square Garden two nights after a Washington performance which the President himself had labeled "extraordinary." Knowing how she pushed herself above her physical condition, that cancellation told him something. Now she was considering marriage, with no assurance—and evident misgivings. Even the jazz aspect worried her.

"Mahalia had the fond hope she could make a perfect marriage," says Dr. Barclay. "She was a lonely woman. She had the adulation of many friends, but she didn't feel she had a real close identity with someone. She hoped for a mate who would respect her as a woman as well as an artist; she wanted a home to be head of, with a man. It was just a kind of impossible American dream. Given her disease, and the demands upon her, I was simply apprehensive that it wouldn't work out."

She was taken aback, he could see. "I can counsel, Mahalia," he said gently; "but I can't dictate to you."

Louise and Snooks Smothers were for it. Hadn't Mahalia been her maid of honor in '55—and asked Rev. Elijah then, joking but maybe not joking, "Reverend, I wish you'd do one thing for me; I wish you'd try to get me a husband." Meaning the right husband—Russell Roberts not even in the picture 'til the next year. How many times since had she called and, getting Snooks' leave, got Lou to come spend the night? "Don't listen to what anyone says," Louise advised. "If you love Minters, marry him."

She had doubts one day, was positive the next, had doubts again. She felt like a grandfather clock. And don't know how much time she got, to decide.

Mildred was against it. Cordie King—quick, devoted—she was for it, if that was what Mahalia wanted. Polly was against it. Boy Baby was for it. It was natural Polly would be not so much in favor of the marriage, Rev. Thurston judged—would see Mahalia as a rich woman, him with no money, and younger; possibly Polly believed the backgrounds were not compatible, and felt close enough to give that advice. Nonetheless, from his several meetings with Sigmond, his impression was that Galloway was good for Mahalia, tried to give her male support. Rev. John felt she needed some interested male. "I believe everybody has something to offer somebody else," he told her in measured, judicial tones. "If you get out of life what you want, there is no harm in also giving, as you receive. If he doesn't have as much to offer in one area, he has more in another area that you can't offer yourself."

Yes! She made up her mind.

And unmade it at the next barrage of outcries. The nays far outweighed the ayes. "The main purpose of some of them talking against it is they're afraid it will cut them out financially," Louise said darkly to Snooks. "You know how Mahalia is—I have reason to know myself: If a person needs assistance, she's going to give it, family or not; but if she has a husband, he's going to come first."

Torn, Mahalia brought Minnis to Dr. Barclay. And brought him again. Dr. Barclay just became more apprehensive. Here was a sick woman who would need a tremendous amount of tender loving care and support. He didn't think Galloway would give her that quality of support.

On the surface, the play of events was proceeding. Martin dropped in for overnight. Unable to sleep, at 1 a.m. Halie heard restless sounds from his direction and called Boy Baby. "We can't sleep over here; come over and talk to us." The three talked until almost 4. Ernestine Washington came for a weekend. Rev. Walter Odom came the next, with the Baptists. She threw herself into cooking for the influx; it was almost a ritual to stop by Mahalia's. The Soldier Field rally was an immense rousing of the spirit: "I'll Be There—I Care" buttons by the thousands. Almost a lifeline in this period—this prescribed rest period—was the gospel singing. No matter what the turn or the time, they ended at the piano. She could not fail to feel the rise. The drop—the body's protest—came after; alone, and trying to stir for the new day. Help me, Jesus. Guide me, Lord.

She gave a dinner party for Minnis for a selected group and basked in their approval. To Albertina Walker, it *felt* like an engagement party. "We had a fine time." If Mahalia didn't say anything—that was her way. She'd say, when she was ready.

It was a yes day.

On any day, missions and messages bounced like dry peas on a slate. An artist offering her portrait; Dorsey offering music; Sallie Martin, Robert Anderson, Sis Frye—all the old gospel crowd, and new; Studs Terkel; strange preachers, known preachers; a godchild; cousins and cousins of cousins. Minneapolis—Benton Harbor—San Antonio—Kansas City wanting concerts; never mind the agent, they wanted to talk with her. Russell Goode called. He was down in St. Augustine, Fla., helping Martin—people were putting alligators in the motel pool to keep the Negroes out. Mahalia listened with full attention.

And shortly, Rev. Leon Jenkins listened to Mahalia. The quiet Greater Salem pastor wasn't one to talk.

Thursday morning, Mahalia called Boy Baby. "Come on over; I want to see you. Come now."

In Mahalia's family room that morning, Lou Mindling was upset. When Mahalia called him in Los Angeles, he'd dropped everything and flown in immediately—for good reason: she said she was going to marry this guy. She'd sent Polly for the license. The minister was coming. Would Mr. Mindling give her away? He'd gone along with her, humored her, called a blind press conference this afternoon—no hint of what was up; but this was the moment of truth. Mahalia, Minters, and he were the only persons in the room. The agent eyed Galloway a moment—a cool cookie, so quiet, so sure of himself—then, ignoring him, turned to Mahalia. "Now look, Mahalia," he said bluntly, "as far as I'm concerned, I don't think it's going to work. I have to be honest with you, 'cause I've never been anything else. So if you want me to hold the license up, have it torn up—I can do anything you want."

Mahalia looked at Minnis—at Mr. Mindling—at the room.

"No," her voice low, "no, I don't think that would be right."

Rev. Jenkins arrived; Cordia King arrived; Rev. Thurston arrived. Polly was somewhere around. The cast was complete. The agent shrugged. He'd tried.

Rev. John was surprised that he'd walked into a wedding, and yet not surprised. Hadn't he advised her to go ahead? It was right that Rev. Jenkins should perform the ceremony; he was her pastor, she was largely responsible for his elevation to the pastorate. But it was right, too, that Mahalia should want him, Rev. Thurston, here as her spiritual adviser.

Mahalia vanished upstairs to ready herself, and Polly joined her. At the last moment, Mahalia was seized with qualms. "There's a burden around my heart." Polly's hopes rose. But Mahalia said, "No, I'll go on," and started out. "Well, go ahead," said Polly, and ran to her room and cried before she followed.

There'd be no ring, Mahalia had told Rev. Jenkins beforehand, so he could be thinking along the lines of the ceremony. What did she need with another ring, she'd assured a smiling Minters. For this major appearance, then, for this smallest audience, the simplest of rites.

"Do you. . . . Love, honor, and obey. . . ."

She was Mrs. Minters Sigmond Galloway. She felt as if she'd burst 21 years' bonds of singleness and gathered a silken cord. Looking at Minnis, her heart said it could only be a silken cord. It was getting onto time for the press reception. Lou Mindling led the way.

IN THE BEAUBIEN Room atop the Prudential Building, a beaming, buoyant

Mahalia introduced to press, radio, and TV her new husband, "in the building contracting business in Gary." Eager for pictures, jostling, happy for Mahalia, the media shared the champagne and the wedding food; they lavished flashguns, questions, laughter, adulation. And for the first time in his life, the giant balloon marked "Celebrity" floated away with Minters Sigmond Galloway.

When all had subsided—reception, dinner over—the check came. Lou Mindling glanced at Mahalia and picked it up. They both knew Minters had no money to pay. "So that's how we start," thought Mindling. As Mahalia moved to rise, Sigmond drew out her chair, took her elbow, kissed her on the cheek. Mahalia glowed. Now let the world have its say.

It did. Fast. It was a full job just monitoring the calls. Teevee was helping out. Sigmond's mother called in first, "to congratulate you both"; shortly, his sisters, and a friend from Los Angeles. Otherwise, the deluge was for Mahalia. Coast to coast, friends and family, even Aunt Hannah caught unaware. Only Aunt Alice did not call; she'd wait on Mahalia's good time. Mahalia always did what she wanted to do. And did: scheduled a dinner a week from Sunday so they could meet Minnis—the aunts and all the main connections.

Elliott and Ida Beal had to learn it from *Jet*. "Now what is this!" said a shocked Beal. "This is too peculiar. She always has confided in me most things about her love life through the years, you know that, Ida. Well! I never heard of him before."

In Los Angeles, Mother Parks was busy defending the match. "No, she did *not*, say, 'pick him up.' He had work, he had a car, and he owned his own house."

In Chicago, among the whole undulating mass for which Mahalia was the rock, only happy-go-lucky Albertina and quiet little Louise had an openly good word for Minters—they and Missie Wilkerson, who was not so much *for* Minters as "if Mahala want him, that's *it;* that's the whole shoot." Halie was prepared for these critics. What she was not prepared for was the deluge from strangers. Hundreds of letters, most fearful that her marriage would rob her attention from the church, or her charities; many sounding offended, betrayed, by one claimed as their own, their spiritual intercessor. Furthermore, from his picture, he looked white. Was he?

THAT FIRST weekend, she was babied as she had never been—certainly not by a male. Minnis got up in the morning, fixed her breakfast, and brought it to her—their—bed. He fed it to her. He put her in the tub and bathed her, to her delight. He petted her. He pampered her. He brought her pills. When he made himself a drink, he made her hot tea. He seemed given over to tending, observing, this rare being, this darling of the press and the world. They talked music arrangements. He was so educated. At night, all hired help gone, he screened the telephone, would not let her be disturbed. His was the voice Dick Yancey heard, calling from Los Angeles, recognizing it. "Hey, Sig!"

"Yes. What do you want?"

"I just called to congratulate you and Mahalia. I heard you all got married."

"Well, anything else? Mahalia's busy." Used to a long run of words, Yancey gulped, "Well, no. I'll call her later."

They began plans for enlarging the house. "We need it, for entertaining," said Sigmond. "And Sigma," said Mahalia. "We need more space for her; she'll be growing up. I want to ask Josephine Davis what's the best school in Chicago to send her; she be old enough for kindergarten, this fall. My baby's going have the prettiest clothes in school."

Monday was oddly quiet of business. That night she called New Orleans. "Laurraines? Me." They hadn't talked since she'd gone to Europe, and Mahalia sketched the tour's triumphs. Then lightly, "Oh, and I'm Mrs. Minters S. Galloway now. He's in the contracting business with his uncle. Yeah, child. The National Baptists all come by my house—I tried to fix dinner for everybody; I was so tired—and I went right into getting married. Oh!" her voice lilted, "we just been rehearsing your song; I like that New Orleans sound, and those blue notes in it. I'll send a special little letter to Townsend and say, 'How you like that number *I Got to Walk—Lord, Hold My Hand*?' I don't want to just do it with piano; I want a full orchestration."

She was out of the cocoon, mind running. Let's see the book: who all out of town called for concerts? Israel Community Church on Cottage Grove want a benefit. Fix a date for Gleason's South Side boys' center. Better call Mr. Mindling. No telling what he got going on.

ONE RIVER YET to cross was meeting Minters' mother. Getting ready, fussing with her clothes, she suddenly grinned: nervous as a schoolgirl, going to meet her mother-in-law. But these were all college people. She didn't want to not fit in.

She needn't have worried. She and Mary Lou Jenkins became close-knit friends. His uncle, all the family in Gary, made her welcome. She could relax that tightness of being on trial. She sang on the way home and Minters held her hand with his free one, the Cadillac purring its own music in his ears.

By week's end, when her own introduction-dinner came around, the whole multilayered sandwich of her marriage felt swallowed, digested, already a part of her being, so she did not so much worry about how the family would take Minnis as say "Here he is." To the two most important persons in her Chicago life—outside of Minters now—that view was all right: Aunt Hannah, the witty, the easygoing, figured never to interfere between husband and wife anyway. "Sooner catch my finger in a car door." Aunt Alice? "I'm a sensitive, you know," says Alice Lawson; "if I see you right—look at you, I can tell. But he was her concern. And that little girl was all right; you know I like children. He didn't strike me as the right person for Mahalie. But she loved him. So."

Friends, ministers were streaming in; some invited, some just dropping by. It was Sigmond's first full immersion in what he would see was the steady swirl and shape of Mahalia's home life. It was *his* home now, and as he emerged from the kitchen with drinks (ignoring Mahalia's warning frowns and signals) a resolve firmed inside.

Aunt Alice saw the drinks, and the signals, and shook her head. Trouble right there. With ministers always around, or probably going to be, Mahalia had a rule against serving whiskey; didn't think it showed proper respect. And here he is bringing it in her living room!

Finally, late—many of these night people, musicians, to whom midnight was apt to be calling time—with the house emptied at last, Mahalia brought up the whiskey. A minister should be offered only coffee. Minters was genuinely surprised. This was today, Chicago, not some backwoods town. Most of those ministers took a drink and she knew it. If they didn't, give 'em the choice. He wasn't going to not drink in his own house. And he certainly couldn't have a drink and not offer it. What sort of manners was that? She could put it on him, he said, suddenly smiling that easy smile that melted her.

Well—she'd wait on the Lord. She kneeled to her praying and read her Bible before putting out the lights. It was a new life for Sigmond Galloway.

54

Within the muddle, Halie was happy. She had what she'd always wanted: home, husband, and child, all at once, together. Now she saw why the Lord had got her to flying. She could be home so much more. If Sigma was a little hard to handle, that much *more* reason: just sing, and get back. She found energy to weed the garden, little Sigma tagging behind.

As the weeks passed, Sigmond was restive. What kind of life was this for a star, all this staying at home? Why waste her time on these nobodies, so-called friends, when she had entrée to the best, would be welcome and given the best table anywhere, be with *real* people? Even off

→27
→22
→16
→17
→11
→12
→13

The Seven Sisters

Duke

Bell

Hannah

Charity

Alice

Bessie

Rhoda

Opposite Johnny Jackson senior, Mahalia's father, nicknamed 'Reverend' because he had been to a Baptist seminary.

Mahalia with her young stepdaughter Sigma Galloway in 1964.

Mahalia's first husband 'Seeing Eye' Ike Hockenhull was a devoted race-goer, but couldn't understand his wife's devotion to singing gospel.

Rev Russell Roberts of Atlantic City, Mahalia's lost love, haunted her even after she chose a second husband.

Minters J. Galloway with Mahalia after her announcement in November 1968 that they intended to remarry.

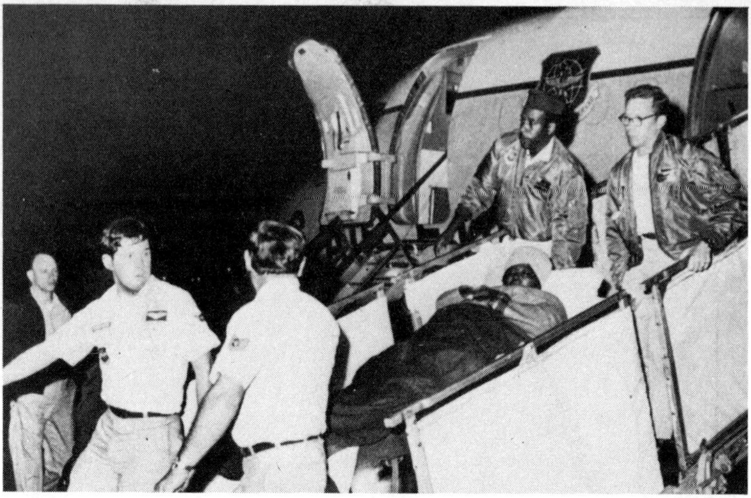

Mahalia is carried from a US medical evacuation plane after a three-day journey home from Germany in October 1971.

Back to the riverside. Mahalia lies in state in New Orleans' Riverside Auditorium with a guard of honour drawn from US and city services.

on concert, all she wanted was the bed to rest, piled up talking to some more of the same she saw in Chicago. Rest. Rest. He'd get her out of that kick. What was her money getting her—getting them?

Unused to public caution, he sounded off on the subject of the moochers eating off her, getting into her for money; he was going to put a clamp on that. He found his words in *Jet.* Facing him, Mahalia was torn between resentment and love, between seeing his measure of truth and the impropriety of his having said it in public. The preachers particularly would feel bad and many were real friends. Hospitality was her very nature. Sigmond was equally certain: Mahalia needed a firm hand; these people were just stealing her blind. They had no claim on her.

At Morgan Park Assembly Church, Margaret Aikens watched Mahalia get caught up. Rev. Golder *was* a dynamic preacher. Margaret was waiting for May to hear Rev. Golder sing her song, *Lord Don't Let Me Fail.* Ah, that was it. Yes! She felt a stir: "Mahalia ran out of the church; I found her standing against a big tree in front, tears streaming down her cheeks, just sobbing, 'Lord, don't let me fail!' "

Of all those watching on the sidelines, lawyer Aldus Mitchell felt he was the most knowledgeable. As a student, he'd played jazz gigs with Minters in Gary and occasionally in Chicago, and knew him as a great partygoer. He couldn't believe the man was prepared to live as Mahalia would want. It was going to be interesting to see what gave. He kept his counsel. Not to, was a great way to lose people. But he saw that as the crux of the matter—not the friends and religion, as some contended; and not Polly, whose power was threatened.

MINNIS, HALIE saw, was making a point to be pleasant to Cylestine—Polly—and to the aunts, even though he was so cool to most of the friends and cousins. Now look like he was putting himself out for Beal and Hogan, up from New Orleans to stay a while, and showing himself very attentive to his bride. That was good. She especially wanted Beal to see Halie'd done all right by herself.

The marriage was some five weeks old when Elliott Beal and Edwin Hogan walked in late Saturday afternoon to a huge greeting from Mahalia. She's just so happy to have us, Elliott saw with satisfaction. Wait 'til we get our heads together; I'll find out about this Johnny-come-lately hooked himself onto her. But as the hours passed, the only heads together were Mahalia's and Sigmond's. "He didn't leave us together no time," says Elliott; "she and I always get off, talk about home; but he covered her too closely." Furthermore, there was entirely too much tea being passed to Elliott's way of thinking, rooted in the paths of Pinching Town. Every time he looked, Galloway was getting himself a drink and fixing Halie a hot cup of tea.

"Child," said Elliott, picking up the cup to have a look, first chance with him out the room, "what you drinking all that tea? Mama says tea is binding. You don't have trouble with your bowels?"

"Beal, you something else. This tea is good for me."

"Yeah? That's what your *husband* say."

"Well, put it on down."

If he didn't have Mahalia, he had Sigma. He went to the front bedroom and closed the door, but the knock came right on. "Where you?" Beal let her in, and talk, talk, talk, as a child would.

Next morning, a knock. The father, this time: "We're getting ready to go." Go where? "To New York. I'm leaving something for you guys."

A fifth of liquor. Hogan didn't even drink. "And you know I don't need no liquor. But I was pleasant. So they went on."

AT THE WALDORF, Sigmond expanded. This was more like it. A suite. Interviews. He naturally sat in, as the husband, and listened to Mahalia's replies to the questioning—correcting her when she made an error in speech. Mahalia took the correction, but she twisted inside with shame, for him. These people *been* knowing her, knew she was just Mahalia and accepted her, went on; but of course he wouldn't know that and she could see where it would be hard for a person with so much education to sit by and let someone he was *responsible* for make mistakes. She knew she had a lot to learn. Still, it hurt. But he meant the best for her. He did.

With no singing that night, Minters was ready to make the clubs. Expense unlimited. Mahalia balked. No. Oh, no. She didn't belong in no clubs, would not set *foot* in a nightclub. When no persuasion would sway her, Minters was out the door with a light "Well, I'm going to have a look around."

"Better be sure they take a credit card before you run up a bill," she cautioned his disappearing figure. "Well, go on, then," she said weakly to the door. Where all this party business come from? All the time they went together in California and the times he'd visited her in Chicago, he'd been bright and full of life but none of this party business. They'd just done simple things. Lord? What is the answer here?

WHEN THEY returned to Chicago, Elliott had made up his mind the man had some sort of spell on Mahalia. He thought to unburden his mind to Polly when the two went on an errand for Mahalia, but before he could work around to the subject, near a Catholic church Polly came out with "I got to stop in there; I'm making a novena and I don't want to break it."

What is this, thought Beal; this is something wa-a-y out, 'cause Polly is a Baptist. 'Course, prayers never hurt anybody. "I'll go with you," said Beal, and asked her what the novena was for. Polly cut her eyes at him. "I'm praying special prayers for them to stay together. She needs somebody to help keep the niggers off her, keep them from resting on her for everything they want. He has broken a whole lot of that up. I've been fighting that battle all of these years. But he's the man of the house now. He can do it."

Elliott bit his tongue. Ooh, my goodness! this woman is definitely in his corner. I better be careful what I say about *him*. Beal's sole satisfaction was when he went with Mahalia to see Minters's uncle about enlarging the house. The uncle asked too much and Mahalia gave the job elsewhere. So she still had her eyes open in some directions.

She opened them even wider as she listened to Bob Miller, one of the few of her Chicago old guard for whom Minters showed respect. The dignified executive secretary and editor for the national funeral directors had just returned from Jackson, Miss.—turbulent territory: three civil rights workers missing and presumed murdered. Hotels and restaurants were newly integrated, and Bob Miller had registered into a downtown hotel for the first time with as much unease as pleasure: no sooner in than he got a call to come out to Charlie Evers's house—Dr. King was there. Mr. Miller set out at once. Three times he was stopped by police. At the half-block mark, some of the civil-rights lookout escorted him the rest of the way. Inside, shotguns were leaning alongside or below every window.

"Well, what have you seen?" Martin asked him.

"I'm a little worried," Bob Miller said in his soft, precise voice, "because the place I'm staying, they got bright lights, and all those white people back there, they might take a pot shot at me."

Martin laughed. "Those aren't whites; those are Negroes. The hotel backs up into a Negro neighborhood."

"Well," said Bob Miller, eyes rolling, "I'm afraid to go up to my room, 'cause those bright lights are shining on the back of that building."

Martin roared with laughter. You learned to live with it.

Halie couldn't join Bob's grin; she kept seeing those shotguns, and Martin laughing and laughing in the danger. That night she prayed for him, and for President Johnson. She'd promised to work for the President the whole campaign—told Lou Mindling to get with his staff on that. That he must win, she devoutly believed; he had too much important freedom work to do to be interrupted.

That August in Atlantic City at the Democratic Convention it was Marian Anderson who sang the *Star-Spangled Banner;* that left Halie free to put her heart and her soul and her God into her hymn for the country. Young Eddie Robinson, at the organ, was thrilled. It was Minters, though, who opened to full flower under the spotlights for Mahalia: "It's Mrs. Sigmond Galloway, remember." *This* was the real thing, where the important people were.

"Look at that guy," Lou Mindling muttered. "He walks in and he's a star—vicariously."

IT WAS HARD then for Sigmond to settle into the humdrum of Chicago. He told Mahalia he had a week's work, that his mother would come stay with her—and off he went. Mrs. Jenkins came eagerly to do for the sweetness of Mahalia. She was startled at the sourness she found alongside. "That whole week, Polly never missed a chance; every chance she got, she would make some crack about a man marrying a woman for her money—digs like that, in my hearing. When Minters came back, I asked him, 'Why does Polly dislike you?' He said he believed she despised him the minute he walked in that house, when they first got married."

Mrs. Jenkins left with a heavy heart. Even Bertha doesn't like him, she thought, nice as he's been about taking her to work when her car broke down. They don't at all appreciate how Minters is caring for Mahalia. Like he took care of Celeste when she was alive, her a welfare worker on days and him on nights—did all their cooking then, and that's how he can do so good for Mahalia. But I see he'll get no credit, no credit at all.

Mahalia's old friend Rev. Joe Campbell showed up the first of September, moved back to Chicago from Washington. He'd seen Mahalia whenever she was in D.C.; usually she was with Bill Davis, the lawyer he'd brought along to the Chester Bowles's *bon voyage*. This was his first look at Minters Galloway. "Sigmond Galloway," extending his hand. "J. Tallefarra Campbell," extending his. "Let me show you the improvements I've made in this house," Sigmond began, when Mahalia interrupted. "You can't show Campbell anything about this house; he's the first man ever stayed in this house." Rev. Campbell was amused to watch the husband's face until it came clear that Ernestine Washington was the houseguest, in from Brooklyn, when Campbell came to call, but the visiting went on 'til he stayed the night. This man was just going to have to get used to Grand Central Station.

AT UNIVERSITY OF Chicago Hospital, fine-tuned to all that affected Mahalia—working constantly on her physical condition to achieve a balance against the pervasive disease—Dr. William Barclay found himself point 4 to a sharpening triangle. Aunt Hannah was out of it; spoke no word. But Polly was his patient too—another paid for by Mahalia as a matter of course—and more pertinently, he had come to see Polly over the years as "a sort of manager, who lived with Mahalia."

At times Mahalia would be very dependent on Polly, he observed. "Polly was very managing, a dictatorial kind of person. But she was a great ally of mine in difficult periods, because I could tell Polly that I wanted something done and she could boss Mahalia around and see it was done. If I wanted to get Mahalia in, Polly would insist that she come. So in a way, I used Polly as an extension of my own authority over Mahalia." Now the husband was in the scene. The physician witnessed the triangle shaping, listened to the conflict between its points. "One of the things Polly resented Galloway for was because he came in and replaced Polly. She had nothing good to say about Galloway. It was a very interesting three-way relationship, with Polly struggling for domination over Mahalia, Galloway struggling for domination, and Mahalia struggling not to let either of them dominate her. I was sort of the sounding board for all three. I'd get a different story from each one."

Now Galloway was questioning him about Mahalia's "real" state of health, but to Dr. Barclay he didn't seem to be really listening, accepting. It was easier to think of Mahalia as a hypochondriac. That wasn't too surprising. Right here at Billings, a new resident or intern would say, "Aw hell, there's nothing wrong with that woman." Then when he went over her history, gave them a little lecture on the problems of progressive sarcoid illness, it was a great education—for some, anyway. Some were no more convinced than Galloway seemed to be now. Dr. Barclay sighed. This just wasn't one of the rare people, the "in sickness or in health, for richer, for poorer, for better or worse, 'til death do them part" people. Unless he was greatly mistaken.

55

"You can't have it both ways, Mahalia. If I'm *in* the house, I'm going to have a drink when I feel like it."

"How 'bout you just not drinking 'til they out the house?"

"Okay—*when* are they out of the house?"

Well, Lord. In Your time. Riding to St. Louis tomorrow. Got to get *some* rest. On her knees to pray. For the family. For Martin. For Sigma. For Minnis. Especially for Minnis. . . . Ooh, this bed feel like cotton to a black baby. Where Minnis? Getting himself a drink, probably. Sleep clouded in. Or did it?

She was passing the little prayer room—not where she had her saints and things now, the little room downstairs she dedicated to a prayer room when she first got the house. She was fixing to leave for St. Louis to sing, and as she passed, a woman was standing in the room. She handed Halie the statue of St. Jude. "What I want with that?" Halie asked.

"Here, you take this," the woman said.

"What I want with it? I'm going away."

"Take this," the woman insisted; "you're going to need it before you're through."

Rousing Sunday morning in her bed upstairs, Halie tried to remember whether she took the statue, but she couldn't call it either way. She dressed, thinking about it, then the car was ready and she kissed Sigma and Minnis goodbye—he wasn't going to St. Louis just for this—and matters of the moment swept away the peculiar dream.

At Kiel Auditorium Monday night, she was full into *I Don't Know About Tomorrow But I Know Who Holds My Hand Today* when she went to make a note and "look like something just—*click*—like that; and my breath was taken from me, for a while. Now the doctors at Billings, when they give me tests for breathing, they give me a hard test. Because I was used to handling my voice, they'd make my test harder, to see if something *was* wrong with me; and by me having those type of tests made, I didn't know if anything was wrong there on the stage. I just stopped singing for a while and nodded to my pianist and my organist and they kept on playing; then I finished the program and came off and autographed. Then I talked to my manager, went up to my hotel room, entertained guests—all of that. Next morning I got up about nine and hit the road back to Chicago. And *then* I began to get coughing spells; just cough, cough; and I began to drink hot tea. Every place we got that there was a restaurant, I would drink something hot; and it wouldn't stop that coughing. Six or seven hours, all the time coughing. Finally the road was getting on into Chicago—95th St. I was trying to make it home, so I could go to Billings in the morning—they all know I got heart trouble—and right there, I began to get like this—(DEEP, HUGE HEAVES). I had been coughing, but not this. Now we were opposite this hospital and you know *I couldn't pass that hospital.* So they backed on up and took me in. And I walked in there."

It was a strange place to her. Little Company of Mary, the sign said. She headed for the Emergency Room. "I think I have indigestion," she told the doctor.

"Yes?" he said, sticking her with a needle. A frightened Mildred gave the admitting information and called Polly and Minnis to come.

As Mahalia walked toward the room assigned her, in one corner she saw a statue. It was St. Jude. Electrified, when a nun came to her room, Halie told her about the dream, and sensation rippled through the quiet corridors. It was almost the last quiet they would know for weeks. If 1952 had been bad for Billings—when save for Ed Sullivan's show, her audiences were almost wholly black—'64 overwhelmed the little hospital in suburban Evergreen Park. Press from throughout the world clamored for news. Photographers sought admittance. Friends, fans, high, low, wanted information or admission or both. A special public relations desk was created. Media bulletins went out several times daily. Wires, mail came by the sackful. Polly took to plastering it on the walls, on the ceilings, for Mahalia to see and feel surrounded by the prayers and wishes. Flowers

Halie dealt with herself: "Flowers in a room smell like embalming fluid to me. Put them by St. Jude, or give them to somebody sick."

The nuns she got along with famously. She had a fondness for nuns anyway, as holy people. Hadn't she gone up the steps of Dominican Convent on her knees when she was 12, to pray for a steady job?

Of all the wires, Halie singled out in her mind those from a "quite upset" Dinah Shore, from Arthur Godfrey, Duke Ellington, Belafonte, Vice President Hubert Humphrey, and of course Martin and Coretta, and Mayor Daley. Then an envelope arrived which created a new stir: the White House. Next day—another.

In Washington, Elizabeth Carpenter had received a note from the vice president of a giant Chicago advertising/public relations firm who wrote, he said, as a close personal friend of Mahalia. On Sept. 29 a cheery personal message went forth: "Lady Bird and I were most sorry to learn of your recent illness and we hope that this note will find you well on the road to recovery. You have always given generously of your talent and energy to our country and your voice has gladdened and uplifted many a heart. All America joins me in warm wishes for your renewed good health and for your happiness in years ahead."

Independently, the next day came a briefer message dated Sept. 30, with a whole other set of initials attached, signed by the President too: "I was distressed to learn of your illness and want you to have this brief note to wish you a speedy recovery. Mrs. Johnson joins with me in hoping that you will soon return to your fine career. Our thoughts and prayers are with you."

The President and Lady Bird certainly were wishing her well.

The Sept. 30 White House file copy had a memo that Mahalia's problem was "slight heart strain" and "exhaustion" (and that the Chicago campaign rally was Oct. 30).

The public relations word, the doctors' word, and Mahalia's word of her condition had some differences. Mahalia's understanding was that "one doctor said I had a blood clot, the other doctor said I had a coronary. I don't know what I had. The most peculiar thing to me was that I couldn't swallow, hardly. When I'd swallow, it was like—look like my tongue was kind of out my head."

"Doctor," she said to Earl Vondrasek, "I got sinus trouble or something like that in my throat. Please get me a bottle of Watkins liniment and some Sloan antiseptic for my throat—I can't swallow."

"All right, Mahalia," he said. Then he never would get to it. She'd figured that. "I'm always diagnosing my case, you know. But the doctor never would pay no attention, and that just automatically healed itself."

Dr. Vondrasek's records showed another story. He'd been called into consultation by Dr. Theodore Gasteyer, the general practitioner on call when Mahalia walked in. "At the time, the impression in consultation was 'hypertensive heart disease manifested by acute coronary insufficiency.' Her symptoms were shortness of breath and easy fatigue, and outbreaks of profuse perspiration. The marked fatigue had been going on three or four days before she arrived. Then there was increasing severity of chest pains and she had some choking sensation in the lower throat. Her blood pressure was somewhat elevated—170 over 100—and her electrocardiograms were definitely abnormal: they were reported out as 'extensive coronary insufficiency'—narrowing of the coronary artery so the flow of blood to the heart muscles is impaired." Actually, he said, in light of later knowledge, "she had a probable myocardial infarction—a plugging, a complete obstruction; a segment of the heart not getting any flow at all, so there are some gangrenous changes in the muscle. This causes pain early, but frequently the pain goes away because the cells no longer are capable of giving rise to pain—the nerves and so on are so badly damaged."

But at the time, they went with "insufficiency." She lay shattered, imperiled, voiceless. The Associated Press issued word that she had been ordered to remain in bed four to six more weeks. Bishop Holmes called from Washington to say his entire church was fasting, on her behalf. Access to her room was limited as strictly as Halie's leanings would permit—and Polly's steady watch decreed. Sigmond and Mildred were there daily, and at night; the aunts came as the car went to bring them, this long way. But Mahalia called for Joe Bostic to come, and he caught the first plane from New York. Then the long haul out to the hospital. It was about 9:30 that night when he arrived, but he explained to the nun in charge. "She let me up, and then there's Minters, acting like he'd never heard of me: '*Who* wants to see my wife? *Who? What's* his name? *What?* Yeah, I guess he can come in.' "

Mahalia hadn't *said* she'd called for Bostic.

Ike, too, won admittance. He wouldn't have left until he had. He'd stayed away since the marriage, although he didn't blame Halie; he knew she must be lonely—but this was different; she was fighting for her life, like the papers said. He simply sat quietly, offering his presence. Margaret Aikens, "Little Missionary," was admitted to pray. Miranda Cox, Missie's slim, quiet daughter who did missionary work for her Spiritualist church, came to pray with her too. No bars for Rev. Jenkins, her pastor, or for Rev. John. And one day, Mahalia directed that her car be sent for Mother Gaye. She hadn't forgotten Mother Gaye's ministrations in 1952 so Halie could make that plane to Europe. And she remembered in 1955 when Mother Gaye prayed over Aunt Berta—in from Cincinnati and happened to be there seeing Halie at Billings; and Aunt Berta's trouble *was* heart trouble, *had* been, and that particular pain went away.

Gentle Mother Fannie Gaye felt it her appointed business to pray for Mahalia at whatever time of day or night it was revealed to her that Sister Jackson was in need of prayer—tell any others present it was time for her prayer, or simply "Let us pray." So many times, in the years, when she saw Mahalia, it was just as it was now. "Mother Gaye, I *felt* you praying for me." Lou Mindling was here in the room. "Now you pray for him."

"Yes," said Mindling, "I'm about as sick as you are, 'cause you're my moneymaker and you're down."

He left. Quietly the two women prayed together; then Mother Gaye alone; and Mahalia felt the clear water of the spirit bathing her, relieving her. Finally, "You have been sick unto death, Mahalia," said Mother Gaye, "but the Lord has rebuked death."

TUESDAY NIGHT, Sept. 29, Mahalia fell into sound sleep and woke startled. "The Lord has given me a song!" Not since her early Dawson days had any but gospel songs come to her, and Dawson's she had made up, with all the precinct people before her. But here the *Lord* had given her a complete song for the President! To the tune of *Onward Christian Soldiers*. 4:30 a.m. She could get Sister Matthew to write all these verses down now; when Minnis came, he could write the music right away.

Two days later, into the mail went a handsome blue velvet folder imprinted *ONWARD PRESIDENT JOHNSON*—"A Song Written by Mahalia Jackson Especially for Lyndon Baines Johnson."

Inside, the neat music manuscript was headed "Words by Mahalia Jackson, Music Arrangement by Sig Galloway."

OCT. 13, DISCHARGED only for strict bed rest, Halie was taken home to a house that seemed strange and to a future that could be stranger. Townsend had just got her a new Columbia contract. It ran five years and the terms were better. But would there *be* Mahalia Jackson? Nobody knew what it took, who hadn't been there.

56

On Delachaise, Doodutz and Brisko's oldest boy Fred, raised by Mama-Duke, visited quietly with friends the end of this New Year's Day, 1965. So said, Friday wasn't too good of a day to start on. Isabell was keeping one eye out for Mama-Duke, low sick and unable, gone senile. Nobody had wanted to tell Mahalia, sick as *she* was. The bells struck for midnight. And Mama was gone.

Now Mahalia would have to be told. It would be her to take care of the funeral. Lord, Lord, Isabell sure didn't want to be the one who had the telling.

WEAK BUT willing herself, Halie made the train. She kept an eye on Hannah, see how she was holding up. Mrs. Lockett and Ida were getting things together; they were used of it by now. She was more numb than not, pushing away thought, but it did pass her mind: good with bad, dark with light. Just Wednesday she's in the papers nominated as one of the Most Admired Women in the World in the Gallup Poll for '64—and she can't get Minnis to come be with her. She could see it being hard for him to be around death, he so loved life. But it would have been a comfort.

She sighed and closed her eyes to pray, for all of them.

She could do without these crowds around Mt. Moriah. They not here to pay respects to Aunt Duke, they here to see Mahalia Jackson, monkey in a zoo—Celie was right, people even up there on the Governor's Fleet building. Inside, Hannah rose up and had to be taken in back. "Please don't leave Aunt Hannah out there moaning," Halie told Beal. Celie made out with not too much commotion until the thought hit—she's finally gone to where her sister Bell; then Celie's scream was such that Beal, in the doorway for a breath of air, saw men running out the barroom a block away. "Please," said Mahalia up front, wholly unable, "somebody see to Celie."

Later there was a feeling to talk it out. Celie told about her last visit to Aunt Duke, when pushing open the side door to her bedroom, Celie felt a pain hit her middle finger and go straight up her arm.

"Come here," said Aunt Duke, "let Auntie saturate your arm with this alcohol. That's probably arthritis." Probably so. Celie started for the kitchen to fix Auntie some lunch, "and the Spirit spoke. 'Go back and look at the door. A snake bit you.' I turned back and there he was, on the door, on that wide board centerpiece, you know? Lying there. I told Auntie about the Voice and the snake, and sick as she was, she sprung up on that bed and 'What you say, baby!' Then I hollered for Fred's children and they took a stick and killed him. God is real."

"Oh, yes," breathed Aunt Bessie. "And you mind how the Spirit gave it to Bell not long before she passed, about Son Baby's daughter? Murdered out in California—somebody had went in and smothered her to death? And we wouldn't tell Bell 'cause she was sick, and next morning she said to this child here, 'Something done happened—' " Celie gasped, "That's right! Mama said, 'Last night I seen Betty coming thisaway, and she's hollering to me, "Gram, come help to save me!" ' And we hadn't told her one thing."

Mahalia shivered. All this talk of death on death.

PAIN, PAIN washing over her and would not go away. She turned to Minnis for comfort but he just didn't see how anything could still be wrong. She'd had all the rest she needed to get over that touch of heart strain, and she'd done nothing but rest two full months past that. Sigmond was almost beside himself: All these invitations for President Johnson's inauguration, and she's lying there saying she can't make it. "Come on, get up from there!" Halie cringed. Mínnis riffling through those invitations like they was thousand-dollar bills. "Well," he said, staring down at her, "I'm not going to let you pass this up, you hear me? You can just stop acting like a child. There's nothing the matter with you."

Halie checked into Billings.

"Mahalia," said Minters, "if you're not going to the inauguration, I am." Halie eyed him. Let him go. "He'll find out he's not going to be a star with me not there," she told Emma Bell.

"That man sure loves publicity," said Emma Bell. She believed Mahalia had just put herself in the hospital to keep from going to the Inauguration with Minters—there wasn't anything particular wrong with her.

"It's all the sarcoid," Dr. Barclay disagreed firmly; "just as it's *been* sarcoid." He'd obtained the cardiograms from Little Company of Mary Hospital. They thought she'd had an occlusion, but he'd consulted some expert cardiologists who went over her history, and it was fairly obvious she had sarcoidosis of the heart. It was rather rare, but it was described in medical literature, so now she had sarcoidosis of the lung and the heart in interaction: a very major problem. "Well," he smiled, "we'll see what we can do to relieve you."

"What'll relieve me is getting back to singing, Dr. Barclay."

"You'll be singing, Mahalia," he said firmly. And hoped to God he was right. He increased her dosage. He'd have to control it very carefully. He kept her in Billings eight days, until she was without the lower back pain which was her dominant problem in her own eyes. "We'll just have to build you back gradually," he said in parting. "But watch out now; remember that extra dosage is going to increase your appetite."

"Not for the kind of food you got on this paper."

He wished all his patients tolerated their physical problems that well. Tremendous malaise, great aching, a dragging fatigue along with enormous range of other sarcoid manifestations, such as her palpitations—all that without prospect of cure. A severe psychological handicap. He wished she had more . . . warmth of understanding at home.

MINTERS WAS GONE almost a week and returned glowing. There had just been this little difficulty with the hotel suite (reserved for her, officially) but he'd straightened that out, as her husband. It was a letdown to come back to the same old sight—Mahalia in the bed.

"Mahalia," he said with a wearied patience, "I believe if you had a toe ache, Dr. Barclay would say it was sarcoid—whatever that is; nobody ever heard of it."

"He said I had heart trouble."

"Well, they say the worst thing in the world for people with heart trouble is to baby themselves. Get out of the bed and go out somewhere with me. People are going to forget you exist."

"They wouldn't if you let 'em up here to see me."

"Now you can't have it both ways: You complain I'm never here; and if I'm never here, then who's keeping the people out?"

Mahalia surveyed him a moment. "Polly."

"You said it, I didn't. Well—you coming?"

"Minnis, believe me—I just can't make it."

"JOHN," SHE SAID glumly into the telephone, "people don't believe I'm sick as I am. Even Hannah and them."

"Hard as you push on the road?" cried Brother John, "and push everyone else you can reach? If you say you sick, you sick."

But from what? Furtive whisperings behind held hands—bolder words when the coast was clear—all these began to take hold. Wasn't it out of common to just drag on, drag on, maybe even getting worse? Was it possible— She began to suspect Minnis was poisoning her food, a little at a time. It was easy for all the tales of Pinching Town to rise up. Doctors don't know everything.

Emma Bell wasn't working, and Halie made her stay in the house with her. If Minters thought it strange she refused the trays he fixed, he gave no sign. That could mean he was just sure he'd get it in her someway. If he suspected— Tears flowed again. It was hard to think Minnis would do this to her. But Beal said he'd had his suspicions right from the start.

Emma Bell didn't believe there was a thing to it, but you can't convince Mahalie once she's got something in her head. It was just embarrassing to see—to be around, first Polly acting like he didn't exist, wouldn't hardly speak to him, her just coming to work here and him the husband, and now this thing of the meals, with him taking such pains. Like this morning.

"I'll fix breakfast for everybody!" said Minters, giving Emma Bell a big smile as she came into the kitchen. "What do you want?"

"Whatever you fix, that's fine with me," she said, and Minters busied himself with steaks, eggs, toast, everything. Emma Bell went back upstairs to see if Mahalia was awake. She was, and wanting something to eat. "Minters is fixing your breakfast," said Emma Bell.

"Oh!" said Halie, "I don't want anything he fix! You go down and fix me something."

"Mahalia, I can't do that. That man is down there fixing breakfast for everybody."

"Well," she whispered, "you watch it; you go on down and watch everything!"

Emma Bell followed Minters upstairs as he brought up the big tray. Mahalia looked at it, and turned her eyes aside. "I don't want this," she said weakly; "Emma Bell, go down and fix me some grits."

Now who, thought Emma Bell, exasperated, has got her stirred up like this? Who is pushing this thing? Mahalia sobbing, going on so, Emma Bell could not stop her in any form or fashion. She called Big Alice. "You all supposed to know so much, from New Orleans," she cried; "why don't you try to find out what's wrong with her?" If there was anything to anything, someone from New Orleans was supposed to could tell.

It took about a month for the thing to run its course. By the time Emma Bell left, after five weeks, got on to her own place, Mahalia had swung back. Minters was even giving her her pills, and she was taking them. Mahalia said it was her sarcoid was wrong. Whatever that was; Emma Bell didn't ask. Truth was, she loved the man.

57

Another month of bed. Sigmond put his foot down, made clear to many who got past Polly he felt their visit ill-timed, unwanted. Word circled that Galloway wouldn't let you in. To some this made little or no difference: Margaret Aikens came to kiss her beloved May goodbye; going to join Celeste. Boy Baby came and cheered her with word of the third generation into the ministry—Stephen John Thurston a theological student now. "I wish Sigma would turn out fine as that," Halie said wistfully. "You know I got her in Howalton School, suppose be the best. Ought to be, for the price!" Rev. John saw the flash of the old humor and was cheered. But it ebbed, and he left soon. Rev. Jenkins limited his calls, too. Mahalia just wasn't gaining back her strength.

Sick or no sick, when President Johnson had his landslide, she wired congratulations and the hope that God would keep, bless, and protect him. The President answered a nice letter back with more wishes for her recovery. Halie, whatever is ahead or is behind, you have this—that through God's will and gift alone, you have stood with Presidents and Kings, as Aunt Bell foretold. What God gives, God can take away—man is but custodian.

But Lord, what about our temple?

MINTERS WAS outdone. Nothing but lack of will holding her down. It was too boring playing nursemaid in a sick house week after week. He began to hunt diversion at night. Restless, unhappy, Halie turned to Aunt Alice. Hannah, in a constant state of sick or half-sick, couldn't be called on for anything past the job she insisted on keeping these long years. But Aunt Alice still had the strength and will for vigil. "I had to leave my house and go out there and stay with her because she couldn't make herself comfortable, her sick and him staying out 'til all hours—some nights 'til in the morning!" Be her, she told Halie flatly, she wouldn't put up with that kind of foolishness.

And yet—mornings when he was there, making her breakfast, bringing it to her, feeding her, his little mustache curving in a smile with that sweetness, that twinkle in his eye, she lifted. And sagged with the first friend who got through whose vibrations gave off the dislike. It didn't help for Polly and him to be struggling—and yet to her mind, it seemed sometimes just the opposite. Missie Wilkerson had no doubts. Watching—the whole scene out of Mahalia's sight—she winced as Minters asked if he had any mail and got "Not unless you're Mahalia Jackson."

Nov. 14, Halie called Dr. Vondrasek to come see her, please. He found "quite an insufficiency." She was depressed. He did what he could to make her more comfortable. Nov. 16, she called Dr. Gasteyer; he had nothing different to suggest. Nov. 20, she went to Dr. Vondrasek's office to be checked. And saw Dr. Gasteyer.

By Thanksgiving she was wandering the house a little but not for long. Yet she couldn't let this first Thanksgiving of her married life go by. She wanted to have a big dinner, have some friends over, have the jolliness she so missed. She'd ask Nettie Irving and her children, that's who. Be nice for Sigma. Minters was against it. If she wasn't well enough to get up and get out, she wasn't up to entertaining company. Aunt Bessie called from home to say happy Thanksgiving, and that just left her pressed in more. Thursday morning, thunderheads gathered but Minnis escaped into his Chivas Regal and would not say more. With a floating population of extra help, fixing the food was no problem. She called Nettie. Minters ought to like her. "Nettie, I want you and your children to come on out here." Nettie was taken aback. "Oh, Mahalia, I'm so sorry; we have plans. I naturally assumed you'd just be with your husband."

"Nettie—be *sure* and come." Something in her voice wrenched Nettie's heart. They came. At sight of Minters, Nettie blinked. Why, she'd picked a substitute for Russell Roberts. About the same height, same color, sophisticated. But this man was *too* smooth; Russell was not. "And that man proceeded to be evil. Actually belittled Mahalia before me—digs about her condition and so forth. *Oh!* My children just loved Mahalia, and they hated him on sight."

A week later, Dr. Vondrasek got a hurry call to the house. She had a fast heart action; it had obviously frightened her. She told him what she hadn't yet said to anyone but the Lord—her fears about never again singing. She was quite emotionally upset.

Bertha (still living with her) taught her embroidery "to keep her together." It was hard to see her so nervous. Mahalia made two dish towels and that was that. Bertha folded them away.

Dec. 18, Mahalia went into Billings. Dr. Barclay was off but Dr. Connelly would take care of her. She stayed five days but no particular thing was coming up so she asked could she be home for Christmas, and left on the 23rd.

Decorations weren't what they'd have been if she'd supervised, but they had the three trees for her and there was a certain glow just from Christmas in your own home, with your husband. But Christmas in Mahalia's world had always meant a bursting overflow. The house seemed haunted by the people kept away. She didn't want it like that, she told Minnis. He didn't listen and she hadn't the strength. Still she told them to bake a Christmas ham and cook some greens and some good old neck bones, "State Street chicken"—she'd never forget that. She was having her some *guests* at the Christmas table; she wasn't going to be that selfish.

Nettie and her children arrived about 4:30; the S. B. Fullers were already there (he owned the *Courier* newspapers and the cosmetics company) and Rev. and Mrs. J. C. Austin from Pilgrim Baptist. Halie'd caught the Christmas spirit and had a big, rich eggnog made up—but she certainly hadn't expected to find Minnis had spiked it. And her having to face it out or make a scene. *What* was she going to do about this man! They were all waiting on Minters, who finally arrived with his sister, his mother and her husband, and his aunt. Mahalia walked to the head of the table. "Nettie, you sit here."

"But this is your husband's place!"

"Come here, you do what I tell you." Mahalia in a mood was not to be brooked. She must have her reason. Nettie shrugged and sat. Mahalia was seating the other guests when Minters walked up; he'd stopped to make himself a drink. He saw Nettie, frowned, and spoke to her—gracefully but pointedly. "Don't speak to me," said Nettie; "speak to your wife. I'm doing what she told me."

Sigmond took another place, made a pleasantry, and the incident passed. But was she wrong, Nettie wondered, or was there enough edge at this table to slice the ham without a knife?

58

It was a lift just to look at Martin, hear his voice—he and Andrew Young in town to talk, to weigh a plan. Minters's mother came to give them "just a lovely meal," to her thinking. Halie and Martin had prayer together, and later Studs Terkel came to tape an interview with Martin at her bedside. "It was one of the most moving things of my life," says the seasoned performer/author. "She was in good form, even though she was still ill. She kept saying, 'Go ahead . . . go ahead.' "

Chauncey Eskridge was still Martin's lawyer, but Mahalia had shut him off. Now Martin urged Mahalia to take Chauncey back, let him work for her again. Well—she wasn't one to hold things, anyway; just let it go. Tell him come on. "So Martin brought us back together," laughs lawyer Eskridge, "and we were all the same again: argue, fuss, squabble, fight, and cuss each other."

BUT AFTER the lift, the letdown. The pressing and the pulling and yet she could—not—make—it. Uncle Porter came. She'd never noticed before how *much* he ran on, 'most like a goose's behind, but you can't say nothing to a good man like this, seeking to keep your mind off. Lord, is it something Halie's not doing that she ought to do?

She sent for Mother Gaye. Evelyn and her husband carried Mother Gaye over. The evening before, hearing she was going to take her mother to Mahalia's, people said Mr. Galloway wasn't going to let them in there. But one of the old circle who was helping out, Luberta Lindsey, opened the door. Mahalia was stretched out downstairs, with Aunt Alice and Willa Jones to keep her company. "Mama," Mahalia said earnestly, "my prayer is that I'll get the Holy Spirit like you have. I want to be *filled* with the spirit like you are, Mama. I want to be able to feel this thing just like it is."

Mother Gaye prayed then, the soft voice gradually reaching inward; and out, out, out. . . . "When I pray," explains Mother Gaye, "I begin just to pray, and *then* if the Lord *direct* me to lay hands, then I lay hands on that place, wherever He direct me to lay it; and I ask the Lord to take away the pain, aches, *and* the thobs, those annoying thobs, and heal whatever the condition is."

The voice flowed. Sigma wandered in, listened, and left. Eyes widened as Mother Gaye moved to lay hands, soft hands, fluid hands. Finally the voice stopped. Mother Gaye looked deeply, directly. "Mahalia, the Lord is going to heal you," she said definitely.

Mahalia caught her breath. "You think so, Mama?"

"Mahalia," injected Willa Jones, "you heard what the Lord said. Just take it like she said it."

Mahalia looked steadily at Mother Gaye, then Evelyn gave a little gasp within herself. "Mahalia got up *rejoicing*. She got up with her hands *up*, high, rejoicing that she felt the divine power. She told my mother she wanted divine healers there by her temple. And my mother told her she knew of this plan; although Mahalia had not revealed it to her, the *Lord* had revealed to her that Miss Jackson was to have such a temple."

In her natural voice now, Mahalia told some of her temple plans, then she put on one of her last recordings—songs cut before her attack. "I want you to hear; Minnis is playing on there." It had taken herself and Mr. Mindling combined, but Minnis was on there. Mahalia vanished once the music started, and when she came back, "Oh, I feel so good!" she exclaimed, clapping her hands. "You know my bowels don't move unless I take something, but after you prayed for me, Mama, my bowels moved." They all nodded, pleased. "I'm going upstairs. Mama, I want you to stay up there and pray for me 'til I go to sleep."

Mother Gaye followed her upstairs, and as they turned into the bedroom, Halie put out an arm to halt Mother Gaye, who could see past her. "Her husband was laying up there in the middle of the bed with nothing on but his shorts," says Mother Gaye, "laying up with his legs crossed, talking on the telephone."

"Wait a minute, Mama," said Mahalia. And into the room, "Get up from there and put your robe on and go into your room." Minters got up "but he didn't put no robe on," says Mother Gaye; "just got up and went in his shorts. So Mahalia called me in there."

"I'm going to get rid of him, that's all it is," Mahalia said bitterly. "I have tried every way I could to have him change into a different kind of person."

Mother Gaye made no comment. That was outside her province. She began to pray. Gradually Mahalia went on off to sleep. Mother Gaye went downstairs, and they got ready to go. She did not tell the others what Mahalia had said.

Mahalia called Mr. Mindling. He could begin to take dates. Not concerts; let's ease into this thing with TV. Yes, if March was the soonest, that was fine. Then she summoned the press. Waiting, she thought on it one last time: she had to remember Minnis had a different upbringing; he said it was nothing to him to act like that if somebody coming in on *him*, and she could see how that could be even if he had shamed her with a pure woman like Mama.

Feb. 10, headlines told the glad news that after five months' recuperation, Mahalia Jackson was getting back to work with a series of TV appearances next month. The accompanying photo showed Mahalia and her husband close together at the piano, beaming with shared pleasure.

So buoyed was she at the prospect of being Mahalia again, that five days later she could take it in stride—jolted, saddened, but not leveled by the death of Nat King Cole. Cancer. She smoothed the warm brown cabinet of the color TV he'd given her. Beautiful as that boy was inside, his soul ought to have no trouble at all getting over. The *New York Post* called for reminiscences of his early days, and it was a pleasure to call him up.

OH, NO. NO. No! The palpitations were back. When she got up to go to the bathroom, she was weak as dishwater. And her trying to get ready to do TV. Lord?

Dr. Vondrasek listened with interest to his most famous patient, this handsome brown woman so diminished—but by what? "Her big symptoms were that she was weak, tired, and would develop these palpitations. She had a lot of engagements and she was concerned that she just wasn't up to it." He studied the summary he'd written University of Chicago for, after her last hospitalization there, which made him aware of their findings of pulmonary sarcoidosis, coupled with a hysterectomy, in 1952. In the light of the changes in her electrocardiogram, he had considered sarcoid—it was a disease he did not treat, but he was aware of its manifestations. "However, we felt that for a patient who was overweight and hypertensive, coronary disease was far more likely." Now her current obvious depression. Her manager, in speaking with him, had felt she should be encouraged to fulfill her engagements—had indicated that she might be "emotionally disturbed"; suggested it might be "more of a psychological problem." Dr. Vondrasek raised this possibility to her. He did discover one specific problem: when she stood up, there was a considerable drop in blood pressure from the reading when she was sitting down. "Now this was a patient who previously was *hypertensive,* a patient with blood pressure 170 over 100. When she stood up, the pressure was 90 over 60—which explained why she felt weak when she stood up to sing for any length of time."

He prescribed the usual measures for such a state—wrap the legs, and use an abdominal corset. Halie accepted them both, but it seemed a mighty frail line to hold back troubles big as hers. Sure enough, the palpitations came back. How she going stand up and sing and maybe keel over before how many million people on TV? Unh-unh. Nooo. She called Lou Mindling. Cancel. "Mahalia will let you know when she's able. God knows, I want to get back. I'm not used of this much inactivity. It works on my nerves."

Nerves. That was it in a nutshell. Sigmond decided enough was enough, and coaxed, wheeled, needled, browbeat her into going to a psychiatrist in Gary. At least, thought Halie, that'll cause less commotion than anywhere she turned up in Chicago. Aunt Alice stood by silently. She had her own notions but she wouldn't say. She just fixed her eye on Galloway; she believed he just might be a little bit afraid of her—and he better be. Polly better be watching herself too.

THE PSYCHIATRIST picked up the dollar bill on his desk and slapped it against the back of his hand. "Miss Jackson," he said, "you're sound as this dollar bill. Whatever's wrong with you, it's not in your mind." Ha! She'd met an honest man. He could have kept her coming, and she might've just been fool enough to do it, to please Minnis.

March winds blew cold as she headed back to Dr. Vondrasek. Her blood pressure was still quite low, taken seated—110 over 60; when he took it standing, he got 94 over 80. She said she'd improved somewhat but she still had the palpitations. Electrocardiogram. Further changes. So these are progressive changes. Nitroglycerin? Mahalia dodged; she was clearly afraid to take it. True, in some people it causes a rapid drop in pressure, and headache. Well— "We gave her stimulants to try to keep her blood pressure up. And then I didn't see her again for over a year."

She better get back to Dr. Barclay.

"Sarcoid changes, Mahalia. All of this. The blood pressure drop is because the heart is not as strong a pump as it was." The disease was obviously all through the heart muscle. He must keep her on her medication religiously. He grinned: that one should have come from Mahalia. "Don't worry, we'll get you back on that stage."

She felt better as she rose to leave. She was used to her sarcoid.

The physician ached for her. This time that impish light wouldn't come, though she managed a joke about her losing weight. And the husband still couldn't credit that she was actually ill. Blocking it out.

SIGMOND DECIDED to plan seriously for her career. It might get her off this sick kick. For one thing, he told Mahalia, refilling his glass, she couldn't expect to go on holding large audiences with the sort of songs she'd been singing. The world moves on, you know. You have to give people something fresh, especially now you've been away. Who did she know in show business who was a big star who kept doing the same act all the time? Nobody. That was a sure way to flop, because people had *heard* that.

"Look, I'm a gospel singer, I sing for the Lord; that's what I am and that's all I'm going be."

A stubborn woman. All right, suppose she could—well, not *kill* two birds—say, fly two birds with one pitch? He could play the flute between groups of songs. That would rest her, and further his career. And if he lined up another good act, he said expansively—not more gospel songs; say, a good dramatic actor—that would go over. These were some of the things he was turning over in his mind, and if she would just accept his judgment—after all, he was a trained college musician.

Sigmond grew a little excited just thinking of the possibilities. Watching him, Mahalia thought, Lord, are you putting something else on me? Just call me Madame Job. But don't forget I'm due a feast.

Turning on TV for the news, her heart gave a thump. It was the night of Sunday, March 7 ("Bloody Sunday" in SCLC annals), when the first SCLC/SNCC voter-registration march from Selma, Ala., toward the capital was broken up by nightsticks, whips, and tear gas. Martin announced he himself would lead a second nonviolent march on Tuesday. Monday morning Halie dictated a telegram to the President: "In the name of the Lord please send protection to Dr Martin Luther King and the civil rights marchers in Selma Ala. Dont let him get killed. God has given you the power to free us and all people. I ask you this in the name of the Lord to send protection to the civil rights workers tomorrow Tuesday March 9th, Selma Ala. Thanking you for the consideration you might give this message, yours in Christ Mahalia Jackson"

She waited tensely for news on Tuesday, and relaxed only when the newscast showed no eruption. A pact had been worked out by Presidential go-between LeRoy Collins: the march went just so far, without defying an injunction. And President Johnson had a joint session of Congress agreeing to pass his federal guarantee of voting rights.

Wednesday, Martin called her from Selma. God is real. She just wished He'd speak what He had in mind for Halie.

She woke with her heart pounding. She had just seen herself in her coffin. Clearly, no mistaking. Then she looked up and the lid was closing down, when she came to. She lay feeling the life drained out of her. Was that a dream, out of *her?* or was it a vision, like the St. Jude statue—the Spirit preparing her so she could get herself in order?

59

Cecile Taylor had her eyes sharp. She was here to spend a month with Mahalia—see to her. It was the first chance she'd had to prise loose from New Orleans; before she'd been her mother's eyes. Now she meant to look just as sharp for Mahalia.

There was a lot to see. The husband seemed to be off; she did not have the straight of that—Mahalia just saying he was on a trip. There was the kitchen. There was this man she's paying $16 a day to clean! Not a one but Polly set that thing up. *She* was another thing. And that gardener. The Lord cut her work for her here in a many-fold cloth. All this was affecting Mahalia's health. And that was the *first* thing.

"Mahalia—" Celie's precise voice was firm. Halie was stretched out in the bed, Celie lying beside her. "Mahalia, you are suffering from the chaos in your life. It is affecting your health. Now—"

"Do you know I saw the coffin closing down over my head?"

"Not so," said Celie positively. Seeing how weak and sick she was, Celie had considered the many times jealous, evil persons had employed potions and powders and other means in an effort to do *her,* Celie, harm, whereon God had brought her out victorious. But considering all, Celie did not feel this was a problem to be dealt with here. The Spirit had spoken to her that Mahalia would get well. "Jesus says not so," Celie said. "He's going to let you get up, and you're going to sing better than ever."

Tears gave a glisten to Mahalia's eyes. "You think so?"

"I know so. You're going to get up from there. And when you get up, I want you to be very cautious. Get close to the Lord. You got a lot of prayers said for you, but you be particular." Mahalia sat up, listening intently. This was Aunt Bell's daughter. "You are like Joseph and you have some that are like Joseph's brothers, jealous of his coat that his father gave him—as God gave you your gift. They can see your coat, and they are covetous. You must seek the Lord and set your house in order." Celie's word caught a dormant thought: "I might sell this big house," said Mahalia.

"Why would you want to sell it? It is a gorgeous home. I simply adore it." Halie's long fingers plucked at the bedspread. "Oh, I've gone through so much in it. And it's a burden."

"We'll talk about that another time," said Celie, getting up; "aren't you supposed to go to the doctor?"

"I don't want to go back to the doctor."

"Oh, yes. I know prayer changes things, and God's going to let you get up, but I don't want you not to go back to the doctor; that is in the *progression.*"

Celie's voice, thought Halie, dressing, was like breathing vinegar; it sure opens your head—even if it doesn't last.

RUMOR HAD IT that Mahalia was dead. Answering the long-distance when she had the chance, Celie was indignant. "Indeed she is not! And you can tell that to anybody." That gave way to the rumor that Mahalia was gravely ill. There was a surge of calls from ministers throughout the country—whole churches and temples were praying. A healer arrived from California. He was shown to the prayer room. He's a nice-looking fella, kind of full eyes, thought Celie, following him—then came up short as she saw the door shutting. "Listen," said Celie, "don't close the door on me, because I know the same God you know, and I'm serving the same God you're serving."

"He took my hand," says Celie, "and the spirit come through me to him. He says, 'You're a Christian.' I said, 'In my heart.' " They both went in to pray.

In the succeeding weeks, Celie was just as direct in dealing with the rest of the problems she singled out one by one, her approach like an arrow from a taut bow.

"There is no need to have this man coming in every day to clean up, paying him $16 a day. The Lord is improving you; you can commence to look around. When this man comes today, tell him you don't need him tomorrow. That's money thrown away. I can take care of this while I'm here; nothing to taking a dust mop and brush."

"That gardener, Mahalia, is not doing his work and you in here sick." Leaving dead grass on the ground! It didn't look nice. "You hear that?" Mahalia cried to Aunt Alice; "see how she notices things? That's the man got $50 from me for crocus and tulip bulbs." Next cutting day, Mahalia went out and told him, Celie saw.

Wilmon Jackson had taken to being by, making entirely too free, to Celie; like it was his place. Look at that! Into the kitchen without a word to anybody and get his dinner. "I have charge of the kitchen," Celie informed him. "You should sit at the table, and I will serve you." He did; and she did. "When has my kitchen had order like this?" said Mahalia.

"I am on alert," said Celie. Now Yvonne's child Bertha, she seemingly took an interest—told Celie how she'd tried to coax Mahalia out of wearing that mink coat on into April. "Mahalia was afraid she'd get pneumonia again," Bertha said. "That's what she had, this last sickness." Bertha didn't mention sarcoid. Mahalia had never used the word to her.

Minters's sister Ruth came early in Celie's visit, while he was still away. He has sent this sister to see who I am, Celie decided the minute Ruth came into the house; she got up and turned 'round and around. "Take a good look, miss," said Celie; "that's why I got up, so you can carry the message back what I look like." Ruth went on to Mahalia, but she didn't stay long and had nothing to say on the way out. Hmph! came fiery and left fiery.

Polly's son Gary Belt was in, but he had little to do with Celie until Mahalia told him to set up her projector so her cousin could see the movies she'd taken of Aunt Bell's 85th birthday party. Celie cried so that Mahalia had Gary take it away. "Oh, Mahalia," said Celie, "you have never had the chance to know a mother's love and yet you are so kind, such a pleasant person. It is hard to understand why people do not do right by you."

Polly did not, to Celie's observations. This woman tried to overpower Mahalia, did not tell her all her own business. And now Polly was definitely, again, throwing away mail Mahalia didn't even know had come—just look at a name and throw it away unopened. "You," quivered Celie, eyes flashing up the height of Polly, "you are not fit to be in this house!" And to Mahalia, "*This* woman is not the right one to have, and her having her hand on all your business." The Lord is with the righteous, thought Celie. Indeed I'm not afraid of her.

It was on Minters, however, that Celie concentrated. Of those coming into the house, she figured Missie was 100% for Minters and Alice was 100% against him. Aunt Hannah was Mahalia's confidante; she didn't appreciate no man mistreating her niece, but she wasn't one to interfere. Aunt Alice was the opposite. If you loved Mahalia, she would be wild about you; but if she found you were not like you should be to Mahalia, she was like a streak of lightning on you. Oh, Alice was something in that house. Minters was afraid of Big Alice, he'd told Mahalia—and Mahalia told Celie—because Alice was so strict. Alice watching over like a hawk watch a chick. Celie's ears popped as Alice spit out, "You just married my niece for what she's got!" He turned it off, though. Just made up to Mahalia, gave her the thought he was trying to keep peace.

"Mahalia," said Celie as they lay on the bed, "you are unequally yoked. This is a man who entertains highly with alcoholic beverages. He has misled you about what his background was—he wasn't no contractor. You are kneeling to this man. You better be very cautious you are not separated from the love of God."

"*Nothing* is going separate me from the love of God," said Mahalia. "Oh, I'm so *anxious* to get well—I want to get to my temple! Do you think I'm overanxious?"

"Wear it as a loose garment and don't just have it in your heart, and you'll find you get well much faster. It's hard to see yourself, but you are improving steadily this minute. That's from eating those *proper* meals like the doctor ordered," Celie said triumphantly. Aunt Alice, never one to keep still, tried to cook Halie's meals when she was off her job with her "second family." But Alice gave in to Mahalia, seasoned her food like she *wanted* it. Celie was determined the doctor's orders be kept. Mahalia was not to have that rich food. But bring her proper meal: "I don't want that! I want my Creole soul-cooked food." "Yeah, but you going to eat broiled steak today." Hannah got a laugh out of the two of them. That was one of the *nicest* things, that earphone Mahalia got Hannah on her telephone since her deafness. It was nothing for Mahalia and Hannah to talk an hour, laying up each in her own bed.

STILL SHE lay diminished, gaunt. The parade to the door increased. And the rancor fell more on Polly than on Minters, since it was most often she who banned the call, who barred the door: Mahalia wasn't to be bothered with people who called to get them on a city job; with new songs; for substitute singers "if she couldn't come"; for money; on "urgent personal business"; to get them started in music; to teach them voice lessons; to share heart troubles or their relations' accidents or illnesses or funerals. Equally at bay were many who felt certified intimates, and even—at point of disbelief—preachers: a category never before balked. Sallie Martin heard the urgency in the white minister's voice calling from California. "Sallie, I can't get to Mahalia. The secretary says she's out, or she's asleep, or she's this, or that—just won't let me talk to her. I'd like to stop on my way to a revival in Ohio. Will you find out if she would let me come in to pray with her?"

Sallie said she'd go see. Mahalia said tell him come. Sallie met him at the airport, carried him to Mahalia—and watched with disapproval: Polly was staying right there and her presence was a distraction, because the man said, "I wonder if she would just let us be alone for a few minutes." Sallie felt sorry for him; he really could not work under that condition, had to let it go.

When Gwen arrived, it was Robert Anderson who took her to the house. Polly barred the way. "Miss Jackson can't see nobody!" Robert did his best. "This is Gwen Lightner, used to be Cooper; she goes 'way back with Mahalia; she—" Mahalia's voice issued from beyond the door with explosive authority: "*Let* that child in here! She come all the way from California. Let her in!" Worried as she was about May, Gwen couldn't help giving Polly a look as she passed—*this* was the woman acted so mean, all the times she'd tried long-distance.

Evenings, Missie was in and out. Cooking, often as not, which Minters seemed to respect. But it was day when she boldly brought a newcomer who for essence of quiet authority was anybody's match. Besides, this was Mahala's *business:* Missie was cooking for pretty, *cafe au lait* Mrs. Jean Childers in the restaurant-lounge Jean and her husband Ken had opened, an extra to Ken's career as architect and Jean's as one of the country's few women building contractors. Mahalia had told Missie she'd get rid of this big place if she could find a nice apartment building to buy. "I know just the person for that," said Missie. Mississippi-born, warm, bright, Jean was a natural for Mahalia. Nothing would come of the real estate search (Mahalia's mind was not really made up), but they were instant friends. Still, Jean didn't run the gauntlet unless there was real reason. It wasn't worth the strain, and if Mahalia really didn't want it that way, surely she would change her arrangements?

Under assault, Polly (Mrs. Cylestine Fletcher, since her marriage) was certain she was the only strong barrier of defense Mahalia had against an encroaching world.

The family itself had no visiting problem. Including a renewed presence —Brisko's daughter Rose: Rose Champagne, married and moved up to Gary. Looking at her, it felt like a hundred years, and no time, since Halie'd tried to keep that child for herself.

AND NOW CELIE had to go. Puddin was pressing her. "I just wish you'd come up and be with me," said Mahalia.

"I would sell out, I just love the neighborhood up here," said Celie, "but Puddin doesn't like Chicago; he just isn't willing."

"Now Mahalia," she said earnestly at the last, "I want you to remember—be very caution, 'cause you know Christ was here and they put down the palms for him—oh, yes—and the next minute they turned around and said, 'Crucify him, away with him.' A lot of obstacles being put in your way, but you can overcome."

Funny, mused Mahalia, lying alone. A small person like that can leave a big space behind.

Celie had wanted a picture, and Mahalia gave her a nice color one of herself and Minters, heads close. "Cut him off," said Son Baby, when Celie gave her brother an account of the trip and showed her souvenirs.

"I don't think so, brother," said Celie, considering; "not just now."

60

Sigmond was off again in mid-June—had some short band dates in California a week after Celie left—when Russell Goode walked into the house he knew so well, to the Mahalia he—oh no. He was shocked. The young Chattanooga teacher called Mahalia every Sunday, but he was not prepared for this sunken figure who only whispered, except when something caught her interest. Russell promptly instituted his own therapy: Lake Michigan. Each day about 11, he drove her to the lakeshore, spread a blanket and pillows on the rocks, and tuned his portable radio to soft music. Often Mahalia didn't want to go, refused, fussed, but he overrode her. Once there, she'd lie easy—munch on the sandwiches, sip the pop they'd picked up, speak whatever came to mind, telling him, with all the rest, about Russell Roberts. I believe one reason she likes me is because of my name, thought Russell; content, knowing Russell Roberts's picture was still up in Mahalia's bedroom, Minters or not. While Mahalia watched the water and took the sun, Russell's quick, light voice ran on until she dozed.

Twice Polly was with them; once, Aunt Hannah. Otherwise, for the almost six weeks he was there, just the two made the siesta. Once some nuns came by, breeze flipping the black habits, and told her they were praying for her. Mahalia thanked them, dozed, woke and, near tears, began "Oh, *why* can't I—" so that Russell hushed her with, "Don't think about it."

At the house, when he could catch her interest and she called up the energy, he'd practice her on new music. His Catholic background had given him no instinct for gospel, but "Keep on practicing, baby; one these days, I'm going shock 'em."

He was upstairs with her when Minters called to tell Mahalia he'd be home in time for their anniversary—their first: he'd arrive the night before. Mahalia hung up slowly, silent. And burst into tears. She'd gotten used to some peace. "If you don't want him to come, tell him," said Russell. "I can't do that," said Mahalia; "oh, I couldn't do that."

Mahalia was in bed, Russell sitting on the chaise longue with his shoes off, when Sigmond arrived. He headed upstairs to Mahalia's bedroom, saw this fellow there, ignored him, and went straight to his wife. "Hey, what you doing in that bed? Get on up!"

"Minters, don't start that mess. I'm sick."

"Oh, nothing wrong with you!" He was kissing her on the cheek when Russell tiptoed out, shoes in hand.

About midnight, Sigmond came downstairs. "Mahalia says you're a great musician; get on the piano, play me something." Russell was shocked. It was too late—they might disturb Mahalia. "Oh, go on, it's not going to hurt her," said Sigmond, but shrugged, accepting it, when Russell held off. Next day, Mahalia told Russell that Minnis wanted to take her out for their anniversary, but she wanted all of them to go—Russell, Bertha, and her friend from Hawaii, Lucius Curry. "I'll tell Minnis," said Mahalia, "and I'll send him down to invite you all, and I'm telling you so you'll say yes. You tell Lucius and Bertha." Russell hadn't got to explain to Bertha privately (since she and Minters didn't get along) when Minters came down and invited them; but he kicked Bertha under the table and she accepted.

The Chicago Sheraton's Kontiki Restaurant was elegant and Russell felt expansive. Mahalia said go ahead, order drinks, she didn't mind; just she wouldn't. The seafood was delicious. It was a *real* party. They'd been there two hours. Sigmond called for the bill, took one look and blanched. "Oh, my God! It's too much!" Mahalia reached over, glanced at it, and handed him her American Express card.

Outside, Sigmond informed one of the hotel staff, "This is Mahalia Jackson. Go get her car." Big shot! glowered Russell. Mahalia said quietly, "Minnis, you get the car." And once settled into it, "Don't go telling people I'm Mahalia Jackson; I don't need people making over me," she said. "Well, you're the queen!" Sigmond protested. "I want the best for you!"

Russell gritted his teeth at this man so careless of Mahalia. July 26, when he left for New York, he was still just very upset at the way Minters was acting, and her ill.

But she'd had a lift. Martin had come, with some of his team—there for serious business, but the house rang with the richness of his laughter. That was maybe the best medicine.

For three days, they worked like beetles to round up some organized support for this first Chicago move toward a face-down with the city's deep-set, often devious segregation. Mahalia did what she could. Then Martin led a march down to City Hall with school demands, although Mayor Daley was in Detroit.

Mid-August brought riots; not in Halie's section, but she sat heartsick at the reports. In Chicago! She prayed for the Spirit of the Lord to prevail. And to help Halie Jackson. Lord, if Halie wins this fight, look like You going have the doing of it. She took refuge in thinking out her temple, of the various ways it could be. But Lord, what is Halie going do about money for the temple, if she can't get back to singing? Mr. Mindling wasn't happy, she knew that. A whole year off now. For herself, the way she'd laid up her store, she was managing even with the big drain off that. Royalties came in from Columbia, and from the publishing on her arrangements. The buildings brought in something. No leg to lean on but her own, though. That cash would peter down to nothing, if she wasn't out there singing. Minnis reminded her of that often enough. Besides the steady payroll, there was the floating help (often more to meet their needs than her occasion). If Minnis could get him some steady kind of work. But he couldn't play jazz here in Chicago, not and married to Mahalia Jackson. Oh, Lord! Lord! my temple!

August's end brought something she could not deny and didn't want to: Archbishop Cody, from New Orleans, was being welcomed to the city—Mayor Daley leading the official welcome. She headed for the dinner at the Conrad Hilton praying for the Lord to sustain—confronted the thousands of faces—and hallelujah! she sang. Not to push. But she sang. Oh glory in the gospel. Thank You Lord.

She sang a little in churches, then. All the big ones were vying for her presence. But she slumped again; she had to pick and choose.

Missie's daughter Miranda was engrossed in the service at her tiny Spiritualist storefront on Racine St. when a stir among the handful in church caused her to focus on the door. Glory to God! Mahalia Jackson had walked in off the street, like anybody. "I want prayer," Mahalia said, getting on her knees at the altar—a worn table. Asking prayer from us humble people! Miranda never thought Mahalia could come, would keep a pledge made near to death at Little Company Hospital. Prayers over, Eddie Robinson helped her to her feet. The voice of the Queen of Gospel Singers brought astounded faces to the door. Restore her, Lord; we need her so. Miranda made it her business that very week to get out to the house and pray again. She left with Mahalia's voice haunting her, asking so low, "I wonder if God going let me sing again?"

61

Lou Mindling was jubilant. "Mahalia, that's just right. It's just what you want, to get back big but easy."

"I wouldn't say easy, Mr. Mindling: after a year out, to start in on the White House? But they asked me, and I don't see how I can tell the President no. But Mahalia's not going in there croaking like no frog. So I got me this little place I'm going to sing first. Then I'll sing for the President."

The agent wasn't disconcerted. Even when they were going gung-ho, Mahalia had the habit of throwing in these little things of her own. "That's fine, Mahalia. I just want you back singing."

Glad and scared tumbled inside like clothes in the washer. Lord, You going put Halie on the line? Will you please be ready with Your pins? Ha! How long since the Lord had Halie make Him a joke.

RADIO, TV could tell her nothing for sure. Halie was beside herself. Hurricane Betsy had hit New Orleans so bad in the night, they said whole sections under water, people lost, whereabouts unknown. Seem like all her people ought to be all right except Celie: Celie right *in* the Ninth Ward, the part out past the Industrial Canal. Levee broke and water come in higher than a man's head, and Celie—God! Help her! Let me see can I find out any more. . . .

CELIE HAD RESISTED leaving all her pretty things for anybody wanted to lay their hand, even though Puddin said some people were getting out just in case. It was a shock when the wall of water hit, penetrated the doors, filled the rooms, coming up higher than standing on a table. "Puddin," she gasped, "I can't swim the first stroke!"—he urging her to make the start into the dark waters. He held her then, keeping her head above the water, making way. She screamed; the current wanted to suck her from him! "Don't panic, Cecile; don't panic and we'll make it," and they did, were rescued, passed from hand to hand and ended in Municipal Auditorium with all the other refugees. To Celie, it was the Tower of Babel, for though there was the one language, you could not understand. Puddin went to see what he could find out. On the outside, the sister-in-law of a nurse heard a message on her car radio: "Mahalia Jackson is trying to locate her cousin, Mrs. Cecile Taylor, and Arthur Taylor. If you locate Mrs. Cecile Taylor, have her call this number—" On impulse, the woman jotted it down and passed it on to the nurse: she was on duty at the Auditorium; she might run into this Mrs. Taylor. Celie was just gathering herself (she had no belongings) to be sent over to the Navy Station refugee center across the Mississippi River when the nurse came up with the message. "There's a pay phone you can use over there," she indicated; "you wait your turn." Celie just looked. When had this ever happened to her in her lifetime. "I don't have a nickel in the world," she said. A lady standing by said, "Here, honey, take this dime, 'cause you may lose the first nickel." Celie reached her brother Allen—Son Baby. "Mahalia says tell you don't worry, all she want to know, if you are alive. She say, 'Don't worry about the material things, 'cause I can replace that, but I can't replace your life.' "

"And she did that," says Cecile. "Yes, she did. And the Lord saw fit to make my damages less than most."

MAHALIA CHECKED with Dr. Barclay. Thin as she was, could she let out? Yes. She marshaled her strongest pray-ers. She and Celeste kept a busy line. But it was Celeste's sister Margaret, her Prayer Warrior, she drew on for prayer *with* her: "Baby," she said on the phone to Los Angeles, "Halie want you to pray like you never prayed before"—"and the Lord anointed the conversation," says Margaret. Now Halie was getting back, just what he'd been urging, Minnis was a strong right arm, right up to carrying out the baggage for them both. He would be at her side. She smiled up at him gratefully.

This is it. Out there was a goodly measure of Port Huron, Mich. Staring into the dressing room mirror, she said one last prayer and nodded to Mildred and Eddie. They went on; the prelude began; she walked on stage, looked out, bowed her head—and felt a surge of power. Oh, amazing grace—amazing!—and amazing to the audience, who knew the drama of this first concert after a long, dark year. Two hours! Cheers. Applause. She brought them to their feet with a message: "It took God to heal me. If you people are really Christians, you'll take inventory on yourselves every day, and ask the Lord for His mercy. Faith and prayer are the vitamins of the soul; man cannot live in health without them."

Minnis guided her outside. She had let him be MC.

WEDNESDAY morning, Oct. 6, 1965, they checked into the Hay Adams Hotel and trooped over to the State Department auditorium for rehearsal. It put her in mind of Kennedy's inauguration—and there was Frederic March, being MC! The morning went quickly. Minnis was buoyed up, his old self the way he was before they were married. He sure loved to be on the go. After lunch, she checked in on Martin's civil rights meeting like she promised. Back at 8 p.m. for the all-cast call. God! listen to that Robert Merrill sing! It was midnight before she got back to the hotel, pulling down on Minnis' arm. She didn't much mind if he went on out "to look around a little." He was still excited, and *he* didn't have a morning rehearsal.

Whoo! since 9 a.m.—50 pounds off a person's singing weight, they's not much to pull up on. 'Til through the night, the first and only chance for rest be about two hours *after* this 3 p.m. show for the press. Help me Lord. Because pictures weren't allowed tonight (and papers always liked to do things ahead anyway), *all* the Washington press was there, it seemed to Mildred. AP. UP. Everybody. She watched the parade of photographers sticking their head in. "Miss Jackson, will you come take a picture with Sheila MacRae?" Mahalia pulling herself up, going on over. "Miss Jackson, can you—" "Miss Jackson, will you—"

"Wait a minute," Mildred said, *"this is Mahalia Jackson.* She's a star in her own right. Don't come hollering all everywhere telling her go take pictures—let them come to her. She's a star! She's the only one we *have* in this field. The greatest one there is!" Out of the side of her eye, Mildred could see Mahalia giving her the hand signal: hush, hush, hush; "but I kept on singing," chuckles Mildred. Just then, a new press face. "Miss Anita Bryant—" Mildred pushed past him. Miss Bryant's dressing room was right next. "Miss Anita Bryant," said Mildred in ringing tones, "would you come in here and take a picture with Miss Jackson?"

"I'd be delighted to," beamed Miss Bryant. When they'd all left, and the door shut, "Ohhhh," winces Mildred Falls, "did Miss Jackson bawl me out!"

AT THE WHITE HOUSE, guests had begun arriving at 7:30 p.m. at the East Gate, greeted by music, flowers, and military aides. Preparations had taken weeks, ever since President Johnson had asked for a "Salute to Congress" gala as a thank-you to the members of both houses. Logistics had been minutely planned. Now Mrs. Johnson stood distressed as her careful schedules scattered to the winds. Cabinet members and their husbands and wives were being served drinks in the Diplomatic Reception Room as planned. But the guests of honor—the Congress—were still in session, debating the Highway Beautification Bill, her own special project, long past the hour the party was to begin. Fortunately dress was informal; they could come directly from Capitol Hill. But there'd be no time for the intimate top-echelon salute in the Blue, Green, and Red Rooms. Vying for Mrs. Johnson's awareness was the President's impending admission into Bethesda for surgery; after the show, he'd go directly to the hospital. He had refused to postpone the gala.

The cast began to be edgy. In her dressing room, Halie tried to gain a measure of peace—read her Bible, meditate. She felt weak. She was glad Minnis was off somewhere. He be back in plenty of time. Do, Lord, remember me. She sat up. It stirred you when the band struck up *Hail to the Chief* and you knew the President was walking in, especially when he's a friend of yours. Frederic March speaking, that means—yes, there's the President thanking the Congress for all their good work. Indeed they *have* made us a better country; have given Negroes their best hope to lift their heads and walk in dignity. Hallelujah! She walked onstage—and soared. Yes, Lord! Mrs. Johnson recalls she felt Mahalia's "deep and abiding belief in the Almighty gave a special dimension to her personality and her performances—a light from within . . . . How could one ever forget being enfolded in that voice. And, because Lyndon was scheduled to have surgery the very next morning, I know the faith and love she radiated was deeply meaningful to him."

The President overruled them all and came back to the White House for the reception. Halie found herself in the East Room talking with him, Mrs. Johnson alongside. She loved that woman; she took such good care of that man. And really backs him up. "And look like," said Mahalia, telling it, "if you're from the South and you get away from it, whether you're white or black, it's a bond between you. It seemed the way with President Johnson and me. He was sort of worried about his condition—and anyone *should* be worried when a knife is concerned. He kept at me to pray for him. So I took his hand and told him everything was going to be all right, that God was on his side." At this point came an embarrassment which seared Halie's memory. "My husband started talking to Lady Bird, broke in and asked her, 'How did your deal go through with the beautifying program?' So she turned around and said to him, (FROSTY TONE) 'It takes time to do things like that, but I'm sure it will go through.' Then she turned back to me and she talked to me, and I was talking so fast, so the President wouldn't hear it.

"And then, do you know the President, he had me to sing *Precious Lord* for him again? I was glad if I could help—except my feet hurt."

THE PICTURE came from Lady Bird within days; Sigmond couldn't get enough of it: himself and Mahalia with the President and the First Lady. She'd had a letter from the President expressing his deep gratitude the next *day*, from the hospital. And something else in the mail was special: Hugues Panassié sent his review of her *Greatest Hits* album from 1963, just now issued in Europe. She couldn't read the French but his note said "Wonderful." It was like a little warm fire. She was not forgotten.

Now let's see what they going think in Hollywood. *Those* people tougher.

62

Ease in cautiously. Church concerts in Montreal, Calif., and San Carlos between the TV. The Dean Martin Show. Such an easy man, he made you easy. Now Merv Griffin, from his hometown, taping at San Mateo College. Just the two songs, after they talked a little, and she liked Merv Griffin.

Halie's voice, her eyes sobered as she told them of her heart attack, the long pull, how she'd lost "100 pounds"—well, it felt like it; then she sang *He's Got the Whole World in His Hands*. She was into her second song when she heard some little stir but it was none of her. She lost herself again in the song; so thankful. When she finished, they told her the tape had broken and please wait while they fixed it, then sing the song again. She stood at the back until she got the signal and started again, reaching in for the essence, the love of God greater than any pink tongue can tell but trying to come close: Righteous victorious! she stood panting, glowing, pleased it was over—and some place back the tape had broken again. Would she— Nobody thought to bring her a chair. She moved around a little. She felt her throat closing and gave the quick little coughs that were her way of piercing the phlegm without rasping. Finally she sang again. The tape held. Thank You Jesus. *Who* said this the easy way? It sure wasn't the way to make a dime. She got ten times as much for a concert as she'd get for this type of show—plenty pay less than this; and you spend just as much of your time. Well, Lord, it take a lots of things to make a sandwich.

They were staying in Sigmond's little house at 3521 Seventh, Mrs. Jenkins taking care of Sigma in Chicago, getting her off to school. His sister Ruth there to help, too. Minters wasn't too sorry for the child to have a spell with his mother, says Mary Lou Jenkins. "He'd tell Mahalia she was ruining the child, by spoiling her. Mahalia didn't want to ever refuse her." Halie was trying her best not to refuse Minnis, either. Out here, on territory he felt was more his own, he took charge. She knew now Minnis was a man with the desire to accomplish great things but hadn't, so it was his nature to somewhat belittle hers and yet there was only hers to work with. Sigmond announced he was Mahalia's manager now. That didn't make him popular with Lou Mindling. "We had a constant run-in," shrugs the agent, "because to me, he was *cruel* to Mahalia and I couldn't stand by and see that. He acted as if he were the star and she, the hireling. And she let him get away with it."

In the long drought of Mahalia's inactivity, Mindling had taken on the leasing of the *Batman* show but that had peaked out; he had plenty of time to put together her comeback tour for spring.

Little Dick Yancey had fallen into close step behind Mahalia again. That he irritated both Mindling and Galloway disturbed him not in the least. He knew he was invaluable to Mahalia; *he* was setting up things and doing the day-to-day managing; Sig didn't know managing from a hole in the ground. "Ha!" It delighted Yancey's soul to hear one of the TV people call Sig "Mr. Jackson." Listen to that high-hat jerk: "I'm *Mr.* Sigmond Galloway, and that's *Mrs.* Galloway and don't you forget it." What a changed guy.

"Mahalia," said Irv Townsend wearily, "have we got to put the man in? He can't play, not with this orchestra." It was a losing game; Mahalia was going to get her way again because he didn't want to upset her. It had taken too long to get her back. He'd even appealed to Dinah Shore one day when he was cutting a special with her—told her one thing upsetting him and everyone at Columbia was that Mahalia seemed to have given up, lost her spirit; that was the reason he couldn't get her to record again. He figured Dinah might do the trick. "If you could just get her excited about recording, then she'll be back in the swing of things." Dinah was worried for Mahalia, but—Mahalia was a wise woman; she'd know when she was ready. *Such* a pity. And now, to Townsend, a pity to be saddled with this guy she'd married. Well—there was an album to do. And there was the black chorus pouring in. This wasn't going to be one of her best efforts, by any count. He'd never seen her looking so worried, so nervous. And where was the *fun* in her? Look at Galloway order her around! Anybody else, she'd "dish him out."

Privately, Minters reverted often to his tender touch, so that when Audrey Franklyn came to the cottage to visit Mahalia . . . "Audrey P., you should find somebody who offers you compassion." She didn't say *passion,* thought Audrey; that was *compassion.* "Mahalia," she answered, "I'm too much a woman for anybody." What could Mahalia see in him? Very polished; very, very sharp dresser; played it very, very cool. But Mahalia was a woman who had gone as far as she could go. What did she need with him?

"Everybody talks so against him in Chicago." Gwen Lightner was sitting with Sister, just relaxing; she could see this thing was worrying Mahalia's mind. She didn't know why people couldn't leave the two of them alone, let a woman handle her own man.

The spring tour was shaping. Lou Mindling said there were plenty of takers. Just let me be ready, Lord. "Yeah, go on; go on, Minnis." He was a man had to be out.

"Mahalia?" Audrey P. "Would you like to go out to eat?"

"Yeah, Galloway isn't here. He's gone with the Cadillac." Oh-oh, thought Audrey P. "Well, I'm with a friend; we'll take you to Chinatown so you can eat up a storm."

It was Chinese New Year. The firecrackers were popping like gangbusters. Oh, my God! thought Audrey: suppose she gets scared and has another heart attack! She didn't look nervous, but with Mahalia you could never tell.

To Halie, the firecrackers put her in mind of New Orleans. Hey! Enjoy the fun and the food; the problems going last past this moo goo whatyoucallit.

SHE HAD TO get back. Never mind February weather. Martin was in Chicago, put himself on the line to do something about the slums, and she needed be there if no more than give him a good meal, try to see nothing happen to him.

She was a welcome sight to the weary black messiah. "This was the house that Martin said was his haven, his favorite place in all the world to relax," says Xernona Clayton. Ed had just left Martin's staff as public relations director to start his own weekly, but they kept in close touch. "Martin got *many* things from her—the freedom to laugh, good food, wit, and a sense of privacy. Just headed toward Mahalia's house, he would start laughing gleefully; just anticipate the moment when he's going to be arriving. It's difficult for many people to comprehend this need for carefree, relaxed *pleasure*. She was unaffected, she would say what she had to say—most times, it was funny; she was such a humorous person—and yet she was deep and serious when she *was* serious. Another thing he appreciated is that when Martin asked Mahalia for an opinion, Mahalia would give him the truth—the truth being her honest opinion. 'I don't think that's such a good idea'; or 'You ought to do this—instead of that.' She respected him to want to *hear* her honest opinion."

Trying to sense the truth of Chicago was complex. Martin questioned her yet again, taking her through the ministers: the key to arousing any substantial proportion of the city's blacks to *believe* enough in the movement to join in. It wasn't too much different from 1963, Mahalia said, even though he had such a big reputation now. With some, that made them more against him. Like a seesaw: if they no more than squeak, somebody heavy getting on going pop them out of sight. What about Dr. Jackson (head of the National Baptist Convention): anything Martin could do to lessen his antipathy? A strong word there— Better not count on that, Mahalia said, especially him having to fight last convention to hold his presidency: let's get Boy Baby over here, see what he think (Rev. Thurston firmly in Martin's camp). Mayor Daley? Mahalia believed he would see the need. 'Course he's got his politics; he'll wait for his step; them slum landlords not going let up on him. Al Raby, he's a preacher you can work with. who'll *do*; yeah, head of the Chicago Coordinating Council of Community Organizations, but that don't mean they coordinating. Who, him? Forget that one; he's just flunking for Jackson.

Outside was wearisome, often bitter work in bitter cold for Dr. King. He was staying in a slum apartment on South Hanlin for the experience, the symbol of it (street-gang territory that made Halie shiver for him). But you got to put that aside, get this food in you with some suption to it; what you think, you going disgrace Mahalia, come to Chicago and turn into a shadow? It was good to see him laugh. Everybody relaxed, Minnis entertaining them too. They fell to singing gospel. "Talk about soul food —*this* is soul food," said Halie. She'd seen Martin go through the door that led off the music area and assumed he was going to the bathroom until she heard him—clear to her ears although the song was in sway—heard his voice from the dark of the middle bedroom: "Father, why? Why me, Father?" His voice pierced Halie, but she made no move. He would want his privacy. First chance, though, she checked Mildred, wondering if she had misheard. "I heard it too," said Mildred, ears fine-tuned by years of on-stage signals. "Honest to God?" said Mahalia. Mildred nodded. Halie stared inward. "There is something peculiar about that man I feel in my soul," she said slowly. "To me he seems like he's always *pressing* to do something, like he had to leave. And yet he'll take time to laugh and joke with us."

And talk with her about her temple. "I want all faiths to study the Bible there, especially for integrated missionary work—where children could be taught love instead of wrath," she explained, feeling Martin look deep into her heart. "And my temple would help young people get an education. We will never have any peace with ignorance. Even ministers: too many don't have enough education in the Bible, they have taken hearsay. There are many things we are confused, perplexed about. All ministers should be versed in the answers. And I want to build this temple all on my own," she finished, exhilarated. Martin was with her all the way, saw it clear. Why couldn't Col. Reilly, down at Mayor Daley's office, why couldn't he grasp what it was she wanted to put up? It was so simple.

She could talk to Martin about Minnis, too. He had prayer with her; prayer for a troubled marriage.

ALL HER PRIVATE concerns were quickening. Every few days, a letter from Mr. Mindling on the newest tour date. Word from Townsend on which two Christmas songs for the single with Percy Faith. A letter from Mrs. Bowles—in India, now Chester Bowles was ambassador—wanting to promote a tour for her there. A wonderful woman. India. She'd tell Mr. Mindling. Mainly Mrs. Bowles was remarking on the death of their friend Shastri in Tashkent; how his wife believed absolutely she could have saved her husband's life had she been there. Not through physical aid, but by strong prayers. "There is an old Hindu legend in which Savitri is caring for her husband who is about to die. The King of Death comes, stays for a few days, and then leaves because of Savitri's strong prayers to her Lord, which succeeded in turning back the King of Death." Mahalia was struck by the wonder of God's weavings; here the Hindu people really believed in God too; in prayer; just had their own ways. She thought about it, humming.

Her pressing problem now she had prayed over and knew what she would do: she'd buy this piece of land at 89th and So. State and put Minnis in business. He couldn't stop talking about his hotel. It was his own idea. He had never loved her more. But peace on this end tipped up the other: Mr. Mindling was really carrying on about her wanting to borrow on the $100,000 privilege from Columbia. She wanted to use that, not her temple money, to build the hotel. "Mahalia," said Mindling, "you call that a 'worthwhile investment'? That's what the contract says, you know; it's got to be a worthwhile investment."

"You explain to them, Mr. Mindling."

"Mahalia," he said, trying not to let his fury at this—this—get into his voice, "Mahalia, what does he know about running a hotel?" That, she wasn't worried about. "He used to run his own house, and you do that, you just add one on, one on." The agent groaned. Sometimes it was almost too much. He started to put together the papers. He'd drag his heels as much as he could.

BEFORE MARTIN'S big announcement, he walked the slum streets accompanied always by the press. Easy to see the plaster crumbling its steady rain of lead poisoning; easy to smell the broken plumbing; harder to spot the big rats but the evidence there in the bitten children, the horror tales. Painters and plumbers were apt to bob in his wake, hurriedly launched by landlords abruptly uneasy about building inspection. Hadn't the mayor said King had the city's cooperation?

But Chicago was a big city. Dr. King could not walk out the big, deep trouble and the mayor could or would not talk it away. March 16, a Halie still gaunt threw herself into a program with Belafonte, Poitier, Dick Gregory, to make sure of a crowd for Martin's Freedom Rally. He committed himself to an anti-slum campaign no matter how long it took or where they had to march, or how often. But *when* they marched, he said, it would be without violence. "Our only weapon is love."

"Yes, Lord!" exclaimed Mahalia. Before he could march, though, Halie must hit a wider road with its own perils: her first U.S. concert tour since spring of '64. Mindling had booked her solid from the end of March into June. She was letting Minnis be MC. She'd never needed one, but that's all right. And he was going to play his flute.

MARCH 31, 1966, Celie was in her kitchen. She could see her flowers in bloom, but she was not light of heart. She had just so recently buried

Puddin. He was in her mind when Mahalia appeared through the back door sudden as a vision; so fast, she stumbled. "Put the house up for sale! Call the junk man! Puddin gone, Aunt Bell gone, you have nothing to live down here for—nothing! I want you to come on up there and live with me."

"Precious," cried Celie, "you come on me kind of hasty. You haven't given me a chance to think it over."

"Nothing to think over," said Halie; "I want you to come by me."

Celie was overwhelmed as realization came. "Oh, we locked arms and we kissed, and we kissed, and we kissed. And when we finished with that, she say, 'I mean it. You have nothing to stay way down here for, and the rest of the family way up in California. And you take such an interest.'

"Well, baby, let me think it over," Celie said hesitantly. "There's nothing to think over," said Mahalia; "do it right now."

Next day Celie was no closer to knowing. The Lord had put her in this place to lead the way to populate the subdivision, but that was long complete. Halie's house was so beautiful. But what if Mahalia should precede her? Still she *did* have a will to go. She spoke it to Aunt Bessie, who went to just crying; she cried very easy since her husband gone. "Sister, don't you go! If you go, I be all alone; they all gone now but me. Oh, who going look after me?" Celie clearly could not go off and leave Auntie crying like that.

By then Mahalia had sung her way up to Virginia, down to Miami Beach, up to Cincinnati; singing hard, with the people look like couldn't get enough. If Mr. Mindling and Minnis just wasn't like two bulldogs.

Lou Mindling swallowed his ire. Again! Just politely reaches in and takes a couple of thousand out of Mahalia's money and she lets him get away with it. If she'd just stop this insistence on cash—

Back to working the East Coast now; Mr. Mindling packed it in there. If she could just make it on to Norfolk . . . Baltimore . . . and oh thank You Jesus! a week home. Waiting was word the First World Festival of Negro Arts, held in Dakar, had awarded its *Grand Prix du Disque* to Madame Mahalia Jackson.

It wasn't really a week *off*. In this one gap, the end of April, she was sponsoring Martin at a church: a fund-raising, but just as much so he could raise more support. Rev. Abernathy, into the Chicago campaign now, found Mahalia about the one warm spot in a cold, cold city. Cold in more ways than one: "It was much more difficult to promote support than we anticipated. The whole tempo had changed—a lot of people were attracted to the so-called militant leaders."

Following Mrs. King off the plane in early morning, Xernona Clayton shivered. Mrs. King must feel it even more. She was singing in Canada the following night; and this was a chance to spend a day and a night, and go to Mahalia's program. BrrrRR! whatever else that slum apartment was, it would at least be warm.

The church was full; they were happy at the response. And wasn't it just like Martin? "Let's go over to Mahalia's." That night, 8358 So. Indiana was oddly clear of others. Nothing but talking, laughing, eating, singing. But it seemed just the *best time*.

IT WOULD BE different, she'd agreed. Minnis had kept on that her program should have more "change of pace" and she'd let him go on, fix it with his friend William Marshall, that he'd grown up with in Gary. The actor would share the bill this June 2, 1966, at Constitution Hall. She was nervous some anyway about this first whole concert in a big *big* hall since she got sick. Could she hold her end for the Lord? She'd get Joe Bostic to come say what he thought. He be surprised to see William Marshall . . . "a great actor; got a voice like a organ. Him and Bradley was big friends in New York in the '30s," she told Louise Weaver on the phone. "But look, Lou, I called to tell you come on, go up with me tomorrow; you can be with me before the graduation." Louise's nephew Sammy would graduate from Howard University the day after Mahalia's concert. Louise said she couldn't leave early, but she'd call Mahalia at the Hilton soon as she got in. There, that's fixed. Lou sure going be surprised when she find out Halie's giving Sammy a commencement party after Constitution Hall. But that's a good boy.

BEFORE THE CONCERT, Joe Bostic came by. Minters was there. And a small white woman: Jeanne Gardner, a psychic woman from West Virginia, Mahalia said. The woman offered to read his palm. Why not? Hmph: "a long life and a violent death." At least it wasn't a heart attack. The palm business had caught Mahalia's eye, he could see, and now she asked to have hers read, too. "The woman just looked," says Bostic; "then she closed Mahalia's palm."

"What it say? . . . Come on, Jeanne, what it say?"

Mahalia couldn't get another word out of her. What Bostic was hoping for was a private word with Mahalia—she'd asked him to come. But it wasn't in the cards. Or the palm. He'd go check on the lights for her. He might have detected a small nervousness there.

Was she that good, or were they just so glad to see Mahalia again? The question was in the back of Halie's head as she made sure Sammy's party got off right. William Marshall enjoying himself. Boy Baby too. And Sammy's friends. Some of these people she didn't know. Look at Minnis hanging on what Eddie Robinson would call a chick. But wasn't Louise proud! Here they go with the pictures. Gingerbread Simmons got a camera, Louise got a camera; more bulbs popping than the *Washington Post*. Where Minnis? She was beginning to— Almost 3 a.m. Just got to turn on in. Once in her robe, stretched out, she phoned Joe Bostic; he's the original night owl: Come on over, tell her what he thought. Joe Bostic wasn't surprised at being sent for, or at finding her propped up on the pillows, in the bed. He *was* surprised that Minters wasn't anywhere around; up to some of his activities, probably. Mahalia didn't waste time. "How did I do?"

"Mahalia, it was a *tremendous* performance," he said earnestly; "you were marvelous. You have certainly had a resurgence of strength." He began going into the fine points where she really thrilled him—he could see she just *feasted* on this kind of thing; she got such a *little* of it. Mahalia was drinking in his words—eyes held by those eyes that fix you like a safety pin on the wall—when Minnis walked in, and frowned. "What are you doing?" he asked Bostic.

"He's talking to me about the concert," Mahalia said. Minters continued to eye the New Yorker steadily. "You know, I don't appreciate your being in my wife's bedroom," he said, and turned to Mahalia. "I'll tell you how good you were when we're in bed together."

Joe Bostic cringed for Mahalia. The lack of decency! With her marvelous, acute sensitivity for the correctness and fitness of things—class all the way, instinctively; like Joe Louis.

He left.

THE TOUR ENDED in Tennessee, and Halie promptly headed for New Orleans for her own date: Union Bethel Church needed money for its restoration after a bad fire. It was Rev. Lutrelle Long's idea to make it a banquet-concert at the Jung Hotel. With William Marshall performing, and Minnis on his flute, and all the eating, it sure wouldn't be no strain. She didn't know the Jung Hotel, but Laurraines said it was a big one right on Canal St., and Laurraines had called the people to be sure they gave Mahalia Jackson a good suite and courtesies. Last place a prophet is honored is in his home land.

Lord! this girl really got them to roll out the red carpet. A real red carpet from the Delta plane on up the ramp and won't let a soul off before she made the walk—like royalty. And Delta's VIP Room for interviews. Just sending out the press something else new. And every sort of drink. Look at the eyes pop. And here a *long* limousine. New Orleans has changed its foot for Halie.

One thing hadn't changed. Family court in session. The main one she had in mind to help now was her own idea: put Aunt Bessie up in a little cafe business right around home, for men who don't have their wives to cook for them. Way Bessie could cook gumbo, that ought to go—and take her mind off.

ELLIOTT BEAL could not believe his ears. Standing in his own dining room, the man his guest, and saying he'd had Beal investigated. "I wanted to find out just who you were," said Sigmond genially, "what kind of a record you had, so I had the FBI investigate you."

I ought to say "What the *hell* do you mean?" thought Elliott, outraged, flabbergasted, but mind your manners. "What do you mean?" he asked formally, as he might in class.

"Mahalia talks so much about you and Professor Hogan—we will be needing men like you to travel with us, and we are prepared to pay. . . ." The amount sounded good but the "we" stuck like a fishbone in Beal's throat. "So first, you see, I had to make sure you were the right kind of guy."

"And what did you find out?" said Beal precisely. "Oh, you were clear," said Sigmond airily; "you're clean." Well! Beal was glad he had at least brought that out, in front of all.

Mahalia could find no place to hide.

63

June 16. Minters was so mad he was almost swelling up before her eyes. Mahalia said it again—low, distinctly. She had prayed over it, and what he wanted to build on that land was no more than a motel, and with what went on in that type place, she could not have Mahalia Jackson associated with it. Didn't he hear what she said? They'd just have to— Yes, she did mean— No, she would *not* change her mind. The Lord— Didn't he see— Don't you yell at me! What little Sigm—

Incoherent with rage, Minters swung at her. Missed. Turned away. Mahalia was astonished. And for the first time, afraid.

THEY MADE it up. It was a big disappointment, but they'd figure something else out. One thing Minters figured out was that he could help produce the album she wanted to cut at Greater Salem. Right in the church. Halie yearned to get back to her root music. She believed if Townsend would hear the real thing in church, Columbia would get rid of some of this extra they wrapped 'round and around her 'til she felt like a roll of cotton and wasn't sure but what she sometimes sounded like it. "All right, Minnis, that be a good thing. That's right, you my personal manager. You can sure help with that album. I'll tell Townsend."

MARTIN WAS HAVING to seesaw up and down the country between Chicago and Mississippi. James Meredith had been shotgunned; protests and marches spewed up, and militant splitoffs. But he would not abandon the whole Chicago investment of time and money and body. Mayor Daley publicly smiled and promised, spoke of "the same goals," cited building programs and vast projects—to most blacks, he was for *them.* A substantial number of whites thought so too. What did King expect? The mayor gave the niggers everything they wanted. Punching at the realities was like punching a giant marshmallow; any dent shortly disappeared and the smooth white surface was as it was. Something dramatic—some catalyst—was missing. Doggedly they worked out a series of open-housing marches through white neighborhoods where blacks were barred: kick off the campaign, give it a newness, with a big Chicago Freedom March and Rally at Soldier Field. Mahalia could be a big help on that; they'd use her name on the posters. The tension, the tired of the days found ease at Mahalia's at night. They came to her like moths, to where beaten wings were mended.

She was supposedly resting from her long tour. Actually, she wasn't feeling too good, but she kept her promise to sing at the women's prison in Indianapolis: got into the spirit and gave them—this must be seven numbers, thought Eddie Robinson. *It Don't Cost Very Much* just tore the place up. Then they went to visit Gov. Branigin, who asked Mahalia to autograph a picture and gave her a key to the state. She made it up to St. Louis, too. Then she checked into Billings. Dr. Barclay shook his head. At least he could make her rest a few days—although here were another couple of visitors: Rev. Joe Campbell and a Washington friend, Bill Davis. Strict no-admittance was the doctor's preference, but by now he knew Mahalia would wither away without other human beings around her.

HALIE WAS SHAKY but the crowd couldn't have told, giving them the shout: yes, Lord! that blazing July Sunday, her cousin John Stevens hard put to keep the umbrella over her head. There were 40,000 in Soldier Field to hear Martin's three-point rally cry: for open housing; for equal justice—scarce in many precincts if your skin was black and your pocket empty and you're noooobody; for jobs—a prickly, dangerous corridor: blacks barred from Chicago's trade unions and most ill-trained (barely dusted with such education as passed their way) for those nebulous "better" jobs even had they been open to Negroes. All this, all this, must be *changed.*

Two days later: the first Civil Rights march for open housing. Mahalia wanted to go, and they wanted her to; got her to go on WBEE to urge the women especially to join in. "Clean your kitchen, clean your house, and then go march for something better!" said Mahalia.

"LOOK WHAT I get paying attention to Martin!" Halie panted, proud and shaken too. They hadn't thought to be loved on that walk, but they hadn't expected rocks and bricks and—worst of all, somehow, to Mahalia, to see Nazi swastikas. Only they were *American*. And more mob against them than marchers: "Do you know I was *out* there, Butch? Crazy as I am?" she demanded, her voice on the telephone recreating the drama; "out there marching with *that man!* You know I haven't got good sense, don't you?" Butch laughed. She knew Mahalia; not going to tell Martin no. Halie turned to Russell Goode. "See why I don't want you mixed up in this thing? I don't want to be calling Chattanooga, giving your mother no consolation message." She wouldn't even let him go see where Martin was staying: "Too dangerous, baby; you can get carved." Mahalia was worried to death because Coretta had come up with the children; staying in there with Martin. Halie sensed something mean, bad in the air.

They marched in sun, and they marched in rain, but they would not again let Mahalia go: "We need you here when we get back." Mahalia wrote Mayor Daley. "In the name of the Lord let them march, but give them protection. We don't have a toothpick to fight with." Mayor Daley wrote back thanking her for her letter "and the comments therein." . . . It was nice to hear she was improving in health each day. "Kind regards and best wishes." Pray, then.

This had to be the worst. They'd all been briefed that Gage Park was a tough, segregated white community. But to Ralph Abernathy this was like a heat wave, the sound and the feel of hate on both sides and ahead as they walked, walked, silent, walked through rocks, bottles, spit, curses, jeers, debris. Police kept the mob from the line of marchers but some dodged in, got in their licks on those black bastards. In the forefront with Dr. King, Dr. Abernathy felt fear—who wouldn't? Martin did too—but he was exultant: here in living color going into the nation's conscience and, they hoped, Chicago's, was proof of what had been kept tamped down, under cover. Dr. Abernathy wondered if they would really be able to win a victory—and was it worth all this? The barrage of screaming was almost harder to take than the rocks and bottles; those you had a chance to dodge. God! Martin was down!

Debonair Chauncey Eskridge was shaken, staring at the front-page picture of Martin, bent, holding his head, struck by a stone; he looked agonized. And Mahalia was giving him a dinner party tonight! Eskridge was invited. It did not occur to him to look for Martin any place else. He burst into the house. "I expected he'd be half-dead in the bed," says lawyer Eskridge, "and there he was laughing and talking. 'What are you doing? Look at the newspaper—" Dr. King guffawed. "That thing really didn't hurt me. I bent down and the photographers thought I was in pain! It didn't hurt me." How could the man laugh!

Nobody wanted to dwell on it, and Martin said it just once: "I have never before seen violence on this scale—hate like this. Nowhere. Not anywhere in the South. Not even in Mississippi have I seen mobs as hostile, as hate-filled."

"This was 'Bad Sunday,' " rumbled Rev. Abernathy. Martin caught Halie's brooding, worried look, and laughed abruptly. They got the message and turned to their party. "Oh, we had a great celebration that night," says Eskridge. "We had champagne. And all this food. And Mahalia! When she was serving us, that's all she wanted." Minters was happy, playing host, joking with Eskridge—his kind of man. Mahalia tried to make sure everybody had everything they wanted. This thing was not ended. She told Martin he better get Coretta and the children out of that neighborhood.

WHEN THE BLACK West Side exploded, Mahalia's first thought was to thank God that the Kings' children were all staying at Rev. John's—his six to play with their four. Martin and Coretta were with Halie, the slum apartment almost unbearable in the heat and its point made. The riot had flamed in an argument over fire hydrants—police and city workers had shut them off. "But they *always* let the hydrants run for the kids in summer!" cried Mahalia. Dr. King decided he'd ride down there, see if he couldn't help calm them down; Mahalia might come, too; nobody in the world held in more esteem there than Mahalia Jackson. Sigmond announced he was going with his wife.

Baby-sitting with Sigma—So. Indiana wholly peaceful—Mary Lou Jenkins was frightened to her core: her son had never been into anything like this, and she hated to see Mahalia in it, either. Of course Mahalia had lived all over those bad neighborhoods, maybe she *could* do something with them. She switched off the radio; she didn't want Sigma hearing that: looting, snipers, fires; what was the world coming to. On the West Side, Martin spoke from the car; Mahalia spoke and sang too, fighting the Devil with the Lord; but what was loose was past words.

When they came back, it was with reinforcements. Mrs. Jenkins checked past the newcomers for her own— Intact. And prepared. They'd stopped by Helen Maybell's restaurant and got a whole mountain of steaks to cook, bringing Mrs. Maybell back with them. Sigmond announced Mahalia was to stay put, he and his mother would take charge. "Me and Minters cooked steaks that night for galore, and when he wasn't cooking steaks, Minters was mixing drinks for the crowd. Rev. Raby came in the kitchen *still* upset; he said he never got pushed like that before in his life."

Late that night, meditating, Halie thought of Aunt Bell—sweetest person who ever walked this earth. "If there's a person," Aunt Bell had told Halie and Celie . . . the cousins sitting under the hackberry tree after Halie jumped those Italian boys meddling her from the neighborhood . . . "if there's a person will give you a stone, you give them bread and leave them in the hands of God, for God can right all wrong. And God can turn hate into love." Blessed Aunt Bell—what would you found to say tonight?

THIS WAY? She'd been searching actively these weeks, praying God to guide her to temple land at a price that would leave something to go on with. And searched it out! Then it was to get. She'd felt burdened because she had to leave that—and Martin. But look like his people going get some action on their program. And listen here, her too! Hallelujah. Go ahead, make them the offer, she told lawyer Aldus Mitchell, assigned to her real estate. "What you mean, am I sure. Go 'head!"

64

The West held its own confusions. Not to match Chicago, but look like peace fled down the road. In Oklahoma City, it's Mindling being fly with Oral Roberts when this fine preacher giving Halie his blessing, promising a long life. "Isn't that beautiful?" Mahalia beamed.

"How does he know," said Mindling, "how long you're going to live? But if it makes you happy, you do business with him." Sometimes Mindling just put her off him entirely. Now Minnis digging her about him—"I wonder if you have noticed—" She noticed a lot of things; not just Mr. Mindling.

Then it's Minnis and the boy Yancey and Eddie Robinson and who all here in Los Angeles picking at each other. Mildred think she hold it in, her not liking Minnis, but it's about as covered as wallpaper. And everybody running to tell Halie tales. Got bad as Chicago. Maybe Halie don't want to hear all that. And maybe some of them signifying wouldn't mind having him themselves. There's a lots to this thing; Halie's not blind. Anyway, why can't the rest be more like Celeste, and Johnny? 'Cause when she *did* know it, she couldn't let it pass, and now Minnis and her had another big fight about him running around and he got that little white-handled silver gun in the bedstand he say for protection but she—oh, it's a mess! And he could talk her around, pet her around every time. What they need is a desert island—but where Minnis going run the streets then?

AND MILDRED—what to do about Mildred? Look like her problem getting worse. Me having to send for Albert Goodson to Portland! And that last session. And can't get her money straight. That's a sickness with that girl.

Now it's Mindling pulling about this date, that date, for Europe. How she going put her mind on all that?

THEY COULDN'T. But they did. Those skunks found out it was Mahalia

Jackson want their property in Chicago and jacked the price up so high she'd have to put it out of her mind. Listening to Aldus Mitchell, she felt like Minnis had actually connected that swing he took when he got so mad this last time. But by the next night, on the phone to Aunt Hannah, "I'm looking again," she said; "I'll find it." God's not going let that temple go. She'd put her mind on this session.

LORD GOD, been worrying this *Not My Will* like a dog with a bone half the night, Celeste and Margaret keeping on, keeping on. 'Course Margaret going to—it's her song. Bad as Oozie Robinson at Mt. Moriah. "May," said Margaret, "now just try to remember it's *If I ask for things*."

"I got to get me something to eat," said Mahalia, "I'm hongry." The sisters snacked, fatigue claiming them, while Mahalia tucked in a substantial portion. "Okay." Mahalia walked back to the piano, the two trailing uncertainly. Listen to her! stronger than ever and we're both worn out. What is it—2 a.m.? Mahalia broke off, not satisfied with her sound. They started again, Mahalia singing softly, tentatively, still half-following Celeste's cues. Suddenly Mahalia gave full voice and Margaret's hair rose on her arms. "That's it!" cried Celeste. No stopping Sister now. They fell in behind her—not rehearsing, singing the song for itself—senses quickening. Hallelujah! When they came down to earth, Margaret couldn't let it pass. "You're still saying *If I ask for a thing*."

"I like it that way," said Mahalia. She would record it tomorrow.

Just as well Minnis missed all that, she thought, in bed and drowsing over her Bible. She wish he'd come now, though. It was lonesome.

Now it's Townsend. Can't stand Minnis, screaming about the session, about the way Minnis conducting it; Minnis mad, nervous as a cat crossing broken bottles and don't know how to act, can't nobody talk to him, leastways Townsend. *He's* mad 'cause we got to finish up the album from Greater Salem out here. Halie had dished him out, where nobody could hear. And look like Townsend would know better than to try to put those white people with Thurston's choir; ain't nothing good going come out of that.

If Sig had just left it at writing the arrangement, thought Dick Yancey, out of flak range. He has just fallen apart; it's too much pressure—and it falls on Mahalia, of course. Look at her trying to cover for him, and Townsend in the booth screaming "Let's go! Let's go!" So mad he's really shaking. Look at the Great Galloway.

GWEN LIGHTNER tried to hear over the whir of the hair driers. Thurston Frazier was talking so fast. He was at Columbia, he had to get right back. "You better get down here right away, Gwen, see what you can do. Mahalia's mad at Mildred, says she's not getting the right chords; and she's mad at the choir."

It was *A Mighty Fortress* causing all the trouble. It wasn't well known to Gwen's group, but the white chorus didn't sound too good either as Gwen walked in. Sister really got the storm flags flying, rushing over there like that, waving her music at Mildred. Mahalia tripped—fell backwards—thrust her arm out to break her fall—took her full weight on that—bounced the rest of her to the floor—and pandemonium broke out. At Good Samaritan Hospital, Halie discovered she'd broken her wrist. And she'd better stay a couple of days for observation.

"MAHALIA, DO I have to?" Yancey grimaced at the hospital tray. He'd no sooner walked in than Mahalia made him close the door and told him to eat up that food. How come he always managed to get there when she had a tray to get rid of?

"Now, that's good, they not going know," said Mahalia. "Celeste and them brought me something fit to eat." Townsend brought her news even better than that: this new album put her at 300 songs recorded, another first for gospel singers. Not too many any kind of singer got 300 songs on record. That's what Townsend said, and he the one knows. Humming a little, easing the cast—ooh, this thing weigh more than she did—she came full round to the thought that that was a long lot of singing. No wonder Halie feel so tired.

Somebody suggested she could sue, get a lot of money—Columbia was bound to have accident insurance. "No, baby, I wouldn't sue them; we been together 15 years. But I sure almost broke my behind while I was breaking my arm.

Home, and this thing really troubling her. Best thing was to get your mind off. She'd rehearse that song she got Laurraines to send airmail special, if she could get the "stars" to come over to play. That young man she just run into was a wonderful pianist; play classical, gospel, boogie. She was keeping her eye on him. If Minnis didn't use the extra ticket to Europe, she might take him along to play a concert on her program. " 'Course what Europeans really like is that I'm an American product, I believe in being completely natural," she reminded Laurraine. "That's why I sing spirituals in dialect." She could speak well as the next when she wanted to. And she was tired of these Negroes looking down on the old folks' ways. She knew some of these young ones calling her Uncle Tom 'cause she was just herself. Like she told Studs Terkel when he got mad about that—let 'em talk; talk's cheap.

Lord, Lord; so tired and Dr. Best come here, woke her up at 10 p.m. and then didn't give her a thing. Where Minnis? He better be seeing about that passport, if he going to Europe with her. Something about his birth record, and he got to get affidavits. It put her in mind of her first passport, in '52: wasn't for that, Minnis be just six years younger. It was 1912 in Aunt Bell's Bible 'til the hurricane washed it away.

EIGHT DAYS after her accident, she went down to Columbia and completed the session—that day, and the next. "Nothing but the grace of God pulling Halie through this," she told Gwen, shifting the heavy cast. And much as she had risen to the two days, that much lower it felt like she'd slipped down the mountain. Maybe she ought to tell Mildred don't come tonight. No, might hurt her feelings and her having trouble with her leg. . . .

Halie couldn't believe it. She could *not* believe it. Of course Mildred was not herself, all her problems crowding her. But that she could have it in her heart! Alone, Halie walked back to the kitchen, the scene still surrounding her like the dark of night. She called Celeste, who came rushing over. Then she went to bed and called Aunt Hannah. Brother John was with Hannah, making his off-season visit, so Hannah held the receiver off a little to let her godchild listen: he was going ask her all about it, anyway. "After all you have done for her!" cried John, breaking into Aunt Hannah's soft, considering response. "I'd have done more than send her on back to Chicago, tell her to get herself together."

Hannah wouldn't tell it. Neither John. She didn't want any to-do. Grieved as she was, Europe was too close to make a change if she didn't have to. After all this time they been together. Maybe if she prayed on it harder. She called New Orleans and talked to Doodutz, got the family goings-on; called New Orleans again, and for a long time Laurraine listened. It seemed more than Mahalia should have to handle.

THIS THING weighed a ton. It did. Almost daily she summoned Dr. Best to So. Norton; she and Minters were staying in a ground-floor apartment. But she was so tired from having to do everything with this one arm. "People say 'can't.' I learned there's no such word as can't," she sighed. "I'm dressing myself with one hand, and combing my hair and everything. But it sure makes you tired." She was on the phone to Laurraine. They wanted to make a TV program on her life down in New Orleans. "Tell 'em I'll come first of November; that be good." It caused her to think back on her life up to this September, 1966. "You can have dollars and cents," she said earnestly, "and if you don't have friends, you don't have anything. This is the very heritage of New Orleans, *my* heritage, and it is dear to my heart; that's the way I was brought up." If Minnis just could see that. "He is a good man, Laurraines," she said, measuring her words, "but I don't know—I guess I'm selfish, I'm used to having my own way for so long, and I'm used to having my friends around. I played the fool and got married. I was lonesome. I wanted to share what I had. Look like sometimes you ask God for something and you don't know what you're asking. I've been with my people so long . . . the whole family fuss at me from the babies on up if I don't do like they think I ought to do. But I'll suffer a long time because of the principles of my religion."

Sigmond was discouraged; if she kept this arm business up, the whole

Europe thing was liable to blow up. And how could she expect him to stick around with her dragging? Mother Parks watched Minters as he sat around with her son. From all Minters would say, he cared for Mahalia, "but she has her way too, you know," he said defensively; "she has a disposition that's hard to get along with. She nags me." He didn't say any more. Mother Parks figured he honored her too much *as* a mother, to be telling her tales on Mahalia. She did notice Minters was drinking more.

SEPT. 24, BACK in Chicago and this cast can't come off yet. They'd been going to leave Oct. 1 for London, Paris, Germany, Spain—soon as the cast was off, she told the reporter. But now— "Mr. Mindling? I'm really sick. You got to tell those people in Europe. We got to put it off." Help me Jesus. Call Dr. Vondrasek—he'll come out.

Dr. Earl Vondrasek came just as soon as he possibly could; he was fond of Mahalia. He found she had a fracture of the left wrist and complained of palpitations. "She was very weak. And nervous. She was taking anticoagulants that somebody had put her on for her heart. I thought she was somewhat depressed, and I gave her a 'mood elevator.' "

BEING AT 8358 Indiana instead of in Europe wasn't helping Minnis's disposition. On that motel business again, she told Boy Baby; she just didn't feel a religious woman ought to be mixed up in that. "And when it came to her religious beliefs, Mahalia was a rock," says Rev. Thurston. He could see it was a major irritant between the two.

And this thing of Minnis chasing around. . . . Aldus Mitchell listened in real disbelief: He knew Bertha; she'd have no part of Minters. Absolutely not. And *that* was why Bertha wasn't living at the house any more? He couldn't get this thing straight. It was the first time Mahalia had mentioned her marriage difficulties.

Just what did Minnis think he was doing to earn $500 salary? With no expenses, everything charged. And all those "food" checks she was writing him—$50 extra every week. At least he was honest about it. Chivas Regal was expensive, and she wouldn't have it showing up on her charge. Funny thing. No matter how much he put in him, he never acted drunk.

RUSSELL GOODE was delighted. He was playing for Coretta King, being presented in concert at Ebenezer Baptist, and since Mrs. King's sister Edythe was with her, Russell excused himself to see Mahalia. There'd be no time later. "Tell Coretta I want to see her," Mahalia said, so, concert over, the three sped out to the house. They hardly had 10 minutes before they had to leave for the airport, but it was something. The only thing was the way Minters was acting. "But I didn't say a word; and I hadn't said a word to Coretta or her sister beforehand. But when we got in the taxi,

Coretta said she did not like the way Minters acted, the way he looked at Mahalia: 'No wonder she can't get well.' "

Oct. 4, Mahalia and Sigmond checked into New York briefly. Mahalia signed for them as "Mrs. S. Galloway." That ought to please Minnis.

Home. She did not feel right. Could be something nobody found yet—

She mustn't crowd her schedule any more, Dr. Barclay said carefully. No point dwelling on "sarcoid." It was already a near-miracle there had been no disfigurement of the skin.

"Minnis, hush; they going stay." The struggle at home over the visitors never went away. Minters was certain they exhausted her; she'd never get going again. He had plans, as manager. The last thing she needed was all these people praying over her. Now Mildred had reason—

Mildred really wasn't in too good of a shape. Sometimes Eddie Robinson had to come ask help for her. Mahalia signed the check for $20 and marked it "salary." She'd try to use Mildred for some dates, when she got back to singing. Maybe the Lord would stretch out His hand, cast out the demons. Right now Halie had her own demons to wrestle.

Oct. 26, Sigmond invited the press to come for a piece of Mahalia's birthday cake. Mahalia explained she'd just been resting at home since she broke her arm, but she was much better now, thank you. Next day the newspapers showed a beaming Mahalia feeding cake to her husband, Sigmond Galloway, in their home. The caption said, "She was born in New Orleans Oct. 26, 1912." Might as well get the record straight while she's stopping up a few mouths.

65

Thanksgiving was a big day to Halie—she'd picked up Aunt Duke's and Hannah's tradition. But this was special: the two families *together*. Minnis's mother was cooking the turkey to bring it over for that evening. ("Cooked all day," says Mrs. Jenkins, "but I didn't mind. I did a lot of cooking for her.") Sigma was with her grandmother for the holidays—spent most weekends with her—so Sigmond came to get Mrs. Jenkins and Sigma and Emma, his oldest sister. Big Alice and her husband were there, and Aunt Hannah, and Bertha. So was Mahalia's friend Rev. Joe Campbell; need at least one minister for Thanksgiving. And Virginia "Gingerbread" Simmons, the manicurist friend who been so nice when Halie was *real* sick, came to do her nails and feet. Louise and Snooks were due if they got away in time from dinner with Louise's first husband's family, the Weavers—they kept up. Some other drop-ins would show. Always plenty of food at Mahalia's. Everybody had to pile in through the rain, but that didn't put a damper on the party, and Mahalia made no objection as Sigmond served drinks . . . and drinks. Watching the Galloways' glasses, Aunt Alice thought it was sure a different way than their family. Time to eat. Let's see this Gary turkey. . . .

They shifted into the family room and sat around talking, laughing. Mahalia was pleased, but she was tired, too; she was ready to go on up. Anyway, it was time for Minnis to take— Minnis was gone. Had not said where, and here his folks to get all the way to Gary in the rain! The Mahalia Jackson information network was excellent. She dialed. "Get back here and see to your mother and child!" Mahalia was close to flashpoint. That he could do her like that! before people! Sigmond came back furious. Calling him like a child, embarrassing him at another party—he was a man, wasn't he? Did he have to account for every minute of his time?

The Lawsons were dropped off first, then he turned onto the broad throughway to Gary, windshield wiper slapping at the rain. It paced Sigmond's temper. He stalked back into 8358. The party had broken up. He rushed upstairs—naturally; propped up on the bed. He was ready to let her have it! He'd show her who was a man! Higher, higher, feeding his fury with pent-up resentments. At its peak, when words failed him, Sigmond swung at her—Halie ducked—and his hand smashed into the dresser beside the bed. He howled, anguish lacing his anger.

HOME FROM Mahalia's party, Rev. J. Tallefarra Campbell decided he'd get his family some ice cream. The way to the drugstore took him past Mahalia's and he saw both Minters and Mahalia outside. He slowed and tooted his horn in greeting and was startled to hear Mahalia cry out his name. He pulled to the curb. As he did, Minters took off like a shot in his Chrysler. "What happened?" Rev. Campbell called even before he was out of his car. He could see Mahalia was crying. "Minters swung at me so hard, he hit the dresser and broke his hand!" Rev. Campbell started to run back to his car; he'd go get that— "Wait a minute, Rev," Mahalia said, "I don't want you to get in trouble. Just go to Billings, see how his hand is."

At Billings, Rev. Campbell and Minters sat almost three hours in the crowded Emergency Room before Minters could get his hand attended to: broken, all right; it needed a cast. When the two returned, cars in close formation (Rev. Campbell was going to see this thing through), they found Big Alice there, and Bertha and Gingerbread and one new element.

ALDERMAN Bob Miller listened, shock turning to anger. In all the years he'd known Mahalia, almost since she stepped off the train, he'd never heard her like this. Sounded scared half to death: Minnis was fighting her—tried to beat her—would he call Mayor Daley or somebody to come out here, keep him from fighting her? And hurry, please? She was calling from a phone booth. She didn't know how soon he might get back to the house. "The man has to be crazy," he muttered. He called the mayor. "Between us, we called everybody," says Mr. Miller, "sent everybody over there: the police department, someone from the ward office, one of my secretaries."

Minters would not leave. He lived here, and he wasn't going anywhere. His wife could do what she wanted to. Shaking, crying, under guard, Mahalia packed a bag and went to the Sheraton Hotel. Downtown. That felt safer. Minters had swung on her before, but tonight—she couldn't explain what it had done to her. It wasn't just the force of that crrrack! She could have had a broken jaw. But worse was what she saw in Minnis's face in that instant. She saw the Devil. In Minnis. Just thinking back, it chilled her blood.

Downtown three days, she couldn't stand it; she moved out to the Del Prado, overlooking the lake, in the same section where she'd busted suds on day's work. She had a special spot to go sit and look at the water, hours at a time. She was still hiding out, but she was closer to Hannah, and Billings, and some of her friends. She wished Emma Bell wasn't away. She called Lou. "You busy?" Louise was giving her last piano lesson of the evening. "I wanted you to come, stay all night with me. . . . Take a cab; I'll pay it when you get here."

Louise left a note for Snooks, who was working nights. He wouldn't mind—especially when his sister Emma Bell was down in Clarksdale, couldn't be with Sister. . . . "Mahalia?" Snooks. "Look, any night you need Louise to stay, it's okay with me; I don't want you to be alone." Friends. A person really needs friends. Good thing Lou was a night owl like her, stay up all night talking. She was so nervous she could hardly be still, but too tired *not* to be. Lou tried to take her mind off . . . talked music . . . old times 'way back. Sister was going to come 'round; in a few days she'd be ready to go by Louise's and go over some music. She had a lot of new music to learn for Columbia, and the Del Prado didn't have a piano. Halie tried not to think of her piano *and* organ sitting at the house. The Devil probably playing her piano, having himself a time. She hoped he didn't mess up— She turned her mind off that. But she had to think about it. She'd told Ming to draw up the papers for a divorce, and she had to go over her grievances with him and Mitchell. Chauncey Eskridge was keeping hands off, "didn't want any part of it"; he was "too close to both sides." Hunh! That told her something about *him*. First thing she wanted, she told Ming, was to get back her house. What right Minnis got to hold her house?

She went to Aunt Alice's a few days, then moved to Aunt Hannah's.

That's where she ought to been in the first place. Misery had topped her reluctance to burden Hannah. "Burden? Burden!" cried Hannah, deep voice rich with welcome. "Who you always come to?"

Dec. 10, 1966, the American Friendship Club gave her an award as Ambassador of Friendship, "in recognition of the friendship and goodwill carried forward by you to all individuals and groups, and the impact of your influence which exemplifies the principle of equality and the best of American ideals. Your daily life has demonstrated a deep sense of responsibility toward humanity."

Dec. 13, the rift and intent to divorce hit the papers. It was big news—and swelled: one paper said Minnis's arm was in a cast. Hand. *Hand*. Dec. 15, a forlorn, dejected Mahalia sat slumped on a bench in the lobby of the Civic Center, waiting for Bob Ming. He was filing her suit for divorce from Minters S. Galloway for "extreme and repeated cruelty." Dec. 19, lawyer Stanley W. Cooke, acting for Sigmond, filed *his* suit for divorce, asking alimony and division of property. The two main points of his petition were, first, that she had induced him "to live in a mode and manner to which he had now become accustomed," and second, that because of her wealth, she "is able to retain the services of the finest legal talent." To a *Sun-Times* reporter, Ming "humbly conceded the second point."

Next day, Mahalia and Ming lost their first legal test in the struggle: the judge ruled against her bid to evict Minters.

AT 8358, Sigmond rolled some white paper into the typewriter, sat in thought, then in fits and starts, ripping out, beginning again, he typed a statement. Finally, he made a clean copy and read it over:

"Mahalia, my wife whom I still love has the greatest contralto voice in the world today.

"Being a college-trained musician, and having worked in all phases of the music profession: jazz and recording, television and movies, for seventeen years, the world and I know this to be true.

"After we were married I gave up the pursuit of my career and devoted my life to my wife's happiness and her career.

"In all tours, I have assisted in securing other talents for the program, master of ceremonies for many programs if it were necessary. Play flute on record dates and arranging and conducting voices and orchestra on two dates for an album, that has been released.

"For someone you love, you don't measure things you do for each other in money. Within my wife's good Christian heart she knows these charges that her friends and employees who have kept rumors in the air ever since we were married, are false and untrue. I deny each and every one. If my wife wants a divorce, I will give it, but not on false gossip.

"And as far as living in our marital home, the judge ruled in my favor because it would be a tragedy to take our daughter out of school in the middle of a semester and move back to California and try to put my life back together again."

He stared at the page and put it aside. He did not issue the statement.

HALIE WAS frantic. After Minnis filed his suit based on how much money she had, *Jet* had come out with all her finances, her property, all her private business. ("That had to come from Minnis—and not but one way *he* could have got hold of all that," she said grimly. "Didn't I tell you?" cried John Sellers, come to nurse Aunt Hannah—she had taken so sick. "Didn't Aunt Hannah tell you?") With her business in print everyone felt free to talk about it—and ever since the judge let Minnis keep the house, people were saying what was sinking at the bottom of her heart like a stone: "That man could end up taking everything you have, Mahalie."

"I'm scared to death of that, Laurraines," she said; "I'm striving against the Devil."

Letters began to come from "divorce experts" soliciting her case. One said he would *guarantee* her husband wouldn't take everything she had.

NOWHERE, NOWHERE was there any escape. Even downtown shopping, where she'd hoped to lose herself a while, a clerk she'd never seen before offered sympathy and indignation at "that no-good husband of yours" in a voice that carried in every direction. It shivered Halie's soul. Among the friends, opinion was almost unanimous—but not quite. Emma Bell Smothers, back from Mississippi, had been keeping Mahalie company most days and many a night for weeks. Not that Mahalie wanted to talk. She spent hours reading her Bible, kept it in her hand, especially the Psalms. That seemed to Emma Bell about the one sure way Halie could stop herself from crying—and what she was crying over was her marriage breaking up. Wasn't a thing but that, to Emma Bell's mind, making Mahalie go down to these hospitals day after day, sometimes from one to another, crying about her heart palpitating 'til Emma Bell knew they were sick of the sight of her, especially Billings. Get back from the hospital nice and quiet, lay down, eat something—and minute it get dark, have to get out, go by somebody house, if not but Alice. Mahalie was hinting something about her "sarcoid" giving trouble, but Emma Bell believed Dr. Barclay and them just humoring her.

Missie Wilkerson was direct as she'd always been since she first stood by this girl when hardly another hand was turned her way. "Mahala, if you love the man, if you want him, take him back, go on back home. Don't listen to any of 'em." No doubt in this world, to Missie; Mahala loveded the man.

Lou Mindling got the story quickly from Polly and, when he came, told Polly he thought Ming could handle the divorce. On his own, the agent got hold of Minters and offered him a deal—cash to vacate—but when he told Mahalia, she was scared, she said; she didn't want Minters mad again.

Mindling dropped it, but he was glad of the chance, when Minters started in, to look at him and say, "I can't believe you're real. You're the phoniest guy I ever met. Don't come to me and tell me all that bunk, 'cause you don't con a conner, you don't hustle a hustler." Treat him like a little six-year-old baby, that's the way to handle him.

Irving Townsend came and found her in tears. He tried to reassure her: the man *couldn't* take everything she had—which she seemed certain was going to happen. He didn't think he'd made any dent in her fears. She knew he had no respect for Galloway; hadn't she married without telling him? Any way you looked at it, it was a mess.

Rev. Thurston found himself a sounding board for both Mahalia and Minters—Minters insisting he was just trying to protect Mahalia, that there was no privacy in the home. He admitted he was angry about not getting the motel, but it was people had come between them, he insisted—people. In her turn, Mahalia slowly sifted the issues and the discords, wondering, measuring, praying, but always she brought up her fear. Rev. Thurston said he didn't think this was Minters' ordinary disposition, that rage.

To Rev. James. Lewis—a devoted satellite—Mahalia mourned it must be God didn't want her to have Minnis, that it was flesh speaking. "Well, Mahalia," he said, "just let it be."

"That's the only thing I can do."

Eddie Robinson brought mail in by batches—mail from strangers, from friends, most berating Minters, offering advice and prayers. It was more than she could take in, but one letter she treasured, pored over. Dinah Shore was going through the same kind of thing—divorce trouble. She was glad she could offer Mahalia a lift, some encouragement. Mahalia had given her a lot of courage at times when she needed it.

Dr. William Barclay was on sabbatical from the university, working with the U.S. medical laboratory in Montana, but he came in frequently to see his family. His medical relationship with Mahalia remained established, but he saw her at her home, "more in the role of friend." He was touched that Mahalia should be consulting him about the possibility of a divorce, but he wasn't surprised. He had seen her in tears during the marriage, too. She wanted him to speak with her lawyer as well, and time and again, when he was in the city, the three talked. The physician was deeply concerned; this kind of pressure was definitely aggravating her sarcoidic illness. He cautioned his team at Billings, to assure empathetic care.

Ming's preparations for the divorce went forward. Halie wrenched her attention to the books Polly brought to Aunt Hannah's to go over with her. Polly had her own system, and she was the only one knew where anything was. Brother John grimaced. He hadn't thought Mahalia still had that woman.

SIGMOND GALLOWAY was tired of the wall of silence. He had expected to hear from Mahalia by now. He telephoned Aunt Hannah's. if anybody would know, she would. "Where's my wife? I want to see her."

"She's here. Wait a minute." Mrs. Robinson walked into the bedroom where Mahalia was stretched out, John keeping her company. "Tell him to come on," said Mahalia. When he came, Hannah, hesitating, came back to ask again. "That's all right," said Mahalia mildly, "I'm not scared of him, you can let him come in."

At a look from Sigmond, John left. Aunt Hannah stayed up front. From the kitchen, John could barely catch the murmur of voices. Minters had been meek and mild when he came. Gradually the sound swelled—his voice got loud, Mahalia's got loud: something about a ring . . . he give her . . . want it back. . . . Aunt Hannah came hurrying from up front to see what was going on, Brother John on her heels. "This nigger done made me mad!" Mahalia flung out. "Minters," said Aunt Hannah, "you better go on out." He left.

"Abusing me," Mahalia glowered. "I don't know nothing about his ring."

"I got the ring," said Aunt Hannah.

AS CHRISTMAS neared, it was hard to stay in Chicago. In the cover of night, she got Eddie to ride her past her house. Seeing it, she cried, she was so sad: her house was lonesome as she was, lonesome and dark. Dec. 22 she went to Cincinnati, to Uncle Porter's. While she was there, the newspaper came out that she was on the Gallup poll nominations for "Most Admired." She came back after New Year's: Ming had another hearing coming up soon on the house.

BROTHER JOHN blinked. He was used to Mahalia pulling him out early, but this was pitch dark. "Come on, get up," said Mahalia, "come go with me to Ming's. We got court coming up."

"Now?" mumbled Brother John. "Mahalia, that man don't want you bothering him now."

They were in the Loop at 6 a.m., Eddie Robinson driving. It was cold, and John was *evil*. Nobody up at Ming's, of course. "See? What you getting—"

"He TOLD me!" They went downstairs to the drugstore and drank coffee; then Mahalia went up and got herself let in and stretched out on the couch in Ming's waiting room, covering up with her old Persian lamb coat. Eddie and John slumped in chairs. About 7:30 Bob Ming walked in, down early to catch up on paper work. "Mahalia! What are you doing here at this hour?"

"You said be here at 7."

"I told you 9 o'clock. Now go on home and get some rest."

"I got these folks to drive me down here!"

"Mahalia, you can't lie here like this, I have clients coming; what will they think? Now go on home."

Trailing behind her in the corridor, "I sure am glad you came," Eddie said to John; "Mahalia's about to worry me to death."

The day did not give her back 8358 Indiana, but the judge did issue a restraining order to keep Minnis from running up bills on her.

IT HELPED to have Celeste in town, with Margaret. Their father had had a heart attack, and one memorable day, the sisters brought Mahalia to spend the whole day at his house. She managed to brighten him—"you so good-looking, *you* the man should have married me"—but as the day wore on, the front wore thin and she wept, great sobs tearing from her. Minnis still in her house! Celeste and Margaret and their stepmother went down on their knees to God, all three crying through their prayers. Mahalia joined them, and the exhortations rose in a great fountain to heaven. When they rose, May felt better, the sisters could tell.

JAN. 12, ABILENE, Kan. She'd brought Win Strache and John to spell her, but even so—weak as she'd been? with her heart pounding? She acknowledged the call, and walked on stage. She was taking few engagements, although she sang a little around Chicago for churches. She was gaunt; at the point of thin, moving toward sunken; and yet—bathed now in the lights and the music and the message, an illusion of strength and surpassing beauty fused with the dignity of her rising passion. The difference in this woman on stage and off! thought John Sellers, the old awe in him again.

Two weeks later, she was glad to be shedding her mink aboard a plane headed for Florida. Better than Ming's idea to "get some sun in the Islands"—with her maybe going to lose everything she had! Mr. Mindling had made a special rate for twin concerts in Jacksonville and Tampa; then the man switched that at the last to Orlando. Halie's sixth sense stirred. And it was a mess, just like she'd thought. Mindling trying make him live up to his contract, promoter shouting, her acting mad—you got to impress some people—him finally admitting he was having to cancel Orlando. Lying man. She was getting too old for this kind of mess. She sang Jacksonville anyway, then flew back to Chicago. Let him and Mindling and that Florida booker fight it out: each one threatening to sue. She'd have done better to stay home and sing her benefit for the East Garfield Park Co-op that she'd postponed to June. Well, the Lord just might be saving her. He works in mysterious ways. Thank You Jesus.

MINNIS ASKED for a *jury* trial? for a divorce? Lord, help me. Why would he do that? Halie pondered it, wakeful, nervous, in the nights. Bob Ming and Mitchell said so much the better for her, but Minnis wasn't dumb—he must see some advantage.

HONOR IN HER own state. That counted. Her spirits rose as she and Louise took the train for Springfield on Saturday, Feb. 11. She was to be formally invested as a member of the Lincoln Academy of Illinois, and receive an extra distinction given only one other among the 19 due recognition as distinguished citizens: as the two laureates, she and Hugh Downs would receive the Regents Award. Nobel Prize winner Charles Huggins was being installed as a member in the Medicine and Health category; Buckminster Fuller, in Creative Arts; but Halie was more interested that her friend "Kup" Kupcinet was being recognized in Communications and Sen. Paul Douglas, in Government—that was nice, especially since he'd lost out last election.

When the train pulled in, they had 30 minutes to change into formal clothes and get to the Governor's mansion, but they made it. Gov. Kerner welcomed Mahalia as an old friend and admirer. Quite a few of those were around, it seemed to tiny Louise, from the crowd swamping them. Louise had hardly got her fill of looking before it was time to leave for the main event: the 6 p.m. convocation.

To Halie, the big picture of Lincoln behind the speaker's rostrum seemed to speak to them all. It brought Papa close—Grandpa Clark, born in slavery. Her citation rolled on . . . "service as an artist in the cause of civil rights . . . without word of bitterness or hate . . . great interpreter of her people's emotions and aspirations . . . lustrous career as a singer . . . but mostly for her impeccable taste in rejecting the unworthy and choosing the high road of fine musicianship, personal dignity, and lofty aim . . . great artist and distinguished American."

The tears inside were joy. She was even gladder now that she'd said what she did when they asked her to speak: "Let Mr. Downs be all the speaker; I'll give my message in the best way I know how."

She sang three gospel songs that seemed to swell beyond the great spaces, hallelujah in every note. And amen in the fervent response; even the reporters. Then as ceremonies ended, she sang them out with the Lord's own news.

THE NEWS in the divorce case when she got back left her shaking. Minnis's lawyer said he'd settle out of court for $150,000 cash. "I wouldn't mind giving him *something*," she told Ming and Mitchell, "but—"

Ming offered $10,000. It was refused. The gauntlet was down.

It was no time to be getting a letter from Stuart Kadison (the lawyer who'd handled the Songs of Praise-T.E.C. business which had become another mess) asking her to tell him directly if she wanted him to negotiate a deal for a motion picture based on her life, as "a Mr. Yancey" had called to request. Well, she'd told Yancey it would be good to have a picture of her life, but— "I don't think I am capable of taking care of such an important matter at this time," she wrote the California lawyer. "I am getting a divorce from my husband and I have been so upset, and so oppressed. I will be out there when Townsend tells me to, and we'll get together then."

BUT THIS—THIS had to be decided; it was affecting her big business. Easter Sunday, Mar. 26, she was singing a doubleheader at Lincoln Center, and Columbia was recording it live. She planned to use Louise and Eddie, but here Lou said she could not find a qualified organist in Chicago who could take the 150-voice massed choir Rev. John wanted for Easter Sunday at New Covenant. No use thinking about switching piano to Mildred —that was finished, for anything big. Eddie said he knew somebody good on organ—studying at American Conservatory. Mahalia was dubious. "You ever heard of Charles Clency, Lou?" He sounded classical. "I know *of* him," said Louise. "He's supposed to be a wonderful organist; gospel, too. And Eddie says he can read." Well, that's what she needed for Lincoln Center. Townsend was putting guitar, bass, and drums to her piano and organ. Bring him, she told Eddie.

Ten days before the big date, slim, reserved young Clency debuted for Mahalia at Ball State College in Muncie, Ind. Rehearsal was one thing, but what she heard that night, under the pressure of her moods and changes, decided her: Clency was staff organist. For his part, when Charles first answered Mahalia's summons, he could not believe it was Mahalia Jackson he was standing before. He had seen her—not met her, but seen her—five or six years before. Could this be the same woman? She was absolutely changed in looks, she had gone down so, he reported to his wife, as excited as he ever allowed himself to be.

A week after Muncie, they were in New York, rehearsing.

On Easter Sunday, 1967, Mahalia drew on a reservoir of power that startled her anxious intimates. Few in New York's Philharmonic Hall—certainly not the critics—knew of her private trauma, and none could have guessed from the performance they shared with her: singing for her soul, singing for the souls on the brink of God's mercy, singing for the glory of her crucified, risen Lord. Whitney Balliet—exposed to virtually all the music there was, as critic for the *New Yorker*—felt his senses stir. "Miss Jackson does not give concerts; she creates an experience. . . . She expresses in her gospel songs and spirituals an ardor . . . that no saint has surpassed. . . . All were stirring, but one, *Were You There,* was nearly unbearable. It was . . full of graceful ascending steps . . . deep, aching, bent notes. She pushed the beat around to suit herself . . . she used husky tones and shouting silences. She *became* the words and music."

Twice that day she made this magic. And, "Thank you . . . thank you . . . thank you . . . it was nothing but the hand of God. I'm the instrument."

Martin Luther King came for the 8:30 p.m. concert; stood backstage watching, listening, with Mrs. Mindling. "Hold onto him," the agent had told his wife, "we'll all go out together later." But, he cautioned, "going out with Mahalia is having a Pepsi, that's a big night out." What Halie really wanted to do was have a chance to just sit and talk with Martin. They could have got something to eat from the hotel room service, but she didn't like to hurt Mr. Mindling and his wife's feelings.

One thing, she wanted $200 cash to buy herself a wig tomorrow. "Just slide it under the door," she told her agent. He did. It wasn't until he was in his own room and in bed that he thought, What if someone walks in the room and picks up that $200. What a stupid thing I did! But if it makes her happy. It was like having a little kid, trying to make Mahalia happy.

She stayed over a couple of days, luxuriating in the Americana's extra appointments. A little refrigerator, and a phone in the bathroom. That was high on the hog as you could get.

Of all those at the Easter concerts, Townsend's was the only acute distress. He'd seen this high and known the low, and he begged her, begged her, to stop doing these concerts alone. "And stop trying to sing for three solid hours at a stretch. There's no need for that; nobody expects it and you're not up to it. They'll pay another act to work with you, for God's sake." He was wasting his breath, but he had to say it. Halie let it be said. No use to tell Townsend it was for God's sake she couldn't stop. She had to sing 'til the Lord come, and when He comes, you sing 'til He lets go.

IT WAS LIKE jumping into a pit to be back in Chicago's troubles. She was tired of trust betrayed, and she didn't just mean Minnis. She was getting of a mind to change some living when she got out from under that. Restless in the evenings, she got Teevee Hall to come: Tee-o hadn't been around in a long while, since after she and Polly had that run-in and Polly slapped her. Teevee brought her dictation pad, and the two worked the night 'til Halie got caught up. She got some of her best ideas at night. "And you put this down exactly like I tell you."

One thing she did not entirely appreciate from Mr. Mindling: While Halie was at Aunt Hannah's, he'd taken to sending her business papers direct to Polly at the house Polly'd got herself on So. Yale, not far from Mahalia's—with little notes to Polly like "Just keep Mahalia CALM! Will talk to you about my conversation Ming!" Treating her like a child. And even before, taken to sending notes "Polly and Mahalia," soandso. Who suppose to come first? Of course, Polly had all the files at her house now—they couldn't be at 8358, with Minnis there. Halie wasn't sure what all was at Polly's.

The waiting for the trial was a trial in itself. When she sang in St. Louis, she didn't linger. Something might come up. Since Feb. 1, Minnis had a job as bailiff for city circuit court, the paper said. He'd tried to pass it off, said he was "down doing a favor for a very big politician," but the sheriff's secretary gave him away to the reporter. $349 a month. Polly made more than that. That wasn't going to make his disposition any prettier.

HER MIND just stayed in a whirl with this thing, John could tell. He was bunched up down at the foot of Aunt Hannah's bed, where Mahalia was stretched out, and he was glad when she got off the divorce at least a while. "John," she said—restless, plucking at her robe—"go get me that book. Let me see what's in that book." Since it come, she'd had no mind to even open that book on her, with all the Minnis business; but the man wrote it said it was going be put out the second time. John fetched the book, got up by the bedlamp so he could see too—and was surprised at Mahalia's cry as soon as she opened the cover. "Look—at—that!"

" 'I dedicate this book,' " John read, " 'to my husband and my daughter —Sigmund Galloway, Sigma Galloway.' Well!"

"This book suppose to be dedicated to *Aunt Duke!*" Mahalia roared. "That's Minnis's doings," she added grimly. "You better read me this thing." John began, Mahalia exclaiming, correcting . . . "John, get me some paper. We got to change this if they going put it out again." John went back —skimming, reading portions, scribbling furiously—until he protested his hand hurt. "Mahalia, you got to fix this *whole thing!* Got your name on this book!"

"That ain't none of mine," said Mahalia, lower lip pushed up; "that's Minnis's and Uncle Porter's book."

"Mahalia," John said firmly, "you should have paid more mind." Mahalia didn't answer. Her mind was back on bigger problems. She couldn't even get a royalty check like this one Townsend's secretary sent—$18,573.32— without wondering how much of it going to Minnis. She had to be worrying with tax papers, too—here *and* Los Angeles. And she wanted to get the second verse of *Until Then* from Willa Dorsey—could no more remember it than walk the waters. She listened to the returns on the mayor's election— hadn't been able to put her mind to it but she hadn't neglected him—ha! biggest margin yet: 73% of the vote. Best wire him congratulations; he be too busy to phone him now, and tomorrow Ming wanted to talk to her again and see some more about her witnesses—be sure who be good on the stand and so on. They went to trial next week. This thing closing in on her.

On Joliet St. in New Orleans, Aunt Bessie just could feel the fearfulness in Mahalia's voice, asking her to pray. "Put your hand in the Lord's," said Bessie, full voice firm with reassurance. "He is going to lead your way. It's going to be righteous victorious; it's going to be righteous victorious."

"Yeah," said Mahalia, "but sometime the Devil gets his innings."

66

Aldus Mitchell ushered Mahalia and her friend Louise Weaver into the lawyers' conference room, Lou Mindling following immediately behind. Polly Fletcher was already there. She'd been very helpful in the lawyers' dealings with a lot of the people surrounding Mahalia, Mitchell reflected. He had a feeling they didn't really trust him and Ming, but Polly had taken over and directed them: "Go ahead and talk to the man, tell him what you know—nothing to be afraid of; they're not going to do a thing to *embarrass* you" . . . that sort of thing. They weren't going to use her as a witness, but she was being very helpful with the interrogations. Very. Polly and Minters at first were supposedly quite friendly, but without a doubt that had changed—he knew from each one that the two definitely did not like each other. So she could put her heart into getting rid of him now—aside from her obvious, to Mitchell, possessiveness about Mahalia. Mm-hm, Polly was getting a fix now on little Louise Smothers. Where were the pictures Louise had taken at Mahalia's commencement party for Louise's nephew in Washington? What pictures did she take? Did she actually have this woman on— What—Louise was stiffening, getting resentful of Polly's manner. Bob Ming took over: Louise would bring her pictures and be a witness.

As a legal exercise, the junior partner was looking forward to the trial as much as Mahalia obviously was not. It was the end of a lot of long, hard work—a big case for the firm, with all the attendant public prominence. Neither he nor Ming could be seriously worried about the outcome. And he was going to enjoy springing their surprise.

Selecting the jury took little more than the expectable time, since Minters's lawyer seemed to share the same aim as theirs: to have a thorough mix; men and women, black and white. With the witness slate they had, however, and whatever the opposition would come up with, Mahalia had to expect the case to stretch at least two days, maybe three or four, both Mitchell and Ming warned her.

Mahalia sat pulled deep within herself. The small courtroom was packed. Not everybody could get in. A succession of ministers came to give support to Mahalia. Allen Clark, Jr., was in from Los Angeles—given urgent summons by Emma Bell, acting on her own when she decided Mahalia needed *family* by her. As he ran a knowledgeable eye over the courtroom, Aldus Mitchell was intrigued to detect the two camps within Mahalia's camp: "Polly and a couple of other ladies; and the musicians and other people such as Missie Wilkerson and whatnot, and the ministers—Mahalia's ministers," he says.

The testimony mounted. Ming is going to take the guy to pieces, thought

Lou Mindling. That's what's needed. But he'd hate to be the husband or the wife in this. All this out in public. It was really getting dirty.

Eddie, Celeste, Louise . . . these and others of the intimates were the expectables, tossing their chips into the fire: an extra hotel room engaged when they were touring the Northwest—a woman brought in; the disputes; jewelry charged to Mahalia, a lot of it, signed for by Minters but not for Mahalia . . . Mitchell had told Mahalia at the time, when she came, bill in hand, asking what she could do about it, that there was nothing she could do except confront him. Mahalia had never mentioned it to Minters, but now the charge slips bore witness. The D.C. pictures told their story, a woman on one identified as one Minters went off with—named by Eddie, not Louise, who said when she left the suite, Minters was still there. The doctor at Billings gave evidence of what Minters said when his hand was treated: that he'd swung at a woman and hit his hand on a dresser. (The cast was gone now, but Minters's hand still had a bandage on it Ming made sure the jury noticed.) Mildred climbed painfully onto the stand and said Minters had a gun at his house in Los Angeles. Mahalia herself recited her woes, voice low, words at a minimum. ("You don't have to go into details," Ming had coached her; "just answer what you're asked.") But the climactic evidence was the surprise witness. Occupation: prostitute—retired.

The legal team felt pretty set up about this one. They'd used a proven technique. They asked the people they knew in the street—the stretch in the area of 63rd and Cottage Grove where a gang of hustlers hung out: Do you know this guy? What has he been doing? Who does he associate with? Fishing. They'd hooked one. She testified now that Minters had some high-placed political friends and she had done business with a group, in a series—Minters included. He was supposed to pick up the tab. He hadn't paid her. She wasn't willing to appear at first, she said—she was no longer in the business, she had a job and she was trying to be a respectable lady. But she had decided Minters was a no-good and nobody should treat Mahalia that way. On cross-examination as to what prompted her to testify, she said she felt it was her Christian duty.

SINCE LOU was past being a witness, Mahalia had asked her to watch one man on the jury. Louise had her eyes on all of them, trying to read *their* eyes, but she paid particular attention to this one Mahalia singled out. Over all, Louise reported, they sat very attentive, but their expressions didn't show any emotion in any way, even when Mahalia herself was on. But this particular man—a black man, stocky, well-dressed—he was with Minters. His face didn't move, but his eyes came to Lou as saying, "Man supposed to come out on top." Lord, Lord, Lord! save me from the pit. Still she couldn't help but feel sorry for Minnis. These people want to help her, but they were crucifying him, coming at him from all corners and him just sitting there, one man fighting his lone battle, taking it. But that didn't mean she wanted him to take *her.*

Minters's lawyer produced witnesses whose testimony mainly said he wasn't a bad guy but never touched on the charge of physical cruelty, Mitchell noted, pen busy on his pad. Minters's own testimony was toward demonstrating that life with Mahalia had thorns among the roses: The night she tapped him with the "His" stick (one of a pair of gag wedding presents) when Minters wasn't answering her as they lay in bed, he half asleep, he said. The night in Los Angeles, eating in their room after a concert, when a chicken bone she'd aimed at an ashtray landed on his plate and he said, "Don't do that again," she got so angry she wouldn't spend the night there—then because her arm was in a cast, he was helping her into a girdle so she could leave and he lifted her off her feet, and she shouted at him.

That was it. It put no weight on the seesaw, that Mitchell could see.

The one surprise witness for Minters was Rev. J. Tallefarra Campbell, subpoenaed from Los Angeles. Minters's lawyer took him over the events of Thanksgiving night and tried to get Rev. Campbell to say Minters had asked Mahalia, in his presence, if he had swung at her and she had answered "No." Rev. Campbell flatly denied he heard any such thing. Later, outside the court, Ming said, "Rev. Campbell, I would have asked you, but I would never have subpoenaed you." Rev. Campbell shook his head. Everyone knew how close he was to Mahalia.

THE SUMMATIONS were over. The jury was out. The tension was so great that when the call came that the jury was ready, most of Mahalia's inner circle stayed outside—unable to bear the impact if the verdict was against Mahalia.

Clear. Unanimous. In her favor, on grounds of adultery and physical cruelty. Judge Holmgren had to rap for order, but the instant he dismissed court, the jury itself poured from the box to surround Mahalia. Her first words were "Thank You, Lord! You won the battle! Saved by Jesus!" Then she burst into tears. Mitchell took her arm to escort her out of the courtroom. "Where Celeste?" asked Halie, looking around anxiously; "where Celeste?" Celeste was outside—one of those who couldn't stand the strain.

Louise Weaver looked over at Minters. He was leaving by himself. He looked—disillusioned.

Sigmond's mother knew the answer the minute her son walked in with his belongings. She'd stayed in court the one day, but that was all she could take. Telling those lies on her son! The only one fair was Louise; she'd called Louise to say she admired her for that. Anybody who had known Minters from a boy knew how sweet-natured he was, and clever. And why would he want to have a prostitute when he had women calling him? She'd asked Minters about that, and he said he'd never seen the woman before.

"Well, son," said Mrs. Jenkins, "that's it. I'm surprised at Mahalia."

"Mahalia didn't do it," Minters said; "those people around her did it. But that's all right; I'm going to write a book." The case had been a field day for the media. Now Minters went to his portable. He ground in some yellow second sheets first to work out what he wanted to say. Finally, he came up with about what he wanted to put in print:

"After reading this week's *Jet*, I couldn't help but spend many hours reflecting on the two years I spent with Mahalia. My wife has gone to great lengths to discredit me as a man. In spite of Mahalia's fame and fortune, she was a lonely, unhappy woman. I too, while not sharing her fame and fortune, was a lonely, unhappy man. . . .

"Our mutual need seemed our main attraction. My happiness in finding a good mother for my daughter, and a wife whom I thought wanted and needed me made me willingly commit myself to most of Mahalia's wishes.

"Giving up my personal pursuits in life and becoming my wife's employee was possibly the greatest mistake of our marriage. With this control, my wife made me the puppet on the string: In many instances being more an employee than a husband. . . .

"I would have been happy to have been the bread winner in my home. Mahalia knew of my financial limitations. . . .

". . . being overwhelmed by the love of the great Mahalia Jackson, I gave up all of my personal pursuits to be worthy of her love.

"I was gainfully employed before my marriage as a jazz musician. Since this pursuit would not add to Mahalia Jackson's public image, I willingly gave up this employment at her request. . . .

"I became devoted to her way of life spending many hours, night and day, helping her in her gospel arrangements. . . .

"I became content just to walk in her shadow. She paid me a salary of five hundred dollars per month even though ordinary musicians are paid twice this amount. I was willing to make this monetary sacrifice just to be a devoted husband and companion to Mahalia Jackson."

Sigmond read it over once more, and put it aside to think about. Mrs. Jenkins had heard the typewriter going, but she didn't know what on. The book, maybe? "I changed my mind on that," Minters said, brushing off the question. "It would just hurt Mahalia."

He'd watched Mahalia's face in court and thought he saw something there.

AT 8358 INDIANA, the first thing Mahalia did was change all the locks. Minnis might be mad enough to come in and kill her. Aunt Alice came to be by her, and Ike showed up, said quietly he was going to stand guard—she needed a man who could handle that fellow. Coming after he left the track, Ike sat up in a chair at night just inside the downstairs bedroom assigned him, the door open. Mahalia told him to go on to bed, he'd hear if anything was wrong, Aunt Alice was upstairs with her; but Ike said no, he'd rather be up. Uncle Porter came for a month; he and Ike could talk old times. But if Mahalia so much as grunted loud, Ike was up the stairs to check. Allen decided he'd come back to stay. Mahalia said he could work for her, she'd pay for moving his things back. He lined up an apartment in Louise's building.

Old friends who'd kept away made a point now of spending time with her—Bob Miller, Willa Jones, Nettie Irving, Louise Parnell, Cordie King, Ann Walker, Butch Thornton . . . these, and more. Mainly the stream filled at night, Polly trying to stem it by day; it was *not* good for Miss Jackson to be too tired and she had Dr. Barclay's word on that, personally. Weekends, Jean Childers often brought Mahalia out to Harvey, where she'd spend hours sitting on the front steps with Ken or just enjoying the three boys. Halie had a special link with Ken—he liked peppermint pickles, which Jean thought weird. The two would empty a pickle jar together, happily poking the candy in the center.

Besides the friends and the ministers came the friends of friends and the strangers. Often it was young singers seeking the magic formula. "I am famous through being disappointed," Mahalia told these, pacing her words. "Accept your disappointments, let them make you wise and help you work. There is plenty of room at the top. New singers come up like fine grass. But you must study your music. There are no more Mahalias. I am the last, and my success is the work of the Lord."

AMONG THE newcomers were some who disturbed Emma Bell, listening on the edge, watching them upset Mahalia's mind: catching her in the late hours and telling her things were wrong about her house, it had bad vibrations for her. Mahalia didn't answer, but she listened. It spooked Emma Bell. Besides, "you-said-and-she-said," that was all was going on; first thing you know, they be carrying tales on her. She backed away. "You know how to get me," she told Mahalie.

Mahalia did not necessarily stay downstairs because people were there; she had to get her rest. And at times, at night, she wanted some business done—done *now*. Then she got Teevee to come take letters. Polly was there some evenings, but she had her house and her husband.

Missie Wilkerson was, as always, in special status. And her husband Tom came to the fore. He loved Mahala—she'd been good to them in every way: paid their house notes, bought clothes, paid their taxes, fed them, helped raise the children, everything. Now since Mahala had a scared on that Minters was going to come kill her, Tom would let Missie stay weeks and weeks at a time, Mahala sending different ones out to pick Missie up on her job to stay the night, then drive her back to work next morning. Tom looked after their house, coming back and forth. For his part, he took over Mahala's garden—got some good greens coming—and he cut her grass, Missie taking her turn at the mower; not on no payroll, and never beg her: because he loveded her, Tom did. Big Alice generally cooked at night, but if she didn't and none of those flunkies around was doing it, while Missie was there she'd take over, get it done. Some of these people hanging around wouldn't wash a dish.

The one person who could not get to Mahalia now was Minters Sigmond Galloway. He tried repeatedly by telephone, but he wasn't going to come crawling at the doorstep.

Aldus Mitchell watched the tide wash back and stuck his foot out from time to time to curb the cash outflow. The lawyer's tactic was the wait. "Mahalia would call me to take care of a crisis but see it done right, and I'd make her wait—see if the people wouldn't work out the problem when it got really late—and somehow, the amount necessary would become reduced or the demand would melt away." It was hard on Mahalia when it was the cousins, spread from Louisiana to California. They thought they were entitled, that Mahalia was responsible for them somehow—and he thought she kind of felt that way. Somebody couldn't make his car note, or he'd lost his job, or whatever, and she'd fuss—say she wasn't going do it again—but she would, if Mitchell couldn't stall her. Curiously, it wasn't the aunts—the legitimate claimants—who made the demands.

Right now, she was furious with Ming *and* Mitchell. The divorce bill had come in and it was more than $20,000. "Some of those 'experts' who solicited you wanted more," Mitchell said defensively. It didn't make her noticeably happier.

Other than rehearsing from time to time, the issue of musicians hardly arose. She sang little more than twice in a month: a concert in Albany, N.Y., then no singing except for Sunday church for two weeks or more before she rose to an Israel Bond Rally at Chicago Opera House.

June. Still struggling to make each day. Subdued. Diminished. She prayed. She *had* to make it. To Europe. After the divorce went through, Mr. Mindling said he was going work up a tour for fall and she hadn't said no—fall seemed a long way off. Then Mr. Calamita and the other people at CBS/Columbia came up with a big TV show in Berlin Aug. 26—a gala to celebrate opening the color television network in Germany. Now Mr. Mindling just sent in a long thing from CBS about the contract conditions and how France wanted her for a festival either Aug. 25—no, that was too close to Berlin—or July 31, so that meant July 31. One thing: Mr. Mindling was still sending her business to Polly's house. That's not all's happening, but she'd wait on God's time. And still writing "Dear Polly—For yours and Mahalia info." Or maybe to Polly "care of Miss Mahalia Jackson—Tell Mahalia—" Like Mahalia can't read.

What Mahalia don't *want* to read is these prescriptions. She's tired taking 'em. But she can't just be sitting around like stale bread waiting for jam. And she was tired of the bed. She'd get Mr. Hunter to come freshen up the house. Get some new wallpaper on, some new draperies up. That's what she'd do.

Lord, please. After Halie falling down on Europe in '66 from that arm accident, she can't be telling these people Mahalia Jackson's not able. Please, Lord, You *must* be going lift the cloak?

67

Hallelujah! She was going make it. Woke up this morning singing, full of the word of the Lord. She'd go on down to Dawson's breakfast club. How many years she been singing for that man!

She sang as she ate and dressed. Must be Dr. Barclay being back to Billings got Halie well. Oh—'scuse me, Lord; Halie knows it's really You . . . but You got to use Your instruments.

What clothes she better take to New York for the movie for Mr. Rasky. They'd want to pick. Then right after, the Kennedy memorial program for CBS. *What could I do if it wasn't for the Lord* . . . that's one great song writer, Dorsey; he has wrote songs that's 20 years ahead of time—coming back again in style, yes Lord! *He's my—*

"Beautiful! Beautiful!" breathed Harry Rasky. The Illinois Sesquicentennial Commission should be happy; it was a beautiful sequence for *I Remember Illinois*. It really had gone off all right. Thank You Jesus. But this now, the program for President Kennedy—there was a sadness, and yet a joy for what he had accomplished; and he was gone to glory! Hallelujah. She was pleased with the letter she got about it from Jerome Schnur at CBS News. And more Europe coming in: Sweden writing Mr. Calamita at Columbia—well, CBS Records, they calling it now—anyway, Sweden want her. All those pretty blond people. She laughed, thinking about those flying teeth.

June 11, she and Louise went to keep her promise to the East Garfield Park Co-operative—the one she'd postponed for that Florida skunk. She liked these people's slogan: "Dear God, Help us to help ourselves." Looking at the long rows of local singers sitting on the high school stage took her back. Days later she went farther back than that, to where Bob Miller had put her up for her first concert out of church—DuSable High. This time for her own project, to help a convalescent home. Missie came with her, and Willie Webb to play—it *was* old times. Mahalia drove the car herself. The house was packed out, and they all got to shouting and had themselves a time. Halie gave them song after song 'til they could all come down—then she was out to that box office in a flash. Wasn't *nobody* going to dip, not if Halie's taking charge. They counted, recounted, proved it, then Halie had the tally of the exact sum written down and the money and the tally on top went into a suitcase Halie had brought. Willie Webb was waiting outside. Missie noticed in the car Mahala didn't say nothing about that money, so she didn't say nothing about that money neither. What you don't drop, you can't break. But Missie was glad *she* didn't have to tote that suitcase. She didn't want *none* of it.

When they got to 8358, there was company from out of town. "I didn't know the people but she knowed 'em," says Missie, "the different peoples that come. Well, she give *me* this money. Me. I went in the bedroom and I taken it out the suitcase, and I wrapped it up in a great towel. And I slept *on* the money. First I put it under me. But it were such a worriment to me, I put it at the *head* of the bed. Well, then it was such a big bundle, I put it at the *foot*. And it was so much money it looked like my foot was coming *up*. See, she couldn't trust nobody *with* this money. So she give it to me. With the note in there how much."

In the morning, "Mahala," said Missie plaintively, looking up to the height of her, "I hope you ain't got nothing for me to do today, 'cause I ain't had nary rest this night." Halie whooped. But she didn't have a hole in the money, like she had to make up for Martin Luther King.

Waiting for the people to come, she decided she'd let Missie's brother Sam go get her a new Cadillac—he was coming around again. She had the cash money in her purse.

IT WAS LAURRAINE's first chance to visit in a long while, and what luck Mahalia had this much time at home. Look at her: barefoot, ironing a cotton dress in the kitchen, singing away. She was natural as the morning. And let's hope she's out of the night.

Halie was in a mood to talk. "That Minnis; he used to embarrass me to death getting up there with that flute. Didn't no more fit than a pea in a pancake." But of his roving eye, "You got to expect that; that's men, baby." She took a telephone call, agreed to see what she could do, and came back to her ironing. "So *many* poor parents call me to send their children to college. They really got me overestimated that I'm rich, but they call and ask me for money and to do things." She hung up the dress. "Of course, what's *constant*, Laurraines, is people asking for advice. They worry me to death. They ask me things about these contracts. Some of them don't know how to get a song published. And they worry me to death about getting them on records. And how to become famous." There was no resentment in her voice; these were the facts of life, spoken as she stirred a pot of grits and settled into a kitchen chair with a cup of tea. She paused for a moment, thoughtful, and when she spoke, it was with a cadence, a flow, another voice, and new language.

"People don't realize that we have this tremendous power in us. Every one. Because Jesus said, 'These things I do and greater things will you do.' But we don't know of the simple things that is so powerful to us. And what's more simple than a man will sit down and get a thought, and that thought is applied into a great thing, as an airplane, or a big battleship, or *some* kind of a great thing comes out of it. But when he first thought of it, he didn't know—he never had seen it before, nobody else had created it before, but he didn't think it was so much. But something inside pushed him, and this thing became bigger than he had dreamed that his thought had brought to him—it just spurted into this huge thing. This knowledge *is* given us: we are the weak vessels. It is our thoughts that do not pull up on the salvation, which is the strength of man, is the life of man. If we would pull up on it and use this strength—it's right there within us. All the materials we need, it's right there; it's just you having the faith and the ability to accomplish what you want, and you will get it. God has already given it to you. It's nothing that man has made himself; it's the thought that brought it to his mind and helped him to magnify and to bring it to life.

"So I always think that the inside, the soul, knows just what's going on. Maybe the flesh is weak, but the soul transmits to our brain just what's what to bring out, to materialize. I believe that."

She returned to the room, to the kitchen. "You hongry?"

RUSSELL GOODE came from Chattanooga while Laurraine was still there. People dropped in from St. Louis. Hogan came weekends, working on his master's at University of Illinois. Beal would be up next week. And Walter Odom. Allen's son Donald came in with a group of ministers; doing fine with his pastorate out West. Louise was in. Nettie was in. Jean was over. The piano stayed warm and the house rang with gospel at night.

Russell played for her at Greater Salem and they went down to CBS to make a voice-piano working tape to send Townsend, to build some orchestrations. Mindling was talking now—talking to her, writing Polly—about more countries for Europe: Paris, London, maybe Spain. He was going to Europe himself next week, he said, to see the man in London doing the booking. He must be getting off from his job he just started at Paramount Pictures: "Director of Merchandising and Licensing," it said on this note he wrote Polly. He had told London to book her everywhere into October, so starting from August, that be another long one like '61. Longer: wouldn't be two weeks being seasick on the ship. That water was just about worth it, though.

Laurraine asked how many of her records had been sold since she started, and after they figured a while, they came up with 22 million singles and albums. Whoo!

They went shopping at Sears for some curtain rods for Aunt Alice, and while they were comparing prices and quality—one dark face, one fair, bent over the counter—a white woman walked over. "You look like Mahalia Jackson." Halie looked up briefly, with a smile. "You know, a lot of people tell me that," she said, bending back to the display. "I try not to let people know it's me wants something," she murmured while they searched out a clerk. "If they find out, the price goes sky high."

Halie was feeling so well, she thought she'd cook her Billings doctors a New Orleans dinner. Soon as she had time. Right now CBS in Germany was worrying her to death for her music for the show in Berlin. She didn't know where all that was; maybe Townsend *did* give her the parts after the session with Marty Paich. Townsend finally came up with *Go Tell It on the Mountain*. He wrote her to see in her files for *Without a Song* and *Let's Pray Together*. Well, if it's found, Polly's going have to find it. Halie can't even get in one closet door been locked and no key to be found. She got S&S Key to come in—and changed the front door lock again. Some people got keys she didn't want prancing in as they pleased.

EUROPE WAS close. A big date in Denver July 23; she went a day early to help the promotion. Then Toledo July 28. It was going to be a tight squeeze for Milwaukee and Oakland and what she wanted to do first in Los Angeles—but the way opened up. Not any way she'd have picked: Milwaukee had "civil disorder erupting." They cancelled out. Oakland was Aug. 7. That's when Mr. Mindling wrote Polly he'd try to be back from this second time to Europe—he said he needed to do the business firsthand. And 11 days after that, *she* had to fly the ocean. No telling where-all those Europe people would book her by then. But before Oakland was Los Angeles. While she was there, she was going do that benefit to help the Committee of Responsibility bring the Vietnam babies to U.S. hospitals. She'd promised Mary Ann Hooper—that sweet girl who booked talent for Steve Allen.

DICK YANCEY's short blondness was invisible; so was Eddie Robinson's toast brown as the two trailed Mahalia like pages. Entering the palatial home in Encino, her long, sequined gown gave off glints. She really looks sharp, thought Yancey, proud. On the grounds, where the entertainment would be held, Mary Ann Hooper stood checking off her list . . . Bob Crane, who would MC; France Nuyen, John Barber, Pat Collins, Robert Culp. More were due, but if just these showed, Dr. Peck should be happy—a real success in a town surfeited with fund-raisings. The $7.50 admissions were mounting beautifully; the guests were cheerfully paying their bar tabs. But more than that—her production sense felt the electricity. It would be a great evening.

It was. Mahalia came as the *pièce de résistance*—but nothing of the preliminary acts had prepared the audience for her. Surely they'll get the spirit! thought Mary Ann, and sounded a "Hallelujah!" She started the clap. Within seconds, the rest were connected and Mahalia turned the sophisticated event into a Baptist revival. The whole place tingling, she cried, "We go to church to have a good time, but I know you all realize that a good time means we have to dig down into . . . wherever you keep it—up here, down here (clowning, miming, making them laugh), wher*ever*. Who going get me something for the collection? Edward! give me my money!" Shy Edward, custodian of the purse, was too startled to move from the piano. "You know, I don't travel with my money too much, but—Edward, get up off the piano and give me my money!" Edward still found movement impossible, all eyes upon him. "Well," said Halie, "that's why I don't pay him very much." As she spoke, she reached down into her bosom, long, practiced fingers rippled, and she waved aloft a $100 bill. Through this, there had been a somewhat bewildered scramble for a receptacle—nothing seemed suitable. Someone thrust the top off a huge trash bin into the sequined arms. "Now I'm putting $100—there—now I want every*body* in here to give me $20!" Into the audience she went. Bills mounted like a crop of lettuce, and when she got back to the stage and counted, they had $700. "That's what I call *church!*" beamed Mahalia.

Through this, Mary Ann, Dr. Robert Peck, the whole staff sat stunned. It was Yancey—always quick to ferret details—who voiced the matter: "Mahalia, those people had already paid for their tickets and their drinks too." Mahalia stretched her eyes wide, voice bland as she drawled, "I didn't know."

"Now give me back my $100," she added briskly to Mary Ann. "That's Halie's temple money."

Lou Mindling took Mildred's call. She thought she ought to be the one to go to Europe; nobody could bring out Mahalia like she could. She was well now, Mildred said. The agent nodded as he listened. Whatever was wrong between her and Mahalia, it shouldn't count. He thought Galloway was at the bottom. But somebody was always squabbling and it smoothed out. He put Mildred's name down for a ticket. Mahalia would let it go, once it was fixed, since Mildred was all right.

Heart pounding again. Fatigue. And Europe so close. Dr. Barclay examined her thoroughly. New sarcoid lesions in the left eye. He'd been nursing a hope—sarcoid could burn itself out, often did; he knew more about it now than he had 15 years ago. Of course, severe damage— Still— He put her back on prednisone and cautioned her. Actually, he thought she'd sought him out as much as anything to mourn her marriage.

Ida Beal felt she'd better tiptoe. She'd planned to stay at the hotel where the Morticians Convention was being held, but Mahalia had insisted no. Now Ida was here, she realized Mahalia was actually *afraid* of being in the house by herself. Oh, she was upset!—just wandered in and wandered out; then upstairs and lay down in her room and stay there. Ida believed she'd bring some tea or something and try to make her come down. . . . Hmph! Took the tea but not the idea. Still, she wanted to have the people from New Orleans over for Sunday dinner. Ida would cook.

Mahalia pulled the bunched-up robe flat under her and poked her middle to see could she tell exactly where it hurt. Ida had such a nice sound, just a nice way to her, and gets things done. She sighed and sipped at her tea.

Sunday Mahalia made it to church, but she went upstairs right after and didn't come down even when Zenobia Lockett and Dorothy Lawless arrived. They went upstairs. When the two came down, Mrs. Lockett said nothing, just gave Ida a look—but Mrs. Lawless was one to speak her mind. "Allen," she said firmly, confronting the second cousin, "you all stop worrying Mahalia. From the looks of her, Mahalia is still in love with that man, and *she*'s going to have to give him up herself. And if she won't, that'll be her road to walk." A startled Allen had no answer. Anyway, these women didn't know Mahalia like he did.

Monday evening, Mahalia watched Ida get ready for the morticians. "What time you going?" Sometime around 6, Ida said. "You not a mortician."

"You know I work with Mrs. Lockett and I work with Dorothy Lawless at times. But if you want company, I'll stay here." Mahalia nodded, satisfied. Ida got comfortable and went downstairs. Mahalia wandered down. Milliard Lester, the live-in houseman now, stuck his head in. "Ida, you going to stay?" Mm-hm. "I was going to take a little run." Mahalia looked up. "Well, get Ida some Chinese food."

Mahalia stretched out on the couch in the family room with the TV on. Ida lay on the floor beside her. Time passed. "What is Lester doing?" Ida asked. "He's been gone so *long*."

"He just out there doing something. He don't have no business."

"I guess not," Ida shrugged. "He don't get out too often." A noise. They both sat up. Mahalia ran to the kitchen and got a big butcher knife while Ida closed the curtain. Mahalia stretched back on the couch, knife hidden from sight, so Ida got down on the floor by her but she didn't lie down. Another noise. Ida gulped and looked at Mahalia: just looking straight out toward that noise. Lester came in. "Oh!" gasped Ida, "I'm so glad it's you. I was scared to death."

"You didn't have to worry," said Halie, " 'cause I had *this*"—the butcher knife gleamed—"and *this*." It was a gun, pulled from under her other side. At Ida's look, Mahalia popped out laughing. It was the only time Ida saw her laugh—really *laugh*—the whole visit.

Europe was on the brink. Ida stayed to see her off, and Polly set about getting her ready to leave. So *many* things to tend before you can go, but

Halie began to hear echoes of "Ma-hahl-ya!" She felt a quickening of pleasure. Those people loved her.

But Mildred. What was she going do about Mildred. She eyed her steadily, with sorrow, hearing her out. She thought a lot of this girl. She just wished it could be another way. When Mildred had gone, Mahalia called Mindling. Three tickets arrived Saturday, Aug. 15, for the Aug. 18 Lufthansa Flight 431 to Frankfurt. They were for Mahalia, Edward Robinson and Charles Clency. Jim Mindling (the agent's son, who was in Paris) would join them there as road manager, for the flight to Berlin.

Shortly before she left, she felt her heart start that fast beat. Dr. Barclay was out of town. She called Jean Childers and asked did she know a doctor who'd come, and Jean called Dr. Quentin Young, who gave her something to quiet her and suggested she rest before she left. She called Mindling and told him about her heart. He told her the best doctors in the world were in Germany.

MAHALIA LOOKED up from checking over her clothes. "Ida," she said, "I need me a white velvet hat to go to Europe."

"Okay," said Ida calmly. "I'll go down to Novak and get a frame and some velvet." Halie grinned that quick grin of pleasure that you remembered. "And get me a brown," she said; "I want a brown to go with my suit."

The two hats were a full day's work, Mahalia looking on with interest. Johnny Jackson called from Los Angeles to wish her *bon voyage* and tell her the roof of the building needed fixing. Halie told him to see Mr. Mindling. And they put her on the plane in the white velvet hat.

CHARLES CLENCY glanced at his pretty young wife. On the plane for Europe! Mahalia had said it would be all right if Bea came. Six months ago the classical student hadn't dreamed he'd be seeing . . . he ran a slim finger down the itinerary: Berlin, Hamburg, Munich, Essen, in Germany; beyond that, Switzerland, Denmark, Finland, Sweden, Paris, London. And more dates might be added. He rose to go sit with Mahalia a while. He didn't mix much with the gospel crowd, but Mahalia liked you to check in. She really had picked up. She'd do herself even more good if she could keep her mind off her main topic of conversation—her divorce. She kept going over all the factors that led to the break. He could see she was rejecting what many people said was the prime cause—greed; she would prefer any combination of the dozen others. But—far be it from him; he preferred to mind his own business. He went back to Bea. It was only five hours to Frankfurt. You could say they were almost there.

EVERYBODY IN Berlin, it seemed, was delighted that Miss Jackson was there—sponsor Kurt Collien; the hotel staff, CBS-Germany, the press. After the interviews on arrival, she was supposed to have two days' rest before rehearsals, but radio people came for separate talks, and people about the show, and CBS record people, and some soldiers who wanted to tell Mahalia Jackson from home hi. More than any of that, though, there were three strange musicians—bass, guitar, and drums—to get with before Mahalia Jackson walked into any rehearsal. They were all right, though; Mr. Muller from CBS picked some good men.

Aug. 22 rehearsal went well enough, the first of four for the complicated show, *Gala Abend der Schallplatte,* presenting an international potpourri. Jim Mindling telephoned his father that Mahalia was okay "*so far.*" The agent relayed the word to Polly with an added "Let's pray together." Mahalia's segment would run just 6 minutes, plus the finale. But she was an old hand at this: four days' rehearsals meant four days' full time put in one way or another. Lights, cameras, orchestra, stage blocking, costume—they'd find a way to fill it up. And did. By Friday she figured it would've been easier to do a whole concert than this waiting around. But after the show she'd have a day off; then the Berlin concert for Mr. Collien and she'd be on her good gospel own.

Friday night her heart was pounding fast. She was frightened. They got a heart specialist in to see her—Dr. Rolf Schroeder. He checked her over and gave her a prescription. An electrocardiogram Saturday was all clear. That night, packed rows for the big event gave act after act high favor, but it was to Mahalia that they gave their hearts and hands: clapping on the off-beat, swaying, barely able to stay in their seats for *Go Tell It on the Mountain.* A sweating, excited Halie made it back to the hotel with Eddie and Jim Mindling and had something to eat in her suite; then Eddie stayed to keep her company.

Sunday morning, Charles and Bea walked over to Mahalia's suite—and stopped, startled at what Eddie told them at the door: an ambulance had been called to take Mahalia to the hospital.

Mahalia wanted Dr. Barclay. Next best, they could *talk* to Dr. Barclay about these pains in her chest. Jim Mindling reached him in Chicago, then had Dr. Schroeder speak. Dr. Barclay explained the medical history and his suggested medication. Monday morning, Dr. Rolf Schroeder, cardiac specialist at West Berlin Westend Hospital, issued a statement: Miss Jackson's European tour was postponed indefinitely, upon his advice. "The burden of performing would have been a great strain on her heart and could have led to a heart attack," he said firmly. In her bed on the second floor, Halie cried. She'd tried.

Cards, flowers, telegrams, telephone calls. Clency and Eddie alternated visits. There was no cheering her. Where was Jim? She was worried about business. What about all the contracts? This hospital was going cost a fortune. And having all these people here on her. She ought to send them back. But then she be here all by herself. Her heart got a lift as Paul Siegel of *Radio-TV Berlin* came in with a conspirator's smile. "You got it?" whispered Halie. "Yess!" He'd smuggled her in a steak. She was tired of this hospital stuff. One of the other reporters had promised to bring her one tomorrow. Ah. This look more like it, got some suption to it. Wish she could have some good old Texas greens. And— No! It could not be. "Boy Baby!" she shouted, bringing an aide running. "Hello, Halie," said Rev. John Thurston and, on his heels, Rev. Frank Sims. Vacationing in Europe, they'd learned just yesterday in Wiesbaden that Mahalia was in the hospital. Seeing them, Mahalia "almost jumped out of the bed," says Rev. Thurston—and started talking.

Sept. 5, Kurt Collien saw her off as Pan Am took her to Frankfurt and Lufthansa flew her to a welcome-home led by Boy Baby. An ambulance took her to 8358 So. Indiana. Thank You Lord! Her bed never felt better. Dr. Barclay came that same evening to check her over and said to be at Billings at 3 p.m. for an electrocardiogram.

Dr. Barclay's associates looked at the tape. That dramatic change, he pointed out, could be mistaken for evidence of a heart attack whereas, in fact, it was consistent with sarcoid disease of the heart. He had a talk with Mahalia about this, praised the care she'd had in Berlin, and said what she needed was a good long rest. He rose to usher her out. "Aren't you going to give me any medicine?" Halie asked. "Oh, you've taken too much already," said Dr. Barclay easily. "You know I'm afraid of dying," said Halie, making a joke of it. Dr. Barclay smiled. "I want to wait about 10 days or 2 weeks and let you get over that plane ride; then I'll bring you in for some tests."

Next day Halie dictated a letter to Polly to Dr. Schroeder in Berlin. She told him she was thankful to God and to him, told him of Dr. Barclay's praises, and asked: "In your examinations did you find any traces of 'SERCOIS' [sic]? I am a little worried, and I would like for you to write me immediately."

She was deluged with flowers—from Mayor Daley, from the Kings, the Hayakawas, from DJs, friends and fans. Get-well prayers through the mail came in a steady rain that was nourishment. She put Allen to work typing thank-you letters, while Polly took care of business.

"One thing certain," says Cylestine Fletcher with satisfaction, "Mahalia knew she could leave her business in my hands and know *nobody* was going to pick nothing out of *me*. I don't believe in all this talking—people trying to make themselves shine. I kept her business in order. Period."

KURT COLLIEN's appeal had been written while Mahalia was still in the Berlin hospital, but Jack Higgins of the Davison agency in London had not forwarded it to Lou Mindling until Mahalia was discharged. Now Mindling sent both letters to Polly and asked her to please discuss the matter with Mahalia: Collien said he was badly hurt financially, and "her doctors in Germany are convinced that Mahalia will be able to work full again in about

6 weeks. She could start the concert-tour in the middle of October." He also said that in fairness to his loss, the fee should be reduced. Lou Mindling wrote Polly he agreed on that, and to payment of some London expenses. "Also can we reschedule Europe and when?"

Mahalia listened, and pushed her lip up. She wasn't going back to Europe in no six weeks or five weeks; she wasn't going back 'til Dr. Barclay and the Lord said go. Tell him go ahead, though, she sighed, and pay the London man his money.

EASING INTO Billings, Missie cradled her pots and pans carefully. She had cooked up a good dinner for Mahala. She knew at the desk Mahala warn't supposed to have no visitors, but she kept immediately upstairs—she had the room number. But that door said "No Visitors." Well! thought Missie, it's *downstairs* "No Visitors"; I never seen no such sign on a *door*. Must be a lady done had a operation. Mahala is tests. Here I am with my ham hocks and greens and where is Mahala? Missie roved, uncertain, until a nurse stopped her and said yes, that *was* Miss Jackson's room. Even opened the door, Missie having pots and pans and whathaveyou. "Where you going?" Polly's voice came sternly as Missie backed in with her load.

"I'm coming to see Mahala."

"Can't you read? Can't you see that sign?" Polly was indignant. "Yes, I see that sign," said Missie, "I'm not thinking about that sign"—just coming on in. "Let her alone, Polly," came Mahalia's voice. "Let her in." Missie could see how glad Mahala was to see her. "I couldn't get *to* you, Mahala!" she said, opening up the dinner. Polly stepped close. "She can't eat that," Polly said firmly. "Yes I can," said Mahalia eagerly, sitting up in the bed. "She brought it. I want it. I'm going eat it." She had finished by the time the doctor arrived. "Missie," said Polly, "you'll have to step out, the doctor's here." Missie sat. "I'm not going no place. I'm sitting right here. What the doctor say, I'll hear." Polly was determined she go. She was determined she stay. The doctor waited. Mahalia grew upset. Missie left. At home, she called Jean Childers. "Mahala is scared of that woman, you hear me? *Scared*. But," she concluded, triumphantly, "I got past the dragon."

But that woman *ruled* Mahala—Missie could see it more every day and had her say to Alice.

BROTHER JOHN Sellers listened with mixed emotions. "John"—her voice sounded mournful, but that could be the long-distance—"people don't believe I'm sick as I am. Hannah and them believe I'm just putting on all the time."

"Yeah, that's what I been hearing, Mahalia," said John, noncommittal; "say, 'Oh, Mahalia ain't got her money, that's what's wrong with her' . . . 'Every time she go, ain't nothing wrong with her.' "

Mahalia stared into the mirror. Her face was full. 'Less she was a scarecrow, it just didn't show when she was sick. Let somebody tell *her* she wasn't sick!

She wasn't talking to people or seeing them much—Polly was right, that was the only way she was going get well, and who didn't like it could lump it. But there was business to mind: Get her clear title back on her land at 89th & State—the judge had ruled Minnis had to give up what was in his name. Get the mortgage note extended on the Los Angeles apartment house. Bills to examine—some didn't seem right, and that included the ones coming in for Mindling's son from Europe but no use talking about that. Statements to check with Mr. Shayne, the accountant. And she was worried about her different insurances: some might be run out and some ahead and Polly wasn't sure. One particular big business made her mad with Ming—and Townsend mad with her: how long this been dragging? Been a year ago last March, Townsend told her the lawyer out there had another offer to settle the Songs of Praise mess, wound up in a lawsuit and owing her more than $40,000 and Townsend probably $10,000, he said; and back *then* Townsend was mad about Ming not settling up 'cause Townsend had his problems and needed the money . . . and here it was still dragging and Townsend madder. Ming was not tending to her business. She wrote him she wanted some action in the next 10 days—"my just debts are resting heavy upon my heart." And she reminded him she had his $20,000 divorce bill to pay. Let him think about *that*. Ming didn't answer; Mitchell did. But whatever he wrote Townsend's lawyer just made Townsend write, "They are obviously making every effort they can to see that I get as little as possible." He did give Halie credit for getting it started again and maybe they were all right, 'cause he'd come up with an idea for her to record with the Mormon Tabernacle Choir in January or February and was hoping before that she could get in an album of her own. Her own? what was the Mormon one? She got Allen to write Townsend what did he want—them to do her songs, or her to do theirs; that when they talked on the phone, she'd thought he meant for them to blend in with her. She reminded him the Mormons had been off to themselves, their songs were not too nationally known. And she just hoped the business would be settled; she didn't want to do any wrong to anyone.

She couldn't say the same for some other people close by. Mitchell said she was wrong on that—part wrong, anyway. Well, she wasn't all that strong on all them down at Ming's office either. "I know more than people think I know," she told Celie, settled into a midnight call. "Whether it's conniving or stealing or deceit or just don't-do, I know; and what I don't know, I'm making it my business to find out. Far as stealing, that's the Lord's money; people are going have to face the Lord on that. But baby, I'm going clean me a few plates. I might not do it all at once, but I'm doing it."

Oct. 10, she had Polly write Mindling to send her copies of all the 1967 contracts he had in his possession and a copy of the check for last Easter's

Philharmonic Hall doubleheader . . . "to give Miss Jackson a total income," wrote Polly. That week when Laurraine came to dinner—quit that fancy food at the newspaper meeting downtown—Halie's mind was on a lot of things, but she told just two: "You know a good manager? Ask some of those television people you know—I want somebody know TV; I don't want to be out on that road too much." She wasn't going have a commotion with Mindling, just get her somebody else. He had his job at Paramount. And, "Laurraines, what I particularly want is a TV special for my foundation. Dinah Shore, Danny Kaye, Bing Crosby, Pat Boone—a whole bunch said they'd be on my benefit, and I want my temple *started*. Talk to that president of Quaker Oats; some people think I'm Aunt Jemima anyway!" She laughed at herself, round and brown. To Laurraine, it was a good sign; and when pert, pleasant Jean Childers drove her back to the Loop, Jean said she believed Mahalia was getting her old self back. "That woman's got me driving her every place!" said Jean. "And I have wined and dined her. Let me tell you, she's eating."

(One of the things she needed driving to was to speak for Councilman Hatcher, a friend of Butch's running for mayor of Gary. "I'm not for a man automatically because he's black," Halie said, endorsing him; "I'm looking at the inner man.")

In Hollywood, as the fact of the severance came clear to Lou Mindling, he shook his head. He didn't really blame Mahalia. Galloway—he was the wedge. And Allen wanted to be manager. From what Polly said, he believed he could probably settle Mahalia down, talk her out of it, but was it worth the effort? He owed Mahalia a deep debt of gratitude just knowing her, and she was kind to him when it counted. Well, Polly would keep him posted, and Ming; they'd keep in touch. Polly was a warm woman—fantastic loyalty. Too bad her son Gary had enlisted in the Navy instead of letting him and Mahalia send the boy to college.

"THE LORD Is My Shepherd, I Shall Not Want" in big letters. To Missie's eye, it was the prettiest Bible cake she had ever seen. She carried it carefully out to Jean's car. Was this the last stop? Jean checked over the list in her head and headed for 8358 So. Indiana. It was Oct. 26, Mahalia's birthday, and the two were giving her a surprise party. Mahalia had slumped; moping in that house again, and the pair figured this night to get her out of it. Missie used her key to get in, and quietly in came the others. When they were all together, Jean got Mahalia downstairs. At sight of the smiling faces around the cake and the pretty party trimmings—at sight of Aunt Alice and Aunt Hannah, one on each side—Mahala's face was a study, to Missie. Alice and Hannah had not set foot in the house for weeks. The two aunts felt they'd lost their welcome. But if Missie and Jean were having her a party. . . . Missie's daughter Miranda Cox had no qualms. She saw the hand of the Lord pointing her path and she took it eagerly. Before the candles were blown, before the cake and ice cream were eaten, Miranda prayed—and *it was a prayer*! Jean Childers felt herself stir: she'd never heard prayer like that before in her life! and coming from this small woman, this calm woman with the soft voice . . . ringing now like a hammer. "We're going to get rid of this devil that's in this house causing *allll* this conflict, allll this mistrust surrounding Mahalia!" cried Miranda. "In order for Mahalia to get well, things have got to get better around here with the help of the *Lord*. We going to *have* to *pray! pray!* you hear me! and bring you close together, and ask the *Lord* to get this devil out of this house, wherever it's coming from!

"Lord!" she cried, arms upreached, "Lord, give us your light this night!"

Miranda had each of them to testify then, to speak her heart, and in her turn Mahalia admitted she had come to believe her aunts just didn't care for her. Everyone at the table was crying now. When the speaking was over, Miranda had each one walk up to Mahalia at the head of the table and kiss her and say, "Mahalia, *I love* you!" Everybody was still crying, but they were happy tears. They were at the cake and ice cream, laughing, joking, having as much fun as babies, when Polly let herself in, bringing a sack of groceries. Seeing the party, she stayed. Mahalia kept an arm around one aunt or the other. Shortly, Allen came in, just back from California. He'd said he'd make it, if his plane wasn't late. The co-conspirators surveyed the scene. "What did I *tell* you," whispered Missie; "Mahala were *confidenced!*"

THREE DAYS later she was in a mood to get a whole bunch of letters off for Allen to type. Most were simple thank-yous for more cards, candy, plants, and, always, prayers. But of various proposals for projects which were daily coin of her correspondence, she could write, "I thank God I am feeling much better. . . . It has always been my desire to help anything for humanity. If you feel that my name will help, I don't mind the use of it." . . . "When I am able to come out I will be over to your church, and when I do, make yourself known to me." . . . "I am not able at present to say when this meeting can be held . . . I know that God will bring me out all right." . . . "I am surprised receiving a letter from someone I met at Lincoln University. We never know what impression we make upon people. . . . I've been so active in my young life, and to set around home trying to get well, it somewhat getting me down. . . ."

SHE HAD prayed. She'd just go ahead now and do it. Enough people been telling her. Even Willa Jones, and she was a person whose opinion Halie respected. It wasn't just from that. No. But. Well, if it's to do, do it. It was Saturday. Missie had stayed over and Willa was visiting too. When Polly came in, Missie could not believe her ears, although Missie had *laid* on it: Mahala was telling Polly that she could not keep her on "because she was not able to pay her." Polly said that was all right, she'd work on. But Mahala said no, she didn't know when she'd be back to work. And asked for the keys.

Next day, says Aunt Alice, she and Willa Jones came by right after church. They were in the kitchen with Mahalia when Polly came in with a bag of something—maybe groceries. Then she heard words she would never forget. She heard Mahalie say, "Polly, I don't need you no more." Like that. And Polly went on. Mahalia said she'd let Polly go. Like that.

Shortly, when Rev. Thurston saw Polly on the street, "she told me she was going back to work for the Internal Revenue Service—she could spend more time with her husband."

Halie put Allen to work sorting through to see what business she had. She was going to work him into secretary, she told Boy Baby. Teevee Hall came some evenings to help. There was one closet with papers in it they couldn't get into, so Halie had S&S Key come Nov. 17—and change locks on the entrance doors. Butch Thornton turned out the closet with her and sorted through the papers and some unopened mail. A couple contained checks. Halie called City Wide Locksmith and changed the rest of the locks in the house.

Nov. 21, Allen typed a letter for Mahalia's signature which she had him register with return receipt, forwarding a certified check for Polly's back salary plus an extra week's pay of $100, and requesting the forwarding of "all papers and books and any other personal belongings of mine to me." Polly replied by letter that she would comply on or before Dec. 7, as she would be out of the city.

Allen had papers spread out all over a table in the family room. Everything felt like it was behind. Jean came to lend a hand, stayed on—and shortly, agreed to function as Mahalia's secretary. The poor lady needed someone desperately, Jean could see, and she couldn't afford to hire the trained staff she needed. Jean would figure out a way to keep an eye on the four buildings she had going up. She accepted $125 a week. It would help pay for driving all the way from Harvey every day. The boys and Ken could get used to getting themselves off.

Allen was still in a mess of sorting and tallying. Could he ever get it straight? Then he'd have to go back to writing those thank-you letters. Mahalia wanted each person to keep on praying for her full recovery.

MR. FLETCHER WAS at the door. He told Mahalia he had her books and things outside, then backed up the car to unload and bring it all in. Big Alice said no, just leave it in the garage. When he had left, Big Alice told Missie she was going to go get some saltpeter, and she wanted Missie to help her wash off all those books and things before they carried them in. They did, wiped every one, then brought it all inside the house. Louise and Ida were there too, but they could see Mahalia wasn't going to discuss it.

"WHEN MAHALIA got disenchanted, got angry, with Polly, I never knew what the difficulty was," says Dr. Barclay, "but this created a problem for me too. Because whereas Polly had seen that Mahalia took her medicine regularly and insisted that she get rest, now this created a rebellion, subconsciously, in Mahalia's mind, against me and the things I insisted on, since Polly was kind of a remote agent of mine. A very interesting situation."

WHILE HALIE WAS cleaning plates, she inspected her building on So. Prairie, told the real estate management to get rid of the resident janitor and hired James Lewis. Mr. Lewis was almost a relative. She had him to clear the rubbish, paint, scrub up. Then she had Jean write the five paying tenants a firm set of instructions. By now she'd changed her house help too; and she got Ming on the phone and told him to *settle* that down in New Orleans—get those people out of the other half of Delachaise. She wanted Brisko in there, alongside Doodutz.

Now the big thing— She picked up the telephone. "Baby, you got me a good manager yet? You tell your friend it's a manager Mahalia wants?" Yes, Laurraine had; "Maybe that's why Kaye Ballard hasn't called me back yet. She says there are plenty of agents, but good managers are scarce as hen's teeth." Laurraine said she'd write Kaye immediately.

Halie sat a while, then she called Joe Glaser in New York. He'd been after her for years. Louie Armstrong, Duke, Dizzie Gillespie—they got nothing but good things to say about him. . . . Joe Glaser listened while Mahalia explained her position and what she wanted in the way of bookings, especially TV, so she wouldn't have to be out so much on the road. When she finished, Glaser made a suggestion. Mahalia then made her third call—to Hollywood.

Bob Phillips, head of West Coast operations for Associated Booking Corp. (the Glaser agency), listened with surprise and growing pleasure. Mahalia Jackson wanted him to book her. Phillips, personally. She obviously had a very good feeling for him, although they'd never met. He accepted promptly. He told her he wanted to put her in touch with their president, Joe Glaser, in New York. "I want Joe's strength out of New York for you," he said. "That's fine, baby," said Halie. He said he believed he could get Mahalia $10,000 per concert. Within the week, in the course of a call, Halie told Laurraine that Joe Glaser's office was booking her now. As soon as she was able.

68

And still she languished. Dr. Barclay said she was the only one who could say when she *felt* well. She told Townsend she couldn't come in to record. She told the civil rights people in Madison, Wisc., she couldn't come for their meeting; Belafonte said he'd go in her place. *Anybody* be glad for the great Belafonte. She did let Bob Phillips book her for Rev. Cleaver in Booneville, Mo., in February. Halie's bound to be all right by February. Won't she, Lord? Bob Phillips wrote her that Mr. Shoofey at the Flamingo Hotel wanted her to just come out to Las Vegas and rest a while as his guest. Be so nice and warm out there, away from all this mess. But that's no way of the Lord; that's the demons poking in.

Lord, what is wrong with Halie?

WITH ALL THE different people tramping in and out, the place needed a good cleaning and Big Alice and Missie set about it. Top to bottom, wash the floors—everything. Missie set her pail outside Mahala's bedroom, flipped up the throw rug inside the entrance in one practiced motion—and stopped dead in her tracks. She got down on her hands and knees and looked close. It was black powder just like gun powder *all under* there!

She called Alice. Alice came, looked, and got her a spoon. She scooped up some of the stuff. "Now I'm going to show it to her." While Alice was off showing it to Mahala, Missie got down close to look again. It warn't body powder.

Late that night, alone, Halie called Celeste in Los Angeles. They had found something like voodoo in her bedroom, she said somberly. Don't know how it got there or how long. When Halie hung up, Celeste called Margaret. "That's the second time she has spoken of that," said Margaret. "Before I came out here, she was laying downstairs in that little room she calls the prayer room, and she spoke about some voodoo she was afraid of then."

Celeste rolled her eyes.

Halie prayed on it and left it with the Lord. She was putting her mind on something better. She was moving on her dream. She felt and believed and had it from God that He was going give her another chance. She'd been too blind to see. He had put the time in her hands, to His purpose. She'd had a vision.

69

The Mahalia Jackson Foundation up to now had been largely a paper show, a path for her $900-a-year church music scholarship to Roosevelt University for a student of its choosing; plus the help given friend and stranger, white, black, and yellow (no Indians had yet passed by) as Mahalia approved the need and the student—or, more often, his parent. Now she saw in the troubled day a need for the Foundation to stretch, to raise its sights, to build. In time, the Foundation would be the foundation for her temple—the fulfillment of Mahalia the evangelist—the teacher of the word—the believer in the ultimate good, the individual worth: how could anyone be little when he had as good a way as every other man to contact God? You can't get any greater than that. But the temple, she saw now, the temple had to wait on God's plan. She rose up knowing *this* was the time she'd been talking about, getting promises on, for years; the time for her Festival of Stars. It would be the cornerstone of the new Foundation. She leaned back, visualizing. With just the stars said they'd come when she let them know, this be the biggest show anybody ever put together. But you can't jump up a wall on a thing like this. It's got to be thought through, it must be done with dignity—and it can't flop.

First, her board. Bob Miller had some thoughts. Bob Ming was too busy to talk about it, but Chauncey Eskridge had the legal side. Nettie Irving had her ideas. She listened, and thought, and prayed; then, huddled with Jean and Missie in the kitchen, she made a list. Willa Saunders Jones, president; Allen Clark, recording secretary—he was working for her already and that was family; Robert Miller, treasurer—though she'd still be the only one to sign checks. The rest would be Judge George Leighton, Ming, Eskridge, and Rev. Lewis for chaplain. She'd be executive chairman. Then the Advisory Board. Carefully they culled 15 names, each with its significance: Aldus Mitchell, Doris Akers for California, Helen Maybell, Josephine Davis, Studs Terkel, Ethel Davenport in Florida, Jean Childers, Joe Bostic in New York, Era Bell Thompson of *Ebony*, and six preachers, headed by Dr. Martin Luther King. In gear now, she lined out the job ahead. To do right, to make some money, a thing like this had as many bits as a dandelion head, but each little bit carried a seed; plant it well and it would grow.

The next step Mahalia prayed on. For the Foundation to work as she visioned it, for the first time in her life she'd ask other people for money in her name. Swallowing her pride, she had Allen write for a non-profit bulk mailing permit—and learned how much doing even that took: city, state, federal. Well, if she had any problems, Mayor Daley would fix it. One thing to make sure of—that people understand not a dime going in anybody's pocket, especially hers. She called Laurraine to write something—she'd know how to put in there about the temple. Purposes, plans, hopes spun over the phone in the soft, earnest, famous voice, the circles widening as Mahalia reached for yet another need. Listening, Laurraine thought of David the psalm-singer: he'd have understood this temple. Alive today, he might have built it for his own. Chicago-Jerusalem. She laughed at her fancy and turned to her typewriter for the first of many drafts.

"Now," SAID Mahalia, "I want to get hold of some famous people, money people, to help."

"I know a *lot* of famous people," said Missie; "I know the Rockyfellers."

"Aw," scoffed Allen from his vantage at one side.

"I *do* know the Rockyfellers," said Missie; "I used to work for 'em."

Allen was scornful. "She don't know 'em."

"Old *you*, making *fun* of me!" cried Missie. "I'll tell you how *well* I know the Rockyfellers. When I was working for John D. Rockyfeller Prentice, I lived with them for *years,* on the place, cooking for them, and you cook for *one*, you're cooking for *all*—John D. Rockyfeller Prentice. All the children born, they named Rockyfeller. John D. Rockyfeller Senior's daughter Alta, that's Mrs. Prentice—that's who I worked for. At Lake Geneva, that's where you'd see them, when you'd have a big party; they *all come*—see?" she glared at Allen. "In '51 I started, 'cause I got a 1951 *Vic*toria *Fo'd* 'cause the Rockyfellers wouldn't hire you unless you know how to drive, and it come up that this big party was going to be, *in* March, and that morning it was the biggest blizzard I ever seed in my life; Mr. Rockyfeller carried me down—we rode the 26th floor down in the downstairs, where you park the car, and he says, 'Missie, I want to see can you drive.' Okay. I drove all around. He say, 'Well and good.' Well, we went upstairs, and my daughter called me. 'Mama, don't get on that highway. You know you never have drove but in the city; you have never *been* on the highway. Don't get on the highway when it's snowing.' I said, 'Look, girl, *I* am working for the *Rocky*fellers and I'm not gonna lose *this job*. I'm *go*ing.' So! It stopped snowing. Mr. Rockyfeller say, 'Missie, think you can make it?' I say, 'Are you gonna drive?' He say yes. I say, 'Is Mr. Hunt gonna drive?' He says yes. Well, Mr. *Hunt* is a man that owned the Morton Salt; the Rockyfellers and them was friends. Well. I say, 'Yes, I'm going.' Well, cutting the story—I made it over, and I cooked this big dinner at Lake Geneva, me and Frieda, and then the Rockyfellers come, Nelson and all of 'em, all of 'em come and they shook hands with me and admired the dinner, and what *have* you. *Then* in Lake Geneva it was so *high,* until it was so bad that night, when we got ready to go home, I couldn't pull the hill because with the Rockyfellers's station wagon it was a *standard* shift, and I didn't know how to put it in low, 'cause I hadn't learned how to drive good. So the *maid*—she was named Roberta; well, she was really jealous of me—she was a maid. So the maid says, 'What you gonna do *now?*' I said, 'I'm going back in this house and ask Mr. Rockyfeller to come out here and pull this hill.'

" 'He'll fire you,' she said. 'Look, Roberta,' I said, 'Mr. Rockyfeller ain't no more than me. Ain't but one thing different between I and him. He got money and I ain' got none.' And I went and rung that bell. 'What you want?' I said, 'I want to see Mr. Rockyfeller—John D. Rockyfeller Prentice.' And Mr. Prentice come and he couldn't—couldn't *none* of 'em pull the hill.

"And *that*'s how well *I* know the Rockyfellers!" Missie concluded, triumphant, head high. With abrupt dignity, she indicated the telephone directory. "Jean, look up there in the book and find John D. Rockyfeller Prentice."

In easy sequence Missie reached Mrs. Prentice, explained the Foundation, got her promise to give, and added, "*Now*, you call *all* of 'em—*all* the Rockyfellers—and you get in touch with all the rest of the rich people."

"Well!" Missie told Mahalia. "Now we got the Rockyfeller I worked for, *everybody* gonna flow in. You watch now."

"What I got to watch now," said Mahalia, "is catch up on this mail before the Foundation begin. Come on, Jean."

IT WAS ONE *among* many, from—where? Endicott, N.Y. She read the man's letter and read it once again. No form reply would do. The dark eyes sought some path beyond the room. Jean waited, pen poised, until she spoke. "In this day and time," she dictated slowly, "when the world is so disturbed and confused and frustrated with things that are going on in our generation that we have never seen before, we must not lose faith or become disturbed. We must go back to the Bible as the children of Israel, and read our Bible, and remember what our foreparents have taught us: how good God was to them, how God made a way, how He led the children through the flood; then we would have more assurance in the New Testament, how God sent His Own Beloved Son who came to a world that rejected Him and wanted Him not. But God brought salvation . . . God brought Love, Patience, and Grace to them who do believe. When man came into the world, that was nothing for him to do but live in the likeness of God, but instead of that man grows weaker because he is constantly drawing off from God and there is always an inner conflict between the soul of man and the flesh. What Jesus said is true, if it were not so He would have told us. Let your heart take hold and continue to trust in God."

She nodded, answering herself, and plunged into the grabbag of the day's concerns. That letter from Ben Hooks in Memphis—but that best wait. Too big to rush. If it was real.

IKE WALKED IN with his same quiet smile and asked if she needed anything at the store or anything, and when she didn't, and he didn't relax, she saw it coming. But she made him say it. He was past curing and he'd have to face his maker, but "$500? You better slow you down and speed up the horses," Halie said drily as she reached for her checkbook. "Tell you what—you been doing things for me, Ike; I'm going to make this $500 'salary,' and write you another one like it; see if you can't get back on your feet." Abruptly, her eyes glinted—that light he knew so well. "You not feeding some woman on Halie?"

"You know better than that," said Ike softly, accepting the two checks. "Nobody else gets a Valentine and never will. And I got a horse coming up," he said eagerly, "that'll get this back and plenty more."

That night Missie was cooking dinner when something suspicioned her and she looked in Mahala's bedroom. There she was, setting there crying at his picture on her dresser—Russell Roberts. Missie eased on out.

The closer it got to Christmas, though, the better Halie's spirits got. Son Baby (Allen, Sr.) wanted her to come down there; Celie, too; and she had part of a mind to until she thought how her house was so lonesome last Christmas with her out and Minnis having it. She got out her great Santy Claus and put him on the back porch upstairs, like he's fixing to climb up. They put up Mary and Joseph and the Baby, and the three wise men coming from afar; then all around they strung the beautiful lights. By the time Russell Goode came, they were decorating the three Christmas trees—one inside and one each on Indiana and 84th.

She got such a lift, she had Allen to dig out all the letters from people wanting to present her—he found one clear back to last February—and say she'd be glad to come now; just contact her agent, Bob Phillips. One letter she fingered a long time, smiling: from Mrs. Vera Bisso in New Orleans, the same ferry Bissos—Bisson, they'd always called it—she'd ironed for as a child, helping her aunts. Who would have dreamed. God is real. And God is love. Those Bissons loved her.

She told Aunt Alice her fatted lamb was going to be two turkeys and ten ducks—and fix every kind of trimmings she could think of. Missie would help her all day Sunday, after church. This was going be a *feast* day! No need even to invite people—the word was out.

Monday—Christmas day—the house was so full there was hardly room to breathe, much less lift your elbows, but Ken Childers figured he held his own. Mahalia looked drawn and somewhat ill to his eyes, but obviously determined to have a good Christmas and stuff every gut in sight, including her own.

It was Missie who made the most excitement. She'd thought and *thought* what she could do for Mahala, and come up with something that couldn't miss: she arrived staggering under a whole pig, elaborately dressed. It didn't even muffle Missie out when Polly Fletcher said she thought that pig looked ridiculous with the apple in its mouth. Missie just looked at Mahala looking at that pig; that was enough.

All week, the good time rolled. There were serious moments, though, when the surface wore thin. The Wednesday after Christmas, her old friend Lloyd Davis returned to HUD headquarters in Washington and wrote Bob Ming he would deeply appreciate being advised if there was anything which he or other friends of Miss Jackson might do to help her: "She gave every indication of a great need to know that long-time friends with whom she had been associated are prepared to do what they can to be of assistance."

NEW YEAR'S EVE, Halie had never been anywhere but in church in her life and she didn't aim to miss out now: "You not going to have *me* out New Year's Eve! I'm going be in somebody's church on my knees!" She let herself be persuaded on one condition: she'd leave at 11 p.m. in plenty time to get to a church. So at 9 p.m. Mahalia and Martin Luther King (pleased with his triumph) plus Martin's traveling companion Bernard Lee, Chauncey Eskridge, and Russell Goode went around the corner on E. 84th to the Maybells' home. It wasn't a big party—*they*'d be the party, their hostess said.

Martin was in a mood to sing. He sang for Mahalia some of the gospel songs he liked best. Then Mahalia sang his favorite, *Take My Hand Precious Lord,* the song that was like a prayer to her. Then they sang together, Russell falling easily into the gospel beat. "Russell, you watch the time!" Halie cautioned, and he nodded. They were having *such* a good time. So was Martin, Russell could tell; he didn't want it to end either. Suddenly Mahalia broke off. "Russell! What time is it?"

"Five minutes to 12."

"Oh my God," said Halie. She ran into the closest place, the bathroom, and got on her knees and said her prayers until midnight. Then she came out. She was in time to hear Martin say something that was completely different from the atmosphere of the room: He lifted his head at midnight and said, "This is going to be a *terrible* year."

Russell made a joke of it, and Martin shrugged it off and started another song. Mahalia came to join him, and they sang together.

It was 1968.

70

Maybe she might be going get it all together. Bob Phillips and Joe Glaser both looking up stars' addresses for her. Committees set up—on paper, anyway; Willa suppose to get on that. They had the place picked and she was turning over in her mind how to price it: those boxes could bring good money. Bob Phillips was doing a wonderful job on bookings and look at that man getting her $10,000 a night—asking $15,000 for Easter Sunday! Joe Glaser said he was working on some TV—acted like it be no trouble at all. Townsend setting up two concerts in July at that French festival for $17,500, and she could have the TV film they'd make, after they showed it . . . Townsend must not know about Bob, asking if she wanted to talk the deal over with Mindling. She'd say when she went to record. Bob had the ABC people down in Miami working up four concerts for March and April, including Nassau and, best thing, a week apart—but that's no mind, God given Halie this second chance. And if this chicken business—oh, Lordy Lord, she could just see, hear, and *taste* her temple! Getting *Halie* in a new shape, too—nobody believed she'd check herself into Wesley Memorial Hospital and have them separate those last two toes on each foot—"fused," Dr. Compere said. Been that way since Halie saw light with her legs curved, but they wasn't no bother 'til she got up on these high heels. They so pretty. And necessary for her "image," like Celeste say. Mm-mh! that girl loved reflected glory like sunshine—or sunburn, one.

Celeste put her in mind of Los Angeles, and that got her on the phone Saturday to Laurraine about something else but "Call Ida Beal and ask her when did I ever owe money that I can't have my hat? Call her today; it'll fix her good when she's busy." (Ida mailed three.)

The chicken business kept nicking around her mind. It sounded fine, but *who* going count on that before she see who's setting in it—and who going make it hatch. She called Bob Miller at his funeral parlor and talked Foundation; then she tickled him with her "hatching"—and what did he think of that proposition? He promised to give it some thought. She better get Judge Hooks up here. Bob Miller asked some questions she didn't have the answers to.

FOR BEN HOOKS, it had begun late last year but in reality, much further back: since 1956, at National Baptist Conventions, when he was a fledgling preacher (and lawyer) and she was a great singer. Then in '59, when he was active in running the Volunteer Ticket for elections in Memphis, Dr. King came and Ben Hooks ended up very quickly on the board of SCLC—from which stemmed a closer tie with Mahalia and admiration for her because "she didn't just sing for the civil rights functions, she would be around, lend her presence," he says. A successful financier now, besides his ministry he was active on TV twice weekly and was a Criminal Court judge, a bench he was preparing to quit to go into a major new business—if he could convince this magnetic, dedicated, absolutely maddening woman sitting before him.

It was so simple, really. He and his associates were prepared, with ample financing, to launch a nationwide chicken franchise business and they wanted to use Mahalia's name. She didn't have to *do* anything, other than contribute a certain public-appearance quotient. They were ready to pay her well for the privilege. "I thought she would jump at the chance." But since he'd first telephoned and got a warm response—then flown to see her and got a warm response—months had gone by. When she summoned him, "I assumed I would sit down, as is customary in any business proposition, with her legal adviser or some other business associate she trusted." But no, they seemed to be spinning out another discussion. Yet she *was* interested. She was a most peculiar person to deal with. They were in a sort of warm limbo.

That was one fine-looking preacher, thought Halie. Too bad he couldn't stay over: she was finally giving her doctors their Creole treat.

ALL THE MEN knew Mahalia well—had cared for her from time to time: Dr. Albert Niden, Dr. Ben Burrows, Dr. John Kasik (each would go on to head a university medical team). But the evening was an introduction to Mahalia for their wives. She had certainly gone to a lot of trouble!

It was an introduction to all of *them* for Eddie Robinson and for lawyer Aldus Mitchell. Mitchell had talked with Dr. Barclay by telephone, had heard "sarcoid trouble" ("although I never really knew what it meant," the lawyer says; "actually, Mahalia got sick when people didn't have her money"). He'd wondered about this white man Mahalia thought was so wonderful. He could see now that the man felt quite affectionate toward Mahalia, that he was relatively young and outgoing; it would be easier to talk to him from here on out. Except don't give him any of this scientific language, this medical jive.

At the head of the table, Mahalia was happy. Just nothing wasn't going down. And the best compliment of all, from the ladies: every one wanted the recipe for every single dish. "Honey, honey," she dimpled at the one who'd just asked, stretching her hands wide, "you can't get the recipes for these things, you got to go through it. You don't learn how to cook greens, you don't learn to cook gumbo, you got to live it. But I tell you what," she added, including them all, "when you want to do it, I'll come out there and do it for you."

"Oh, I couldn't ask you—a grand lady!" protested the medic's wife.

"Baby," Halie said, "I scrubbed me enough floors and ironed me enough shirts 'til I can't never get grand."

UUGH! IT WAS a grand evening, but she was wore out. Halie got no business enjoying her own cooking that much, either, 'specially when she's getting back into her singing business. And has Halie got any business going into business with somebody want her to put out such a thing as Glori-fried Chicken?

71

Back to work. She was just singing for the one hour at Emory University and that was in Glenn Memorial Church, so she could sing easy if she felt like it; and she had Russell Goode bringing over some children from Chattanooga to sing a few numbers first. It ought to be all right.

The music. Halie panicked. "The music! Did anybody—Jean? Eddie? Charles?" Nobody had the music and they were how many thousand feet in the air on their way to Atlanta?

WHO WAS PULLING her off her job, Missie Wilkerson wondered. Must be something bad *bad*. She ran over the members of the family until she picked up the receiver and heard Mahala. "Missie, you got to go get it and put it on the plane. I got to have it right *away!*"

"I'll get it, Mahala," said Missie, "if I have to fly it." But Monday, and she can't find a car. "Alll them people, nobody ho'p me," says Missie. "Finally I call my daughter Miranda, she *got* to ho'p me. Can't find her. I call her church, I call all over. I call back her church and tell them this for Miss Mahala Jackson! My daughter's deacon come got me, we went and found the music, then the deacon got me out to the airport, but he took me to the wrong place. I'm running all over. Finally I'm at the right place and the plane done loaded and took off—'taxiing down the field,' what they told me.

"It *can't* go! This is Mahala *Jackson!* Much as she does for this city, much as she does for *everybody*; you can't *let* it go. This is Mahala *Jackson!*" Missie danced up and down, a brown gyro before the towering might of the airline. " 'Just a minute, lady!' The man reached for the phone; he called the field. 'Hold the plane!' he told them. We scuffles out on the field, they put down the steps, and I runs up. 'Here the music,' I told them, 'for Mahala Jackson.' They took off. That's how she got her music, that particular time."

"MISS JACKSON— Would Miss Jackson like a drink?" Jean Childers looked at Mahalia. So far, so good. Atlanta had been relatively easy and she'd liked stopping by the King house. Now, aboard the plane for Los Angeles, Jean didn't have to wake Mahalia to answer the stewardess's question. "Yes, she drinks Scotch," Jean smiled, and as the stewardess obliged with the complimentary liquor for first-class, "Ooh, this is terrible!" Jean told herself.

Eyes closed, Mahalia listened to the exchange. Jean knew what she was doing; she'd bring those little bottles to Allen. She knew how to get along.

In Los Angeles, Johnny Jackson had followed Mahalia's instructions and freshened up Apt. 106 that he'd been holding for her. Celeste and Eddie, Doris Akers, Doris Simmons were getting it comfortable—renting the furniture, hustling the extras and so forth. He was glad Mahalia had her close buddies here, especially Celeste. "She very seldom did bring up Galloway's name, but I knew the girl had had a rough time," says Johnny. . . .

"Everything here but the piano, Jean. Listen, Minnis got that piano setting right there in his house—I ought to call and ask him to let me have that. And some of them big pots he got. He wouldn't mind." Jean knew better than to answer. This was a subject Mahalia had to handle by herself. She certainly was on it enough: Minnis this, Minnis that. She ate, drank, and slept the man's name. "When we go down to Columbia, Jean, I'll take you by and show you his house." Halie guessed she might as well go on, rent a piano. Eddie and Albert Goodson going make the session, but Gwen coming over to rehearse her.

SHE CERTAINLY wasn't at her best, that was clear to Irv Townsend. But she was rid of Galloway—and it was interesting that Mindling wasn't booking her any more. He'd never had any real personal problems with Mindling except the guy had reamed him good on the T.E.C.-Songs of Praise thing, whether Mindling admitted it or not. Anyway, now he wouldn't be in for both sides of the Mahalia-Mindling problems: there always were two sides; no villain, no saint—and that applied to Mildred, and Polly too. Mahalia'd said nothing, but from what he got from *them*— Polly had been one of the few people who really knew what was happening. Bob Phillips just *thought* he'd only be booking: as if anybody could stay out of Mahalia's personal life once you started doing business with her. Yet the toughest people in show business— "It was almost like speaking against motherhood, saying anything against Mahalia," says Irving Townsend. Now this Foundation again—God! he wished she'd save herself. They'd been a long way together. Well—they had a long way to go, after a whole year with no recording. Better get started.

HALIE WAS worried. The cramp in her leg had come on her, bad, and this hoarseness hadn't broke like it always did. She'd see if she could get through one more song, and if it didn't clear up, she wanted to see a doctor. She didn't care if Townsend *did* think she was a hypochondria.

Dr. Lincoln Best examined her carefully, listened to the long recital, and looked at the array of bottles she'd brought to his clinic. She certainly had more than her share of medication. But none covered the three immediate problems: A muscle relaxant should take care of the cramps; bed rest and care should clear up the respiratory infection. The other would take more treatment: she had diabetes, which she had not known. He wrote a prescription for diabenese, to control it, and explained she would have to watch her diet very carefully—and revise any idea of 200 pounds as her "singing weight."

At Apt. 106, Jean Childers plumped Mahalia's pillows compassionately.

She'd done everything she could think of—given her medicine, cooked her something light to eat, made tea, given her an alcohol rub, brushed her hair: my God, it was coming out by the handsful. Mahalia was convinced the worry during the divorce was making it fall out. She should ask Dr. Best about that next time. If Mahalia would just stop feeling sorry for herself. What she really was doing was worrying herself sick about Minters.

DIABETES. Oh, Aunt Bell. Does it run in families? Mm-*mph!* This cramp eased off, now it come back bad. She'd let Yancey give her a rub when he got back. He got stronger hands. He can do that and talk about getting hold of stars at the same time. Halie's got to beat this thing of the way she feels—got a Festival of Stars July 1 and no stars. Except the main one: Dinah. They *all* said they'd come back when I asked them. But you got to give stars time. If Dr. Best—he seem like a good man, but it won't hurt to call Dr. Peck, ask him just to stop by. He really liked her when she helped him for the Vietnam babies. And studied under Dr. Barclay! "Yancey! Come here, boy. Jean baby, get your notebook. We got to send some telegrams to these stars I asked the addresses from Bob Phillips and Joe Glaser. All right now, we got Ella Fitzgerald, Ray Charles, Pearl Bailey—but Joe Glaser say she won't be able to get off *Hello Dolly*—tell her, anyway; Lou Rawls, Dean Martin, Red Skeleton, Jimmy Durante, and Moms Mabley—she's real big now. Send all them telegrams, to start."

Mar. 2, for the Johnny Carson show, it was Foundation she talked. And Mar. 5, for Steve Allen: "Somewhere there must be another Pearl Bailey and another Marian Anderson who seeks to come forth. Somewhere there's another Mahalia—one better than me. Through my foundation I will find them, and they will find their open door."

That sounded fine, to Dick Yancey, but what he wanted to hear was her *voice*. She just hadn't been letting out. Afraid to, he figured—thought she didn't *have* a voice any more. He didn't believe it, himself. Through Mary Ann Hooper, he'd told the Steve Allen director just how he wanted Mahalia set so she'd be near the band to pick up the vibrations. Eddie Robinson was playing, and since one of the options he'd got Mahalia to list for music was *Come On, Children, Let's Sing* and Yancey had a pretty good idea that or *Elijah Rock* was one of the two she'd do, he primed Eddie: "Right off, give it everything you've got." He'd planted Bill Duncan and some other friends and told them, "The minute she hits that chorus, you start clapping. The audience will get with you, and that's going to pull her." He stood offstage now with Celeste and Jean and wondered if it would work. *Work!* She tore up that theatre. To Yancey, his reward was when Mahalia came off glistening with tears and sweat and whispered, tickled—"I really did it!" Her second song was *Just a Closer Walk With Thee* and that did something for her too: it was as close as she'd come yet on getting a network to let her sing a song with Jesus in the title, on the air. "God's moving the world," she said. "Don't let them think He's not."

One other thing they thought of was an ad in the *Hollywood Reporter* announcing a meeting to explain her foundation and get ideas. Mary Ann Hooper came to that, and some other production people, and they all had ideas of what she ought to do.

"MAHALIA, THOSE people aren't getting the telegrams." Yancey was spending most of his time at 106 now. Often he slept on the couch. He wasn't working, and there was just so much interesting going on around Mahalia. Besides, she needed him. There wasn't anything he wouldn't do for her if he could, and break his neck trying. This minute, she was lower than a snake's belly, as she'd say it. And no wonder. Not a single star had answered her telegram. "They're just not getting them," he insisted, jumping up. "I'm going to phone them."

"You won't get *to* them," said Mahalia, eyes narrow, pushing up her lip. "I will—I'll just say it's Mahalia Jackson calling. Stay right by. When I get them, you get on the phone." He dialed the number he'd got for Bob Hope, said Mahalia Jackson was calling Mr. Hope—and Bob Hope came right on. Mahalia's eyes were eager as a child's as she grabbed the telephone. Jean hurried close to take notes. Oh. Bob Hope had a commitment on July 1. But she'd talked to him. "Boy," said Halie eying Yancey, "you have the nerve of a brasstailed monkey." But this white boy was a do-er.

No other star was around to answer, it seemed. "Let's go down and see Lorne Greene at Paramount," said Yancey briskly; "you like him."

Lorne Greene was really pleased to see her—was just as nice as he could be—said he'd like to—but it developed later he "had a commitment on July 1." So did Eva Gabor and Buddy Ebsen, that they ran into and Mahalia went ahead and asked. Yancey got on the phone to some local talk shows: free work, but maybe building up the Festival of Stars as a big thing would get more action.

Hollywood hadn't seemed so spread out since she and Ed and Babe promoted Martin, but she made the miles—including the KMPC Radio show at Universal's commissary. Somebody spread the word that Mahalia Jackson was on the lot and minutes after she walked in, she was surrounded, Helen Hayes and Chuck Connors in the forefront. Yancey stuck close, not to miss anything. Why, people was flocking around like they was worshipers! When things thinned down, a man introduced himself as Elvis Presley's public relations man. Mr. Presley would like very much to meet Miss Jackson, but they were filming. He'd sent a car: would she come to the set? Mahalia hated to leave right then; she'd done her air time but she wanted these stars' autographs. Still, she didn't like to be impolite. Climbing into the back seat of the limousine, Yancey was elated. Presley kept a closed set, and here he was going in with the queen.

"Mahalia!" Elvis Presley's face lit up as he rushed to greet her. He led her to meet Col. Parker, and had his personal chair brought next to the camera. "Now sit right here; I don't want you to *move*." Between each take, then, he came over quickly and took her hand and stared intently at her, smiling. It made Halie a little nervous, him just staring, but he went on staring and he's the great star. Finally, "Mahalia," he said softly, "you're just like my mama."

"Oh!" Halie said, "was your m—" She broke off. He hadn't noticed, he was so set on what he was thinking. Well, you never know in this world. (Later on, somebody told her Elvis had sneaked into one of her church concerts in Mississippi when he was a child. And he'd grown up Pentecostal. That explained a lot about that boy's singing.)

And still, sitting in the Brown Derby waiting for air time, Mahalia peered past the line standing behind the camera and asked TV host Jack Barry, "Isn't this where all the movie stars come? You think there's any here today?"

"Well, I'm sure there are, if we look around."

"Do you think I can get their autographs?"

Jack Barry stared, incredulous. "Mahalia," he said, *"this whole line* wants *your* autograph!"

72

Six weeks and Mahalia seeing Dr. Best the entire time but she never stopped doing—Jean certainly had to hand it to her. Too bad she hadn't gotten more definite commitments for her benefit. Jean turned her head just slightly in the plane seat—Mahalia seemed asleep. Jean ran her watch ahead from San Francisco time to Chicago. At least Mahalia had Celeste and Margaret's Ladies of Song with her at the Opera House last night—and Yancey; Jean hadn't known he had it in him. The way Mahalia kept urging Celeste to sing more numbers, she *must* have felt tired. Or something. That sponsor didn't help.

Halie put her mind on the Lord—the only way she's going keep down this tightness in her chest. Lord, *You* going have to get on this benefit. Look like Halie's poor hands not big enough for what she's grasping. 'Course, I still got April to see stars when I go back, but that's going be it, Lord—we got to do it by then. You know I'm going *try;* I just want the assurance that You with me. Bob Phillips talking going to Japan, but how I'm going get my money in Japan when I can't even get it in San Francisco? It was good seeing Strawthford, though. Bob says the Japan man's all right, but—oh, Halie can't be studying Japan; the most I want to know now if Martin's settled what day in April for his Poor People's campaign on Congress.

Halie's sure going *be* there, and I'd hate to mess up on Bob Phillips. If it's Townsend, he'll shift a day. May be a message waiting home. Oooh, Halie going be on that bed like a chicken on a raft. First thing tomorrow, get Jean to call Dr. Barclay. If he's not in town, maybe Dr. Vondrasek. Jean thought a lot of him. . . .

She was quite disturbed, Dr. Earl Vondrasek could see. This long story of where she'd been in California . . . of Dr. Best discovering diabetes . . . even back to her experience at Billings last August when sarcoid was discovered in her left eye, although she knew Dr. Vondrasek didn't do that kind of work. Of course, this was her first visit to him since . . . October, 1966. Poor Mahalia. Her search for health seemed never-ending—and ever-widening, medically. Hm. "Your blood pressure's pretty good this time, Mahalia." Halie brightened. "But your weight is 208½; that's too high." Halie's face fell. Didn't have a thing for her except cut-down-your-weight-follow-your-diet.

She was going to lose some weight and lose somebody else some, if this Baltimore promoter she never heard of on these coming-up three dates turned out like the last Florida one. Her voice carried easily from the bedroom to Jean's typewriter. "Jean! You got off that letter to Freddie Williamson?" ABC in Miami better check up. It was already causing her to put off the Step Foundation in San Francisco for the convicts—poor Frisco, look like it and Halie never get straight—but Celeste and them going in her place. Halie was sorry to miss Pat Boone; that's a nice boy. And he was coming for her benefit; said he wanted to and he'd see if he could clear July 1 and she felt he would 'cause she be counting on him. Dinah was sure, sure. Lord, You ever hear so much talk and no do?

"Did you all hear me? A lot of talk and no do around here!" Halie was up in arms. Middle of March and these people just loaf 'less she's here to drive 'em. No notion how much promotion you got to do to put on a success. And promotion nothing but *detail,* not sitting around looking grand "helping Mahalia Jackson." When she got back from Florida and Nassau . . . no, she better go right on out to Los Angeles to see some stars. Right now, she was going see Lou Mindling. He was in Chicago.

JEAN AND KEN Childers had got a late start; they wouldn't be able to stay long. They were going out to celebrate their anniversary. But even when Jean had explained, Mahalia still insisted she come. Lou Mindling was just leaving. He'd been calling Mahalia, but Jean hadn't met him before; he was *gruff*. Or was he upset? After he'd gone, it was clear *Mahalia* was upset: something about Columbia still sending her record business to him; and when he thought he was still her manager; and even on things he didn't book, he—if that *was* it. Ken tapped his watch; they had to go. Once in the car, "I don't know why Mahalia wanted us to stop," Ken said.

FLORIDA, now. Mahalia on the road was like contracting a whole building;

there were just that many people to deal with. She'd sing here in Jacksonville tomorrow, Mar. 24; then immediately to the Bahamas; then into Mobile for Mar. 31; Tampa was April 6. Maybe they could get some sun in that Mobile-Tampa gap. It was still so cold at home. It was also hard to imagine just lying still, around Mahalia. It was a pleasure to do for her, though, she was so appreciative of the least little thing.

Waiting to give interviews, Halie still couldn't get over Jean Childers: do everything for her on the road, even to trim her toes, and Jean a *well*-educated woman. Rubbing on that cramp helped. Thank You Lord. Jean had been on her about all her sackful of medicine 'til she had to tell Jean she had these lumps in her chest—these sarcoids . . . "even if the doctors take 'em out, they going come back, but they won't get no worse, I'll just always have 'em . . . they take some out every now and then." She just always had to take her prednisone—like cortisone. Jean said that made her "moon face—filled out so beautifully." That Jean. She'd already called the press—that's why Halie'd come early, to help the promoter. But before this thing was through, she'd have to do battle. Her vibrations told her that 30 seconds after she *met* that promoter. "He does seem a little bit devious," said Jean. "Devious?" said Mahalia; "baby, that's a snake trying to walk."

He almost didn't get off the ground the next night. Just *did* come up with the money, and Fred Williamson had warned her not to set foot on stage unless each step of that whole contract was followed. He could just get the rest together while she's in Nassau. Now those people know how to do, with dignity. Sending a lady senator, Sen. Doris Johnston, to greet her in Miami and escort her over.

FROM THE MOMENT they stepped off the plane, Jean knew it was a happening. A giant sign was flapping in the breeze—"Welcome, Mahalia Jackson"—with an eager crowd massed, waiting for a glimpse. All the island dignitaries greeted her formally and presented flowers. A band was playing island music; radio was there for her to speak. Jean was asked to introduce Mahalia, Charles, Eddie and herself on the air; then they rode in procession to the hotel for a reception. Everywhere, everyone seemed ecstatic over her presence, almost awed. Upstairs, finally, to rest, Mahalia was excited, happy. "And it's so *beautiful*. Why did I wait this long to come here!"

The concert, they knew, was to be at the Hangar Auditorium—that's what ABC's letter said. Wednesday evening, Mahalia was ready early. The people said it was a good bit out of town, and she wanted to check the mikes and instruments. It seemed a good *long* way. "People walk a lot on the roads down here," Halie murmured, noticing. "They are walking in from all over the island to hear you, Miss Jackson," assured their escort. At this point they turned into the airport, which was puzzling until they discovered "Hangar Auditorium" was, in fact, an old airplane hangar on Oakes Field. Nothing on the island was big enough, so they'd converted the hangar for the night, fitting it with rows all around like a circus. They'd fixed a makeshift dressing room for her, too—including bedroom furniture: they knew she'd want to rest. Before she changed, Mahalia stretched out on the bed, picked up the program left for them—and burst out laughing. "Listen, Jean. This is the 'charity' we come for: 'Entire proceeds to the P.L.P. Election Campaign Fund.' You know something?" Halie said, eyes gleaming, "I think we into some politics." Jean had been looking too. "Mahalia!" she cried, pointing—"Look who's MC!"

"Sidney Po'tier. Sidney *Po*'tier!"

"I didn't know," Jean said, reading, "he's from the Bahamas!" She helped Mahalia change and went to check the house. One sweeping look showed the huge hangar packed solid—no way of telling how many people were there. Ordinarily, Jean might have lingered; it was a colorful sight. But she didn't want to miss meeting Sidney Poitier.

She not only met him—after he gave Mahalia a beautiful introduction, he came back to keep Jean company until intermission. Which didn't come. Number after number, rising in the spirit, the islanders with her every note, sweat streaming off Mahalia despite a chill wind, hair beginning to tumble. Still she didn't break. Jean was puzzled and she felt sure Sidney Poitier was —he was due to go on. He was certainly putting himself out to entertain her—even dancing! But why— She went to have a peek. No, Mahalia seemed all right; just very much with it.

After two hours and more—encores after encores—Mahalia exited to cheers and came in reaching for dry clothes. "Baby," she panted, "with this night breeze sweeping in here, wet as I was, I didn't dare come off in here and change."

EVERY MINUTE she could, she wanted to soak up sun. Except go find a church and thank God for all this beauty and this fine reception, and sing to the glory of His name. Hallelujah. Outside of that, she wanted just to relax. And here Eskridge followed her from the States and talking chicken business! Look like he'd have better sense, better *instinct*. Well, she wasn't going let Eskridge mess up Nassau on her. Let him talk to Jean.

Chauncey Eskridge felt more than a touch exasperated. You couldn't get a definite word from Mahalia. He'd done his best to settle this thing for Ben Hooks and his crowd before she left Chicago. They insisted he follow her around until he got a yes on *paper*. It was just his good luck that where she had to be followed was Nassau.

FOR JEAN, IT wasn't only Poitier's brother, who was headwaiter at the hotel: maids, waitresses, porters, all had come, a steady trickle since they'd arrived, knocking at Mahalia's door, wanting her to know about their political problems. Earlier, Mahalia had been busy or resting, but this time on an impulse Jean said, "All right, come on in and talk to Mahalia, tell her about it."

In they filed, several, and humbleness gave way before their eagerness for Miss Jackson to know the story of the past political uprising and how now they were trying to elect some people who could identify more with themselves, the natives. Sen. Doris Johnston was with them, leading them. (Jean knew this to be true; Sen. Johnston had asked Jean privately to approach Miss Jackson about getting involved in their cause.) Mahalia listened to the words tumbling out, one topping the other. She searched the faces. She nodded. Jean sensed it was time to usher them out. With the two alone, "Mahalia, you *got* to help these people!" Jean was surprised at herself; listening, she hadn't known she was that committed. She knew what they wanted, but hadn't really made clear, was for Mahalia to come to their meeting in the park the next night. Mahalia nodded, thoughtful. "I'll come," she said.

THE CAR MADE its way through the park to a roofed pavilion strung with lights. It was on a hill. Everybody would be able to see her. Mahalia got out. "Chauncey," said Jean, "you go up and help Mahalia." Mahalia gave him her elbow with a certain elegance, and the two proceeded upward, the mass of people parting to let them through. Expectancy flickered through the night. The great Mahalia Jackson had sung for those with $5 or $10 at the hangar, but tonight she would sing for them free.

My God, *how* she's singing! Jean felt it on her skin. The other concert was fine, but this—this surpassed anything, ever. The black figures were almost lost in the night, but the black faces upturned glistened, glowed, with more than electric light. When she stopped singing, Mahalia spoke, her voice soft, yet carrying to the outmost, arms outstretched, mother to her children, shepherd to the flock . . . no, for what she told them was that they should tend their own affairs. They should not let themselves be run over by anyone. "God has given you this beautiful land and it is yours to keep, to run just like you want it run, and you must *work* to run it that way. Black people in the United States have had to fight for their rights, too; everything there is still not just like we want it—everything there isn't as great as you may have heard; but the thing is—like the song says—" and she led them in *We Shall Overcome*. Jean was shivering now, and it wasn't the chill night.

Afterwards, the problem was to get her out, to part the crowd. The people just wanted to touch her; if possible, to have her hand. "It was just like Jesus himself had come to the islands," says Jean.

Saturday, it took several planes to get from Nassau to Mobile. From Miami, Jean telephoned Joe Glaser, who said yes, the rest of the Mobile deposit was in, go ahead. But here at the auditorium, Mahalia had yet to see half the $2500 still due. She was fully dressed, waiting. Jean hunted down the promoter. "I'm going to count the house tonight," Jean said, 5′4″ of indignation. "We're going to turn stiles and what have you, before she goes on." She stalked the long route to the front office and started counting cash. Money wadded in hand, she hurried what seemed three city blocks, dim-lit, back to the stage entrance. My God! she thought, it would be just like me to get knocked on the head in Mobile. Now what to do with the money? She didn't want the man to think *she* had it. It was too big to stuff into Mahalia. They finally planted it on Charles Clency, safely on stage.

Next day they waited over: if the man didn't send Tampa's $1500 deposit in to Glaser— Forfeited! Hallelujah. She'd have all the time in the world for Nashville, Tenn., like Ben Hooks and them wanted. It was a clear sign.

Halie was going in the chicken business.

73

She was Sarah Ophelia Colley Cannon, but to Mahalia she was Minnie Pearl. They hadn't met before, but they were mutual admirers and about to be partners-in-stock.

Mahalia and Jean had flown in Monday night. Tuesday, Gov. Buford Ellington made her an honorary citizen of Tennessee. Now today they'd all eaten Minnie Pearl chicken and gone back in the office for business. John Jay Hooker, Jr., of Nashville—president and board chairman of the Minnie Pearl's Chicken System, Inc.—was sitting down with Judge Ben Hooks and his primary partner, A. W. Willis of Memphis, plus various aides on each side, to talk about the Minnie Pearl corporation's taking 50 percent of Mahalia Jackson's Chicken System, Inc., by matching their cash investment: Starting a national franchise would take capital until its stock could go public. Mahalia was visible evidence of the value and integrity of the plan, and its essential difference: all Mahalia franchises would be black-owned and managed, just as the national management would remain black. Halie listened as the figures and plans rolled on. Gulf Oil was interested in a station tie-in . . . the talk branched to a future Donut Shop chain . . . to Mahalia Jackson's Parlors, budget-priced ("You could make 'em like New Orleans," Halie injected eagerly; "put in some Creole food.") . . . then back to the concrete present: the chicken system. And ultimately, what it offered Mahalia Jackson.

Mahalia heard it all out. And—the meeting over—heard out Eskridge too. Then she called Bob Miller and made Chauncey tell him. Bob Miller didn't think it was enough front money. Chauncey was furious. "You're not a lawyer," he grated; "you have no business interfering." Bob Miller didn't care; he was only interested in Mahalia.

Even before Mr. Miller told her, Mahalia read the story in Chauncey's face. Jean said Chauncey had a conflict of interest; he could not be representing both sides—so he could just get his pay from them.

One thing she wanted was for some of the chicken money to go to her Foundation.

Next morning Mahalia woke brooding. She looked out of her hotel window and said, "I ain't flying." Jean was really disappointed. Mahalia had told Dr. King she'd be in Memphis for his meeting April 4 and Jean was looking forward to it. Mr. Hooker had arranged for them to be flown to Memphis in his personal plane. "Mahalia," Jean coaxed, "come on, let's go. The weather's not all that bad; it just *looks* stormy. Besides, Mr. Hooker's plane has two engines."

"That's not enough engines for me. I'm not flying today," Mahalia said flatly. Eskridge came by and talked contract some more and left. Mahalia was restless. In the afternoon, they went to see J. Robert Bradley at the National Baptist Convention offices; then he took them to his apartment. Toward evening, he and Jean got some dinner going. Then they all settled to TV. It was a bombshell. Martin Luther King was shot. All three sat shocked, exclaiming, moaning. "Mahalia, they killed him!" Bradley cried. "No they *didn't,* Bradley!" she said sternly, "they shot him in the behind; didn't you hear? Now be *quiet*." She crumpled, rocking. "I got to know; I got to know how he is, I got to know." She wish Bradley wouldn't carry on so; make a exhibition of every thing, got to *dramatize.* Please, God, don't let Martin be too hurt.

"Mahalia!" gasped Jean, "do you realize if we'd flown that's right where you'd have been? Right *with* him?"

"I know it, baby; I know it. Now let's just listen. Oh, my God, Martin—Martin!" She wept, praying it wasn't bad as that crazy woman in New York; that woman hurt him *so* bad. . . . This time Bradley had no doubts. "Mahalia, he's *dead,"* he shrieked. She refused to accept it. He *required* her to listen to what the man on TV was *saying* . . . and Mahalia collapsed. Finally, "Jean, let's go back to the hotel."

Already, radio and television told of rioting in Chicago—rioting everywhere. "What shall I do? What shall I do?" Mahalia was so *piteous,* thought Jean, unable to advise—certainly Chicago wasn't the place to be. Nashville, too, was breaking into violence. Halie was distraught. Where was there to be? To get to Atlanta from? Suddenly she knew. "Jean, call Russell come take us to Chattanooga; we can be there with him and his mother."

Early Sunday morning, Russell Goode drove Mahalia, Jean, and Bradley directly to Ebenezer Baptist, Dr. King's church in Atlanta. They were led up front. Martin's brother A. D. was delivering the sermon. Martin's father followed him. Then Mahalia stood and, alone, sang her sermon—a song out of the gospel whose spirit of love had been Martin's and was her true religion; the heart might break—the faith in man that God created could not. Evil was loose, but God was on the side of the angels. Hallelujah.

As they neared the desk at Regency Hyatt House, Jean's heart sank: "The clerks were turning people away—'no rooms, sorry, sorry, sorry.' But when Mahalia walked up, magically two double bedrooms were ready and waiting." Shortly, a boy brought up an entire meal—turnip greens, sweet tomatoes, ham, corn sticks, everything. On top was a big box of roses. The card said, "Coretta King." Bradley looked at the food, looked at the roses, looked at the card. "It was a sight I'll never forget," he says. Coretta wasn't one who took to everybody, but she liked Mahalia.

Bob Miller was in Atlanta, waiting, by the time Mahalia arrived. He knew there'd be things Mahalia would want him to do. Yes—transportation for the musicians playing in relays while Dr. King was lying in state. Mr. Miller leased a car. Mahalia needed him herself to meet Mrs. King, coming from some kind of memoriam in Memphis: "Everybody thinks Coretta's coming in to the airport, but she's coming to the Southern Airlines hangar. So let them all run and we'll just leave after them and they won't know." Mahalia had her own way of doing things, and Mr. Miller never questioned it. And he had a chance to talk to her again about that chicken business.

5 A.M. WAS a terrible time to get up, but this was a terrible time. Jean helped Mahalia into the navy and white knit she'd bought in Chattanooga for the funeral. They were ready at 6, when it was necessary to leave to get into the church. Already there was a crowd, but entrance was by invitation: Bradley couldn't come, space was so short. Mahalia was ushered to the pulpit to sit with the ministers. Jean went to the balcony. She could spot some of the names she knew were down there: Eartha Kitt, Belafonte, Poitier, Gov. Rockefeller—that must be his wife; he was giving her his seat and moving to the wall to stand; Mayor Lindsey from New York and—George Romney? That was Bobby Kennedy—it must be his wife sitting next to him. Oh, Mahalia's face was strained. Thank God she didn't have to sing here. Considering the state she was in at the hotel, Jean didn't know *how* she'd be by the time they got to Morehouse. . . .

She was all right; reasonably so; at least she was staying on top of what had to be done, which at this minute was trying to get through to the car, at least two blocks off. Impossible to connect with anybody to get Mr. Miller to come closer now he could have. Ooh, another walk—at least a block pushing through the crowd to the building on campus. Jean knew Mahalia's feet hurt just as much as hers did.

Juanita Abernathy was concerned. Standing downstairs in the foyer of the Morehouse library, Mahalia was obviously ill; almost out of breath, could hardly reply when Mrs. Abernathy spoke although her smile was greeting enough. What a great spirit she was. Even though she had risen above many of the injustices that a lot of her people experienced, even though *she* was not in the grass roots, she had a deep concern for change. Martin loved her.

It was a relief to see Mahalia escorted upstairs. She could get a little rest up there, until time for the service.

Dr. Benjamin Mays looked up and greeted Mahalia warmly, but the Morehouse College president was still working on his speech. Jean tiptoed to a chair. Mahalia walked out onto the balcony to get some air. She'd do better to sit down, Jean thought. "Jean! Open that door!" Mahalia's voice was sharp. "Let President Kennedy through there!" Mahalia had spotted Bobby Kennedy. "Mahalia!" They rushed to greet each other, then drew aside to speak quietly. Several people came in and out, but Jean found herself watching only Bobby Kennedy: "His manner was so unusual. He seemed to be concerned about open windows and doors. He was constantly looking back over his shoulder when he heard someone approach the room. I'd never seen him in person before, but on television he hadn't seemed that way—more of an outgoing, easy person; certainly not a nervous type."

Time. Jean gave the new assignment to her feet and followed Mahalia.

The speakers' stand was on the entrance level but the piano was on the ground, a few feet from Martin's casket. Mahalia was disturbed: scarce as seats were, Edward had brought some woman with him from Chicago and got her seated on Mahalia's name. Not only that, the woman had on a headful of white feathers stood out like a cock. Hard enough to get her mind on her singing. Lord, give me breath.

He did. He *did*. She sang out her sorrow, sang a plea for forgiveness of mankind, sang for the soul she knew was sitting at Jesus' side. Save me a place, Martin. Save me a place. But don't you people go trying to make him a saint. Martin was a human man—and that's the whole thing of it. Can't they see?

WEDNESDAY morning, almost the whole planeload to California was sleeping when Jean roused and headed for the washroom past James Baldwin, Clara Ward and her mother, Brock Peters, Tony Franciosa. The stewardess was kneeling by some man's seat, and as Jean waited to get past, "Hi," he said. Jean gave a guarded hello. "I know what kind of cologne you're wearing. Yeah, that's Nina Ricci's *L'Aire du Temps*." It was. "I wonder if you would introduce me to Mahalia?" Jean glanced ahead. Mahalia was nodding, asleep. They'd do it when the plane landed, Jean compromised. She had a feeling she ought to know him. But who? On putdown, the man walked up immediately. Jean had no choice. "Please forgive me, I *know* I'm supposed to know you, but I can't recall your name and I want to introduce you."

"Well, Jean, I'm Marlon Brando." Jean's jaw dropped. But he seemed so tiny—she'd have looked for a big guy! And listen to Mahalia: "Oh, honey,

I'm so *glad* to meet you!" After they were off, and Yancey was bustling the luggage, it was Mahalia's turn. "Jean," she asked, "who Marlon Brando?"

74

The Easter concert at the Forum in Inglewood had been in the works for months, a big one for the Foundation. Celeste, Margaret, Robbie Preston, Gwen, Yancey, Allen Clark, a whole squad had worked with churches, choirs, handed out placards. When Dr. King was killed just 10 days before, Mahalia converted the program to a memorial and had his portrait painted to put on stage. It stood there now on an easel, spotlighted. Already Thurston and Gwen's Voices of Hope had won their response . . . the Staple Singers, theirs . . . the Ladies of Song, theirs with Celeste's *This Same Jesus* sending the Forum's white owner to his feet clapping to the beat. Mahalia had called Edwin Hawkins, James Cleveland, Yancey to the stage. Emotion was lapping the house like a rising tide, and now Mahalia—hair loose, face contorted with the agony, the ecstasy—strode to the portrait and began *We Shall Overcome.* Yancey rushed to Mahalia as she struggled with the heavy frame and together they held the painting high, Mahalia singing all the while. The audience was into a shout. Women screaming. The white folks in the audience won't know what to do with this, thought Yancey. He could see Mary Ann Hooper; she was crying. Mahalia was improvising, exultant, handing the microphone to first one then the other to take a verse, drawing them together for a chorus, reclaiming the lead. On the line *We shall all be free,* something pierced through her voice that exploded the teetering dam and the audience went up! out, over, onto the big stage in a screaming, shouting, crying, hollering, jumping mass. The singers were out of it themselves. It was a jubilee. Mahalia was pitched high . . . *Weeeeeee shall over—yes!—we'll overcome! Yes! Lord!* The police were trying to hold a path to get her off. Yancey was trying to pry loose the painting—she would not let go (her friend, her friend), still singing. Yancey finally tugged it loose and with the guards, pulled her off, Mahalia nowhere in this world. Gwen was still playing, tears streaming, not realizing Mahalia was gone 'til Yancey shouted. Giant Thurston Frazier was jumping up and down in a trance, the stage shaking as he landed. Margaret took off down the aisles and had to be caught. Yancey and one guard were guiding Mahalia down the long hall to the dressing room. She was still singing, echoes bouncing back on echoes in the narrow corridor, and under this, shouts from the stage abruptly peaked again—something had set them off. Almost to Mahalia's dressing room. Suddenly Margaret rushed past, shouting, high in the spirit. Yancey broke away and chased to grab her, afraid she'd hurt herself crashing into something. One by one the principals made it into the dressing room, aware again—then without warning, the spirit took over. Up went the song. Down went Mahalia into a chair, and up again, thrust high. Gwen is running up and down. Margaret is running up and down. Yancey is trying to hold onto Thurston, who is spinning, all 300 pounds, little Yancey spinning with him, trying to slow him down. An hour and a half later, calm had come.

Remembrance held through the week. By then Mahalia had recorded for Townsend—Charles Clency's first exposure to the perfectionist who made the session wait while a score was changed; who slapped a slim hand on the piano imperiously to pick up the beat; whose "Hallelujah" let you sense she was pleased (later, privately, not so pleased to have to apologize to Townsend for Mitchell's not settling the Songs of Praise) . . . had done three talk shows, talking benefit . . . and had got herself a Festival of Stars. The minute she got home, she had her placards printed, her squads out to tack: Dinah Shore, Moms Mabley, Dick Van Dyke, Pat Boone, Peter Lawford, Della Reese—who hadn't hesitated a second once they caught up with her: she'd *positively* be there for mama. Besides, she had the Staple Singers, the Caravans, Red Saunders Band. That didn't include all the smaller acts they'd back up with.

"Now let's sell it," said Mahalia. They had May and June. She'd taken time out to do right by Ralph Abernathy, speaking April 28 at Boy Baby's church in his first public address since he was named SCLC president hours after Martin was killed. "Andrew Young called to ask particularly that Mahalia give the same courtesy she had given Dr. King, to focus attention on him," says Rev. Thurston. Coretta came too. With Mayor Daley's help, they were met by special limousine procession with police escort to the church and a protection squad assigned. Mahalia sang and afterward she had a dinner for him, some 25 leaders, and the police. Missie had stayed home to cook—and chase cars to keep the whole block clear.

Rev. Abernathy's name went on her Advisory Board to replace Martin's. Then Nettie Irving got hold of Duke Ellington for her, and she put both of them on. "Now let's concentrate on this show." The house was a warren of workers. Mahalia roved—asking, prodding—Jean at her elbow. The Friday after Rev. Abernathy's dinner, everything had to be cleared again for a kick-off luncheon for the Indiana group of, hopefully, buyers for the $50 and $100 box seats. Tiny Barnes helped cater the food, and Albertina Walker did a Halie and sang *a cappella* when things seemed a little slow. She'd have the big, big kick-off for Chicago in two weeks: so big they'd have to make a patio party and not feed the people. Everybody worked on names to invite. She didn't need to put down Mayor Daley; she'd spoken to him when she sang for his annual Prayer Breakfast.

It wasn't easy to keep track of who actually did what when because from time to time she had to fly to sing—to Los Angeles, to Portsmouth, Va., to Winston-Salem—$10,000 a concert nothing to treat lightly when you're pulling hair, teeth, and nails to sell $10 tickets. She'd told ABC not to book her for June—except for Washington, D.C., and the three days in British Columbia—going to let Albertina sing on that. She had some little ones in Chicago. Maybe if Mildred all right, she could take her to the Palmer House . . . she's not able to help Louise too much anyway. Lord Jesus! Look at what still need doing. This minute write Lady Bird—Halie sure want her on the benefit; *she* would understand the need to help these young people prepare. "The world is so battered and torn up," she dictated thoughtfully, "it seems that love has gone. So many people I come in contact with, I hear their cries of their condition. My heart goes out to them. . . . If you can't come, you have two lovely daughters I believe love me very much. . . . I'll be praying and asking God for your decision." Well, that's the best she could do. This place around here like Babel. She didn't know if they understood much more.

A new figure was a free-lance public relations man brought in by Willa Jones; he'd worked on her pageant. Brown, brisk, a born front-man, Harry Dale reminded her a little of Al Duckett, only this boy did a lot more fetch and carry—including hauling her to the doctor. More and more, her heart beat fast. Harry could see to Mildred, too. She wish Mildred hadn't of called Celie to get Celie to ask her to take Mildred back. Mildred couldn't admit she wasn't able, and Halie wasn't going to tell Celie Mildred's business.

Harry Dale was fascinated by the whirlpool he'd stuck an arm into. The cross-currents were such that he figured he'd better go cautiously. Mildred Falls was one. He'd overheard Miss Jackson and her former pianist get into—misunderstandings—behind closed doors, but "Mildred was with me when we was eating hamburgers, baby, bumping along in those cars," she said, having him "see Mildred gets where she's going"—maybe to cash Mahalia's check, or to the doctor.

Polly Fletcher was another. "The oldtimers really buzzed afterwards, the couple of times she came around," he says. Apparently she usually was in touch with Miss Jackson at night, by phone.

A lot to learn around here. But worth it.

Bobby Kennedy! Jean hoped by all means to go. It would be an exciting evening: "You could tell just from the people calling Mahalia to come, begging her—Peter Lawford first and then all the others when she didn't say yes. Of course, whenever political people called to ask Mahalia to sing, or go anywhere, she always cleared it with Daley's office to see if they were backing it." But this Hollywood rally May 24 for Bobby Kennedy for President was almost nonpartisan, there were so many stars going; some Mahalia would want to speak to, too. And she was waiting on what Mayor Daley thought. "Call Col. Reilly, Jean," Mahalia said at last, "see what Daley's going do." The "second mayor" wouldn't know her from Adam, Jean knew, although her name was on the Democratic political-dinner list. "We're not sure yet we're going to back Bobby Kennedy," said Col. Reilly, "I'll have to get back to you." Damn. "What he say?" asked Mahalia. "He said yes," said Jean. It could not possibly injure Mahalia in any way.

THEY WENT a day early so Mahalia could do a Steve Allen show, but nobody's mind was on anything but Friday night's rally at the Sports Arena. Ordinary seats cost $25; it ought to make a mint for his campaign, Dick Yancey thought, sizing up the house. Of course, he didn't have to pay; he was with Mahalia. So were Bill Duncan, Bobbie Harris (Mahalia's half-sister Yvonne's stepson) and his wife Geri, besides Clency and Eddie Robinson. Johnny was on his night job.

Jean was elated; it was as special as she knew it would be. Jerry Lewis came in and clowned around, sat on her lap, and kidded Mahalia—Mahalia really liked him; he was the one could make her relax. He promised he'd take three pages in the Festival of Stars program because he couldn't break his July 1 commitment. When Peter Lawford came he said no, he wouldn't forget *her* benefit and Mahalia said she'd send his plane tickets.

Watching another and another star come, Clency did a mental blink. Possibly he had not really valued Mahalia's stature as highly as he might, growing up in the same town with her.

After the show, Bobby invited them to his private reception room. They walked in on some 600–700 people. Both Bobby and his wife Ethel managed to get through to greet Mahalia warmly and thank her. Jacqueline Kennedy spoke too, but she seemed naturally more reserved, to Jean's eye. Yancey wanted Mahalia to speak to some of the stars for her benefit—Rosey Grier, Shirley MacLaine, Raquel Welch, Gene Barry, so *many* were here. But Mahalia said not to bother them.

Next morning it was Jean's job to turn in the car they'd rented at the airport, and what with one thing and another and too much business at the rental desk, time melted. Mahalia was aboard; so were Edward and Charles—*always* the last. No Jean. The engines started. No Jean. The door slammed shut. Mahalia rose up 10 feet tall in her stocking feet, planted a fist on each hip and roared, "Don't you move this plane! Jean's not on! Don't you MOVE this plane—don't you dare move this plane—Jean's not ON!" The crew heard it even in the cockpit. The captain looked at his copilot quizzically—they were 10 minutes late. That was Mahalia Jackson. They'd idle just a few more seconds. . . . Jean ran for the closed, quivering, roaring jet although she knew she'd missed—they'd told her she missed it—but instead of rolling, it opened like Aladdin's cave, swooped her up and inside, slapped shut and took off, and as Jean entered the cabin, the entire length of it burst into laughter and applause. "I told them not to move this plane 'til you was on, Jean," Mahalia said comfortingly. It was Jean's most embarrassing moment since she hadn't known Marlon Brando.

Twelve days later Robert Kennedy was killed. Mahalia shared her memories and her voice for television in Chicago and New York; but when it was time for the requiem mass at St. Patrick's Cathedral, she was too stricken to attend. She prayed in her hotel room—for his peace and for the Lord to smite what was fearful in the land.

CHICAGO HELD its own fears. Her benefit was falling apart. The stars were backing out: She called Ann in Hollywood (Mary Ann Hooper) to please, please see what she could do. Besides that, the tickets weren't moving, couldn't get nothing contributed, couldn't get the right publicity—nothing. The Democratic Convention was coming and Mayor Daley had the city locked up. Nothing but politics. Anything else, just dump. She didn't even have Jean—come back from Bobby Kennedy eyes all swollen, and still sick. Mahalia dialed Col. Reilly, unburdened herself, listened, nodded, put down the receiver, and jumped up. "I'm going downtown," she said firmly.

Supplicants to see the mayor were many and entrants were few. But when Mahalia came to see the mayor, she came to see the mayor: "Mahalia could walk into anyone's office and upset the place," says Col. Reilly; "she didn't stand on dignity. But then, she always had entrée. The mayor was proud of Mahalia; he loved her. And she loved the mayor."

That was not her mood of the moment. She walked close, fixed the mayor's eye and said, "Look, I'm having this program and you got everything tied up. I need you to turn it aloose. Turn this city *loose!*" The mayor gave his pledge of anything she wanted—told Col. Reilly to find out what Mahalia wanted and get it for her—then wrote a $5,000 check as his contribution.

"The next *day*," says Allen Clark, awed, "things began to move like clockwork. Tickets were popping; press, radio, TV, everywhere you went, the talk was about that affair."

COUNTDOWN was close. Tickets were selling (all except the $50–$100 ones) but where was the show? The best Halie could do was pray—and call Sherman Oaks again. "Ann—?" It was not a good time to have to sit and wait in Ming's anteroom, trying to ask him about the extension on her record contract. She'd given it to him in April, and now the Columbia people thinking it's her fault. Jean Childers grew indignant. "The business you give these people! To sit out here and wait! Isn't there anyone else who can handle your affairs?" Halie looked at her, and rose. "That friend of yours, that lawyer who came to my kickoff," she said, "I liked him. Take me to see Mr. Superior."

Dark-haired, fair, forceful, with an attractive vitality, Gene Shapiro was surprised and delighted. And after a three-hour talk about the general state of her business (contract muddles, property mismanagement, percentage squabbles, displaced or misplaced funds, no portfolio, "people in cahoots"—Jean contributing overpaid credit-card bills, lapsed checks, a years-old savings account with no interest ever paid, forgotten small-bank deposits, and currently a $13,900 check returned, reissued, and now misplaced) Shapiro was appalled. "I told her I'd be happy to serve her in any capacity she wished, with two reservations: no Mahalia Jackson Foundation and no chicken system"—for which Mahalia had just signed in a flourish of goodwill in Memphis.

For a long time Mahalia would keep her Great White Lawyer a secret. And for just a little longer than that, Shapiro could keep his reservations.

75

Mary Ann Hooper wasn't sure how she got here, or what she was doing in a setup where she was "Whitey from Hollywood." Mahalia's call .earlier in the week had seemed so artless: "Why don't you come over this weekend, Ann? You can help me put the show together." Mary Ann hadn't liked to just dash in and out, so she'd arrived Friday morning.

It was an abrupt awakening. The star search on her end had gone reasonably well, she'd thought: Robert Culp and his wife, France Nuyen, were coming to Chicago for Jesse Jackson's ordination Sunday; they'd both do the show Monday. She'd found James Baldwin at Columbia Studios working on a film script, and he was positively coming for dear Mahalia. That should fill the major name gap.

But as of this appalled moment, Moms Mabley had canceled for illness, and Marlon Brando, Dick Van Dyke, Sarah Vaughan, Pat Boone were all out. Mahalia was clinging to the hope that Aretha Franklin would give in and come work with the Saunders band, but Aretha insisted she needed her own troupe. When Jean added up costs, that came to over $2300 for transportation, hotels and meals, and Halie said no, it was too much out of the benefit. Bad enough things crop up like $1,000 to the artists-union people (Theatre Authority), or else they wouldn't let her hold the show. Mrs.

Spachner at the Auditorium Theatre explained it had to be. Eskridge messed up on that; she just *did* get it in three days ago. Him and his ski accident; she dished him *out!* Mary Ann said all right, Mahalia, but it's the talent we're talking about. Forget Aretha; that wasn't going to work. But the show was all out of shape—*had* no shape—and she was afraid Mahalia was going to have a heart attack. They needed one socko name. "Yancey," said Mary Ann abruptly, "who's in town?" No! The two raced off. (Mahalia said she had to stay on the phone to sell those $100 tickets, baby.) At the Palmer House, "I was ready to go on my knees," says Mary Ann. No need. "I love the dear lady!" beamed Jimmy Durante; "of course I'll do her show." His one proviso was that they take him whenever he showed: he was flying daily to Battle Creek, Mich., to make commercials. All her problems should be so small, breathed Mary Ann.

They rushed back to the Albert Pick Hotel. Willa Jones had rented a two-bedroom suite at Dale's urging, "so Mahalia can get some rest before the show." Mahalia sputtered about the cost, but it was handy—downtown, and right across from the Auditorium Theatre. As for rest—who going sell these $50 and $100 tickets? Mary Ann shook her head; Mahalia really was not well and yet Mary Ann could hardly tear her off that telephone day or night for a serious conference about the show. And it needed it. As Mary Ann gathered from bits and pieces of information, among them they had graciously accepted offers of about 90 local acts. Something had to give. A *lot* had to give. Mahalia was more worried about James Baldwin's being on the show: he was a good man but what would he say? She didn't want nobody messing up her show. "Mahalia," said Mary Ann firmly, "stop worrying about Jimmy Baldwin; worry about the 90 acts. They've got to go."

Slowly, just by arithmetic, she convinced Mahalia that some, indeed, had to go. "But not *too* many, Ann; I promised these people." And she put a bodyguard on Mary Ann. Mary Ann demurred. She realized there was resentment of her coming in and usurping authority and so forth, but a *bodyguard?* "Listen, baby," said Mahalia, "you got to understand that being black don't mean you're good. There's bad black and good black and in-between black; just like there's good white and bad white and in-between white. And we've got some rotten niggers!" The word shocked Mary Ann; it implied a highly prejudicial state of mind even from a black person. Mahalia just shook her head at this white child. "Ann, you don't understand. If you was black, you'd use the word 'nigger.' But you're not, and you're very fancy in your sensitiveness." Mary Ann stared. Given Mahalia's enormous compassion and understanding of her people, Mahalia couldn't be wrong in this. Mary Ann knew she'd been put down.

BUT PUTTING out—that was the issue: For two days they warred, Mahalia wanting her way, Mary Ann insisting "You sing, I'll produce." At

6 a.m. Sunday, Mahalia knocked on her door. "Ann?" Mary Ann had just finished working out the logistics of what was still left on the boards. She threw down her pen. "Mahalia, it won't work. You'll be run out of town on a rail." Mahalia stood and looked at the pale, determined face, the small figure thin as a whip. Finally: "Okay, go ahead and do it your way." Mary Ann would never forget the look on her face.

IN THE JACKSON suite, Yancey and Russell Goode had been added. Mahalia didn't feel easy about Yancey in Chicago, anyway—she'd given him a butcher knife and shown him how to hold it and warned him about standing with his shadow showing on the bedroom blinds, which he was to keep pulled at all times. It was easier to guard him here at the hotel. Yancey and Willa were at each other's throats, but you got to expect that; everybody nervous. But she warned Yancey to pick who he tangled with: "Boy, they be over you like grease on gravy."

The one key person missing was Jean Childers. She'd collapsed a week ago and was in the hospital. Yancey waited as long as he could to say Peter Lawford was missing too; he wasn't on the plane when Yancey went to meet him. Now the show was in the hands of the Lord.

And Mary Ann. Mahalia was at the hotel Monday, still making $100 calls. Ben Hooks and John Jay Hooker were in. Townsend too; she asked him to go help Mary Ann but he came back saying it was a madhouse. Rev. Franklin, Aretha's daddy, was here. And Rev. Bentley, who got her out of jail in Philadelphia and never let her forget it. She was waiting for the main one.

DINAH SHORE had broken into her summer tour, but she wouldn't *not* have come for anything. "Mahalia had talked about this for at least three years. Now she'd hired this big hall and so many of the names I expected weren't there—probably didn't realize the significance to Mahalia. Hardly *anybody* was at rehearsal, and the orchestra was weird." A union pickup, if she knew Mahalia; nobody would be paid and that's as it should be. But what a shame, the only complete section was the rhythm section. Her boys would just work with that. Part of her was keeping an eye out for Mahalia. She really loved that woman. "We talked on the telephone every once in a while, and wrote, but it had been years—"

Mahalia tried not to hurry too fast, but the second she hit the entrance and saw Dinah up on that stage, she rushed down the aisle and up the steps to throw her arms around her. Dinah! This was the show. When she could catch her breath—got no business acting like a child on skates—they rehearsed the numbers they'd do together, Eddie Robinson and Charles Clency quick to grasp what Mahalia wanted. Mildred Falls was down there watching; had, in fact, said, "I don't think Mahalia's going to let me play for her tonight," as if she expected an ally; but Dinah felt at that moment *Mahalia* needed an ally, "because there had to be a reason and this had to be dragging at Mahalia, but you'd never guess it. Mahalia disliked scenes as much as I did; we both had a very slow fuse."

Singing with Dinah, arms about each other's waist, Halie's joy was like a bubble inside—but she wish her heart wouldn't beat so fast. Like a hammer on the rails. When Dinah went to work on a solo, she left. "I got to get back to the hotel," she gasped to Yancey. He helped her across the street and called the house doctor from the lobby. Mahalia was almost grey. The doctor prescribed a sedative he said would knock her out for about four hours and rest her heart. He wasn't willing to say whether she'd be able to sing.

Dr. Barclay listened to the familiar recital. He had been seeing Mahalia so often recently, he knew precisely the shape she was in. He sensed her fear—and he knew how high she had built herself for this night. "You're the only one who can tell how you feel, Mahalia. Possibly after you rest—" She wanted him *there.*

"All right, Mahalia, I'll come to your show. I'll come check you."

"I DON'T KNOW why I answered the phone," says Missie Wilkerson. She was alone in Mahala's house; it was the last thing before the program; Allen and Allen's daddy and Jerome Burks—working for Mahala now—taken the money *and* the tickets and she had nary a ticket to sell. *Wrong* to take those tickets, *she*'s the one Mahalia trust. All right. She's just waiting for a ride. So why did she pick up the phone? No tickets. It was Minters. She knew he was scared it was one of his enemies. "It's me, Missie," she assured him. "This is Galloway. I want two tickets for tonight for me and my daughter. Let me talk to Mahalia, Missie."

"She's at the Albert Pick, Minters, but I doubt if you get to speak to her. And Minters, they ain't a ticket in this house. But you can get one downtown—the $10 and all them's gone, but they's $50 tickets."

"Missie," he said, "I don't have *ten* dollars." The best Missie could think was for him to come ride her downtown, see what they could scuffle. "But watch—if I make a wave at you, keep going, 'cause your enemies will be here." While she was waiting, Missie phoned her granddaughter and she phoned Jean; nobody had a ticket, but Jean said she'd give Missie a lift. Jean had signed herself out of the hospital to go to the show.

Minters came first. "Minters," hissed Missie, "I'm going to hide you in this house 'til Jean and Ken come." Just then they pulled up. The upshot was Childers said, "Follow me, Galloway; I'll give you my ticket," and he lit out, Missie no more than inside and the door shut. It was late.

And now Minters was lost. Jean wrote "For Galloway" across Ken's ticket and scooted and ducked through the crowd, then Missie and Jean went inside. Galloway was not to be seen until—"That's him!" Jean said. The ushers were arguing with him; he had just taken whatever seat suited him. He came on up, laughing, waving. "I'm in!"

THANK GOD. Jimmy Durante. Mary Ann pounced on him. It was curtain time and Albertina and her Caravans weren't here yet. Surprised applause swept the audience as the Great Schnozzola entered with his entire show. He entertained them for 30 minutes. Mary Ann used the respite to confer with Kup Kupcinet, who was MC, Mary Ann having decreed that *two* MCs was too much. Studs Terkel said he'd introduce Willa Jones and bow out. All Mahalia's scholarship winners would get was an introduction, too: operatic arias were *out*. Those of the audience with programs were a little bewildered; nothing listed seemed to be what they were seeing, but nobody minded—Mahalia was full of surprises. Mary Ann gathered the show was going well but she couldn't stop to see. She was tending lights, giving directions, getting the next act ready, and typing cue cards in time to hand them to Kup one by one. Fortunately, the big newspaperman seemed calm; all he wanted was a nice, smooth show for Mahalia. Della Reese had to get on quickly, too—she had her own show at the Sherman House. Still, Jerry Butler, the Staples, the Shape—it was working, thought Mary Ann, daring a little elation even as she tried to soothe the temper of one more scissored act.

MAHALIA WAS in Dinah Shore's mind as she stepped on stage determined to give it all she had. She'd left Mahalia in the dressing room lying ashen, exhausted; the fact that she had her hair and face all fixed just made it more touching when she said, "Darling, they're not going to let me go on tonight."

"Well, don't worry about it," Dinah said; "the show's going to be wonderful." She hoped nobody would tell Mahalia that half the orchestra hadn't showed up. And hoped now that the audience wouldn't mind too much when just *she* showed up, without Mahalia. But she won a really warm reception and was just about to make her exit when she had "one of the most memorable moments of my life. I looked up and here comes Mahalia, exquisitely dressed in a beaded gown; she was slimmer, and so proud of herself. I ran over and I hugged her and I thought, I'll help her over, and she walked out proudly, with all her dignity. She bows very quietly to the audience, and we do *Down by the Riverside* and all the other numbers we'd rehearsed, and then she says, 'We'll do *Elijah Rock*.' I did the biggest take I've ever done—it had been *years* since we'd sung that. So I said, 'Okay, we'll do *Elijah Rock*.' She bows to me, and I bow to her, and she signals and the organist plays this chord and it's in the right key and we start to sing. I don't know *what* I'm doing. Mahalia sings *Elijah Rock, shout, shout, Elijah Rock*—and I sing *coming up the Lord* . . . but I get a word in there. Now we do this whole thing and when I tell you I sang Hallelujahs, *ave*'s,

Elijahs, whoooo-whoooo's, any way I could fit 'em in—hand claps, *anything* to distract from what I'm *not* singing—and she kept singing and kept looking over at me and the audience goes wild at the end. As we finished, she takes my hand and we bow to each other, and she says, 'You forgot your part, didn't you, darling?' "

BACKSTAGE AT intermission, Dr. Barclay saw that after that remarkable exhibition on stage Mahalia had folded again. Her pattern. How long she could keep it up, he didn't know. She seemed literally to draw strength from her singing. Now she was worried about her solo section. "You want to go on, Mahalia, and you can," he assured her; "sing. But rest now. Don't talk." Mahalia nodded, dubious. He was right, but she didn't know if he was *really* right.

Outside, Yancey was standing beside the policeman Mayor Daley had assigned, helping the man keep people from Mahalia's door. The mayor himself was standing to one side, waiting to be introduced on stage; *he* knew the doctor was in there and *he* wouldn't go in. Yancey sure wasn't going to let this person in insisting she was "Polly Fletcher, Miss Jackson's secretary." Yancey knew better; Jean Childers was Mahalia's secretary. "Lady," he said, "if you was the Angel Gabriel, you couldn't go in that door." Mary Ann called him just then and when he came back, the policeman shrugged and said she *knew* the doctor.

Working with Mary Ann, Ken Childers was suddenly aware that poor bastard Galloway was trying to get through backstage. On an impulse, Ken went to the outer door, beckoned him in, and pointed him in the direction of Mahalia's dressing room. Sigmond started off with assurance—and was blocked by the police guard. No visitors. No. No! "LET HIM IN!" roared Mahalia's voice from inside.

Shouts, laughter, screams. Jean Childers, hurried up because she'd heard Mahalia was ill, pulled open the door—and backed out. They were kissing, hugging, having a ball. "Who let that man in?" Allen Clark said sternly. Ken drew on all his Indian ancestors. "I did, with my bow and arrow," he said, hoping he looked fierce. "And you done the right thing, honey," called Mahalia, swinging open the door, Minters beside her. "Now I can sing, 'cause I got my man and I got *another* voice!"

Charles and Eddie walked on to signal her entrance—and Mildred darted after, making as if to sit. Eddie did not budge. The tableau held for what seemed minutes, then Mildred retreated. Mahalia gave her a scathing look and walked on (she'd deal with Miss Mildred after—humiliating her!) but right now, she had *songs* to sing. *Hallelujah!* "She's singing like she never sang before!" thought an awed Dinah Shore, listening, scalp prickling with the thrust of it. "This is her night."

IT WAS 4½ hours before the curtain rang down, and longer before goodbyes were said. Mahalia had a 7:45 a.m. plane to catch. She'd spend what was left of the night at the airport hotel. Her luggage was already in the limousine Bob Miller had lent her this week. And when she pulled away from the crowd, Minnis was in the limousine too.

". . . and that's what he done, Ida," Elliott Beal reported, voice quivering. "That man is *so* fly—say like the old folks, 'fly as the shithouse rat, never can catch him.' "

76

Why had she thought it would be any different? In Minneapolis she had helped dedicate something remarkable, a chapel in the tall new Midwest Federal Savings & Loan Building—with a surprise helper: Mitch Miller, in town to conduct the symphony. She'd fallen on his neck; hadn't seen him in *years*. And the bank people just so nice. Then Minnis had to be up to his old tricks. Embarrassing her, correcting her, acting grand. Then right after, at Old Milwaukee Days, him running after some little old girl and staying out. She smoothed a finger on the framed photograph she was staring at, and tears stood in the dark almond eyes. Like she told Ben Hooks when he come in here to talk chicken business: there's the man she should have married. Russell Roberts. But Minnis was her *husband*.

She went downstairs at 4:30 a.m. and woke Yancey to help her strip the furniture in the pink bedroom and call her niece—she was making Bertha a present of it; be ready for it at 7:30. For the life of him, Yancey could not figure what prompted Mahalia to buy new.

In the weeks that followed, Minters became a frequent adjunct. Allen was there, Beal and Russell Goode were still guests, so when Minters stayed the night, that routed Yancey. He didn't really mind, especially after he opened his eyes one night and saw a huge man looking as startled at seeing a white fellow sleeping in Mahalia's house as Yancey was at seeing Cassius Clay.

But Mahalia had more on her mind than Minnis. The closer Democratic Convention came, the more politics was rising. She wasn't bothered that McCarthy headquarters was calling; she *knew* where Daley stood on that and Daley *still* doing the most for her people, in her book. No, it was the violence going up like a balloon. Now Bayard Rustin said something in *Jet* set her to more than thinking: said the black-power people who didn't believe in America would be turning against the black people who did. And *who* in front more than Mahalia? Lord, Lord, Martin was missed; nobody else around could lead them out of the wilderness. Halie best be looking to Halie. She called Nettie Irving and Jean Childers (no longer secretary since she'd fallen ill; Allen was). She gave each a different reason, but her request was the same: see can they find her a condominium up high. Harry Dale drove her around looking. But Halie had music to rehearse, and Jesus Lord! the Mormon ones enough to make Beal *and* her sweat, both. She better send this boy Yancey home. She had to go to Europe soon. And she sure wasn't taking him to Harlem.

THE PLANE to Tony Lawrence's Harlem Culture Festival swung over New York the better part of an hour and Edward wasn't even on it, had missed, but Beal could play with Clency so they rushed to the park, police sirens wailing a way . . . only to have the police back out: crowd too dense to risk Miss Jackson. It was all to do again Sunday. Some whichaway, to Beal, things naturally got excited around Mahalia. She'd offered to take him to Europe—just a quick trip—if he got his birth certificate up and a passport. "But it was so jumped-up I couldn't get myself to *figuring* it—all to do in a week and she was just now getting her own shots." He better go home and relieve Ida taking care of his daddy, gone senile.

THE ANTIBES Music Festival at Juan-les-Pins had even agreed to stop selling liquor during her performances, July 20 and 25. She had time and the mood to enjoy the water and the flowers and the sun and do something nice like going to visit Princess Grace. Minnis would *die,* much as that man love celebrities; with him, it's like having TB.

It was a private call. Grace of Monaco had admired Mahalia Jackson for many years and she was looking forward to their meeting. She received her in the palace, then shortly they went into the garden to sit and talk: of her reactions to the festival . . . her Silver Dove award at the Monte Carlo Festival in '61, and how she treasured it . . . the deaths of Robert Kennedy and Dr. King and occasions they had shared . . . her foundation, her hopes for youth. "The afternoon passed much too quickly," says Princess Grace. "Mahalia Jackson was a very rare and wonderful person and gave one the feeling after a few moments in her presence of having known her a lifetime." She felt grateful to have been in her presence.

At the hotel, Mahalia reflected on what a nice girl the princess was, with a depth to her, and how she hadn't been spoiled by changing from Grace Kelly. That was more than she could say for a lot of them in Hollywood. Look like when most people get famous, they forget how to be natural, their lives change . . . and they lose something.

One thing she had to think through and pray over before she got caught up in something make people think *Mahalia* changed: Minnis was after her to put him up in a record company. All kind of records. Halie had seen some them jazz sessions at the studios and she couldn't see Minnis *not* bringing in the bottles. But she wouldn't say no. She'd pray on it. When she got back, she was going to ask Bob Phillips to book her in Nassau again, and tell him she's ready to do some more Europe festivals—this was nice, short like this. She was in a hurry now to get back, see if they found her a condominium. And she wanted to see what plaques and trophies Dale got for the Festival of Stars workers and the big contributors. She wanted a nice one for Sammy Davis, Jr., and Daley, Judge Hooks, Mr. Hooker—and of course the Rockefellers! And nice trophies for the entertainers. She wanted the biggest and best for Dinah—Dale said he saw a nice one three feet tall.

NETTIE DID. Found her the condominium. Cornell Village, 2601 So. Lakeshore Dr. right *on* the lake. Beautiful! And just finishing. She called Ken Childers to come see the penthouse and draw up a plan to fix it for what she wanted. . . . Too small, said Ken, appraising the conversion he'd sketched out for her. No way. "But I can put together those two apartments on the 26th floor and give you everything you want, baby. Including the den for Minters and a suite for the little girl and that big living room you want for his 'lifestyle.'" Halie looked around quickly, alarmed. "Okay, okay, it's our secret," grinned Ken. "Now let me show you what I mean."

Milwaukee, Beloit, Rochester, then California to record and don't tarry. Townsend said don't bring her pianist; he wanted to use this man out here to work with the Mormons' music, but Halie just couldn't get with those arrangements and the studio man couldn't get with her so they put him out and the Mormons got put off but how about Gwen Lightner stepping in—ended up finishing that Christmas album in three hours! And Lord, please don't mind me using Yancey's notebook for a Bible for the photographer—You know they wasn't another thing around and the man said in the candlelight nobody could tell. Old Townsend sure couldn't say Minnis bothered him. 'Course they didn't use the orchestra; Townsend was going add Marty Paich on after she left. Anyway, Minnis got his mind on a trio. Bob Phillips might help but that was between them: she didn't want Minnis messing her *big* business.

FOR BOB PHILLIPS, it was something to take into account. "I realized I was not the first in line, I was second, because Galloway had more time with her than I did and he was in a much better position to assert himself with Mahalia." The gall of the man, trying to pump him, trying to act as a personal manager. And hinting for "compensation" for what he could do for Bob with Mahalia! Bob had erased that idea pretty quickly. But it should be possible to get along. He wanted very much to, not just for business but for Mahalia's sake. She'd begun looking to him for all sorts of matters in her personal life and he appreciated that, as a mark of trust and friendship. Even this about her condominium.

"YEAHHHHH," breathed Halie, looking at the sketch. It was Sept. 13, 1968, and Ken Childers had just spread the rough sketch before her with a flourish: A 28-foot master bedroom ("that's where you receive most of your company anyway," laughed Ken) with a walk-in closet that was a room in itself "for all those stage gowns and furs." A 29-foot formal living room. ("That's Minnis's," injected Halie.) A 17-foot music room ("That's mine") with an outlook on the lake. A soundproofed den so Minters could play his saxophone, with built-in stereo system. A suite on the west side of the foyer for Sigma: bedroom, play space, bath, a room for a governess or whoever was taking care of her, and a guest bedroom. Closed-circuit TV linked to the downstairs entrance so she could look over callers. "My peers would say this is bad planning," said Ken, "but I'm trying to hide you away from people—your *own* people, Mahalia. And because you don't trust anybody," he concluded triumphantly, "I'm putting in an intercom system that you can turn on from your bedroom and listen to anything that's happening in any of the rooms."

"Yeahhhh," said Halie. "Now tell me again how you going do Minnis' den, and then I got to go." In this one day, she had the dedication of the Mahalia Jackson Room at Greater Salem and a *This Is Your Life* kickoff to build a $200,000 Mahalia Jackson Wing on the new South Side YWCA. It was Friday the 13th. Halie knocked on wood and thanked the Lord for her blessings.

INTERWEAVING three musicians now—Eddie Robinson, Charles Clency, Louise Weaver—sometimes she took all three. Charles, still a student and minister of music at his church, flew in just in time—came right to the hall; "the Grey Ghost," Mahalia called him. Dr. Barclay thought she should do no more than two concerts a week, but Halie felt like she could do more and told Bob so.

Much as they were in and out, Halie made it her business to keep clear one date for Chicago Stadium: Hubert Humphrey's rally for President. He was a good man, a friend to his people, her friend, and Daley's man. Hush about that mess-up at the convention; Daley told her he had advance word those white militants and the black ones too were going fix it so there'd *be* no convention and Daley had the job to see that didn't happen. South Side *still* for Daley. And now look at this turnout! Mahalia Jackson on the program for Humphrey wouldn't surprise Chicago—she'd come out strong for him at the rally for Dawson. And went right from that to endorsing Fannie Jones for the first black Clerk of the Illinois Supreme Court. Whoo! and Halie not even a politician. But she been knowing Fannie Jones since she was a child in a gospel choir.

She spied Odetta, and Odetta threw her arms around her, so glad to see her. Then Halie noticed Tina Choate, the pretty blonde secretary Harry Dale got in to help the last of the Festival, when Jean collapsed—been around one way or another ever since, like Dale. Halie stayed a minute talking to her and her fiancé when she noticed Dale off to one side with a really big black boy: you could see his muscles even under his coat.

The shy young man had seen Harry Dale talking to Mahalia in between Dale's running around taking pictures, and in a soft, Southern voice had finally spoken. Could Dale introduce him? "No problem," Harry assured him, and presented George Foreman, who had that summer won the Olympics heavyweight boxing championship over the Soviet and helped the United States take top honors at Mexico City. "Oh, baby, I heard a lot about you," Mahalia dimpled. "Mm! you got big old arms, big old fists—baby, you going be next champion of the *world*. Come here, what's that around your neck? From the Olympics?" Mahalia clasped the gold medal in both her lean, long hands and pressed hard. "I'm going to ask the Lord to bless this." She opened her eyes. "Baby!" she said, handing back the medal, "you going be the champ. But you got to keep practicing, now; you keep on practicing."

It was time to sing, and sing she did. Her heart and her voice were in it as she went into *He's Got the Whole World in His Hands* . . . began to feel the spirit and moved into another chorus . . . suddenly was struck, backed off from the microphone, and electrified the entire stadium belting *Humphrey's Got the Whole World in His Hands!* The crowd leaped to its feet, roaring; Hubert Humphrey was catapulted to her side to throw both his arms around her while Halie, exhilarated, sang on, improvising. Below, Harry Dale glanced at the mayor and nudged the Daley son next to him: the mayor had a look of intense satisfaction on his face—this was his very own.

Afterwards—"Child, but we had 'em rocking. Now I hope the man get to be President. I just wish," she added, "Dick Gregory would stop playing the fool, taking black votes."

Then it was white votes to black she was concerned with, not that she had too much business running to Brooklyn Academy, but two ways she couldn't turn it down: It was a rally for James Farmer, and Gov. Nelson Rockefeller was backing him—nice as that man and his family been to her Foundation! And before that, with that Marine Band. Besides, Al Duckett had put it together and she liked that boy, much as they fell out and made up. Shelley Winters, Brock Peters, they all had a time. Then nothing but out to Oakland for Jodie Strawthford, to sing for a preacher friend who was a candidate—and introduce the Mahalia Jackson Foundation by letting Strawthford hand out the four West Coast scholarships Doc Hayakawa had helped her organize. She'd come out a week earlier, but Aunt Hannah took a bad turn and Halie rushed back to Chicago but hallelujah! the Lord brought Hannah back. Now Mahalia was at Oakland Auditorium by special sufferance of worried authorities: the city was crackling like an electrical storm from tensions of the Huey Newton trial and Hayakawa's defiance of the militants on the campus across the bay. Mahalia's alliance with him had brought Black Panther threats. The place was under guard. And lo! the spirit came. It was Easter all over again. Edward got happy and took the organ from Charles, who switched to piano . . . then Eddie rushed back to the piano, dodging the shouting singers. Halie was enraptured no matter *who* played what or didn't. Tiny Doc Hayakawa felt it too, clapping, jumping up and down as if he were on a spring. Halie seized his hands, and "the up and down of the two was a sight to behold," says Yancey, who'd learned his lesson: he didn't try to calm anybody. Afterwards they sat until almost 4 a.m. listening to Hayakawa.

All this business of planes and Panthers and Hannah got Halie to thinking. When Jean drove her down to Humphrey headquarters to talk over the loudspeakers, she was ready to make her move. She'd tried to see Ming; too busy again. Now she told Jean, "Let's go see Superior." It had been a long time since she made a will; it didn't near cover now, and she'd changed her mind about some people, both ways.

HALIE WAS IN a towering rage. *Who* told that? She accused Dale, but he wouldn't admit it. *Somebody* told the press she was going remarry Minnis and gave him a Lincoln Continental ("how they dream these things?") when right now she wouldn't give Minnis the time of day. "He been trying to get back with me since the day of the divorce," she said with infinite scorn to *Jet*—although *Jet* hadn't printed the story.

Three weeks later, *Jet* got confirmation that she and Minters were "discussing" remarriage. Minnis had tended her like a baby when she had to cancel San Jose, Calif. That was a $10,000 flu, but she could count her blessings: Townsend and Frank Calamita at New York CBS working up a Europe tour for spring with just two concerts a week like she asked them both. Townsend had got a copy of her Columbia contracts from 1964 on like Superior said he needed—all that been to Mindling. And Minnis was just like when they first got married.

But she couldn't take him with her to the Colgate Rochester Divinity School dinner. Take a drink, with Martin's folks and Rev. Ralph and all them there for Martin's memorial scholarship? It caused her to have second thoughts. Oh, Rev. Ralph spoke out that night—served notice *he* was carrying on; that he couldn't fill Martin's shoes but he had some sandals of his own. "Mahalia gave them glory from within that night," says Louise . . . and when she sang *Precious Lord,* they wept.

Five days later, at the New York Hilton, at a CBS Records party to debut *Christmas With Mahalia* (getting her first major promotion in years) before some 200 DJs, critics, reporters, and assorted industry people including Joe Glaser and Joe Bostic, Mahalia gave her news: she would remarry Minnis Galloway ("Sigmond," murmured Minters) within the month. "I prayed him back," she said, eager, laughing at the buzz of reaction; "many of our problems before came because I was used to my own way; but I realize I still love him . . . I decided a piece of a man is better than no man at all."

A hush fell as though sound had been wiped out. The MC hastily brought Sigmond forward to say a few words. "I don't have anything to say," he said, managing a smile. "I just want her to retract that statement."

Next morning Albertina Walker came into Mahalia's room. Sigmond was there, and Louise. "Mahalia," she said, striking a pose, "Tiny got his bags ready but he wants to know if you're going to pay this bill so he can tell these people to let him out of here, 'cause he ate some ice cream and it was $5 a scoop, and he *know* that rent has to be $50 or $60 a *day*. He's scaaared to leave. But he's 'shamed to come in here. So can he go or is he going to be arrested?"

Mahalia rolled the floor; Sigmond, Louise, Albertina all were convulsed. "Tiny," roared Mahalia, "come in here. . . . You ought to be ashamed of your-self." Huge Tiny Barnes looked at them all, still on the floor. "No," he said, "you the one ought to be ashamed, bringing us poor folk up in this kind of hotel."

"Right!" cried Albertina, "you get mad, *all* of us go to jail. So whatever you want, honey—you want me to fix you some juice? you want your house shoes? I'm ready to flunk like a *dog,* 'cause I *refuse* to be embarrassed and I sure can't pay this rent!" They were all rolling helplessly on the floor again. "If I get this much exercise all the time," gasped Mahalia, "I wouldn't *have* to reduce."

THE MONTH passed. No one dared ask. Mahalia got the flu; Louise got the flu. Wednesday, Dec. 4, they were due in Memphis for several days' promotion for Grand Opening ceremonies Saturday at the national headquarters of Mahalia Jackson Chicken Systems. No way. The staff had been working toward this week since October. A stand had been erected and decorated outside the building. Saturday the crowd showed, the governor and other dignitaries showed—and just before despair seized Judge Hooks, John Jay Hooker and A. W. Willis, Mahalia and Louise burst into sight, straight from the airport. Saved! Sunday afternoon the company had a reception inside what had been the six-story Adler Hotel, long past any glory, a block off Beale St. Eight or ten months from now, announced Board Chairman Willis, this would be a first-class office building with the Mahalia Jackson offices, management training center, and soul-food dispensary as head, heart, and soul, as it were, of the structure. Already in Memphis the first retail outlet was in business.

Flu or not, Mahalia was really elated, Judge Hooks decided. He felt good about that. "The life of a black woman in this country had not been easy, and from the many, many talks we'd had since this chicken business was suggested, I knew she felt that black men really never went to bat for any black woman and, more particularly, never for her—her experience had been rather bitter." And now they were a group of black men putting money in her hand: $15,000 to seal the deal plus $10,000 to the Foundation. Yes, she felt good about it, he knew, looking at her.

Alongside Mahalia was Minters. He had surprised her, Saturday night. That last fuss wasn't so much after all.

Mahalia called a doctor as soon as she reached San Francisco. His antibiotic helped. Edward and Charles flew in and she managed to perform. Hayakawa, acting president now of troubled San Francisco State College, called to say that if she felt well the next day, or the next, possibly she could come on campus and speak and sing; it might break the tense mood. He was thinking also of asking Duke Ellington. What did she think? Mahalia was somber—somebody going get her killed yet—but she said yes, she'd look those Black Panther boys in the eye in the name of Jesus. Next day Dr. Hayakawa surveyed the campus and called to say he thought she'd better forget it. Thank You Jesus!

Two days later from the Imperial Hawaii Hotel (a three-day run for a concert) she telephoned Minters to say she still had the flu and how was he; and he said he really loved her, not Mahalia Jackson. His words hung in the air like an inverted question mark as Gene Shapiro sat before the two in Los Angeles two weeks later.

77

Sigmond was wary. Mahalia was silent, watching, her breath shallow. It hadn't been an easy two weeks. As soon as she got back from Hawaii, she'd been X-rayed in Los Angeles and advised to stay here to recover; she was in no shape for Chicago weather. She spent a strange Christmas in a furnished apartment at the Fountain View West on La Cienega. She called the family; in New Orleans they said Ike was trying to reach her, had a stroke, so she called and told him to get a nurse, get two, whatever he needed, she'd pay. She called Dinah Shore . . . reached other friends—caught Laurraine in Georgia. She sat down to a crowded table with Mother Parks. And still there was a lonesome place inside. Russell Goode came for two days before New Year's—he helped Yancey drive her car and her furs from Chicago. New Year's day, Jean and Ken Childers visited, with Gene Shapiro and his fiancée.

Then Minnis came. He said he'd had to spend Christmas with Sigma. It'd been hard waiting 'til he could hear what Superior had figured out for her to hush this unease about jumping back into marriage: each time she got close that divorce pulled inside like a scar and something said, "Be sure."

Sigmond knew something was up when Mahalia made sure just they three were in the living room with no listeners. He wasn't happy to be dealing with a lawyer about their marriage as if he weren't man enough to handle it. Still it would be a relief to stand solid after this seesaw where, when his foot slipped, he had no hold. But he'd never heard of a proposition like *this*.

Patiently Gene Shapiro again spelled out the nature and terms of the prenuptial agreement which would stipulate that in the event of their marriage, Sigmond relinquished all claim to Mahalia's existing property—all assets of any nature—and she relinquished all claim to his. "In effect," he concluded, "it's a quit-claim contract."

Sigmond stared, debating. He might jump off a seesaw onto a tightrope. But Mahalia was at the other end. He wondered if— "Go ahead and draw it up," he said. As Shapiro left, Mahalia murmured quietly, "Now don't forget about that other—"

MARY ANN Hooper couldn't believe she'd actually caught Mahalia with a stretch of time in Los Angeles when she was both able and willing to talk two and three hours night after night, tapping her memories, as the first step toward an NBC-TV special for which Mary Ann had go-ahead as writer/producer. And Mahalia was in such good spirits! It must be the Japanese plum wine she'd brought along the first evening as a pleasantry: Dr. Barclay had advised a glass of wine or some brandy at night—"for my heart," Mahalia explained. Apparently, quite religious black Baptists had their own liquor code. (As Mahalia's Aunt Bessie would say, "Nothing wrong with taking a drink at home, baby; just don't go sneaking into bar rooms and mix with the sinners. Not church people. How you going bring somebody in, and you joining the sinners?") The sweet wine became a ritual of the sessions. Mary Ann just had to be careful to space it. Two glasses and Mahalia was gone. Thank God she was enjoying something! The bickering of this in-and-out claque was enough to shatter glass.

EDWARD WAS overdue and you never knew what was coming up, so Mahalia told Lou to come on, get out that terrible weather. Mahalia had one bedroom and Louise the other—but the white boy Yancey had moved in on the couch, more or less on his own as far as Louise could tell—even having his friends in. Louise wondered if this boy knew when Mahalia said, "Nigger! come here!" she was cutting him to size, letting him know he was getting a little too important to suit. He and Allen were a dogfight at sight. Of course, Yancey did just anything for Mahalia; it was just his *way*, to Louise . . . and to Sigmond.

"MAHALIA," said Dick Yancey, blond hair bristling, "I don't like him; I don't like anything about him."

"He don't like you," Mahalia said calmly.

"Well, just don't ask me and Sig to work together, that's all; keep him out of my way." Mahalia didn't look up from her Bible. The Lord got a way of working things out; this boy had that to learn along with learning about gospel music operations. She wish Minnis had that much push for gospel. Well, if wishes had wings, she'd win the Kentucky Derby. Be glad Minnis got one of his "gigs," even if it put him back in Gary for three weeks . . . and that just might be the Lord's doing to get him with Shapiro about that marriage contract. If the man would just give her the *evidence*. Lord Jesus, Halie can't get on that now; got to think what to do if Edward don't get here. Got more excuses than a river got fish—and Halie's just about fished *out* with him. All these shows to do—Donald O'Connor, Joey Bishop, Rosey Grier, TV movie at Bakersfield, Long Beach benefit; and an album before any of that. Louise's specialty was organ; Clency's, too. *Eddie* was her staff pianist. She telephoned. "Where you?" she asked, plaintive. "Miss Jackson," came Eddie's soft voice, "I got me a job here in Chicago." Mahalia's heart thumped and she was on the point of pleading when—it hadn't happened in some time but it happened now: the Voice spoke. "Wait." It was a peculiar time. Still holding the telephone, Mahalia said, "Lord, You know I'm out here in this water knee-deep, and You say 'Wait'?" She heard then, "WAIT." Edward's voice on the line was puzzled. "What you said, Miss Jackson?"

"Oh, nothing," said Mahalia, abruptly vague; "I'll write, then—I'll be talking to you." Anything to get off the line, so she could ask again. "Lord, what You mean 'wait' and I'm in this water and I got nobody."

"I SAID WAIT," she heard. She argued again that night before her prayers. And heard the word: "WAIT."

Next day Gwen came, as she did most days, to rehearse Mahalia for the new album. Suddenly she was aware Mahalia was looking at her peculiarly, as if she'd never seen her before.

GWEN LIGHTNER was shivery proud. The Lord had shown Mahalia it was time for a new direction and Mahalia thought *she* was the instrument! And to start with this particular album Mahalia had wanted such a long time: *Mahalia Right Out of the Church!* Mr. Leonard Feather was there to write about it and he said it was Mahalia who had influenced popular music and jazz with her gospel—and this man had written a whole *encyclopedia* about music. Mm-mh! she and Clency fit like one glove . . . and *everybody* at home backgrounding: Celeste, Robbie, Margaret, Doris, the whole chorus . . . oh-oh, Halie's getting happy . . . it's church!

MAHALIA HAD to rehearse, Mrs. Robert Peck knew, but she was getting a little nervous about the state of her dinner—a formal sitdown dinner. So eager were her friends to meet Mahalia Jackson that she'd extended her table to her last dinner plate. Of course, Miss Jackson had said she would be a little late, but it was so long past a little and—ah, the doorbell. Dr. Peck hurried to open it, and in walked the missing guest of honor. With two extra persons, a Mrs. Lightner and Mr. Yancey. Mrs. Peck's heart dropped. Her hospitality could stretch, but her place settings couldn't. "Yet somehow it all worked out," she laughs. "The one thing was that nobody wanted to have conversation with his neighbor; they all wanted to listen to Mahalia. It was extraordinary, the power that flowed from her simply in a dining room setting."

It meant all the more, then, when Mahalia agreed to sing for a Beverly Hills dinner to raise funds for a black alderman who had dared declare for office against Mayor Yorty. Great! With Mahalia, Dr. Peck felt they'd get a good turnout. And did—all white, primarily wealthy Jewish liberals. On the way home, Mary Ann asked Mahalia, "Well, what do you think?" It was very good for Los Angeles to have him running, Mahalia said, and he was one bright man. "But he probably won't make it. He doesn't have enough fire. He speaks well, but—I don't know anything about politics, but the people seem to make it, they all have fire. Lots of fire." It would be another four years before Thomas Bradley, with a new stance, defeated Samuel Yorty as mayor of Los Angeles.

MINNIS WAS BACK, but he just pinched her chin and said they'd have to wait on *her* lawyer; Shapiro said he'd see them out here. She wasn't happy about that, but she had to let it go because Halie had got herself into something. It didn't start that way—all she told Rev. Esters was she'd give a benefit in Long Beach for a day-care nursery for working mothers: he said it was a sore need. He had somebody to promote it. It came about, then, that the city council of Long Beach declared Mar. 23, 1969, would be Mahalia Jackson Day, her first concert in this city of a million people. Pleased, Halie called and invited Dr. Hayakawa. Gwen began rehearsing a Long Beach/Compton massed choir. But the closer it came to Mar. 23, the more Halie's vibrations told her it was going to flop. "We got to get on this thing ourselves," she told Yancey. They ranged the newspapers, large and small; TV, radio, were pleased to find Mahalia Jackson at their doors. Halie put up a $5,000 kitty and ads, handbills, air spots appeared. The choir was extended to Los Angeles, to bring in more congregations. Mahalia began a series of talks at elementary and high schools and junior colleges—and got in a blow at the Devil. "Laurraines," she said, "I faced those young people, and I talked about how you've got to help yourself do what you can do if you expect help from other people. I stood there, a woman without formal education who had made a name for herself through hard work and asking God's help every day. And none of those people could say a word back. There just wasn't anything to say.

Excited, Gwen and Yancey appeared at the apartment with a surprise: a $500 gown they'd picked out at Lane Bryant which made Louise gasp: they'd better take it back right now; Mahalia *never* spent money on her clothes. Gwen meekly showed it to Sister, just saying it was a dress for Long Beach but not whose, and after Mahalia turned the yellow gown this way and that, admiring it, Gwen added with a gulp, "By the way, you just bought it," and braced herself. "They got any more like this, Gwen?" Mahalia said. "Can you go back tomorrow?" ("I didn't know she had money, Gwen," said Yancey, excited, when they went back to get the dress in pink too. "I thought all this time the woman was broke.") That was for the stage, but for Halie was something else. These two tricked her, embarrassed her before all those white people at Bulloch's 'til she had to take a $80 hat just 'cause she liked it—"Halie! who never paid more than $6.50 for a hat in her life!" she protested in the car. But she wouldn't take it off all day and Gwen knew a new era was born.

So was a new program: Mar. 23, they entered Long Beach Arena with Rosey Grier, Della Reese, Steve Allen, Peter Lupus, Tom Lester, and six supporting acts. City, county, and state officials and ministers bloomed about the stage. Allen Clark and Yancey hawked Mahalia's pictures with practiced success. Dr. Hayakawa was so elated by Mahalia's lengthy paean, introducing him, that he sang with Gwen's choir. Mayor Wade presented Mahalia with a gold watch on a chain, and set her off. She gave them a concert in the full glory of voice and passion and when she reached *Guide Me Over, Thou Great Jehovah,* Halie got happy, into her holy dance and in another world. People were pouring down and around the arena's central stage. Yancey pulling, Bill Duncan pushing, got her off. "I tried to tell May what she had made us feel," says Margaret Aikens. Mahalia looked far away, and deep. "Little Missionary," she said softly, "I'm just the instrument. Don't never forget it. I can't help my people individually, every one, but one of these days my works will be of benefit to my people. I feel this. Just as I know I am an instrument, used by God." She turned then to all of those crowding to see the watch, but it was only later she could tell it: "When they gave me that watch on a chain, it was just like Mama had sent it from the grave. One of my earliest recollections is admiring somebody's watch hanging on a chain like that and my mother saying to me, 'That's all right, honey, you'll have one some day.' "

For a week she wore the watch even to bed, trying to make sure it wouldn't vanish, and it had not yet disappeared by April 16 when Gene Shapiro once again sat in her living room. Her mind was bent eagerly to the future now: Shapiro had placed before her and Minters a copy for each to follow as he read the formal prenuptial quit-claim document he had prepared. The lawyer was hoping Galloway wouldn't question the blank lines. "I knew how much Mahalia wanted this, and I wanted at this stage not to fully magnify for Galloway all that he would relinquish claim to—that could be filled in as the final moment's work before signing and witnessing." There was so much else open to the man, but it would defeat Mahalia's test to point that out.

Sign, Minnis, sign; sign. Halie's heart stretched with the need to have him mean it. Sigmond was fixed and staring, held by blind instinct and memory of that last bad advice that made him leave a divorce court with nothing but a red face and a lawyer's bill he still owed. Suddenly, "I don't have to sign this!" he flamed; "I'm not a fool; I'm not going to be pushed around. I'm not going to sign anything *like* this!"

This won't do; it's hurting Mahalia, Gene Shapiro saw. "Sigmond," he said matter-of-factly, "I think what you want is for your own counsel to look this over; then *you* can proceed and we can all get together again." Sigmond calmed and they fixed another date, in Chicago. Well, that took one matter off Gene's agenda tomorrow. "If Galloway had signed, Mahalia had instructed me to come the next morning to draw up a will leaving everything to him."

Minnis was so sweet after they had some time alone together, and Superior had this other idea to fix what he thought was troubling Minnis, that soon as she had the chance, Halie had Yancey drive her around to look at some nice houses; one on Rossmore took her eye. Minnis wouldn't want a place too small, and she ought to buy one out here, much time as she was spending. And now this big film deal coming up.

SHAPIRO FELT the atmosphere shift from warm to lukewarm to cold to bitter, but he wasn't perturbed; he enjoyed a good fight. These Hollywood types throwing their special language at him did not in the least obscure his view. Here in their offices—which looked like a loft to him—it boiled down to his insisting upon enough money for Mahalia so it didn't matter if this particular ship sank. He'd shocked them good with his figure; the next meeting could come to equitable terms.

Gene, Mahalia, and Minters had barely walked into her apartment when Townsend was on the line. Mahalia looked as if she was getting pretty shaken.

Irving Townsend was totally, wholly, completely in a fury. Mahalia asks him to find her somebody to do an hour's TV film for syndication, and though he doesn't know a damn thing about the movie business, he lines up something he's assured is a good deal, and now this lawyer who's so damned pleasant at lunch yesterday—he'd even told the man he was glad Mahalia "finally had somebody to help her," for God's sake—that's yesterday, and now the man's turned into some sort of monster and the people here are alienated from *him*, and who ends up with his foot in a tub of cement who didn't ask for it in the first place?

"YOU BETTER come on back here," Sig said, "there's a meeting going on." It was 6:15; the scheduled meeting at Mahalia's was 8 p.m. Shapiro went. By the time the session broke, the film was off. "A deal that bad you don't want; we can get better than that," he assured Mahalia. But he couldn't stick around—he was getting married day after tomorrow. Mahalia said she couldn't leave, but Sigmond and his sister Ruth came to toast him in wedding champagne in Chicago—and added another bit to the drama Shapiro was helping script: Gene's last analysis to Mahalia was that Galloway apparently felt he'd be stripped; no resources and no prospects if he signed—so why not create a capacity? Shapiro had drawn up papers for M-G Investment Co., funded by shares from the Mahalia Jackson Chicken System. Gene hadn't had a chance to hear Galloway's reaction, but now at his wedding Galloway was asking Gene's opinion about a South Side location for an M-G shopping center with a Chicken System take-out, ice cream parlor, and laundromat. Since M-G Investment Co. was a reality only if they were married, that meant—

IT WAS CLOSE to Europe and Mahalia felt like she had a four-layer sandwich that wouldn't cut. These twelve days since Superior left, she'd asked Bob Phillips to set the TV movie right, whatever was wrong, and signed a contract on that . . . lit out for Chicago but had to chase right up to Montclair, N.J., to do the concert she promised Rev. Coleman . . . hit on back to Chicago for chicken business—Ben Hooks and his people in Florida want to start up frozen soul food and cans too and Judge Hooks said could she get up some recipes for a premium? . . . then right out to Oakland to open their baseball with *The Star-Spangled Banner;* the people actually put "bombs bursting in air" when she got to that part and with the noise and the dark, they nearly had a riot on their hands . . . chased home to see Dr. Barclay and present Daley his Festival of Stars trophy she was ashamed to still be having and get Allen to pack her California clothes and Europe clothes and her fanciest clothes for the White House . . . but even before she could leave for D.C. got to fool with denying she's mother of some girl got herself free shoes in Norfolk claiming she is—*told* the *Jet* people Halie's a barren woman and she can't even remember all the girls claim they her children, 'specially that child in Nashville . . . called Ken Childers *please* jump those folks suppose to have her condominium ready for August and the way it's dragging she be too old to ride the elevator . . . gone right into D.C. a day early so HEW can talk to her about a job and still don't know if she got any business messing with Washington but this was for her to talk to the children wherever she was singing; she *would* welcome telling them not to have a retarded mind about their opportunities—Harry Dale sitting in the meeting with her and Minnis 'cause Dale figured to be advance man; but it was all up in the air when they left and *next* night was the White House, Duke Ellington's 70th birthday party that you had to hand Nixon he gave Duke in style with everybody in the country wanting in and Nettie there too as a close friend of Duke's and Minnis in his glory and glory-fried, both, but you never could tell, it was a world's wonder . . . and *then*—these days feeling like months—right up to New York to check with Mr. Calamita at the CBS Foreign Department and Louise hurrying in again from Chicago, Charles due just in time for the concert for Bishop Johnson on Long Island: Louise excited as a child with going to Europe—her and Gwen and Charles—and yes indeed, she brought her hot and cold clothes, both, like Allen said pack since now they'd be leaving out earlier, to Los Angeles to do some work and go from there for Europe . . . and in all this time, all these days, Minnis had not signed the marriage agreement and wouldn't say and what was *wrong*? Superior had promised her. She told Lou not to bother about not having her shots, get that in Los Angeles, it just took no more than a few minutes. It took a lot longer to check with Mr. Calamita because when look like Townsend got it all started but it wasn't all *set* by spring and she asked Bob Phillips to talk to Townsend and get it fixed like a regular agent would—whatever was holding anything up—and Bob had the tour starting now May 14, she had to just make sure the CBS people in London and Paris and so forth was still keeping to their part: something was telling her something and she wasn't getting it clear. She called Superior and told him she was going to California before Europe because Bob Phillips had fixed it for her to make this film in L.A. they going package for distribution; and then she asked him about Minnis and he said let him think about it, he'd get back to her and he did, and she listened, and she figured to think about his new idea and ask the Lord on the plane to Los Angeles.

She tried to just breathe a while so she could meditate, after they got up, but look like she had to run on, run on. She told Lou she was going make some changes in her working when they got back from Europe; Dr. Barclay said the dates coming too close . . . and another thing— Louise fell asleep with Mahalia still talking.

At Hyatt House, Louise thought she'd pull out one dress to be unwrinkled in case the movie man wanted them right off tomorrow. The knock at the door surprised her. It was the house man from the apartment across the street where Mahalia was. Her phone must not be working yet. "Miss Jackson says come on over." She crossed and Mahalia was really in a talking mood: mostly about the condominium—Louise had seen the plans and walked the littered shell—and about remarrying Minters. They talked furniture, and Mahalia fried some bacon and eggs, and Louise crossed back happily tired to think of Europe—nine days off!

All the while she'd been talking Mahalia didn't know her mind had been studying, but when she was alone she knew and she was hooked up now for a phone call. It was a long one. When she hung up, she read her Bible a long time before she went to sleep.

Sigmond Galloway could think fast and move faster when he needed to. He'd let this quit-claim marriage thing float, just float, while he tested it. One lawyer he put the question to looked at it and said go ahead and sign, he didn't think it would stand up in a divorce; but another one said yes, it was valid under Illinois law—if he could marry without signing, more power to him. If two lawyers were that far apart, what was a man to think? But this that Mahalia said tonight: stock in the chicken system in his own name, an executive position, and an immediate lump sum "so you'll have something in your pocket, baby." Plus the M-G Investment Co. in both their names, drawn up and waiting. He could operate with that even if— Offhand it sounded good and he'd told Mahalia so . . . and this woman he could never keep a jump on said get on the plane then, right now, tonight, and she'd take him to Europe.

Louise was a late sleeper when she could, so she was blinking when she answered the phone. Mahalia. Minnis was in. "When are we supposed to play?" Louise asked. "I haven't heard from the man yet," Mahalia said. Louise was just getting her head together when Minters appeared. "Louise, I came to tell you you're not going to Europe—it's Gwen, Charles, and me who're going." Louise just stared, unbelieving. Minters seemed uneasy and said something about Mahalia could have told her sooner, but— "In that case," Louise said, "I can just leave out of here today; it's my wedding anniversary." Minters came back with Louise's pay and money for her ticket and considerable extra. He waited when the phone rang and Louise told her godmother she couldn't see her this afternoon: "I'm going back to Chicago. I'm not going to Europe." She turned to Minters. "Tell Mahalia I'll see her when she gets back to Chicago. I have to make my plane." She was glad she hadn't unpacked too much.

WHEN MAHALIA first said "Europe" to Gwen, she couldn't believe it; and when Mahalia said, "Get your passport," she was leaving and said, "I'll send for you to come go to Louisiana with me" and Gwen had nothing more on that, so she couldn't seem to get set with a passport. Then Kay Saunders from ABC Booking called and said, "You're going to Europe—where's your passport?" Europe! Gwen's husband said he and the kids would manage. She'd have to get her some clothes in a hurry. The people better hurry and make that TV movie, too, if they wanted to catch Mahalia. She had a concert in Portland, Ore., the 11th, and in Orange County the 12th. By May 14, all they could film was bye-bye.

MARY ANN Hooper was in shock. Bob Phillips had signed with a syndicate for an hour TV special on Mahalia. She didn't know whether to laugh or cry or curse or get drunk and dance around a bonfire of her scripts and tapes. God! Why hadn't she got her whole package signed and sealed first.

"WELL, HAVE a good time," Shapiro said genially; then his ear went to alert: "Who? Who did you say was going along to film your concerts? Miner? For the State Department!" Trying to keep your finger on Mahalia was like grabbing at rolling ballbearings.

78

Down at Heathrow at 10:30 a.m. Thursday, through Customs and in to the hotel, and no time even for a cup of hot tea—big press conference at 2 p.m.: the press so sweet, they love her, but *who* did that; she *told* all those people she didn't want no trouble in Europe, make it easy, two concerts a week at the most with her already feeling like a lily done bloomed . . . and Lord, what You think about what's happening to Halie just from the middle of Thursday? Press, then radio, then conferences on the film and Lord God! the London sponsor having a fight with Mr. Miner on that, and the BBC TV Friday morning and *another* press conference for 1:30—they sure press over here—and more fussing about the filming and *she* didn't have the straight of it; Bob Phillips and them switched that around at the last minute, but she had to tell the London man finally to keep peace that Mr. Miner was filming for the State Department but he wasn't nice about it at all, even looking at that letter Mr. Miner carried; and now it's Saturday and Clency better get his behind off that plane, can't even have a rehearsal and the concert tomorrow night and them on film—if Mr. Miner don't get shot. 'Course Charles in school but where Minnis? How long it take to get his passport through, even having to dig up a birth certificate—there was such a thing as emergency issue.

Well, all right—Minnis, Charles, his wife all on the same plane from Chicago, if you please, and heaven help Halie and the heathens, it's good to lay eyes on this man.

Gone. No more than hello and her laying up here not feeling good in this dreary old room, no flowers nor nothing, and don't even stay with her—gone sightseeing. She was ashamed for Gwen to see Minnis do this way; it was belittling him in Gwen's eyes. Ungh! This cramp gaining on her. "Come on, Gwen, rub harder." Strong hands, this girl, and fingers itching this very minute to get onto that piano "where Chopin played." That's all she say. And *Halie* say, our American gospel good as Chopin and Gwen can hear it from the critics themselves. Miss Gwen going have her eyes, ears, and mouth opened tomorrow night.

EXTRAORDINARY! thought Max Jones of the *Melody Maker.* A commercially organized concert, not a vacant seat in Albert Hall, and Mahalia turns it into a spiritual event that is yet extravagantly successful for the audience. A spiritual magician; a stupendous gift, and withal, the utter simplicity. He made his way to her dressing room after the last rousing response. He found her overflowing a chair, looking rather flaked. She rummaged through what seemed to be a miniature medicine chest and swallowed something. "I wish I was as young as I was when you first met me, Maxie," she sighed; "there's so much to be done and it's always me—if they want someone to ring the bell at church, they call on Mahalia." It wasn't the concert tired her, she insisted—she was tired when she came, and with all the to-do here and this film— "We were supposed to make it out in Hollywood, but then they decided to make it in some of the big places over here—London and Sweden and maybe France. But it's all been so heavy, I hardly had time to eat properly. I love the singing, though," she roused; "I sing because I love to sing."

It was clearly not the time for an extended interview. Before she left, perhaps.

The pains! She lay frightened. Felt like her heart going squeeze right out her throat. Gwen got hold of Mr. Miner, and a doctor came—a top heart man, they said—and now after all the examinations, she couldn't help crying, Europe crashed down on her. The London doctor said she'd had a heart attack and she would have to go home, but who she wanted was *her* doctor. How this man know to do for her, never saw her before in his life? Oh, Dr. Barclayyy—

IT WAS SO good to get out of reach of the pressures, William Barclay exulted as he stowed his skis and entered the lodge of the remote little ski village in British Columbia. With utter astonishment he learned he had a call from a doctor in London. He recognized the name—an eminent cardiologist, who said he was calling at Miss Mahalia Jackson's insistence, but clearlv she had had a coronary occlusion. "Of course, I haven't seen her," said Dr. Barclay, "but I think you're wrong. If you take your cardiograms—as I'm sure you know, I've diagnosed she has sarcoidosis of the heart; look up the literature on this, and you might agree with me that she has sarcoid of the heart, and what you'd better do is boost her cortisone—her prednisone—up to very, very large doses." He specified precisely. That was extremely high, the cardiologist said dubiously, but he would do that. "He called me back," says Dr. Barclay, "and said, 'Yes, you're right. I increased her cortisone and her cardiogram has come back to normal, and it is certainly consistent with sarcoid of the heart.'" Score one for us, thought

Dr. Barclay. When Mahalia herself called, crying about her broken trip, he told her to go on—just rest a few days to get over this episode; she wasn't going to have any more trouble now.

And didn't. Not heart trouble. Not even when she got flaming mad on discovering the CBS man in Paris had canceled her concert there instead of waiting to see if she really *did* have to go home. To prove she'd done her part, she had Gwen take her picture in front of the *Salle Pleyel* to show that Mahalia Jackson was there the day she was supposed to be, and then they picked up the tour in Sweden. Stockholm . . . Malmo . . . Lund: in a cathedral, so Mahalia had special red choir robes flown from California for her and Gwen . . . then, cutting Deauville, back to Paris for standing room only. On to Berlin—oh! Mr. Miner got in trouble in Berlin, Mr. Collien saying Mr. Miner needed a contract to film at *his* concert and "U.S. Government" didn't mean a thing to Mr. Collien; but next stop, in Hamburg, he gave her and Sigmond each a beautiful watch to show he knew it was none of her. Frankfurt, Basel, Zurich . . . closing in on her; she *told* them not to book her so close together and now riding these trains in Switzerland, no way on God's earth she was going make Vienna, so cancel it. Sing Munich, then the last, back in Stockholm. And everywhere, everywhere, love, cosseting, hospitality, wild enthusiasm. The Swiss wouldn't let her off the stage; one critic kept tally, said she'd sung 35 songs. An outdoors crowd in Stockholm sat through a downpour and Halie sang on, protected by a shell. French monks were so carried away, they came next morning to quiz her about gospel music—they wanted to try it in their mass so people would get *involved*. "They gave me the 33rd degree and I took it," she laughed, telling it. "And Laurraines, you know all through every bit of that—rain, everything—I had to come back to Chicago to even catch a cold."

"Mahalia wouldn't tell it on herself," says Gwen, "but the most beautiful thing was that young German girl thumbing her way around Europe who sneaked in backstage at Zurich." She got caught once but managed her way past somehow and just dropped to her knees before Mahalia, crying. Since she was a little girl, she had wanted to meet Mah-hahl-ya. "They will take me out when they find me here, but I have meet you!" Mahalia reached her dark arms around the thin shoulders. "That's all right, baby; you're safe here." And when the guard came, hunting her, Mahalia told them to let her stay. Then Mahalia had her to walk with them to where she could watch. And when they came off, she whispered it was the greatest moment of her life. Little white girl.

So *much* to tell, thought Gwen, easing contentedly in her plane seat. And Mahalia so happy to have Sigmond with her; just admired the man so. Although he put her through some changes! Gwen peered up ahead. Yeah, he's got his Chivas Regal. First man she ever knew personally who drank Scotch first thing in the morning. He was really cool.

Luxuriating in first class beside Mahalia, Sigmond felt broadened—any man of intelligence was, by foreign travel. He had a new insight on what life could be if you had the class and the cash to make it. And one short stop in Chicago would be the hinge on the door.

"I'M READY to sign—where's the paper? I'll sign it right now." Sigmond felt beautiful. Even Shapiro looked beautiful. What man wouldn't who was about to put in your hands a beautiful hunk of money—not *too* great, but enough for the beautiful life for a while, with nothing but a thank-you due?

Thank God, an end to the business, but "I think I want Mahalia to be present," Gene Shapiro said genially. He needed to complete the document, but he wasn't about to tell Galloway that. There was the matter of incorporating the extended terms as well. And Galloway's surprise present: the subsequent will in his favor, which he still knew nothing about. They'd fix the earliest possible day, the two men agreed, and Sigmond left for Gary: His standing there was about 20 feet tall since the fellows heard how he and Mahalia had been received in Europe—with his engraved watch to prove it.

SEE JUDGE HOOKS about the chicken shacks and the new food business . . . catch up with Allen on the mail and Missie on the gossip and see Aunt Hannah and Aunt Alice—both all right, thank You Lord . . . tell Bob Phillips how *bad* those CBS men in London and Paris did and all the trouble Mr. Miner's camera stirred up—but he was a *nice* man . . . get the new contracts . . . tend the people's problems saved up while she's gone . . . and *when* she going get in her condominium? She and Minnis could get married there; they'd have that grand living room and her music room both for people to circulate in and Minnis wanted a big one this time "to show he was more than a piece of a man" (oooh, she bit her tongue off many a time about those words). . . . Things rushed into 10 days off like water into a hole, and then she was up to something nice: being a family. Sigmond brought Sigma up to New York when she went to sing again for Tony Lawrence's music festival in Harlem, and he brought Sigma to Tanglewood, too, when she went for Gov. Rockefeller. Afterwards Step'anie Barber had them all for dinner at her beautiful resort estate on the water. Halie couldn't do much walking—her feet had begun to swell so bad—but Minnis acted proud of her that evening. Even his excuse for never taking the plane with her seemed all right: said if anything happened to one or the other, Sigma would still have someone to look after her. They said September now, for the condominium.

Townsend came then, and she had a job on her hands to work out the *structure* with the feeling of this one song, *Abraham, Martin and John*. She saw Yancey had brought in Geni Fox and her family, come all the way from Spokane, Wash., just to meet her. She'd been so touched the night before at the ABC panel show, she told Mrs. Fox for them all to come go eat with her tonight. That was a beautiful blond boy, her son Michael, to be blind—had all those operations. If she got the chance, she was going let him play for her, see what he had. "Yeah, let's take it again, and Charles—"

WHAT HAD to be set *right* was SCLC. Rev. Ralph had put her on the board and this meeting down in Charleston was important. Since Martin's death, all the comers were grabbing for the top, and Mahalia was going stand behind Martin's No. 1 lieutenant. Rev. Abernathy wasn't Martin, but she didn't see a Martin in sight, either. Wednesday, Thursday, Friday, she made every session. Gwen was there but not at the business, so, she says, she didn't know what was going on, "but something was—Mahalia and Judge Hooks with their heads together." Something going on with Sigmond, too; the night of the big banquet Sigmond wanted to sit at the speakers' table and Mahalia wouldn't let him—made him sit down on the floor level while Gwen and Charles sat up with the important people. Gwen wanted to step down, but Mahalia flashed that don't-you signal with her eyes and Gwen kept still. That was the night Coretta King spoke and had the beautiful African clothes on, from her trip with Dr. King. Wouldn't *that* be a trip to make! With Mahalia, you could dream big.

A "SALUTE to Black Women." Halie wanted to do it and something about Charleston made her want to do it even more: right at the top—Lincoln Center. And for the Foundation, which made it more right because it was black women been trying to push black children higher all these years and black men too, and who ever come out and give black women the *recognition?* But it would have to be big. It couldn't flop. It was on her mind as they flew to Montreal for *Expo,* and Gwen listened in the long hours when Gwen kept her company so she wouldn't be alone—Sigmond out "looking around," he said. Gwen decided it was a real obsession with her even before Mahalia knew she was definitely going to do it.

Halie sent Al Duckett some expense money to get started. Saturday, Nov. 8, would be the date. He had two whole months. You could elect the President in that.

AND SHE WAS going cut this album this one day. She'd *been* here—come to give Celeste a big benefit at Embassy Auditorium because she was worried sick about that girl: doctor said she had a brain tumor and Halie was praying hard for the Lord to remove that—always remember Aunt Bell telling how the Lord had spared *her* as a baby without the knife. So she *could*'ve been at the studio earlier and no use Townsend acting up; she was going leave town *in the morning.*

Irving Townsend felt he actually didn't have the physical strength today to argue with Mahalia, even though he was bitter about that European tour and hadn't seen a cent of commission yet—and even though this was a major album for Mahalia. How major, he didn't particularly want to make clear yet. He'd dub in much of the sound and special effects later, in peace after Mahalia was out of the way. Mahalia and Mr. Big. If going to sing for some school benefit in Memphis tomorrow was more important than cutting an album—it was her reputation, not his.

DICK YANCEY shook with rage, but he wasn't going to make a scene backstage. He'd driven Nettie Irving, Mahalia's niece Bertha, and Allen Clark in Mahalia's car for this program at the Colosseum for Judge Hooks and his wife's school project. Sigmond flew—*he*'s too grand to drive. Yancey had been in Chicago since Mahalia sent him back with the car from California when she got mad at Allen for being late. Mahalia needed God-all things done for her, and Galloway certainly didn't know nothing about things a real personal manager would be doing; actually, it was Yancey doing the duties and Galloway getting the glory. Like now, just countermanded Yancey's order: "Leave those lights alone; he's nobody; I'm in charge of Miss Jackson!"

NETTIE WAS impressed with the Salute idea; she'd help all she could. She was sorry Mahalia had to go into another big thing with the bad taste of having a good bit of Foundation money vanished into thin air, from all Nettie could gather. When, where, how: with all the talk, there was no proof; but one thing, Mahalia made clear she was reshuffling the whole Foundation structure before she went into Salute, and Superior was to see *that* kept straight. They were due at Shapiro's office now, actually; Nettie had come by to go with Mahalia—there'd be Jean Childers, Sigmond, and herself plus Gene Shapiro and Aldus Mitchell. "Mahalia even hired a legal secretary to come take a transcript of the meeting," Nettie says, "or maybe that was Shapiro's idea." Sigmond came in as Nettie was mulling the whole muddle-up and said he was hungry; before he went to any meeting he had to go get something to eat. "Plenty in the kitchen," Nettie told him, but "No, I'll go out," Sigmond said. Someone claimed he was afraid to eat there for fear of being poisoned, the way people had the run of Mahalia's; this was the first Nettie heard of *that*.

THE ONLY THING faster than time is trouble—just time runs off and trouble runs in. Halie stood planted in the middle of her bedroom on Lennox Terrace four weeks before Salute to Black Women. She shut out the chittering and chattering and twittering in the rooms beyond, came to some decisions, and moved. Some 48 hours later she was minus the man supposedly organizing; had Gene Shapiro committed to help and to call Mary Ann Hooper; cried "help" to Joe Bostic to see if he could placate the ministers, miffed because they hadn't been sought out before she came into their town; had Harry Dale on a plane to come work publicity and preliminaries, whatever they might be; had Tina Choate—Dale's suggestion—as secretary for a month on condition she come that night. (She came next morning. Her fiancé was just back from Vietnam, but an urgent Mahalia was a gale force not to be denied.) Albertina called to say she'd let the man into the condominium with the last furniture due—Allen and Yancey had stayed behind to clean up—and Mahalia told her to get Tiny Barnes and drive up here—she needed the car and she needed them. She assigned Gwen and Albertina to canvass churches: perform and then talk Salute. She assigned herself to maximum visibility with the media; and Tiny and Yancey, "to-do"—whatever there was. All this supportive to her New York co-chairmen, Dolly Dickens (Dickenson, to Mahalia) and Alma Johns, plus longtime friend Melissa Young. The apartment got so it reminded her of Harpo Marx and his crazy running, only this didn't make her laugh. "It didn't make me laugh, either," says Mary Ann, when she flew in to make a survey of the situation and discovered they didn't want one show, they wanted two—one for children and one black-tie. The old trouble had reared its head: "All the agents wanted to foist losers on the show, on top of Mahalia and Very Important People committing spots for various personal reasons." Okay, Hooper turns heavy. Except she didn't even have a telephone. No office. She talked a good friend into turning over his office for four days which became nine, including some $2,000 of long-distance calls which she sincerely meant to have repaid as legitimate production expense. Talent didn't come easy; it was a sort of search-and-arrest process. Typically, she caught Muhammed Ali just making tracks out of Las Vegas, after training; then he was taken with the idea. He'd be in New York anyway, which was the first thing Mary Ann had had to uncover. Miriam Makeba she got on sworn oath that her appearance would not be advertised, since Makeba was going into Lincoln Center herself the night before at triple the ticket price. (Mary Ann aged rapidly when an irate agent called to say whatthehell, Mahalia Jackson just said on the air Miriam Makeba was going to be on Salute Nov. 8 and Mary Ann could expect a lawsuit forthwith, individually and jointly.) Shapiro came in for two days and left, pleading business in Chicago but with "Coward!" in his ears as a parting word from Mary Ann. Sigmond was rarely to be seen. Tina's fiancé came, but this was no place for him, either. "Card—card—who's got my credit card" was a continuing chase. Natives and imports circled like strange cats and periodically tangled. One threatened to throw another out of the window; a frustrated performer threatened Mahalia; Yancey ran scared—whitey in Harlem; Mary Ann had a bodyguard. And one morning, Mahalia had a collapse. In the days prior, she'd had ABC concerts in Newark and Kansas City and Dayton: she didn't mind getting off from the New York confusion; and she saw more of Minnis than she did at the apartment and they were all right together. It wasn't 'til they got back to Lennox Terrace that he played the fool and she sent him home. Oh! that man going be the death of her, but she felt fine in Philadelphia and now here at the apartment can't catch her breath, stomach cramping like a spasm and her chest—Lord, her heart. "I feel like I'm going die," she gasped and Albertina and Dolly Dickens turned white as Tina, all trying to chase down the doctor who lived in the house until Harry came in and called Harlem General. "An ambulance was there in five minutes," says Dale, "but Mahalia stopped in her tracks and said, 'Not me. If I get in there, I'll die in there; you get me a cab or hire somebody in the building.'" It was a relief but almost a letdown when the medical verdict was gastritis. Five doctors asked for her autograph.

All the while they'd poked and pictured, Halie'd had in mind those stories she saved from the Sunday paper—two in one paper about heart transplants. One was a priest had it done; he'd died, but he said God would have nothing against it. When this confusion was past, she might talk it over with the Lord. She shivered and put her mind on the program. And Missie with her Rockefellers.

LAYING UP at the New York Hilton Hotel, Missie was in bliss. "Go on, have everything you want," Mahala said; "it's your boss worked you so hard who's paying for it." That was Mahala's joke, but Missie was proud the Rockyfellers was the biggest part of Mahala's backing for the Salute: Nelson Rockyfeller paying for the Philharmonic Hall and, from what Mahala say, this bed she's laying up in; and Mrs. Prentice say the rest of the family was coming in. MMMMh! Tonight Missie Wilkerson is going to play millionaire.

It was really quite an impressive program, Mary Ann thought, rubbing at the ache in her neck: Mrs. King as guest speaker—she and Mahalia seemed quite close; Rosa Park ("the first lady of civil rights," Mahalia called her, because she touched off the spark in Montgomery), Mrs. Jesse Jackson, and Rep. Shirley Chisholm to be introduced; Willa Dorsey to sing *Lift Up Your Voice and Sing,* which Mary Ann now knew was the Negro National Anthem; thumbnail histories of black women and then the entertainment—black and white—that had got the black-tie audience into the hall: Muhammed Ali (Mahalia insisted on calling him Cassius Clay, "but I don't think he could get angry at anything that came from Mahalia"), Rodney Dangerfield, the Les McCann Trio, Miriam Makeba (no lawsuit, thank God), the lady herself, and the half-dozen other acts Mary Ann had pared the program down to with steel jaw and iron fist . . . although Mahalia won on the young blind boy Michael Fox's performing both shows instead of simply the youth concert. Well—he had an appeal. In any event, the die was cast. And if Mahalia started trooping people up on stage like a church revival to bear witness, that was the dear darling's own doing. Mary Ann was going to put on a long dress and enjoy herself.

This Green Room party before the 9 o'clock curtain was a good idea, thought Shapiro, steering his wife through the crush as best he could. Nelson Rockefeller there—good; and David Rockefeller, equally good—thinking Foundation. "Back off, fella, you're breathing down the back of my neck!" Gene backed off; that was Muhammed Ali. Ha! Tony Bennett, being objectionable; Gene offered to throw *him* out. Looking around, he thought Mahalia had done it again. And he'd take care of that matter of this fellow she fired who'd filed an unfair-labor-practice charge with the District Attorney. He and Nat Borah could heave that out; no sweat.

Backstage, Kurt Kaiser was sorry he couldn't make the Green Room party but—that's the business. As director of music for Word Records, he was here to look out for Willa Dorsey. Most of the artists were certainly bustling about, nervous and anxious, but look at Mahalia Jackson! An island of calm.

WELL, LORD, You did it. We got us a *salute*. She just hoped Minnis wasn't off saluting some other black woman. She checked—Gwen had the music—and beckoned to Brother John Sellers, who'd got himself back from Paris just in time to enjoy the show without doing any work. John stepped over Cassius Clay, stretched out on the floor resting—"I can rest here as well as any place," he'd said, and Dolly Dickens said it was too crowded back here for anybody to lay down on the floor but Mahalia said, "Oh, let him lay," so lay he did and John stepped over him to Mahalia. "John—" she whispered. John nodded. And he sure wouldn't tell.

"WELL, I'M at home so take my coat and give me some pajamas or whatever you got, honey, 'cause I'm going to *bed*." It tickled John; he knew Halie would and he kept those extra big ones. Like old times. She and Gwendolyn had slipped over after the program. "I'd spent so long in Australia, and then again in Paris, I had catching up to do," he says. "And had to go right cooking corn and okra." Mahalia was still sleeping when Coretta King stopped by for Mahalia; she left a letter with John. "Shapiro was over, and the look on his face at Mahalia in these big pajamas eating gumbo for breakfast at 11 a.m.! She sure trusted that man—said she had put everything in his hands; Ming was out." Jean Childers was no more than in the door when she had to call Ken. Dolly Dickens came. And Albertina, for a check to replace one she lost. David Rockefeller called; he had a check for the Foundation. He came by Monday and ended up giving them a ride to the airport. "Falling down dead as she was, said she *had* to go to the Veterans Day program in Washington because she'd been quoted on some things about the war she didn't say; she was upset about that," says John.

OH, IT WAS a grand affair! Arlington Cemetery. Halie felt proud, fatigue pushed aside and all this bother of missing tickets from the Veterans and mussed-up arrangements about limousines and the organ so she bit at poor

Yancey like a cottonmouth moccasin, but he had it straight now—been at it almost since he drove in from New York with Dolly and Melissa. And here Halie was, up from a little old black girl running when the police come busting heads at Cherokee and Ann, sitting in dignity as honored guest beside the Chief Justice of the Supreme Court, Mr. Earl Warren. Aunt Duke, I hope you watching. You see I didn't come up no wet devil—the Lord has taken me, every step. She looked around for the President—he was due—but the Secretary of Defense was here, and he was chief man for Veterans Day, when you look at it that way. She was glad Superior had come too, to support her. She wanted to sing *The Lord's Prayer* first—nothing going happen without the Lord—then *Let There Be Peace.* Yes! Lord, let there be peace.

My God! thought Yancey, you can be mad at the woman and then listen to something like this and—something's come *over* her! . . . *and let it begin with me!* The audience to its feet, cheering, cheering; Mahalia rising and once more, the prayer for peace: for the world . . . for her . . .Great God Amighty! let there—let there be *peace.*

IT WASN'T at home. Even with a new beginning. Allen had finished moving her, so she went straight to the condominium, to the 26th floor—and carried the same lowdown problems like a satchel of old clothes. She meant to wait her own time on what Hannah phoned John about in New York for him to tell Mahalie. First off, got a houseful of people and nothing to eat with. She sent Yancey to 8358 to bring some tableware and Albertina and Snooks and Tiny all at the house—where Allen's staying to watch it—and can't wait to tell what happened, but here's Yancey yelling and carrying on, has tied in with Allen—two tempers; and Superior says if she wants something *he*'ll go get it, and now the kettle's on the boil about neighbors complaining, been partying while she's gone and next thing, Allen is packing for New Orleans. Missie can watch the house. "Don't talk, Missie, just do; you know you too poor to paint and too proud to whitewash, and this way you can rent your place and keep the money 'cause this won't cost you a cent. I'm going send you food every *day*; and you need that change with you and Tom split up." Not past that when Ike rides up; can he have $500 to go get some horses he has down in Virginia. She told him she would put him in any kind of business but she wasn't going to be a partner to his gambling. Then it's a call she would not have believed if they tied her to a post: Aretha talking so bad she put John on the extension 'cause *he*'d never believe it; and what Halie know about this child's business? Not messing in it, no matter what people say—her own business enough to crack a Christian: all this time in New York and Allen gone; Eskridge saying the Foundation checks stolen from New York and Yancey say he packed up all the records in the car and they did turn up, but oh! she was in the waters without a line but the Lord. And what to do about Minnis. Made him president of her Foundation and told Ben Hooks he got to have a good job with the chicken business 'cause they going get married again, and she didn't even know did she *want* him to sign that paper after New York. She'd about lost track of the chicken business, too, but you couldn't ask for a more faithful friend than Ben Hooks and he said they just hired on a new man to take the kinks out so that was good; but Lord God, mercy on high, here come the IRS saying she's in deep tax trouble from 1968: Talk about the frying pan and the fire—*this* how the new man do after she fired the old one for cahooting? How come Aldus Mitchell didn't keep an eye? Don't come telling her "he didn't hire the man." How she know what the accountant put on that paper? She just signed it, like anybody would; that's what you pay people for; but Superior say she didn't make that much, cool down, it's 'cause she keeps checks so long and go split some into cash and cashier checks and sometimes look like *twice* from different checks on the same money. She didn't know what that meant, but she been saying ever since she got 15 cents above 10 that she rather pay the government too much 'cause Halie Jackson can't stand stripes; and she never *could* get her papers out of Ming. But Superior say if Mitchell and them that got the tax business just add up her W-2s to show what she *did* make, the government going pull back; "this was just a routine audit." Routine? Don't that mean regular? One thing, at least Superior trying to help her save money: said that little State St. bank she got all that in might collapse any rainy night and had her put it in a big bank downtown going give her bigger interest . . . but oh! those people so mad at her, give John trouble with cashing a check of hers not but $200 but he should've had better sense than take it there. Him talking about crossing the Atlantic ocean to marry some white girl in Paris and got the nerve to sit here and ask her for the money to do it on. Whoo! she dished him out and Halie's not through scraping that plate yet. Lord Jesus! If there's peace in the valley, lead me on.

Dr. Barclay was seriously concerned about Mahalia's depression—no little quips, no twinkle. And it took relatively little now to completely exhaust her. She was quite short of breath and aware of heart irregularity. She was frightened. With reason. Definitely, the sarcoid was progressing—the cramps, the eye lesions, the heart, the chest, God knew where else by now. Important as any medication was keeping full awareness from her consciousness. If she ever truly understood, it would break her spirit, and her spirit was Mahalia. Even now, she knew her singing was going to be compromised, that she was going to get more and more short of breath. Of course, he didn't think she'd been taking very good care of herself. "But part of her depression was due to a feeling of desertion by persons close to her," he says. "It hurt to know that she included me in this category: I was deserting her by going to the A.M.A." She couldn't understand this. "Mahalia," he said, "I've got to be coming back and forth to Billings. I'll meet you here, unofficially." Halie felt her burden lift. She could still see Dr. Barclay! Thank You Lord. "Just try to stay on regular medication, Mahalia, and see if you can't keep away from some of these tensions."

TOP ROCK 40!! " 'Her most radical,' producer Townsend says." Wait 'til she get hold of Mr. Irving Townsend. And wait 'til her people get hold of this record. With all that rock noise Townsend sneaked in, you can't even hear the words half the time—and gospel *is* the message! *What the World Needs Now!* Took Halie 25 years to make a flop. Halie's not going say it in public, not going embarrass Columbia, but there won't be but one Mahalia Jackson record like *this*. In fact, she just might— Hm. See what Ben Hooks think. She'd see him in two weeks to open another chicken shack, but call him to come up now. Then he could be thinking about it. While she's praying on it. That's one thing she hadn't lacked to do that peculiar Thanksgiving right after Constitution Hall, singing at a barbecue in Mississippi where Charles Evers was mayor. Halie prayed her thanks to God with every note she sang: even for her burdens, for they make you strong. The Lord never gives you more than you can withstand.

And he always shows you a door, if you have the sense to open it. She'd just opened one, and it was overdue, even without this fuss. Yancey had grown up and he'd learned the business. He was a worker and he was fast on his feet. But not but *one* way to stop him getting those feet in *her* way—doing her business without asking her, calling Superior on his own: She had bought him a ticket and had John and Bertha take him to the plane. Like she told John, Yancey wanted to do publicity for Della Reese and some of them; he could operate for himself in Los Angeles.

Now here it was Christmas, 1969, and she didn't know whether she was opening a door or shutting it, but what was inside was grand. Christmas dinner with the table loaded and sitting to it was Minnis, Sigma, John Sellers, Aunt Alice (she'd get dinner to Hannah), Rev. Branham and his wife, Russell Goode, Robert Anderson, Josephine Davis, Bertha—with more due. And not a cross word or look. Maybe it was the food. Robert Anderson could purely cook a turkey. But she did believe, from the way they dived, that it was the chitlins got everybody with such a good face. Even Minnis having some. He caught her look and winked. Christmas was beautiful.

79

She'd thought Bermuda would be warm and do it, but it was cold and wasn't doing it. Lord, give her strength. *Told* Mr. De Mello when she come she had the flu, and still the interviews. Well, that's their business . . . and it's Halie's business to get on that stage tomorrow and her struggling with this chest trouble ever since Memphis. That's 10 days and she's better, but how come the islands wasn't warm?

No, she did not want that hot tea, go on take it way, she told Sigmond crossly. Gwen Lightner lay low; Sister's mood was going to calm soon as she was shut of the demons. Charles was wondering if Mahalia would be able to take two concerts in one day, but Gwen said you watch, the Lord takes care of His own.

Promoter Eddie De Mello had his fingers crossed, but there she was—had sung the one-hour matinee in marvelous form and now tonight His Excellency the Governor, Lord Martonmere, and Lady Martonmere were lending patronage and homage—yes, homage—to the Queen of Gospel, who was being fantastic. One-hour provision forgotten, she was responding to "Encore!" again—and now again. Oh, indeed, she was fantastic!

"THEN TRY the Americana," Mahalia whispered. Gwen fumbled through the Manhattan directory again. They were at the airport hunting a hotel reservation, and both the Hilton and the Waldorf were full, even for Mahalia. Nothing here, either. "What shall I—" began Gwen. Mahalia heaved and thought a moment. She knew Minnis thought she was putting on, anybody getting over the flu didn't ought to take on like that, but she knew well as she knew her name she couldn't make it on in to Chicago; *got* to get to a doctor. "See the Wellington, then; I used to stop there years ago." At the Wellington (grown musty with indifference and small by comparison) Mahalia knew by morning it was not a doctor's office, it was a hospital she needed. Gwen helped Minnis check her in, then Gwen had to fly to the funeral of *five* grandchildren of a friend, lost on a boat; but she said she'd be right back.

John Sellers swung between pain and frustration: Mahalia in the hospital and him in town and can't even tend her because he's laying up here with a bad burn from when a big wheel off a Con Edison truck hit his building, and he had to be holding a pan of hot grease. But he knew sure as he was born that so-called husband wouldn't tend Mahalia properly.

SIGMOND SAT at Mahalia's bedside. She was napping, knocked out from the sedative probably. He wondered why he didn't go on and sign that marriage quit-claim like Eskridge and Mitchell both said he was a fool not to. Mitchell said Christmas Day it wouldn't hold up—but that was the man who'd put him through that divorce trial. Eskridge said go on, "Mahalia will tear it up after you've been married a week," and Sigmond laughed and called him a dirty old man but that meant Eskridge saw it as *valid*. This thing had too much difference going on it. Sigmond couldn't make up his mind to trust it to look out for Galloway, and if he didn't, nobody else would. He knew he was bored with this bedside business when all was wrong with Mahalia was that she loved to be babied.

"SEE, IT'S easy," said Tina Choate, "you just put it all in the blender and it's instant juice."

"What all we got?" Halie sorted it on the kitchen table: spinach, beets, carrots, alfalfa, apples. "Yeahhhh, that's going cleanse our body." Harry Dale shook his head. Had him run to 71st to buy all this stuff—and within an hour they'd both run for the bathroom like they'd seen a mouse.

Tina watched Mahalia drink hers down and pretend she liked it. What a woman. "When Curt and I drifted apart," says Tina, "I spent more and more time with Mahalia. She was still pushing me to marry Curt." Well—time to get Aunt Hannah to Billings. While she was waiting, she could slip over and ask Gene Shapiro about this mail before she showed it to Mahalia.

GENE SHAPIRO looked at Allen Miner across his desk, working up a sweat. So this was who'd called him last June from Europe: "could Shapiro help a guy out?" Gene had got right on it—Mahalia said the man was from the U.S. government making some sort of film. Now it develops he's also working for the outfit Gene had the knock-down, walk-out session with. This poor fish apparently got a fast hook too. Well, well. He'd get the contract from Mahalia and see what they'd bilked her into. "I was fairly sure I could force a better deal," he said, "because from what Miner was telling me, the whole project had got royally fouled up and at the very least, in Mahalia's name, I could refuse to allow its release on grounds of inadequate presentation of the artist, her story, and her personality." He'd prepare Mahalia—she seemed well enough since she'd canceled out and rested.

MAHALIA SIGHED. She ought to be working on music. Especially after having Hogan send a tape of those songs of Laurraines. Supposed to know *Who Made the Great Plan* and *I've Got to Walk—Lord, Hold My Hand* for 10 days from now with Beal and Lord knows she could feel that walk one—Halie's through running, just let her walk, Lord; hold her hand. Poor Ike. No more even *walking*. Just sit in a wheelchair at Rev. Cobbs' rest home. She'd told them be sure and give Ike everything; she'd pay. She better call Dr. Barclay to come meet her. Out of town. Dr. Spaulding. then; this flu just hanging on, hanging on.

SHE WAS GLAD she made it—and started not to, with having to take the plane to New Orleans tomorrow: come down to see John H. Johnson get his honorary Doctor of Journalism at the Blackstone, and what does Halie hear whispered around? That Mahalia Jackson's the next one going be honored like Duke at the White House. She wouldn't be the one to tell it; whispers are like the wind, and just as numerous.

MAHALIA RAPPED one wall, then another, of her room at the Royal Orleans. "This real plaster; they don't make many new buildings like that any more. Where I am now, what's going on on the first floor, you can hear clear up on the 26th." She was in a fine mood. Laurraines had her in this grand hotel and the people sent up welcome fruit that no time ago they'd put the man in jail for letting her in. It was nice to receive people in dignity. Jerome Burks was with her as valet to tend her needs, and except for interviews and rehearsal, she had three days off before the concert. Allen had got it together for New Orleans scholarships from the Foundation, with Beal's chorus and Ida's beauticians selling the tickets. It had caused her to take another look at Allen: blood's thicker than water. Minnis be in tomorrow. Still got to come late and stay behind, every time.

JOHNNY JACKSON looked around Loyola Fieldhouse, enjoying even the waiting. When had the Clarks and the Jacksons come together like this? Yvonne, Pearl, Wilmon, and himself plus his two kids and their mother; and Allen, Isabell, Manuel, Bessie, George, Allen Sr., Celie—well, too many Clarks to count. Came near not being counted himself: "I had to talk somebody into finding Professor Beal to verify all this was members of Miss Jackson's family, to be passed in," he said. He was interested in the opportunity to assess Galloway as a musician. What he thought of him as a man made no difference, it was Mahalia's business; he *was* in the family—or just before. Johnny wasn't sure which and wouldn't pry. But he'd never seen him on stage . . . well, that was all right, the man can MC. Oh! listen at that girl. Mahalia made him want to stand up and say "That's my sister!" Now Galloway with the flute, to play what he calls a "standard." Say, the man can play. He can really *play* that thing.

One way, Halie just as soon Minnis go on and play some more; that much less for her to pull. But another way, she was lifted with the Lord in bringing her so high with her own: that was more than kings and queens. Must be the tail end of the flu made her sweat like popcorn out there. "And come off drenched again! That takes something out of you, baby!" Halie was standing in the apartment kitchen, an apron tied firmly around her waist—it didn't much reach across, but that's all right. She'd accepted the dinner invitation from Laurraine's nephew Roger, who'd helped her figure some business though he'd never laid eyes on her—that was a family. She'd told his little wife what she wanted was shrimp Creole and then found the child was from Oklahoma, so she said what ingredients to have ready; she'd come cook it herself. She was washing the rice the third time now: "see, 'til there's no starch." In the living room, Roger Winters was almost gagging on his Scotch. One of the world's most fascinating women in his own kitchen, and the husband insists, "Come on out here with me, you don't want to talk to those women."

When the dinner was in the pots and pans, Halie washed up the sink, wiped the counter, washed her dishcloth, and smoothed it on the sink to dry. "That's the way my Aunt Duke taught me, baby," she overrode Katie's protest; "the Lord likes a clean kitchen."

"GWEN, YOU GO represent me. I don't think I can make it this morning." If Mahalia was skipping church, she wasn't well; Gwen would hurry back. Maybe she could do something to make Sister feel better; they had the concert to do tonight.

Mahalia had come Saturday to Salt Lake City hoping the dry climate would help. She'd had just two days in Chicago after singing for Ida in Baton Rouge on top of New Orleans. She'd hardly had chance to go into her special business with Superior they'd been on and off with since October, but it was in her mind and caused her to say, "Gwen, I want you to get you some E bonds." They'd eaten in the suite, and Mahalia had out her bras, girdles, wigs to sew on. She explained what E bonds were, and told Gwen soon as they got back from this islands tour coming up, she'd give Gwen a *This Is Your Life* to have something to get the bonds with. "You got those children, your husband with heart trouble— What I'm talking about—I don't know how long I'll be on this road. When I leave, I'm going leave you at the top of the ladder, all you have to do is walk in the door. Ain't no Negro going be able to stop you."

Even in her excited gratitude, Gwen took a close look at Mahalia: She didn't *seem* depressed. Just a deep thinker.

NOT ANY MORE! She'd come home in time to sing for the $100-a-plate dinner for Adlai Stevenson II, and next day she felt so terrible she got Dr. Barclay to meet her at Billings. And after he'd listened and told her her medication, he said, "This can't go on." She'd never forget those words. He wasn't supposed to any more, he said, now he was vice president of the American Medical Association. Billings knew her case, he said; they'd take care of her. Then why is it these three days and nights she's been crying and carrying on something terrible? Ashamed of herself and can't stop. A grown woman, crying her eyes out like a little girl because Dr. Barclay wasn't going take care of her. "I'm here," the Voice said. Just as plain. "I'm here." Halie sat up, contrite and apologetic. "Oh Lord, forgive me for forgetting You," she said. "I won't do it again."

"The Voice spoke," she said, telling it, "and I dried my eyes."

NO ONE COULD have told two nights later at Brooklyn Academy of Music, when Mahalia "really got into something"—and into a packed week she was just as glad Dr. Barclay—oh, excuse me, Lord: It was Brooklyn, the 8th; Dick Cavett, the 10th; Mike Douglas in Philadelphia, the 12th; to Portland, Me., next day and over to Bowdoin College in Brunswick: where Clency finally got in trouble. Breathless, he'd made it to the organ in Philadelphia when Gwen was starting the first song. He dashed back to Chicago for one day's classes, missed his connection in Boston—and missed the Bowdoin concert entirely, despite a desperate taxi ride. Things didn't rise until next day—a major civil rights benefit in New York. When Mahalia saw the hall's pipe organ, she told Charles he couldn't play that—go on home. Sigmond took him aside and reversed the order. At the Hilton later, with thunder and lightning rising over money due and orders given, Gwen escaped to her room. Next morning, Charles was gone. And they had played like one instrument.

Who now? The Caribbean was days away: Erie, New York, shots, and fly. Ralph Jones was the answer; the Ralph Jones of the first Columbia recordings. All of them were excited. New territory, exotic black territory. Sigmond was coming—he traveled with them regularly and this contract spelled out "Mahalia Jackson and her husband." So was Jerome Burks, to look after Mahalia. Aunt Alice would look after the condominium. Gwen just knew this trip was going to do Sister a world of good.

JAMAICA, get straight with the sponsor, a day's rest, and off to St. Croix to begin. Six concerts, two one-hour shows daily an hour apart, the contract said. That sounded all right; there'd be some rest days and she sang about that long for one concert—the man just collecting two tickets for one night. It was kind of a peculiar contract, though. It took about six technical pages to say—far as she could get it straight from Bob—that they might want to go into South America (both sides would have to agree), in which case they'd cut the Caribbean short and begin South America on April 18 for 19 dates, about every other day: sing one, travel one. Or, if they didn't do that, it said she was supposed to go to Australia. And there was something about TV and radio. She stopped trying to figure out all that and just sang: St. Croix, St. Thomas, Trinidad, honored by the governor on each island, cheered by the crowds, the natives crowding in as if to be blessed and, lacking the language, "Sis-tah! Sis-tah!" was their amen and hallelujah when the gospel carried them away. In Trinidad, a troubled island, she was the guest of Prime Minister Eric Williams—resting after her concert when a black-power mob gathered and in all the shouts could be heard her name too. It was frightening, she couldn't understand how she figured in; but when she was asked to go outside and speak to the crowd, she did. There was some misunderstanding about this "black power," she told them; what they wanted to go after was "good jobs and the vote": if they had those, they had *real* black power, "not something to be manipulated." She thought she'd got her point across pretty good and still they didn't leave and the shouts started up again. Then it came: one of their main grievances was that her concert had been too expensive for the people to attend. ("Money's thin here, just at the top," murmured Gwen.) She agreed—and the sponsor agreed—she would return and give them a concert free. There was one free concert for the underprivileged somewhere in all those contract pages anyway, unless she was wrong about that. On then to St. Vincent, Guayana, Barbados . . . the islands began to run together; there were three more but nobody could remember where, they were extra, and then it was Trinidad for the poor people and Halie learned from Ernestine Washington (at convention with her husband) that Halie's old friend Becky Nelson that she'd given her flower shop, who'd helped Emma Bell with the beauty shop Grand Opening when Dorsey kept her away—Becky was dead. She was so upset that finally Sigmond and Gwen got a car and drove her up into the quiet of the mountains. She came down into a fight: The sponsor owed her money for all these extra concerts. The sponsor said he'd been giving it to Mr. Galloway. "He's not my manager, you're dealing with me!" stormed Mahalia. Sigmond shrugged that he'd turned over what was given him. Somewhere in there was a lie and Halie didn't know whose but she had more than sung the six concerts on that contract and she wasn't going into Jamaica, she was going home. The sponsor was livid: all these little islands didn't make up for Jamaica; that was where he planned to make money. "You the one messed up; I still don't see my money," said Mahalia. Sigmond tried to dissuade her; Ralph kept quiet; Jerome dare not speak. Gwen was so upset over missing Jamaica that she tried to be peacemaker. "You're talking to a made-up mind," said Mahalia and told Jerome to pack. Sigmond shrugged; he was staying. On her cards.

She was home Monday, April 19, when Laurraine called. "Can you call me back in two hours, baby? I'm cooking dinner for Aunt Hannah. She's sick and I can't do it all tomorrow." Cook and pack too, that is; she was flying to New Orleans Wednesday. Laurraine noticed Mahalia was panting, as if she'd been running—but there was a telephone right in the kitchen. . . .

Wednesday night when she checked into the Royal Sonesta she was bone-tired, she told the girl from the paper. The reporter was there when ABC Booking in New York called to see she was in all right; she said yes, she just got in from the islands. New York set up the Caribbean but the one she's going tell the story to is Bob Phillips—since Joe Glaser died, he's head of all the ABC. They didn't have the end of *that* yet. Going get that Jamaica sponsor on the phone while she's this close. Or get Laurraines to. This girl here now, Betty—Anding?—she was asking about her husband, and she might as well give Minnis the satisfaction: "he's my business manager." They didn't get this paper in Jamaica. She was waiting to see what tale Minnis had to tell about staying down there all this while.

Early Thursday she was heading uptown to the high school where Ellen Blount's daughter Robin was a student. "I got to go," she said; "the child been telling the other children how she knows Mahalia Jackson and she'll be through at school if I don't." She was only to speak, but looking at the mass of dark young faces, she broke into song, with a flustered, hurriedly recruited teacher at the upright piano. Into the noonday sun to Canal St. "for something cotton to wear," but diverted at Krauss's by an armload of pretty dresses which she tried on, then dashed the clerk's hopes by concluding, regretfully, that she couldn't wear that kind of party clothes; just give her the seersuckers. "Now let's go down to Congo Square, see what George Wein's got for his festival" . . . and coming upon the Eureka Brass Band beginning *Just a Closer Walk with Thee,* she climbed onto the makeshift stage and gave them a chorus for the fun of it. "I got no better sense," she panted; "now let's go get us some jambalaya." Whatever had been wrong with Halie, Laurraine decided, she must be well now.

Minnis came, but she didn't want to spoil things and there wasn't a note off until she was in the dressing room at Municipal Auditorium Friday night. The room was full of people but only Gwen knew what it meant when Mahalia started on a moan—fixing herself at the mirror but moaning low to herself, looking from one direction to the other. Gwen came close and Mahalia said, "Death is right around," and went back to moaning. Gwen opened her eyes wide, funny, striking a pose: "Ooh, is it me?" She made Mahalia laugh, and then it was concert time, but when it was over, Halie called home. It wasn't the aunts.

That night Minnis vanished and Beal, Ida, and Doodutz volunteered to keep her company until he got back. At 4 a.m. they gave up. At 5 she woke Jerome: pack.

"Checked out? We had an appointment about her business!" cried Laurraine. "What is this? We had an appointment to go shopping!" cried Ida. "She can't be gone; she was spending the weekend with me," cried Doodutz.

"Well, Ida," said Beal, "he has succeeded, he has disgraced the woman in her own home town."

She wasn't in town, then, for Duke Ellington's surprise. The premiere of his *New Orleans Suite* included four musical portraits, and one of them was "Portrait of Mahalia."

"Dear Lorraine," the letter said, some days later; "please forgive me for leaving so unexpectedly. I was tireder than I imagined. . . . My blood-pressure went up to 256 and I'm feeling very weak from it and my head is very sore. . . . Let me know about the record business, whether to distribute or sign."

THAT WAS THE question. Halie had made up her mind to a lot of things, and one of them was to quit Columbia and get back to her own sound. Which way to go was the only question. She'd let Superior sign that two-year extension to October, 1971, because it would take a lot of time to get the different opinions and information and, if she made her own records, to get set up. She'd asked Ben Hooks what he thought, and she wanted to ask John Jay Hooker. Minnis had been after her again to put *him* in the recording business. One more ditch too wide to jump.

Two days later she was in Hartford, Conn., to sing, Minters with her. The Lord give her the strength. She had to go down on her knees against the demons from Minnis, though—Nettie had caught her so mad when the April charges came in from the credit cards and she *saw* what Minnis had done that she popped it to Nettie—thousands and thousands! look at this American Express alone; but what you going do? If he'd go on and give her *proof,* sign the quit-claim, Sigma and him could move up in the condominium. All those rooms. But go on, let him play his flute and tonight with two shows on the contract one after the other, the space is a blessing. Lord, You know what You doing, but I'd appreciate it if you'd reveal it to me.

Then she sure didn't want Gwen to know she felt like death warmed over when the girl got herself built *so* high on her *This Is Your Life,* so it's Los Angeles with the show to do May 24. Celeste's Ladies of Song, Thurston's group, James Cleveland, a whole bunch of California people and nobody but her to try to line the thing and Minnis getting people upset backstage, acting grand, giving them instructions 'til she had to cut him off with "Who's the star?" Help me, Jesus! Superior would never know how she appreciated him coming out to support her. . . .

Gene Shapiro shut out the bar babble and listened. He'd been chiefly listening for quite a while, with growing sympathy. The man was pouring it out, and it came out bitter. Even when he played the flute, she introduced him as her husband. He was Sigmond Galloway, flutist, husband of Mahalia Jackson. *He* had no identity.

June 1. It was getting *started* with some main one since Dr. Barclay stopped but no putting off now; not with the chicken shacks going open about one every weekend someplace. No, she didn't want to be hospitalized. Dr. Earl Vondrasek called in his associate to proctoscope Miss Jackson. "Primarily," he says, "her blood sugar was out of control—quite high—and prednisone is somewhat antagonistic to insulin, so her diabetic control was going to be a little bit difficult to achieve. She insisted upon the prednisone for her sarcoid." He increased her diabenese dosage to 250 mgs. twice a day and put her on a reduction diet of 1200 calories daily.

"Mahalia Jackson tries some 'Glori-Fried' chicken prepared at a Mahalia Jackson Chicken Store opened this weekend at E. 83rd and So. Evans," said the *Sun-Times* caption. The June 6 opening was the first of five in Chicago; Judge Ben L. Hooks, president of the franchise corporation, and C. W. Lutz, vice president of Gulf Oil's midwest marketing region, made the joint announcement, said the paper. It did not say Mahalia had been in Detroit at Mayor Gribbs's mansion that day as the main attraction of a fete to promote her Foundation benefit there July 11. As more and more lined up to meet her, she grew worried—nervous—frantic—and was finally raced under screaming escort from the sheriff's department and flung aboard a plane in time to eat fried chicken for the press.

DR. VONDRASEK was encouraged. In just 10 days her blood sugar was more balanced. He'd like to get her into the hospital for closer control, but—yes, come back Saturday. . . . Better. Now come back Monday. . . . Splendid! June 15, blood sugar normal, weight down to 211 pounds. Come back in—say, 10 days. That sure was good news; got chicken business tomorrow. Then before she had to get back to concerts, she wanted to hunt a place for her temple—get *on* that, especially now she's got this $46,000 from the land at 89th. Nettie said she'd take her looking every day this summer if she wanted to; and Dale said *his* car had gas—he well knew she'd fill it up. But now she had Allen back as her secretary, and Teevee coming in after her job to help catch up, she could do more looking. Just not to let the people find out who it was. But Superior would handle it. And no cahooting. One thing about that land sale—and working on her house now too—did Mitchell think he can call Polly about where her different papers and things without Polly telling her—and Polly calling sometimes every night?

PACKED AND ready. July 4, Omaha; July 8, New York; July 9, Philadelphia; July 10, Newport; July 11, Detroit; New York July 14; Berkshire Music Barn right after. "Jerome—let's go."

July 4 was just to sing at the Omaha baseball stadium for 20 to 30 minutes to begin and then close. They wanted *God Bless America* but she didn't know that by memory; she'd substitute *The Lord's Prayer*. It was a night game, but still she could get back.

MISSIE JUST didn't know. She had *never* asked Mahala to do nothing that she wouldn't do. Still, with Mahala off in Nebraska *any*thing can happen and she's scared to say "Mahala" except to tell the boy at the gate to let her *in* if a lady name Miss Mahala Jackson come. This big company picnic, all the big bosses, and nobody see Missie the scrubwoman when all of a sudden people start running and *scrambling*. Missie wondered if these people got to fighting. Then she went and looked and it was her. Everybody taking pictures. And Mahala asking, "Where's Missie?" Luberta Lindsey, Russell Goode, Harry Dale all with her. "Where's Missie?" and they start the page. Missie acted like she didn't hear, she wanted it paged a *long* time. Mahala had *thrilled* her. And the bosses. One had never spoken to her, didn't care for colored, but it was "Missie, can I take her picture?" Everybody forgot the scrubwoman. "Missie, can I take her picture with me?" And when Mahalia said, "I want some *watermelon*," one of the bosses took out and got her a whole half from somewhere, that she ate.

It was Aunt Hannah's birthday, too, and Mahalia had a dinner for her that evening—it wasn't often she got the chance, with the family.

And how long since she had a chance to see Louie Armstrong! They fell in each other's arms at Newport—red beans and ricely! nicely! Bill Russell was up from New Orleans: to him, not even the rain could dampen those smiles. Elliott Beal felt the same way; but he wished it wouldn't rain *every* time Mahalia took him up here with her. Halie offered to cook Louie his rice and beans, but if he'd come, it would've had to been Detroit next night for her Foundation—and she might've put him to work. She'd never forget the programs arriving under Russell Goode's arm at the last second because Harry's wife died suddenly and it was Tina and Russell had them to put together. . . .

Dr. Vondrasek was disappointed. She was hypertensive. Chest pain was recurring; she had intermittent diarrhea; her weight was 219.

Bob Phillips grimaced at the phone. Just because Mahalia didn't feel well today, how could she tell she wouldn't feel well a week and 10 days from now? But if she could back him up with a doctor's report, all right —he'd cancel.

California wasn't doing her much good either. She'd come out to get away from the heat wave in Chicago, but here she was at Dr. Peck's office July 27, waiting for a prescription for sudafed. She couldn't record like this—or make Toledo. Instead, Aug. 9 she was in Billings Emergency Room with severe chest pain. Dr. Lloyd Ferguson, the young black doctor they'd put her onto since Dr. Barclay, came and said the pain was hypertension and prescribed valium. She flew to Toronto the next day to do the Barbara McNair show she'd canceled two weeks before, and the next night she was in Detroit. She couldn't fail the benefit for Joe Louis, fighting his toughest fight since his son put him in the VA in Denver. It wasn't a sad night, though; so many old friends together for Joe—Red Foxx, Billy Eckstein, *so* many. Halie's heart lifted with joy in the Healer. Watching offstage, Sigmond shook his head. At the hotel, she's groaning, so sick, no breath; and next you know, she's belting a song so the whole hall is in an uproar. Most of it had to be her mind.

What was *all* her mind was the Swedish Club, just off Stony Island—beautiful dining room, ballroom, kitchen, offices, parking space. She was the only one taken with it. Nettie thought it was fine for wealthy Swedes, but not for a church. Jean said it wouldn't hold but 500 at most. "We want some place that will hold 1000 or 1500 people," said Mr. Miller. "You could get yourself into a lot of trouble with that," said Aunt Hannah—and she had a lot of sense. Well, what Halie really wanted anyway was to have it on Martin Luther King, Jr. Drive, that used to be So. Park. That would be like having him a part. She'd ask Gene Superior if he couldn't find her something there. That's one thing could take her mind off how she felt.

Three weeks, but when National Baptist Convention came, she had to cancel—in New Orleans, too. She stayed on her knees and with her Bible. *They that wait upon the Lord, He shall renew their strength. . . .* And did, in Monroe, La. Halie got so joyous they had to lead her off the stage. Two days later it was hallelujah for back-to-back dates . . . gave James Lee a benefit because he was ailing and needy and Two-Finger-Picking James Lee, right on; when he got out the hospital, she was going see to an apartment and some furniture . . . and Oct. 10, at the Blackstone for her Foundation fashion show, she was good for whatever was needed.

It was beautiful. Ivory Wilkerson, president of the Mahalia Jackson Foundation Guild, had had the thought, guided the doing, and Halie approved, looking out over the well-dressed crowd, the flowers, the laden table that might seem out of place at any fashion show but this: can after can of Mahalia Jackson Butterbeans, Mahalia Jackson Pinto Beans (should have been "red beans," but they told her nobody outside New Orleans would know), Chopped Turnip Greens with Diced Turnips. That was all so far, but fixed in pyramids it looked plentiful. You could buy them in the A&P. The silver cover of the program gleamed, its names a judicious mixture of personal, political, and religious: Bob Miller, Alderman Ralph Metcalfe, Fannie Jones; Gene Shapiro, Aldus Mitchell; Revs. John Thurston, Clay Evans, Frank Sims; and her cousin Steve Stevens. Music by Mr. Sigmond Galloway and His Pied Pipers.

As MC, Bob Miller was trying to keep it off the mike: Minters fussing about too much talking, Mahalia saying tone down the music, forgetting they each had a live mike in front of them, sending messages back and forth by this Dale fellow. Of course, with these two it was always something, though it didn't seem to mean anything—they were engaged to be married again. The music was really rather loud. He didn't know why Galloway needed such a big band.

Sigmond was pleased. The way to handle Mahalia was to just do your thing and talk about it later. Did she have any idea 500 grown men and women would stick around a fashion show if he hadn't set up a bar upstairs as a favor for people? And it made him a nice piece of change.

"FOR LIQUOR! On *my* bill! Liquor on Mahalia Jackson's bill!" Ultimately, Allen would write a check for total expenses minus the sizable sum for liquor; the hotel would threaten to sue the Foundation (which pointed out it had not ordered liquor); and Minters Sigmond Galloway would be off Mahalia Jackson's list. Off!

"I don't want to talk to him," Mahalia told Gwen flatly. They were in Mahalia's Oakland, Calif., hotel room three days after the fashion show—

Mahalia had sung for Rev. Jodie Strawther the night before. Gwen relayed the message. "Tell Mahalia I said come," Minters's voice on the phone commanded. But she wouldn't. There was a spare ticket, then, for the scheduled concerts, and Oct. 31 when Gwen arrived in Phoenix for a Tempe concert next night, Polly was with Mahalia. Gwen didn't recognize her—so *long* since the beauty shop. "Polly need a change," Mahalia explained. When Mahalia went on to Los Angeles—got to see these real estate people been having So. Norton since back when Polly was secretary —Polly stayed over a day there before she went back to Chicago. Gwen wasn't asking any questions. Mahalia was feeling all right, doing all right, and they just had two concerts before Africa. She knew one thing had helped Sister: Butch Thornton gave her a birthday party in Gary and a lot of old friends who showed up showed her they loved her.

DEAD. Dawson, the man who first ever tried to do something big for her, a girl not old enough to vote . . . "Dawson will show you the way." All through these years. It saddened Jean Childers to see Mahalia grieve so deeply. She sang at his funeral the day Allen packed her for Africa, with a concert to sing first in Virginia the next night.

It didn't help Halie's mood, when she left town, to know Bob Ming had been convicted for not filing income taxes and was going to the federal pen. Lord, You sure looked out for Halie when You sent Superior. And Lord, do remember me, over that ocean. *Some*thing wrong; too many changes before this trip: Ralph Jones sick and got to get a new musician in a hurry three weeks ago. Joyce Lampkin, the girl Teevee's pastor knew, turns out fine but she's a student at Oral Roberts University and can't stop school, so here she has Edward, had asked to go. And instead of Minnis—his name down and everything when that business started—she's taking Harry Dale. It ought to be Bob *Phillips* coming; she *told* him.

Bob Phillips checked the hour: she's off. He'd had a time at first convincing her: "I don't want to go there, they have them big black snakes and I'm scared of snakes." It took him a little to realize she thought she'd be carried through the jungle by barefoot native bearers. "Liberia is very modern; the capital's a beautiful city right on the coast," he'd assured her. "You won't have to go into a jungle, and you'll be treated like royalty." He wasn't sure she believed him—especially when he turned down going with her, but she'd begun to concentrate on the honor of being invited to this giant fete for President Tubman's 75th birthday.

AMBASSADOR Samuel Westerfield was there; Vice President William Tolbert was there; pomp and circumstance were expansive and so was Mahalia as the welcome motorcade moved out of Roberts International Airport, Monrovia, for two fairytale weeks in which she felt like a princess and was treated like a queen. She and Gwen were installed in the ambassador's residence in a second-floor suite with a sun porch overlooking the Atlantic; they could watch the ships as they breakfasted. Nowhere was there *not* something to watch, even the way the women moved on the street. The chic of the ladies at the functions was eye-opening. ("And look, Gwen, not a bush around and this is Africa!") They were guests at a Calendar Tea—a hospital benefit—and discovered this meant an astonishing array of cookies and cakes, intricately decorated, the work of weeks (some had been soaking in rum that long, Gwen decided). The wives of the Vice President and the Bank of Liberia president had made for each of them a wondrous, long Liberian garment—a *grand bubu.* Mahalia's was a silken white lace threaded with gold which cascaded from its flowing headpiece. The ladies presented their gifts at intermission and drew a gasp from the audience when the curtain rose. Stephen Tolbert (who arranged Mahalia's coming) and his wife had them to dinner, and Mahalia was showered with intricately worked 24-karat gold jewelry. Gwen received gold earrings and "a nugget to match." Some days later a group of admiring ladies presented Mahalia with ivory jewelry because she had responded so to the elephant symbol. Ambassador Westerfield escorted Mahalia to the executive mansion for a private visit with President Tubman, who said her singing "thrilled his soul" and extended the courtesy call so he could tell her of his hope of making a sort of economic United Nations for his country, so the nations of the world would help develop its rich potential. Mahalia left deeply moved and excited to share his vision. His Presidential dinner and ball showed her the other side of the coin. Dignitaries from a number of neighboring states were in attendance; so was the global diplomatic corps. Everyone stood for the President's entrance and could not remain seated any single time he rose for any purpose thereafter. The 75-year-old President led the grand march and started the ball with a little dance around the room by himself, to horns, sticks, and hand drums. "He could pass for 40," Mahalia whispered. "Whatever Miss Jackson wants" was the standing staff instruction at the embassy. On Thanksgiving, there was a candlelight dinner with turkey and trimmings flown from the States. In all this Harry and Edward were sometimes present, sometimes not; they were quartered downtown at the Intercontinental Hotel. To some functions only the two men went, when Mahalia gave out and took to her room, Gwen keeping her company. They went shopping, got lost in the fabrics, and Mahalia had 12 dresses made. (If you had a few moments, they'd run a dress up for you on the spot.) They went sightseeing into the countryside. Mahalia balked at just one thing: She would not leave the car unless it was at the top of a hill. "I know about that mamba snake that's one bite and you dead, and I see dead snakes at the *bottom* of the hill, so that must be where they cross."

All this and more in one week. Then a U.S. Navy plane flew them to Maryland, the capital of Cape Palmas, the island where President Tubman was born. By now Mahalia thought if she had to stand for one more toast at anything, she was going disgrace her country; and when they were taken to a children's presentation of the President's life f-r-o-m b-i-r-t-h, Mahalia, in the Presidential box, just naturally eased off her shoes. An aide hurried to find Dale down below and urged he get Miss Jackson's shoes on before the President noticed; it was a serious breach of protocol! Climbing over what seemed about 20 people, Harry whispered to Mahalia. She fixed a stare in his direction and said, "I take off my shoes in the White House, I *know* I can take off my shoes in Africa, for the same reason—my feet are killing me!"

And she could have killed those people waking her at 4 a.m. giving her a serenade—just like Mardi Gras—but since she was awake, she looked and—"Gwen!" Gwen hurried from two doors away to find Mahalia hanging over the balcony. Below, old and young were dancing to the drums and they saw the upstairs maid, on the stoop, tuck her baby into her back sling, dance down the steps, and merge with the crowd, the baby gurgling with his ride.

They watched a walking funeral, too, from that window, and Gwen remembered Mahalia at the ambassador's house the other morning when she grew still and said, "I smell death." Gwen tried to convince her it must be some perfume but "I smell death," said Mahalia with that look of a sphinx. Gwen turned the talk. Sister wasn't having her to call home; it wasn't too close.

Cape Palmas was Mahalia's final concert—so heart-felt, so soul-full that first President Tubman, then his wife, flung their arms around her as she stood drenched and disheveled but to them, they said, beautiful. Then the final big event—the dinner for visiting heads of state. Mahalia had had it. She did not want to go. And after she got there, she didn't want to stay; every *one* of those people got to toast the President, one at the time. "Stay!" said Harry, "they're going to give you an award!" Oh. She couldn't be impolite. So she was on hand to receive Liberia's award of high distinction: the Grand Banner of the Order of the Star of Africa. "We are all one, from America," said a beaming Mrs. William Tolbert.

Two weeks to the day, back in New York and Halie hadn't really been sick a time. Thank You, Jesus.

She believed she'd go on out to California and fix up that upstairs apartment she had Johnny holding vacant for her since October—really fix it up. Look like warm climate agreed with her, and she better gather her store: Bob Phillips had booked her out again. And if Halie's fool enough to take Jesus' gospel to the Buddhists, she better be strong. She might have to contend.

If anybody there to listen. They sure don't know Mahalia Jackson in Japan.

80

"What's Mahalia doing, Johnny?" Galloway's voice was casual, but on the other hand he'd never called Johnny Jackson before. "What's she up to?" Johnny was pretty general in his reply; Mahalia hadn't brought Minters' name up to him, and one thing he never did was pry. "Just setting up a second-floor unit, that's about it."

Celeste was high on the hog, helping her spend, and Halie was afraid it might be catching; she was enjoying it herself. The major pieces had been waiting, shipped from 8358 in Chicago, but they'd bought carpeting and a new chandelier and fill-in pieces and they weren't through yet—but then she'd taken time out for Christmas. That was something different. Had to come to California to have her first white Christmas; well, Christmas Eve. She'd spent it with Ann Hooper and her friend—big handsome Johnny Meston who wrote *Gunsmoke*—and a lot of their other white friends, and Johnny couldn't get over her telling him "they don't make Jews like Jesus any more." Well, they don't. Christmas Day at Mother Parks it was the other way around: all the old gospel bunch, the only white face was Yancey—she'd brought him. Oh, they had a time! Robbie Preston got at the piano and they had the old house rocking so nobody noticed for the longest that in the yard and all up and down the street everywhere the people stood listening—Halie's voice carrying Christmas clear down the block. ("Next day," says Mother Parks, "a boy said he'd have given $100 if he could just shake Mahalia Jackson's hand. I said he should have knocked, Mahalia would've said come on in.") There was Johnny's family to be with, and Bertha came by to see her and Uncle Johnny—just *had* moved here from Chicago. And with staying at Celeste's 'til her apartment got fixed to move in, there was all their house going on. She hit into New York of 1971 with a fresh mind and some business on it. She definitely wasn't going to sign with anybody else, she was going make her own records. Hallelujah! That was the very name for her label: Laurraine said anybody heard Mahalia, heard "Hallelujah!" whenever the spirit moved, and that's the God's truth. That Laurraine; tell her Halie's going to tour Japan and right off she wants to write some official in Japan she knows, see if they want to give Halie government honors like Liberia and Europe. That girl got a restless mind . . . good thing; Halie can use *all* the thinking, on this record business. You don't just up and press. There's whether to rent a studio and where, and what quality they got, and the prices—or get your own equipment; run mail order, or lease the distribution; figure the best way to promote for the money, and find out air charges for different parts of the country; and how could you halfway make sure you get your money when you sell dealers: record business was bad about that.

More angles to this thing than a dog has fleas and you can't scratch 'em all at once—and sure not by yourself. Money didn't look like the problem. Ben Hooks and Mr. Hooker both say they want to be a part. Superior going help when it come to that. She had Laurraine's nephew Roger Winters figuring the best way the Foundation could be in, so the government don't get her crying the blues after holding out 58 years. She wasn't worried about the records selling; she'd prayed on it and she knew her old sound—the good old sound that was the depth and breadth of the meaning—was going to reach into young *and* old like an instrument from Jesus. And not just her to be singing. Plenty good voices; she'd groom them how to take hold. Lord, You better help Halie with this thing—You got her wading in the waters.

She didn't know what she was wading in when she got started on this thing Celeste got her up to, magnifying about her snaggled teeth 'til Halie's getting planted and that's just what the dentist call it—planting. But she was fixing Miss Celeste good; make her wag Halie back and forth and see this thing through. But Lord, did Celeste back up when Halie passed clean out on the dentist. "Stop! Oh, don't go on!" When did she know Halie to call quits halfway? She ought to call Celie right now, tell her wait 'til she see her teeth: even as a picket fence. Johnny Cash could just pay her a compliment when she got herself to Nashville day after tomor—

She broke off her meditation. She sat awhile, then she telephoned. Maybe she was off. Maybe— Not Little *Alice!* But she wasn't hardly sick! Halie *told* Little Alice go to the doctor any time, she knew Halie would give her anything she needed. Lord a'mercy, keep us; it was like losing her own. Poor Aunt Bessie, all that's wrong with her, she never dreamed her own daughter would go first. . . .

Mahalia sang *Amazing Grace* on the Johnny Cash show, the old long-meter never so drawn to the outmost stretch of bearable endurance of emotion. When she finished, the audience gave her a standing ovation. Then she and Gwen left for Little Alice's funeral.

Before they went, Halie called J. Robert Bradley at 3 a.m. and told him she was thinking about that pot roast Gwen come raving about (Halie too much in a heap to move) and bring her some. Bradley dressed and got the pot hot and explained to the guard at the Ramada Inn he was "just taking Mahalia Jackson some meat, mister!" which he didn't think the policeman believed but he got past and up; and Mahalia took one little piece—one little piece!—and said she believed that was all she could eat.

"MAHALIA, I just don't have one." Polly had come down to Little Alice's funeral, and Mahalia told her to call Ida Beal, say she needed a white hat for the service. "The only white hat I have isn't finished," Ida said, explaining she was about to go to the wake. "I don't care if it's not finished, I want it; bring it with you," said Halie. "A lining's the least of my worries."

What those were, she didn't tell in the next two days visiting with the family. George's wife sent some food down by Carol Ann, grown already from the time Halie tried to get her in black and white so they couldn't change and George's wife wouldn't. When she was ready to leave, she said to Zenobia Lockett, "You don't know what it means, to go out and work, come home and put your key in the door and find an empty house, nobody to greet you."

AT 6:01 A.M. Feb. 10, 1971, a powerful earthquake wrenched the northern end of the San Fernando Valley, the Associated Press reported: 64 dead. Over 2,400 injured. Some 850 homes and 640 buildings severely damaged. Another 4,800 homes, 265 apartments, and 1,125 commercial buildings had appreciable—

Halie was profoundly rocked. Her own building had been damaged but it could be fixed; that was not it. "God just picked us up and *shook* us. He is reminding man of his might," she told Laurraine, a fearsome awe still upon her a week later. She was just stretched with her Bible when the yelling came through. People calling her name. She opened her front door and found a strange man lying there half-naked, and half-dead from his look. She called the rescue squad, told them to put him in the hospital, she'd pay. Why had he come the long walk and made the steps? This place getting bad as Chicago for upset. Now she's up, she better phone Laurraine, tell her she's going get a call from St. Paul and please give that child Sue some help. She could do it on the phone. To think of Sue—a beauty queen, from a well-off, educated family—leaving all that to work with Rev. Gleason in Chicago and go pick greens, work in the fields, with white and Negro, all those children, on that farm they got now. "That's Sue's hometown. I'm going there and give that boy a benefit. I told Sue go to Humphrey, tell him Mahalia said get that auditorium free—much as I worked for him. Yeah, baby, I *am* trying do my utmost for humanity. 'Course I got to make something to keep all this going. What Roger say about the record people? And are you getting any sense, Laurraines, and resting? I'm praying for you. Tell Ida I say get somebody to fix you some ham hocks; you got to get the suption, get all the noxion out. You get yourself well enough, I'll take you to Japan with me. Then we *really* get chance to talk."

"I'm well enough," Laurraine said instantly. "I'll go see Dr. Robinson tomorrow."

"Tell him the itinerary's spaced out; we get plenty rest time." Now *Halie* better get her rest.

"BURIED ON HIS 75th birthday, Celeste; the Lord's giving Dr. Haynes his biggest celebration." Mahalia, Gwen, Celeste, Rev. Strawther, and J. Robert Bradley made a group up front, with Dr. Hayakawa. The big church was overflowing. Licensed to preach at 17, Dr. F. D. Haynes had been president of the California Baptist Convention for 52 years, up to 1968—a top minister of the National Convention and ran its oratorical contest to the day he died. The biggest Baptist funeral since Dr. Jemison. It had to be Mahalia to sing; she just thanked God she wasn't already off in Japan. Bradley, "Mr. Baptist," would come first. He told her what he'd sing and she said, "No; *Amazing Grace*." Bradley shook his head. Mahalia didn't argue. But when he was all set to begin, Mahalia told the boy at the organ "*Amazing Grace*" and that's what Bradley sang. Then it was she who sang an old friend to his glory. Outside, a dense crowd was gathered, waiting to see Mahalia. She turned and made for a back door, but the crowd had guessed, shifted, and there was no option. Jodie Strawther took one elbow, Dr. Hayakawa the other—and as he did, a murmur rose: some in that crowd didn't want him near her. The air was tense. Mahalia looked about and said quietly, in a voice that carried, "This is my friend." The crowd fell back. "The fire," says Rev. Strawther, "hadn't quite gone out from his campus."

"THEY SURE?" Turn your head on the demons, and they'll leap in your pocket. Here she is making ready for a strange land, trying to prepare her heart and her mind, looking to another region of God's creation—and her organist can't go. The worst of it, Joyce had leukemia. In the hospital. Halie prayed for God's healing hands to touch her. But meanwhile she's already past her time to get back to Chicago—trying to make sure fixing the outside the building was anyway started right—and the Lord hands her this problem. Now what is this, Lord?

Gwen said Clency. "I'm glad to be peacemaker, Sister, and I do believe Charles would love to go." And he would. He would. His passport was still good from last time. No, he laughed, nothing wrong with *him*. He'd have to join them late, but—oh, yes, by the first concert.

Mar. 24, in his Los Angeles office, Dr. Peck gave her some gamma globulin to prevent infectious hepatitis and a new prescription for her diabetic control.

Mar. 29, at Billings in Chicago, Dr. Siegler gave her a new 5 mg. prednisone prescription and an extra supply.

That same day, Drs. Vondrasek and Rosi kept their habitual late hours, and Dr. Rosi saw her. She had some epigastric distress—gas pains—which apparently had developed in the morning. He gave her something to relieve the condition. She was somewhat apprehensive, anxious about this forthcoming trip.

USUALLY, WHEN look like Mahalia was in a deep, deep study, Aunt Bessie wouldn't want to burden her with her thoughts. Especially when Halie hadn't hardly got back to Chicago when she's doing business—got Judge Hooks there—and now she's wore out by the time they left. Bessie had just been waiting in another room, come over from Alice's; Bessie was visiting between her "Gold Dust Twin" and Hannah since Little Alice's death. But here, now! Bessie offers to cook her food and she say she done let that biggity woman up here and *ate* the food she had brought her. "I wouldn't eat *nothing* from her!" rumbled Aunt Bessie, the soft, deep voice wrathful; "I wouldn't even accept a *bouquet* from her! I would never have let that food down *my* stomach! If she was up here *hounding* me, I wouldn't eat what she brought me. I'd have told her, 'Put it back on the stove.' 'Cause way I figure—a person that did me dirt give me something, I'll put it in the garbage can! Yes, I will! Oh, yes!" Bessie was outdone. Mahalia was in a dream. She'd overdo: she just had that kind of *heart* in her body; she didn't believe nobody would do her harm.

FRIDAY, Apr. 2, Mahalia was back in Dr. Vondrasek's office. He prescribed an antibiotic as a general travel precaution. Saturday, in Los Angeles, Mahalia took a call from Laurraine. They'd been supposed to fly today, but it got set back to Tuesday. Good thing: Laurraine's ticket wasn't there and no more mail delivery until Monday, when she was due in L.A. from New Orleans. The airlines people, the girl in George Wein's office in New York, none of them had it traced. "Don't worry, baby," Halie said calmly, "I'll call, and call you back."

Tuesday, 6:30 a.m., after a frantic marathon to materialize her ticket and getting it Monday through the grace of Pan American (which they weren't flying), Laurraine fastened her seat belt for Los Angeles. At least the fuss and fury was over. Everything was programed now.

WHERE *was* Mahalia? Delta's VIP agent kept lookout with Laurraine as long as he could, then positioned her at the one strategic two-way spot to see both routes to the Japan Air Lines take-off area, so swarmed it might be possible to miss even Mahalia. It was past time to enter the restricted area for outbound passengers. . . .

"She'll get killed," gasped Celeste, but she couldn't help laughing at the picture of Mahalia standing *in* Century Boulevard, all those lanes of traffic whizzing by, shouting, "I'm Mahalia Jackson! Take me to the airport!"—waving at taxis, cars, anything moving but it all kept moving, and the minutes went by. She'd *been* to the airport; got there early and thought to check for her shot record and it wasn't there. Nobody had it—not Gwen, not Celeste—and there wasn't time to go all the way back to So. Norton, miles and *miles,* to get it, so nothing but to rush in a taxi with Celeste to the closest doctor and get the shots over again. Now she had the shots, she had the record, but she did not have a way back. "Come on off there," gasped Celeste, wiping her eyes; "these people don't know about you, baby; come over here and wait for the cab I called."

They were holding the plane door open, the stewardess beckoning,

Gwen and Laurraine waiting to get on board, when Mahalia churned in sight, pulled up panting, and walked aboard under escort, dignity intact.

"It's a long way without that Honolulu layover they cut," sighed Mahalia. "This sure is one beautiful plane, though," she brightened; "look like they feed you every 20 minutes, and that—what they call that? suki-dashi?—it's *good.* And the stewardesses—they're like little porcelain dolls." Silence. "I'm not singing *I've Got to Walk—Lord, Hold My Hand* yet, Laurraines; they might steal it—I'm not singing anything I haven't recorded yet until I get it on my own label." Silence. Both almost asleep—so Laurraine thought. "You know what?" said Mahalia. "It struck me just before I left, reading my Bible, and I had never noticed it before. Solomon was black! The wisest man! And *he* didn't go to a university!" Laurraine grinned at the dear, almond eyes gleaming wide. "I've been trying to tell you, honey," she said gently; "none of the wise philosophers in ancient times learned in a schoolroom—they *thought* and listened; just as you think and listen."

"I do like to be around people who know more than I do; that way you learn something."

"You won't listen to *me*—I keep telling you: you've educated yourself. It's harder that way, but you're *self*-educated. You're a wise woman." Halie nodded, but—all right for Laurraine to talk. Still—look at Solomon! That gave her the confidence for the Buddhists. She stayed cheerful through the hour's halt in Honolulu, when they tramped the airport to get rid of cramps and a reporter dashed out to interview her. But when she climbed aboard again, she asked for some brandy and a teaspoon. She didn't explain even to Gwen, who had swapped places with Laurraine now to keep Mahalia company awhile up in first class.

Thank you Jesus; You got us here. At least there's no people around. Just get Halie to a *bed!* Customs. "Ah *yes!* Miss Jackson." Mahalia through; Gwen through; Laurraine—stopped. Her name wasn't on the big semi-circular JAL manifest of flip cards. Everything else was in order, but did she arrive correctly? Dekko Teruya of International Artists Booking (the Japanese sponsor) suggested Miss Jackson come along; Miss Goreau could follow. "I'm not going anywhere without Laurraines," Mahalia said and sank onto a bench.

Over an hour later, near midnight Wednesday, the weary party straggled into the night—and a welcome burst upon Mahalia like "bombs bursting in air": a happy mass of cheering fans, flowers, flashing lights, reporters, with a giant welcome banner hoisted high. Yoshiki Inomata of NHK, the government television system, waded through to inform Mahalia she was a "national honor guest"; would she accept formal greetings and introduction to the nation tomorrow morning? She would be called for at 7 a.m., he added hesitantly. Mahalia accepted instantly; fatigue gone, she laughed with pleasure as Taisuke Ohnishi, CBS/Sony Records promotion director in Japan, escorted her to a waiting limousine. And she thought Japan didn't know her!

Next morning at the Imperial Hotel, Laurraine was grateful Mahalia had ordered her to stay in bed and rest while Halie went to the studio. She checked the desk—no mail, no message for Mahalia. Too bad. Well, Gary warned there might not be enough time.

Exactly three weeks ago, Mar. 17, out of all context of conscious thought, she'd been prompted to call the Public Library and ask when Emperor Hirohito's birthday was. Just days from the period they'd be there! and a significant one, his 70th. U.S.-Japan relations were scratchy just now; a drawn-out squabble over textile regulations. Wouldn't it be nice if Mahalia offered to give the Emperor a birthday gift from America: a gospel concert? She called Mahalia. "Yeah, honey, that be nice," Halie agreed mildly, "if it's for America." She called Washington to Hale Boggs, Majority Leader of Congress and an old friend, a New Orleanian. Hale wasn't in, but Gary Hymel, his administrative aide (a former New Orleans *States-Item* reporter) was eager about the idea: "I'll call State right now, since there isn't much time, but get a letter off to Hale right away with all that about Mahalia, so he can send it over. I know he'll go for it." He had. But diplomacy wasn't a daily newspaper; it had its ritual dance. At least the move had evidently alerted State Dept. Office of Cultural Presentations Director Mark Lewis to hook on a piggyback tour by Mahalia as *envoi extraordinaire*—to India! The last-minute arrangements had killed their Honolulu stop. They didn't even have an India itinerary yet. But India! Too bad about the Emperor's concert, though. And the Japanese envoy she'd known was in another area of government now, no help to add a new honor for Halie's collection.

"WHAT! REALLY!" They were in Mahalia's room having brunch when the call came. For Laurraine, by name: startling in itself. But this— "Yes, I'll caution her. Please do!" Halie was standing impassive, ready for what might come. "Honey, that was the American Embassy. The Emperor may invite you to the Palace!" Betsy Fitzgerald, young U.S. Third Secretary, had warned it was still uncertain. "Dealing with the Imperial Palace is a most delicate business," she explained. "You don't make a direct overture of any kind. It's done *sub rosa*. We have one contact to the Palace, a Mrs. Matsudara. She will propose everything quietly. Then, if it is approved, we back up and proceed openly; then you'll get an invitation from the Empress. It won't mention the concert, but that's what it will be about. But for heaven's sake, don't say *anything* about it to anyone; that would end it. The ambassador, the minister, everybody over here is all excited about it," she added in a burst of enthusiasm. "If the invitation comes through, Miss Jackson will be the first Western entertainer ever to be invited to the Imperial Palace."

"Honey," said Laurraine, telling it, Halie and Gwen drinking it in, "I didn't even know what I was asking."

"We don't have it yet," said Halie, stretching out, wig off, settling down with the Buddhist Bible she'd been telling them about that she found in the night table. A knock. Reporter and interpreter. Just a few words for radio? Yes, they knew the press conference was on Saturday, this was a rest day—but just a few words. . . . "Tell 'em come on in," said Mahalia, clamping her wig on, slightly askew, "but I'm not moving from this bed."

Dekko ("Cuckoo" to Mahalia "because she's like a little bird") returned. The bright young secretary was Mahalia's liaison with Katsuhiro Ataka, the tour sponsor, who spoke no English and was rarely in evidence. Dekko was excited with her news. Princess Takako Shimazu—Princess Suga, to the people, the youngest daughter of the Emperor—would be present at the first concert Sunday. (As it developed, her son had an accident, but she sent flowers and a greeting.) Tai Ohnishi was in to say 20 million viewers had seen Mahalia welcomed as a national honor guest. A smiling magazine editor and his photographer appeared and trooped out with Miss Jackson to see the cherry blossoms. At one shrine whose double blossoms were breathtaking, Mahalia turned away from the cherry trees to try and try—words, gestures—to communicate with the tender at the shrine entrance . . . with the vendors at its trinkets stall. Nobody understood that this tall brown woman wanted to talk with their priest.

At the New Otani—shifted there as soon as accommodations were ready—Sister was oppressed. Really bothered, Gwen could see, in a way that made Gwen tense. "Aunt Hannah is sick, Gwen," she said at last. "But it's more than that. Call home." From Chicago, Allen said Uncle Porter in Cincinnati had had a stroke. No, no need to come home; do what she got to do there.

It was a busy rest. At least they'd have a nice breakfast in the room, and— Phone already. "Laurraines, get it, baby." Laurraine didn't know if her feet touched the floor or not as she whirled to Mahalia. "It's yes! You're invited! You're going to the Palace!" Mahalia's flash of smile was the brightest light she'd ever seen on a human face, and the quick hug was all the answer needed. "Miss Fitzgerald says she'll be in touch." She was, within hours—and would be, almost daily. There was protocol and proscription: "Don't wear white; that's the color of mourning. Don't wear yellow; that's the Imperial color. Her Majesty the Empress will wear a short silk suit. Let me know what Miss Jackson is wearing, so that I can be sure it's approved. Give us a list of 15 songs Miss Jackson is willing to sing so the Imperial Household may request eight. There will be no encores. NOTHING is unscheduled. And Miss Goreau—"

"What's the matter?" Mahalia broke in sharply. Laurraine asked Betsy Fitzgerald to hold on a moment and told Mahalia, "She says I can't go; only those directly in the performance may enter." Mahalia didn't even blink.

"Well," she said, voice distinct, formal, "it seems to me you'll just have to be there, because you are my stage producer."

Yes. But that was far ahead—Apr. 23. First came the business of the tour. The second rest day, Halie crossed the vast city to the CBS/Sony Building and rehearsed. photographers snapping. There were people to meet. Arrangements with Dekko. Father Joseph Love came by—he would interpret her songs Sunday. Japanese Baptists called. She began to have hand cramps; her legs too. And yet she had not a sick feeling. Thank You Jesus.

Saturday she walked into the New Otani ballroom for her programed press conference—and confronted some 200 writers and cameramen from all media at the ready; seated, standing, crouching. Facing them, microphones set, a banquet-length table was neatly covered with cloth, chairs there for interpreters, sponsor's representatives, Tai Ohnishi (directing publicity) and—"Come on, baby, sit by me," Halie told Laurraine, who looked over the mass and thought there were more here than for any Presidential press conference. At 1 p.m. on a Saturday. If they only knew the *big* news! But the Embassy had warned it was absolutely private; no word to be said.

Commonplaces about travel and Japan were barely over when a voice called from the rear, "Miss Jackson, do you have any plans to sing before the Emperor?" So the Imperial pipeline had a leak. Mahalia looked at Laurraine, who gulped. This accounted for that electricity in the room. The Emperor might be officially demoted to "hereditary symbol of the nation," but you don't legislate away divinity entrenched for centuries; Hirohito was the 124th in his line, and to gain the Presence must be—"May I answer that for Miss Jackson?" Laurraine said quickly; then, groping—"There was only some . . . discussion; this is not—anything to be discussed because there is nothing to be discussed. But if something of this comes to be, Miss Jackson will be very happy to let it be known." Whew. Now it was all Mahalia's. And *listen* to her. . . .

The question was about her first concert being on Easter. Mahalia had been struck by this herself. It wasn't on purpose, not for commercial purpose, she knew: there wasn't one percent Christians in the whole country. That's nothing but God's work. "I hope I can share this glorious feeling that I feel about Easter with Japan," she said, hands reaching to cup it. "We can share each other's love, you know, and I believe that this is one of the greatest ways to share our *appreciation* of love—not only Easter Sunday but every day for what Easter stands for . . . love of your fellow man . . . love for the world. Easter is the *redemption*—redeem man back to his rightful place, and that place is to be happy between himself and his creator. That's why we make a big ceremony and a very sacred ceremony. It is a prop to so many millions of people's lives."

Translation, Mahalia sipping water. Now where did I get those words? I had not these thoughts. Her voice resumed its steady course. No fumbling, no groping for a phrase, vocabulary ready. Extraordinary! thought Laurraine.

Questions tumbled together, but "What is gospel?" topped the clamor now. "Frankly," chided Mahalia (Halie for the moment) "you should know more about gospel than I do because you're older than America and it was created in the old countries—" Pause for translation. A puzzled silence. "That's the foundation," Mahalia explained—since they didn't know. "It goes back from alpha and omega. The word *gospel* means 'good news and glad tidings,' and 'Well,' you say, 'what's going to make us glad?' Since the fall of man, the gospel came to redeem man and lift him up and bring him back to his paradise. Now, God being our creator, we don't know how many forerunners He sent before Jesus came. You got yours, and other nations got theirs, and I think that it's left up to the Almighty to be the one to make the decision with you and with me and our personal beliefs about one God. We *sing* the gospel, which is songs of savior. We *teach* the gospel. Then there is a *gift* of the gospel which comes under—as Paul says—under salvation. So we settle it all up, it's a very wonderful group, to sing of love that God—whatever name you call your God, whatever name I call my God—that one God so loved us, you and me, that He sent His son to bring us back to be united in love and peace. . . ."

"My God, she's real," breathed the blonde American listening intently. UPI bureau chief Albert Kaff had sent his wife; she was a singer, she'd know what Mahalia Jackson was all about.

"Oh," said Mahalia, living it, "sometimes we get happy, we get a joyful feeling and we sing and we sing, and we have a great imagination and a great belief about the beyond, tomorrow. Some people call it reincarnation. I can't go that beat. It's not here. But we believe in living after death because we are taught that in death we live eternally. So we have no fear of having trouble," she smiled, quietly triumphant. "This goes back to the promise of the spirit which God giveth His own forever. So we make a joyful noise sometimes when we feel that we are oppressed. We say, 'It's not going to be like this always. There's a brighter day ahead if I can just hold on; there's a brighter day ahead, not only in death but here where we live.' We keep this hope and build upon that, that life can be beautiful through all obstacles. The most beautiful flower in the world is the rose and it's full of thorns. So sometimes oppression makes us beautiful . . . because there's something that's bigger than you are. It's a *force,* it's an inner power that you've just—just got to go on and feel like you can make it. And that goes for you, whatever you call it—Buddha or Allah or Guru, I don't know—whatever—that same one man does all that for you and for me."

She sat back; but there was no stopping. They got her to the blues, and she patiently explained its birth with "the man who did not have faith and hope in God" . . . onto early spirituals "born out of oppression

—divine songs of inspiration, such as *I'm Gonna Walk the Street of Glory,* and *A-Low Down Chariot and Let Me Ride"* . . . into jazz "born out of spirituals, down in New Orleans where some were very poor and yet they were happy, happy with feeling" . . . to rock 'n' roll: "every generation has its interpretation of expressing itself; the young people are doing their thing, as they call it, the best they know how, and I think the young people are doing a fine job. . . . It's something that's locked in them and they're letting come out, and they're not ashamed. People want to be themselves. Now, because I don't have a soft, sweet voice like yours, do I have to try to speak like you? Let me speak like *me*—and that's what the young people are doing." She said firmly that Bessie Smith did *not* influence her, she was a product of the church . . . that she didn't choose a program in advance because that was stagnant . . . that— Pop gospel? For the first time, Halie's eyes snapped. "There's no such thing as 'pop gospel'! Men and women have given their lives—you don't want people to blaspheme."

She embraced them again, and the room relaxed—chastised. "Gospel is the salvation. You can sing it, you can teach it, you can preach it, and you can live it. If the gospel applied, there would be more love, with your brother, your fellow man. But because we have not this real love, we have fallen away from what we really are. We are in the image and the likeness. I was reading in one of your books, from your Bible, the Buddha, that explains the same thing. Love you each other—and when you have this love, it brings this truth, that nothing else in life can do. It brings this joy. And it gives the satisfaction that is in here," she said, long fingers pressing her heart; "not the lust of the flesh, but in *here.*" The room was hushed. "Without love there will always be wars and confusion. Without love, there will always be discrimination. One nation against another. And who knows how many years, millions of years, we have been having these signals to love even one another? Until we do this, we are going to destroy ourselves."

On, on the questions went, insatiably, Mahalia never faltering, sipping water in the gaps while the translator caught up, until finally . . . her happiest moment? "Oh, there've been so many, I—" She stopped and seemed to be sifting her crowded life. Then she answered slowly, surely, "The only thing I could say, to me, is when I found favor in the sight of the Lord. Then I felt happy. And this was not any big ovation, nor nothing; it was a quiet moment; and to me, in the solitude, by myself, being accepted as a Christian—I consider that the most happy moment in my life."

LAURRAINE HAD been called away and returned, and now in the break for translation, she whispered to Mahalia, who nodded. "You tell 'em, I'm talked out." The word brought pandemonium—confirmation of the Emperor's birthday concert. Somehow, somewhere, the decision had been made: it was to be announced. "No, no, no!" said Mahalia's impromptu spokesman; "it will be completely private. It is a completely private birthday greeting from America."

Two hours, and they were reluctant to let her go. "Can you give us a short personal message for Easter Sunday?" asked UPI's Mrs. Kapp. Mahalia straightened, eyes glistening. "Ohhhhh yeeeeees! There's no way for me to have words to *express* to you what Easter Sunday means personally to me, and to all Christians all over the world, because—we believe that Christ died because he loves us, Christ gave his life that we might have life a*bun*dantly, while we live, and *after death* we shall live on," she said earnestly, searching for their understanding. "The world is very small today. Everywhere I go, man wants to be free; he wants to be free. And he has found out that material things does not give you this freedom—you already have it within; but you must pull up on this inner power that your creator gave you and you *shall* be free. Please believe me. And so Easter—we fast for forty days, to resurrect our sinful bodies—get the spirit of God—through the spirit of Buddha, the great prophet before Christ came on the scene . . . this is what I think. Some of you people that have been to school and have studied somebody else's thought—God gave you a brain and a mind—think for yourself, and *see if you can outthink God.*

"There have been some very, very intellectual people that have gone around saying 'God is dead.' Well, He's not dead," said Mahalia, voice intimate as if they were sharing a cup of tea, "because I talked to Him this morning. And He tells me He loves me, and He calls me His own and we rejoice because man has a chance to be back in his rightful place—in paradise. Love the Lord with all your heart, with all your mind, all your soul. . . . *God* is *soooo* big. You that don't know me, don't form your opinion about me, 'cause I'm weak like you . . . I need your help, and you need mine, because we all one." A Japanese writer rose to thank Mahalia in lilting English. Then Mahalia smiled—tender as a mother with a newborn babe—stretched her arms wide and upward, said softly, "Let's have the blessing," and in utter stillness from the crowded room sang four lines of *His Eye Is on the Sparrow.*

There was little left of her for the conference into which she must walk immediately with the director of a Japanese Christian children's choir who would precede her Sunday. He wanted to check his repertoire. "Oh, no . . . oh, no . . . oh, *no*," she said. He had *her* songs down there. When he left, the director's list was reduced to Gregorian chants.

"GWEN, SEE if Charles in yet, and check *his*." Mahalia had been resting after the conference, but now she and Gwen were staring at their passports at Laurraine's insistence: ah-hah! none of them had a visa for India. Charles was in but he didn't have an Indian visa either. Well, somebody was fixing it, probably.

BETSY FITZGERALD conveyed as tactfully as she could that Miss Jackson's list was needed; and now there was a request from the Palace for a thumbnail gist of the meaning of each song. Laurraine would try. "By the way," she said, "I just noticed that none of us has a visa for India. Of course, we still have two weeks."

"My God!" gasped Betsy Fitzgerald. "Get over here *first* thing Monday and I'll ask the consul to see what she can do. India takes a minimum of four weeks and usually six!"

HALIE WAKED almost sick unto death. "Lord," she said, "touch me and heal me; since I'm off on this trip, touch me and *heal* me. I can't find—" She broke off; get up and look for your medicine, Halie. She searched, searched everywhere, could not find it. "Lord," she said, in tears now, "Lord, I can't *find* this medicine. Lord! You told me You were here. Lord? Lord?" The Voice spoke. "I'm here." She searched again and found her remedy and knew what she must do. "And finally the Lord touched me," she said, telling it, "and I fell asleep."

She woke well—but her voice was hoarse. And by the time she was backstage at Bunkyo Kokaido, her hands were painful with cramps. She stuffed splayed feet into the needle points of her stage shoes—Jeeesus! save me; her corns hurt; then she stared into the mirror—not into it, through it—praying, fingers touching her wig here and there. She flexed her fingers. Husked her voice. That hoarseness. All this way. With all those people.

Time. She nodded to Gwen and Charles, charged Laurraine with her huge purse, and walked onstage to one of the major triumphs of her life. "Wonderful . . . fantastic . . . speaks to the spirit . . ." said the reviews. "Her first concert gave me so deep impression as I have never felt at any concert of classic, popular and jazz singers," wrote the dean of Japan's music critics, Hisamitsu Noguchi. "Her gospel songs have not only the perfect musical beauty but also the very persuasive power by her belief. . . . Though I am not a Christian, I could not stop running tears; tears of joy." So entranced was the critic, he returned to the night performance at Koseinenkin Hall.

Backstage, greeted by her elated troupe, Mahalia shook her head. "That's God. He gives it to me or He don't. Sometimes I'm good, sometimes I'm bad."

THE BAD was back at the Otani. "Don't hand me that stuff," grated Mahalia, flinging back a bundle of yen and returning to paring her corns. "I want my *money*. I *told* you, and I *trusted* you, and I *sang*—AND I DON'T HAVE MY MONEY!" Wire-thin Marie St. Louis had arrived to represent Mahalia in fulfillment of the contract terms—which said American dollars. "Mahalia," said Marie, "you don't need ten thousand American dollars over here. Dekko says Mr. Ataka says he can't get all the dollars yet—they're scarce here. You can change the yen easily at home. Why don't you—" Mahalia leaped from the bed. *"You get my money!"* she roared, brandishing her penknife, Marie St. Louis's tawny skin blanched and she fled down the hall. "You get my money, or I'll make Hell a present of you in a basket!" Mahalia flung at the disappearing figure. Then she rapped on Laurraine's door, doubling with laughter. "You ought to see me scare Marie St. Louis! Child, I waved my corn-knife at her. 'Course, I wouldn't use it but she don't know that. Ohhhh, baby, I was evil."

Back in her room, Halie grew quiet. Then abruptly she rose, stood ramrod-straight, eyes flashing, and in a voice like a clap of thunder cried, "Satan, I *rebuke* you! In the name of Jesus—in the *blood* of Jesus!" She stood breathing heavily, then subsided onto her bed. He'll catch you out when you weak. But he can't stand against the blood of Jesus.

Monday, 11 a.m. The train for Nagoya left at noon. "They're looking for dollars," Marie said quietly. "I'm going home," said Mahalia even more quietly; "Gwen, find out when's the next plane for L.A." Marie pleaded for time, vanished, returned, and a temporary cease-fire was arranged. "Until 6 p.m.," said Mahalia matter-of-factly. Laurraine brought word that Consul Florence Adamson would personally convoy their passports in time for the India visas—if they were going to India. Gwen debated whether to telex her husband to meet her at the airport. Mahalia read her Bible. In the afternoon Tai Ohnishi spirited the whole group off to see the Meiji Shrine and Gardens, Mahalia in high spirits at their beauty.

She clapped her hands at the beauty of water, fish, flowers, trees. She broke into song after she drank from the dipper at the sacred Shinto spring said to have magical powers of health . . . *"Drink from the fountain of life*—ho-ho!—*Drink of the living water,"* she caroled. "You need a whole bucketful," she teased Laurraine. "And I should put some on my head." (To make her hair grow back.) But—"What time is it? Take us home," said Mahalia. "I don't want no disappointment." On the long ride back, she alternated between singing *Who Made the Great Plan* ("You know, it come to me, God *is* science") and discussing everything from the price of a full "sound-studio setup" with Tai ("Could you handle my records?") . . . to having a kimono and obi made for Carnegie Hall ("I want to look just like a black Japanese") . . . to the virtues of Leonard Bernstein and Laurence Olivier . . . and as the car turned onto the Ginza, inquiring where the Oscar Peterson Trio was playing ("That be a lovely place for you and Gwen to go").

At 8 p.m. the night train for Nagoya pulled out. At that moment Laurraine, summoned to witness, was confronted by Mahalia at one end of the bed, Marie St. Louis at the other, and between them stacks and stacks of dollars. "Count 'em," said Mahalia. "Don't you trust me?" said Marie St. Louis. "This is business. I counted, you counted, now Laurraines, you count."

Counted. Tallied. Proved. $10,000. Marie went to recover. Laurraine went to bed. Mahalia went to Gwen. The cash went into Gwen's purse (a fact known only to those two; at each concert Laurraine would carefully guard Mahalia's vast purse—kept incredibly jumbled, she thought, until Halie explained it was harder to steal from that way). It was not until shortly before they left that Laurraine chanced upon the regulation that Japan forbid more than $200 in yen to be taken out of the country.

A WAVE of adulation swept the country. Nagoya's Prefectural Hall was surrounded with a dense crowd an hour before the doors opened. In Osaka's Sankei Hall, they shouted their own Japanese phrases for the amens and hallelujahs, and rang the hall with the right off-beat. At an NHK-TV special, a weathered Japanese grip in faded black cotton squatted on a stool with tears streaming as his eyes clung to Mahalia's face. Photographers flickered like fireflies, almost unseen by day and barely at night but there, as a stream of photostories evidenced. Interviewers whispered respectfully in and out. Mahalia was stimulated, chatty, mind ranging wide. She was entranced with the cleanliness of Japan's streets and ready to start a campaign for Chicago when she got back . . . tramped through ancient palaces, gardens, Buddhist temples—absorbing . . . spent endless energy searching out a natural-hair wig styled "no, not that way" (rejecting the modern guise offered by mystified clerks), "I mean the real *Japanese* way!" Getting film for her 8-mm movie camera became a quest, renewed at every stop. She pored over tea sets for all her aunts and succumbed to pearls for herself (although her standing joke was that the huge, faceted ring she wore—the object of lavish compliments—cost $1: "you don't think I'd wear something like this if it was real—I'd be scared to death it be stolen") . . . lingered after dinner with Father Love (*ex*-interpreter: none needed, it was evident) and some 60 of his fellow Jesuits at Sophia University, where one priest cheerfully hand-pumped an ancient organ so Clency could play for them all to sing, and Gwen's recipe for "destroyers" had the Jesuits reeling. She kept Gwen busy with a stream of letters back to the States about the tour and possible TV shows she'd like to do—starting with Pearl Bailey, most of all, and Flip Wilson. But one thing Laurraine could not get her to do was sit down and name 15 titles for the Emperor's concert.

"Honey, there's no choice. We have to do it. Now." Laurraine sat balancing a wad of hotel stationery and looking determined. Calls from the Embassy in Tokyo had reached out like ribbons—details must be precisely worked for the historic performance. The ambassador was drawn in—he and his wife would be the only guests outside the royal circle. One call was a correction. "It's not the *first* Western performance ever; we understand a European harpist performed shortly after World War II." Mahalia pushed up her lip. "That's all right," she brightened; "I'm the first singer." But no titles—no concert. With Gwen's help, Mahalia roving the room, for the first time in her life she was pinning down her psyche. They had 14 and were pressing her for the last. "Deep River," said Mahalia finally. "I haven't sung that since Kennedy died." All right. "Now give me one sentence," said Laurraine, "that tells what each song means." Mahalia's look was a sufferance.

"DID YOU GET it?" Mahalia asked eagerly. She wanted the Emperor to have some actual memento and the Embassy had arranged to have a scroll made of the words of *Who Made the Great Plan*: the Emperor was a scientific man, and this song was about science and religion, one of the eight the Palace had selected. Mahalia planned to hand the scroll to His Imperial Highness in lieu of an encore. But, "you don't hand the Emperor gifts," Laurraine reported with a sigh. "They're sent in advance, and screened for suitability. So I couldn't bring it—an Imperial messenger took it from the Embassy—but they say it was beautiful."

What Laurraine *had* come back with, Halie and Gwen bent over: an address in English and Japanese and an envelope with a slip clipped to it bearing two final, green-inked injunctions: "Give to Abe-san. Don't mention the Emperor." Mahalia patted Laurraine's arm. "You'll do all right," she said.

NEVER BEFORE, thought Laurraine, has an Imperial Palace guest arrived *this* way. The taxi driver she hailed in front of the New Otani was so flustered by the address she showed him—Kunaicho, East Gate—that he wouldn't go up the long approach to the stern iron-studded gate where soldiers guarded the high forbidding stone walls beyond the moat . . . so flustered that he landed her beyond the *wrong* gate and she must tiptoe over millions of small black stones to the East Gate—about a football field away. She longed to mop her forehead. Instead, waiting, she smoothed her kid gloves and studied the stone wall as if it held some mystic message until, several people later, a gleaming black limousine crossed the moat bridge and impeccable Daisuke Honda of the Imperial Household Protocol Section—secretary to the Hon. Shigenobu Shima, Grand Master of the Ceremonies—escorted her within. The official envoy of Miss Mahalia Jackson. They drove decorously past various of the buildings which jointly were "the Palace," Honda-san explained—all tucked discreetly among serene grounds and gardens . . . entered a modern façade . . . walked past an area of ancient elegance whose small, low, square stage was roped in crimson and gold, ringed about by floor cushions—court dances were performed here, Honda-san explained, the dances unchanged for centuries

. . . down corridors with exquisite single art objects suitably spaced . . . into a small utility room, to confer.

Master of Music Abe had joined them: a lean elder with wise eyes peering from a face out of an ancient print. He spoke no English. But through Honda-san, Laurraine learned with dawning horror that Mahalia Jackson must not only abide by a set of songs for the first time in her life—she must move minute by set minute. The quiet, gentle voice was stipulating the Empress's schedule as well—the movements alternating, never meeting. "At 2 . . . at 2:05 . . . at 2:18 . . . at 2:25 . . . at 2:27 . . . at 2:29 . . . at 2:30. . . ." He spoke only of Mahalia and the Empress. Laurraine remembered the injunction in green ink; probably to foreign commoners, one didn't speak directly of the Emperor's movements, especially since now they were going through the motions of the schedule's being "approved." When Halie heard!

She listened in utter calm. "You know *I'm* going be on time," she said. And it wasn't Mahalia who breached the schedule.

SHE JUST WISH the Embassy'd had a little American flag she could pin on like she asked—never thought they'd be without. Well, she was carrying Jesus' banner. *Mine eyes have seen the glory of the coming of the Lord*—Ha! Clear as a bell. Thank You Jesus. Knocks, scrapings, murmurs, giggles, laughter as she considered the finishing touches for the pink silk dress-and-jacket outfit she got approved for their Majestyships days ago. They'd said short or long, but this seemed more right, with the Empress in a suit. "What you think? Do I need to curtsey? Just bow? Do I wear the pearls? Or you think it look better without?" She pirouetted. "I pass this way but once. Mrs. Gore, where is the historian?" It was a fine day. Little David, play on your harp. It was right there in his Psalms: *By my God I can leap over a wall* . . . good thing she *didn't* have to jump this one. Mm-mnh! beautiful . . . all this peace . . . and look at this beautiful new building for the music! Their Majesties might be back here behind walls, but they sure kept up. So the acoustics could be *very* good.

Into the "resting room" on the stroke. "Help me out of this jacket, baby, so I don't wrinkle." Touch her hair. Out by the watch for "rehearsal moments" . . . this auditorium like a *jewel*-box! Microphone, piano, organ . . . fine, fine. But what is this? She wasn't surprised to have Cuckoo along as interpreter, but Mr. Ataka? all this crew? Oh. Emperor Hirohito had a business appointment with his Prime Minister—well, business first—so all this was to set up for taping so he could hear the concert after. "Return to resting room"—right by the watch. ("Millions of people will never believe this," Laurraine murmured to a Gwen compressed with excitement.) Exactly at 2:30 p.m., Gwen and Charles in position, the curtain opened to a packed court. Seating, like everything else, had been prescribed—by diagram.

She stood a moment, in natural dignity, letting the music's introduction run on. What's she thinking, Gwen wondered, fingers on their own course. She saw the head bow, the signal, and slowly, softly, Mahalia began to sing *The Lord's Prayer* in a totally hushed house. We'll have to be ready, Gwen reminded herself, in case they don't applaud—it might not be the custom, if the Empress doesn't first, and an Imperial Majesty might not applaud.

Applause firm! felt! Into *To Me, He's So Wonderful*—and isn't it wonderful, Lord, that these people would pick this song? . . . *Abraham, Martin and John . . . Who Made the Great Plan*—Gwen lifting the tempo, Charles's organ like white water rushing, happy, Mahalia exultant in her message. Heads began to nod, feet to tap—the Empress herself was actually smiling, ear to ear! By *Didn't It Rain,* Halie was just short of a holy dance.

Off. Still applauding out there. Thank You Jesus, no encores. She sprawled in the one seat, a straight chair in the crowded little space; got shed of those spike shoes and into slippers—panting, arms and legs flung out 'til she had it in her to walk . . . and a gray little man bent double in his hurry shot through the corridor door. "Her Majesty the Empress wishes to know, will Miss Jackson sing one more song?"

Shortly, Empress Nagako received her in private audience, escorted by her ambassador and his lady. Mahalia tried, but she could never remember what the room looked like, just it was filled with the Empress's family —she just as quiet and simple in her little silk suit, look like the clothes the rich white women used to wear in New Orleans. The Empress smiled warmly. A lovely, quiet voice, too . . . "Miss Jackson, your music was very moving of the spirit. I thank you so much from my heart."

"I thank you *so* much, Your Highness," said Mahalia. "To me, it's a great honor to be singing for Your Majesty and for the Emperor, even if he isn't able to be here, and for such a great and old and spiritually minded country as Japan."

They were being somewhat reserved, Mahalia felt—us older people— but you can't keep the young people down; listen to this! Over and over how much they had loved the American gospel music—Crown Prince Akihito, Crown Princess Michiko, Prince Mikasa, Princess Mikasa, Princess Chichibu . . . the names ran together, and all so enthusiastic they were wearing their mother out, Mahalia could see. The Empress made it clear the audience was ended, and Mahalia went to the resting room holding close a lapis lazuli blue porcelain vase with the Imperial crest and a box of Japanese tea-ceremony candies in a brocaded box.

Fragrant hot tea cooled in fragile Imperial porcelain cups while Mahalia rounded up subjects for her movie camera. It was hard to settle down. A jubilant Ambassador Armin Meyer injected one serious note for himself and his wife Alice: "Really," he said earnestly, "this was a great honor. We've been here two years, and I've never been here before."

"They gave me the honor," said Mahalia, dimpling, "but it's for all."

In the cool depths of the New Otani Arcade, having Kobe steaks, Charles asked, "I was wondering what you were thinking about—*I* could not have stood before the Empress, and sang like I was at Fellowship Church in Chicago!"

"Well—" said Mahalia, "when I walked out, I bowed as usual to my audience, whether they are a large or small one . . . but after I began to sing, I said to myself, 'Lord—Lord, get Your glory,' and then my mind drifted off back down to Loosiana. I forgot the people was there, for a moment, and I saw myself as a child, coming down the tracks with a sack, picking coal, from Greenville up to where I stayed. And I saw myself out on the Mississippi River bringing in wood that was drifting down the stream, putting it on the banks and letting it dry, and then later on, taking my saw or my ax, cutting the wood and bringing it home and putting it in the bin. Then I saw myself taking care of the little sweet babies, the white people's babies, that amazed me. Then I saw myself setting on the levee—Clifford, Stella, Herman, and a big *bunch* of us around the fire . . . look like some was eating sugar cane and some was baking sweet potatoes, and we was singing and the train was passing. Oh, we were having a glorious time. And then I come out of that . . . it dawned on me where I really was, I was in the palace of the king, and emperor, of Japan.

"But it wasn't any happier feeling there," said Mahalia, matter-of-factly, "than it was at the storefronts of State St. where I had sang so often for a nickel and a dime. It wasn't any different, Charles. People may not believe that, but it wasn't any different. I never saw the stiffness of those people" (long hands sketching the court decorum) "because I discovered long ago that the world is seeking something, the same thing I am, and that's peace and contentment and joy. And no matter whether they are millionaires or what, they cannot buy this perfect gift of God, and they have to trod this same road that I do to achieve it.

"Now will you let me eat my steak?" said Halie.

While she was eating it, the wires of AP, UPI, Reuters, the world, were humming. Within hours, Hollywood's Mary Ann Hooper looked at the headlines, listened to the news, and exclaimed to John Meston, "My God! I'm sure most people in show business weren't even aware that she was giving concerts. After this in Japan, they know!"

Surely, nothing could top this?

April 25, the last concert day in Japan, Mahalia came to the Sunday matinee at Shibuya Kokaido tired and hoarse. She came off gasping, wide-eyed with awe. "Did you *hear* them?" She'd started off slow, worried . . . heard her voice suddenly come clear and true . . . and *stronger,* lifting the audience with her. Applause now was heavy, on and on. "Then—I don't know what moved me. I stood there quiet a minute, my head down, and the audience got all still too. Then without even telling Gwen, I started off *a cappella* with a song I hadn't sung in 20 years, *I Woke Up This Morning with My Mind Stayed on Jesus*. Singing so quiet. I knew I was in the spirit, on the Lord's Day. And all of a sudden that audience started talking in *tongues!* Not Japanese—I *been* hearing that—in *tongues!* Look like everybody screaming, praising God . . . just like the Bible say, right there in Acts 2: the uttering of an *inner* divine language, coming on up in unknown tongues. It happened out there tonight! I could hardly believe my ears!"

AT THE AMERICAN Embassy, they could hardly believe their eyes. In the past two weeks, priority cables between Delhi and Tokyo on Mahalia Jackson had taken on aspects of a solar stream. The incredible fact was that Prime Minister Gandhi wanted to attend the concert. Now she wanted to meet with Miss Jackson privately! Veteran Asian/Eastern envoy Armin Meyer and his staff looked at the thickening file through diplomats' eyes: This was the world's most powerful woman, politically—leader of one of every seven people on the face of the earth, of the largest free nation in the world, wooed by both the Soviet and the U.S. and still, she insisted, "unaligned." Serious, complex, tough-minded, her pyramid of crises was teetering dangerously. Millions of East Pakistan civil war refugees were pouring into India's West Bengal State—already about to explode under militant Communist-party goad. She had sent West Pakistan three warnings in one day about armed incursions into India. They could easily stumble into war. Cholera raged. Hunger was rife. Just voted unassailable power for the first time, the pressure wasn't off Indira Gandhi with her voter landslide; it was on. She was known to be working from dawn to midnight. And she wanted to attend Mahalia Jackson's concert. And now—to come backstage at intermission! Was this agreeable with Miss Jackson, the cable asked?

"Tell them that be all right, that's fine," said Mahalia, "and the people's hospitality—that's fine too." Just Lord, let me last. Oooh, these cramps. And give me breath. Be no leaving tomorrow, make it the next. "Gwen, get you some paper, girl. I'm writing Daley be on the lookout for something for me to do; I'm getting tired of being on this road." And after India, she believe they got to go to Egypt. She wasn't sure.

81

The Bangladesh border was just forty miles away . . . the people covering parks and paths like white ants were war refugees . . . the sickles and hammers splashed in red paint on stone walls were Communist incitement that did not, after all, wash out when the monsoons came . . . the uniformed men clustered at the entrance of the high-walled enclave of the American Consulate in Calcutta were armed Indian soldiers posted since a bomb was thrown over the wall during the election. But what Mahalia saw were giant frangipani trees covered with white flowers like the ones hung around her neck when she landed . . . tree bark spread out—to make paper, the consul said . . . men squatting by woven trays heaped with fruits and vegetables . . . so much! this *all* a strange land . . . men bicycling people around like a Chinese rickshaw . . . great bales of hemp passing by on carts . . . and the clear, direct, smiling eyes of Mrs. Herbert Gordon. There wasn't a thing about the wife of the consul general that Halie didn't like at sight and sound, and the more she was around her house, the more Halie knew her vibrations were right. *This* lady was a wonder. She was a friend. And it was a pleasure to watch her work. This the type of person that when she works, *it* works.

Selling tickets wasn't the consulate's business: it was the concern of the Indo-American Society, which 1½ hours after the concert was announced found it had a problem: would-be buyers were using every known pressure to get a ticket. None to be had. "They say sellout wasn't much longer than that anywhere—about two hours," said jovial Herbert Gordon, rubbing his hands with pleasure. (Mahalia was astounded—where did these people know of her?) No, it was the social side where the work was and that was Mrs. Gordon's department, to Halie's eyes. Right now, with all that energy that never seemed to cost her good humor, she was waving a pink telegram for Mahalia to notice: "GRATEFUL KIND INVITATION VERY HAPPY TO ACCEPT YOUR INVITATION OF TWENTYEIGHT EVENING STOP REGARDS—CHOGYAL AND GYALMO."

"That's the ruler, the king, of Sikkim," Mrs. Gordon explained gaily; "the Gyalmo is his queen—and she's American! Hope Cooke. I knew her when she was a girl at Sarah Lawrence. They'll fly in. That's the only way to get in and out of Sikkim, anyway." It sounded like the fairytale books the white people's children in New Orleans used to have with the pictures in there of people in strange costumes. And this was *her,* right here, *in* it!

The Chogyal wasn't well that evening, but the Gyalmo came, draped in some of the most beautiful cloth . . . all these saris were beautiful; she was going ask Mrs. Gordon to help her get some. The Gyalmo came to where Mahalia was holding forth on a chaise longue (more comfortable than that high-backed chair she started in) and the child had the whisperingest voice Mahalia'd ever heard. Beautiful dark eyes—something to this child, except you had to lean to hear her; and when she said come see *her,* seemed like she meant it. It was hard to concentrate on any one individual, though; so *many* to pay attention to. The top of everything in music, dancing, actors, newspaper editors, foreign diplomats, the government—just everything—and a swami. Swami Nityaswarupananda—he repeated his name several times until she could say it. He was much interested to learn of her American spiritual gospel, he said. Mahalia was sorry she had to turn to this new gentleman, Mr. Ashok Mehta—and he was? The only company licensed to press foreign records! She was making her own, she told him enthusiastically; they could do business. Lord, You sure work in mysterious ways. Then it was his wife Ruth's turn, and she was from a part of India that *was* a mystery, she said—the women ruled, and the children took the *mother*'s last name; they were all very musical there, *all Christians!* And imagine, a deity in the Bengal religion named "Ma-hahl-ya"—she was just as glad the spelling was off: "Meghalaya." But these were very spiritual people, close to God . . . and here now! they have Indian *gospel.* She listened entranced to Purna Chandra Das, and when finally his soft drum and lilting voice and dancing feet were still, she said she wanted to put him on her records.

Just been shopping with Mrs. Gordon, but her legs cramping and her heart going fast; pulling it to St. Paul's Cathedral was a job for Halie and the Lord. Then she sang. To the *Statesman* critic, "The near-legendary singer . . . almost hypnotized her audience." "Inspired; between a high-pitched vocal cyclone and the softest, almost inaudible cadence . . . matchless," to *Amrita Bazar Patrika.* She had a standing ovation and she appreciated it, but what she needed most she got at Mrs. Gordon's: a good dinner and *bed.*

If I'm going, Lord, You gave me a grand send-off, thought Halie, staring out of the Air India plane to New Delhi next morning. Plane been searched—*every* passenger searched—but they sure didn't find the bomb supposed be on board and finally took off, saying everything all right, but human beings are not perfect and Lord I'm the last to complain except I thought You wanted me to get the temple.

Touchdown and the welcome committee were more welcome than they knew. Halie was happy these flowers going over her head were for the living. To tall, handsome USIS Director Daniel Oleksiw and, shortly, to silver-haired Ambassador Kenneth Keating, she gave her biggest smile. And she assured the ambassador she appreciated his thinking of her heart: Roosevelt House—the gleaming white residence in the famous embassy design—had no way for the unwell. It was walk the circular staircase or never lay your head, and Halie hoped to do that as soon as possible, at Mr. Oleksiw's. . . . Ahhh, she really liked his better anyway. Mrs. Oleksiw said it was Indian, but it look like one of those great *big* old St. Charles Ave. mansions, been lived in. There was time for lunch before the schedule started, and Halie tried to analyze the spices. She'd meant to get her some in Japan; she'd sure find out about these ones in India. She was almost sorry she liked the food so *well*.

One nice thing about America, they sure look after you. Brought the TV camera *to* her, for the interview; so maybe—if You help me, Lord, help me pull up on the inner power—maybe I'm going get through this too.

"OH! LORD HAVE mercy." The time and the talking had gone on after the interview, and to tell the truth she was enjoying herself and didn't have sense enough to go lay down; and first thing, got poor Mrs. Oleksiw scared and a doctor in. . . . From superficial examination, it appeared to Dr. Thomas Wiegert to be hypertension and fatigue. He knew the heart history, but there seemed no immediate problem there. He gave her a relaxant and recommended rest and possibly a massage. Ram Lal, the head bearer here, was very good.

"Can I get that fellow back in to massage them?" Neither Laurraine nor Gwen was really *worried* about Mahalia. She *lived* tired, and they'd seen her come up and down and up so often. It was rest she needed. But she was in pain and something ought to be done about that. "Let me get him in," urged Laurraine. They were trying to get Mahalia's girdle up for her, but Halie kept trying to help herself. It's odd, thought Laurraine, no matter how heavy her thighs get, her legs from the knee down stay really slender. So do her arms and those long, mobile hands—cramping badly now, poor dear. "Shall I?" Laurraine asked. Mahalia shook her head. "That don't do no good. As soon's you pull up on something—" If she could just dress slowly, she believe she could make it to the dinner. Dr. Clapp had gone to a lot of trouble to honor her. "No, that's all right, leave your recorder on, baby; it takes my mind off—what was we talking about? Yeah," she grinned, diverted. "Frank Sinatra is an onery man when he gets mad. I was glad at President Kennedy's it wasn't me. . . ."

A GARDEN party. That's one thing she missed in that condominium. Can't even grow her greens. Watching, Gwen decided Sister was getting better. Good. And after dinner, back in her room, didn't Mahalia keep her and

Laurraine up until all hours, keeping her company, the three of them just talking? Then that big lizard showed up and they all chased out until somebody got rid of it and that got Gwen and Laurraine to bed. Halie did not like to be alone, no two ways about it, even when the one thing she needed most was to *be* alone and rest.

JIM ASCHER, deputy information chief, got the word. Cancel Roosevelt House. All of it: Voice of America and the New Delhi press interviews. Dan Oleksiw could see that either Mahalia was ill or a very slow starter of a morning; she hadn't gotten herself in to breakfast yet and by now she should have been on her way and her people said she wasn't even close. Well, you win some, lose some.

Ah. Well enough for breakfast and she wants to go shopping with Lois Flanagan. Good. I'll tell the ambassador he can count on his guest of honor for tonight, and see if I can pin the lady down on what's needed for the Prime Minister. Such a funny beginning. That simple first newspaper announcement that Miss Jackson would appear in four cities—and a call from Mrs. Gandhi to the ambassador asking to buy tickets! "Not at all," the ambassador gulped; "you're my guest!" It had been so out of all belief that the P.M. would attend that nobody had thought to invite her. Then the business of wanting to meet Miss Jackson privately at intermission—the woman who *never* wasted time. His opposite number at the Soviet Embassy must be green. Now her office was calling again—twice, in fact: "Would the concert actually begin at the announced time? How long would the first half of the program last? At what time would Miss Jackson leave the stage?"

Mahalia heard Oleksiw out, slowly consuming breakfast at the long dining room table; then she said serenely, "Now that's one thing I can't tell you. I sing what the Lord wills me to sing; I don't know if it's going to be a two-minute or a three-minute or a five-minute song. And I don't know about encores. Just as the spirit moves me. But I'll start on time; *they* can tell you that." Gwen and Laurraine, sharing the table, simply swallowed. What could they say?

"YOU GOT TO get the doctor back. I'm sick." After doing so fine for the ambassador's party with all the high dignitaries. Lord? But when the doctor came, all he had for her was "rest and keep on with the medication." Well, he was doing the best he knew how, without knowing her case. All right, she wouldn't go check the auditorium this morning like she ordinarily would; she'd leave it to Gwen and Charles. Oh, Lord, touch me. I can't explain to a living soul how I feel.

Dan Oleksiw had seen his schedules disappearing like water in sand. And now— "I'm sorry," he said, "you better prepare your lady. The Prime Minister has just fired a good part of her cabinet and she has a meeting tonight with the rest. It's doubtful if she will attend. And if she does, it can't be for long." It was Mahalia who comforted *him*. "That's all right," she said, "that woman has a lot on her mind."

PANTING, MAHALIA shucked her sweat-soaked dress like an ear of corn while Gwen held her change and Laurraine took her discard. A room in this wing of big, plush Vigyan Bhavan (a conference hall) had been especially fitted for her as a dressing room, even to a chaise longue for resting. But this was no time for rest. Indira Gandhi was waiting. Outside, Oleksiw paced. He'd asked Miss Goreau to see what she could do—warned that the P.M. had a hair-trigger temper, that *no one* kept her waiting, she hadn't the time to waste—particularly tonight.

Laurraine still thought she was right. Halie had asked if she thought she ought to change first, and Laurraine said yes—Mahalia would be at such a disadvantage with her hair disheveled, her dress soaked; it wasn't even courteous. It wouldn't take two minutes. "Help me with this zipper, baby; I don't want to keep that lady waiting." One motion and already Mahalia was quickly, carefully mopping sweat beads from her forehead and nostrils . . . pressing in a moist red rubber sponge dense with powder . . . tidying her mound of glossy black curls. Laurraine saw pain arrow her face. Hand cramps again. The tension. She rose immaculate in white chiffon—smiling, strangely youthful for her 58 years.

It looked a lengthy mile across that stage. She could hear Gwen and Charles close behind. Why did the other room have to be on the wrong side? These shoes killing her. She could feel Oleksiw and Laurraines just willing her to hurry without wanting to seem to. She knew they were worried the lady might be mad, but she'd done the best she could.

THERE WAS applause as she entered—there were others in the room, but it was clear Mahalia really saw only the one who had risen with Ambassador Keating: a small, fragile-looking woman whose skin seemed olive under the lights, dressed in a figured sari that looked humble. Her dark wavy hair had a wing of gray, and her eyes were the most compelling they'd ever seen—huge, black, lustrous, intense—locked now with Mahalia's own in shared, smiling communication. They sat to talk, their voices low. Finally, "When you coming to America?" Mahalia asked, eyes never leaving Mrs. Gandhi's own. "I don't know just yet," smiled Mrs. Gandhi. "Well, when you do, you come stay with me in Chicago," said Mahalia. Mrs. Gandhi dimpled—the offer so simply put—and as simply nodded.

Laurraine could not believe Oleksiw was whispering what he was whispering. But wouldn't Mrs. Gandhi herself— Well, if Laurraine *had* to— "I'm going to have to be the ogre who says wouldn't you all like to hear some more of Miss Jackson?"

DAN OLEKSIW wrote the words down immediately. He wanted to be sure he would have them exactly right. He had heard Mrs. Gandhi say to Ambassador Keating, "I will never hear a greater voice; I will never know a greater person."

THE SECOND half of the concert was just—inspired, thought Lois Flanagan, listening backstage. She wished the Prime Minister could have stayed to hear this song . . . *this* song . . . oh, this one! On, on, Mahalia went, the Indians by now clapping with the beat. Off dripping with sweat. On for an encore. The cheers wouldn't stop. She was almost staggering now. In the audience, Dr. Wiegert had qualms. So did Laurraine, who saw familiar signs. Lois sent out the word: after this encore must come the flowers—the traditional Indian salute which signals the "real" end. Over the footlights poured a stream of young Indian beauties in saris, arms filled with baskets of blossoms. Puffing, triumphant, Mahalia headed for her rest. But there was an eerie silence on the other side of the curtain; you should have heard the shuffle and murmur of the exit. One peek—and an indelible memory. The entire audience was standing. Not asking. Just standing in tribute. "Open it," said Mahalia, and she was back on stage to thank them, bless them, and offer one more song "for the young people" . . . which turned into another and another and . . . she was off again and running.

STARTLED OUT of her absorption, Laurraine stared at the white envelope. No mistake—her name was on it. Who— A note from Dan Oleksiw: "The Prime Minister not only stayed until the end, she left and came back for the encores. She's standing in the fire exit to listen. For God's sake, please tell Miss Jackson."

Mahalia blinked in alarm at seeing Laurraine on stage. She ducked her head to take whatever was coming, Lord . . . and lifted a happy face at the news. She caught Laurraine as she turned to hurry off. "What's her name again?"

"Just call her Madam Prime Minister."

Mahalia grasped the lectern—but she might have been pulling up a chair to the kitchen table. "I have been gospel singing for 42 years. Maybe I have got 42, 52, or 62 more years to do it. (Applause) But today I have so *much* to be grateful to God for, and when *Madam Prime Minister,* a very *busy* woman, with many things to do, many things on her mind, stayed—is still *here*—that is a blessing from God. (Applause) That's why she's the Prime Minister. (Applause and laughter) When people learn to *serve* their fellow man, and be a *part* of them, and don't worry about titles, that's what makes you great. For a fine, fine lady to stay here after the program—

"You know, they can say what they want about us women—and I

say this all over—but really, it takes a woman to really *do* something. (Huge applause while Mrs. Gandhi, standing under a red "Exit" sign, grins broadly.) Now ladies, and all the good men too— Men are proud of great women; they are, you know. They don't always show it, but behind their back, child, you ought to hear them brag! (Whoops of laughter and applause) So I think everyone ought to stand up and give her a great big ovation, give her a great big hand—men and women and children and all." (Huge sustained applause, led by Mahalia, which goes on and on, wave after wave folding back, while Mrs. Gandhi stands, clearly delighted. Mahalia's practiced ear notes the first level of subsidence.) "And while you're standing, don't forget the American ambassador. He's *so* nice and sweet and kind." (Mounting, sustained applause from the entranced listeners)

Somewhere along the way, a slight Indian man in nondescript cotton homespun sitting in one of the cheaper row-end seats by the exit realized with a start just who was standing nearby. He scrambled to his feet and offered Mrs. Gandhi his seat. Her security cordon hurriedly regrouped. But nothing bad could happen this night in Vigyan Bhavan. Revolt and plague and the cabinet could wait for the one enchanted evening. Mrs. Gandhi had left reluctantly when the flowers came over the stage and was almost at the main entrance with Ambassador Keating at her elbow when she heard the ringing applause of Mahalia's re-entrance and the music. She hurried back down the long side corridor to the entranceway nearest the stage, to stand and listen.

The last note of the last encore was the song most shouted-for through the auditorium when Mahalia asked them to decide upon one final choice: In the lilting English of India, they joined her for *We Shall Overcome.* Mahalia made clear that it held a broad, broad meaning; that "with God's help, we shall overcome the evil raging through the world."

THE ELECTRICITY could be felt through the reception rooms of the Oleksiws' post-concert reception. "My God, what a diplomatic coup!" gasped a Yugoslav envoy. "I said the same thing," trumpeted a West German diplomat, walking up, "and I didn't consult him!"

"And did you notice," said a smiling Indian woman, "the Prime Minister had her head uncovered the whole evening? That is most unusual; she usually has her sari draped over her head, even indoors."

Across the hallway, in her small wing, Mahalia lay writhing in pain. Her heart. It was almost like England—but was it like England? She'd got up and gone on from *there*— Dr. Wiegert hurried in and said he thought she'd better give up tomorrow. She wondered what she had said up there tonight—could not remember a word. But that's like always. It's given to her.

At 4:30 a.m., Rev. Hendrix Townsley—district superintendent of the Methodist Church in Southern Asia—began typing a letter to the President. In his more than 28 years in India, he wrote, "never before have I experienced anything like the good-will engendered by this one lady last night. . . . Send her back."

She was half-groggy with sleep or whatever the doctor gave her last night when she had the second spell of pain. Dan Oleksiw had canceled the film crew for the Taj Mahal. "Do you all think I can go out there today? The doctor told me not to, but what I was trying to think . . . well, call 'em, and—we'll go . . . I don't know *how* I feel . . . but if they going work, say I'll go."

She made it, brightening to be driving on a road where there were camels and a black dancing bear and an elephant and a snake charmer—unh-unh, she wasn't getting out by no snakes!—but for the film, she did . . . and trudged the brilliance of the Taj Mahal in hot sunlight . . . bargained for souvenirs . . . seemed better when she returned than when she left. Nobody could understand it. She was no more than worn out.

At the airport next morning, waiting for the plane to Madras, Om Prakash—the silent young man who had been Mahalia's constant security guard—knelt and asked that she touch his head . . . and seeing this, others asked, too. Mahalia stretched out her arms. "Just remember it's nobody on this earth, it's God's going to bless you."

Madras was easier, staying at just a house with Mr. and Mrs. George Henry because the new Consul General, Stephen Palmer, hadn't settled in yet. In 48 hours, *they* entertained her, Mr. *Palmer* entertained her in his garden—"like a fairyland, all strung with lights showing up these temple flowers and flame trees and bougainvillea!" she caroled, making it come alive for Laurraine, laid up with a fever . . . they took her to one of the great wonders of her *life*, Mylapore Temple—"All the activities of the community carved in there just as the people lived it, Laurraines; it spoke to me; it's better than the Taj Mahal—that's a tomb!" . . . she got into a mess with the pay—rupees, not dollars? (but this was America's, it would straighten out) . . . she had back-to-back press and radio interviews and a 30-minute Air India Radio concert besides the sold-out concert at the hall . . . and got through it all. And *wasn't* she an instrument, heard herself telling those smart young intellectuals, "God always spoke to you; He's always been able to lead you and tell you what to do . . . what makes it so puzzling for you to accept such things? It's just since man has been able to talk and not send mental thoughts to each other, he's been a hypocrite. But when man was strong, couldn't talk, and I knew what you were thinking about and you knew what I was thinking about—you had to be truthful with me." Some people have that quality yet, she hinted to them; "it's not yet gone."

Bombay was a big city, she saw, and that consul general wasn't in his house either—wasn't even in town yet, but they stayed in the beautiful old place had been an Indian prince's marble palace. "Ask the doctor to see me, please, when he's through with Mrs. Gore." Halie's got to get in *shape.* This is Whitney Young's memorial concert—sat at her table many a time. She liked the concert's being in a cathedral—built before America was even a country—but ooh! wasn't this a hornet's nest of Indian ladies been stirred up: The Time and Talents Club had set up 500 seats on the grounds to hear by loudspeaker, so great had been the clamor for attendance Friday and Saturday; thousands turned away. And now the Canon of St. Thomas forbid applause. Not even a clap! The ladies were outraged and vocal. "Really, ladies, it's *all right,*" Mahalia kept assuring Mrs. Rose Mehta and her committee backstage, "I don't mind." And she could have told them: don't argue with this one. Ah, but he was a sweet old man. His tribute at the end was beautiful . . . but those people sure had to work to sit on their hands. The world over, got to argue with the preachers.

The hospitality was wonderful. Bob and Ginnie Murphy, Arnold Hanson and his wife Lorraine laid themselves out the two nights with beautiful parties. This second day she had taped a Voice of America, filmed at Rajkamal Studios, gone looking for a silk shirt for Uncle Porter, and at the cathedral again, after having a time even to heave herself up off a chair, walked into the pulpit and been *transfused* with the spirit 'til she made a fool of herself crying—and this was a wonderful dinner party up here now. But Halie still had to go. The schedule had said tomorrow night but Halie had to go *now.* Got the tickets on the bags? Was 19 pieces; believe it's 24 now. All right, we ready.

Bea Thompson from Pinching Town days was on her mind as they flew through the night May 9 from Bombay to Bangkok. That was a friend . . . like she'd told those press people yesterday. Those were *friends,* and real people back there, and she was still looking for real people like that in her life today . . . and love like that. Ohh, Lord, You know I'm so tired I'm 'most sick just from that. "Let's see if we can't get us a quicker through flight at Bangkok," she murmured . . . and did . . . and one more scramble later, excited Thai officials left behind, she, Gwen, and Laurraine (Charles was flying the other way around) were in the air with 50 minutes due in Guam—when they finally would ever get there—then no stops 'til L.A. Jesus, pilot me.

In those 50 minutes, they had to leave Laurraines in Guam for her niece Missy Mann and her husband Lee to nurse—just the Lord's wonder they were there—no luggage but she wouldn't need it in bed. Halie climbed back aboard, carefully holding a seashell little Russell and Debbie Mann had brought, bought with their own money. It was nice for families to be close. She thought of her own hopes she'd built so high—26 stories high—but her mind was so tired it wouldn't hold, and she slipped off.

Headlines in *every* newspaper—a whole page in the L.A. *Times*—clippings coming in like a paper parade and thank You Lord but don't parade Halie *nowhere* for a while, please. *Two* of 'em! Two different colleges, white colleges, want to make her an honorary doctor—of music. Lord, I thought You had served me the whole cake and now You piling up the icing. Wait 'til Townsend hear. Bob Phillips' eyes going pop. He had not *yet* got her the rest of her money from Japan. Just don't let him get any big ideas now about. . . . "Yeah," she told Leonard Feather, "want me go over there again for eight weeks. I don't want to go—then again, there's something about this work possesses you. Long as I love what I'm doing." Hadn't she told those people in India she'd be back? If she could just hold *off* a while. What possessed her to tell Bob Phillips she would go to Europe? So soon. Like a cork on a pond. Lord, if Halie don't have no better sense, would You please make her—for a while—no more than *breathe?*

82

"Dear Mahalia: Per your request when we spoke on the phone yesterday morning, I advised New York that you will accept the dates for Madame Adolfi in Sweden and Norway, as well as the Aug. 19 date in Palermo, Italy, and Sept. 4 or 5 in Tel Aviv, which I had already confirmed . . . but that you definitely will not play the additional dates in Europe for Collien since we feel it would be injurious to your health; and as a consequence, we will have to play for Collien at some other time. . . ."

Bob Phillips paused to let Kay Saunders's pen catch up. The trouble with Mahalia was that she didn't much want to work. Tell her about a contract, and the money, and she says yes. Work on it, let a date get close enough to see—and she cries wolf.

HALIE SHIFTED, seeking her ease. This little time in L.A. after India gone *so* fast. And so nice. Just be around the apartment . . . keep an eye on how they fix that copperteen outside the building: be nice, especially since Margaret and Celeste and them come to rededicate the building to God, ask Him to send the kind of people He want in here . . . and didn't Celeste play the fool! got Laurraines and her both *crying*, laughing so hard at Celeste being Halie counting the house in the old percentage days: "*When my work is done, set the setting sun*—she's got the first four rows counted; *I'm going to my home over there*—she's got the next four; *I shall walk the golden stairs*—she's got the balcony. Why you think she opened with that song?" That crazy Celeste! And how about Laurraines when Halie showed her the piece out the paper about the divorced man gone berserk, come murdered his ex-wife—*told* her I was afraid to make Minnis mad, him so excitable. Good thing I'm shut of that Indian; no telling. But *look at this man* Celeste pushing at me, think she so roundabout! Persian man; don't know a thing about him—all right to take you to the dentist, but here he want to get Halie off down at some strange restaurant at night! Could be some Communists want to kidnap her, all that publicity about her representing the government . . . *pay* something to get Mahalia back. Wasn't that man's face a study when Halie's whole bunch walked in, didn't know I'd called them? Ha! Rather be home, let Johnny's Geri fix something. . . . That's not so far off about the Communists; anything can happen in this life and most of it *happened* to Mahalia. Like I told Laurraines—Gwen just nodding, knows Halie's right—"Write the *real* book of me, baby; don't make me no saint. I'm just a frail human being wrestling demons every day, trying to make my way with the help of the Lord." That's what I tell 'em about Martin; don't make him no saint. That's the whole thing of it!

So now Chicago, hit on into all that—but Halie's got to get her *temple.* Ohhh, she's glad she told Celeste tell Mayor Yorty if Ted Kennedy want her at his luncheon, Ted Kennedy can call her himself; that's what his brother Jack did—Bobby too. Ted didn't call and that's one less thing Halie got on her dish with a bent spoon—and the up and down track record. "Laurraines! you got yourself together, girl? They ready to take your bags; and don't let 'em forget my big red one in there too." Halie's going see Dr. Vondrasek *tomorrow*; this thing been going on long enough, it's embarrassing. And it's sure got to be fixed before Marymount College. . . .

Dr. Vondrasek was a little puzzled. May 21, and Mahalia said this diarrhea started in Bombay, India, and was of three to four weeks' duration. But nothing showed up in the tests to account for it. Well, they could give her some treatment for it. She was still taking the medicine for her diabetes—good; and prednisone—stayed on those two.

"WAIT'LL YOU see me in a cap and gown, Mrs. Gore," said Halie, crinkling eyes betraying her haughty voice. "Whoo-ooh! it's cold here at night—where *is* this? Tarrytown, New York. Girl, you going freeze in that; here, take this flannette . . . see how it do to always have extra?" Woman had not the sense to look out for herself. But Halie sure appreciated her coming to support her at this strange place. The nuns— "Laurraines, what you think about that nun had the lipstick, and bare knees and spike heels, and *earrings* dangling! I wonder if the Dominicans down home changed like that? Listen, the whole *world* is changing."

That's what the speaker said, but he'd been saying it so *long*, and all the other ceremony. Halie fought to keep her eyes open, sitting up there with all the dignitaries, only black woman on the stage, representing her race—but some pretty colored girls in the students. Just . . . she snapped her head up, thank You Jesus, before people pay attention. Ohhhhhh, that's Mahalia Jackson he's talking about . . . heaping her name; but it's for You, Lord. Isn't this beautiful! And all His doing.

"Will you send me some pictures?" Eager as a child, Bob Shepherd thought; she certainly doesn't act the celebrity. "And Mrs. Patt, you think I can take my cap and gown home with me? I want to show off to my friends." Mrs. Robert Patt was a bit nonplused—no one had ever asked before; but she was definitely not going to tell Miss Jackson the things were rented; there must be some way to simply purchase them and send them as a present.

"Well," Laurraine grinned as they exited, finally, from the reception—and Mahalia still in *fine* form—"aren't you glad I dogged you into wearing those sensible shoes?"

HOW SENSIBLE else could she be? She wish she could sensible herself out of Europe, but Bob Phillips popping that whip like cat-nine-tails and say the same thing—"It's for your own good." Well, it worked from Aunt Duke. Might be easier to go to Europe than get this benefit for Gleason on here, though. That nice banker who got her up to dedicate his chapel, he was going help Gleason—they in there talking now . . . *what* that he say about Sunday being a holy day? "Every day's a holy day!" Halie bellowed without stirring or interrupting her train of thought. Gleason was owed a lot of credit—South Side wouldn't let you touch that man now. She hoped Sen. Humphrey would give them a hand with the farm. But wasn't that sweet of Humphrey, send her flowers to welcome her and then take the *time* to call, a man got as much business as he has to accomplish . . . and how many these people in this room got any business they *can* accomplish? Standing in her hotel suite in Minneapolis, Halie had heard quieter henhouses when the eggs was being snatched. Well, let 'em scrabble. When they through, she'd go sing. She just hope she didn't have to disgrace herself.

Visiting from Wisconsin, Iris Day thought she'd see if her New Orleans friend was by any chance with Mahalia Jackson—the newspaper said she was at the Leamington, right on the heels of being given an honorary doctorate of music. Yes. "And Mahalia says come on up in a few minutes and meet her."

"Dr. Jackson, I presume?" said Iris, smiling at the beautiful, tired face she so admired. Instantly, Mahalia reached out, hand dark against the Norwegian whiteness. "Just Mahalia, baby," smiled Halie, leading them in. Her bedroom was a swirl of people; dirty dishes stood ignored on a hotel tray; everyone seemed to have business but that business didn't seem to be Mahalia. A man came in with an armload of dresses—it must be time for them to go. Iris rose. "Come on, go with us," Mahalia said comfortably; "everybody got they hands full—you can carry my purse; and bring my slippers, baby, my feet killing me. *No*, Laurraines, I am not going to wear my slippers on the stage. Did Gleason give you those pictures so you can help him with his story?"

She'd promised herself an easy concert—declared it; but the spirit touched her and there was no holding. Off at intermission drenched with sweat—not a piece of Kleenex in the place and this strange girl Iris got to grab up a handful of toilet paper for her to go back on stage with . . . dear Jesus! it was hot; sweating like popcorn. Halie's going cut this part short, now. But she didn't—couldn't—and gave them a sermon besides on the love of God and one another: all these young people here, white and black.

"Oh, baby, keep these people back from me; just let me get to the rest room and get out of here tonight." Embarrassed again. Dr. Vondrasek got to do something about this. It was robbing her strength.

RIGHT INTO running revival at Salem all week. Never mind tired—she promised God. Good she could tell Mildred to bring her singers one night. Let her be a part. Oooh, it's a small bed this week for Halie: Can't invite Rev. Bentley all the way from Philadelphia to preach and not give him the best, her queen-size; she sure wasn't going take Minnis's bed; got Laurraines in Sigma's or she wouldn't mind being in the little girl's. Anyway, Laurraines need to be there 'cause that's the closet where Allen keep the stationery and Laurraines writing the important people for her in India. Halie was ashamed to let it run this long. So *much!* But it was good to have people fill up some this space. "Allen, you found Joyce yet?" Joyce Lampkin was better from her leukemia and in town; she could come rehearse this TV commercial for New York next week and go with her to CBS tomorrow. They didn't *say* bring a pianist, but she liked to be prepared. Soon as she got past that, she's going take her India and Japan pictures down to show Daley she been associating with the *cream*. He be glad to know she told Mrs. Gandhi about him. And see has he got that job lined up for her yet. Something with young people. They're the hope.

COL. JACK REILLY—Mahalia's "second mayor"—listened. "Whatever Mahalia wants, we'll try and find it for her," the mayor said. As far as Col. Reilly could understand, he says, "she was getting tired and she wanted to get away from traveling and perhaps take a position with the city teaching young people. She could have anything in Chicago that wasn't nailed down—but you never could pin Mahalia down to exactly what she really did want to do. Of course, she always had this ambition to start a gospel singing school." And she did say this trip to Europe would be her last. Maybe she could come up with something *concrete*. There was only one Mahalie.

THANK YOU LORD for putting DePaul University right here in Chicago; don't have to move a foot to get their honor: Doctor of Humane Letters. She liked the humanness of that. But it was when they presented her with the St. Vincent De Paul medal "for serving God through the needs of man" that Louise Weaver saw the tears really flow.

Lord? Where is my *strength?* Not moved nor sung hardly but in church for a week and it's a pull to make it to Little Rock. Strawthford got her on the same program with him for the Sunday School Congress—and wouldn't you know, got a mixup on rooms: "Nothing for Rev. Strawther"—so Strawthford end up staying with her 'til she can raise enough Cain to get the boy his own. It took her back.

IT TOOK HER back when she meant to be *forward*, this business of it not being the White House, and not being the President, and not being the astronauts, and got her piled up in Washington in a room must've come *over* with the Mayflower, to shoot the first TV show to the Congo by satellite. Bob Phillips got that part right. That and the day—June 29. It did end up fun, but Lord! You looked after Halie when that man didn't come up with the money for Texas and Loosiana; otherwise been down there, up here, down there like skipping hots and Halie's too tired for that. What she *ought* do is see some these people about her Foundation benefit she was going start on for Washington after Europe. Know Duke Ellington and Dizzy Gillespie going come—*who* paying any mind to Bob and his "Who's going to work for free?" He'll help her get the people together. But dear Jesus, Halie got to go see the doctor tomorrow; every time she sing, still running like a goose. He could give her something for the swelling, too. Allen say she's running a drugstore now. Lord, Halie's too *tired* to go to the doctor. But can't do it day after; they all coming up to talk about the thing for Daley.

JEAN CHILDERS was indignant. Putting Mahalia in that position! Jean only published a little construction sheet with Ken, but she'd had enough dealings. Use Mahalia as head of a youth-newspaper project and have those columns wide open for dropout kids who were supposed to be "learning the media"? She'd never be able to control it. Just because Mayor Daley had said come up with an idea didn't mean she should jump at this proposal. Gene Shapiro was looking at it with a lawyer's eye. Harry Dale was naturally defending his concept—he had put a lot in on it. But if Mahalia asked *her*— "Jean! come in here with me a minute." Trust Mahalia's vibrations. . . .

Laurraine was certainly glad Mahalia called. Good Lord. She'd be crucified. Retraction had never yet been known to have the impact of the first— "Honey, absolutely not. Tell them no. It's tough enough to control the writing when you know the newspaper business."

"That's what Jean said. So look, put down a good program for me for drug control for my city work. Don't go into all the details, just the general outline. Send it air mail special delivery."

Judge Ben Hooks was pleased. Mahalia thought sufficient of his acumen and of him personally to call and ask him to outline a program for her to combat the drug menace. He'd get it off today as she asked. As a judge he certainly had ideas on the subject. With her multiple appeal, she could be a tremendous force; there had been so much in her life. And even with this other, she hadn't lost sight of her temple.

SHE COULD TELL it was close. She hadn't found it, but she knew. She had so wanted it to be on Martin Luther King Dr. and look like Superior *had* it for her that one time. Got the one piece and able to buy all around it to put up a highrise with the government program, so all the bottom could be housing to help finance her temple, school and everything, up on top; Superior figured that out . . . but then that one woman would not sell at any price, not even giving her a place in the new and any cash she want in her hand—said she was *willed* her place. So that was bad. Or was it? The Lord works in mysterious ways—had withheld—and now she felt it coming close, the *right* one. Might get Dale to ride her around this morning after he took her to Billings for her heart, going fast again. That might be from finishing up with Superior yesterday and laying awake last night with second thoughts—or third, or fifth—how many times they been working on this new will? Seem like the Lord pressing her to get it accomplished. She was ashamed to say "change" to Superior. It wasn't the *main*; got that since she saw in Acts 2, from Paul: "I have showed you all things, how that so labouring, ye ought to support the weak." No, it was just the particulars of some of the individuals. She'd ask Russell Goode; right here now. He could work with her 'til she had it *sure* for Superior to type up new. One thing with Russell—he'd never tell. Yeah. Soon as she got back from Los Angeles.

ELDER RALPH Lewis was amazed. To think! Margaret Jenkins and Celeste Scott bringing *Mahalia Jackson* to Mt. Zion Apostolic—hardly a church more humble. And back again tonight! Working around the altar with the young people, helping give the call to come to Jesus, had witnessed and singing now to the Lord completely lost in the spirit—really *enjoying* Jesus; caught fire on *I Have Decided to Follow Jesus* and hadn't come out yet!

That refueled her, getting through to God in a small place without no crowd around. Now she had Oral Roberts to rehearse Monday, tape Tuesday; next two days Flip Wilson rehearsals, tape next day; she just *would* make it back the 31st for Miracle Tent. She was praying for her own miracle, that the Lord would save her from going to Europe. Hadn't He already got the lady in Sweden to mix her dates—or Bob—or anyway pull out, so it's not 'til September and still time to pray?

"LORD—" Russell had met her at the plane this afternoon and she had not even changed; "—Lord, grant me strength to sing for You tonight," her prayer a yearning that made the huge crowd fall silent. She leaned against the piano . . . *Precious Lord, take my hand, lead me on* . . . and the power came, the strength surged, and Mahalia launched Rev. Don Stewart's "Compassion Explosion" revival and faith-healing crusade under the billowing canvas: the first revival tent permitted in Windy City since 1958. If Halie couldn't get a revival tent up in Chicago when the need be great—

HAND ME *Down My Silver Trumpet, Gabriel!* She felt like shouting in the middle of Drexel Blvd. She had found it. Marble and stone. Look like a temple in Rome. And the size—over two stories high! And the building in back! "Just drive around again, Bob; don't stop." Mr. Miller obediently shifted gears. Couldn't get out, people bound to see her and know it's Mahalia Jackson and the price go up but just looking, you could tell. And the Lord caused it to be just in the right place for her people, and all people: Drexel at E. 51st—on the South Side, in Hyde Park, close to University of Chicago and not 15 blocks from her condominium. K.A.M. Temple. *How Great Thou Art!* Now Lord, make these people move on out, like they talking. See how it pay to have friends—what you pick up on?

"What they take, Doc?" Gene Shapiro could hear the eagerness. His first contact had been neutral; the synagogue hadn't fully decided to sell. Now the day before it was to be listed, he'd had a call to give first chance to his client—whoever that was. The property wasn't cheap. The listing was $450,000. He'd checked the appraisal value—$350,000. Now he was trying to get Mahalia to name an offer, and it was a round-robin. "What they take?" . . . "I don't know. What will you offer?" . . . "How much it take?" All right, he'd call her tomorrow, when she'd had time to think.

First thing, she wanted Judge Hooks up here. It wasn't his fault the food and the chicken shacks fell through. He told her the technical explanations: "market fell through, overextended production requirements, financing"—but to her it came down to too much to shove with the push you got. But he hadn't taken a dime from her; put money in her hand—though mostly it ended up stock; and the whole business was good if it no more than brought her this man she believed in: dropped his business and came whenever she called. She wanted Ben Hooks, Jean Superior, and

Bob Miller. They'd go meet at the funeral parlor since Bob could hardly get away with his partner so sick.

BOB MILLER came back to the car. "Mahalia," he whispered, "I've sworn the caretaker to secrecy; you've got to come take a look at this thing inside with this lawyer from Memphis and me—we can't advise you until you see inside."

Ohhhh. Seat over 1200 people in the church. Stained glass windows. Balcony, pipe organ, sound system, choir room. Toilets for men and women . . . and look at this in back! Community hall with a stage and a grand piano, chapel, *big* kitchen, schoolrooms—"how many you count? six?"—desks, chairs, everything all equipped . . . library, nice big office, rest rooms. "Basement, too?" Oh, Lord! You do provide. Look at this: four-room apartment and a mailroom down in all this quiet. Make the records in the basement, charge off the rent and help support the Interdenominational Temple of God. Hallelujah!

Ben Hooks thought it better be a separate corporation, and he was right. Ever since she found out people distrust foundations (that hurt, when she first was asking, from the benefit)—since then, she had shied away in her mind . . . although she told Bob Miller she didn't think the Foundation met enough. Funny how she got off on Ike, sitting there talking with Bob. Poor Ike. Before she left for Europe, say once more: do him *right*. People forget.

Lord, this fast heart. . . . Aug. 9, she woke with a pain and went to Billings, scared. But Dr. Ferguson said she checked out all right—EKG all clear. He gave her a prescription for valium three times a day, to calm her. Next day she went to Connecticut. She'd promised.

June Havoc was elated. Mahalia on her Youthbridge TV show in the center of the children—the way she answered their questions was bound to get support for her theater project for disadvantaged children. She hoped it had impressed the children, too; particularly Mahalia on blacks and whites working best together, not apart. This woman radiated love. Now June wanted her to *rest* here in Weston these extra days. Not even up to being with anybody after the show. A pity, especially since Miss Eva had agreed to come. Maybe walking up the road this morning was better. Mahalia couldn't realize what a tribute to her it was that *LeG* had wanted to meet her—was receiving her as she was, working in her garden. Miss Eva LeGallienne was almost a social recluse these days.

Mahalia, regal in a housedress, and the small patrician slapping earth from her garden gloves in the little greenhouse were like two exotic birds disguising their rareness in small talk, murmurings. June wouldn't have missed the scene for anything. But now "I don't want to *go—pray* for me I don't go!" Mahalia moaned, face contorted with dread, head twisting from side to side in June's sunroom. My God, if she felt like this about a tour, why was her agent forcing her to go? *How* could he force her to go, this woman of almost mystic power . . . bending now over an odd-cut antique metal necklace June had given her. It needed towering majesty such as Mahalia's, someone queenly. "There is a power in this," Mahalia said, brooding over it; "it has a history. I don't know . . . there is a power." She took a call from Montreal and announced she had to leave. The promoter had been counting on her early for his publicity; it was a big open-air show at the Expo grounds.

MAYBE JUST as well Laurraines couldn't come (Celeste using the Montreal plane ticket and so pleased) but how had she forgot to ask her? Halie's half-crazy with this Europe trip; something about it. When she called Joe Bostic from Connecticut, he said she was crazy if she *went.* Bob said unless the EKG *showed* her heart was bad so he could prove it—

Canceled Montreal. "First time a man put this kind of money in my hand for not working," Mahalia laughed. Gullywasher washed the show clean off. "Come on, Gwen, Celeste; we going home tonight." See Superior. Get Russell to rehearse her Daley's program. And see can Ben Hooks come up here.

It was easier face to face, Ben Hooks agreed. He hesitated to dampen Mahalia's enthusiasm, but she was moving ahead and as a lawyer and businessman he had to advise her very strongly against it. Mahalia heard him out, but when she answered at length, he knew truth: "Her real love was evangelistic work, revival work; this temple would be the sum, the culmination of her life—to *concentrate* her time on bringing sinners to the altar for conversion." He wasn't the only one trying to change her mind, she said. "Everybody trying tell me. I've got enough money to do it on my own; and if I want to do it, I'm going do it. The *Lord* told me to do it."

"If the Lord wants you to do it, Mahalia," said Judge Hooks gently, "you do it."

"It won't cost *me* nothing." It's His money. "I just want to live to see the day," she said, almost in tears. "If I go to Germany, I'll die." She really believes it, Ben Hooks decided. At first he'd thought this business of not wanting to go was some sort of talk-up. But no, she was convinced. "I couldn't get clear why."

NO. HERE SHE's ready to fly, got to go to Germany if it kills her, and this preacher say— Call Superior. "Doc, he say he can get the church for $250,000. How he can do that, and you say I got to pay $450,000?"

No, Shapiro explained, clearly this time, he hoped: $450,000 was the *asking* price; it was a question of her making them an offer, a definite sum. "Do you want to offer them $235,000?"

"Yes, but *he's* going buy it and I *wants* it!"

"We'll see."

GWEN CAME, and Sunday morning Mahalia got her to call her mother, known to be very deep. "Will you pray?" Mahalia said heavily; "I have to go, and I don't think I'm going come back alive."

"Oh, God is able. When you get back, I'll come spend a couple of weeks with you."

That evening. Missie called Jean for a doctor who'd come see her. Dr. Quentin Young gave her a prescription for her back pain, which seemed severe. Next morning, "Mahalia," Jean said lightly, getting into the elevator behind her—come to take her to the airport but with Harry Dale available and Rev. Lewis's car too, she'd decided to avoid the terrible traffic in the rain and say goodbye here—"Mahalia," handing the bag over, "why don't you throw away half these pills?" Mahalia didn't even rise to the bait.

"What's the matter, love?" Harry Dale squatted beside her in the waiting room so she could see his grin. But he couldn't jolly her up. Neither could Tina. She was in a real slump.

LAUGH! 'TIL they cried, the two of them, Gwen fishing out the Kleenex. That was the funniest comedy. And the 747 so nice. "This all I'm going fly, from now on," Halie said. Gwen got her onto Gwen's children, then—that always took Sister's mind off. . . .

Gwen called the hotel doctor in Hanover. Mahalia had been depressed almost as soon as they checked in, and now she sounded really frightened. "These pains—and like terrible *knots* in my chest—an oppression." Gwen said she was going to feel better as soon as— "I don't mind dying, Gwen; God knows I'm a Christian; I just don't want to die alone." Gwen moved into the spare bed in her room. The doctor gave her something to relax her, to let her sleep. He didn't hear any irregularity of the heart. Next morning Mr. Schaeffer, the sponsor's road manager, came for her. She dressed and held a press conference. The next night she sang, giving them all they sought from her . . . "Mah-hahl-ya!" Schaeffer sighed with relief. Next morning Mahalia shook her head to "How do you feel?" and they traveled on to Düsseldorf . . . Nuremberg . . . the pattern repeated: travel—pains, weakness—doctor, pills—dress, press—sing. Mahalia openly resisting, pulled protesting, insisting *she* knew how she felt. The sponsor getting an EKG—all clear—determined this would not be another 1967 when what they felt was too-hasty, too-cautious hospitalization had collapsed their tour. Yet there were times when she roused, was cheerful, got "Little Split" (Gwen) to write to the family, Ike, Daley, Superior—what's happening to her temple?

GENE SHAPIRO sat down with Sheldon Good, but before he could begin, the broker asked, "Aren't you the people who offered me $225,000? Isn't this man in your group?" Gene heard instant echoes of Mahalia's "preacher" call. "Do you have any correspondence?" Gene asked casually. "I sent a letter to him at the address he gave me," said Mr. Good, "but it came back. I thought I had the wrong address. I had 1456 E. 67th St."

Shapiro adjusted his $235,000 offer to $225,000. It would be relayed to the owners. As quickly as he could, he talked with Bob Miller and Allen Clark, and they checked the address: 1456 E. 67th *Place* was the address of a basement church of yet another preacher—one often in Mahalia's home. Possibly the basement church was merely being used as an accommodation address by the "buyer" preacher, the one who'd called Mahalia—the one, the three men agreed, who was trying for a skim on a sale *to Mahalia.* That would be one less thing to worry her.

Sept. 17, Allen and Mr. Miller handed the broker Mahalia's check for $15,000. So it was *Mahalia Jackson!* The owners would check out her offer.

That night, in Gütersloh, Switzerland, Schaeffer was astounded: this was the sick woman? this was the woman unable to stagger on? wanting to break contract and go home? For an excited, stomping, clapping, chanting auditorium jammed with college students, Mahalia soared high . . . came back for six encores . . . "Mah-hahl-ya!" pulled her back for four more . . . and hundreds of students swarmed on stage and swept her into a second line of *When the Saints Go Marching In*, Mahalia in her holy dance. Schaeffer had never seen anything like it. And he could certainly report to Mr. Collien the *Fräulein* was in good shape.

In Frankfurt next day, she seemed rejuvenated. She greeted Laurraine at the Hotel Intercontinental with her old zest—chided her on being the one who'd called off four days before flight time: "she couldn't pull it," she pointed out to Schaeffer, "and got herself able two weeks late" . . . ate a good dinner in the hotel restaurant—amiable, interested: "Mayor Daley's going give me a big welcome home program; *Belafonte*'s going MC" . . . walked a couple of blocks outside for the fresh air.

She woke with a low pain, and the pressure. "Doctor?" No, the heart is all right. More relaxants. Wary, at bay. "Laurraines, you be me for the *Stars and Stripes.*" And that night out of all belief was suddenly transfused with the spirit, gave a packed audience of demanding admirers four encores. "Mah-hahl-ya!" The drum of the unison-chant still sounded when—flung in a chair, ill now—she roused enough to change clothes and get to the hotel. Dear Jesus, deliver me.

Berlin. So much that was pleasant. A blonde child named Mahalia bearing flowers . . . courtesies from Capt. Gentry . . . a 24-karat gold medallion struck by Heinz Wipperfeld ("Mr. Tiffany of Germany") to commemorate her first concert at the new *Philharmonie* . . . Reiner Schroeter (a Mahalia satellite at Chicago U., a tax lawyer now) wanted Hallelujah Records for Germany . . . the temple hers! $40,000 paid in and binding. But Sept. 23, a major scare: to the hospital with a doubting Schaeffer. Electrocardiogram clear. Two doctors. Persistent pain in heart area. Mahalia in tears, a gray cast over the brown—fearful of strange doctors, strange medication . . . pain forcing down one pill . . . another . . . the pain subsiding, but—cured or covered up? Weak. "We going home tomorrow. Be ready."

Into the dressing room heaving, exhausted. A quiet opening. Easy, easy . . . Collien, Jr., offstage, watching: "cut it short"; Mahalia willing. Then the spirit takes hold, her head comes up, her body surges, praise His name! I am the vessel; He's pouring His spirit right through me out to these people . . . thought flowing over and under the voice which is sending the Berlin audience into its own ecstasy. Off, heaving, clutching for air. How will she have to pay?

Mrs. Ilse Reichel, State Minister for Family, Youth and Sports—here by appointment. But not Mahalia's, the stern "Tell that lady my audience is waiting; she needn't think she's so grand!" a measure of her fear and frustration. Down the long, long corridor, up the steps and onstage again; surmounting, climbing, not just in fullness but beyond . . . young Collien half-calling "Stop, stop." But there is no way-stop off the mountain . . . up, up . . . *Didn't it rain, children—didn't it? didn't it?* face awash with sweat and light and swimming eyes, *didn't it?* into the holy dance—that's it—that's it—blithe in her lightness and the glory of a voice loosed from all bounds *didn't it rain*—a child of her Maker, come to fill the Ark, make the Covenant, tell the Story, gone straight to everlasting sweet blessed Jesus! and she was offstage still dancing, skirt hem lifted, head down, eyes closed, face in-drawn with her vision . . . a half-shake of her head and Laurraine pulled young Kurt Collien's arm away: "She's in the spirit, she has to work it out," the merest whisper: Do Not Disturb . . . following at a distance as Mahalia passed through plastic and chrome in the grip of an ancient spell. Moments. She returned. She dwindled. She sank. There was only a whisper of her to say, "Gwen, take the bow; tell the people I'm sick and thank you." But one more effort: mind your manners, sweet and low—the lady is waiting and tell her it's youth that matters; but there's been too much talk, Mahalia aims to do.

SHE WENT to Munich. And got her bill. Friday night, Sept. 24. A huddle of misery. A small yellow pill on her stretched pink palm: the newest prescription to magic away pain and exhaustion. She could match it by the bottleful: librium. "I want an *American* doctor!" If she can hold on— She is clinging to Gwen's call to Bob Phillips; if it's broken, she can go home on that. . . .

Foreign city . . . midnight . . . weekend . . . no answer—no answer— In Chicago, Shapiro strained to hear Mahalia . . . it seemed the contract was breached—by failure to deposit second funds in New York before Berlin; his lawyer's mind was already mapping the moves; they couldn't push

Mahalia around . . . then as he listened to Laurraine, her tone as much as her words convinced him Mahalia was in fact seriously ill . . . "but I can't find an American doctor and we need one *now!*" He had an answer: the American consulate in Munich had a 24-hour duty man; he'd had to call on them once.

"—no one. Not one doctor. It's the weekend, you know. Well—you might try calling the U.S. Army Hospital at McGraw Kaserne; but if anybody comes, it would be out of the goodness of their heart. Yes, I realize it's Mahalia Jackson but they're not supposed to treat civilians. . . ." 3 a.m. The ambulance backed into position and Capt. James Schlie admitted Mahalia to the emergency room.

CLOSED CARE. Tests. 24-hour EKG. *No* visitors. Yes, Washington called. EKG clear Saturday; clear Sunday; more tests: you may be just exhausted. . . . "If it is just exhaustion, Herr Doctor, could she sing on Wednesday?" . . . EKG running. *No* visitors. Well, three minutes only but don't let her talk—no! one person; *one.* EKG clear Monday; EKG Tuesday—irregularity. Severe pain. Better fly Major Santos from Frankfurt; *he's* the chief cardiologist. And set up a Public Information Desk. See if you can get Major Foster in from Heidelberg.

"—electrocardiographic changes which supported a diagnosis of coronary artery disease with angina. . . ." The release was fed to hungry media around the world. In his A.M.A. office in Chicago, Dr. William Barclay shook his head. "Sarcoid," he said. If she didn't stay on the prednisone, the sarcoid would go completely out of control. "Can't I just go home, to the hospital?" Mahalia's eyes anxious. "Possibility of early medical evacuation has been discussed with Miss Jackson but in the interest of Miss Jackson it has been decided best for her to receive more conservative care." Col. A. A. Howard, MC, commanding officer, read it over and approved. He sighed. They weren't equipped for a celebrity situation.

Flowers. Calls. Cables. Letters. Cards. The meek and the mighty. The saved and the seeking. A reporter came from Holland but was barred. Pearl Bailey cabled; Mayor Daley called (and deputized Col. Reilly to follow her care). Commander of U.S. Army Europe Gen. Davison wrote; the President wrote; Hubert Humphrey wrote . . . the Gordons cabled from Calcutta; Dan Oleksiw, for the New Delhi Embassy; Rev. Abernathy for SCLC. Prayer cloths came; she pinned one inside her flannette—*And God wrought special miracles by the hands of Paul: so that from his body were brought unto the sick handkerchiefs or aprons, and the diseases departed from them and the evil spirits went out of them.* Troops, schoolrooms of children, in English, French, German, Dutch; from Austria, New Zealand, India, Belgium, Japan—500 missionaries. "I am a 16-year-old boy" . . . "I am just a 65-year-old white woman" . . . "I love you very much" . . . "you are my idol." Neat printing, labored scrawl, elaborate cards, ruled tablet paper. All word relayed, messages taken; she was forbidden to talk.

Alone in the intensive care unit—not another patient there—she fingered the one cable she'd kept by her. I'LL COME IF YOU WANT ME. LOVE SIGMOND. And named the money he'd need. No one else be here tonight—would not let her own *people* keep her company. She coaxed the orderly into rolling her bed close to a telephone. No answer. She lay back considering. Who would? Superior. "I can't find Minnis, Doc; he's not home. Call his sister Ruth—get her to find him; but you find him and buy him a ticket to come." . . .

Galloway was still not home. Gene reached Ruth and asked her to tell Minters that Gene Shapiro wanted to talk to him. "I didn't say why. I wasn't in the habit of discussing Mahalia's business."

THE QUESTION was, what did Mahalia want them to do? The Grand Hotel Continental was elegant, expensive—the tour sponsor's choice. But now the cost was Mahalia's. For her room and Gwen's; for Charles and his wife down the street; for meals—none of them prepared for this. A taxi to the hospital and back cost $10. With Halie losing this money from the concerts, having heaven knows what medical bills— Laurraine had never forgotten what a Chicago newspaper friend, Alma Locke, said when Laurraine had just met Mahalia—said indignantly: "Mahalia makes a lot but people get it all away from her, or she gives it to the church." So was Mahalia wishing now they'd go home, or some of them—spare her this expense—but too delicate to say "go"? They weren't being allowed to see her but moments at a time, a relay of one each, three times a day. . . . "I guess you all better go on and go," Mahalia sighed. She was obviously worried about this contract business, with the Collien people insisting she was obligated to continue the tour when she was well or she owed them money—although Shapiro said not. "I'm in *their* country, that's the trouble, Laurraines," she said, low, not wanting it around. . . . Gwen was philosophical; she'd be home in time to play for church. Charles and his wife prepared to go.

"Doc?" IT WAS two days after her first call. "Doc, why Minnis not here yet?" Shapiro hesitated but had to confess his failure to find him so far. "Then you come," said Mahalia.

"Are they giving you problems, Mahalia?"

"Yeah, they don't believe I'm really sick; they think I can go on. So you come. And bring my coat. It's getting cold over here; I need it to go home." He couldn't drop everything and leave. But if it would make her happier to have her coat . . . "Do you want Allen to bring the coat?" Not yes and not no; it wasn't always easy to figure Mahalia's scenario. He called Allen to see if by any chance Galloway had contacted *him* and to tell Allen about the coat. "I'll take the coat," said Allen. Well—why not? Her Aunt Alice thought so. Shapiro called the McGraw Kaserne adjutant general's office and asked that the tour management be barred from disturbing her; that only such persons as she named be admitted to see her at all.

HALIE'S VOICE was glad, on the telephone from the hospital: "I asked the doctor and they going let you all stay out here at the bachelor officers quarters. I told them I needed you for my business. You all can come *now.*"

Almost four weeks. Peculiar weeks, right from the first day in a different room when the bird come to the window. (Gwen shivered when she came in—Mahalia seemed a little upset but not enough for it to be anyone *too* close; and when word came, it was an old friend from early gospel days.) Her two doctors, Major Thompson and Major Hansen, they both were nice, but she couldn't get anything good to eat unless the dietitian—thank You Lord he's black—smuggled her up something a little seasoned; or maybe Allen fixed something with some taste at the kitchen over there. They would not say what was keeping her here so long: just "rest." Rest better at home. And her temple sitting there; no telling what. Now finally they talking letting her go—but what kind of a way was this *to* go? "Can't I just use the ticket I got?"

No. Col. Howard said they wouldn't risk sending her by ordinary commercial flight where she'd be without medical attendance. In fact, with the eyes of half of Washington on them, apparently, they didn't want to release her from Army medical care until she was in the States: she would be flown home by Air Evacuation plane. "What that means?" Mahalia asked cautiously (all this relayed to and fro by intermediaries Allen and Laurraine). "Col. Howard says they'll take you by helicopter Tuesday to Frankfurt Air Base; you stay overnight there to be checked at their hospital. Wednesday they fly you to Andrews Air Force Base in Washington; you stay in their hospital overnight. Thursday, they fly you to Great Lakes Naval Hospital. But you have to have an ambulance waiting to drive you from there to—Billings, you want, don't you?—to be signed over to a particular doctor. You tell them who, and they contact him in advance."

"Dear Jesus," said Mahalia. "That's instead of flying straight to O'Hare?" Great Lakes must be 30 miles away. They nodded. "It's regulations. They have to land at a military field and that's the closest." There'd been no persuading past the rules. "And Col. Howard says," Laurraine added with a sigh, "that it's stretching regulations enough to send a civilian this way; that he's not going to ask permission for somebody else simply to ride with you."

Sunk into the white pillows, Halie just looked. *Jesus, Savior, Pilot Me.*

The old song ran along the page of her Bible. Thirty miles in an ambulance. Might be my hearse.

83

"MAHALIA JACKSON arrived late Saturday night—" Press, radio, TV were at the ready to record a Mahalia being lifted down on a canvas stretcher by Army medical corpsmen, flanked now by Allen Clark and Gene Shapiro, with Aunt Alice, Tina Choate, Harry Dale, and Gene's wife beyond—the impossible at Munich suddenly possible at Washington: Mahalia had been landed Oct. 23 at O'Hare Airport, Chicago.

And at her condominium Monday, Oct. 25—out of Billings for her birthday, as she'd asked. In Munich, she'd thought to go to Aunt Alice's ("*she* won't let people in to bother me, Laurraines") but the longer that trip stretched, the tireder she got. Big Alice could come up *here* and not let them in. All the tests at Billings said nothing wrong; still, she got three more prescriptions. One was valium. (At Billings Hospital the Mahalia Jackson medical record was filed away, its newest diagnostic notation, "sarcoidosis.") Dr. Thompson in Munich said even if her heart had been weakened, all she needed now was "rest and light exercise and she could sing in six months if she started easy." Easter in her temple! But rest—so how Dale take this into his head, her just back from planes and hospitals and a heart attack and the way she feel this minute? All she ask him do was go down, see Col. Reilly for her at Daley's.

Tina Choate was edgy for Harry's call. He was on the run, arranging Mahalia's surprise birthday party; had worked so hard. They had all the ice cream, cake, Cokes donated; he'd spoken to the mayor (he was coming—had already sent red roses) and Col Reilly, and a lot of important figures. It was 1 p.m. and if he didn't call soon— "Listen, stop! Harry, she doesn't want *anybody!* No—she's real cantankerous; adamant. *No people!*"

Call Dr. Young—this pain in my back *and* my heart; suppose I'd let those people come? . . . Her EKG at Michael Reese registered clear. Next day, to Dr. Vondrasek. "—back from Munich . . . 'coronary insufficiency.' *Still* got the pain . . . all right, I'll try this and come in Tuesday." Jesus! But she sure was glad to see Russell Goode this evening. Ha! knew he would: this boy have the sense to bring his yellow tablet got her new will they working on any chance she get without Teevee or *somebody* seeing what they at. Uh! got to run in the bathroom and lock the door—

now, you know! Well, the boy be back Thanksgiving, they can work on it then. So long as he take it back; don't leave it around here. But the temple, now that won't wait. Lord don't ask "do it hurt?" when a mother birth a child; He sure ain't waiting on Halie to take her ease. It's get up and *do.*

Now we getting somewhere. Daley going get her some children—nursery school, kindergarten, like that—and Nettie Irving going run the school with the different arts: Duke and her other entertainment friends, when they in town they can come give a lecture and that will help the interest and be educational. For the preachers, be Strawthford; Allen's boy Donald —*sure* got to have the family preacher; Preacher Gaye, Mother Gaye's child, represent the young Pentecostal. That's besides the different ones for guest preaching—*need* a lot to have continuous prayer meeting day and night; people come in any time and find service. Robert Anderson be Minister of Music. Robert not half crazy as he acts and he know the *original* gospel choir sound. Write Josephine Davis, ask her and George to paint inside the church auditorium—that's all the place actually needs. And send out a choir call. CBS want a Mahalia Jackson Christmas Special, from her temple! 'Course the money question still up there. Superior got the temple corporation but they saying—

"Ask your brother-in-law if anybody can forge certificates." Long-distance, she sounded weak and worried. "I mean—no, wait; first I want you to listen to this wire I sent Mrs. Gandhi in care of the President and see if you think I did right ('Allen! bring me that wire to Mrs. Gandhi') then I want know how can I be sure she going get it? Listen: 'Welcome to our country. With the world on the brink of war, God has given you the power to lead men. He is leading you through a divine plan. All things work together for the good of those who trust in God.' And I put my phone number. You think so? You going call the India embassy for me? Yeah. Well, listen—different people trying discredit Superior with me. But I had Judge Hooks to come check over Superior's work on the temple and he said it look all right. 'Pretty high for the property,' he said, 'but everything seems in order.' Superior want me to put the temple in the church's name, not mine—say the people can help raise the money. Oh, I have confusions and doubts, Laurraines. And I don't feel good. No, I still can't have no visitors. I got my brother Johnny to come stay."

It did seem a consolation he was there, Johnny thought. Even though most of the time he just sat in the kitchen shooting the breeze with Big Alice, Allen, sometimes Rev. Lewis, maybe her neighbor nextdoor, Chere Strong. The big thing was whether to tell her about Celeste, and they'd decided not yet. Mahalia's progress was the first concern, and *what* would she do when she knew Celeste had dropped dead of a heart attack while

Mahalia was in Germany? Close as Celeste was—and Mahalia not strong enough to eat a thing but food ground up like a baby's.

"SHE REALLY didn't seem all that sick, to be eating this ground-up cooked food—looked like liver paste," says Ben Hooks. Not digesting well, apparently. Although it could be she took what the doctor said and went a little further. "Talking about her CBS Christmas special and whether I was going to participate, she sounded fine. And when we went down for her first choir call, she seemed in good spirits, actually healthier. Possibly—doctors do say about 45 percent of all illness is psychosomatic." There was this setback now about the temple; stripped it clean, beyond the agreement, which only allowed for removal of the organ and the Judaic objects. But he and Gene Shapiro had done sufficient point-by-point arguing; plates, knives, chairs, the whole gamut, it was all going back. "All except the grand piano, which unfortunately was someone else's property, but this had not been pointed out to Mahalia and she was affronted, really, that it should be gone." Still, she'd gone ahead on the replacement. In a project this massive— He still wished he could talk her out of it before the deadline. "But she was positively defensive about it."

GENE SHAPIRO was pretty pleased with himself. The temple was clear on the two key fronts. As he'd told her, she must have control of this temple *by herself*. She could appoint a board, if she wished (and apparently she did, immediately starting on "Aunt Hannah and Aunt Alice and Bob Miller") but she must always keep control. So he'd structured it that way. Then he'd done quite a bit of shopping to come up with a loan at 6% when they were paying her 5% on certificates of deposit, so her money was costing her 1%. Neat.

"Talk louder! I can't hear you!" The men around Mahalia's breakfast table obediently raised their voices: Bob Miller, Gene Shapiro, Judge Hooks, Rev. Parnell, Rev. Lewis, and the key visitor, Roland Burris of Continental Illinois National Bank. "Talk up! I still can't hear what you saying!" Mahalia was in her bed, attending the temple finance session two rooms removed. Judge Hooks and Bob Miller rose as one and walked into her bedroom, but Ben Hooks singlehandedly picked her up, brought her in, and deposited her in a comfortable chair. She looked gratified, but not unduly. "I'm the one going have to pay this thing, you know," she said to Mr. Burris, "so go ahead and talk." When all her questions were answered—first mortgage, second mortgage—she signed the waiting papers: The remaining $185,000 of the $225,000 purchase was secured. Mr. Miller was glad Mahalia would have revenue right off from leasing the school, with the mayor's help.

". . . the Mahalia Jackson group is to take possession of the K.A.M. Temple Dec. 15," the newspaper read. "Reported purchase price is $2,225,000, personally guaranteed by Miss Jackson."

"Great God in the morning!" said Mahalia. "They off two million dollars."

COL. JACK Reilly had distinct qualms. Once again the mayor had given him the project of helping Mahalia. There'd been talk about this temple they were plotting, talk about the school, but in kind of boxcar figures that didn't seem right. He'd have to know a lot more about it.

"CONTINUED chest pain when she wakes"—Dr. Rosi made notes steadily as she spoke—"aggravated by walking"; that was frequent with coronary disease. She was afraid to stay in bed because it was weakening . . . "but that's the only way I get relief." Pain also present in bed. Some pain in left arm. Definitely not hypertensive. No evidence of cell damage. Blood sugar normal. Continue same medication. She was on a coronary dilator, diabetes medication, a tranquilizer. And the prednisone she'd been on through the years.

Nov. 18. "Still weak," Dr. Vondrasek wrote. Heart pounding. Appetite improving; gained six pounds in two weeks—213. Tolerance for sugar improved. The doctor reduced the diabetes dosage and gave her something to help her sleep.

DOODUTZ stayed clear of all this big temple finance, but she was relieved to see Mahalia getting up and going some. She seemed in pretty good spirits since she'd called for Isabell to come do for her, right after Johnny Jackson left . . . taking her little ride around with Dale. And *all* excited about her temple. Still, "I don't care what you and those doctors say, I know how I feel and I'm going to bed!"

And they needn't think she don't know they keeping her best medicine from her. She know. She's just waiting. Some people going be surprised—and she don't mean Doodutz.

"THE LADY ACROSS the hall say she'll cook dinner for us. Let's stay here." Mahalia had walked into Isabell's room Thanksgiving morning, Doodutz not up good yet. Oh Lord, thought Doodutz, here's a mess. "You know Allen's got all the dinner cooking; let's go—you told him you'd come." Mahalia just did not *want* to go for some reason, but she gave in. Isabell was glad. Peace at any price if you can. And Allen was cooking for Mahalia, Isabell, the two aunts, Rev. Lewis, Russell Goode, Teevee Hall, Allen's friend Bobbie Singleton, and Mahalia had made particular point she wanted John Stevens, their cousin Steve—about third cousin, said Mahalia had wanted him to come work for her, live with her, after she divorced Galloway.

LORD, HALIE ain't got Job's patience and You might as well accept that now 'cause there's no fighting the demons sometimes and there's times you wrestling with the Devil. She was home and shaking and sick and just everybody leave me be, leave me alone, just leave me in my bed.

She changed the locks on the condominium next day. And called Johnny Jackson to unburden. Johnny considered a bit, and called Allen. "Put your pride in your pocket, man; go on back, she's sick; she needs you and she sure ain't going *ask* you, mad as she is."

"RUSSELL, YOU brought the pad? Well—I told you when I called, I wanted make some changes and I *want* some changes now but I'm just too sick. Take me over to Billings Emergency, Russell; I got to have help. You bring it back Christmas, hear?"

Isabell blinked awake. She'd been up late, packing. Mahalia was whispering. Her will! "Hear, read this, read it good. Read it *good*." Speechless, Isabell nodded; Mahalia went back to bed . . . came back. "You understand? All right. I want you to take this home, show it to Brisko, and put it in a safe deposit box. You send me a key, and tell Brisko what bank you got it in. *Nobody know this but you, me, and the lawyer*. Nobody. *Nobody*. Aunt Alice or nothing."

Isabell was ready to say goodbye. "You still want me to take this?" "No, leave it. I got to make some changes." She went out—to the bank, she said—before Isabell left. In that terrible weather.

"MISS JACKSON, we can't find anything wrong and. . . ." "No, Miss Jackson, nothing wrong that we can see. . . ." "We're just taking your money, Miss Jackson; we can't. . . ."

She sure couldn't put on a Christmas special in this shape. Give it one more week. Oh, Lord. Call New York, get Ernestine to come. Anybody about to get their Lord's temple ought to be joyous, instead of oppressed by— Bishop Washington! Ernestine's husband be the very one to actually pastor it, thank You Lord. At least Superior said they sold 8358; that be something more in the bank. He going see where else can he get me some more interest. . . . "Doc, I don't *know* where the key is to my safety deposit box. I ain't had that thing in— Polly might have a key. Yeah, I believe that's where the deed to the house is, and that's where the annuity certificate is—that I.D.S.? I know it's a lot of money, but I ain't had my hands on that certificate; it must be still in the box. I'll call and ask Polly."

"Miss Jackson had to go to Billings Emergency again, I'm sorry; she left a note for you." Mrs. Washington had wanted to go with Mahalia—so weak, couldn't hold anything on her stomach—but she'd asked her to stay behind and hand this over; it seemed important. Poor Mahalia. Trying so hard to make her dream come true. She still could. If she could get over this spell. Bishop Washington was going to come out and look over the church.

THURSDAY, Dec. 9. Realtor Sheldon Good, Gene Shapiro, Judge Hooks,

Mahalia. Everything settled? No more questions? Friday, Dec. 10, Gene Shapiro's voice was firm. "We're ready to close." Yes, on Wednesday, Dec. 15.

ALL WEEKEND she wrestled. Prayed. A brown finger traced Psalm 83. *O God, do not keep silence; do not hold Thy peace or be still, O God!* Monday morning, she called Superior.

Sheldon Good was shocked. "Thursday evening—Friday—nothing was brought up of this!"

"Miss Jackson decided she did not want to buy," said Gene Shapiro, "due to the state of her health—which is obviously not good—and that she does not have her own source of funds."

"You'll forfeit the $40,000!"

Almost out of a clear blue sky, as far as Ben Hooks could ascertain, from *her* viewpoint; she suddenly just *that quick* changed her mind. It had certainly caught them all by surprise. She was in a real frenzy now about that $40,000. He was glad he was here so he could talk to her about it with Gene Shapiro. Now she'd got him off and pulled out her will to show him—worried about her will. Still, she was moving around, going in the closet, telling them what to cook, picking up things. It was odd about her best friend, Celeste: Even after she was told, Allen said she just blanked it out—never asked about the circumstances, about the funeral; not even "Won't ever see her again."

ALBERTINA WALKER didn't know if her luck would stretch to actually getting in. She'd maybe see Mahalia at church, sick or not, but that was no place to visit, Mahalia need to get on home, out the way of all those people. 'Tina just *happened* to be at a girl friend's when Madame Washington had called from Mahalia's, and Mary handed 'Tine the phone: "Somebody wants to talk to you"—and it was Mahalia. Why hadn't Albertine come see her? "Girl, ain't no problem my *coming* to see you, way I flunked for you, your driver, your chauffeur, your maid and I sang the gospel myself, flunkying for you" (she waited while Mahalia hollered with laughter); "no problem my *coming*, and calling—been calling—'no visitors, no guests, no company'—regardless what paid help or whatever of help you got, you got friends who really care for you other than you being Mahalia—they like you for just you—but girl, can't *nobody* get up in there!"

"Oh, baby, they do me so bad around here, I didn't get your messages. I wish you'd come."

"I know how you do"—'Tine rolled it out—"you tell folks to tell folks you ain't ho-ome, or you sick . . . no, you never did it to me, but what go 'round, come 'round." Funning aside, Albertina decided Mahalia wasn't so much sick as she needed quiet; she'd wait.

"COME ON, GET up, sit in the sun," Allen commanded, "if you don't feel like going for a ride. Come eat in the kitchen."

"Oh, get up and let the bed rest and walk around, girl." Aunt Alice believed all this bed was so weakening.

AUNT BESSIE nodded to the long-distance. She could see what Big Alice was contending with—say so many come, phone, talk, want this, all sitting on side the bed, telling, kneeling; Big Alice felt like they was pulling Halie down. She taken to sleeping in the bed with Mahalia, keep them off. But she had to leave it to some these other folks, her two days she was working; they *supposed* to not let her talk and *keep out*.

"You need any money, James?" James Lee was thin as a rail—knew that would worry Mahalia much as she cared about him and he'd started not to come, but she probably heard he was out the hospital and would wonder. James wrote the check like she asked but when he handed her the book to sign, she said that wasn't enough, tear that up, made one out herself for $135. He started to massage her shoulder blades—big knot up there—and Mahalia pulled her housecoat up and made him look at her legs, how they'd fallen off. First strength, he would tape her those inspirational messages she wanted, to listen by her bed.

"MISSIE? OH, MISSIE!" Missie Wilkerson had finally made it. Been blocked, but late this night Mahala caught the phone herself and had not even had the *message* of Missie's phoning, neither her nor Jean. They set it that Mahala would fix it with the doorman to get Missie up . . . and now look a-here, Missie slides in past Teevee while they arguing and Big Alice will not let her past the den! Missie settled down, prepared to wait the *night* . . . tried to follow the tray as Big Alice went but blocked there, and here is Mr. Lewis—Mr. *Lewis* carried on up there . . . and Missie right on up with Mr. Lewis. Tears *rolling* from Mahala at sight of Missie. Mr. Lewis had the strength to help that gas out, true enough . . . but Mahala with not even a bell! Okay. Get her in the whirlpool—Missie can *fix* the whirlpool. . . . Big Alice *got* to give the enema, hurt or not. Doctor come, couldn't find nothing ailed her: *nothing! nothing!* Okay. Missie climbed in the bed like Mahala asked and, whispering secrets, got at it: Mahala want Minnis so *bad*—he been calling but they got him blocked! Missie and her made it up that Missie would call him and *hit* on him—not say she want him so *bad*, just *hit* on him to come on, never mind phoning, just come, but then they figured he might not get up. Mahala afraid he be insulted and he *going* with a woman in Gary got money; and the best thing—the best thing, meet at some place; see will Jean let us go there . . . *hit* on him and ask Jean . . . or tell him come next Wednesday when Big Alice working and Allen be gone to New Orleans . . . Mahala all this while trying to smuggle down his telephone number—or else his sister Ruth's, if she's not remembering his right—in between somebody coming in the bedroom. "Mahala, I will get Minters for you if it's the last thing I do *alive*, I will get him," Missie promised in a whisper before she let out to hunt him down. . . .

Found him! And no "hit on him," told it like it was, Mahala want him so *bad* but didn't want him to *know* and sure enough, he had *been* calling. He said he was not afraid, he'd go straight on up. . . .

Mahala was where? In the *hospital!* Warn't in no hospital yesterday. *What* hospital? Mean to tell me you don't know which one?

DR. QUENTIN YOUNG had come as often as she called and would continue to do so as long as she wished, even though he was particularly discomforted by this round of doctors, these panicky assaults on emergency rooms whose staffs didn't know her case at all—there could be only *one* caretaker in health. But here was an extremely energetic, vigorous person deeply threatened, extremely anxious about her palpitations, her constipation. She had an irritable colon, true, but he could not get her to deal with the primary problem he felt was important to her survival: to lose weight. He had scheduled her for exhaustive tests now, but unless they turned up some new specific here at Michael Reese—

LIKE PROVIDENCE, Missie's state police friend calling her up, and now *he* checking the different hospitals for where Miss Mahala Jackson, saying who he *is*. Even Hannah could not get where, from the house. Missie had sat while Hannah phoned— All right. Okay. *Now* she can tell Minters.

NO DECORATIONS. And no Christmas dinner. When has Halie had this in her grown life? But they just let her out of Michael Reese yesterday, and with Allen taken off to New Orleans almost the minute he left from getting her certificates at the bank, to hear Allen tell it—"snow, blizzard, man waited late at the bank," like of that, and still not in her hand and she would not feel safe until they were. But here the boy Russell come so faithful from Chattanooga while she's in Michael Reese and now no Christmas dinner to feed him; she was ashamed. . . . Well, sure, they could eat *out*, got a good place close—him and Teevee and her; nobody else know she's home: word out she's at the hospital, from all who showed up when she *wasn't* supposed to be there; or if—'no visitors'; but *that* don't make no difference when the one person in this world she most want to see. . . .

Look at 'em now, poking in her important Christmas cards—President Nixon, Lady Bird Johnson and the President. Let 'em look; Halie's still looking for her *best* Christmas message. . . . Yeaaaaaaah. She could just about say hello to Rev. Lewis, 'cause right with him at the door was Minnis, and his sister Ruth.

REV. LEWIS greeted Mahalia and left the room. Coming up at the same time as Galloway—the two elevator doors opening at once! He had a strong premonition something was going to happen, and he didn't want to be involved.

NETTIE WAS glad Mahalia had Russell call to say come and bring the children. No one barred *her,* but it was Christmas and Mahalia must be drained. The two sat close now, red chairs pulled up together to look onto the water. Mahalia was worrying: her illness might be a judgment. "I just wonder what it is I have done wrong? What I'm being punished for?" God wasn't that kind of a God, Nettie reminded her. This wasn't Mahalia talking; someone was putting this into her head. Mahalia checked to see the two were private and told her about Minnis—been up to Michael Reese every *day* after his work; Nettie had just missed him now. Well, yes, *maybe,* but the family— Nettie listened with her senses as well as her ears and thought of what her daughter Gail said: "Aunt Mahalia always tries to please everybody and you can't."

Halie didn't tell (except to Minnis's mother, Mary Lou, next day) that she'd told him bring Sigma. The child had wanted to come but he'd thought it might tire Mahalia. She didn't tell Mary Lou she'd given Minnis a key—not going have him insulted at the door. And she sure didn't tell a *soul* they going get married again, paper or no paper—she didn't even tell *Minnis* that.

SIGMOND TURNED away. He'd just consulted lawyer Bob Tucker about the marriage quit-claim. The lawyer said it would hold; it was valid. Now say he signed and married Mahalia and she threw him out again for some reason. It wasn't easy to get a job. But still— She sure had perked up at the idea.

RUSSELL GOT Mahalia and her *Ebony* friend Era Bell Thompson to pose for pictures, and just talking to Miss Thompson, he said the doctors said they can't find anything wrong with her; they want her to be *quiet,* but—he wondered if she'd ever be able to sing again. "Oh, I'm going sing again!" said Mahalia. "Well, good," was all Russell could say—and suddenly Mahalia opened up her mouth and started to sing. Just as *strong* as could be. Russell leaped to the piano and she sang something else—kept it up about five minutes. She was so happy and pleased. She probably couldn't make Martin's birthday memorial service in Atlanta on Jan. 15, but she could be there Apr. 19 for his Memorial Center board meeting.

Dec. 28. Good thing Billings just 10 minutes away.

Jan. 1, 1972: "Dale, you hear the way they did me?" Wait 'til Hannah hear, she won't believe it . . . "and Hannah, you heard anything from Bertha? I been looking for her in from L.A. all day. I thought maybe she called and they didn't let her through." *Told* Bertha she'd have a good job with her, live right here. "But I'm thinking of getting married," Bertha'd explained when Mahalia called. "Maybe you could be married here," said Mahalia.

"MARY LOU, these people about to worry me to death. If Minnis and me can get together one more time, I'm going move away from here and go to Jamaica or Hawaii or somewhere these folks can't afford to follow."

"That man worrying her to death!" Allen hated to see him come in; just get Mahalia all upset, put her back. Big Alice agreed. She'd almost rather see Mahalia dead than go through all that mess with that man again; bad as he did her, he'd *be* the death of her.

"Albertine, I got news for you—Minnis and me going get together again! I'm ready now, but Minnis say, 'Wait, they'll say I tricked you while you sick, your mind's not together.' But I got all my sense—I *know* what I want to do."

Russell Goode could not imagine what Sigmond Galloway was doing calling him. He'd just left Chicago, and Galloway had never called him before. Oh. Mahalia herself on the line and wanting to know where they'd hid the will Russell had been wagging back and forth for them to work on 'til this time she said leave it, she knew he was tired of carrying it so leave it 'til he come back next month, and now she couldn't remember where they hid it. "In that big straw pocketbook you got in the islands, remember? In your big closet?" Showing it to Galloway! The man was worrying her to death, and she said she was sick as a dog.

Robert Anderson helped her to the bathroom and sat on the side the tub to make sure she was all right, and she told him how she loved her husband and she was going have him no matter who said—"now will you get out my face and let me set here in peace?" When she came out, they diagnosed each other.

Ida Beal was thoughtful as she hung up. Poor Mahalia. She'd been supposed to come at Christmas and postponed for some cause, but now she said she'd come soon as she could get away, to recuperate . . . said then Beal could get on the road with her, end of June.

SO THEY'D MADE it. Gene Shapiro knew the birds had been whispering. It was Jan. 4, and Mahalia was on the line. She wanted to cash in *all* her savings certificates. "I want my money and I want it now and I want it in cash." The lawyer had Allen meet him at the bank in Melrose; got a cashier's check for the $100,000 certificate; drove down to Cornell—up to the 26th floor—gave her the $100,000 check and every certificate of deposit—and insisted she note they were every one in her name, *not* his. He then went to his office and resigned as her lawyer, by letter. Jan. 6,

Mahalia called: please, please come see her. Jan. 7, with Big Alice and Hannah beside her, Mahalia in tears, he agreed to resume as her attorney. "Doc, you the only one I got!" He refused to take back the certificates of deposit. Once was enough.

"Doc, THEY THINK I'm crazy." Superior knew her—*he* knew better. She'd called Monday morning to Dr. Rosi, since Dr. Vondrasek wasn't due 'til afternoon ("abdominal pain, nausea, vomiting," Dr. Rosi noted; "developed after ate some organic foods") and Dr. Rosi said she'd better get into the hospital for tests. She did, that same day: not to his; Minnis brought her to Billings—*that* was her hospital. Emergency room wasn't the whole hospital. But since then— Dr. Ferguson was sick himself. He'd seen her but mostly she had these other people, had all these tests, and now here this woman doctor saying she need a psychiatrist! Telling Allen it must be something on her mind she won't talk about, making her feel like this. Well—she didn't like it and she'd never like it but she told him go 'head on, they can do what they want to do—been through every other department in this hospital. . . .

Cylestine (Polly) Fletcher was startled. And irate. She'd come Friday to keep Mahalia company on her lunch hour and found her furious. She had *submitted* herself to these psychiatrists, but she said it wasn't just the psychiatrists—it was a lot of people in there and *one* of them she recognized from his doing newspaper stories on her years ago; dressed like the doctors but he was *not* a doctor and that let Mahalia o-u-t. Polly had found her in her room trying to leave—would not wait even until Allen got back. All right, Polly would take her, lunch hour or not. There was no keeping her even long enough for Polly to get things together properly to leave.

"I WANT TO write Dr. Harper a letter; I want him to know exactly why I walked out of Billings after I been going there all these years." Dr. Harper knew she loved him, and he *knew* her—been her surgeon from way back, the first time. "And call Ann Walker." Her son was vice president at the University, *he* ought to know about this. Polly reached Ann Walker, and the two old friends talked a long time: Halie wanted to go back to Billings, if she could straighten this thing out.

Polly wrote the letter and sat with her that Sunday night. Minters Galloway and his sister and her husband barged in. Polly did not leave until they had gone.

RUSSELL GOODE was grim as he listened to Tevelda Hall from Chicago—said he had better get up there, that man, that ex-husband, was killing that woman, driving her crazy. Russell couldn't just pick up and fly—he had to teach school—but he'd go just as soon as he could.

JOHNNY JACKSON listened sympathetically. He knew Mahalia didn't like being in the house by herself, even full strength. He'd hoped when he sent his daughter Gyrlie out that she'd more or less stay, something might work out there, but Gyrlie's boyfriend had persuaded her home just—it develops now, listening to Mahalia this Sunday—just before Mahalia had to go *into* Billings. Johnny figured he could be there about Feb. 1. Seemed Mahalia just wanted someone to talk to; she was tired, and she was sick. Well, he'd be there in two weeks and make it a good stay.

BESSIE KIMBLE woke frightened. The *second* message on Mahalia inside a week. First time, look like she could see Mahalia off in a place. Sad-looking. She'd called Doodutz then—"Isabell, you all say Mahalia ain't sick, but Mahalia is sicker than what you think. I know. I had a dream." She had said that, and now in *this* dream she had lost a piece of jewelry. That means somebody you love, you going miss them. They going die. It was the same before Little Alice passed. They laugh now, if she tell them; it's not like she used to be—used to could just sit down and vision, 'most as bad as her sister Bell.

"HERE IN ARIZONA, that's where *you* need to be, Mahalia; it would do you the world of good." Nettie hoped she could persuade Mahalia. She'd scheduled herself for a month, and already she was so much improved. "No, California's too foggy—damp; meet me here in Scottsdale: . . ." Oh, my Lord, no sooner off the phone than Mahalia got hold of Duke this same *night*, telling him "Nettie's down there sick! That woman's gone down there to die!" Got Duke so upset, *he* called. That's Mahalia—worrying about somebody else. It was that kindness plus that steel-trap mind that made her so remarkable. If she could just solve this problem.

8 A.M. TUESDAY. "I feel like I'm dying, doctor." Nauseated and vomiting throughout the night. Pulsations. The prescription Dr. Vondrasek had phoned hadn't helped. Dr. Rosi studied his X-ray. There was gas within the small bowel and he considered the possibility of an early, incomplete bowel obstruction. He gave her three prescriptions and stressed to her nephew Allen the time factor in taking them. If she wasn't appreciably better tomorrow, he'd put her in Little Company of Mary Hospital for observation.

Wednesday, Jan 19. Psalms 114–115, the hymn of praise by one who was mortally ill, who prayed at death's door and was heard by God and cured—her Bible lay open there, left behind. There'd be one at Little Company of Mary.

Admitting diagnosis: intestinal obstruction and coronary heart disease. Abdomen somewhat distended. She was installed on the second floor south. Where St. Jude? They began intravenous feeding. "She's asleep, they've given her something," Allen whispered to Jerome, one eye on the window —it was snowing against the dark. "I'm so hongry. I feel better, but they ain't giving me nothing to eat." A little Jello—they'd lean that far, Dr. Rosi said. She took two spoonsful from Allen and that was it. Thursday, Allen brought the checkbook. "That's all you know, to spend my money," she said, signing. "She's feeling better, talking like that," Allen told Jerome, and the two got to gossiping with her, Mahalia laughing at the latest. "Well, I guess you be going home pretty soon; that's when the rat race—riot—going start, 'cause you ain't going give nobody no rest," said Allen, eyeing her. "You ain't doing nothing for my money but sitting down noway," said Halie, pushing up her lip. In good spirits! good spirits! Allen assured Jerome as they left.

MINNIS. THAT'S who she been waiting for; soon as he get off his city job in Gary—right here. He said he'd talked to Dr. Vondrasek—knew him from back when they were married—and the doctor wanted him to talk to her about running a suction tube down to help clear out her intestine and the gas and so on. ("This is the conservative approach to incomplete intestinal obstruction, or to paralysis of the bowel," Dr. Vondrasek had said. Sigmond could grasp that.)

"Ohhhh, no! Unh-unh. Not down *my* throat. Ruin my vocal cords? That would be the *last* thing— I told that doctor," she fretted, smoothing over her swollen stomach. "Minnis," she whispered, "you know, we could get married right up here—we don't have to wait. Call Missie and Jean, they can be witness, and Jerome—he on your side. Jean could go down with you to get the license; they'd give it."

Sigmond shook his head. "Let's wait until you're home. We want to do it right." He wasn't having anybody charge him with undue influence. "All right," said Halie, "we'll do it the day I get out of here. Ought to be out by Friday, latest."

CELIE WAS IN a state again; her brother Allen sighed on it. Enough upset about Mahalia without her insisting, *insisting*, she had seen— "Mahalia's first and second burial, I tell you. A revelation. I saw her burial by water, and I saw it by clay. And the birds! Sang all *night* in the crepe myrtle tree, and you know that's a valuable tree: in the Bible—and those birds were in that tree and sang all night *long*. That has never happened before. I said then those birds are singing me a message from God—they's something coming . . . Father, able me to stand it. And then I had the revealation. First and second burials."

"Sister," said Son Baby, "you just keep Mahalia on your mind."

REV. JOE CAMPBELL was amazed he reached Mahalia directly Saturday when he telephoned the hospital—he and Rev. Thurston had been turned away at her condominium when he passed through town Monday. Thurston had to leave for Jamaica on his vacation Tuesday, but now Rev. Campbell was back, and—amazing grace—Mahalia was full of plans to remarry Minters. A good sign. He told her not to pay any attention to those talking against it—although he well remembered the night she'd sent him with Minters to see about his hand, when Minters swung on her. Looking out for him then. If she loved him, that was her business. They were talking operation to her, she said, because she wouldn't let them go down her throat with a tube. She was afraid to be cut—but she was more afraid about her throat.

"RIGHT HERE, Rev. Jenkins." Mahalia showed her pastor where all the hurting—the misery—was and said she'd made up her mind to the operation. "I got to go through with it, to unlock my bowels." She seemed pretty calm, resigned to it, sitting in a chair talking with him. He got as far as the door when she said, "Reverend, come on, pray with me before you leave."

He'd heard rumors about her and Galloway but she didn't mention it, and he wouldn't—she was too sick for that.

MAHALIA HAD obviously been doing some thinking, Shapiro thought Sunday, surprised at her call from the hospital: "Get my money from the church, sell all my property, get the money for Indiana, and sell the condominium —I'm moving to Arizona," Mahalia said distinctly.

"Is anybody giving you trouble?" Gene was ready to take on any comers.

"No," she said, and went on to ask him about the baby, about his wife Jo Ann. He broke in to discuss the certificates of deposit—he wanted to make sure she understood that matter thoroughly. And then she gave him his second surprise: she was going to be operated on tomorrow. He tried to pin her down on exactly what was to be done, but she really didn't seem to know, just "unlock her bowel." He'd check with the doctor. Then she gave him his third surprise: she was going to marry Minters; it was all set; he'd be there today and— She broke off. "I can't talk any more," she whispered. "Polly and them, they're coming in."

Polly Fletcher found her rather weak—her voice was weak, anyway. They arranged for Polly to take the papers on 8358 Indiana over to the lawyer tomorrow—to Mr. Tucker. Mahalia did not mention operation. Nor Minters. He came, though, and so did Mahalia's two aunts—she lived for those aunts.

IT WAS SUCH a *distance* to this hospital—past the city limits into Evergreen, Ill. And January so bitter. Big Alice had been sick with her diabetes, and Hannah with her pressure; this was their first visit. Louise Parnell had given them a ride. Mahalia seemed to be all right—looking out the window, talking nothing special. It was growing dark early. She thought they should go before it began to snow or something. As they gathered themselves, Mahalia said quietly, "I want you all to kiss me before you leave."

She didn't mention operation.

"EMMA BELL—" Hannah's low voice was troubled—"Emma Bell, I am so disturbed. I don't expect Mahalia to live." Emma Bell had been through so many of these sick spells, knew how Mahalia pulled herself out. She did her best to talk Hannah around—especially since Hannah didn't have a single thing to name for a reason.

MISSIE AND Jean eased into the lobby. Minters had said he'd be going back at 6 p.m., to meet him there and they could go up with him. They found him waiting behind a pillar—said they'd just missed the relatives. That was luck. Mahalia's even being here was a big secret.

An old, worn cover on the bed, Mahalia in a hospital gown, not a flower in the room—Jean didn't know what she had expected, but not this. For somebody of Mahalia's magnitude. Minters opened the bathroom door to wet a towel to bathe her head and a man was standing there—not even a private bath.

MISSIE WAS happier than she'd been for days, since she lost Mahala—nary *trace* until yesterday, from Minters—and now Mahala want her to comb her hair. *Look* at it; look like it had not been done for months; a *time* to get the braids loose. Now. This is nice. Jean combing the wig, Missie combing the hair, Minnis ready to give her a rub when they through. You could see Mahala's spirits just lifting. Even to teasing "What we going do about Missie?"—Missie saying she want a *man*, trying get her a *man*; Mahala just cracking up. Minters had told Missie downstairs that Mahala would probably ask what she thought about an operation, and talk it down—try to get her to avoid it if she can; there was something about a tube they could do. But—"Minnis, you going let them operate on me tomorrow?" She had told about the people come to roll her out yesterday, said she was scheduled for a operation and she said "No! I ain't got no operation coming!" and *fell* trying to get out the way—and sure enough, man come in, said it was the wrong room, they was sorry . . . so now Missie didn't truly heed this talk. It was still up in the air. Got this tube.

Cut on her tomorrow, Mahalia told Jean. She asked Minters if he'd stay all night, being she was to be operated in the morning. He had a band job at the Holiday Inn in Gary that night, but he said he'd be back tomorrow as soon as he could—before she was out of surgery.

THERE WAS NO option, Dr. Vondrasek agreed with Dr. Nester Martinez, the surgeon. He was deeply concerned. X-ray did not show anything causing the obstruction, but it existed. One other problem was that for some reason, her pulse was getting very fast. Ever since she'd entered, Dr. Vondrasek had found her morose, just lying there; he hadn't been able to cheer her up—or get permission to use the tube. With this cardiac problem, she just wasn't in good condition. They couldn't wait, he agreed. Monday, Jan. 24, Dr. Martinez performed abdominal surgery and cut adhesive bands for release of partial intestinal obstruction. Intensive care unit. The problem was not post-surgical, in that sense, but this severe tachycardia, this rapid heart action. Tuesday, "We're encouraged—she seems brighter." Her blood pressure began to fall. Minters Sigmond Galloway, taking his customary route, found himself barred. Family only. Allen had decided this man was pestering Mahalia enough; he'd just fix his drinking self. Wednesday, circulation failing, kidney malfunction, very fast heart rate. Where Minnis? Where— Early Thursday morning, a sudden increase in blood pressure, followed by zero. Mahalia Jackson died.

Alone.

There were headlines around the world—even in Brazil, where sh never set foot but was revered. In Jamaica and in Nassau, her music wa poured onto the streets by loudspeakers for 24 hours of mourning. In Calcutta, Duke Ellington sat for hours with Mrs. Herbert Gordon, reminiscing their own eulogy. In New Delhi, Prime Minister Indira Gandhi—visibly moved—spoke her tribute. President Nixon issued a statement of mourning for the nation. In Hollywood, quiet Ella Fitzgerald startled her publicist by declaring that she was flying on her own to the funeral of "a great lady," even though she must fly back the same night. Three Mahalia records were chosen for the White House Library. A posthumous Grammy award was designated. In Paris, Hugues Panassié asked Madeleine Gautier to prepare the magazine's tribute. Max Jones shared his memories for London. In Chicago, Studs Terkel shared his. The bitter wind of January did not keep 40,000 from standing in line to file past her figure in Greater Salem Baptist Church. *Oh, Hand Me Down My Silver Trumpet, Gabriel.* Six thousand more filled the place of Mayor Daley's choice—Aerie Crown Theatre in McCormick Place—where there was weeping with her tributes but more joy with her gospel. Hallelujah! Then the majestic figure in a blue concert gown which had known the currents of the world came back to the Mississippi, to the Rivergate Auditorium in New Orleans, where through a day and a night and a morning over 60,000 would wait hours to file through—many of them children, white and black, brought by school bus. For her memorial service, 4,000 filled every seat and yet another 4,000 outside silently pressing were let in to stand, to sob and sing and, some, to shout in glory. A choir of 550; color guard of the U.S. services; a mixed honor guard (black/white/men/women) of city police; the mayor, the governor . . . and next morning, gleaming limousines past Mount Moriah where once there were no shoes for Sunday School, on eight miles to the grassy green of Providence Memorial Park.

Halie had her silver trumpet, Gabriel.

Sing aloud, O daughter of Zion;
shout, O Israel;
Rejoice and exult with all your
heart.
—Zephaniah 3:14

Epilogue

Four months after Mahalia's death, Minters S. Galloway died of cancer (detected only shortly before his death). Isaac Hockenhull died within the year, and successively, Mildred Falls and Aunt Hannah Robinson. Their contributions for the book have been left intact in the present tense, as they were given.

All her life, Mahalia reshaped names to suit some inner sense, but she never knew the import of her own. Rabbi Julian B. Feibelman of New Orleans has provided an arresting translation from the Hebrew:

Mahala—melodious song.

And in an extended form:

Mahalaleel—the one who praises God.